ROUTLEDGE HANDBOOK OF
SPORT AND NEW MEDIA

New media technologies have become a central part of the sports media landscape. Sports fans use new media to watch games, discuss sports transactions, form fan-based communities, and secure minutiae about their favorite players and teams. Never before have fans known so much about athletes, whether that happens via Twitter feeds, fan sites, or blogs, and never before have the lines between producer, consumer, enactor, fan and athlete been more blurred. The internet has made virtually everything available for sports media consumption; it has also made understanding sports media substantially more complex.

The *Routledge Handbook of Sport and New Media* is the most comprehensive and in-depth study of the impact of new media in sport ever published. Adopting a broad interdisciplinary approach, the book explores new media in sport as a cultural, social, commercial, economic, and technological phenomenon, examining the profound impact of digital technologies on that the way that sport is produced, consumed and understood. There is no aspect of social life or commercial activity in general that is not being radically influenced by the rise of new media forms, and by offering a "state of the field" survey of work in this area, the *Routledge Handbook of Sport and New Media* is important reading for any advanced student, researcher or practitioner with an interest in sports studies, media studies or communication studies.

Andrew C. Billings is the Ronald Reagan Chair of Broadcasting and Director of the Alabama Program in Sports Communication at the University of Alabama, USA. He has published eight books and over 80 journal articles and book chapters, with the majority focusing on the intersection of sports media and identity.

Marie Hardin is Professor of Journalism and Associate Director of the John Curley Center for Sports Journalism at Penn State, USA. Her research concentrates on diversity, ethics and professionalism in mediated sports with a focus on gender. Her work is published in sport- and communications-focused journals.

Natalie A. Brown worked as Assistant Editor on this book.

ROUTLEDGE HANDBOOK OF SPORT AND NEW MEDIA

Edited by Andrew C. Billings and Marie Hardin

Routledge
Taylor & Francis Group
LONDON AND NEW YORK

First published 2014
by Routledge
2 Park Square, Milton Park, Abingdon, Oxon OX14 4RN

and by Routledge
711 Third Avenue, New York 10017

Routledge is an imprint of the Taylor & Francis Group, an informa business

British Library Cataloguing in Publication Data
A catalogue record for this book is available from the British Library

Library of Congress Cataloging in Publication Data
Routledge handbook of sport and new media / [edited by] Andrew C Billings, Marie Hardin.
pages cm. – (Routledge international handbooks)
1. Mass media and sports–Handbooks, manuals, etc. 2. Sports–Computer network resources–Handbooks, manuals, etc. 3. Social media–Handbooks, manuals, etc.
I. Billings, Andrew C.
GV742.R68 2014
070.4'49796–dc23
2013028822

ISBN: 978-0-415-53276-1 (hbk)
ISBN: 978-0-203-11471-1 (ebk)

Typeset in Bembo
by FiSH Books Ltd, Enfield

Printed and bound in Great Britain by
TJ International Ltd, Padstow, Cornwall

CONTENTS

PART IV
Audiences: Fanship, consumption   **211**

PART V
Identities in the digital realm   **297**

Contents

LIST OF ILLUSTRATIONS

Figures

Tables

CONTRIBUTORS

María Arauz is Olympic Studies Centre (CEO-UAB) Junior Researcher and PhD candidate at the Department of Audiovisual Communication and Advertise, Universitat Autònoma de Barcelona.

Kathy Babiak is an Associate Professor of Sport Management in the School of Kinesiology at the University of Michigan. Her research focuses on organizational governance and leadership, sport policy, social responsibility and individual and organizational philanthropy in elite and professional sport.

Vincent L. Benigni is an Associate Professor and Director of Graduate Studies in the Department of Communication at the College of Charleston. His research interests include sport, media and public relations.

Andrew C. Billings is the Ronald Reagan Chair of Broadcasting and Director of the Alabama Program in Sports Communication at the University of Alabama, USA. He has published eight books and over 80 journal articles and book chapters, with the majority focusing on the intersection of sports media and identity.

Kimberly L. Bissell (PhD, Syracuse University) is the Associate Dean for Research and a Professor of Journalism at the University of Alabama's College of Communication and Information Sciences. Her research interests lie in the intersection of media, sport, health and children.

Nicholas David Bowman (PhD, Michigan State University) is an Assistant Professor of Communication Studies and Research Associate in the Media and Interaction Lab at West Virginia University. His research focuses on new media technologies and their influence on human interaction.

Raymond Boyle is a Professor of Communications at the Centre for Cultural Policy Research at the University of Glasgow. He has published widely on sport and the media and his latest book *The Television Entrepreneurs* (with Lisa Kelly) was published in 2012.

Kenon A. Brown (PhD, The University of Alabama) is an Assistant Professor of Public Relations at The University of Alabama. His research interests include sport image and reputation management and media coverage of trends and issues in sports.

Natalie A. Brown is a doctoral student at The University of Alabama. Her primary research interests involve crisis communication, sports communication and social media use.

Toni Bruce is an Associate Professor in the Faculty of Education, University of Auckland, New Zealand. Her research critically interrogates media representations, particularly the influence of dominant discourses of gender, race/ethnicity, disability and nationalism on the production and consumption of sports media texts.

Michael L. Butterworth is Director and Associate Professor in the School of Communication Studies at Ohio University. His research examines the relationships between rhetoric, democracy and sport, and he serves as the founding Executive Director of the International Association for Communication and Sport.

Austin Stair Calhoun is a doctoral candidate in the School of Kinesiology at the University of Minnesota and the director of the School's eLearning and Digital Strategy unit.

James L. Cherney (PhD, Indiana University) is an Assistant Professor in the Department of Communication at Wayne State University. His investigation of ableism in rhetoric and media appears in such journals as *Disability Studies Quarterly* and *Argumentation and Advocacy*. His work with Kurt Lindemann on disability, masculinity and sport is published in various articles and book chapters including those in *Western Journal of Communication* and *Examining Identity and Sport Media*.

Thomas F. Corrigan is an Assistant Professor in the Department of Communication Studies at California State University, San Bernardino. His research examines the intersections of Political Economy, Digital Media and Sports Media. His peer-reviewed work has been published in *The Political Economy of Communication, Journalism: Theory, Practice and Criticism, Cultural Studies Critical Methodologies, International Journal of Sport Communication,* and *Journal of Sports Media.*

Gregory A. Cranmer (MA, West Virginia University) is a doctoral student in Communication Studies at West Virginia University.

R. Glenn Cummins (PhD, University of Alabama) is Director of the Center for Communication Research in the College of Media and Communication at Texas Tech University. His research employs a variety of methods and measurement techniques to examine viewer response to structural and content properties of mediated sports as well as other entertainment genres.

Joshua Dickhaus (PhD, The University of Alabama) is an Assistant Professor of Sports Communication at Bradley University.

Stephen W. Dittmore, PhD, is an Associate Professor of Recreation and Sport Management at the University of Arkansas. His research interests are in social media, sport public relations and sport media rights. He previously worked 10 years in sport public relations in the Olympic movement.

Andrew Ellis (MA, Florida State University) is a doctoral student in Mass Communication at Florida State University. He is currently studying the function of stereoscopic 3D technology in various training applications.

Emilio Fernández Peña is Olympic Studies Centre (CEO-UAB) Director and Professor Titular at the Department of Audiovisual Communication and Advertise, Universitat Autònoma de Barcelona

Melanie Formentin is a fourth-year doctoral candidate at The Pennsylvania State University. With a professional and academic background in public relations, her primary areas of interest are corporate social responsibility and crisis communication, particularly in the professional sport context.

Walter Gantz is Professor and Chair of the Department of Telecommunications at Indiana University. He's particularly interested in how sports fans fit their passion into their daily lives.

Marie Hardin is professor of journalism and associate director of the John Curley Center for Sports Journalism at Penn State, USA. Her research concentrates on diversity, ethics and professionalism in mediated sports with a focus on gender. Her work is published in sport- and communications-focused journals.

Robin L. Hardin is an Associate Professor in the Department of Kinesiology, Recreation and Sport Studies at the University of Tennessee. His research interests are within the areas of sport communication and intercollegiate athletics focusing on consumer behavior, fandom and the holistic care of student-athletes.

Richard Haynes is Professor of Media, Communications and Culture and member of Stirling Media Research Institute at the University of Stirling. He has published widely on media sport including work on the history of sports broadcasting, sport and film, digital media sport, the media representation of sport and sport communication management.

Brett Hutchins is an Associate Professor in the School of Media, Film and Journalism at Monash University in Melbourne, Australia. His latest books include *Sport Beyond Television: The Internet, Digital Media and the Rise of the Networked Media Sport* (Routledge 2012, authored with David Rowe) and *Digital Media Sport: Technology, Power and Culture in the Network Society* (Routledge 2013, edited with David Rowe).

Jeffrey W. Kassing (Phd, Kent State University) is a Professor of Communication and the Director of the School of Social and Behavioral Sciences at Arizona State University. His work explores parents' behavior at youth sporting events, coach–athlete interaction and athletes' and fans' use of social media.

Edward (Ted) M. Kian is the Welch-Bridgewater Endowed Chair of Sports Media at Oklahoma State University. A former sport journalist, his research focuses on sport media, specifically examining areas such as portrayals of gender in print media articles, new media, attitudes and experiences of sport media personnel and marketing of sport to LGBT consumers.

Pamela C. Laucella is Academic Director of the National Sports Journalism Center at Indiana University School of Journalism – Indianapolis, IUPUI and is an Assistant Professor there too. Her research investigates socio-cultural-historical issues in sports media and specifically the intersections of race and gender.

Nicole M. LaVoi, PhD, is a senior lecturer in the School of Kinesiology at the University of Minnesota, where she is also the Associate Director of the Tucker Center for Research on Girls and Women in Sport.

Nicky Lewis is a doctoral candidate in the Department of Telecommunications at Indiana University. She's interested in media psychology as it applies to media consumption behavior.

Kurt Lindemann (PhD, Arizona State University) is an Associate Professor in the School of Communication at San Diego State University and an affiliated faculty member with the SDSU Center for the Study of Media and Performance. His work on disability, masculinity, media and narrative have appeared in the journals *Text and Performance Quarterly*, *Qualitative Inquiry and Western Journal of Communication*, among others, and various book chapters co-authored with James L. Cherney.

Pirkko Markula is a Professor of Socio-Cultural Studies of Physical Activity at the University of Alberta, Canada. Her research interests include poststructuralist analyses of media representations of dance, exercise and sport in addition to women's experiences of practices within physical activity industries.

Shannon T. McCarthy is a PhD student in Marketing in the Sam M. Walton College of Business at the University of Arkansas. She has research interests in sport branding, social media and relationship marketing.

Lindsey J. Meân (PhD University of Sheffield, UK) is an Associate Professor in the School of Social and Behavioral Sciences at Arizona State University. Her research examines the intersection of identities, discourses, ideology, language and representational practices with an emphasis on sport, gender, race and diversity.

Andy Miah is the Chair of Ethics and Emerging Technologies and Director of the Creative Futures Institute at the University of the West of Scotland. His research engages with the aesthetics, ethical, cultural and policy issues that arise from emerging technology.

Scott Morton (MA, University of Alabama) is a doctoral student in the College of Communication and Information Sciences.

Jed Novick is an author, journalist and Senior Lecturer on the BA (Hons) Sport Journalism course at the University of Brighton. He has written for *Sport and Society* and has worked on all the major newspapers in Britain in addition to writing and editing more than 12 books, including *The Cambridge Companion to Football* (co-editor and contributor). His next book, *Crossing The Line*, is a study on ethics and cheating in sport.

Paul M. Pedersen, PhD, is Professor of Sport Management and the Director of the Doctoral Program at Indiana University. Pedersen, who has published seven books (e.g. *Contemporary*

Sport Management, Routledge Handbook of Sport Communication, Strategic Sport Communication) and 80 articles in peer-reviewed outlets. He is the founding editor of the *International Journal of Sport Communication* and an editorial board member of 10 academic journals.

Lance V. Porter directs the Digital Media Initiative in the LSU Manship School of Mass Communication. He studies the effects of digital media on culture and creativity.

Natividad Ramajo is Olympic Studies Centre (CEO-UAB) Senior Researcher and Professor Titular at the Department of Audiovisual Communication and Advertise, Universitat Autònoma de Barcelona

Arthur A. Raney (PhD, University of Alabama) is the James E. Kirk Professor of Communication and Director of Doctoral Studies at Florida State University. He studies entertainment psychology, with particular interest in issues of media and morality.

Steve Redhead is Professor of Sports Media and Associate Dean Research, Faculty of Education at Charles Sturt University in New South Wales, Australia. He publishes in sport and journalism in popular culture and has published 15 books along with hundreds of book chapters and journal articles.

David Rowe is Professor of Cultural Research in the Institute for Culture and Society, University of Western Sydney, Australia. His recent books include *Global Media Sport: Flows, Forms and Futures* (Bloomsbury Academic, 2011) and *Sport, Public Broadcasting and Cultural Citizenship: Signal Lost?* (Routledge 2014, edited with Jay Scherer).

Brody J. Ruihley is an Assistant Professor of Sport Administration in the School of Human Services at the University of Cincinnati. His primary research interest revolves around fantasy sport motivation and consumption.

Jimmy Sanderson (PhD Arizona State University) is an Assistant Professor in the Department of Communication Studies at Clemson University. His research interests include the influence of social media technologies on sports media, sports organizations, identity and social/parasocial interaction and how health and safety issues in sports are discussed and framed in the media.

Brad Schultz is an Associate Professor of Journalism at the University of Mississippi. He specializes in sports media and has written five books on sports and broadcasting. Dr. Schultz focuses his research on the impact of new technologies on sports media, and is also an award-winning sports documentarian.

Mary Lou Sheffer is Associate Professor/and Head of the Broadcast/Multimedia Sequence at the University of Southern Mississippi. Her research area includes social media and journalism practices, sports media and media management. She has published in numerous journals such as *The Sports Journal, Journal of Sports Media, Journal of Communication Studies, Newspaper Research Journal, Electronic News, Journal of Computer Mediated Communication, The International Journal of Media Management and Berkshire Encyclopedia of World Sport*. Currently, she's the editor of the *Journal of Sports Media*.

Rob Steen is an author, sportswriter and senior lecturer on the BA (Hons) Sport Journalism course at the University of Brighton. He has written for Sport and Society and for major newspapers in Britain, Australia, India and South Africa since 1983 in addition to writing and editing more than 20 books, including *Sports Journalism: A Multimedia Primer* (Routledge; updated in 2014) and *The Cambridge Companion to Football* (co-editor and contributor). His next book, *Touchlines and Floodlights: A Brief History of Spectator Sport* (A&C Black) will be published in 2014.

John Vincent, PhD is a Professor and Coordinator of the Graduate Sport Management Program in the Kinesiology Department at The University of Alabama. His main research line focuses on how newspaper narratives portray elite athletes competing in major international sporting events, particularly in relation to their gender, race and national identity.

Brandi Watkins (PhD, The University of Alabama) is a Visiting Professor at The University of Alabama. Her research focuses on studying consumer-brand relationships and the use of social media to establish and maintain those relationships.

Erin A. Whiteside is an Assistant Professor in the School of Journalism and Electronic Media at the University of Tennessee. Her research focuses on organizational diversity, workplace routines and evolving industry practices in sports media professions.

Chris Wood is the President of JWA Associates, an advertising and public relations firm. His research interests include sport, public relations and fan identity.

ACKNOWLEDGEMENTS

Any book project requires the efforts of many people with different backgrounds, roles and postal codes. However, the *Routledge Handbook of Sport and New Media* required even more work in virtually all manners. The project encompassed 50 different authors across a half dozen nations. It required two years of planning and the good fortune to include many of the top scholars in sport media research. We feel incredibly fortunate to have had the opportunity to work on this project.

First and foremost, we must thank our Assistant Editor, Natalie Brown, whose expertise and organizational skills kept the entire project running smoothly. She answered hundreds of queries and navigated much of the clerical terrain and still managed to do so with a positive attitude and winning smile. We were immensely thankful to have her work on this project.

Second, we have to thank Routledge for its support of this project from beginning to end. Simon Whitmore and Joshua Wells were specifically very helpful in all aspects of this work, aiding us in everything from author suggestions to manuscript delivery guidelines. Routledge has established itself as a leader in publishing academic work in sport studies, and we hope this volume represents a worthy addition to that legacy.

Third, our contributors to this volume were terrific – not just with their insights, but also with their willingness to adapt to the various moving parts of the project all while staying on a finely hewn manuscript delivery deadline. With a topic such a new media, we were constantly pushing authors to think in the moment, as even works of just a few years ago often require a contemporized context. The terrain was ever shifting – even as our authors were finishing their drafts. They added and updated material without complaint.

Fourth, we wish to thank our institutions, the University of Alabama (specifically the College of Communication and Information Sciences) and Penn State University (specifically the College of Communications), for their support in this project. Having academic structures in place where one can agree to say "yes" to a project of this size and scope was an immense benefit, and one that we do not dismiss as standard in all university settings.

Finally, we must thank our family and friends for their support of our work even if they are not always sure what exactly that entails. It has been a great deal of fun working on this project together, and we loved that we each had the personal support system to make it happen, even when the hours became quite demanding.

Acknowledgements

In all, we leave this project with a great deal in which to be thankful. To everyone who touched this work over the course of the past two years, we hope the result makes you proud.

Andrew C. Billings and Marie Hardin
June 1, 2013

DEFINING UBIQUITY

Introduction to the *Routledge Handbook of Sport and New Media*

By definition, a Handbook covers a great deal of intellectual terrain. However, the *Routledge Handbook of Sport and New Media* canvasses not just a great deal of scholarship, but also – perhaps more importantly – attempts to provide academically sound bridges between past, present, and future conceptions of what sports media have been, are, and could or should be. When dealing with something as innovative and malleable as new media, providing such connections can be difficult; yet, within these pages lies a great deal of noteworthy advancement of the intellectual discussions surrounding sports media in the twenty-first century.

While the focus is obviously on new media, it is impossible to discuss new media inventions without discussing traditional media formats and standards. Indeed, one can tout increased web streams of games and online discussions of their outcomes, yet one must also acknowledge that this tends to be *in addition to* traditional media consumption rather than *instead of* it. Television consumption remains the top leisure activity of all age demographics, with the average person watching 4 hours and 39 minutes per day in 2012 (Stelter, 2012). Sports media, in particular, continue to dominate; 31 of the 32 top-rated programs on US television in the fall of 2012 were sports programs. Thus, this volume frequently employs words such as "integration" and "convergence" to most aptly describe the state of modern sports media: ubiquitious, significant, mobile, and increasingly simultaneously consumed through second (or more) screens.

It is also important to clarify what this Handbook does and does not do. We encouraged authors to deconstruct notions of "new media" into sub-classifications of formats that do similar things. Thus, a plentitude of important distinctions are made between social, mobile, user-generated, and beyond. We encouraged contributors to frequently discuss what applications and websites *do* more than relying on assumed knowledge about specific websites. Other than web behemoths like Facebook, Twitter, and YouTube – which seem to have left an indelible mark on modern culture regardless of their long-term prognosis for sustained growth and financial viability – we limited references to other forms of new media that may not exist a year from now, or may exist under a different name. The focus instead is on what new media allow people to do and consume, how the interaction between media, athlete, and fan is markedly changed, and the new conglomeration of partnerships and cross-promotions that could still be referred to as Wenner's (1998) *MediaSport*, but perhaps with a twist: MediaSport 2.0.

What this Handbook also does not seek to do is offer value judgments about various forms of new media, as those are inherently limiting, both in scope and in broad-based understanding

1

of the magnitude of what constitutes the sports media complex. Authors largely refrain from value judgments about whether something is good or bad, better or worse than its predecessor. Any time one attempts to say he or she loves/hates a given media format, the argument is overstatement at best; hopelessly myopic at worst. Traditional media formats such as television can provide incredible insight via comprehensive news investigation and unparalleled artistic programming or, conversely, can be shown as catering to the least common denominator, highlighting the decay of society in what is shown on screen. The same is true for new media inventions. Depending on one's stance, one can either classify Twitter as the great equalizer of modern democracy or the facilitator of snark, reducing complex arguments to 140 characters or less. YouTube can be positively regarded as an outlet for watching hard-to-find speeches, or merely as the mechanism for delivering debatably funny cat videos. Facebook can be positively viewed as the greatest web of social connection, reducing traditional notions of six degrees of separation to 4.74 (Markoff and Sengupta, 2011), or it can be regarded as a place where people post the mundane, pictures of meals they are about to consume. Regardless of the web-based format, one commonality pervades: these outlets are too expansive to be reduced to any one conception or classification.

The same tenets are true when discussing new media specifically within sport. The chapters featured in this book offer a great deal of nuance as they highlight what must predominantly be labeled as advancement in terms of the overall number of communication channels afforded to all participants in the media sport complex, even while one could ably argue for whether the increased channels raise or lower the discourse surrounding sport. While scholars in North America contribute the majority of the chapters, samplings from other continents such as Europe and Australia provide telling glimpses into the new media sports complex.

Rather than focusing on specific chapters or providing 31 mini-synopses of the work embedded within this volume, we instead want to ponder on what some of the macro-level messages are when taking the full Handbook as a composite. Such arguments offer more questions than answers, such as:

- Will traditional and new media soon be so blended as to make such divisions virtually obsolete?
- Are increased new media sport platforms offering more breadth (e.g. niche sports) or depth (e.g. offerings of minutiae within established mainstream sports)?
- How are sports organizations interacting with fans and other stakeholders in the sports media complex? How are fans responding?
- Does mobile media make first-person fandom (e.g. people in stadiums) more or less likely to occur?
- Which aspects of new media should be regarded as hard-wired linchpins to future sport consumption? Which ones are fads or, at the very least, cyclical in nature?
- If new media change the equation, is sport about to become even more central to the public lives of people who consume it?

Many additional questions could certainly be proffered, but the truth is that while sport and new media have existed for several decades, this burgeoning academic field is still in its relative infancy. Moreover, academicians must be cognizant of the latest trends, as new media and sport can change in an instant. The heuristic value of such work cannot be understated, and future work must begin from pre-established tenets surrounding the new media sports complex: MediaSport 2.0. To do that, one must survey the intellectual landscape. It is our sincere hope that such a survey is offered in the pages of the *Routledge Handbook of Sport and New Media.* Enjoy!

Andrew C. Billings, University of Alabama, Co-Editor
Marie Hardin, Penn State University, Co-Editor

References

Markoff, J. and Sengupta, S. (2011, Nov. 22). Separating you and me? 4.74 degrees. *New York Times*, p. B1.
Stelter, B. (2012, Feb. 9). Youth are watching, but less often on TV. *New York Times*, p. B1.
Wenner, L. A. (1998). *MediaSport.* New York: Routledge.

PART I

Foundations

1

GLOBALIZATION AND ONLINE AUDIENCES

David Rowe

UNIVERSITY OF WESTERN SYDNEY

Brett Hutchins

MONASH UNIVERSITY

Introduction: Going online, becoming global

The concept of globalization appears to fit perfectly with the phenomenon of the online audience. In reflecting on this seemingly natural affinity, we can first take a standard glossary definition of globalization as "a process through which space and time are compressed by technology, information flows, and trade and power relations, allowing distant actions to have increased significance at the local level" (Miller, Lawrence, McKay and Rowe, 2001: 131). Here the critical elements of flow and fluidity that are integral to any conception of globalization articulate smoothly with what we generally conceive as "being online," which involves connection to the Internet and the World Wide Web anywhere across the globe. Online audiences for sport and other mediated content would, therefore, seem to be perfectly suited to the globalization process in receiving and dispatching communication, free of hitherto awkward constraints of time, space and technology. Thus, for example, an online sport fan ought, at least technically, to be able to access any mediated sport text that they desire, and to interact freely via computer mediated communication with any fellow fan, irrespective of their physical-spatial location.

The use here of the conditional tense, though, signals the need for some caution in making such sweeping claims. The gap between what might be possible in the abstract, and actual material conditions, may be considerable in empirical terms. For example, the so-called "digital divide" (Norris, 2001) can be highlighted as demonstrating the extent to which the process of globalization is uneven and hierarchically ordered. As Curran (2011: 89) has noted:

> In the late 1990s, the richest fifth of the population had 86 per cent of the world's GDP [Gross Domestic Product], while the poorest fifth had just 1 per cent – an enormous disparity that has broadly persisted. This disparity is reproduced as a structure of access to the Internet, with the world's poor being largely excluded. Their voice is muted, and their participation limited, by poverty. This is illustrated by the fact that the entire continent of Africa hosted fewer websites than London in 2000.

Although the digital divide consists of a complex series of measures of access, capacity, use and so on, and there is considerable variation in its extent between and within world regions, a recent report by the International Telecommunication Union (2012) showed continuing considerable global disparities. The composite ICT Development Index (IDI) involving 11 indicators that it applied across countries revealed that, "European countries generally rank very high in the IDI, with a regional average of 6.49, which is clearly outstanding in international comparison," (p. 45) while "Africa remains the region with the lowest average IDI (1.88), less than half the global average (4.15)" (p. 48). Increasing variation in ICT development "in the Arab States, CIS [Commonwealth of Independent States] and Africa," it found, indicated "that regional differences are widening. This is a rather alarming trend, which suggests that the digital divide, both globally and regionally, is widening" (p. 48).

However, even if such structural inequalities impeding online access did not exist, theoretical and conceptual debates about globalization would not be rendered irrelevant. Notably, there are considerable differences about how the process of globalization, if it is accepted as valid at all, can be characterized. The "grand narrative" of an unstoppable wave that annihilates temporal and spatial barriers is interrupted by many less conclusive accounts of change, continuity, adaptation, resistance and uncertainty. For example, George Ritzer (2011: 2, original emphasis) advances a definition of globalization that resists some of the blander summations of the process, seeing it as:

> ...a transplanetary process or set of processes involving increasing *liquidity* and the growing multi-directional *flows* of people, objects, places and information as well as the *structures* they encounter and create that are *barriers* to, or *expedite*, those flows.
>
> In contrast to many other definitions of globalization, this one does *not* assume that greater integration is an inevitable component of globalization. That is, globalization can bring with it greater integration (especially when things flow easily), but it can also serve to reduce the level of integration (when structures are erected that successfully block flows).

This is not the place to examine competing theories and conceptualizations of globalization in great detail, but it is clear that there are considerable differences over the nature and extent of globalization, including the degree to which the nation state retains its potency (Hirst and Thompson, 2009); the relationship between global power, nations and cosmopolitanism (Beck, 2005); its positioning among other complex processes (Urry, 2003) and, indeed, the validity of the concept itself (see various contributions to Held and McGrew, 2007a). These differences, at their starkest, produce utopian and dystopian analyses (Rowe, 2006), with the former emphasizing the process of globalization as an advance for humanity in promoting universalism, trade, movement, and communication. At the same time, it can be seen from this perspective to have a positive effect in eroding a narrow introversion and even ignorance that obstructs human progress by compulsively erecting material and symbolic borders between people based, in particular, on nation states (Ohmae, 1995). By contrast, the dystopian view sees globalization as a homogenizing force that undermines socio-cultural difference and nation-based self-determination in ways that weaken resistance to supranational capitalist exploitation and political domination, and further empowers elites (Starr, 2005). Between these polar positions can be found more mixed analytical appraisals of globalization (Held and McGrew, 2007b) that qualify both the totalizing nature of the process and its actual implications in material environments as opposed to abstract models.

The institution of sport, alongside the audiences attached to it in various ways, is very well suited to exploring these questions of globalization and online constituencies. Sport is both practiced and followed in specific spatial-temporal contexts (such as the "live" event at the stadium), and yet what happens within that limited space and time can be experienced and monitored in very different contexts. Thus, for example, only 80,000 people could have watched Usain Bolt win the men's 100 meters athletics final "live" at the Olympic Stadium in Stratford, in the east of London in the UK, during the 2012 Summer Games. Yet, for those unable to "be there," the race could be viewed in an array of viewing environments (sometimes in high definition and in 3D) – for example, at a "live site" elsewhere in London or in any other public space across the globe with a satellite link; in a hall, pub, cinema or some other public or commercial building, or via television broadcast or otherwise conveyed into the private space of the home. By means of these media arrangements, the "live" audience can be measured in billions rather than thousands. However, it is not only audiences and their spatial locations that have proliferated. Broadcast television is now supplemented by an array of other platforms, including Internet-enabled television sets, mobile (also known as cell) phones, tablets, game consoles, desktop, laptop and notebook computers. This impressive mediated "live" audience, although it is large and aspires to be "global" in terms of reach and simultaneity, is only one manifestation of audiences in the global "media sports cultural complex" (Rowe, 2004, 2011). Despite the "accelerated culture" that can be said now to be integral to the contemporary world (and which Steve Redhead, 2007, relates to sport "on behalf" of the theorist of speed, Paul Virilio), media sport audiences do not form and disappear in the less than ten seconds that it takes sprinters such as Bolt to run 100 meters.

Sport audiences have never been constituted only around the time of the live event. Indeed, before the advent of radio and television broadcasting, they were largely reliant on the print media to provide information about sportspeople, clubs and other fans, and to preview, report on and discuss sport contests and their implications in ways that could not overlap with those contests as they happened in real time. In contrast, broadcasting was able to intensify the focus on sport events as they occurred, but did so in ways that would facilitate even more media coverage through highlight programs, replays, panels, quiz shows and so on. Furthermore, sport fans have never been wholly reliant on the professional media to communicate with others beyond their own neighborhoods – the rudimentary newsletters of sport fan clubs, and the small-circulation, amateur "fanzines" (Haynes, 1995) that were printed, sold and circulated among fellow fans as a "labor of love," are examples of sport audiences also becoming minor producers of media sport texts in the pre-digital era. Fanzines, which were especially popular in British association football in the 1980s and 1990s, could take the form of "garage-style" fan publications devoted to their favorite teams, like Manchester United's *United We Stand*, or more sophisticated and widely distributed works, often with contributions from "moonlighting" professional sports journalists, such as *When Saturday Comes*. The crucial change is that new media technologies – or what we prefer to call the emergence of "networked media sport" (Hutchins and Rowe, 2012) – has created a dense, rich media environment in which sport can be viewed, discussed and, in some cases, organized among online sport constituencies in ways that challenge the traditional distinction between audience and participant. One of the characteristics of this networked media sport *milieu* is that, while place and space are still important aspects of the experience of sport, the globalization of the sport industry and of new information, communication and media technologies has created many more opportunities both to "attend" to sport in traditional terms and to intervene in its discourses and modes of organization. As a consequence, what is commonly regarded as the audience acquires new properties and possibilities.

Media sport audiences in transition

The media audience has been the subject of intense academic debate for many decades, with initial concerns about audience manipulation by media challenged by those who have emphasized that audiences are active rather than passive (Ruddock, 2001). With the rise of "new" or "social media," the concept of the audience itself has been thrown into question, with the capacity of individuals to communicate via blogging, Twitter, Facebook and other forms of "chat" suggesting for some that the institutional media are now outmoded in their capacity to create, maintain and influence audiences. As Virginia Nightingale (2011: 2) has noted in her introduction to the compendious *Handbook of Media Audiences*:

> ...some new media commentators argue that because people can now broadcast themselves online, the need for audience research is at an end. This view is based on a narrow understanding of broadcast media audiences as passive recipients of broadcast messages, and it overlooks the emphasis on the "active audience" that has been so influential in audience studies for the last quarter of a century and more.
>
> Still, many media scholars today do feel impatient and more than a little bored with the term *audience*, and by implication with audience research. There is a sense that the term is inadequate to explain the sorts of things people do with media now that social media and web 2.0 have transformed the media landscape.

It is ironic that, with media and telecommunications corporations continuing to expend vast sums on acquiring the rights to premium sport in the quest for large audiences for exposure to advertising and/or paying subscribers (Rowe, 2011), some media scholars should have become "bored" with the idea of the audience. In 2012, the US media corporation NBC (owned by Comcast) successfully bid US$4.38 billion for US media rights to the four Olympic Games between 2014 and 2020, having spent US$5.55 billion on the seven previous Games of the twenty-first century (*Huffington Post*, 2012). Unlike "some media scholars," media companies like NBC, Fox, CBS and ABC, and even public service media corporations like the UK's BBC and Canada's CBC, are not indifferent to the size and composition of audiences. Sport is becoming increasingly important as a TV program genre that is far healthier than most others at a time of falling aggregate viewer ratings. As Gregory (2010) has noted in the US context:

> It's no secret that with an array of cable channels, video games and the Internet competing for viewers' attention, the audiences for network television are eroding. These days, even the biggest hits are suffering: average viewership for the Wednesday-night broadcast of Fox's *American Idol*, for instance, was down 14% from last season. The audience for *CSI*, on CBS, dropped nearly 19% from 2009 to 2010; the Tuesday-night broadcasts of ABC's *Dancing with the Stars* fell 9.2%, according to Nielsen data.
>
> But amid these sagging performances, television appears to be experiencing a resurgence in a surprising place: sports programming. Of the 13 television programs that drew more than 30 million viewers over the past year, 11, or 85%, were sports-related, according to a new research report from Horizon Media, a media buying and planning agency. The only non-sports-related shows were the Oscars and the first episode of the CBS reality show *Undercover Boss* – which debuted immediately following the network's broadcast of the Super Bowl.

Given the popularity of sport as a key form of "appointment television," it is unsurprising that the media sport industry consensus is that "sports media rights are rich and getting richer, and profitable to the networks paying the money, thanks to huge consumer demand and the DVR [Digital Video Recorder]-proof nature of live sports programming" (Van Riper, 2012). Instead, media and telecommunications corporations are purchasing comprehensive sports rights, including online and mobile, in order to find and form audiences anywhere among the technologies that they possess and the spaces that they inhabit.

Media sport audiences are heterogeneous – that is, they consist of people with very different relationships to the sport that is being represented to them (Solberg and Hammervold, 2008; Whannel, 1992). Aggregate audiences range from *aficionados* who are deeply interested in some sports (or are devoted to sport in general) to those who intermittently or "accidentally" encounter sport texts, and may be attracted by tangential aspects of sport, such as the dramatic presentation of the Olympic Opening Ceremony, the half-time music shows at the Super Bowl, celebrities spotted in sports crowds, or the human interest "back stories" of particular teams and athletes. Media companies that pay for rights attempt in some way to cater to all potential audience fractions depending on the platform. For example, specialist subscription sport channels address the *aficionado* and assume advanced sporting knowledge and interest, while free-to-air programming of major events is more oriented towards audience maximization and so capturing the casual, often uninitiated viewer. Even the latter audience, though, is not generally addressed in global terms – the worldwide Olympics audience, for example, is in fact split into national and regional broadcasters, each of which addresses an audience in cultural and linguistic terms and seeks to "connect" with them via a common – though by no means "watertight" – identity. Emphasizing this point, major events featuring national teams generated the largest sports television audiences in the European markets of Denmark, France, Germany, Italy and Norway during 2011 (Sport Business Intelligence, 2012), while the men's ice hockey final between Canada and the US at the 2010 Winter Olympics was the most watched broadcast in Canadian history (Hutchins and Rowe, 2012: 123).

The ongoing cultural potency of the nation demonstrates that the "global audience" for mega sports events is mythological, as it is global only in the abstract (as noted above, meaning notionally available to anyone with the necessary technology and resources) while, in fact, being "decomposed" by interpellating (that is, "calling out") audience members in terms of their assumed identities. Indeed, because sport is an inherently competitive activity, existing and potential audiences are almost compulsively divided into rival "camps" supporting and opposing teams, sport clubs and athletes, and drawing on national, regional, local, class cultural, racial/ethnic, historical and other factors that have a bearing on identity and subjectivity. This has always been the case regarding, for example, sports television, but, as we have seen, this medium's signals – and so audiences – have usually been organized around national jurisdictions.

Non-broadcast digital technologies, on the other hand, are more widely accessible to global audiences, even if media companies "speak" largely to their national audiences (including those diasporas located far from the "home" country). Therefore, in discussing the "global" in relation to media sport audiences, the term might be used in a more restricted sense to refer to platforms and reception modes. Thus, NBC, in discussing its 2012 London Olympics coverage, also highlighted the many media platforms with which it engaged:

> The London 2012 Olympic Games not only generated record television viewership (219.4 million viewers) and digital traffic (nearly two billion page views and 159.3 million video streams), but also unprecedented social media chatter, making them the

most social Games ever for NBC Olympics. According to social media research company Bluefin Labs, NBC Olympics' coverage of the Games were more social than the 2012 Super Bowl, the 2012 Grammys, 2012 Oscars, 2012 Golden Globes and all seven games of the 2011 World Series combined [the measure of how "social" an event is corresponds with the number of Facebook comments and Tweets posted during its television coverage]. Bluefin also concluded that 99% of all social TV buzz between the hours of 7 p.m. through midnight was attributable to NBC Olympics' primetime coverage of the Games.

NBC Olympics partnered with Facebook, Twitter, YouTube and Shazam [a mobile music identification service that, among other functions, can identify music played as part of a television broadcast] to promote its coverage of the Games onto these popular social media platforms. It also populated Google+, Instagram [a photosharing and social networking service], Tumblr [a blogging and social networking service], and GetGlue [a television-focused social networking service] with Olympic content. These social media partnerships and efforts allowed NBC Olympics to communicate directly with fans of the Olympics and celebrate the Games with viewers in new and unique ways.

'Actively joining the social conversation through our partnerships with these platforms, as well as calling out Olympic social trends and highlights in our linear television coverage, aided us in reassembling the ever fragmenting media audience, most notably among that elusive younger demographic,' said Gary Zenkel, President, NBC Olympics. 'Going into the Games, our social media goal was to be the life of the big Olympic viewing parties thrown by Facebook and Twitter over the 17 days of the Games…it appears we succeeded.'

(*NBC Sports Group Press Box*, 2012)

There is a further irony evident here in that that the purchasers of sports broadcasting rights were initially concerned that new/social media would splinter audience attention and so reduce the size of the "audited" audiences on which they rely. However, it was subsequently appreciated that conversations between people using social media could actually draw them to an "appointment" with the live, televised sport event being displayed on the biggest screen in the house – still usually the conventional television set connected via microwave, satellite and cable (Schechner and Ovide, 2010). Indeed, this pattern of viewing and interaction has seen Twitter referred to as a "next generation broadcasting platform" because of the way that it organizes information and audiences around major events (Bohn, 2012).

Despite the apparent openness of its communication with audiences, NBC only permitted its cable and satellite subscribers to watch its live Olympics online streaming (apart from the Opening and Closing Ceremonies), and delayed its most in-demand free-to-air broadcast coverage in order to maximize advertising revenue (Baker and Adegoke, 2012). Resentment at this communicative control, and other complaints about the quality of NBC's coverage, including its overly nationalistic commentary and coverage, led to extensive online criticism of the company via the #NBCfail Twitter hashtag. These critical tweets have continued to be posted long after the Olympic Games finished, addressing both the London Paralympics and a range of other non-sporting topics concerning NBC, such as its 2012 US presidential campaign coverage (thus, #NBCfail now functions as a more general online space for ongoing criticism of NBC). The encouragement of engagement with social media such as Twitter by broadcasters such as NBC brings with it a degree of reputational risk and greater opportunity for rapidly circulating, often vitriolic criticism of the network. However, the calculation is that social media traffic, whether positive or negative, will direct and draw viewers to its TV program content, and so be counted within the audience ratings surveys that generate a substantial component of NBC's income.

The Twitter–NBC connection also produced its own "media scandal," following the temporary suspension of the account of a journalist who had tweeted his dissatisfaction with NBC's handling of the Olympics, and following a complaint from NBC that he had breached Twitter's privacy policy concerning one of its executives:

> Twitter has brought down a hail of critical tweeting on its own head by suspending the account of a British newspaper's Los Angeles correspondent following his acerbic reporting of NBC's coverage of the Olympics.
>
> The social media network hummed with the indignation of thousands of its users after the Twitter feed of Guy Adams of the Independent disappeared.
>
> *(Pilkington, 2012)*

Here it can be seen that, having harnessed social media to enhance its overall audience engagement, NBC has found those same media used against it by disgruntled members of that online/mobile audience. At the same time, global media technologies enable some audience members to circumvent NBC's proprietorial control over sport content, the rights to which it had purchased from the International Olympic Committee (IOC), by accessing coverage provided by other media companies free of charge (through tapping into the live feeds from other countries, such as that produced in the UK by the BBC (Baker and Adegoke, 2012), or through various "pirate" Web services). Such infringements of intellectual property rights may in some circumstances be illegal, but they are difficult to prevent given the existence of virtual private networks (VPNs) that redirect Internet traffic beyond the territories over which the rights holder has control. This aspect of global media convergence – the bringing together of previously separate broadcast, computing and telecommunications technologies – highlights the contest for control over nationally delimited and globally unlimited media sport audiences.

Thus, while NBC was "partnering" with "Facebook, Twitter, YouTube and Shazam to promote its coverage of the Games onto these popular social media platforms," the search engine Google was receiving information from NBC and many other sources in providing customized national medal counts and "updates, news and photos from the Olympic Games on Google+," and also providing trending topics by monitoring its search traffic (Google, 2012). While television and online audiences are likely to remain nationally oriented in most cases, a sport media landscape is emerging that is a far cry from its dominant form of only a decade ago, when live TV sport was delivered by tightly controlled broadcast channels, and sport fans could only communicate with each other on the sidelines.

Expansion and containment

The supplementation of nationally delimited print and electronic sport media by online "global" technologies has created many new sport audience forms and arrangements, with sundry sports entities able to bypass or harness the usual media outlets by setting up elaborate websites (sometimes multi-lingual) containing substantial information and both moving and still images. Various organizations can communicate with – and so develop – audiences across the globe: for example, (1) the governing bodies of the Olympics (IOC and local organizing committees) and association football (Fédération Internationale de Football Association [FIFA]); (2) leading sport clubs like Manchester United, Real Madrid, Los Angeles Lakers, New

York Yankees, and Dallas Cowboys; and (3) associations and leagues such as the English Premier League (EPL), the National Basketball Association (NBA), Australian Football League (AFL) and the Indian Premier League (IPL). Global access to sport websites means that fans can be catered to irrespective of their embodied location, while stimulating enthusiasm for sports, clubs and athletes when they physically travel to where new fans can be found. Thus, for example, both the EPL and NBA, in leaving their "respective" home bases in the UK and USA on "goodwill tours" to establish and reinforce followings in the fastest growing region of world sport, the Asia-Pacific, engage in integrated multimedia promotion and marketing campaigns involving the branded merchandising that is highly visible on their websites (Rowe, 2011).

At present, the containment of live media sport via the sale of intellectual property rights means that these sport websites cannot ordinarily compete with the media companies with which they have exclusive contracts, meaning that their own television services tend to be limited to interviews with players and coaches, studio discussions, highlights and archive material, "candid" coverage of dressing rooms and club facilities, and so on. However, it is possible that sports entities will produce their own live coverage and sell it themselves across multiple media platforms, although in order to maximize monetization this would require the exertion of their own content control via closed subscription for premium sport material (that is, the live event). Thus, as was demonstrated in the case of NBC and its online sport provision, there is no necessary relationship between non-broadcast delivery of live sport and "free" access for audiences. Nonetheless, in an area of mediated discourse that is not dependent on commodified sport action, sport audiences can evade the constraints of both media companies and sports organizations through more direct communication with athletes. Here, by means of blogging, micro-blogging and other social media regimes including video- and podcasting, sport fans can receive and respond to messages from sportspeople without intervention by external bodies (Hutchins, 2011; Hutchins and Mikosza, 2010). Once again, the "global" reach of online communication comes into play under such circumstances – for example, a Japan-based fan of a Japanese baseballer playing Major League Baseball (MLB) in the United States can follow them on Twitter. Such an arrangement gives an impression of being "closer" to the athlete, bringing with it a sense of conversational intimacy that is quite different from, say, a televised or radio broadcast live interview with a media professional. In such a case, online technologies can produce a paradoxical sense of proximity for audiences apparently honoring globalization's promise to override constraints of space and time.

Unsurprisingly, though, the institutional order of sport and media, which is characterized by increasing image and information control, is not altogether comfortable with this development. Professional sportspeople have been "disciplined" in their dealings with the media – and so their communication with most sport fans – by formulaic media training and the "rationing" of their interactions with sports journalists in order to avoid difficult questions and controversies, to ensure that only official sponsors' messages and logos are featured, and so on (Boyle, Rowe and Whannel, 2010). Because it would be draconian for sports organizations to deny athletes use of these widely available technologies of communication, they have sought to control content by setting out regulations that they are expected to follow. Thus, for example, among the IOC's four-page "Social Media, Blogging and Internet Guidelines for participants and other accredited persons at the London 2012 Olympic Games" is the following injunction:

2. Postings, Blogs and Tweets

The IOC encourages participants and other accredited persons to post comments on social media platforms or websites and tweet during the Olympic Games, and it is entirely acceptable for a participant or any other accredited person to do a personal posting, blog or tweet. However, any such postings, blogs or tweets must be in a first-person, diary-type format and should not be in the role of a journalist - i.e. they must not report on competition or comment on the activities of other participants or accredited persons, or disclose any information which is confidential or private in relation to any other person or organisation. A tweet is regarded in this respect as a short blog and the same guidelines are in effect, again, in first-person, diary-type format.

Postings, blogs and tweets should at all times conform to the Olympic spirit and fundamental principles of Olympism as contained in the Olympic Charter, be dignified and in good taste, and not contain vulgar or obscene words or images.

(IOC, 2011: 1)

This is no mere statement of the IOC's preferred form and quality of online communication by "participants and other accredited persons" at the 2012 Games. The Guidelines, which also cover photography, video and audio, use of the Olympic Symbol (the five rings), and unauthorized advertising and sponsorship of "any brand, product or service within a posting", also contain significant penalties for their infraction. In addition, there are constraints and sanctions that might be imposed by National Olympic Committees (NOCs):

13. Infringements

The accreditations of any organisation or person accredited at the Olympic Games may be withdrawn without notice, at the discretion of the IOC, for purposes of ensuring compliance with these Guidelines. The IOC reserves all its right to take any other appropriate measures with respect to infringements of these Guidelines, including issuing a Take Down Notice, taking legal action for damages, and imposing other sanctions. Participants and other accredited persons may also be subject to additional guidelines and sanctions in respect of social media, blogging and the internet, from their relevant NOC.

(IOC, 2011: 1)

These highly prescriptive and punitive interventions in communications between athletes and their online audiences provoked complaints by, for example, US runner Nick Symmonds that it was "ludicrous" and "stupid" to "handicap a form of media that only increases exposure for your event." His teammate Ricky Berens contrasted the direct nature of athlete-initiated communication with audiences with the filtered approach of television, observing that "Twitter and social media are how we can get our word out, and fans kind of want to see what things look like from behind the scenes. TV portrays things the way it wants to, and we can give a lot more that [sic] that" (quoted in Laird, 2012).

Such frustrations among athletes with the highly structured and "processed" nature of communication with audiences are often couched in terms of an "authentic," unmediated connection. However, their social media messages may be as carefully crafted for commercial advantage as those of the institutional media. For example, in 2012 the UK's Advertising Standards Authority upheld a complaint that footballers Wayne Rooney and Jack Wilshere had tweeted messages referring to Nike's "Make It Count" campaign that failed to identify them as a marketing communication (Dresden, 2012). The harnessing of apparently spontaneous utterances of sportspeople to the campaigns of global brands indicates another stage in the development of sport audiences. However, the same media that have been used by sport and media organizations to exploit the passions of sport fans have also been used by fan groups to organize their own resistance, which has included campaigning on issues ranging from improving stadium facilities to incorporating fans in the ownership and running of sport clubs (Rowe, 2011, Chapter 4). The most audacious (though small and faltering) case so far is that of MyFootballClub, which was established in 2007 as "the world's first Internet community to buy and takeover a real-world-football club" (MyFootballClub, 2012, n.p.). Although this experiment in fan ownership of an English football club, with members across the world voting on organizational matters ranging from player budgets to playing strips (the original intention to "own the club and pick the team" did not eventuate), has not been a striking success, it has at least revealed the possibilities of online "crowdsourcing" (Hutchins and Rowe, 2012, Chapter 5), which can take advantage of networked media to enable a much deeper involvement in sport by its fans. By such means, spatially concentrated audiences can be transformed into globally dispersed "activists," with significant consequences for the cultural politics of sport.

Conclusion: Audiences of the future

It is clear from the developments in mediated sport and its relationship to online audiences and globalizing processes that nothing stays still for very long and that, in fact, the extent and pace of change is accelerating. The next frontier for investigation is the growth of mobile media audiences, reflecting the popularity of 3G and 4G smart phones and tablet computers in developed economies. Signifying the rising power of telecommunications carriers across the globe and multinational technology monoliths such as Google and Apple, these devices alter the organization of audiences in time and space, introducing the idea of the "always on" audience that accesses and uses media in more places than ever before and with far fewer temporal and spatial limitations (Goggin, 2011: 130). Audience members are positioned as both consumers of content and the users of mobile social software in a manner that reshapes media in sometimes surprising ways. It was noted in a corporate blog, for example, that AT&T customers at the 2012 NFL Super Bowl uploaded nearly 40% more data than they downloaded, with video content and photographs heavily featured (Goggin, 2013: 33). In this case, the active user is also the energetic producer of content for "personalized audiences" of variable scale on Twitter, Facebook and Flickr. Such activities are indicative of new forms of media practice, time- and place-shifting enabled by mobile devices (Hutchins, 2012). Audiences are reconfigured in highly localized formations in stadiums during sports events, as well as nationally and globally when using tablets and smart phones to follow major events such as the Super Bowl and the Olympics. Over the course of the 2012 London Games, for instance, the BBC received 12 million requests for video served to mobile phones and tablets, and 9.2 million browsers for their mobile website and Olympics app – a huge increase when compared to the 2008 Beijing Games (O'Riordan, 2012).

At each major communication industry convention, new ways of finding and accommodating global online audiences – while still preserving "linear" television – are being devised. These include the use of screen apps, with tablets orchestrating communication and media use and interaction in ways that can create multimedia events in which live sport has an obvious, prominent place (Graham, 2012). The more digitally networked and online these arrangements become, the more global the potential audience or user constituency. Global, though, does not necessarily mean large, so for every mega media global sport event there will be many more small networks of dispersed *aficionados* exchanging information, images and ideas unhindered by media schedules and planetary location. The sport media industry and scholars of media sport are still struggling to grasp the implications of this transformation in what we mean by a global sport audience, and how – if ever – it can be stabilized for long enough to understand.

References

Baker, L. B. and Adegoke, Y. (2012, July 31) Olympics fans find ways to circumvent NBC's online control. *Yahoo!News*. Retrieved September 24, 2012, from http://news.yahoo.com/olympics-fans-ways-circumvent-nbcs-online-control-010417267 – oly.html

Beck, U. (2005) *Power in the Global Age: A New Global Political Economy*. Cambridge: Polity.

Bohn, D. (2012, January 31) Twitter CEO Dick Costolo navigates its next stage: A broadcasting (social) network. *The Verge*. Retrieved from http://www.theverge.com/2012/1/31/2760338/twitter-ceo-dick-costolo-broadcasting-social-network

Boyle, R., Rowe, D. and Whannel, G. (2010) "Delight in trivial controversy?" Questions for sports journalism. In S. Allan (ed.), *Routledge Companion to News and Journalism Studies* (pp. 245–255). London: Routledge.

Curran, J. (2011) *Media and Democracy*. London: Routledge.

Dresden, M. (2012, July 4) Advertising in social media: Wayne Rooney, Jack Wilshere and the ASA. *The Guardian Media Network*. Retrieved from http://www.guardian.co.uk/media-network/media-network-blog/2012/jul/04/advertising-social-media-asa-nike

Goggin, G. (2011) Going mobile. In V. Nightingale (ed.), *Handbook of Media Audiences* (pp. 128–146). Oxford: Wiley-Blackwell.

Goggin, G. (2013) Sport and the rise of mobile media. In B. Hutchins and D. Rowe (eds), *Digital media sport: Technology and Power in the Network Society* (pp. 19–36). New York: Routledge.

Google. (2012) *London 2012 Olympic Games*. Retrieved from https://www.google.ca/campaigns/olympics/

Graham, F. (2012, October 1) Television finds salvation in the zombie apocalypse. *BBC News Business*. Retrieved from http://www.bbc.co.uk/news/business-19790348

Gregory, S. (2010) Why sports ratings are surging on TV. *Time Business and Money*. Retrieved from http://www.time.com/time/business/article/0,8599,2010746,00.html.

Haynes, R. (1995) *The Football Imagination: The Rise of Football Fanzine Culture*. Aldershot: Arena.

Held, D. and McGrew, A. (eds) (2007a) *Globalization Theory: Approaches and Controversies*. Cambridge: Polity.

Held, D. and McGrew, A. (2007b) *Globalization/Anti-Globalization: Beyond the Great Divide*. Cambridge: Polity.

Hirst, P. Q. and Thompson, G. (2009) *Globalization in Question: The International Economy and the Possibilities of Governance* (revised 3rd edn.). Cambridge: Polity.

Huffington Post (2012, August, 10) What NBC paid for US Olympic rights over the years. Huffington Post. Retrieved from http://www.huffingtonpost.com/2012/08/01/nbc-paid-us-olympics-rights_n_1729726.html

Hutchins, B. (2011) The acceleration of media sport culture: Twitter, telepresence and online messaging. *Information, Communication and Society*, 14(2), 237–257.

Hutchins, B. (2012) Sport on the move: The unfolding impact of mobile communications on the media sport content economy. *Journal of Sport and Social Issues*. Advance online publication. doi:10.1177/0193723512458933

Hutchins, B. and Mikosza, J. (2010) The web 2.0 Olympics: Athlete blogging, social networking and policy contradictions at the 2008 Beijing Games. *Convergence*, 16(3), 279–297.

Hutchins, B. and Rowe, D. (2012) *Sport Beyond Television: The Internet, Digital Media and the Rise of Networked Media Sport*. New York: Routledge.

International Olympic Committee (IOC) (2011, August 31) Social media, blogging and internet guidelines for participants and other accredited persons at the London 2012 Olympic Games. Retrieved from http://www.olympic.org/Documents/Games_London_2012/IOC_Social_Media_Blogging_and_Internet_Guidelines-London.pdf

International Telecommunication Union. (2012) *Measuring the Information Society 2012*. Geneva, Switzerland: International Telecommunication Union.

Laird, S. (2012, July 17) Some Olympians chafe at IOC's social media rules. *Mashable Entertainment*. Retrieved from http://mashable.com/2012/07/17/olympics-social-media-rules/

Miller, T., Lawrence, G., McKay, J. and Rowe, D. (2001) *Globalization and Sport: Playing the World*. London: Sage.

MyFootballClub (MFC) (2012) Retrieved from http://www.myfootballclub.co.uk/

NBC Sports Group Press Box. (2012, August 14) NBC Olympics media partnerships contribute to record viewership and digital traffic. Retrieved from http://nbcsportsgrouppressbox.com/2012/08/15/nbc-olympics-social-media-partnerships-contribute-to-record-viewership-digital-traffic/

Nightingale, V. (2011) Introduction. In V. Nightingale (ed.), *Handbook of Media Audiences* (pp. 1–15). Oxford: Wiley-Blackwell.

Norris, P. (2001) *Digital Divide: Civic Engagement, Information Poverty and the Internet World-Wide*. Cambridge: Cambridge University Press.

Ohmae, K. (1995) *The End of the Nation-State: The Rise of Regional Economies*. New York: Free Press.

O'Riordan, C. (2012 August 13) The story of the digital Olympics: Streams, browsers, most watched, four screens. *BBC Internet Blog*. http://www.bbc.co.uk/blogs/bbcinternet/2012/08/digital_olympics_reach_stream_stats.html

Pilkington, E. (2012, July 30) Twitter suspends British journalist critical of NBC's Olympics coverage. *The Guardian*. Retrieved from http://www.guardian.co.uk/technology/2012/jul/30/twitter-suspends-guy-adams-account-nbc

Redhead, S. (2007) Those absent from the stadium are always right: Accelerated culture, sport media, and theory at the speed of light. *Journal of Sport and Social Issues*, 31(3), 226–241.

Ritzer, G. (2011) *Globalization: The essentials*. Malden, MA: Wiley-Blackwell.

Rowe, D. (2004) *Sport, Culture and the Media: The Unruly Trinity* (2nd edn.). Maidenhead: Open University Press.

Rowe, D. (2006) Coming to terms with leisure and globalization. *Leisure Studies*, 25(4), 423–436.

Rowe, D. (2011) *Global Media Sport: Flows, Forms and Futures*. London: Bloomsbury Academic.

Ruddock, A. (2001) *Understanding Audiences*. London: Sage.

Schechner, S. and Ovide, S. (2010, February 7) Record draw for Super Bowl: An audience of 106.5 million bucks trend of declining viewership for networks. *The Wall Street Journal: Media and Marketing*. Retrieved from http://online.wsj.com/article/SB10001424052748703615904575053300315837616.html

Solberg, H. A. and Hammervold, R. (2008) TV sports viewers – who are they? A Norwegian case study. *Nordicom Review*, 29(1), 95–110.

Sport Business Intelligence. (2012) National heroics attract top audiences across Europe in 2011. *Sport Business International*, 176 (March), 5.

Starr, A. (2005) *Global Revolt: A Guide to the Movements Against Globalization*. London: Zed Books.

Urry, J. (2003) *Global Complexity*. Cambridge: Polity.

Van Riper, T. (2012, February, 3) Sports media rights keep rolling – for now. *Forbes*. Retrieved from http://www.forbes.com/sites/tomvanriper/2012/03/02/sports-media-rights-keep-rolling-for-now/

Whannel, G. (1992) *Fields in Vision: Television Sport and Cultural Transformation*. London: Routledge.

2

FANSHIP DIFFERENCES BETWEEN TRADITIONAL AND NEWER MEDIA

Walter Gantz and Nicky Lewis

INDIANA UNIVERSITY

For those who love to follow sports, this is a great time to be a sports fan. Thanks to advances in technology, lucrative transmission rights contracts and a responsive fan base, sports are available 24/7 throughout the year on an ever-expanding number of platforms. Sports fans can and do follow the action across platforms, their use driven by love of sport rather than loyalty to outlet. When a fan's favorite team is battling for the World Cup or vying for a Super Bowl victory, he or she will seek out media content wherever it is available. Yet, in both obvious and subtle ways, platforms matter and can shape the nature of the reception experience. In this chapter, we will examine sports fan use of traditional and newer media platforms and how these platforms influence uses and responses to mediated sports content. Traditional media platforms include broadcast, cable, and satellite television and radio, as well as hard-copy based newspapers and magazines. Newer media platforms include computers, mobile based technologies and the Internet. Sports content extends beyond games and matches and includes pre- and post-game shows, sports journalism (e.g. ESPN's *SportsCenter*), as well as outlets for sports statistics and fan commentary.

Platform use is both complementary and competitive. In at least four ways, it is complementary. First, consumption of sports media is not a zero sum game: Fans spend more time following sports than they did before and now follow sports using multiple platforms simultaneously (Gregory, 2010). Fans are encouraged to do that when sportscasters urge viewers to check the network's website, Tweet, or turn to the network's Facebook page for information while they continue to watch the game. From the network's perspective, this keeps viewers involved and more likely to stay with the contest, even if the match-up or action on the field is not particularly exciting. Second, sports content varies across platforms in non-competitive ways. Fantasy sports fans, for example, watch NFL games on TV yet turn to online sites for player statistics that TV play-by-play announcers do not have time to provide. Third, mobile technology platforms permit fans to follow games when they are not at home, at a sports bar, or near an available TV. At the same time, these platforms provide additional "eyeballs" for advertisers trying to reach an increasingly elusive target audience. Finally, online and mobile platforms provide fans with sports content when games are not aired.

Within content domains, scholars have documented complementarity in news consumption (Dutta-Bergman, 2004). Long-standing interest in a topic area like sports often leads fans to turn to traditional *and* newer media for sports news and increases overall sports news consumption. Yet, in at least three ways, platform use is competitive as well. First, as most of us ruefully acknowledge, there are only 24 hours in each day. Fans have a finite amount of time for sports, even when wedged into work or etched out of sleep. Second, platforms fight for – and often have to split – the fan's attention. Many sports fans use two screens while following action on the field – although multitasking such as this comes at a price (Bowman, Levine, Waite and Gendron, 2010). Learning decreases and it takes longer to complete tasks when attention is diverted or split across activities such as, with sports, watching a game, checking statistics online, and texting a friend. Finally, networks, websites, and social media outlets like to trumpet their triumphs and proclaim they are Number One in any form of usage – be it total users, amount of use, frequency of use, or first source turned to. Collectively, they spend tens of millions of dollars promoting their product so that fans turn to them for sports. However, it is difficult for ratings companies like Nielsen to track the ways in which fans simultaneously use traditional and social media to follow sports. We do not expect spending constraints to have media displacement effects suggested by McCombs (1972). Sports fans seem quite willing to purchase media hardware, reception and connectivity services – and to buy into fantasy leagues – to stay in touch with sports.

Platform factors that influence the reception experience

While they may have favorites, fans routinely turn to a variety of electronic and print outlets to follow sports and offer their own points of view. Fans are likely to prefer some platforms over others based on their intended use (e.g. large-screen TV to watch live sports; Twitter for updates as a game transpires; websites for fantasy league statistics) although we know of no study documenting this. Nonetheless, we expect fans to quickly, routinely – and perhaps subconsciously – consider a series of factors that lead them to select one platform from the rest, factors that are likely to maximize the value of their experience. In this section, we will describe a series of non-orthogonal factors likely to come into play as fans select platforms. These factors are also likely to influence how fans respond to sports.

Locus of control

With traditional media, content developers and distributors control the message and the timing of its distribution. NFL games on television illustrate how this works. In accord with transmission rights agreements, NFL games are aired on specific networks at predetermined times; are covered by play-by-play announcers, color commentators and sideline reporters selected by the networks; showcase establishing shots, close-ups and replays determined by network producers; and are interspersed with advertising and promotional messages paid for by marketers and selected by the networks. In turn – and with four small caveats that follow – viewers tune in when the games air and watch the externally determined product. With remote control and record devices in hand, viewers do have a modicum of control. They can mute the sound and, instead, listen to their team's announcer call the game on the radio; they can easily skip non-programming content by flipping channels; and, if they dare, they can record the game and watch it later at their convenience. Those who pay for special satellite packages are not bound by the game selected for their market.

In small and larger ways, newer media share or hand control to users, to fans of the content

– in our case, to sports fans. Fans who watch games streamed on their computers often have the ability to pick the vantage point /camera angle they prefer. Internet websites encourage fan input, at times without any content filtering mechanisms in place. Blogs, Facebook pages, and Twitter accounts give fans free reign to express themselves and, in the process, develop loyal – and at times large – fan bases.

Traditional media content providers and distributors recognize a central liability associated with the control they exert: If potential users are disinterested in the sports fare presented, they'll turn elsewhere for programming and content that better suits their interests and needs. To counter this, providers now offer multiple channels. In the United States, ESPN is the clear leader, offering at least seven distribution channels (ESPN, ESPN2, ESPN News, ESPNU, ESPN Classic, ESPN Films, and ESPNDeportes). Diversification such as this will attract and keep users but it still falls short of providing the sense of agency users have with newer and more interactive media. Furthermore, while new media producers have multiple options when it comes to content creation (e.g. message boards, forums, games, apps), traditional media producers can only rely on programming to satisfy their audiences' needs.

Level of interactivity

Traditional media feature a one-way flow of communication. Circulation figures and program ratings data do provide critical feedback but these are delayed and have more immediate value on the revenue, rather than programming or content, side of the ledger. Calls to station personnel and letters to newspaper and magazine editors offer a limited avenue for feedback. These feedback loops may represent a release valve for those steamed by the content but they do little to shape the content that follows or the pre-set overall agendas of those producing the content. Newer media are inherently interactive and increasingly are called out for use when traditional media outlets need (near) immediate audience feedback. Rafaeli (1988) noted that interactivity empowers users and increases the consumer's level of control. Indeed, new media allow users to become participants, not just consumers of mediated content. Widely popular programs like *American Idol*, *Britain's Got Talent*, and the Netherlands' *Big Brother* integrate audience calls and texts into their decisions; televised sportscasts routinely ask viewers to vote, using mobile technologies, on the top plays and players of the week. Even ESPN's annual sports awards show relies heavily on fan voting to determine the winners. On their own, newer media outlets solicit and expect input. Reader reactions to online columns quickly number into the hundreds; online fan forums hosted by NFL clubs routinely generate thousands of comments each week during the season. Countless fans turn to mobile phones and Facebook sites to tweet, text, or type in their reactions to games while they are being played. In short, newer technologies provide fans with an outlet to express themselves and shape the conversation or, at a minimum, to "lurk" and observe what others have to say.

Temporal constraints

As suggested earlier, traditional media outlets operate with hard and fairly inflexible boundaries. Sportscasts and games start at predetermined times; all pre-programming preparation has to be complete when the opening video is rolled and the announcers are cued. Regularly scheduled sports news programming (e.g. *SportsCenter*, *ESPNews*) also start with on-the-hour and half-hour start times. Newspapers and magazines have fixed deadlines that demand final copy as well. Newer media feature more flexibility. Websites like ESPN.com continuously rotate story headlines and can be updated as often as warranted. There are no temporal constraints to fan reactions on web-based forums although there is likely to be a cyclical pattern to such responses. Newer media offer anytime/all-the-time convenience that fits with contemporary, overscheduled life. Yet, temporal constraints may be less important with sports than with most entertainment content. With few exceptions, sports contests air as they are being contested; the games are unscripted, the outcomes unknown as the games unfold. One reason fans watch sports is because they enjoy the suspense associated with not knowing what will transpire. As a result, sports are watched live and represent "appointment' viewing, where fans set their schedules to coincide with game times dictated by the networks and leagues. Sports programming is the programming genre least likely to be time-shifted (Nielsen, 2012), Ironically, fans unable to watch the game live at its appointed time – and hope to watch it later – are better off not using social media like Twitter and Facebook, where the outcome of the game is likely to be widely disseminated and discussed among users and friends.

Fidelity

Consumer electronic devices are simultaneously getting larger, smaller and more faithful to the images they convey. Televisions, computers, tablets, and mobile phones offer a dizzying array of size and picture quality options. Consumers are bombarded with information about pixels, screen size, surround-sound options, and whiz-bang componentry such as 3-D. Fidelity is still an important reason why people spend money to see a movie at a movie theater, with debates existing over the quality of true 70 mm IMAX versus digital IMAX (Scrietta, 2011). Fidelity appears to matter with sports, too, especially with the games themselves. Marketers certainly think so, witness large-screen and 3-D television set promotions and sales prior to major sports events like the Super Bowl (Chang, 2012).

For the most part, fidelity is strong across platforms. Newspapers lag behind here. For those without cable or satellite, TV (and radio) signals can be frustratingly fuzzy. The same is true for those reliant on wireless technology for laptop and other mobile communication technology. Despite Verizon's campaign of "Can you hear me now?" commercials, weak (or dead!) wireless spots curtail fidelity. Broadly speaking, these are the exceptions rather than the rule. Nonetheless, an element related to fidelity still may influence platform selection as we will see with the next factor.

Screen size / presence

Millions of people still go to movie theaters to watch newly released films at least in part because sitting in a darkened space in front of a huge screen, surrounded by sound, significantly enhances the experience. This is especially the case with movies where the action sweeps across the screen and the sound score is rich and fully integrated into the film. Researchers describe the phenomenon of complete focus on content and a feeling of 'being there' as presence (Bracken, 2005; Lombard, Reich, Grabe, Bracken and Ditton, 2000; Reeves, 1991). Sports programming can fully engage and engulf fans, too, especially when the contests are taut and the outcomes important. Sports programming is a key factor driving the sale of large-screen high definition television sets (Keating, 2006). Fans want large-screen TVs so they can immerse themselves in football, basketball or other sports action that highlights movement, sound, and spectacle.

Presence is less likely to occur with smaller screens as well as screens with lower resolution quality. Viewers experience more presence when viewing higher quality content and content on a larger screen (Bracken, 2005; Lombard, Ditton, Grabe and Reich, 1997). Even among sports fans, the salience of screen size and the immersive experience associated with it should vary across exposure settings. Here, programming content and gratifications sought are likely to trump screen size. Watching pre-game prognostications, gathering post-game statistics – actually, anything other than watching actual sports – is not likely to require big screen technology. And, for those on the go, any screen may do.

Accessibility

In this context, accessibility incorporates proxemics, availability, finances, and cognitive demands. Users turn to and value communication technology that is by their side, available for use, affordable, and easy to use. Traditional media fare well here with television illustrating this point: Large-screen HDTV sets are reasonably priced and are in two-thirds of households across the land (Winslow, 2011); remote control devices require almost no training and are easy for everyone to use; signal coverage is virtually universal. Yet, television sets are clunky and hard to transport. Those on the go who want to watch sports have to turn to public locations (e.g. sports bars) or smaller screen technology to get their fix. Newer media are portable and often no more than an arm's length away: cell and smart phones are in our pockets (for some, under pillows overnight, too); laptops, notebooks, and tablets conveniently fit into pocketbooks, attaché cases and backpacks. Yet, mobile technology is beyond the means for many who want these products but cannot afford the initial cost or monthly carrying charge for the convenience or downloading and streaming speed they provide. Geographic location may also factor into access and speed. Finally, users have to learn how to take maximum advantage of their features and, in addition to paying for apps, have to learn how to download and fully utilize those features as well. Not everyone has the cognitive capacity – or willingness – to do so.

Accessibility issues may divide sports fans along demographic and socioeconomic lines. Older, less educated, less affluent (and more risk-averse) fans may be more likely to turn to traditional media for sports consumption. Their counterparts may be more likely to incorporate newer media into their patterns of mediated sports usage.

Fanship and the reception experience

In common parlance, the term sports fan is used quite loosely. And, when asked, most Americans say they are sports fans (Gallup, 2009). We see fanship as a multidimensional concept, one that incorporates knowledge, affect, and behavior (Gantz and Wenner, 1995). While one may be a fan of a player, a team, a league, or a sport, fanship entails more than merely attending a game or watching it on television. Fans know sports, keep track of the standings, care and root for players and teams, carve out and spend considerable time following sports, and put their money where their heart is by going to games, purchasing player and team paraphernalia, and participating in fantasy leagues. Fanship actually runs along a continuum from those who could not care less about sports (and cannot quite understand why anyone would!) to others whose lives revolve around sports. Most everyone is likely to pay attention to megasport events such as the Super Bowl and the World Cup (Eastman, Newton and Pack, 1996). These events routinely draw the highest television ratings of the year, easily surpassing the ratings for any other programming. Ratings diminish for less prestigious sporting events, with those on the lower rungs of the fanship continuum dropping from the ranks of viewers. For purposes of this discussion, we will use the term fan to describe those on the high side of the continuum (described by others as avid fans; ESPN, 2009; Wann, Friedman, McHale and Jaffe, 2003) and non-fans as those on the low side.

There are two critical differences between fans and non-fans relevant to this discussion. First, fans are much more likely to watch televised sports because they are deeply interested in following the action (Gantz and Wenner, 1995). They care, root, want to know who is going to win, and expect to integrate the game in activities and conversations with others. Non-fans may find the outcomes interesting but they are not truly vested. Instead, they are more detached emotionally when they approach the set, are more likely to watch because their friends and families are watching, and more likely to *not* give a second thought to the game when it (finally!) concludes. In short, fans and non-fans approach sports with different motivational structures and expectations.

The second relevant difference is that for non-fans, contact with mediated sports is likely to start and end with watching the game itself. They have better things to do – almost *anything*, really. The opposite is true for fans: Watching games represents the tip of an iceberg's worth of activity associated with following sports. Fans turn to television because it offers the games and matches they want to watch. But, fans also want to gather, share, and create information; they want to understand, prognosticate, and pontificate; they want to express glee, indignation, and sadness. For all this, they also turn to newer media.

Fanship and traditional media

With good reason, television has dominated the mediated sports environment for decades. It offers live sports with production values and practices designed to maximize – and maintain – viewer attention and interest. At the same time, televised sports extend well beyond the games and matches themselves. Indeed, it may be that television features more hours of programming about sports (e.g. pre- and post-game shows, sports newscasts and magazines, sports fiction) than of the sports themselves (Brown and Bryant, 2006). It is difficult to determine which of the remaining traditional media fans turn to next. Newspapers provide extensive daily coverage of local professional, collegiate, and high school teams. The sports section in *USA Today,* for years the nation's mostly widely circulated daily newspaper, was deliberately designed to appeal to sports fans across the country. Radio often features home team announcers for games aired on that medium. Sports talk radio has become a widely used format that attracts an otherwise hard-to-reach audience that advertisers covet. Sports magazines continue to draw audiences of fans. Yet, no single outlet across these platforms draws the numbers that TV routinely attracts. In Britain, 18 million watched the 2010 World Cup Final on television whereas Britain's most popular daily newspaper, *The Sun*, had a readership of 7.8 million the same year. US viewership of the 2012 NFL divisional championships averaged 53 million while *USA Today*'s print circulation hovered around 1.6 million and circulation for *Sports Illustrated*, the nation's best-selling sports magazine, rested at 3.2 million. Few sports talk radio stations are rated in the top five within their markets, a function of narrow niche and use of AM rather than FM channels.

As is the case with any genre of content, there are a variety of reasons why audiences follow mediated sports. These include uses germane to the content as well as those for which any genre of content would suffice. Not surprisingly, almost all of the research on audiences and mediated sports focuses on television. Raney (2006) nicely summarized that work and identified affective, cognitive, and behavioral / social sets of motives driving consumption of mediated sports. In this section, we will cover three clusters of uses of traditional media and discuss how traditional media shine or may fall short in light of newer media.

Entertainment and eustress

Even though enjoyment varies on the basis of loyalties and game outcomes (see the disposition theory of sports spectatorship; Zillmann, Bryant and Sapolsky, 1989), fans attend to sports contests because they truly enjoy following their favorites. Fans actively root for – or against – players and teams. They relish the anticipation and suspense associated with unknown outcomes and revel when their side scores a touchdown or goal, makes a key defensive stop, knocks the ball out of the park, or hits nothing but net on a last second, game-winning three-pointer. Rooting comes from the heart and the brain: It is physiologically and affectively exciting. Because television captures the details, nuances, and intensity of every play with startling clarity, fans turn to it to watch games and matches as they unfold. They want to see athletes, coaches, and spectators experience "the thrill of victory and the agony of defeat." For fans, following sports is a visceral experience that television facilitates. Television provides the fidelity and presence fans expect; no other medium comes close. And, since fans want to watch the action as it occurs, factors that might otherwise work against television in today's digital, newer media environment (e.g. locus of control, interactivity, temporal constraints) are likely to carry little weight. Radio is the only other traditional medium that delivers play-by-play entertainment and eustress value. While it does not quite as easily offer presence, good radio play-by-play announcers are able to describe the action in ways that fans can easily visualize. Beyond that, the intimacy of listening to radio may help listeners feel connected to the action in ways traditional or online print platforms cannot.

Learning

Fans are veritable warehouses of information about players, teams, and leagues. Many have crammed in so many facts, figures, rules, and statistics it seems they worship the deity of sports data. Sports knowledge helps viewers understand the games and matches they watch but it also provides social currency during and apart from following the action on TV. The widespread popularity of fantasy sports has elevated the value of sports knowledge and is used by fantasy sports players to draft athletes for their teams, make trades during the season, and make game-by-game decisions as they arise.

Televised games routinely sprinkle player statistics and personal data. Sportscasters use these factoids and tidbits to provide perspective – and, when the games aren't close, to keep fans tuned in. Pre- and post-game shows as well as daily sportscasts are filled with player and team statistics as well. Yet, because television is a visual and fleeting medium, fans who crave data also are likely to visit print platforms which feature more detailed data about each contest and athlete. Hard copy print platforms like newspapers and magazines may end up on the losing side of the ledger for fans who want immediate, continuous, and fan-directed access to sports data. Newer technologies have much more to offer here, including databases designed for information-obsessed fans, and are increasingly turned to by those fans (Otto, Metz and Ensmenger, 2011). Use of these interactive platforms also points to an increasingly well-informed and information-savvy fan base (Block, 2012).

Group affiliation, companionship, and sense of personal identity

Most fans watch games and matches at home. For some, it is a deliberately solitary experience: They want to completely focus on the action. Many watch with family members or friends, a mix of happenstance and planning. Co-viewing patterns in the home vary by gender and age

(ESPN, 2009); compared to men, women are more likely to view sports with others. Married couples see televised sports viewed as a shared experience that plays a small but positive role in their relationship (Gantz, Wenner, Carrico and Knorr, 1995). Watching televised sports at home by oneself is unlikely to provide companionship (even though having the set on makes the home feel less empty). However, for those who are watching alone at home, it is now easy to share the experience with others using newer media technologies; many viewers routinely text friends about their excitement – and their personal take – on the action (Gantz, Fingerhut and Nadorff, 2011). Fans who seek the communal roar – and rowdiness – of stadium attendance but want to spare themselves the costs and hassles of going to games turn to sports bars. Every city has them; it is great business for bar owners and an ideal setting for fans who want to be surrounded by those who share loyalty to a team.

In and of itself, television as a content delivery platform does not provide group affiliation, real companionship or the sense of identity that sports offer fans. Instead, because viewing can be so easily shared, sports on television afford the *opportunity* for fans to feel they are part of a larger group. It may be one reason why young adults enjoy watching televised sports at bars – along, of course, with the chance to imbibe and let loose.

In two ways, radio may more directly offer listeners companionship and group affiliation as well as let them establish and share their identity as sports fans with others. First, and at its best, radio is an intimate medium. Sportscasters behind the microphone have the ability to make listeners feel that the play-by-play and commentary are directed to them. Moreover, many radio sportscasters are permitted to be partisan. Over the years, the best sportscasters become extended members of the listeners' families. Listeners develop parasocial relationships with these announcers (more on this later) and may feel an important sense of connection when-ever they tune in. The second way focuses on radio as an interactive medium. Sports talk radio features highly knowledgeable and decidedly opinionated hosts who share their views, field phone calls and banter with those who call in. Because it is radio, these shows promote a sense of intimacy – the hosts and listeners are in it together. Audiences listen to talk radio for infor-mation, excitement – and companionship (Armstrong and Rubin, 1989). Many who call in are regulars known by the hosts; regular callers develop and cultivate their own radio-based iden-tity. Newer media provide more interactive technology and permit users to much more fully develop their identities as sports fans. Yet, sportscaster skill, coupled with the intimacy of radio and the immediacy of sportscaster–fan repartee, is likely to keep fans listening.

Off-line print media vehicles offer little here. Newspapers feature letters to the editor but few get published each day. Even fewer relate to sports. Online, though, newspapers and maga-zines encourage feedback for all to read.

Fanship and newer media

Newer media allow fans to *extend* their fanship in different and meaningful ways. Newer media complement and supplement traditional media. At least right now, they do not replace watch-ing games and matches live. Many fans turn to newer media screens while watching sports on TV so they can follow multiple games at the same time. Here, though, we would like to focus (a) on the ways in which fans use newer media platforms to create content and (b) on the networks and websites that fans access for existing sports content online. So, for example, fans use their mobile phones to 'check in' on Facebook and other social media applications, report-ing their location at a sports stadium or arena as well as a sports bar; they use notebooks and tablets to access team and fantasy websites before, during, and after games; when in transit or simply not near a TV, they turn to their mobile phones, tablets and notebooks to catch the latest scores. In this section, we will describe five ways that fans make use of newer media to create a richer, more fulfilling fanship experience.

Digital self-expression and identity

Newer media create an environment where sports fans can convey and widely disseminate their support for teams and athletes not possible with traditional media. Using the networked device of their choice, fans can share their anger over an official's call, cheer for an 80-yard touchdown run, or berate a coach for poor play-calling. In fantasy leagues, team managers "talk smack" by disparaging the opponent's line-up or performance and gloat when their team fares well. Fans who use message boards do so to exchange information and interact with fellow fans (Clavio, 2008). Sports message board users bask in the reflected glory (BIRG) of their team after a win, all the while disparaging opponent teams (End, 2001). Fans, of course, can express themselves in the privacy of their dorm rooms, apartments and homes or in the company of other revelers at sports bars. Newer media simply extend self-expression to countless others and provide an extra dose of satisfaction for those who want and like their voices widely heard.

Social networks allow users to create representations of themselves and connect with others (Boyd, 2004). Fans establish their own digital identity and then use social networking sites, fantasy leagues, fan boards and forums to share their online identities and narratives. They become active agents by joining fan groups on Facebook, creating user profiles in team forums, and generating avatars in their fantasy leagues. Some fantasy players go to great lengths to create their managerial personas by uploading pictures, crafting clever team names, and earning and adding trophies to their profiles. In these activities, the focus of media production and consumption shifts from broadcast-centered to emerging digital fan networks (Hutchins, 2011). Fans use websites and message boards to both associate and identify with their team (End, 2001).

Extended fanship networks

With the advent of the World Wide Web, people were able to connect across distances and time zones in ways previously unseen. However, it took the arrival of digital social networks to create and facilitate social interaction in a truly massive and nearly boundless way. From online dating websites to massive game environments, social networks connect people across the globe. Team websites, sports boards and forums, and fan blogs connect fans and amplify their networks as well as their fanship experience. Social networks such as these give fans the feeling that they are keeping in touch with other fans (Hutchins, 2011). Team and athlete Facebook pages created by "super fans" have steadily gained in popularity among users; in 2012, the NFL Green Bay "Packers Everywhere" page boasted 17,000 likes (Broughton, 2012). Major cities have long featured and hosted team bars where groups of loyalists would gather to watch their favorites in action. Now, with Facebook pages and Twitter feeds, these establishments reach fans that would have not been privy to their locations in the past. Business networking sites provide lists of these bars and direct team fans to a singular location to watch their favorite teams play. Sites such as these connect fans, extend fanship networks – and are good for the bottom line of sports bars, too.

Information expertise

From statistics to insider analyses, fans have access to an ever-increasing amount of information about their favorite players and teams. For those so inclined – many fantasy sports players fit here – fans can use new media to develop specialized information expertise. Here, fans control what they know, how much they know, and the means by which they acquire that information. Facebook, Twitter, and YouTube continue to grow as primary sources of information for sports fans (Broughton, 2012). Each of these platforms features extensive search capabilities where fans can tailor their information-gathering experience to their individual needs. Instead of receiving sports information from newspapers, magazines, and broadcast networks, fans select and consume specific sports data online, including extensive statistical information (analytics, sabermetrics), player salaries, contracts, and labor disputes (Block, 2012). It seems reasonable to conclude that fans using online sources will be better informed than those limited to traditional media outlets, with knowledge differences even greater between fans and non-fans. Although it has not been tested with sports, the availability of sports information databases is likely to extend the knowledge gap between fans and non-fans, perhaps making it more difficult for members of these two groups to fully enjoy watching sports together.

Parasocial interaction

Athletes, teams, sportswriters, announcers, and reporters use newer media to interact, expand, and inform their social networks. This creates the opportunity for fans to connect with their favorites and heroes. Parasocial interactions are one-sided relationships where one member knows a great deal about the other, but the other does not (Rubin and McHugh, 1987; Perse and Rubin, 1989). These often occur between celebrities and their fans, thanks to television programs and celebrity magazines that, with or without the stars' blessings, provide fans with intimate details of their lives. New media have opened the doors for celebrities, including those associated with sports, to reveal personal and at times intimate information about their daily lives. Sports fans, especially teenagers and minorities, interact with teams, leagues, and players through social networks instead of using traditional media sources (Broughton, 2012). Many have their own Twitter feeds and often respond to fan updates, providing an experience of pseudo-engagement with the player. According to tweeting-athletes.com, over 7,000 athletes have active Twitter accounts. Furthermore, all NFL, NBA, MLB, and NHL teams have Twitter accounts and social media policies for their employees and players. These fan-to-sport interactions showcase the intricate and interactive aspects of newer media; fans are not just interacting with each other, but with their beloved players and teams as well.

Competitive ambitions

The world of fantasy sports has created a way for fans to engage in competitive activity that also serves as an expression of their fanship. Fantasy sports turn fans into managers who exert control over their rosters and line-ups. Interacting with the user interface and other players involved, fantasy users are able to stoke their competitive juices in a game-like environment that utilizes the teams and players they love.

Farquhar and Meeds (2007) described three distinct groups of fantasy sports players: casual players, skilled users, and isolationist thrill-seekers. Fantasy sports players participate for both competitive and social identification purposes (Lewis, 2012). Those who play enjoy the camaraderie of participating with their friends and with those they have gotten to know through fantasy sports leagues. They also use fantasy leagues as a vehicle of self-expression as league interfaces offer message boards and live chats during player drafts. But, fantasy sports players also compete to win and, even if there is no money in the pool, revel in victory. Fantasy sports leagues allow able and less-able bodied fans to simultaneously satisfy their competitive impulses and enhance their enjoyment of following real life games.

Fantasy sports players need information to make smart managerial decisions. It now appears that participation in fantasy football increases overall media consumption (Dwyer and Drayer, 2010): Fantasy players turn to traditional and newer media outlets for game results and statistics about their fantasy teams – and also watch the games live on TV. Televised sports producers understand this and have taken measures to seamlessly transition their broadcast content for new media applications. The networks that air NFL games provide fantasy updates during games. Cable and satellite companies carry special channels devoted to providing statistics and score updates. Direct TV's Red Zone Channel was created as part of its NFL Sunday Ticket package to provide live television coverage of NFL teams once they cross the 20-yard line. Those who participate in fantasy football use specialized channels like this to get updates in real time about the status of current players and as a scouting tool for picking up players (Swingle, 2009).

Final thoughts

Fans follow sports because it adds a dimension of enjoyment, excitement and meaning to their lives. They turn to sports as a way of connecting with the larger world and creating an identity in that world that is shared and valued by others. Traditional media, led by television, will continue to be prominent providers of sports content. Smaller screen technologies cannot compete with the presence, immediacy, and encompassing spectacle that modern HD and 3-D TV offer for game and match coverage. Down the road, smaller screens (embedded, for example, in eyeglasses) may be able to provide presence but the intimate nature of the experience will fall short on the social dimension of watching sports. At the same time, fans are likely to make increased use of newer media for news, insights, analysis and fantasy games – and for the opportunity to share their voice with like-minded others. Having grown up with accessible, interactive technology, younger fans may lead the charge here. They also may be the first to discard or – perhaps more appropriately – not even consider traditional, non-interactive platforms for sports news. In all, the attributes associated with traditional and newer media coupled with the expected cognitive and affective outcomes associated with exposure point to continued widespread use of one-way and interactive media platforms for sports.

References

Armstrong, C. B. and Rubin, A. M. (1989) Talk radio as interpersonal communication. *Journal of Communication*, 39(2), 84–94.

Block, J. L. (2012, September 15) Who knew that sports could take it this far? *JLBSportsTV.com*. Retrieved from http://jlbsports.tv/who-knew-sports-fans-could-take-it-this-far/

Brown, D. and Bryant, J. (2006) Sports content on US television. In A. A. Raney and J. Bryant (eds), *Handbook of Sports and Media* (pp. 77–104). Mahwah, NJ: Lawrence Erlbaum.

Bowman, L. L., Levine, L. E., Waite, B. M. and Gendron, M. (2010) Can students really multitask? An experimental study of instant messaging while reading. *Computers and Education*, 54(4), 927–931.

Boyd, D. (2004) Friendster and publicly articulated social networks. *Proceedings from ACM Conference on Human Factors in Computing Systems*. New York: ACM Press.

Bracken, C. C. (2005) Presence and image quality: The case of high-definition television. *Media Psychology*, 7(2), 191–205.

Broughton, D. (2012, July 16) Survey: Social media continues to fuel fans. *Sports Business Journal*. Retrieved from http://www.catalystpublicrelations.com/wp-content/uploads/Catalyst-2012.pdf

Chang, A. (2012, February 3) TV prices plunge ahead of Super Bowl. *The Los Angeles Times*. Retrieved from http://articles.latimes.com/2012/feb/03/business/la-fi-super-bowl-tvs-20120204

Clavio, G. (2008) Uses and gratifications of Internet collegiate sport message board users. *Dissertation Abstracts International*, 69(08). Retrieved from ProQuest Digital Dissertations database (Publication No. AAT 3319833).

Dutta-Bergman, M. J. (2004) Complementarity in consumption of news types across traditional and new media. *Journal of Broadcasting and Electronic Media*, 48(1), 41–60.

Dwyer, B. and Drayer, J. (2010) Fantasy sport consumer segmentation: An investigation into the differing consumption modes of fantasy football participants. *Sport Marketing Quarterly*, 19(4), 207–216.

End, C. M. (2001) An examination of NFL fans' computer mediated BIRGing. *Journal of Sport Behavior*, 24(2), 162.

Eastman, S. T., Newton, G. D. and Pack, L. (1996) Promoting prime-time programs in megasporting events. *Journal of Broadcasting and Electronic Media*, 40(3), 366–388.

ESPN. (2009) *The Life Cycle of the Sports Fan – 2008*. Bristol, CT: Author.

Farquhar, L. K. and Meeds, R. (2007) Types of fantasy sports users and their motivations. *Journal of Computer-Mediated Communication*, 12(4), 1208–1228. doi: 10.1111/j.1083-6101.2007.00370.x

Gallup (2009) Retrieved from http://www.gallup.com/poll/4735/Sports.aspx

Gantz, W., Fingerhut, D. and Nadorff, G. (2011) The social dimension of sports fanship. In A. Earnheardt, P. M. Haridakis and B. S. Hugenberg (eds) *Sports Fans, Identity, and Socialization* (pp. 65–77). Lanham, MD: Lexington Books.

Gantz, W. and Wenner, L. A. (1995) Fanship and the television viewing experience. *Sociology of Sport Journal*, 12, 56–73.

Gantz, W., Wenner, L. A., Carrico, C. and Knorr, M. (1995) Televised sports and marital relationships. *Sociology of Sports Journal*, 12, 56–74.

Gregory, S. (2010, August 14) Why sports ratings are surging on TV. *Time*. Retrieved from http://www.time.com/time/business/article/0,8599,2010746,00.html

Hutchins, B. (2011) The acceleration of media sport. *Culture. Information, Communication and Society*, 14(2), 237–257.

Keating, T. (2006, January 25) Sports fans drive HD TV sales. *TMCnet*. Retrieved from http://blog.tmcnet.com/blog/tom-keating/home-entertainment/sports-fans-drive-hd-tv-sales.asp

Lewis, N. (2012) *Trait and Motivational Differences in Fantasy Football Participation*. Unpublished master's thesis, Indiana University, Bloomington.

Lombard, M., Ditton, T. B., Grabe, M. E. and Reich, R. D. (1997) The role of screen size in viewer responses to television fare. *Communication Reports*, 10(1), 94–106.

Lombard, M., Reich, R. D., Grabe, M. E., Bracken, C. C. and Ditton, T. B. (2000) Presence and television. *Human Communication Research*, 26(1), 75–98.

Nielsen. (2012) *2012 Year in Sports*. Retrieved from http://www.nielsen.com/content/dam/corporate/us/en/reports-downloads/2013%20Reports/Nielsen-2012-Year-in-Sports-Report.pdf.

McCombs, M. (1972) Mass media in the marketplace. *Journalism Monographs*, 24, 1–104.

Otto, J., Metz, S. and Ensmenger, N. (2011) Sports fans and their information-gathering habits: How media technologies have brought fans closer to their teams over time. In W. Aspray and B. Hayes (eds), *Everyday information: The evolution of information seeking in America* (pp. 185–216). Cambridge, MA: MIT Press.

Perse, E. M. and Rubin, R. B. (1989) Attribution in social and para-social relationships. *Communication Research*, 16(1), 59–77.

Raney, A. A. (2006) Why we watch and enjoy mediated sports. In A. A. Raney and J. Bryant (eds), *Handbook of Sports and Media* (pp. 313–329). Mahwah, NJ: Lawrence Erlbaum.

Rafaeli, S. (1988) Interactivity from new media to communication. In R. Hawkins *et al.* (eds), *Advancing Communication Science: Merging Mass and Interpersonal Processes* (pp. 110–134). Newbury Park, CA: Sage.

Reeves, B. (1991) "Being there:" Television as symbolic versus natural experience. Unpublished manuscript, Stanford University, Institute for Communication Research, Stanford, CA.

Rubin, R. B. and McHugh, M. P. (1987) Development of para-social interaction relationships. *Journal of Broadcasting and Electronic Media*, 13(3), 279–292.

Scrietta, P. (2011, December 21) How do I know if my IMAX theater is real 70mm or lieMAX (digital IMAX)? *Slashfilm*. Retrieved from http://www.slashfilm.com/qa-imax-theatre-real-imax-liemax/

Swingle, B. (2009) The red zone channel hooks up fantasy football players. *EzineArticles.com*. Retrieved from http://ezinearticles.com/?The-Red-Zone-Channel-Hooks-Up-Fantasy-Football-Players&id=2454060

Wann, D. L., Friedman, K., McHale, M. and Jaffe, A. (2003) The Norelco sports fanatics survey: Examining behaviors of sports fans. *Psychological Reports*, 92, 930–936.

Winslow, G. (2011, June 15) Nielsen: Two thirds of all TV homes now have an HD set. *Multichannel News*.

Retrieved from http://www.multichannel.com/internet-video/nielsen-two-thirds-all-tv-homes-now-have-hd-set/131314

Zillmann, D., Bryant, J. and Sapolsky, B. S. (1989) Enjoyment from sports spectatorship. In J. H. Goldstein (ed.), *Sports, Games, and Play: Social and Psychological Viewpoints* (2nd edn.). Hillsdale, NJ: Lawrence Erlbaum Associates, pp. 241–78.

3

SOCIAL MEDIA, SPORT, AND DEMOCRATIC DISCOURSE

A rhetorical invitation

Michael L. Butterworth

OHIO UNIVERSITY

The 2012 National Football League (NFL) season began amidst a labor dispute between the league and its officials. NFL officials are unionized, and a contract dispute between the bargaining unit and the league resulted in Commissioner Roger Goodell's decision to lockout the officials and begin the season with a crew of marginally qualified replacements. During the preseason, the lockout received significant coverage in sports media but there was little evidence that the presence of the "replacement refs" would affect fans' interest in the game. Moreover, much of the attention granted to the lockout emphasized salaries as the dominant issue, thus defaulting to the common perception that all of the constituents in professional sports eagerly prioritize money over competition, integrity, and, most importantly, the fans (Cole, 2012). Throughout the first three weeks of the season, however, fans, media, players, and coaches grew increasingly frustrated with the poor quality of the officiating, and many worried that the non-NFL officials would eventually cost a team – or teams – a game.

By September 23, when the Sunday night game between the Baltimore Ravens and New England Patriots was harshly criticized for "excessive flags on plays, frequent reviews, confusion over challenges and numerous debatable penalties" (Evans, 2012, ¶ 11), it seemed the league had reached a tipping point. The very next evening, during a *Monday Night Football* game between the Green Bay Packers and Seattle Seahawks, an apparent victory for the Packers turned into a 14–12 defeat to the Seahawks when receiver Golden Tate secured a "Hail Mary" touchdown pass from quarterback Russell Wilson as time expired. Tate's reception was contested, however, and the replacement officials on the field struggled to reach an agreement on the correct call. While one signaled interception, another more emphatically signaled touchdown and the referee ruled it was, in fact, a Seattle score. Few observers agreed with the call, however, with nearly everyone in agreement that the game – quickly earning the nickname, "Fail Mary" (Serby, 2012) – was an embarrassment for the NFL.

In any previous era, the outcome of the Packers–Seahawks game would have sparked controversy. There is little doubt, however, that the controversy was magnified by the present era's fascination with new media forms commonly understood as "Web 2.0." As Parmelee and Bichard (2012: 3) indicate, this label "refers to websites and social networking platforms that enable users to create their own content and share it with other users." The boundaries of Web

2.0 are not always clear, but most commonly they entail sites such as Facebook, Twitter, and YouTube, as well as other blogs, newsfeeds, and wikis. The rapid growth of these sources has generated an entirely new vocabulary, including phenomena on Facebook such as "liking" or "friending," or the "Tweeting" that defines communication on Twitter. In the aftermath of the blown call on *Monday Night Football*, social media sites exploded with commentary and highlights of the play were readily available on YouTube. Players and fans "generated more than one million Tweets" (Ashtari, 2012, ¶ 2), and this Tweet from Packers offensive lineman T. J. Lang – "F – - it, NFL. Fine me and use the money to pay the regular refs" – was retweeted approximately 98,000 times, becoming the most shared sports post in Twitter's six-year history (Bennett, 2012). The subsequent public firestorm was largely filtered through conversations generated by social media, and within the next 48 hours the NFL settled its contract dispute with the officials.

On the one hand, given the sheer volume of commentary in response to a single NFL game, we might lament that the public's attention is fixed on something that is, ultimately, of minimal importance (in the context of the 2012 presidential election, no less). Indeed, much of the Twitter conversation was grounded in the passionate and often crude language typical of sports fans. Yet, on the other hand, there were more substantive conversations facilitated by the platforms of Web 2.0. In particular, millions of fans attended to the source of the problem in the first place – that is, a labor dispute that resulted in the NFL officials being locked out and prevented from doing their jobs. Set against the backdrop of growing efforts from state governors, especially in Ohio and Wisconsin, to curb the influence of collective bargaining for public employees, the plight of the locked out officials was not something to be understood only in the context of sport. Rather, it was a political issue, one that suddenly provoked considerable public sympathy on behalf of the officials' union. In short, the controversial ending to the Packers–Seahawks game opened a dialogue about the lockout, labor, and collective bargaining. In the words of Dave Zirin (2012, ¶ 3), "the entire country received a High Def, prime time lesson in the difference between skilled, union labor and a ramshackle operation of unskilled scabs."

At the risk of over-stating the political potential of social media platforms such as Twitter, I want to take this *Monday Night Football* moment as an invitation to consider the role of new media through the lens of public advocacy and rhetoric. It is no criticism to note that the pages in this volume are mostly dedicated to analyses situated in the traditions of mass communication and media studies. This makes a good deal of sense, especially because media scholars have been quick to recognize the communicative potential of new media and Web 2.0. However, given the rhetorical tradition's focus on discourse that is *public* and *persuasive* (Lucaites and Condit, 1998), it is in our academic interest to consider the role of sports rhetoric in new media. More to the point, I want to suggest in this chapter that rhetoric offers scholars interested in sport and new media a lens through which we may conceptualize a form of active and engaged citizenship. To make this case, I first provide a brief review of rhetoric as a discipline. I then consider the ways that observers have greeted the Internet and other more recent forms of new media with optimism about new forms of democratic engagement. Next, I address the role of new media in sport, with particular emphasis on moments of political awareness. I conclude with some reflections on the relationships between citizenship and sport that is enabled by new media.

A rhetorical view

Rhetoric, as an academic discipline, has the misfortune of being associated with the vernacular usage of the term in contemporary society. Popular definitions of rhetoric commonly feature references to demagoguery, bluster, or hot air. At its best, it is elegant but empty language; at its worst, it is manipulative and deceitful. From Plato (1986), who viewed it as "cookery," to John Rawls (2001: 92), who decries "mere rhetoric or the artifices of persuasion," rhetoric has been conceived in the most negative of terms. This conception is regrettable, for the rhetorical tradition is grounded in classical theories of politics and citizenship that resonate to the present day. A more productive starting point, then, can be found in Aristotle's characterization of rhetoric as "the faculty of discovering in any particular case all of the available means of persuasion" (quoted in Booth, 2004: 4). Although the emphasis on "persuasion" is mostly retained in contemporary discourse, too often forgotten is the commitment to citizenship found in ancient rhetorical theory and practice.

This focus on citizenship spotlights the interdependence found between rhetoric and democracy. Timmerman and McDorman (2008) observe that "democracy is impossible without the practice of public discourse and dialogue among citizens" (p. xiii). In contemporary American politics, getting citizens to engage in public discourse and dialogue is a challenge. As Hogan (2008: 80) laments:

> With the proliferation of special-interest groups, the rhetoric of public relations has displaced the collective voice of ordinary people deliberating over matters of shared public importance. Principled leadership has given way to appeals shaped by polling and focus groups, and we see more and more of the techniques of the propagandist and the demagogue in our mainstream political talk. . . . No longer are we a nation of citizens deliberating among ourselves, committed to discovering the common good through the process of collective deliberation.

Although Hogan is perhaps guilty of romanticizing the extent to which previous generations of Americans fully embraced this rhetorical conception of citizenship, his observation nevertheless reminds us that when citizens disengage from public discussions of politics democracy is diminished.

If a disengaged citizenry is detrimental to a democracy, what does engaged citizenship look like? The contemporary political culture of the United States has largely restricted citizenship to the private sphere. Although political campaigns and elections, for example, are exceedingly public, democracy itself is too often reduced to the act of voting, something that Americans do mostly in isolation from others. The *act* of voting is therefore deemed sufficient for citizenship, whereas discussions about what voting *means* are typically understood as impolitic. As Asen (2004: 195) describes, "The act of voting exhibits a uniformity that is independent of the attitude of the individual voter. Yet it matters greatly in understanding the social significance of voting, whether voters regard their actions and the actions of others as a sham, a duty, or an expression of the voice of the people." As opposed to thinking of citizenship in this individualized fashion, he seeks to cultivate a rhetorical view of citizenship, one that is grounded in "tireless, passionate advocacy" (Asen, 2004: 200). Identifying the proper conditions for advocacy has led rhetorical scholars to theories of the public, something that is equally relevant to scholars of new media.

Public engagement

Classical rhetoric provides an important foundation for imagining democratic citizenship as an active and engaged practice. Motivated by critiques of a disengaged citizenry, contemporary rhetorical theorists have turned to the possibilities for *deliberation* as a means to enliven and enhance citizenship. This is also true of political theory, a discipline historically suspicious of rhetoric but one that has experienced a "deliberative turn" (Gutmann and Thompson, 1996), through which rhetoric has become increasingly prominent (Garsten, 2009). The optimism about deliberation as a tonic for democracy's ill health is based on the principle that if citizens engage in reasonable discussions about matters of shared public importance, then more equitable and just decisions can be achieved. Deliberation, therefore, is a "democratic method to help citizens deal with political differences" (Childers, 2008: 458). To the extent that deliberation fosters reciprocity, publicity, and accountability, it "contributes to the legitimacy of decisions" made in a democracy (Gutmann and Thompson, 1996: 41). This expands confidence in governance because the "chief rhetorical principle of liberal democracy is of course the commitment to consensual decision-making" (Hanson, 1985: 51).

Whether or not rhetorical and political theorists openly acknowledge it, the emphasis on deliberation is largely grounded in Jürgen Habermas's (1991) concept of the "public sphere." In Habermas's terms, the ideal bourgeois public sphere that facilitated democratic deliberation in eigtheenth- and nineteenth-century Western Europe was grounded in the principles of "critical-rational debate" (Calhoun, 1991: 3) and access to an "ideal speech situation" (Habermas, 2001: 97), wherein citizens deferred their individual interests to the collective good. These conditions facilitate "communicative action" over "systematic distortion" (Habermas, 2001: 97) and thus allow decisions to be reached based upon the "force of the better argument" (Hanson, 1985: 32) rather than the influence of those with greater resources and power.

Habermas's model provides an ideal type against which the contemporary deficiencies of democracy can be assessed. His theories have provoked considerable academic discussion, made all the more relevant by another development from the early 1990s: the advent of the World Wide Web. As the revolutionary potential of the Internet became clear, media and communication scholars eagerly turned to it as a site for imagining an ideal public sphere. As Papacharissi (2002: 9) observes, "The utopian rhetoric that surrounds new media technologies promises further democratization of post-industrial society." Dahlberg (2007) identifies three dominant interpretations of the Internet's democratic potential. The first is an individualistic model that privileges access to information for private citizens, and the second is a communitarian model that envisions the Internet as a vehicle for mobilizing collective values and interests. Dahlberg's focus, however, is on the third model, one that "posits the Internet as the means for an expansion of a public sphere of citizen deliberation leading to rational public opinion that can hold official decision makers accountable" (p. 48).

Such idealistic conceptions are clearly rooted in the deliberative principles of access, discourse, and decision-making. Yet for all of this emphasis on *talk*, deliberative models of democracy commonly default to the Platonic suspicion of *rhetoric*, thus eschewing issues of power. What this reveals is that deliberative democracy concentrates on traditional norms ("rational-critical debate") and institutions (voting) in ways that affirm, rather than minimize, entrenched power interests. Habermas's ideal conception of the public sphere, for example, has long been critiqued for marginalizing the voices found within "subaltern counterpublics" (Fraser, 1991: 124), wherein those who do not adhere to White, masculinist norms are most likely to be located. Indeed, democracy in reality is messier and more complicated than it is in ideal deliberative terms. As Ivie (2002) states it, what is required is a much more agonistic or "rowdy" conception of democratic discourse. It is such a conception that returns us to the rhetorical theories of citizenship that emphasize democratic *practices* over *institutions*. Moreover, despite the many ways that the Internet has failed to enrich democracy, it is through the messy, rowdy, and unpredictable forms of discourse that we might consider its democratic potential after all.

Democracy, new media, and sport

In many ways, new media technologies, especially Web 2.0 platforms such as YouTube, Facebook, and Twitter, quite effectively demonstrate rowdiness and unpredictability. These social media sites encourage unfiltered communication, offering users a chance to interact directly with each other or, as is often the case, with public figures of fame and influence. This is especially the case in the context of sport, wherein fans, players, and some members of the media routinely engage in boisterous chatter and "trash-talk." This discourse is highly interactive, passionate, and partisan. I want to suggest here that it also has the potential to be democratic.

Before I continue, I should clarify that I am not making another version of the argument that claims the Internet as an ideal public sphere. It is safe to say that expectations for the democratic potential of Web 2.0 have been appropriately tempered in recent years, and in our focus on sport, it is clear to any casual observer that social media too often enables or even facilitates discourse that can be offensive, prejudicial, and undemocratic. Such discourse occurs all too frequently, especially in the "Comments" section of nearly every online article, but an especially relevant example can be found in some of the Twitter comments that greeted President Barack Obama's December 16, 2012, nationally televised address to memorialize the victims of the Sandy Hook Elementary School shootings. The speech preempted NBC's coverage of *Sunday Night Football*, thus provoking the ire of many devoted sports fans. *Deadspin.com* assembled a collection of some of the more shocking comments, which openly expressed hostility and transparent racism toward the president (Burke, 2012). In this case, new media served both to facilitate (the Twitter comments) and critique (*Deadspin's* condemnation) hateful speech. This example reminds us, therefore, that any discussion about democracy and the Internet must resist the temptation to make grand declarations about the total effect of new media technologies. Rather, in the more measured terms of the rhetorical tradition, it is important to identify moments and spaces for the emergence and cultivation of democratic discourse.

Simone (2010: 122) argues that "participatory digital technologies, not traditional media such as print or television, afford a level of interactivity, flexibility, and adaptability that is most conducive for supporting the ideals of deliberative democracy." Far from simply repeating the utopian visions of the Internet as an ideal public sphere, however, Web 2.0 scholars recognize that new media may enable more robust forms of democratic expression. Papacharissi (2004), in particular, represents a perspective that articulates well with an agonistic approach to rhetoric. As she notes, skeptics of Web 2.0's democratic potential often cite the lack of civility evident in online discourse. However, she suggests that "it is not civility that limits the democratic potential of conversation, but rather, a confusion of politeness with civility" (p. 260). She finds that "incivility and impoliteness do not dominate online political discussion" (p. 276), in part because she is willing to incorporate heated disagreement into the definition of civil discourse. The point to emphasize here is that, despite the trolling, flaming, and other antagonistic behavior that often diminishes online discourse, new media offer compelling opportunities for citizens to engage with one another and to communicate across their many differences.

These opportunities have led to new forms of political engagement. Early in 2007, for example, YouTube launched a channel, "Citizentube," designed specifically for user-generated conversations about politics. Later that year, YouTube collaborated with CNN to sponsor the first presidential candidate debate to feature completely user-generated questions. Although media and political gatekeepers kept many questions from being asked, "the simple fact that the CNN-YouTube Debates took place at all is noteworthy" (Dietel-McLaughlin, 2010: 51). By the 2012 election, narratives created by social media users paralleled those of traditional news media. After the first presidential debate between Barack Obama and Mitt Romney, for example, conventional stories about which candidate "won" the debate were matched by social media conversations and memes based on a brief reference made by Romney – "I love Big Bird" – after he claimed an interest in eliminating federal support for public television (Judkis, 2012).

Given that Facebook now has over one billion users (Smith, Segall and Cowley, 2012), and Twitter is expected to reach one billion sometime in 2013 (Dugan, 2012), it is of little surprise that "political leaders now consider social media vital to many aspects of the job" (Parmelee and Bichard, 2012: 19). Much the same could be said of sport. As Sanderson and Kassing (2011: 115) suggest, "Perhaps no other group has more prominently adopted blogs and Twitter as communication tools than athletes, whose recurrent use of these social media sites appears to be redefining sports media practices." In light of this popularity, scholars have attended to the use of social media in sport, focusing primarily on the most trafficked sites such as Facebook and Twitter. Sanderson (2013) reviews this emerging literature and concludes that most of it relies on either parasocial interaction or uses and gratifications as a theoretical framework. To supplement this scholarship, then, he recommends that scholars give further attention to theories of framing, predicted outcome value theory, and communication privacy management.

Much of the present literature is insightful work, and Sanderson's recommendations are well taken. Yet, regardless of theoretical approach, I think there is another limitation to much of the work on sport and new media. Overwhelmingly, scholars approach new media on its own terms, assessing it from the perspective of branding and marketing. Consider the following: "We contend that blogs and Twitter afford athletes more control over the release of sports news while also increasing their *self-presentation management*" (Sanderson and Kassing, 2011: 114, emphasis added); "Unlike traditional media, social media present unique and distinct advantages for sport entities because they are able *to communicate unfiltered messages directly to consumers*" (Wallace, Wilson and Miloch, 2011: 423, emphasis added). "Sport industry groups including athletes, teams, and leagues use Twitter *to share information and promote their products*" (Hambrick, 2012: 16, emphasis added).

I do not cite these passages because I think there is something necessarily *wrong* with them. However, I do think they reflect our present tendencies and, given the robust scholarly discussion about the political potential of Web 2.0, I argue that communication and sport scholars should be doing more to feature democracy and politics, as well as rhetoric, in their studies of new media. Although popular wisdom maintains that athletes should simply entertain the public and shy away from political expression, the reality is that athletes have access to media and audiences few can match. More importantly, the degree of dedication required to succeed in sport, especially at the professional level, does not "occur at the expense of other social identities. Although they may spend inordinate amounts of time pursuing excellence in their chosen sport, athletes are also consumers, tax payers, parents, patients, voters, and above all, citizens" (Kaufman and Wolff, 2010: 167).

There is a powerful history of athletes embracing their role as citizens and using their sport as a platform to address economic, political, and social concerns. Much of this history is tied to the upheaval of the 1960s and 1970s, of course, and it is easy to reduce political activism from athletes to powerful figures such as Muhammad Ali, Arthur Ashe, Billie Jean King, and John Carlos and Tommie Smith (Khan, 2012). As much as there is to learn from these legendary figures, social movements and political activism have changed, with new media playing an increasingly prominent role in protest and political resistance (Atkinson, 2010). For example, when popular uprisings in Tunisia and Egypt erupted in early 2011 – now commonly known as the "Arab Spring" – new social media contributed to "communicating, coordinating and channeling this rising tide of opposition" (Cottle, 2011: 648). Similarly, in the United States, social media were instrumental, especially during the "initial mobilization phase" of the Occupy movement (Juris, 2012: 261). Both of these prominent examples should remind us that social media's marketing and information dissemination potential tell only part of their communicative story.

Nothing in sport has taken place in the social media era to rival either these movements or the landmark protests of the 1960s and 1970s. However, it is clear that athletes and other individuals recognize that social media can enable sport to be a platform for important political discussions. The *Monday Night Football* controversy with which I opened this essay quickly became a political issue, for instance, in part because it was perceived by candidates as a means to identify with frustrated fans. Politicians have a long history of using sport this way and, while they may facilitate occasional conversation, these gestures are far more symbolic than they are substantive. Both Democrats and Republicans eagerly take the opportunity to throw out a ceremonial first pitch or publicly celebrate the triumph of American athletes during the Olympics.

Timing is everything, however, so it is worth returning for the moment to the *Monday Night Football* example with which I opened this chapter. Since it occurred in the final weeks of the 2012 presidential campaign, officials from both parties made statements about the controversy. While Democratic President Barack Obama declared on Twitter that "NFL fans on both sides of the aisle hope the refs' lockout is settled soon" ("Obama: Disputed," ¶ 2), Republican Vice-Presidential nominee Paul Ryan, delivering a traditional stump speech on the campaign trail, was more partisan, stating, "I half think that these refs work part-time for the Obama administration in the budget office." ("Obama: Disputed," ¶ 6). More interesting, though, was the social media response from Wisconsin Governor Scott Walker, a vocal critic of organized labor, who used the hashtag, "#Returntherealrefs" in a tweet that referred to the Packers' loss as "painful" ("Wisc. Gov.," ¶ 5). This brief comment sparked a more substantive conversation, based on the irony of a governor whose policies had largely stripped collective bargaining rights from public employees in Wisconsin suddenly declaring his sympathies for the NFL officials whose union was subjected to a lockout. The actions taken by Walker generated significant controversy during the 2010 midterm elections and remained a hotly contested issue during the 2012 campaign. To a degree, the discourse that emerged out of the *MNF* game provided an avenue for a timely reinvigoration of the debate about labor and collective bargaining in the United States.

While this example spotlights the role of non-athletes, I think there is considerably more potential in the long run in the democratic expressions of those directly involved with sport itself. I have focused in this chapter more on the conceptual terrain, but I do want to ground my argument in at least one example that demonstrates how athletes can creatively and persuasively use social media for political effect. New media of various types have been resources in recent years for advocacy on behalf of equal rights for gays and lesbians. The Human Rights Campaign, for example, has produced several videos arguing in favor of marriage equality for same-sex couples. These videos feature athletes such as basketball star Steve Nash and hockey player Sean Avery, and are available online ("Steve Nash," 2011). This campaign has also been supported by NFL player Brendon Ayanbadejo, whose advocacy has contributed to a growing perception that sport is shedding, albeit gradually, its more homophobic and intolerant tendencies.

Ayanbadejo plays for the Baltimore Ravens, and in 2012 he continued his vocal support of same-sex marriage in anticipation of a November ballot initiative. In response to Ayanbadejo's advocacy, a Baltimore politician, Emmett C. Burns, sent a letter to the Ravens' management demanding that Ayanbadejo be silenced. It is worth quoting the letter at length:

I find it inconceivable that one of your players...would publicly endorse Same-Sex marriage, specifically as a Raven football player. ...Many of your fans are opposed to such a view and feel it has no place in a sport that is strictly for pride, entertainment and excitement. I believe Mr. Ayanbadejo should concentrate on football and steer clear of dividing the fan base. I am requesting that you take the necessary action, as a National Football League Owner, to inhibit such expressions from your employees and that he be ordered to cease and desist such injurious actions.

(Burns, 2012, quoted in Wetzel, 2012, ¶ 6–8)

There is much to say about Mr. Burns's letter, but what is most striking in the context of my argument here is the request to "inhibit such expressions." Public responses to political advocacy are rarely so transparent in their efforts to suppress freedom of speech.

Mr. Burns's request, it turns out, had exactly the opposite effect of its intended outcome. He was widely criticized for his attempt to shut down, rather than encourage, deliberation (Wetzel, 2012). For his part, Ayanabadejo indicated that his teammates were supportive not only of his right to speak but also of the message he conveyed, observing that the emergence of a more accepting locker room culture in the NFL "has happened faster than I ever thought it would happen" (quoted in Linskey, 2012, ¶ 15). Perhaps the clearest, and the most entertaining, validation of this claim came from Chris Kluwe, the punter for the Minnesota Vikings. In an open letter to Burns published by *Deadspin*, Kluwe (2012) unleashed a profane yet argumentatively sound missive against what he deemed to be the Maryland politician's lack of intellect and appeals to fear. The letter was promptly republished on several prominent websites, posted repeatedly on Facebook, and tweeted and retweeted on Twitter. As of February, 2013, the original letter on *Deadspin* has been "liked" on Facebook nearly 105,000 times (Kluwe, 2012).[1]

Kluwe's language certainly evokes the "rowdy" and "heated" discourse referenced earlier in this chapter. To be sure, saying, "I can't even begin to fathom the cognitive dissonance that must be coursing through your rapidly addled mind right now," is not especially *nice*. Nevertheless, his letter detailed the flaws in Burns's argument, from the misguided effort to suppress free speech to the veiled attacks against gays and lesbians. In addition, Kluwe premised his counter-argument on an essentially *democratic* claim: that gays and lesbians should be treated as "full-fledged American citizens just like everyone else, with the freedom to pursue happiness and all that entails" (2012, ¶ 5). It is not a perfect letter by any means. That Kluwe resorts to gratuitous profanity and insults – for example, suggesting that Burns "might want to hire an intern to help you with the longer words" (¶ 1) – undermines to a degree his more humble effort to identify the shared humanity that Burns has neglected. The risk, of course, is that Kluwe will simply reverse the direction of vitriolic discourse, thereby rendering his advocacy for marriage equality less meaningful. Nevertheless, there is something provocative and encouraging about his willingness to use new media outlets for something more substantive than crafting his "brand."

Numbers of page visits and Facebook likes tell us only a portion of the story, as it would be a mistake to conclude definitively that because Kluwe's letter was read by millions of people that he necessarily inspired dramatic social change. Rhetorical effect is not measured particularly well by such standards, and to limit our understanding of impact to such numbers reveals little about democratic practice. After all, it is one thing to get a public's attention; it is quite another to affect a public's perceptions or alter its behaviors. At present, conversations about new media among journalists and academics alike are too often limited to quantifying content instead of evaluating it. It simply is not sufficient to acknowledge that T. J. Lang's Tweet was retweeted 98,000 times. Rather, it is important to identify Lang's comments as a contribution to a more deliberative public discussion about labor and the NFL officials' union. Similarly, we should be concerned not with the number of likes Kluwe's missive received, but whether or not he promoted an engagement with a matter of shared public importance. In other words, did he facilitate deliberation? By this standard, it is clear that not only did he do so, but that it he was able to do so primarily through the channels of new media technologies. This moment, therefore, serves as an invitation to scholars of new media to attend more actively and critically to the rhetorical dimensions of new media and sport.

Rhetorical reflections

This chapter has operated primarily at the theoretical and conceptual levels. My aim here has been to provoke a little deliberation of a different kind, in this case among scholars of new media and sport. The rapid growth of new media scholarship in communication and media studies in general, and in the area of communication and sport research in specific, is entirely warranted. Daily life in the industrialized world has been altered in too many ways for our academic community to ignore the role of new media technologies, especially those innovations known as Web 2.0. Yet, in the rush to account for these emerging trends, I fear that communication and sport research in this area has been too content to quantify new media uses and explore applications for branding, marketing, and information dissemination. As I hope I made clear earlier in the chapter, I do not mean to suggest that the present work lacks quality. Yet, if we take seriously the discourse that emerges from the social media/sport intersection, discourses about collective bargaining rights, marriage equality, and numerous other issues, we would do well to view the terrain through more varied lenses. Given its emphasis on political deliberation and citizenship, the rhetorical tradition provides just such a lens.

Note

1. *Deadspin* itself is a compelling site for making sense of new media's impact on sport. Founded in 2005, it is one of the most popular and influential sports sites on the Internet. By featuring bloggers and other writers not trained in the conventions of traditional journalism, *Deadspin* has been criticized for being unprofessional and less credible than mainstream sources (Sandomir, 2008). At the same time, it has also been credited with breaking legitimate news stories that mainstream outlets failed to cover and is seen by many as a meaningful alternative either to previous generations' standards of print journalism or the contemporary dominance of ESPN (Freedlander, 2013).

References

Asen, R. (2004) A discourse theory of citizenship. *Quarterly Journal of Speech*, 90, 189–211.

Ashtari, O. (2012, September 25) NFL week #3: #OnlyOnTwitter edition. *Twitter Blog*. Retrieved from http://blog.twitter.com/2012/09/nfl-week-3-onlyontwitter-edition.html

Atkinson, J. (2010) *Alternative Media/Alternative Politics: A Communication Perspective*. New York: Peter Lang.

Bennett, S. (2012, September 27) Revealed: Twitter's 10 most retweeted tweets of all time. *AllTwitter*. Retrieved from http://www.mediabistro.com/alltwitter/twitter-most-retweets_b29141

Booth, W. C. (2004) *The Rhetoric of Rhetoric: The Quest for Effective Communication*. Malden, MA: Blackwell.

Burke, T. (2012, December 16, 2012) "Take that nigger off the TV, we wanna watch football! Idiots respond to NBC pre-empting *Sunday Night Football*. *Deadspin.com*. Retrieved from http://deadspin.com/5968935/take-that-nigger-off-the-tv-we-wanna-watch-football-idiots-respond-to-nbc-pre+empting-sunday-night-football

Calhoun, C. (1991) Introduction: Habermas and the public sphere. In C. Calhoun (ed.), *Habermas and the Public Sphere* (pp. 1–48). Cambridge, MA: MIT Press.

Childers, J. P. (2008) Deliberating rhetoric: Review essay. *Quarterly Journal of Speech*, 94(4), 455–467.

Cole, J. (2012, August 29) NFL moving on with replacement referees. *Yahoo!Sports*. Retrieved from http://sports.yahoo.com/news/nfl – nfl-can-go-on-with-replacement-referees.html

Cottle, S. (2011) Media and the Arab uprisings of 2011: Research notes. *Journalism,* 12, 647–659.

Dahlberg, L. (2007) The Internet, deliberative democracy, and power: Radicalizing the public sphere. *International Journal of Media and Cultural Politics,* 3, 47–64.

Dietel-McLaughlin, E. (2010) *Remediating Democracy:YouTube and the Vernacular Rhetorics of Web 2.0.* (Doctoral dissertation). Bowling Green State University, OH.

Dugan, L. (2012, February 21) Twitter to surpass 500 million registered users on Wednesday. *All Twitter*. Retrieved from http://www.mediabistro.com/alltwitter/500-million-registered-users_b18842

Evans, S. (2012, September 24) Belichick in trouble as criticism grows on stand-in referees. *Yahoo!Sports*. Retrieved from http://sports.yahoo.com/news/nfl-belichick-trouble-criticism-grows-stand-referees-160033160 – nfl.html

Fraser, N. (1991) Rethinking the public sphere: A contribution to the critique of actually existing democracy. In C. Calhoun (ed.), *Habermas and the Public Sphere* (pp. 109–142). Cambridge, MA: MIT Press.

Freedlander, D. (2013, February 5) *Deadspin* rides Manti T'eo hoax story to renown – and keeps heat on ESPN. *The Daily Beast*. Retrieved from http://www.thedailybeast.com/articles/2013/02/05/deadspin-rides-manti-te-o-hoax-story-to-renown-and-keeps-heat-on-espn.html

Garsten, B. (2009) *Saving Persuasion: A Defense of Rhetoric and Judgment.* Cambridge, MA: Harvard University Press.

Gutmann, A. and Thompson, D. (1996) *Democracy and Disagreement.* Cambridge, MA: Belknap.

Habermas, J. (1991) *The Structural Transformation of the Public Sphere: An Inquiry into a Category of Bourgeois Society* (T. Burger, trans.). Cambridge, MA: MIT Press.

Habermas, J. (2001) *On the Pragmatics of Social Interaction: Preliminary Studies in the Theory of Communicative Action* (B. Fultner, trans.). Cambridge, MA: MIT Press.

Hambrick, M. E. (2012) Six degrees of information: Using social network analysis to explore the spread of information within sport social networks. *International Journal of Sport Communication,* 5, 16–34.

Hanson, R. L. (1985) *The Democratic Imagination in America: Conversations with Our Past.* Princeton, NJ: Princeton University Press.

Hogan, J. M. (2008) Rhetorical pedagogy and democratic citizenship: Reviving the traditions of civic engagement and public deliberations. In T. F. McDorman and D. M. Timmerman (eds), *Rhetoric and Democracy: Pedagogical and Political Practices* (pp. 75–97). East Lansing, MI: Michigan State University Press.

Ivie, R. L. (2002) Rhetorical deliberation and democratic politics in the here and now. *Rhetoric and Public Affairs,* 5, 277–285.

Judkis, M. (2012, October 4) Big Bird: Romney loves him, but social media loves him more. *Washington Post*. Retrieved from http://www.washingtonpost.com/blogs/arts-post/post/big-bird-romney-loves-him-but-social-media-loves-him-more/2012/10/04/e3ff789a-0e26-11e2-a310-2363842b7057_blog.html?wprss=rss_style

Juris, J. S. (2012) Reflections on #occupy everywhere: Social media, public space, and emerging logics of aggregation. *American Ethnologist,* 39, 259–279.

Kaufman, P. and Wolff, E. A. (2010) Playing and protesting: Sport as a vehicle for social change. *Journal of Sport and Social Issues,* 34, 154–175.

Khan, A. (2012) *Curt Flood in the Media: Baseball, Race, and the Demise of the Activist Athlete.* Oxford, MS: University Press of Mississippi.

Kluwe, C. (2012, September 7) "They won't magically turn you into lustful cockmonster." *Deadspin.com*. Retrieved from http://deadspin.com/5941348/they-wont-magically-turn-you-into-a-lustful-cockmonster-chris-kluwe-explains-gay-marriage-to-the-politician-who-is-offended-by-an-nfl-player-supporting-it

Linskey, A. (2012, September 9) Burns backs off bid to silence Ravens player. *Baltimore Sun*. Retrieved from http://sports.yahoo.com/news/nfl-maryland-politician-out-of-line-for-attacking-brendon-ayanbadejos-support-of-gay-marriage.html

Lucaites, J. L. and Condit, C. M. (1998) Introduction. In J. L. Lucaites, C. M. Condit and S. Caudill (eds), *Contemporary rhetorical theory: A reader* (pp. 1–18). New York: Guilford.

Obama: Disputed call means NFL needs regular refs. (2011, September 25) *Sports Illustrated*. Retrieved from http://sportsillustrated.cnn.com/2012/football/nfl/09/25/barack-obama-replacement-refs-packers-seahawks.ap/index.html

Papacharissi, Z. (2002) The virtual sphere: The internet as a public sphere. *New Media and Society,* 4, 9–27.

Papacharissi, Z. (2004) Democracy online: Civility, politeness, and the democratic potential of online discussion groups. *New Media and Society,* 6, 259–283.

Parmelee, J. H. and Bichard, S. L. (2012) *Politics and the Twitter Revolution: How Tweets Influence the Relationship Between Political Leaders and the Public.* Lanham, MD: Lexington.

Plato. (1986) *Gorgias* (D. Zeyl, trans.). Indianapolis, IN: Hackett.

Rawls, J. (2001) *Justice as Fairness: A Restatement* (E. Kelly, ed.). Cambridge, MA: Belknap.

Sanderson, J. (2013) Social media and sport communication: Abundant theoretical opportunities. In P. M. Pedersen (ed.), *The Routledge Handbook of Sport Communication.* New York: Routledge.

Sanderson, J. and Kassing, J. W. (2011) Tweets and blogs: Transformative, adversarial, and integrative developments in sports media. In A. C. Billings (ed.), *Sports Media: Transformation, Integration, Consumption* (pp. 114–127). New York: Routledge.

Sandomir, R. (2008, May 1) A confrontation on "Costas Now" worthy of a blog. *New York Times.* Retrieved from http://www.nytimes.com/2008/05/01/sports/football/01sandomir.html?_r=0

Serby, S. (2012, September 26) Goodell, owners to blame for Seahawks' Fail Mary. *New York Post.* Retrieved from http://www.nypost.com/p/sports/more_sports/goodell_owners_to_blame_for_seahawks_XPqTqDDrjgTuQaWS1gNBEI

Simone, M. A. (2010) Deliberative democracy online: Bridging networks with digital technologies. *The Communication Review,* 13, 120–139.

Smith, A., Segall, L. and Cowley, S. (2012, October 4) Facebook reaches one million users. *CNNMoney.* Retrieved from http://money.cnn.com/2012/10/04/technology/facebook-billion-users/index.html

Steve Nash for HRC's NYers for marriage equality. (2011, May 20) *Human Rights Campaign.* Retrieved from http://www.hrc.org/videos/videos-steve-nash-for-hrcs-nyers-for-marriage-equality#.UHcW5duF8ls

Timmerman, D. M. and McDorman, T. F. (2008) Introduction: Rhetoric and democracy. In T. F. McDorman and D. M. Timmerman (eds), *Rhetoric and Democracy: Pedagogical and Political Practices* (pp. xi–xxxv). East Lansing, MI: Michigan State University Press.

Wallace, L., Wilson, J. and Miloch, K. (2011) Sporting Facebook: A content analysis of NCAA organizational sport pages and Big 12 Conference athletic department pages. *International Journal of Sport Communication,* 4, 422–444.

Wetzel, D. (2012, September 6) Maryland politician out of line for attacking Brendon Ayanbadejo's support of gay marriage. *Yahoo! Sports.* Retrieved from http://sports.yahoo.com/news/nfl-maryland-politician-out-of-line-for-attacking-brendon-ayanbadejo-s-support-of-gay-marriage.html

Wisc. Gov. Walker calls for return of union refs. (2012, September 25) *Sports Illustrated.* Retrieved from http://sportsillustrated.cnn.com/2012/football/nfl/09/25/scott-walker-packers-seahawks.ap/index.html

Zirin, D. (2012, September 27) It's over: The NFL's union referees return to work in style. *Edge of Sports.* Retrieved from http://www.edgeofsports.com/2012-09-27-779/index.html

4

THE POLITICAL ECONOMY OF SPORTS AND NEW MEDIA

Thomas F. Corrigan

CALIFORNIA STATE UNIVERSITY–SAN BERNARDINO

The political economy of media

The political economy of media is a theoretical perspective that seeks to understand the inter-relationships of wealth, power, and the media and cultural systems in societies – including sports and sports media. While much of media and communication studies focuses on textual representation and reception, political economists situate those processes in relation to broader political, economic, and socio-cultural structures of power, particularly class struggle (McChesney, 2008; Mosco, 2009).

Political economy's preeminent theorist, Karl Marx predicted that capitalism's contradictions and crises would compel the working class to overthrow this exploitative system (Marx and Engels, 1848/1998). Capitalism has proven remarkably dynamic and resilient, though, remaking itself in the face of existential crises while maintaining its constitutive (if contradictory) structures (D. Harvey, 2006). To explain capitalism's perpetuation during the twentieth century, critical political economists point to the structuring role of modern cultural institutions, such as education, commercial sports, and – particularly – the mass media (Jhally, 1989b; Mosco, 2009; Murdock, 1982).

Ideologically, private ownership and corporate subsidy of media and culture afforded capitalists platforms for advancing their interests by controlling public "consciousness." Materially, the commercialization of the cultural sphere facilitated capital accumulation processes. Commercial media generated demand for consumer goods and services (through advertising), and media firms provided reinvestment opportunities for keeping capital "productive." As this chapter explains, sports and sports media's rich cultural meanings and massive consumer interest factor prominently in these ideological and material processes.

New media technologies destabilize media's role in wealth and power asymmetries (Benkler, 2006; Castells, 2009; Shirky, 2010). For instance, social media tools allow athletes, fans, and sports activists to directly communicate with one another and the public – a development that threatens commercial sports media's (relative) ideological closure and scatters valuable audience attention. Capitalism, again, is dynamic and resilient, though. From a political economy perspective, a full understanding of new media's relationship to wealth and power requires attention to both change and continuity. How are (sports) media's long-standing relationships to wealth and power disrupted by new media's affordances? And – just as important – how are powerful interests using new media to *extend* class and corporate control?

43

Using instrumental control and structural constraint as an organizing framework, this chapter outlines a political economy of so-called "old" sports media. Then, change and continuity associated with new media's digital and interactive affordances are explored. While new media are undoubtedly transforming the sports media landscape, they are also being used to extend established relationships of wealth and power.

Instrumental control

The mass media are the principal institutions through which citizens make sense of the world and their place in it; however, the rich and powerful exercise inordinate influence over these accounts. Wealthy families and major corporations have long owned the lion's share of US media outlets – a tendency that has intensified in recent decades. Moreover, corporate media are embedded in relationships with major non-media corporations and political elites (Bagdikian, 2004; Herman and Chomsky, 1988; McChesney, 2008).

This dense web of relationships means that media workers are regularly tasked with presenting accounts of the world that may negatively affect their owners' and associates' interests. So the argument goes, corporate media's owners and directors exert instrumental control over media content not by directly intervening with "the red pen," but by allocating resources to some projects rather than others and by hiring and firing key media personnel. Further, employees self-censor to protect their jobs (Herman and Chomsky, 1988; Jhally, 1989b).

Historically, sports organizations, leagues, and personnel have all exerted instrumental control over sports coverage. During the 1940s, most Major League Baseball (MLB) franchises employed their own radio broadcast teams (McChesney, 1989), and announcers' full or partial payments by teams remained commonplace for decades. Broadcasters could critique a player's technique or manager's line-up – that was part of the show; however, blaming losses on management or highlighting sensitive franchise issues could jeopardize one's employment (Stewart and Newhan, 1988).

Commercial sports' influence over content has also been institutionalized in the broadcast contract's "no-criticism clause." In 2000, Philadelphia sports radio station WIP suspended talk radio host Mike Missanelli for critical comments about Philadelphia Flyers executives. The station's broadcast contract included a "no-criticism clause" that prohibited "personal attacks" on the team and personnel (Panaccio, 2000).

Newspaper sports beat reporters have faced their own *de facto* no-criticism clauses. To meet their deadlines, reporters must continually cultivate sources within sports organizations – and the sources know it. To discourage critical coverage, sports organizations or personnel can temporarily cut off access to the beat reporter (Lowes, 1999). As *The Dallas Morning News'* Gary Jacobson explained, "If you piss people off, they shut you out" (Strupp, 2006: para. 35).

Such examples attend to sports organizations and personnel advancing their specific interests by exerting influence over media production and resulting content; however, political economists also theorize instrumental control at more general levels, particularly class struggle. Whereas pluralist accounts stress capitalists' pursuit of narrow self-interests, political economists argue that members of the capitalist class coordinate on matters of policy and ideology, advancing their collective interests, in part, through ownership and subsidy of media (Murdock, 1982).

The political economists' argument is two-part. First, the capitalist class articulates shared values and policy positions through elite institutional mechanisms. These include a strategic policy-planning network, corporate and non-profit board memberships, and exclusive social clubs (Domhoff, 2005). Sports-stadium luxury boxes also function as business and social spaces for team owners, politicians, and the corporate elite (Schlueb and Damron, 2011). In the media and technology industries, power brokers meet annually in Sun Valley, Idaho, for Allen & Company's exclusive industry conference. Executives strike mergers and deals in Sun Valley; however, the media elite also use this meeting to "[build] a consensus regarding the primary mutual concerns of Big Media and big business as a whole" (Bettig and Hall, 2012: 81).

Second, political economists document the ways media content reflects capitalist class values and policy preferences. Specific media "biases" are of less concern here; rather, attention focuses on broad content patterns that normalize and naturalize system-maintaining worldviews. As Croteau, Hoynes and Milan (2012: 48) explain:

> Ownership by major corporations of vast portfolios of mass media gives us reason to believe that a whole range of ideas and images – those that question fundamental social arrangements, under which media owners are doing quite well – will rarely be visible.

Conversely, media firms widely distribute system-maintaining content, such as sports news and game accounts. Sports and sports media provide a two-part ideological service to the capitalist power structure – as distracting spectacles and as socializing agents. As an "opiate of the masses," sports spectacles have long served as sanctioned escapes from the alienation of industrial and postindustrial capitalism (Jhally, 1984; Kellner, 2003). And "sports chatter" – ongoing conversations about sports – keeps spectators distracted from more pressing social and political issues well after the game has finished (Chomsky, 2011; Eco, 1983). More than an "opiate," sports also socialize spectators into capitalist production and consumption processes. Media accounts accentuate and celebrate sports' idealized capitalist structures, particularly labor's bureaucratic subordination, rationalization, specialization, measurement, and sale. Players and teams that attend to these processes are rewarded and celebrated. Codes of sportsmanship and fair play reinforce sports' meritocratic precepts, legitimating capitalism as fair, just, and democratic (Jhally, 1984; Kellner, 2003; Real, 1975).

The trouble with instrumentalist frameworks – in both specific and general variants – is that empirical evidence for ideological control is challenging to come by. Power relationships can be mapped, interests inferred, and logically correlating media content documented. But those data points do not necessarily indicate causality. Detailed case studies and insider accounts provide telling, if anecdotal, detail; however, the best of political economy interrogates instrumental control while acknowledging structural constraints that both enable and place broad limits on power (Jhally, 1989b; Murdock, 1982).

Structural constraint

Political economy's structural accounts follow from two basic observations: first, that capital accumulation is fundamental to the system's perpetuation; and, second, that capitalism's inherent contradictions make it prone to accumulation-threatening crises. The wealthy and powerful actively pursue their individual and class interests; however, their actions are ultimately bounded by the structural imperative to perpetually generate ever-larger returns on investment in a crisis-prone environment (D. Harvey, 2006).

"Underconsumption" and "overaccumulation" crises fundamentally shaped the twentieth century's transition from competitive to monopoly (or oligopolistic) capitalism. Rapid expansions in productive capacity often outpaced consumer demand for goods, resulting in underconsumption. Meanwhile, huge corporate profits in mature, oligopolistic industries outstripped the development of new reinvestment opportunities, resulting in overaccumulation (Baran and Sweezy, 1966; Mandel, 1972).

Capitalism is remarkably adaptive, though, and the media industries played important roles in mitigating these crises. Since the 1920s, corporate advertisers have addressed underconsumption by harnessing media's broad public attention and rich social meanings (e.g. youth, love, power, beauty, community) to generate demand for goods and services. Sports' popularity and cultural resonance made it ideal for these purposes. Meanwhile, an influx of advertising dollars made media companies, themselves, viable investment opportunities for overaccumulated capital (Andrews, 2009; Goldman, 1992; Leiss, Kline and Jhally, 1997).

In the newspaper and broadcast industries – those most relevant to a political economy of sports media – advertising sales historically constituted 75 percent and 100 percent of revenue, respectively (McAllister, 1996). Because of this, media companies gave audiences entertaining content, such as sports, primarily as a means to an end; profitability hinged, instead, on giving advertisers *who* they wanted (Bagdikian, 2004; Smythe, 1981). Sports media have a track record for attracting hard-to-reach, "demogenic" consumers (McAllister, 1996) – young, brand-conscious males with disposable income and the willingness to spend it. Sports fans also expose themselves to advertising in an upbeat editorial context that is conducive to consumption (Bellamy, 2006; Lowes, 1999; McChesney, 1989).

Media outlets have traditionally paid sports entities handsome sums for exclusive sports broadcast rights. Since audiences went to specific broadcasters to watch live events, broadcasters maximized audience size, and advertisers paid accordingly (Hutchins and Rowe, 2009). In 1961, the US major professional leagues successfully lobbied Congress for an anti-trust exemption in order to centrally (and lucratively) sell television rights (McChesney, 1989; Rader, 1984). Competition from cable and satellite networks created upward pressure on this market (Eastman and Meyer, 1989; Ourand, 2011). With these huge rights fees, television revenue accounted for large shares of total revenue in commercial sports (Cave and Crandall, 2001).

Sports news, information, and commentary outlets also heaped valuable attention on commercial sports entities. For newspapers, daily coverage of men's commercial sports fed and fomented Americans' "insatiable" appetite for sports coverage (Rader, 1984). This was as much a "push" as a "pull" dynamic, though. For sports franchises, daily newspaper coverage and programs such as ESPN's *SportsCenter* provided valuable "news-as-publicity" (Lowes, 1999). Resource-rich men's commercial sports teams employed media relations personnel to arrange press conferences, compile media guides, and otherwise "facilitate" sports journalists' work. In this, Lowes (1999) argued that sports news was, effectively, a promotional vehicle for commercial (male) sports entities.

With sports delivering large audiences to media, and media providing attention and revenue to sports, McChesney (1989) described the sports–media relationship as "symbiotic." Indeed, commercial sports and media are so intertwined that Jhally (1989a) described the industry as the "sports/media complex"; Wenner (1998) referred to them as "MediaSport."

New media

To what extent have new media disrupted or extended these relationships of wealth, power, sports, and media? To answer this question, it is helpful to identify what exactly is "new" about "new media." The matter is contested; however, *digital* and *interactive* affordances are two characteristics that distinguish new media from traditional media's analog formats and one-way structural relationships (Rideout and Reddick, 2001). Using these affordances as an organizing framework, the following discusses some ways in which new media's uptake by producers and consumers is (re)shaping processes of instrumental control and structural constraint in sports media.

Digitization

Traditional analog media formats were characterized by relatively distinct technological affordances and constraints. For instance, television's live visuals facilitated its "dream marriage" with sports (Real, 2011). And newspapers delivered text-based background, analysis, and statistical minutiae (McChesney, 1989). However, real time newspaper accounts were as impossible as reading long text on television was impractical. Such affordances and constraints made it practically and conceptually useful to talk about media indust*ries*, rather than *a* media industry (Croteau *et al.*, 2012; Hesmondhalgh, 2007).

Digital media are different, though. Compared to analog formats, digital media's basis in binary code means content is more easily reproduced, transferred, and manipulated. Moreover, the Internet's networked infrastructure means that text, photographs, moving images, audio, and live content can all be produced, distributed, and consumed on the same multimedia (or converged) platform and devices (Croteau *et al.*, 2012). For instance, multimedia journalism makes use of the best available medium (or combination of media) for telling stories on the Web. With its emphasis on speed, visuals, and analysis, sports journalism has been on the leading edge of multimedia innovations (albeit sometimes reluctantly). One sports editor explained the demand for journalists who "Talk like ESPN, write like SI, move it like AP" (Brown-Smith and Groves, 2010; Murray, McGuire, Ketterer and Sowell, 2011: 84).

The ongoing shift from media indust*ries* to a more fluid digital content industry has created troubling power asymmetries, though. With the help of deregulation, such as the 1996 Telecommunications Act, media conglomerates have aggressively pursued horizontal integration strategies once restricted, technologically, to specific sectors (e.g. newspaper chains, television networks). Through cross-media acquisitions, large and powerful transnational media corporations (TNMCs), such as Disney, News Corporation and Time Warner, aim to reduce costs, erect barriers to entry, and facilitate cross-promotional synergies (Croteau and Hoynes, 2006).

Given sports' popularity and cultural relevance, conglomerates see sports media and even sports franchises as valuable cross-promotional content for their other media properties and corporate advertisers. Famously, Disney founded the Mighty Ducks hockey franchise in 1993 to exploit synergies between the team and its namesake films, cartoons, and related merchandise (Whitson, 1998). More recent sports synergies revolve around Disney's ESPN brands (e.g. ESPN, ESPN.com, *ESPN The Magazine*, ESPN Mobile, and many others). These properties aggressively cross-promote one another's content, especially live sports programming.

As broadcast rights fees escalated in the mid-to-late 1990s, more media firms acquired professional sports franchises to gain access to those teams' valuable broadcast rights. By 2001, the media and entertainment sector constituted North American professional sports' largest ownership bloc – a full 31 percent of major league teams. Media interests included the "usual suspects" (Disney, News Corp., and Time Warner), regional media firms, and new media moguls, such as Microsoft's Paul Allen. These developments threaten to marginalize remaining non-commodified sports, as well as critical, independent accounts of commercial sports (J. Harvey, Law and Cantelon, 2001; Law, Harvey and Kemp, 2002).

By the mid-2000s, though, some TNMCs divested of their sports franchise holdings. Sports' and media's vertical integration did not disappear, though – it inverted (Bellamy and Walker, 2005). The NFL, MLB, Big Ten Conference, New York Yankees, and Texas Longhorns (among others) all created television networks for distributing live games (Ourand, 2010b). Individual athletes also communicate with fans through web sites, blogs, and social media (Sanderson and Kassing, 2011). And some teams even employ their own beat reporters

("Making the team," 2009). These arrangements provide sports entities and athletes greater control over their media coverage. In its Longhorn Network partnership, for instance, the University of Texas can fire ESPN announcers that do not "reflect the quality and reputation of UT" (Hiestand, 2011, para. 6).

Direct communication with fans shifts the sports/media complex's organization (Sanderson and Kassing, 2011); however, assertions of radical change deserve critical interrogation. As noted, commercial sports interests have long influenced their coverage through broadcasters' employment, "no-criticism clauses," and access to sources. And industry symbiosis meant that sports coverage was largely promotional, anyway. Indeed, sports entities create these new outlets to secure control over new and existing revenue streams; control over "the message" is a welcome byproduct of the profit imperative (Ourand, 2010a).

Unlike free-to-air broadcasts, digital television and online services can operate as "electronic turnstiles" (Whitson, 1998), generating new revenues for media firms and sports entities from pay-per-view and subscription purchases. High consumer demand for live sports makes telecasts a "killer application" (Hutchins and Rowe, 2009) for entering and exerting control in emerging markets (Andrews, 2003). For instance, cable operators use sports content to market "TV Everywhere" packages. After "authenticating" (i.e. passing the turnstile), cable customers watch premium TV content on computers and mobile devices. In 2011, ESPN stated it would not consider rights deals without broadband and mobile rights for TV Everywhere (Ourand, 2011).

Stiff competition for digital rights contributed, in part, to an aggressive 2011 rights market-place, with annual payouts more than doubling previous deals (Ourand, 2011). Quite simply, in a fragmented media landscape of "digital plentitude" (Hutchins and Rowe, 2009) and prolifer-ating ad-avoidance technologies (e.g. DVRs, AdBlock software), few programming genres can still reliably aggregate mass audiences for advertisers like live sports can (Bellamy, 2006; Rowe, 2011). In 2010, live programming with uncertain outcomes – sports, awards shows, reality specials – accounted for 99 of the top-100 rated telecasts. And in 2012, TV advertisers invested 23 percent of their budgets in reaching audiences for sports events (Nielsen, 2013).

Rights holders seek more than advertiser dollars, though. Since live sports may be the last programming to keep cable subscribers from "cutting the cord" and migrating to online serv-ices, cable providers pay handsomely for sports channels ("The incredible value of live sports," 2012). According to SNL Kagan research, ESPN commanded a $5.13 per subscriber monthly carriage fee from US cable companies in 2012, far outstripping the basic cable channel aver-age of 26 cents per month (Badenhausen, 2013). Regional sports networks averaged $2.49 per subscriber – an increase (like ESPN's) of roughly 8 percent, annually (Sherman, 2012). In this, live sports' proliferation is as much – if not more – a function of consumer demand for content as it is advertiser demand for demogenic audiences.

Fans' new technology uses destabilize these processes, though. Most importantly, fans can now share high quality, unauthorized live sports broadcasts using peer-to-peer (P2P) networks, undermining the traditional broadcast model's lucrative exclusivity. This portends, perhaps, media's next big intellectual property (IP) battle. Sports with international fan bases, such as soccer, are particularly susceptible to P2P's global reach (Hutchins and Rowe, 2012). In 2009, the English Premier League (EPL) urged officials to make Internet service providers responsi-ble for users' activities and to appoint an "IP tsar" (Gibson, 2009). Sports organizations only recoil over P2P streaming because live sports rights are so valuable, though. Sports organiza-tions tolerate, if not encourage, other non-commercial IP infringements for their promotional benefits, such as in-stadium photo sharing and the creation of YouTube highlights (Belson and Arango, 2009). This underscores needed attention to new media's second key affordance: interactivity.

Interactivity

Most traditional mass media were characterized by high production costs and low reproduction (or copy) costs. This meant, first, that media production was restricted to a small numbers of wealthy individuals and well-capitalized corporations. And, second, that profitability hinged on maximizing audiences for successively cheaper copies. These economics incentivized a largely one-way, one-to-many communication model focused on the creation and distribution of escapist fare, such as sports (Benkler, 2006; Hesmondhalgh, 2007; Shirky, 2010).

New media radically reduce production and distribution costs, making everyone with a networked phone or computer an instant creator and global distributor. In this, traditional mass media now operate alongside and in conjunction with new media's two-way, many-to-many communication model (Benkler, 2006; Castells, 2009). New media are interactive and participatory in that users can now talk back to traditional media gatekeepers and collaborate with one another. Claims of new media's democratic or revolutionary potentials hinge on these interactive, participatory affordances (Jenkins, 2008; Shirky, 2010).

Some women's sports advocates saw blogs as opportune tools for challenging mainstream media's marginalization and trivialization of female athletes (Maxwell, 2009; Messner, 2002). In 2009, women's sports advocates launched the Women Talk Sports blog collective to promote visibility and issue advocacy around women's sports (Women Talk Sports, 2012). Progressive sportswriter Dave Zirin, and fan advocacy groups, such as the League of Fans and the Sports Fan Coalition, also took to the Web in the late 2000s to challenge entrenched interests, publicize their agendas, and organize for policy changes ("Dave Zirin: Sports columnist," 2009; League of Fans, n.d.; Sports Fans Coalition, 2010).

More common and visible are sports blogs and "Fan Based Internet Sports Communities" (FBISCs) where fans satisfy their sports information and identity needs (Porter, Wood and Benigni, 2011). In the late 2000s and early 2010s, independent commercial sports blog networks, such as SB Nation, Bleacher Report, and Big Lead Sports, amassed hundreds of blogs and FBISCs and sold advertising against these sites' collective traffic figures. Beyond their roughly ten million unique visitors each per month, advertisers also liked these networks' "young, tech-savvy, affluent male" audience (Corrigan, 2012: 131). This "sports-tech" demographic includes "high-information" media consumers (Carmody, 2011) and new technology "early adopters" (Ourand, 2011). Many are also fantasy sports participants – a group characterized as "hyper-consumers" (Fisher, 2008). Moreover, blog networks and FBISCs operate with substantially lower cost structures than the majors. As of 2012, even SB Nation's most prolific bloggers were minimally compensated – if at all. Instead, they write for the pleasure of interacting with appreciative fellow fans (Corrigan, 2012).

Lines between outsiders and the mainstream media increasingly blur, though. Industry leaders, such as ESPN.com, offer discussion areas where fans show off their analytical expertise (Meân, 2011). And establishment sports journalists maintain blogs to engage users, if reluctantly (Schultz and Sheffer, 2008). In 2012, Turner Sports paid $175 million for Bleacher Report, providing Turner a deep well of needed (if largely amateur) Web content. Turner also announced plans to have Bleacher Report talent appear on its CNN and Headline News television properties (Fisher, 2012). Thus, fan production – an ostensible threat to the sports/media complex – is increasingly incorporated into MediaSport's familiar commercial structure.

Interactive media experiences can also intensify fan passions for teams and athletes, as well as media and advertisers' brands (Oates, 2009). Fans that follow the NFL and MLB on social media report increased avidity for these leagues and more time watching and following events (Broughton, 2011). Similarly, by interacting with athletes' blogs and Twitter feeds, fans can experience parasocial interaction – heightened levels of perceived closeness and involvement with an athlete (Sanderson and Kassing, 2011). Many sports fans also augment their televised sports experience by using a "second screen" to search for sports information and chat with other fans. Indeed, fans' historical proclivity to "chatter" positions live sports well for social TV practices (Pardee, 2012).

For advertisers, interactivity creates opportunities for inserting brands into users' meaningful sports media experiences (Corrigan, 2012; Meân, 2011). For its Captain Morgan's "Captain of the Tailgate" sponsored blog posts, SB Nation asked readers to recount tailgating¹ tips and experiences; the process (ideally) created greater resonance with the Captain Morgan brand (Corrigan, 2012). Other campaigns involve even more intensive "consumer co-production" – putting the consumer to work (Ritzer and Jurgenson, 2010). The year 2013 marked the 6th iteration of Doritos' "Crash the Super Bowl" campaign, in which public advertisement submissions compete for possible inclusion during the Super Bowl. The ads – also voted on by the public – circulate widely on social media. As Frito-Lay's Ann Mukherjee explains, "your consumers actually become your billboards . . . They're the ones who become the ambassadors, who talk about the integrity and authenticity of the brand" (Blair, 2013: 9).

Monitoring and measurement of sports media use for behavioral targeting deserves greater attention and critique. Media outlets and metrics companies build user profiles based on visit, clicks, and purchases. With these profiles, media and marketers tailor content, offers, and advertising to us during future sessions, on other websites, and even in offline consumption contexts (Turow, 2011). With a few exceptions (e.g. Corrigan, 2012; Hutchins and Rowe, 2012) sports media research has not explored these processes.

Finally, interactive media have largely extended sports media's broad ideological processes. The expanding live sports menu, and the even larger user-generated content universe means that there are simply more sports events, updates, and conversations competing to distract us from social and political issues than ever before. There is more critical coverage of the sports business and social issues in and around our games; however, the expanding plentitude of commercial sports content dwarfs these critical accounts. True to their insatiable appetite for sports, fans have continued to commit inordinate amounts of time to sports consumption, particularly sports "apps" and fantasy sports games (Chaffin, 2007; Nielsen, 2013).

Interactive media place users in new subject positions, reorganizing socialization processes. Traditional media audiences passively watched sports work play out. Sports video gamers, fantasy sports contestants, and "mock draft" contributors, on the other hand, all actively participate in the "vicarious management" of the capitalist labor processes (Oates, 2009). Fantasy sports participants enact pro sport's managerial processes, and they learn to identify with its ownership class. As managers, fantasy sports participants exercise control and authority amid a crisis in (white) masculinity (Davis and Duncan, 2006).

Conclusion: Property and promotion

Media companies and sports entities face a challenging dilemma. Digital media present opportunities for monetizing live sports through pay services, and for driving fans to content and brands through multi-media distribution and cross-promotion. Generating new revenues (e.g. TV Everywhere) and maximizing existing ones (e.g. advertising sales) requires a degree of corporate control and coordination in production, distribution, and consumption. As TNMCs expand their sports media holdings and sports entities move into the media business, so, too, are opportunities for instrumental control extended and expanded.

On the other hand, fans now interact with sports media, sharing their experiences with others in more participatory ways. Sports entities, media firms, and corporate advertisers all stand to benefit from gains in fan avidity and actionable marketing data, not to mention fans' ideological identification with powerful institutions. To make the most of these opportunities, though, sports and media organizations have to cede to fans a degree of control over the mediated sports experience. Some interactive fan practices, like P2P streaming, undermine key revenue streams, and entrenched interests may not always like the way sports are discussed on the Web. How these tensions are negotiated remains to be seen. What is clear, though, is that incongruities between digital property and interactive promotion permeate and will continue to shape contemporary sports media for years to come.

Note

1. "Tailgating" is the practice of hosting picnics and parties from the tailgate of a vehicle, often on the parking lot of a sports stadium, which originated in America.

References

Andrews, D. L. (2003) Sport and the transnationalizing media corporation. *The Journal of Media Economics,* 16(4), 235–251.

Andrews, D. L. (2009) Sport, culture, and late capitalism. In B. Carrington and I. McDonald (eds), *Marxism, Cultural Studies and Sport* (pp. 213–231). London: Routledge.

Badenhausen, K. (2013, November 9) Why ESPN is worth $40 billion as the world's most valuable media property. *Forbes.* Retrieved from http://www.forbes.com/sites/kurtbadenhausen/2012/11/09/why-espn-is-the-worlds-most-valuable-media-property-and-worth-40-billion/

Bagdikian, B. H. (2004) *The New Media Monopoly*. Boston, MA: Beacon.

Baran, P. A. and Sweezy, P. M. (1966) *Monopoly Capital: An Essay on the American Economic and Social Order.* New York: Monthly Review Press.

Bellamy Jr., R.V. (2006) Sports media: A modern institution. In A. A. Raney and J. Bryant (eds), *Handbook of Sports and Media* (pp. 63–76). Mahwah, NJ: Lawrence Erlbaum Associates.

Bellamy Jr., R.V. and Walker, J. R. (2005) Whatever happened to synergy? *NINE: A Journal of Baseball History and Culture,* 13(2), 19–30.

Belson, K. and Arango, T. (2009, August 19) Leagues see bloggers in the bleachers as a threat. *NYTimes.com.* Retrieved from http://www.nytimes.com/2009/08/20/sports/ncaafootball/20rights.html

Benkler, Y. (2006) *The Wealth of Networks: How Social Production Transforms Markets and Freedom.* New Haven, CT: Yale University Press.

Bettig, R.V. and Hall, J. L. (2012) *Big Media, Big Money: Cultural Texts and Political Economics.* Lanham, MD: Rowman & Littlefield.

Blair, E. (2013, February 1) For Super Bowl ads, more social-media savvy. *All Things Considered.* Retrieved from http://www.npr.org/2013/02/01/170753460/for-super-bowl-ads-more-social-media-savvy

Broughton, D. (2011, June 27) Survey spots social media trends among fans. *SportsBusiness Daily.* Retrieved from http://www.sportsbusinessdaily.com/Journal/Issues/2011/06/27/Research-and-Ratings/Social-media.aspx?hl=Research and Ratings&sc=0

Brown-Smith, C. and Groves, J. (2010, October 7) Newsroom innovation leaders: The sports department. *The Changing Newsroom.* Retrieved from http://changingnewsroom.wordpress.com/2010/10/07/newsroom-innovation-leaders-the-sports-department/

Carmody, T. (2011, May 23) Both the short and long of it: How sportswriting is taking over the web through innovation and adaptation. *niemanlab.org.* Retrieved from http://www.niemanlab.org/2011/05/both-the-short-and-long-of-it-how-sportswriting-is-taking-over-the-web-through-innovation-and-adaptation/

Castells, M. (2009) *Communication Power.* New York: Oxford.

Cave, M. and Crandall, R. W. (2001) Sports rights and the broadcast industry. *The Economic Journal,* 111, F4–F26.

Chaffin, J. (2007, November 20) All to play for in fantasy sports. *Financial Times.* Retrieved from http://www.ft.com/cms/s/0/0c114760-970c-11dc-b2da-0000779fd2ac.html - axzz1AU9W3wo9

Chomsky, N. (2011, August 15/22) Sports and spectacle. *The Nation.* Retrieved from http://www.thenation.com/article/162388/sports-and-spectacle

Corrigan, T. F. (2012) *Manufacturing Sports Blogs: The Political Economy and Practice of Networked Sports Blogging.* Doctoral Dissertation, Pennsylvania State University, State College, PA.

Croteau, D. and Hoynes, W. (2006) *The Business of Media: Corporate Media and the Public Interest* (2nd edn.). Thousand Oaks, CA: Pine Forge Press.

Croteau, D., Hoynes, W. and Milan, S. (2012) *Media/Society: Industries, Images, and Audiences.* Thousand Oaks, CA: Sage.

Dave Zirin: Sports columnist. (2009, November–December) *UTNE Reader.* Retrieved from http://www.utne.com/Politics/Dave-Zirin-Sports-Columnist-Thinking-Sportswriting.aspx#axzz2ezBD3RN7

Davis, N. W. and Duncan, M. C. (2006) Sports knowledge is power: Reinforcing masculine privilege through fantasy sport league participation. *Journal of Sport and Social Issues,* 30(3), 244–264.

Domhoff, G. W. (2005) The class-domination theory of power. *Who Rules America?* Retrieved from http://www2.ucsc.edu/whorulesamerica/power/class_domination.html

Eastman, S. T. and Meyer, T. P. (1989) Sports programming: Scheduling, costs, and competition. In L. A. Wenner (ed.), *Media, Sports, and Society.* Newbury Park, CA: Sage.

Eco, U. (1983) Sports chatter. In U. Eco (ed.), *Travels in Hyper Reality: Essays.* San Diego, CA: Harcourt Brace Jovanovich.

Fisher, E. (2008, November 17) Study: Fantasy players spend big. *SportsBusiness Journal.* Retrieved from http://www.sportsbusinessjournal.com/article/60598

Fisher, E. (2012, August 13) Bleacher sale: Another indie hit. *SportsBusiness Journal.* Retrieved from http://www.sportsbusinessdaily.com/Journal/Issues/2012/08/13/Media/Bleacher-Report.aspx?hl=bleacher report turner&sc=0

Gibson, O. (2009, January 21) Premier League goes to war on internet pirates. *The Guardian* [online]. Retrieved from http://www.guardian.co.uk/football/2009/jan/21/premier-league-cracks-down-on-illegal-broadcasts

Goldman, R. (1992) *Reading Ads Socially.* London: Routledge.

Harvey, D. (2006) *The Limits to Capital.* London: Verso.

Harvey, J., Law, A. and Cantelon, M. (2001) North American professional sport franchises ownership patterns and global entertainment conglomerates. *Sociology of Sport Journal,* 18(4), 435–457.

Herman, E. S. and Chomsky, N. (1988) *Manufacturing Consent: The Political Economy of Mass Media.* New York: Pantheon.

Hesmondhalgh, D. (2007) *The Cultural Industries* (2nd edn.). Thousand Oaks, CA: Sage.

Hiestand, M. (2011, August 12) How Texas is steering college TV sports. *USA Today.* Retrieved from http://www.usatoday.com/NEWS/usaedition/2011-08-12-1A-cover-Longhorn-network_CV_U.htm

Hutchins, B. and Rowe, D. (2009) From broadcast scarcity to digital plenitude: The changing dynamics of the media sport content economy. *Television and New Media,* 10(4), 354–370.

Hutchins, B. and Rowe, D. (2012) *Sport beyond televison: The Internet, digital media and the rise of networked media sport.* New York: Routledge.

The incredible value of live sports (2012, May 25) *On the Media.* Retrieved from http://www.onthemedia.org/2012/may/25/incredible-value-live-sports/

Jenkins, H. (2008) *Convergence Culture: Where Old and New Media Collide.* New York: New York University Press.

Jhally, S. (1984) The spectacle of accumulation: Material and cultural factors in the evolution of the sports/media complex. *Critical Sociology,* 12(3), 41.

Jhally, S. (1989a) Cultural studies and the sports/media complex. In L. A. Wenner (ed.), *Media, Sports and Society* (pp. 70–93). Newbury Park, CA: Sage.

Jhally, S. (1989b) The political economy of culture. In I. Angus and S. Jhally (eds), *Cultural Politics in Contemporary America* (pp. 65–81). New York: Routledge.

Kellner, D. (2003) *Media Spectacle.* London: Routledge.

Law, A., Harvey, J. and Kemp, S. (2002) The global sport mass media oligopoly: The three usual suspects and more. *International Review for the Sociology of Sport,* 37(3/4), 279–302.

League of Fans. (n.d.) *The Core Principles of League of Fans.* Retrieved from http://leagueoffans.org/cor/

Leiss, W., Kline, S. and Jhally, S. (1997) *Social Communication in Advertising: Persons, Products and Images of Well-being,* 2. New York: Routledge.

Lowes, M. D. (1999) *Inside the Sports Pages: Work Routines, Professional Ideologies, and the Manufacture of Sports News.* Toronto, Canada: University of Toronto Press.

Making the team (2009, October 9) *On the Media.* Retrieved from http://www.onthemedia.org/2009/oct/09/making-the-team/transcript/

Mandel, E. (1972) *Late Capital* (J. De Bres, trans.). London: NLB.

Marx, K. and Engels, F. (1848/1998) *The Communist Manifesto: A Modern Edition*. London: Verso.

Maxwell, H. (2009, October 29) Burden, buzz or both? Reflections on social media and women's sports. *Tucker Center for Research on Girls and Women in Sport*. Retrieved from http://tuckercenter.wordpress.com/2009/10/28/social-media-womens-sports-burden-buzz-or-both/

McAllister, M. P. (1996) *The Commercialization of American Culture: New Advertising, Control, and Democracy*. Thousand Oaks, CA: Sage.

McChesney, R. W. (1989) Media made sport: A history of sports coverage in the United States. In L. A. Wenner (ed.), *Media, Sports and Society* (pp. 46–69). Newbury Park, CA: Sage

McChesney, R. W. (2008) *The Political Economy of Media*. New York: Monthly Review.

Meân, L. J. (2011) Sport, identities, and consumption: The construction of sport at ESPN.com. In A. C. Billings (ed.), *Sports Media: Transformation, Integration, Consumption* (pp. 162–180). New York: Routledge.

Messner, M. A. (2002) *Taking the Field: Women, Men, and Sports*. Minneapolis, MN: University of Minnesota Press.

Mosco, V. (2009) *The Political Economy of Communication* (2nd edn.). Thousand Oaks, CA: Sage.

Murdock, G. (1982) Large corporations and control of the communications industries. In M. Gurevitch, T. Bennett, J. Curran and J. Woollacott (eds), *Culture, Society and the Media*. London: Methuen.

Murray, R., McGuire, J., Ketterer, S. and Sowell, M. (2011) Flipping the field: The next generation of newspaper sports journalists. *Journal of Sports Media, 6*(2), 65–88.

Nielsen. (2013) State of the media: 2012 year in sports. Retrieved from http://www.scribd.com/doc/122600857/Nielsen-2012-Year-in-Sports-Review

Oates, T. P. (2009) New media and the repackaging of NFL fandom. *Sociology of Sport Journal, 26,* 31–49.

Ourand, J. (2010a, October 11) Leonsis: Properties' desire to launch networks only natural. *SportsBusiness Journal*. Retrieved from http://www.sportsbusinessdaily.com/Journal/Issues/2010/10/20101011/Media/Leonsis-Properties-Desire-To-Launch-Networks-Only-Natural.aspx?hl=leonsis&sc=0

Ourand, J. (2010b, August 16) Tune in tomorrow. *SportsBusiness Journal*. Retrieved from http://www.sportsbusinessdaily.com/Journal/Issues/2010/08/20100816/SBJ-In-Depth/Tune-In-Tomorrow.aspx

Ourand, J. (2011, June 6) How high can rights fees go? More bidders, solid ratings, attractive demos and 'TV Everywhere' fuel a red hot market, but could the bubble burst? *SportsBusiness Journal*. Retrieved from http://www.sportsbusinessdaily.com/Journal/Issues/2011/06/06/In-Depth/Rights-Fees.aspx

Panaccio, T. (2000, June 23) Hemmed in by Flyers, some WIP hosts fume. *Philadelphia Inquirer*. Retrieved from http://articles.philly.com/2000-06-23/sports/25602051_1_craig-carton-wip-flyers-general-manager

Pardee, T. (2012, May 9) How social TV is changing the field for sports. *Ad Age*. Retrieved from http://adage.com/article/special-report-social-tv-conference/social-tv-changing-field-sports/234664/

Porter, L. V., Wood, C. and Benigni, V. L. (2011) From analysis to aggression: The nature of fan emotion, cognition, and behavior in Internet sports communities In A. C. Billings (ed.), *Sports Media: Transformation, Integration, Consumption* (pp. 128–145). New York: Routledge.

Rader, B. (1984) *In its Own Image: How Television has Transformed Sports*. New York: Free Press.

Real, M. R. (1975) Super bowl: Mythic spectacle. *Journal of Communication, 25*(1), 31–43.

Real, M. R. (2011) Theorizing the sports-television dream marriage: Why sports fit television so well. In A. C. Billings (ed.), *Sports Media: Transformation, Integration, Consumption* (pp. 19–39). New York: Routledge.

Rideout, V. and Reddick, A. (2001) Multimedia policy for Canada and the United States: Industrial development as public interest. In V. Mosco and D. Schiller (eds), *Continental Order? Integrating North America for Cybercapitalism* (pp. 265–292). Lanham, MD: Rowman & Littlefield.

Ritzer, G. and Jurgenson, N. (2010) Production, consumption, prosumption: The nature of capitalism in the age of the digital 'prosumer'. *Journal of Consumer Culture, 10*(1), 13–36.

Rowe, D. (2011) Sports media: Beyond broadcasting, beyond sports, beyond societies? In A. C. Billings (ed.), *Sports Media: Transformation, Integration, Consumption* (pp. 94–113). New York: Routledge.

Sanderson, J. and Kassing, J. W. (2011) Tweets and blogs: Transformative, adversarial, and integrative developments in sports media. In A. C. Billings (ed.), *Sports Media: Transformation, Integration, Consumption* (pp. 114–127). New York: Routledge.

Schlueb, M. and Damron, D. (2011, May 12) Orlando leaders often play host in Amway Center luxury box. *Orlando Sentinel*. Retrieved from http://articles.orlandosentinel.com/2011-05-12/news/os-amway-city-boxseats-20110512_1_orlando-leaders-suite-city-leaders

Schultz, B. and Sheffer, M. L. (2008) Blogging from the labor perspective: Lessons for media managers. *The International Journal on Media Management, 10*(1), 1–9.

Sherman, A. (2012, April 5) For sports networks, you gotta pay to play. *Bloomberg Businessweek*. Retrieved from http://www.businessweek.com/articles/2012-04-05/for-sports-networks-you-gotta-pay-to-play

Shirky, C. (2010) *Cognitive Surplus: Creativity and Generosity in a Connected Age*. New York: Penguin Press.

Smythe, D. W. (1981) *Dependency Road: Communications, Capitalism, Consciousness, and Canada*. New York: Ablex Publishing Corporation.

Sports Fans Coalition (2010) *Agenda*. Retrieved from http://sportsfans.org/agenda/

Stewart, L. and Newhan, R. (1988, June 14) What's fair or foul in broadcast booth? Announcers walk a fine line when reporting controversial incidents. *Los Angeles Times*. Retrieved from http://articles.latimes.com/print/1988-06–14/sports/sp-4297_1_baseball-announcer

Strupp, J. (2006, October 1) Caught (not) looking. *Editor and Publisher*. Retrieved from http://www.editorandpublisher.com/PrintArticle/Caught-Not-Looking

Turow, J. (2011) *The Daily You: How the New Advertising Industry is Defining Your Identity and Your Worth*. New Haven, CT: Yale University Press.

Wenner, L. A. (1998) Playing the MediaSport game. In L. A. Wenner (ed.), *MediaSport* (pp. 3–13). London: Routledge.

Whitson, D. (1998) Circuits of promotion: Media, marketing and the globalization of sport. In L. A. Wenner (ed.), *MediaSport* (pp. 57–72). London: Routledge.

Women Talk Sports. (2012) Women Talk Sports mission statement. Retrieved from http://www.womentalksports.com/p/about

5

FOUCAULT AND THE NEW SPORT MEDIA

Pirkko Markula

UNIVERSITY OF ALBERTA

In his introduction to the special issue on new media and sport in the *Sociology of Sport Journal*, David Leonard (2009) called for further research on how sporting culture might have been changed by new media users, how new media has changed sport knowledge production, and how to challenge the binary between old and new media in sport studies. Michel Foucault's work can offer one avenue for addressing these directions as it opens possibilities for analyzing auxiliary connections with global sporting cultures. In this chapter, I illustrate some ways that Foucault's theory can inform studies of new media and sport. I begin by introducing Foucault's concepts of 'Panoptic surveillance' and 'governmentality.' These concepts will then pave a way to an analysis of knowledge production, technology, and political strategies enabled by and embedded in the new media of sport and physically active bodies.

Panoptic surveillance and the new sport media

Foucault's work is often understood to culminate in three major dimensions: power relations, knowledge production, and the self constructed within the nexus of the other two dimensions. While the issue of power relations was dominant throughout Foucault's work, *Discipline and Punish* (Foucault, 1991) is often used as a basis for examinations of disciplinary control of individual bodies. Foucault (1978) indicated that this type of control occurred through an operation of what he labeled as anatomo-political power: individuals are manipulated by controlling their bodies. His concept, 'Panopticon,' refers to the way of sustaining the anatomo-political control of bodies. Originally, the Panopticon characterized Jeremy Bentham's prison design where guards in the central tower could survey the prisoners in prison cells surrounding the tower. The cells had windows that enabled the prisoner to be visible (even if against light) at all times. In contemporary society, however, the 'panopticism' can also be understood as a more abstract form of control that imposes particular conduct on a particular human multiplicity. We need only to insist that the multiplicity is reduced and confined to a tight place and that the imposition of a form of conduct is done by distributing in space, laying out and serializing in time, composing in space-time. (Foucault, 1978: 141).

The panoptic surveillance has been a central focus of studies of sport and exercise media (e.g. Cole, 1996; Duncan, 1994; Dworkin and Wachs, 1998; Jette, 2006; Markula and Pringle, 2006). These studies typically indicate how the media controls consumers by portraying a narrowly defined ideal of the sporting body. The ideal body type results in oppressive identity construction. For example, the thin, toned, and young body is closely connected to the production of narrowly defined feminine identity, and the muscular, strong, aggressive sporting body to masculinity. For many women, particularly, the narrowly defined ideal body is impossible to obtain. Media consumers engage in particular conduct, sport and exercise in an attempt to obtain such bodies and to demonstrate that they belong to the accepted, 'normal' gender category. This requires constant self-surveillance to avoid possible deviations from the 'normal' and continual engagement in bodily discipline through diet, exercise, and other behaviors. Because a 'normal' body is defined externally, the self-imposed body disciplines exemplify a panoptic power arrangement where an invisible gaze is imposed on individuals through media representations.

Digital technologies can serve as an effective means of imposing a particular taste or conduct on individuals similar to the 'old' media technologies of analog television, videotapes, or DVDs. Digitally based technologies such as video games, Internet, and digital television have created multiple, globally accessible, virtual sport and physical activity information sites. These can be used to discipline individuals to diet, to obtain an ideal physique, to learn competitive individualism of contemporary neo-liberalism, or to consume sporting services and goods more effectively. For example, Millington (2012) illustrated how 'exergames,' video-based exercise gaming such as Nintendo Wii Fit, can act as techniques that discipline individual bodies. The games guide participants through various workout programs, but also model the correct 'lean and gender-appropriate body aesthetics' (p. 7) parallel to the 'old' media workouts. The players also record various body 'metrics' (such as the BMI) through which it is possible to constantly self-survey one's progress toward the 'normal,' fit body. Such monitoring extends 'outside' the actual exergaming when the consumers are asked to reflect their health behavior such as sleeping patterns and eating (Millington, 2012).

To further highlight how Foucault's panoptic power can be used to understand contemporary digital environments for sport and exercise, I draw from 'surveillance studies' (e.g. Best, 2010; Elmer, 2003; Lyon, 2001) that focus on increased surveillance, including digitally based surveillance, in society. While the theoretical impact of the Panopticon has been profound in surveillance studies (see, for example, Elmer, 2003), there are also a number of critics who aim to expand Foucault's concept to better capture the contemporary environment of multiple media uses and users. Elmer (2003) categorized these attempts based on the concepts – 'dataveillance,' enticement, and synopticism – that these scholars derived from Foucault's thesis.

Dataveillance, a term coined by Clarke (1988), refers to 'the systemic use of personal data systems in the investigation or monitoring of one or more persons' (p. 499). With this concept, Clarke aimed to decentralize the spatially and architecturally defined Panopticon to encompass data spaces located in the virtual universe. In terms of sport studies, dataveillance analysis could, for example, examine how computer matching and personal profiling of sport websites are used to direct consumer behavior and how web users' personal information can be employed to control individuals without their knowledge about where their information is spread.

The second strand of Foucauldian applications to surveillance questions the automatic disciplinary effect of the panoptic digital system (Elmer, 2003; see also Best, 2010). These scholars argue that individuals, such as sport website users, voluntarily and knowingly offer their personal information for personal gain. Therefore, 'this "enticement" model helps to qualify the process of surveillance as ultimately an act of solicitation and exchange' (Elmer, 2003: 232). The model could inform qualitative research on sport fans' and consumers' awareness of the surveillance through the use of digital sport information.

The third group of scholars argues that instead of few guards watching many prisoners, the contemporary information system allows many to watch the few. Elmer offered a rare sport example from John Fiske (1993) to further illustrate this 'synoptic' surveillance arrangement. Fiske argued that a football stadium is a reverse Panopticon where the fans can watch few players in detail through various camera lenses. Digital television has now added multiple options for simultaneous, detailed surveillance of players by spectators and thus, a focus on 'synoptic surveillance' can open new directions for audience researchers interested in new media and sport. Fantasy sports, such as the North American Football League (NFL) 'Fantasy Football,' offers fans a similar chance to reverse the control of footballing bodies through drafting and transferring players to create 'fantasy' teams of their own. The NFL Fantasy Football website exploits the dream of managing a successful football team:

> Do you have what it takes to put together a winning football franchise? NFL.com Fantasy Football gives you the perfect chance to find out. Fantasy football, like other fantasy games, puts you in the front office and on the sidelines as General Manager and Coach of your team. You select from the best of the best in the NFL and they compete on a weekly basis for your team.
>
> *(http://www.nfl.com/fantasyfootball/help/whatis)*

By offering this illusory control, the NFL has created a new media industry around the fantasy of being a football coach/manager with apps, blogs, predictions, and statistics during telecasts to satisfy fantasy football participants. While Fantasy Football can be examined as a type of 'reverse Panopticon,' it must be remembered that fans have not gained any tangible opportunity to interfere with the actual team ownership, management, or coaching practices. The NFL remains in strict control of Fantasy Football, which provides an increased fan base with relatively little cost. From a Foucauldian perspective, it is also important to examine the (gendered) need to dream of managing a football team. Most Fantasy Football players are men and, thus, its founding dream is likely to reaffirm 'normal' masculinity in North America.

The multiple uses of the Panopticon provide interesting and unused opportunities to examine digital sports as forms of surveillance enabled by access to individuals' personal data. Scholars using multiple adaptations of the Panopticon emphasize forms of control through surveillance and individuals' reactions to control facilitated by various forms of technologies.[1] Employing Foucault's later concept, governmentality, researchers can access further possibilities for accounting the interplay between the media and its users.

Governmentality and the new sport media

Foucault (2007) introduced his concept, governmentality, in his lecture series at the College de France in 1977–1978, and it has inspired interdisciplinary interest as well as a field of research titled 'governmentality studies' (e.g. Lemke, 2007; Senellart, 2007). Similar to Panopticon, governmentality refers to a way of using power. While the new media can be analyzed as a part of this type of power network, governmentality can also serve as an overarching framework for situating new media within the apparatuses of neo-liberal society. I draw from the works of two prominent 'governmentality' studies scholars, Thomas Lemke and Nicholas Rose. While neither focuses on studying media (or sport), their readings of Foucault's thoughts about neo-liberal society can help researchers of the new sport media, which have, in large part, developed within the contemporary neo-liberal condition. In his elaboration of Foucault's work, Lemke (2007) distinguished three analytical dimensions on the analysis of governmentality: the central importance of knowledge, the use of the broad concept of technology (including 'the technologies of the self'), and the strategic use of power. New media can be located in the center of these dimensions. It is a tool for strategic knowledge production and dissemination in a technologized contemporary society where privacy is continually renegotiated in the virtual realm at the expense of access to a global audience. I will discuss each of the dimensions separately.

Governmentality and knowledge production

Lemke (2001) affirmed that Foucault's 'the arts of government' points to government as a discursive field in which exercising power is 'rationalized' by defining concepts, specifying objects of government, argumentations, and justification. A certain type of knowledge is needed to support this reasoning. However, this is not neutral knowledge (despite the often repeated requirement for evidence-based, objective research as a basis for decision making) that 'simply "re-presents" the governing reality; instead, it itself constitutes the intellectual processing of the reality' (p. 91). These forms of knowledge are partly produced and proliferated by state agencies, but as Lemke concluded, also constitute broader 'discourses, narratives, world-views and styles of thought that allow political actors to develop strategies and realize goals' (p. 48). The media, whether directly a part of governmental apparatus or privately owned, are intertwined with these strategies as distributors of discourses and styles of thought.

In Foucault's work, the term discourse assumes multiple meanings, and he refined his understanding of the relationship between power/truth/language as his scholarship evolved. While it is not clear what he meant by a 'discourse,' it is evident that this term does not refer only to a discussion or language use per se, but rather something that is an event of itself and, thus, in need for specific analytical attention. Nevertheless, Foucault (1972) was interested in how certain statements link together in a discursive event that has specific effects. Discourses are types of ensembles of discursive events, yet their effects are always at the material, corporeal level. For example, in my own research of traditional fitness media (fitness magazines, fitness videotapes), I have demonstrated how certain statements regarding health and fitness turn into 'knowledges' that have material effects on how exercise is practiced and how fit bodies are shaped at fitness clubs (Markula, 1995; Markula and Pringle, 2006; Markula and Kennedy, 2011).

Foucault (1972) emphasized that the aim of analyzing statements is not to discover their hidden elements or secret meanings. In this sense, Foucault's approach differs from Marxist- or Gramscian-inspired readings of ideological systems of beliefs masking oppression. Such ideologies, although ostensibly beneficial for everyone, are circulated by certain individuals for their own benefit. Foucault contended, instead, that discursive events are created through a complex and unpredictable linking of statements, not by an 'original' creator. Foucault (1972) established a method of analyzing 'ensembles of discursive events' by identifying organizations of concepts, groups of objects, types of enunciations, and how these combined into themes or theories. The 'theories' strategically construct certain knowledges or discourses such as economics, medicine, psychology, or sport studies. Central to Foucault's understanding of discourses is that they also belong to a network of power. The enormous amount of knowledge now accessible for mass consumption is not comprised of neutral facts or innocent entertainment, but has broader effects that move across a web of power networks often in unexpected and uncontrollable ways. For example, mobile phone text messages can form statements that while seemingly personal and disparate might link together in a discursive event and have specific effects. For example, text messages allegedly played an important role in bringing political change to the Arab world. These text messages linked into a discursive event of people's uprising, a discourse 'new' to previous forms of governing, and had material, corporeal effects on people's everyday lives. For a possible starting point to an analysis of a discursive event in the new media, I offer my own role as a blogger for *Psychology Today*.

I am part of the *Psychology Today* blogger team as an expert on femininity and exercise. Foucault (1978) (as well as Miller and Rose, 2007) detected that a series of experts have become a dominant force in power relations grounded on knowledge production. While the blog assigns me a dual role as producer of 'truths' (that potentially control people's everyday actions), I also can reach a much broader group of people than through my research alone. I recently blogged on the 'buzz' of barefoot running, which inspired a series of comments regarding the nature of 'evidence' and connections of 'true knowledge' to broader power relations of academic knowledge production and neo-liberal commercialization. One reader accused me of relying on 'hear say' as I did not cite 'the three scientific studies' that supported the use of orthotics. This commentator, however, did not provide the sources for these studies. While I was astonished that only three studies existed to validate this industry, another reader suspected that the previous comment was inspired by a fear of losing a contract with companies providing orthotics rather than any claims of the 'truth' of using these devices. This brief exchange illustrated how commenting on such a personal issue as running in bare feet through a blog created a discursive event linked to several networks of power. First, I was a suspicious 'expert' as I did not use medical research to support my comments, but second, it became evident that medical research is deeply immersed in the commercialization of health in North American society. Medical knowledge, it turned out, was no longer objective, independent 'truth.' It was evident that the various discourses in the blog gave rise to a set of concepts, statements, and themes. For example, such concepts as running, shoes, landing, feet, orthotics, arch, and natural would most likely emerge from the text. These concepts then assumed meaning in the context of specific statements of the blog (e.g. 'it is natural to land on the forefoot when running'). Such statements, for Foucault, formed group relations that belonged to a specific discursive formation (not to a universal system of meanings) and, thus, it is important to analyze the rules of their co-existence within a set of statements. This means identifying theoretical formations that evolved from concepts and derived their functions from statements making these formations possible. The theoretical formations aligned strategically with certain knowledges or discourses. For example, my blog drew from anthropology, anatomy, biomechanics, and sociology of sport. A Foucauldian is interested in why such a combination of knowledges had united into one message. What does this strategic alliance mean in terms of neo-liberal power relations? How were these promoted through the discourses and the material practice of running technique?

In summary, an analysis of statements as events in the context of the new media would mean excavating how concepts assume meanings within the context of their statements, and how statements assume meanings in connection to other statements by forming themes and theories. These statements need to be analyzed within their institutional context that enables practices based on statements to take place. This can present a challenge in new media, where such context is not always immediately evident. However, as a part of governmentality, knowledge formation plays a tactical role in the strategic use of power: it is possible to sustain dominance by the support of certain discursive formations. For example, the issue of health and wellbeing constitute a significant part of population control in neo-liberal society and, thus, the evidence supporting barefoot running is also part of the politics of knowledge production and power relations for defining 'truth' in contemporary society. Foucault (1978: 101–2) further asserted that

> discourses are tactical elements or blocks operating in the field of force relations, there can exist different and even contradictory discourses within the same strategy; they can, on the contrary, circulate without changing their form from one strategy to another, opposing strategy.

Discourses, as tactical elements, always manifest in material life: they are 'embodied in routine action, cultural self-evidence and normative orientations' (Lemke, 2007: 48). When connected to discourses governmentality becomes 'a lived and embodied experience' (Lemke, 2007: 48) that shapes the ways new media users understand themselves.

The technologies (of the self)

Foucault did not limit his concept of 'technology' to 'material' technological innovations such as those supporting communication in new media. His technologies included, more broadly, symbolic devices that shape individuals' conduct. Foucault (1988) distinguished between the technologies of domination (such as disciplinary techniques of the body through the Panoptic self-surveillance) and the technologies of the self. Foucault used his concept of governmentality to further investigate the relations between domination (by others) and the construction of the self (Lemke, 2002; see Foucault, 1988). Both Lemke (2001, 2007) and Rose (1999) emphasized that Foucault defined 'government' as 'the conduct of conduct' ranging from 'governing the self' to 'governing others.' Foucault termed 'governing the self' as the technologies of the self (Lemke, 2001). Consequently, Foucault's analysis of governmentality can help comprehend how new media can be applied to shape the decisions of others, but also how the media discourse is used to construct 'a self' in a (neo-liberal) cultural context. According to Foucault, the technologies of the self:

> Permit individuals to effect by their own means or with the help of others a certain number of operations on their own bodies and souls, thoughts, conduct, and way of being, so as to transform themselves in order to attain a certain state of happiness, purity, wisdom, perfection, or immortality.
>
> *(Foucault, 1988: 18)*

Because technologies of the self and technologies of domination co-exist in different forms of power relations (sovereignty, Panopticon, governmentality), each form offers different opportunities for self-construction. Therefore, Foucault's concept of the technologies of the self does not denote a self constructed outside of power relations (a resistant, agentic self), but rather it refers to how human beings understand and recognize themselves as humans within particular formations of power relations and morality. Through his concept of governmentality, Foucault demonstrated how the rationality sustaining the modern neo-liberal state necessitates a certain type of individual – or in Foucauldian terms: how power relations and processes of subjectivation are interlinked (Lemke, 2001). Lemke (2007: 49) summarized: 'an analytics of government examines how forms of subjectivity, gender regimes and life styles are produced in practical terms by distinguishing a plurality of governmental technologies.' Thus, a self is constructed through the technologies of the self; but, because a certain type of self is made desirable within a broader cultural framework of power relations, the self is simultaneously shaped by governmental technologies of discipline. New media is one operator that facilitates the construction of a self within different technologies.

Francombe (2010) and Millington (2012) analyzed how the Nintendo Wii exergames constructed a type of identity specific to neo-liberal context. Francombe found that 'We Cheer' constructed a neo-liberal girl norm of heterosexy, middle class, white, and young consumer citizen. Similarly, Millington discovered that 'Wii Fit' provided for a neo-liberal consumer citizen who calculatively seeks to enhance her/his existence through disciplined 'self-care.' These studies were based on the researchers' readings of the games and did not include the voices of actual players. They demonstrated, nevertheless, how new media can be used as a governmental disciplinary technology through which an individual is directed to construct a desirable, 'normal,' identity. Although Francombe or Millington did not use the term 'the technologies of the self,' they referred to forms of self-regulation within a particular form of governmentality: neo-liberalism in current Westernized societies.

Foucault demonstrated that neo-liberalism promoted forms of government 'that foster and enforce individual responsibility, privatized risk-management, empowerment techniques, and the play of market forces and entrepreneurial models in a variety of social domains' (Lemke, 2007: 45). For Foucault, 'freedom' in neo-liberalism meant a voluntary responsibility for one's self-care (Lemke, 2001): Neo-liberal government prefers an individual who is both a rational economic actor and responsible for his/her self-care. Lemke (2001: 201) explained:

> As the choice of options for action is, or so the neo-liberal notion of rationality would have it, the expression of free will on the basis of a self-determined decision, the consequences of the action are borne by the subject alone, who is also solely responsible for them. This strategy can be deployed in all sorts of areas and leads to areas of social responsibility becoming a matter of personal provisions.

The different technologies of governmentality enabled Foucault to examine the process of 'conduct of conduct:' the 'complementarity and conflicts between techniques which assure coercion and processes through which the self is constructed or modified by himself' (quoted in Lemke, 2001: 204). Foucault's concept of the technologies of the self differs, nevertheless, from the idea of building a 'resistant identity.' I use an example from new media that, while not directly sport related, addresses the issue of building a body-based Internet identity in a neo-liberal context.

The Internet offers enhanced opportunities to build so-called 'deviant,' anonymous identity communities. One example is the 'pro-ana' (pro-anorexia) community. While there have been repeated calls for shutting down these 'dangerous' websites, they continue to promote communication, information, understanding, and support of a pro-ana lifestyle (e.g. Boero and Pascoe, 2012). These websites challenge many of the medical and psychiatric assumptions of anorexia as a pathology and, thus, as some researchers argue, disrupt the medical model of eating disorders. As a web-based supportive community (Tierney, 2006, 2008), anorexia could be seen to act as a foundation for resistant identity. For example, according to some research, 'participants often explain their behaviors in ways that are more positive and agentic' (Boero and Pascoe, 2012: 35): through the increased sense of control, accomplishment, and attractiveness, their 'eating disorders in many ways transform from individual pathologies to collective actions they enact through their communal identity work' (Boero and Pascoe, 2012: 35). Based on this approach, the 'pro-ana' websites could be seen as promoting 'empowerment' through the practice of anorexia that deviates from the medical norm of healthy behavior. From a Foucauldian perspective, this type of 'self-care' would not be assigned as resistant (or oppressive), but as a form of 'self-conduct' specific to its neo-liberal context. It would be necessary to analyze how 'empowerment' is dictated through neo-liberal ideals of 'freedom.' From this perspective, a pro-ana website could be analyzed in terms of how its statements construct a self-determined individual and how the freedom to refuse food aligns with the technologies of the self provided by neo-liberalist strategies. For example, the thin, disciplined body, the trademark of anorexia, still conforms to the neo-liberal feminine ideal. The websites still draw, albeit selectively, from the medical discourse (e.g. Boero and Pascoe, 2012). In addition, the pro-ana identity could be analyzed based on the (neo-liberal) compulsion of creating a distinct identity based on bodily discipline: Why might such a 'risky' practice be considered to lead to a certain stage of happiness in a neo-liberal context?

From a Foucauldian perspective, the self-determined, free-willed individual is the result of the intersecting rationality of neo-liberal governmentality and the technologies of the self. This does not denote that Foucault promoted 'individual freedom' practiced by an active subject or configured 'resistance' as 'a matter of "self-reflexive" choice or personal motivation to opt out, ignore or dissociate from particular technologies of practices' (Campbell, 2010: 39). The active, self-determined individual, as Foucault demonstrated (e.g. Lemke, 2001; 2002), is self constructed as part of the political project aiming to create reality, not his understanding of 'ideal' personhood.

Using Foucault's theoretical tools, it is possible to repeatedly demonstrate how new media connects neo-liberal rationality with the 'active,' responsible consumer identity (e.g. Francombe, 2010; Millington, 2012; Rich and Miah, 2009). In addition, it is important to consider why it is effective to mobilize 'individualism' to govern effectively in our current cultural condition. As Rose (1999: 10) proclaimed:

> Hence it seems relevant to try to analyse the conditions under which these ideas of freedom and these practices in the name of freedom have come into existence, and to try to clarify the lines of power, truth and ethics that are in play within them.

Instead of individual 'agency' that operates outside of power relations, Rose preferred to consider how 'the values of freedom have been made real within practices for the government of conduct' (p. 11). For example, why has starving, the main conduct defining the pro-ana identity, become an act of freedom within neo-liberalism? Adopting such a standpoint, for Rose, meant abolishing a set of binaries dominating social research. This leads to the final dimension of Foucault's governmentality.

Strategic use of power in governmentality

In his lecture on governmentality, Foucault (1994) outlined the major changes in forms of governing from antiquity to contemporary society. He concluded that the current purpose of the government[2] is understood as the improvement of the welfare, wealth, longevity, and health of the population. For example, life-long participation in (competitive) sport, and accompanying programs such as Long Term Athlete Development (LTAD) endorsed by Sport Canada, are considered to improve population health and longevity. The LTAD is further considered as an integral aspect of a larger population health initiative (Canada Sport for Life). Foucault added, however, that while 'the needs and aspirations' of the population represent the reasoning for governing, individuals have been turned into objects of its control. He asserted that the population is 'aware vis-a-vis the government, or what it wants, but ignorant of what is being done to it' (1994: 217). For example, many citizens who are encouraged to take up sport do not consider the social and political connotations of governmentally based initiatives. The LTAD programs, in addition to physical health, advance such ideals as individual competitiveness located at the center of neo-liberal thought and, thus, serve the government's agenda.

The governance of the population, according to Foucault (1994), is nevertheless conducted effectively and rationally. What is 'rational' is defined based on the ideals of the current era. To analyze rationality of the neo-liberal 'governmentality,' Foucault reached beyond 'state' control to include 'the ensemble formed by the institutions, procedures, analyses, and reflections, the calculations and tactics that allow the exercise of this very specific albeit complex form of power' (Foucault, 1994: 219–20). Foucault (1994) further demonstrated that the neo-liberal government operates within 'new networks of continuous and multiple relations between populations, territory, and wealth' (p. 217). New media allows these networks to connect. For example, the LTAD website, Facebook, and Twitter provide information nationally as well as outside of Canada. At the same time, as the researchers of Panopticon have already demonstrated, technology has also enabled storage of personal information and a flow of data among networks.

Foucault (1978) later used the term 'bio-power' to describe how governmental apparatuses (appareils) together with specific knowledge production operate within 'governmentality' (Foucault, 2007).[3] Miller and Rose (2007) added that 'bio-power' has enabled 'government at distance' in spaces not immediately connected to government. For example, through new media all types of information can indirectly reach individuals even if they consider themselves removed from the government's direct control. In a Foucauldian sense, expanded access, increased speed and coverage of new media can effectively function as a part of neo-liberal governmentality. Their users, thus, construct a self within the widening global influence of complex power relations, not outside of them.

Foucault's governmentality framework 'conceives of the state as an effect and instrument of political strategies and social relations of power. The state is an effect of strategies since it cannot be reduced to a homogeneous, stable actor that exists prior to political action' (Lemke, 2007: 50, bold in the original). However, the state, in which Foucault found much of the neo-liberal power concentrated, acts also as an instrument establishing strategic distinctions between inside and outside, state and non-state, private and public according to its rationality of governing (Lemke, 2007). Paradoxically, distinctions between the different forms of governing conduct are vanishing, because these binaries are maintained through a set of practices that utilize soft and hard, material and symbolic technologies (Lemke, 2007). Within this framework, the distinction between old and new media might become increasingly redundant as both forms of communication now utilize the same material (digital) and symbolic technologies within the governmentality of neo-liberalism.

It is important to acknowledge that the maintenance of certain boundaries through a more complex use of technologies of governance is an effect of neo-liberal rationality. The binary logic of identity politics, for example, is maintained through mediated information, knowledge, and representation due to its strategic alignment with the neo-liberal rationale. Nevertheless, the Foucauldian perspective reveals the binary structures as parts of neo-liberalism that are not real but attempt to create 'reality.' Foucault's thinking departed from Gramsci's concept of hegemony because such concepts as '"compromise", "consent" or "contract" are the result rather than the origin of strategic articulation. These categories are in need of explanation rather than given facts' (Lemke, 2007: 51). Consequently, governmentality is not based on revealing 'abstract ideologies' behind dominance; it construes neo-liberalism not just as ideological rhetoric or as a political-economic reality, but above all as a political project that endeavors to create a social reality that it suggests already exists. Neo-liberalism is a political rationality that tries to render the social domain economic and to link a reduction in (welfare) state services and security systems to the increasing call for 'personal responsibility' and 'self-care' (Lemke, 2001: 203).

Rose (1999: 279) further suggested abandoning, central to those schooled in Marxism or critical theory:

> those binary divisions that have structured our political thinking and our theorizing about the political for so long: domination and emancipation; power and resistance; strategy and tactics; Same and Other; civility and desire.

Through Foucauldian analytics it is possible to focus, for example, on the relationships between governmental technologies in new media. For example, a scholar might focus on how the technologies of the self and the political government are articulated with each other in creation of 'virtual' sport communities.

Conclusion

I have demonstrated how Foucault's theoretical tools might be used to analyze new media knowledge production and the production of users' selves against neo-liberal forms of governing the conduct of conduct. Foucault did not provide examples of individual practices that might change the dominant technologies of governmentality to establish different ways for the 'conduct of conduct' of the self. Consequently, theorizing how to transform neo-liberal governance remains a constant challenge for Foucauldian scholars. Incorporating change into the Foucauldian agenda might be possible by a further reading of Foucault's definition of power relations.[4]

In his later work, Foucault (1978) conceptualized power as relational, productive, mobile, and local. This type of power is not an essence or an attribute that 'would qualify those who possess it (dominators) as opposed to those on whom it is practiced (dominated)' (Deleuze, 1988: 24). Instead, 'power must be understood in the first instance as the multiplicity of force relations immanent in the sphere in which they operate' (Foucault, 1978: 92). This means that all individuals, upon entering relationships with other humans, become a part of a multiplicity of force relations and can use 'force.' Power relations are not all invested with the same amount of force, but rather 'power is exercised from innumerable points, in the interplay of nonegalitarian and mobile relations' (Foucault, 1978: 94). At the center of analysis should be how individuals use their power, not identifying who is without power or who is a resistant agent operating outside of power. Consequently, a Foucauldian analysis of change might focus on the points invested with a significant amount of force to examine how mobility takes place in such interfaces. For example, one might investigate practices of company owners and creators of new media products to understand their effects on larger markets and users' actions. Alternatively, one might focus on the interface of governmental decision-making, knowledge production, and the commercial sector provision to the productivity of these forces onto the new media. For example, governments can shut down certain websites (such as pro-ana websites): What was the process that led to this change? What are its effects? How will this mold neo-liberalism?

In a Foucauldian sense, power is productive rather than purely repressive: It produces relations that have effects, some of which might be disciplinary. Governmentality implies that power relations are present at every level of the social body and utilized by diverse institutions. Consequently, Foucauldian scholars could begin to map some of these dense networks to determine how continually changing power relations might, also from below, impact the divisions within larger cultural forces. All individuals are users of force and can affect the rationales of power use and transform, in theory, neo-liberalism by using different ethics. What this ethics might be and how an individual might begin to 'think differently' within the large neo-liberal media networks are interesting challenges for further Foucauldian research.

Notes

1. See Elmer (2003) for a more nuanced critiqued of these applications of the Panopticon into surveillance through information technologies. Elmer advocated a Deleuzian-inspired model of Foucault's Panopticon. This 'diagrammatic view of panoptic surveillance' assumed that 'subjects are not simply

surveyed, monitored, or solicited for the purposes of automating a self-medicating acquiescence to social norms and rules (as some Foucauldian scholars might argue)' (p. 245). Consumers 'are both *rewarded*, with a preset familiar world of images and commodities, and *punished* by having to work at finding different and unfamiliar commodities if they attempt to opt-out' (p. 245). In this diagram, any changes in 'consumer demand–sales–consumption–distribution–production can drastically affect the whole system' (p. 245). Elmer is not alone. There seems to be a tendency within surveillance studies to expand Foucault's work with Deleuze's contributions (e.g. Best, 2010; Hardt and Negri, 2000; Lyon, 2001; Wise, 2002). One example in sport studies is Sluggett's (2011) Deleuzian inspired study of athletes' increased control by information technologies in doping prevention by WADA.

2. In this chapter, the term 'government' refers to 'the state' that governs populations in its national territory. Governmentality, however, refers to a way of using power, the operations of bio-power through which the conduct of large populations is rationalized.

3. As bio-politics refers to the control of large populations in open spaces, it requires regulatory practices assigned to a continuum of state apparatus (law, medicine, political economy, education). Foucault (1994) did not, however, advocate that 'governmentality' has replaced the previous forms of using power – sovereignty or disciplinary anatomo-political power – but rather we live in 'a triangle' of these forms that now target the population (p. 219).

4. I am drawing from Deleuze's interpretation of Foucault's work to further illustrate the issues of transforming power relations. My approach is not unique as, parallel to surveillance studies, there seems to be a trend towards Deleuze when issues of change are discussed within governmentality studies (e.g. Campbell, 2010; Rose, 1999). Campbell (2010), for instance, lamented that 'Foucault leaves us no analytical tools to think through how…we can overcome the submission of [neo-liberal] subjectivity' (p. 42).

References

Best, K. (2010) Living the control society. Surveillance, users and digital screen technologies. *International Journal of Cultural Studies*, 13, 5–24.

Boero, N. and Pascoe, C. J. (2012) Pro-anorexia communities and online interaction: Bringing the pro-ana body online. *Body and Society*, 18(2), 27–57.

Campbell, E. (2010) The emotional life of governmental power. *Foucault Studies*, 9, 35–53.

Clarke, R. A. (1988) Information technology and dataveillance. *Communications of the ACM*, 31(5), 498–512.

Cole, C. L. (1996) American Jordan: P.L.A.Y., consensus, and punishment, *Sociology of Sport Journal*, 13, 366–397.

Deleuze, G. (1988) *Foucault*. London: Athlone.

Duncan, M. (1994) The politics of women's body images and practices: Foucault, the Panopticon and *Shape* magazine. *Journal of Sport and Social Issues*, 18, 48–65.

Dworkin, S. and Wachs, F. L. (1998) Disciplining the body: HIV positive make athletes, media surveillance, and policing of sexuality. *Sociology of Sport Journal*, 15, 1–20.

Elmer, G. (2003) A diagram of panoptic surveillance. *New Media and Society*, 5(2), 231–247.

Fiske, J. (1993) *Power Plays, Power Works*. London: Verso.

Foucault, M. (1972) *The Archaeology of Knowledge and Discourse on Language*. New York: Pantheon Books.

Foucault, M. (1978) *The History of Sexuality: Vol. 1. An introduction*. London: Penguin Books.

Foucault, M. (1988) Technologies of the self. In L. H. Martin, H. Guttman and P. H. Hutton (eds), *Technologies of the self: A seminar with Michel Foucault*. Amherst, MA: University of Massachusetts Press.

Foucault, M. (1991) *Discipline and Punish: The Birth of the Prison*. London: Penguin Books.

Foucault, M. (1994) Governmentality. In J. D. Faubion (ed.), *Power: Essential Works of Foucault 1954–1984* (Vol. 3). London: Penguin Books.

Foucault, M. (2007) *Security, Territory, Population. Lectures at the College de France 1977–1978*. New York: Picador.

Francombe, J. (2010) 'I cheer, you cheer, we cheer': Physical technologies and the normalized body. *Television and New Media*, 11, 350–366.

Hardt, M. and Negri, A. (2000) *Empire*. Cambridge, MA: Harvard University Press.

Jette, S. (2006) Fit for two? A critical discourse analysis of *Oxygen* Fitness Magazine. *Sociology of Sport Journal*, 23, 331–351.

Lemke, T. (2001) The birth of bio-politics: Michel Foucault's lecture at the College of France on neo-liberal governmentality. *Economy and Society*, 30(2), 190–207.

Lemke, T. (2002) Foucault, governmentality and critique. *Rethinking Marxism: A Journal of Economics, Culture and Society*, 14(3), 49–64.

Lemke, T. (2007) An indigestible meal? Foucault, governmentality and state theory. *Distinktion: Scandinavian Journal of Social Theory*, 8(2), 43–64.

Leonard, D. (2009) New media and global sporting cultures: Moving beyond the clichés and binaries. *Sociology of Sport Journal*, 26, 1–16.

Lyon, D. (2001) *Surveillance Society: Monitoring Everyday Life*. Buckingham: Open University Press.

Markula, P. (1995) Firm but shapely, fit but sexy, strong but thin: The postmodern aerobicizing female bodies. *Sociology of Sport Journal*, 12, 424–453.

Markula, P. and Kennedy, E. (2011) Beyond binaries: Contemporary approaches to women and exercise. In E. Kennedy and P. Markula (eds), *Women and Exercise: The Body, Health and Consumerism* (pp. 1–26). New York: Routledge.

Markula, P. and Pringle, R. (2006) *Foucault, Sport and Exercise: Power Relations, Knowledge, and Transforming the Self*. London: Routledge.

Millington, B. (2012) Amusing ourselves to life: Fitness consumerism and the birth of bio-games. *Journal of Sport and Social Issues*. doi: 10.1177/0193723512458932

Miller, P. and Rose, N. (2007) *Governing the Present: Administering Economic, Social and Personal Life*. Cambridge: Polity.

Rich, E. and Miah, A. (2009) Prosthetic surveillance: The medical governance of healthy bodies in cyberspace. *Surveillance and Society*, 6(2), 163–177.

Rose, N. (1999) *Powers of Freedom: Reframing Political Thought*. Cambridge: Cambridge University Press.

Senellart, M. (2007) Course context. In M. Foucault (ed.), *Security, Territory, Population: Lectures at the College de France 1977–1978* (pp. 369–401). New York: Picador.

Sluggett, B. (2011) Sport's doping game: Surveillance in biotech age. *Sociology of Sport Journal*, 28, 387–403.

Tierney, S. (2006) The dangers and draw of online communication: Pro-anorexia websites and their implications for users, practitioners and researchers. *Eating Disorders*, 14(3), 181–90.

Tierney, S. (2008) Creating communities in cyberspace: Pro-anorexia web sites and social capital. *Journal of Psychiatric and Mental Health Nursing*, 15(4), 340–3.

Wise, J. M. (2002) Mapping the culture of control: Seeing through *The Truman Show: Television and the New Media*, 3(1), 29–47.

6

SOCCER AND SOCIAL MEDIA

Sport media in the city of the instant

Steve Redhead

CHARLES STURT UNIVERSITY

Sport and sport media culture today are an integral part of what Paul Virilio, dromological theorist of speed, power and technology, terms the city of the instant. In this dromoscopy (Virilio, 2005a), amidst what he sees as the contemporary collapse of time and distance, Virilio positions the city of the instant (Redhead, 2004a; Virilio, 2005b) in a rapidly shrinking world of what I have labelled mobile city cultures (Redhead, 2011). For Virilio this prescient concept of city of the instant connotes a live audience of millions or, possibly billions, watching sport events like World Cups or Olympics or Paralympics anywhere around the world, on various devices, all at the same time (give or take a little bit of digital delay). But it can, equally, signify all the social networking sites of new media, globally millions or billions, of connected users all over the world, often in real time. In Virilio's writing ever since the 1950s, it is frequently television that has been the main platform for such a broadcasting community or city of the instant. In recent analyses, however, sports media analysts are increasingly writing about global sport going beyond television (Guilianotti and Robertson, 2009; Hutchins and Rowe, 2012; Millward, 2011; Redhead, 2010a, 2010b; Rowe, 2011), a situation where multiple different platforms exist. There has been to some extent a move, as Brett Hutchins and David Rowe put it, from a state of broadcasting scarcity to what might be seen as digital plenitude (Hutchins and Rowe, 2009). That state of overproduction of information is what characterises social media sites and their connection to global sport media. For Virilio, though, a theorist who sees in every new technology the possibility of the accident, apocalypse is only around the corner. An "accidentology" (Matthewman, 2013; Virilio, 2007, 2010a) is required so it can all be put into a theoretical, cultural, political and even military perspective (Virilio, 2005a, 2012).

Today avid consumers watch Premier League soccer games live on smart phones on the move, or on flat screens in bars, anywhere in the world, all at the same time, eroding artificial time zones. Through constant yearly practice over a very short period, there has been a redefinition of what the mobilities in mobile city cultures actually mean (Redhead, 2011; Urry, 2007). We certainly live, à la Virilio, in something of an instantaneous culture – what I call "accelerated culture" (Redhead, 2004a: 1–10). Accelerated culture denotes the permanent now, though there is so much more to tease out in this concept, pregnant with possibilities for a claustropolitan sociology of the apocalyptic future (Redhead, 2011). More than ever in human history we inhabit the "now" – academics are anxious to capture Virilio's cryptic idea of instantaneity with collections of essays entitled *Virilio Now* (Armitage, 2011). But it is an instant present which is catastrophic, claustropolitan, a museum of accidents (Virilio, 2003b), a university of disaster (Virilio, 2010b), in what Virilio has come to re-envision as the futurism of the instant (Virilio, 2010a). The greatly accelerated communication in the culture of what Virilio sees as the "great accelerator" (Virilio, 2012: 1) of the twenty-first century, symbolised by smart phones, laptop computers, Twitter, Facebook, Google, Flickr, Academia.edu, QR codes, tablets and YouTube is, perversely, "Virilian". Twitter has 500 million users and Facebook over a billion, and these numbers are accelerating daily. Seemingly, suddenly, what has arrived is a globalised, shrunken world devoid of solids, and through an aesthetics of disappearance that Virilio heralds in his writings (Virilio, 2003a), maybe even a globe without a future. For Paul Virilio, dromologist extraordinaire, "to live every instant as though it were the last – that is the paradox of futurism, of a futurism of the instant that has no future" (Virilio, 2012: 1). Sport and new media, especially my specific focus in this chapter, which is soccer and social media, fit into this global accelerated culture in myriad ways. I want to explore some of these here. Let us first bring Virilio into focus.

Paul Virilio: Old painter, new media

At the turn of the millennium, John Armitage, editor of several influential collections of essays and interviews on Virilio (Armitage, 2000, 2001, 2011), hailed him as "perhaps the most provocative French cultural theorist on the contemporary intellectual scene" (Armitage, 2001: 1). Armitage more recently stated of Virilio that "at his finest he is one of the most thrilling and insightful cultural theorists writing today" and "his analyses of contemporary cultural life are nothing than first-rate" (Armitage, 2011: 25) and reviewed one of his most recent books as "indispensable…thought-provoking and contentious". Virilio though is a strange theorist for today's accelerated culture of new and social media in many ways and as a self-defined "Anarchistic Christian" personally at odds with many of the questions academics would normally ask about sport and media cultures. In some senses his work comes with a health warning for today's universities, however provocative and interesting it may be. Insights do pervade his work however. Although there is little about sport media, and media sport cultures specifically mentioned in Virilio's burgeoning writings, in two of his recently translated books *The Futurism of the Instant* (Virilio, 2010a) and *The Great Accelerator* (Virilio, 2012) there is the conspicuous development of his productive idea of "exodus" from the cities *and* the country, and even the planet, including forced mobilities of populations as a result of what he sees as the proliferating speed accidents and global mega sport events (Olympics, World Cups, World Championships). Also, in *Pure War* (Virilio and Lotringer, 2008) Virilio has much to say on specific sport events in history, such as the Moscow Olympics in 1980, where he asserts that those absent from the stadium are always right, foreshadowing the importance of broadcasting rights to sport and sport media. Virilio trained as a stained glass painter with Braque and Matisse before studying under phenomenologists like Maurice Merleau-Ponty at the Sorbonne. He suffers from claustrophobia, rarely travels, has largely given up watching television, stopped driving his beloved Jaguar, and describes himself as that "old painter" who sometimes ranges over "tiny details from the history of painting, engraving and architecture from the eighteenth century" (Redhead, 2004b: 121). Virilio holds on doggedly to old media such as photography, a form he first pursued in the 1950s, a long time before Jean Baudrillard, his long-time friend embarked on a late camera career which would see his photographs lauded by the US art world and witness lavish coffee table publication of his images. Virilio has distinguished his work on media from Baudrillard in specific ways:

The big difference between Jean and me is that he worked on simulation and I worked on substitution…I would like to relate a small anecdote about Baudrillard and simulation and substitution. When we found ourselves at the *Revue Travers*, I had just finished my photographic campaign, which took ten years, on the wall of the Atlantic. Baudrillard hated photography at the time. I went to the *Revue Travers* because before, in the *Revue de L'esprit*, they didn't have photos or images. At the *Revue Travers*, I could publish my photos and I told the revue, "I am coming". When I saw Baudrillard, he said "Tisk, tisk, tisk". And now he is dead and I am still alive…It's been quite a long time now since I have stopped taking photos, but he, he began taking photos. He even finally became a photographer. This is typical in our movement.

(Virilio, 2009a: 68–70)

Virilio's positive value for cultural theory and cultural politics in understanding contemporary communication is not in question, despite being offline most of the time in his personal life. Especially, as we have specified here, Virilio has implications for the study of social media with its manifest dimensions of the city of the instant. It is this live communication that Virilio discusses in conversation with Bertrand Richard (Virilio and Richard, 2010) in a series of interviews published in French under the title *L'Administration de Peur*. This volume of conversations with Richard is replete with everything from Virilio's views on Facebook to his usual diet of war technologies (for example, the Manhattan project), the spreading fear of the title and the catastrophic state of the planet we inhabit, whether it be environmental, social or economic. In another volume recently translated into English (Virilio, 2012) Virilio nails his colours to the mast on the speed of live communication technologies today, perceptively noting the "overexposure" of private life through new media, especially social media. Virilio asks:

Why don't we take this deadly OVEREXPOSURE of private life that is spreading as far as the eye can see just a little bit further? Imagine that, following on from the fixed cameras set up at major intersections to ensure road traffic safety or the entrances to buildings to ensure security, couch surfing is already taking us to the next, the ultimate level of revelation. This is where the Google Home inspector turns up on your doorstep, covered in portable cameras designed to reveal to all and sundry the level of comfort of the bathrooms on offer to low-budget tourists benefiting from the hospitality of the Internet's social networks!

(Virilio, 2012: 52)

Virilio, often seen as a prophet of doom, is in fact increasingly opening up our study of the global flows of the catastrophic, a world where cosmopolis is slipping speedily into claustropolis.

Soccer and new media: The case of Twitter

Globally and locally, sport and new media in the city of the instant is awash with possibilities for interdisciplinary analysis. In the rest of this chapter I want to look at the case of soccer and social media in the context of Virilio's theories of the city of the instant in the futurism of the moment. There are plenty of examples of new media – always already, of course, old media because of the sheer speed of change of modern instant communications and speeded up planned obsolescence, which Virilio writes about so pertinently. Live streaming of soccer matches, illegally consumed in many cases by fans using various sites or illicit software, or online message boards for fans, either new consumer spectators, carnival fans or those tending towards hooliganism (Pearson, 2012), are two examples of areas where research has started to be pioneered over the last few years. However, there is relatively little sustained research in general in this field, either into recent aspects of social media like Twitter, especially in terms of audience reception and participation (Deller, 2011), or into the connections and possibilities of specific sports and other new media forms, such as online supporter message boards or the telepresence of micro blogging sites used by players and fans (Gibbons and Dixon, 2010; Hutchins, 2011). What is uncovered in the research that has been done so far is the process of globalised acceleration, a rapid speeding up (Hutchins, 2011) of sport media taking place in what is seen as a new digital age (Millward, 2011). There is also the possibility to take more seriously the whole panoply of the culture of virtual fandom in media sport culture (Gibbons and Dixon, 2010), at least as seriously as the pre-digital fandom of the 1980s and 1990s (Pearson, 2012). We can also update the idea of a playful, self-reflexive, ironic soccer fandom inherent in soccer fanzine culture (Haynes, 1995; Millward, 2008; Pearson, 2012; Redhead, 1993, 1997), which is pervasive in social media and often mistaken as dangerous and deviant in the moral panics which have been generated in social reaction to the practices of social media.

The most pertinent example of this new global media sport culture is soccer on Twitter. I will take this as a general instance of sport and social media. Although research into soccer and social media is often interesting and rigorously carried out, there are alternative theorisations of globalisation, acceleration and instant communication buried in the work of a theorist like Paul Virilio that might be more productive in the long run. I want to concentrate on Virilio, social media and soccer culture and the potential extension of its importance for the study of sport media in general. My examples are from soccer and media culture in Britain but the themes and processes identified are global.

Soccer and social media such as Facebook and Twitter have changed the nature of sport journalism in a matter of a few short years. Phone-in programmes on radio largely consist of reading out Twitter feed and allowing such pithy comments to set the agenda of the programme for incoming phone calls. A radio programme like BBC's *Six O Six* in Britain, known for its intimate discussions with former players or journalists who take calls immediately after matches, has altered its focus in recent years to take into account the influence of Twitter as an immediate, real-time agenda setting site. Again tweets are read out in the course of the programme, setting the tone and parameters of the conversations. On Twitter, online anywhere in the world, life is lived instantly in one hundred and forty characters, for fans and players alike. Journalists increasingly depend on the instantaneity, ubiquity and simultaneity of Twitter feed, simply filing their copy *after* going online on Twitter and collecting tweets. Soccer players as celebrities are followed by millions on Twitter, though it should be remembered not all accounts in their names are authentic, and much is hidden behind anonymity in all social media, enabling cyberbullying and racism and sexism, and moreover illegal defamation, on a widespread scale. Moral panic about social media, in other words "right thinking" members of society creating social reaction to a perceived problem bringing into focus "folk devils" who bear the brunt of the panic, has started to become widespread (Cohen, 2011).

In sport media, the climate of moral panic created a momentum for regulation of the issue as a social problem – either through intervention using the criminal law by the police and prosecution authorities or disciplinary action by football clubs or the governing bodies of the game. Such moral panics, or law and order campaigns, concerning behaviour of soccer players or football fans, what I have called speeded up systems of "panic morals" (Redhead, 1997: 9), are not new although the digital platforms, and the rich research possibilities and implications they contain, certainly are (Deller, 2011; Hutchins, 2011; Ruddock, Hutchins and Rowe, 2010). Much of the authoritarian discourse in these moral panics, however, is opposed by an equally problematic widespread libertarianism, which holds the World Wide Web and the Internet as essentially *the* progressive technological developments of the late twentieth and early twenty-first century, with companies like Twitter and Google seen almost as humane agencies of intervention in social justice rather than profit-making capitalist companies (Brabazon, 2008). For a writer like Charles Leadbeater (Leadbeater, 2009) social media are a case of mass innovation and creativity. Let us take some instances from the soccer-on-Twitter scene and its weird and wonderful world of trolls, citizen journalists and political activists:

Player and fan misconduct

In July 2012 the media reported that a 20-year-old Arsenal player, Emmanuel Frimpong, was charged with improper conduct by the Football Association for tweeting the words "Scum Yid" from his Twitter account. Tottenham Hotspur, the club aimed at in the tweet, have a considerable Jewish following and also a hooligan firm who self-label themselves as the "Yid Army". An anonymous journalist for *The Guardian* reported that:

> The Premier League yesterday revealed new guidelines for social media by players, on the same day the Football Association charged Arsenal midfielder Emmanuel Frimpong with improper conduct relating to recent comments on Twitter. The 20-year-old responded to a Tottenham fan on July 15 and although he shortly removed the comment from the social networking site, it did not escape the attention of the FA. Frimpong is recovering from a serious knee injury sustained while on loan at Wolverhampton Wanderers. After posting a message on his official Twitter account earlier this month which read "if you are going church today Pray for me Giving today a Miss", the Gunners midfielder retweeted a response from one Tottenham fan which read: "I prayed you break your arms and legs" to which Frimpong replied "Scum Yid". It sparked a debate on the social networking site among supporters from both Arsenal and Tottenham. One was retweeted by Frimpong which read: "You can't go around wanting players to break limbs, no matter who you play for. Embarrassed to be a yid right now!" The term has been used for decades to identify Tottenham supporters because of the proportion of Jewish supporters at the North London club. Last year comedian David Baddiel launched a campaign to stamp out use of the word in football chants, which can be viewed as anti-semitic. However, many Spurs fans use the term 'Yid Army' themselves as a "badge of honour" and claim they are not offended by it. Nevertheless, the FA took a dim view of the matter and Arsenal confirmed the player had been "reminded of his responsibilities when representing the club". Frimpong has until Friday to respond. While many top flight clubs have their own social media rules, after requests from some teams, the Premier League – following several months work which included consultation with the Professional Footballers Association and FA – have now put together guidelines which set out clear direction to players on the use of social media. Those focus on a number of areas including understanding that it is possible to commit offences online via social media, advice on the endorsement of brands, goods and services and also guidelines on disciplinary action that can be taken against players who make improper comments.
>
> *("Arsenal's Emmanuel Frimpong", 2012: 41)*

This incident, picked at random out of hundreds of examples of soccer players and fans misusing Twitter accounts, is significant because it came at the end of a sustained period of moral panic about the issue of misconduct on social media sites, especially in the pages of old media such as newspapers.

Criminal law

It is useful to take more of the incidents of Twitter use by soccer fans and players in this period of moral panic, and note the kinds of disciplinary or legal action taken within this discourse. Coventry City suspended a player for pro-Irish Republican Army (IRA) comment. Bolton Wanderers' Francis Muamba nearly died on the pitch after suffering a heart attack against Tottenham Hotspur in an FA Cup match at White Hart Lane (Spurs' ground in North London). He was technically dead for a period of seventy-eight minutes but was eventually revived in hospital and made a miraculous recovery, although eventually, after a few months, he had to officially give up the game that was his chosen profession. In the immediate aftermath of his heart attack, while he was very ill in hospital, a Swansea University student was charged by police after he racially abused Muamba on Twitter. In another incident, Ched Evans, a Sheffield United and Wales player, was convicted of rape and sentenced to a five-year prison term. Ultimately his contract of employment was terminated by his club. Teammates of Evans at Sheffield United tweeted the name of the rape victim (who was supposed to remain anonymous) amidst comments about the case that strongly favoured Evans' role in the event. They were disciplined by the club and charged by the police under the criminal law. In another well-publicised event, Stan Collymore, former professional footballer and journalist with talkSPORT radio station, reported tweets insulting towards him to the criminal law authorities and the offender was subsequently prosecuted by police. A Serbian footballer was sent home from the 2012 Olympics in London after tweeting racist comments against recently encountered South Korean opponents. Racist Twitter messages directed against Carlton Cole of West Ham United were met with the arrest by police of a 22-year-old man.

Another highly publicised case of Twitter and soccer players and fans in this moral panic period involved the internationally known professional players John Terry and Ashley Cole of Chelsea and Rio Ferdinand of Manchester United. Ferdinand incidentally has 3.7 million Twitter followers while his Manchester United colleague Wayne Rooney has 5.5 million followers. John Terry had allegedly racially abused Ferdinand's brother Anton in a match between Queen's Park Rangers and Chelsea. Following a complaint from a member of the public who was at the game, police prosecuted Terry. After a long-drawn-out court case, the Chelsea player, who was supported before the magistrates by his teammate Ashley Cole, was acquitted. Twitter became a forum for instantaneous debate amongst hundreds of thousands of fans in the immediate aftermath of the court's judgement. As part of the bitter Twitter recriminations where opinion was unusually fiercely divided, Rio Ferdinand retweeted a suggestion that Ashley Cole was a "choc ice" – slang, as Ferdinand subsequently explained, for someone who is "black on the outside but white on the inside". Ferdinand was as a result charged by the Football Association with a disciplinary offence and fined £45,000. The issues of racism in soccer culture (Burdsey, 2011) underlying this use of social media are persistent problems in soccer culture more generally (Redhead, 2013).

Civil law

Twitter has frequently become intertwined with civil law as well as criminal law. A prime example, in this period of moral panics about use of Twitter, involved Ryan Giggs of Manchester United. Giggs, a married man, had an affair with a TV Big Brother contestant Imogen Thomas. His lawyers obtained a superinjunction from the high court, which banned the media from reporting anything to do with the alleged affair (and even that an injunction had been obtained) which was widely speculated upon (though without the names of the participants). When Twitter was eventually used to broadcast the name of Ryan Giggs as the footballer involved, almost instantly millions of people were informed without the need to have recourse to conventional media like television or newspapers. Giggs' lawyers' subsequent action was to launch a civil action against Twitter as a company, a classic case of trying to close the stable door when the horse had bolted.

Fan protest

It is noteworthy here, too, that Twitter, like other social media, is often used by participants to express various forms of "protest" – for example in soccer fans' case the issues range from not being able to stand up at grounds (which are all-seater) to police brutality in crowd control inside and outside grounds (Pearson, 2012).

On all the dimensions of soccer and Twitter that I have presented here, the issues of instantaneity, ubiquity and simultaneity are uppermost. The work of Paul Virilio, though flawed in many ways, allows chinks of what I term theory at the speed of light (Redhead, 2004b, 2011) to illuminate these issues.

Pithy passwords: Soccer and Virilio in 140 characters

As we anticipate the multiple global sports media futures (Rowe, 2011) to come, we need, in my assessment of the contemporary scene of social media specifically and new media in general, to have in our back pocket, however difficult it may be in the application, the work and thought of Paul Virilio as a guide. This is a guide to what panic theorist Arthur Kroker sees as the "trajectories of the catastrophic" (Armitage, 2011: 160–1). These trajectories in sport media culture show themselves in the incorporation of new media age upon new media age (speeding up so fast that they almost catch up) within a very short time of each other. In sport media terms we have experienced a whole series of new media age formations over the last decade such that a serious and rigorous academic book by Raymond Boyle and Richard Haynes entitled *Football in the New Media Age* published in 2004 (Boyle and Haynes, 2004) can be radically out of date within a couple of years because of the emergence of new and social media forms that were not even conceived of when the first edition was written. The overload of information in the social media networks which have shrunk the globe are capable of imploding in a similar way in the speeded up present that Virilio analyses. They may well make the live event, which is Virilio's main focus in his notion of the city of the instant, a potentially redundant phenomena in the relatively near future. David James, former goalkeeper with Liverpool, Manchester City and England, has asked, mischievously, the question: why bother watching soccer when you can follow it through tweets? As a convert to Twitter himself James applauded the regulation of social media like Twitter through club disciplinary regulations and changes to the governance of the soccer authorities as sensible and welcome guidelines (D. James, 2012). However, he has also questioned whether people will actually leave the house in the future – to watch the live event such as a soccer match in the city of the instant – so utterly absorbing and all encompassing is Twitter's hold. James is essentially agreeing with Virilio's more apocalyptic prophecy that 'Those Absent From The Stadium Are Always Right' (Redhead, 2007).

Any snapshot of accelerated culture is dependent on key concepts created by Paul Virilio, and, to some extent, the milieu of their production. The city of the instant and the futurism of the moment are extremely pertinent in the exploration of sport media and social media formations and help to make sense of the moral panics and calls for media regulation, which are currently so pervasive. But they are concepts that are rooted in an art and architectural history that is relatively obscure (Virilio, 2009b, Virilio and Parent, 2010), even arcane. At the end of the century, Paul Virilio's late friend, Jean Baudrillard wrote a short book entitled *Mots de Passe* (Baudrillard, 2000) in which he discussed many of his own concepts – the object, value, symbolic exchange, seduction, the obscene, the transparency of evil, the virtual, the perfect crime, impossible exchange, duality, and so on. The book (Baudrillard, 2003; Redhead, 2008) comprised Baudrillard's passwords. The "passwords" of Paul Virilio, this rather out-of-time "theorist for an accelerated culture", available in a literature of short, pithy books (I. James, 2007; Redhead, 2004a: 1–9; Virilio, 2002a, 2002b, 2003a, 2003b, 2006, 2009a, 2009c), are worth considering here. They are aphoristic, pithy passwords, oddly suited to a social media site like Twitter with restrictions of one hundred and forty characters. Paul Virilio's near-tabloid habit of capitalising his concepts in the middle of paragraphs lends itself to this type of communication, too. Virilio's interviews with Bertrand Richard (Virilio and Richard, 2010), Sylvere Lotringer (Virilio and Lotringer, 2002, 2005, 2008) and Phillippe Petit (Virilio and Petit, 1999) are similarly cryptic, and because of recent developments the reader can also now make forays further into the as yet ill-defined field (Armitage, 2011) of Virilio Studies – an online *International Journal of Virilio Studies* is just a matter of time. The words of Paul Virilio form part of a conceptual vocabulary of a key, if overlooked and misunderstood, theoretician of the contemporary world and the immediate future to come. As we have seen in this chapter, sports media analysts are looking way beyond television in their conceptualisation of globalisation and acceleration (Guilianotti and Robertson, 2009; Hutchins and Rowe, 2012; Millward, 2011; Rowe, 2011). The transition from broadcasting scarcity to digital plenitude (Hutchins and Rowe, 2009), which some commentators have noted as a recent phenomenon, is illuminated by Virilio's concepts of city of the instant and futurism of the moment. The overloading of social media and its overwhelming hold on our senses, increasing our claustrophobia and decreasing our willingness to leave the house, threatens to outstrip the arguments about whether we should bring in new legal regulation to control Twitter, Facebook and the new media to come. Meanwhile we attempt to catch up with the shrinking of time and distance and jack into the trajectories of the potentially catastrophic and claustropolitan future.

References

Armitage, J. (ed.) . (2000) *Paul Virilio: From Modernism to Hypermodernism and Beyond*. London: Sage.

Armitage, J. (ed.) (2001) *Virilio Live: Selected Interviews*. London: Sage.

Armitage, J. (ed.) (2011) *Virilio Now: Current Perspectives in Virilio Studies*. Cambridge: Polity.

"Arsenal's Emmanuel Frimpong charged with improper conduct after tweet." (2012) *The Guardian*, 25 July, p. 41.

Baudrillard, J. (2000) *Mots de Passe*. Paris, France: Pauvert, Editions Fayard.

Baudrillard, J. (2003) *Passwords*. London: Verso.

Boyle, R. and Haynes, R. (2004) *Football in the New Media Age*. London: Routledge.

Brabazon, T. (2008) *The University of Google: Education in a Post-Information Age*. Aldershot: Ashgate.

Burdsey, D. (ed.) (2011) *Race, Ethnicity and Football: Persisting Debates and Emergent Issues*. London: Routledge.

Cohen, S. (2011) *Folk Devils and Moral Panics*. London: Routledge.

Deller, R. (2011) Twittering on: Audience research and participation using Twitter. *Participations: Journal of Audience and Reception Studies*, 8(1). Retrieved from http://www.participations.org/Volume%208/Issue%201/deller.htm

Gibbons, T. and Dixon, K. (2010) Surf's up: A call to take English soccer fans interaction on the internet more seriously, *International Journal of Sports Performance*, 11(5), 599–613.

Giulianotti, R. and Robertson, R. (2009) *Globalisation and Football*. London: Sage.

Haynes, R. (1995) *The Football Imagination: The Rise of Football Fanzine Culture*. Aldershot: Ashgate.

Hutchins. B. (2011) The acceleration of media sport culture: Twitter, telepresence and online messaging, *Information, Communication and Society*, 14(2), 237–257.

Hutchins, B. and Rowe, D. (2009) From broadcasting scarcity to digital plenitude: The changing dynamic of the media sport content economy, *Television and New Media*, 10(4), 354–370.

Hutchins, B. and Rowe, D. (2012) *Beyond Television: The Internet, Digital Media and the Rise of Networked Media Sport*. London: Routledge.

James, D. (2012, December 22) Why bother watching football when you can follow it through tweets? *The Guardian*. Retrieved from http://www.theguardian.com/football/blog/2012/dec/22/david-james-twitter

James, I. (2007) *Paul Virilio*. London: Routledge.

Leadbeater, C. (2009) *We Think*. London: Profile.

Matthewman, S. (2013) *Accidentology: Towards a Sociology of Accidents and Disasters*. Houndmills: Palgrave/Macmillan.

Millward, P. (2008) The rebirth of the football fanzine: using e-zines as data source. *Journal of Sport and Social Issues*, 32(3), 299–310.

Millward, P. (2011) *The Global Football League: Transnational Networks, Social Movements and Sport in the New Media Age*. Houndmills: Palgrave.

Pearson, G. (2012) *An Ethnography of English Football Fans: Cans, Cops and Carnivals*. Manchester: Manchester University Press.

Redhead, S. (ed.) (1993) *The Passion and the Fashion: Football Fandom in the New Europe*. Aldershot: Ashgate.

Redhead, S. (1997) *Post-fandom and the Millennial Blues: The transformation of Soccer Culture*. London: Routledge.

Redhead, S. (2004a) *Paul Virilio: Theorist for an Accelerated Culture*. Edinburgh: Edinburgh University Press.

Redhead, S. (ed.) (2004b) *The Paul Virilio Reader*. Edinburgh: Edinburgh University Press.

Redhead, S. (2007) Those absent from the stadium are always right: Accelerated culture, sport media and theory at the speed of light. *Journal of Sport and Social Issues*, 31(3), 226–241.

Redhead, S. (ed.) (2008) *The Jean Baudrillard reader*. Edinburgh: Edinburgh University Press.

Redhead, S. (2010a) [Review of the book *Beyond the Box: Television and the Internet*, by S. M. Ross]. *Leisure Studies*, 29(3), 343–344.

Redhead, S. (2010b) [Review of the book *Better Living Through Reality TV: Television and Post-Welfare Citizenship*, by L. Ouellette and J. Hay]. *Leisure Studies*, 29(2), 229–230

Redhead, S. (2011) *We Have Never Been Postmodern: Theory at the Speed of Light*. Edinburgh: Edinburgh University Press.

Redhead, S. (2013) "We're not racist, we only hate Mancs": Post-subculture and football fandom. In L. Duits, K. Zwaan and S. Rejinders (eds) *Ashgate Research Companion to Fan Cultures*. Aldershot: Ashgate.

Rowe, D. (2011) *Global Media Sport: Flows, Forms and Futures*. London: Bloomsbury Academic.

Ruddock, A., Hutchins, B. and Rowe, D. (2010) Contradictions in media sport culture. *European Journal of Cultural Studies*, 13(3), 323–339

Urry, J. (2007) *Mobilities*. Cambridge: Polity.

Virilio, P. (2002a) *Desert Screen: War at the Speed of Light*. London: Athlone.

Virilio, P. (2002b) *Ground Xero*. London: Verso.

Virilio, P. (2003a) *Art and Fear*. London: Continuum.

Virilio, P. (2003b) *Unknown Quantity*. London: Thames and Hudson.

Virilio, P. (2005a) *Negative Horizon: An Essay in Dromoscopy*. London: Continuum.

Virilio, P. (2005b) *City of Panic*. Oxford: Berg.

Virilio, P. (2006) *Speed and Politics*. Los Angeles, CA: Semiotext(e).

Virilio, P. (2007) *The Original Accident*. Cambridge: Polity.

Virilio, P. (2009a) *Grey Ecology*. New York: Atropos.

Virilio, P. (2009b) *Bunker Archeology*. New York: Princeton Architectural Press.

Virilio, P. (2009c) *The Aesthetics of Disappearance*. Los Angeles, CA: Semiotext(e).

Virilio, P. (2010a) *The Futurism of the Instant: Stop-eject*. Cambridge: Polity.

Virilio, P. (2010b) *The University of Disaster*. Cambridge: Polity.

Virilio, P. (2012) *The Great Accelerator*. Cambridge: Polity.

Virilio, P. and Lotringer, S. (2002) *Crepuscular Dawn*. Los Angeles, CA: Semiotext(e).

Virilio, P. and Lotringer, S. (2005) *The Accident of Art*. Los Angeles, CA: Semiotext(e).

Virilio, P. and Lotringer, S. (2008) *Pure War*. Los Angeles, CA: Semiotext(e).

Virilio, P. and Parent, C. (2010) *Nevers: Architecture Principe*. Orleans, France: Hyx.

Virilio, P. and Petit, P. (1999) *Politics of the very worst*. New York: Semiotext(e).

Virilio, P. and Richard, B. (2010) *L'administration de peur*. Paris, France: Editions Textuel.

7

THE CYBERSPORT NEXUS

Andy Miah

UNIVERSITY OF THE WEST OF SCOTLAND

> Exercise machines increasingly incorporate computer-controlled motion and force feedback and will eventually become reactive robotic sports partners.... Today's rudimentary, narrowband video games will evolve into physically engaging telesports.
> *(Mitchell, 1995: 19)*

Mitchell's vision of sport's future was one of the first to foreground the integration of digital systems within a broader context of technocultural change. His articulation of how sports would be played within *cities of bits* reveals the intimate connection between organized, competitive sports and the urban environment, where digital innovation is embedded within the build environment. Yet, Mitchell's attention did not attend to the wider context of the digital future he foresaw, where other aspects of the sport experience would be transformed by digital technology and where the convergence of physical and virtual worlds reveals the radical challenge from sport's new media.

As digital environments and sports cultures develop, humanity comes closer to an era of digitally constituted sports experiences, where the primary medium of participation need no longer be a physical playing field or arena, but is a virtual space. While it may seem a long way off to a world where sports take place entirely within digital worlds, this chapter considers how far toward this era sports have come and what may come next. A number of questions arise from this prospect. How are such conditions changing sports experiences, physical activity, and people's experience of their own embodiment? How does digital space change the meaning attributed to sports, their function, and the way in which they give rise to communities of participation? Alternatively, digital innovation invites us to consider whether sports will occupy a different place within our social and cultural lives. Furthermore, one may ask about the consequences of making corporeality a surrogate to a virtual presence, which subsequently may create a physical culture that is defined largely by digital interactions. What distinguishes answering these questions today from when Mitchell imagined the future of sports is that we know and can observe some of the initiatives that will shape these emerging realities.

The future is not quite how it looked back then, but this chapter reveals some of the striking resemblances between these periods and the implications presented by the last two decades of digital innovation around sport. In so doing, it describes the *CyberSport Nexus* as the interface of digital technologies with sport, from virtual realities to social media, arguing that this comprehensive consideration of the new media within sport most adequately explains what is at stake within this transformation. It aims to understand the implications of sports becoming digital enterprises. Experiences within virtual worlds have already become inextricable from many other forms of social and cultural encounters within twenty-first-century living, especially for people within nations that have a digital infrastructure. From remotely conducted surgical procedures in medicine to the global economy, life online is a constitutive element of many societies and, in varying fashions, participation cuts across other technological divides. Yet, life online remains the subject of popular controversy, with continuing allegations of computer game-playing leading to violent, anti-social behavior (Anderson, Gentile and Buckley, 2007; Comstock and Scharrer, 2007), or screen time promoting sedentary lifestyles or more risky childhoods (Byron, 2008). These allegations are often advanced against specific, prominent examples of digital experiences – such as computer games that depict criminal or anti-social acts – but they contrast with other studies of digital culture, which reveal the capacity of computer games to inspire creativity, physical activity (Marshall *et al.*, 2004), and engagement with the world around us (Ott and Pozzi, 2011).

Furthermore, there is considerable mistrust in the idea that a more digitally mediated future lends itself to a better world, a more just society, or richer personal relationships. In part, this is why the debate about new media and sport is critically connected to debates about ethics, morality, and the good life. At a time when the onslaught of digital technology appears to be all-consuming, it is useful to consider claims about what might be won or lost in the process. To scrutinize these competing claims, it is necessary to locate them within a context of digital participation. Whereas media consumption 20 years ago took place in quite isolated, discrete physical spaces, such as public theatres and home living rooms, today's media experiences operate across social spaces, from aircraft to trains, from mountains to swimming pools. Content is delivered across platforms, making it possible for someone to listen to a waterproofed personal music device while swimming and use the same device on a home music system. These possibilities change the debate about the social consequences of media consumption, since the habitus of media exposure is disrupted. Media participation may take place pervasively across an individual's life, creating multi-layered social experiences where previously separate activities become more intimately connected, and where there is blurring of physical space. A person may be watching a film in a cinema while playing a game on a mobile device and sharing what is happening with friends via instant messaging.

In some cases, the social commentary around the benefit of such innovation is made moot by widespread adoption, which marks a significant change in consumer habits. For instance, while e-book readers may present challenges for the book industry, the Amazon Kindle has transformed how people interface with books. Even if there is some compromise to the book's value, e-books provide convenient solutions that appeal because of their adaptability. However, in other cases, there is concern over the potential loss these new media experiences may bring, and it is these considerations that focus our attention in the context of cybersport. For instance, does our evaluation of the worth of digital technology change, if physically demanding elements of game-playing are introduced? Alternatively, do we regard new media differently if it can be shown to have a bigger impact on promoting certain values that we care about, such as greater accessibility, technological equality, or participation?

This chapter provides a more extensive insight into how the *cybersport nexus* will operate by examining some of the key trends. It considers the ways media industries operate through digital technology around sport while also discussing how media technology changes the parameters of what it is to be a participant within the sports world – whether as an athlete, spectator or official. In so doing, it also considers the ethical and moral dimensions of this landscape, discussing how these transformations challenge our understanding of sports, what sports may become, and what value *cybersports* may have. This chapter also exposes the creative use of emerging digital technology within sports culture in order to reveal the ways in which such practices are undergoing significant revision as a result of new technological changes, but also how the culture of physicality that surrounds digital experiences is transforming how we make sense of these developments as either dystopian or utopian. More precisely, I discuss how the advanced use of digital technologies in sports is transforming these practices into new cultural experiences, which are defined by different values and expectations, along with new populations of practitioners.

To further focus the chapter, I examine three dimensions of the sport experience: athletes, spectators, and officials. In each case, I consider what are some of the new digital innovations that are changing the landscape of new media within their field, the key social, moral and ethical challenges this provokes for the world of sport, and what outcomes may arise from such innovation in the long term.

The athlete

For as long as organized sports have existed, new media technology has been utilized by athletes, either for training, performance data capture, or through the technology used within the playing field. In a pre-digital era, timing technology, video capture, and simulation devices were among the many examples that describe the sport's world as a space of creative technological innovation, focused on simulation and measurement. Today, athletes benefit from shoes or even prosthetic devices that are created using foot-scanning technology to ensure their equipment perfectly accommodates their unique physical form. Alternatively, athletes have trained within virtual reality environments, as was true of the US Bob Sled team in Nagano 1998, who practiced their sled run in a simulator (Huffman and Hubbard, 1996; Levy and Katz, 2007). Simulators have now been used in countless sports, from sailing (Walls *et al.*, 1998) to handball (Bideau *et al.*, 2004) to swimming. For instance, before the London 2012 Olympic Games, computer scientists built a computer game called 'Open Water Warfare' to help swimmers navigate during competition. The game simulates the official Olympic open water venue to help swimmers train, which was not possible to access before the Games.

Today, athletes experience their sport within a data-rich environment, which provides insights into their development and performance, mostly for their expert advisers. In this sense, the knowledge systems that surround athletes are highly dependent on new media, which is an ongoing asset to improve performance and our understanding of it. These apparatuses are utilized within established sports practices. Sometimes, they may yield the creation of new sports. Already, a new generation of elite athletes is emerging through the use of new media. *Cyberathletes* who compete within computer game tournaments undertake activities that are often highly demanding physically and, perhaps more importantly, are co-produced by media broadcasters in ways remarkably similar to the media staging of traditional, elite sports events.

Equally, developments in mobile technology allow amateur athletes to redefine their experience of sport via digital devices. The rise of ExerGaming[1] and Bio-Games (Millington, 2012), which involve anything from downloading a mobile app to monitor one's daily runs, to GPS-enabled devices that allow users to gain insurance credits for physical activity, speaks to the shifts in how physical activity is being altered through new media. It also has shown how new media can create new physically engaged sub-cultures, as might be said of the *Dance Dance Revolution* style games that are found within arcades (Andrews, 2006, Smith, 2004). In these cases, the category of sport stretched via new media raising questions about the future interests of and populations within those communities.

One possible future involves the inclusion of computer games sports within mega-event programmes like the Olympic Games. After all, the synthesis of digital technologies and physical bodies – evident in technology trends – coupled with the emerging synergy between sports and new media makes this a scenario worthy of consideration. With the introduction of relatively rudimentary technologies like the Nintendo Wii and its derivatives, playing computer games is now very close to the physical and skill demands of many Olympic sports. In a boxing simulation game, players must throw their arms in similar ways to boxers in a ring. At the opposite end of the scale, in some games the simulator is the primary environment for learning the real activity, not just a substitute. Pilots may train for weeks within game simulators. Thus, the world of simulation is bringing the amateur and elite athlete closer and, when those worlds become indistinguishable, some aspects of the physical experience may be brought into question. Closely allied is the way that all aspects of the elite athlete's body today are monetized and digitized within simulation games. Computer games sports titles are among the most lucrative, not least because every season brings a new opportunity to re-sell a product. For instance, if one looks at FIFA Football games, it is apparent the players' biographies and histories within the game resemble actual players and the sponsorship present within the Game is also tied into wider relationships that exist around the presenting sports federation.

A number of challenges arise from these transformations, which threaten changes to the sports business. First, there are questions about equity and fairness, which often do not generate much public controversy, unlike unfair advantages that athletes may derive from, say, doping. Yet, athletes with access to the latest simulator or most sophisticated form of data capture may increase their chances of doing better in sport. For instance, consider the recently launched Google Glass, a thin device that would allow skiers, for instance, to wear goggles and have a built-in display into the glasses helping them anticipate turns, via GPS-enabled mapping built into the display. Would this kind of technology compromise the skills required for the sport, or might we see its use enrich the competitive experience in a way that technology has so many times before? In some respects, the acceptance of such use is part of the range of knowledge that is accepted as an enriching part of an athlete's development. In the same vein, one may argue that having a better coach, nutritionist or masseuse may also provide advantages that are unfair, insofar as not every athlete will have them.

Second, the increased use of ExerGaming or the development of serious games that effectively *gamify* physical activity may be incentives for people to take part in sports or other forms of activity, but may also become subject to wider public expectations. For instance, it is already apparent that some private insurance schemes and even gymnasia offer incentives for activity (Finkelstein and Kosa, 2003). One might imagine further that digital surveillance of physical activity could become an even more appealing route through which to minimize risks taken by insurance firms, perhaps even a compulsory part of a policy. Companies might even require clients to wear health monitors to ensure they do all they can to avoid health risks. In such a world, one might have serious concerns about solidarity and individual liberty. Yet, there may also be a strong public health argument for providing such incentives.

The ability of new media to generate new communities of athletes is also a challenge for the sports world. While it is reasonably common to see sports with long histories being pushed out of mega-event programmes like the Olympic Games for newer sports such as BMX biking, these are no small matters for either sports federations or athletes. An athlete might have spent an entire career training in one sport and lose their means of competing on the basis of such a decision. Yet, the growth in *computer game sports* and the creation of new demographics of sports participation may force organizations and sponsors to reconsider what the landscape of sports participation should look like. Whereas today's sports funding remains dominated by male athletes in many countries, sports nurtured within digital worlds may create different kinds of competitions that are better at stimulating equal participation. They may even enable men and women to compete alongside each other more easily. Should this be possible, there would be a compelling argument for why funding should be directed to sports federations that prioritize these kinds of disciplines over others, in order to preserve other important values.

Finally, new media presents challenges over the means by which sponsorship is secured and generated around athletes and teams. On the approach to the London 2012 Olympic Games, this issue became particularly controversial around the freedom of athletes to mention non-Olympic products and brands within their social media profiles, which the IOC forbade in the interest of core financial sponsors of the Games. Rogers (2012) reports how athletes were using Twitter to protest against the IOC's rule, which specified that athletes would not be allowed to undertake actions that were associated with commercial organizations. By using the Twitter hashtags #Rule40 and #wedemandchange, athletes expressed their concerns about not being able to promote their individual sponsor relations within personal social media platforms. Athletes may even take into their own hands their financial futures by utilizing social media in publicity and funding campaigns. For example, in 2012, the USOC track athlete Nick Symmonds built a campaign around auctioning space on his arm through eBay, where the winner would have a Twitter account name temporarily tattooed during the Olympic period. The example speaks to how sports may need to adapt to the new media world. More individual athletes may act as their own brands, rely less on a club's negotiation of sponsors, and generally have a greater capacity to act as their own mediators of financial support. Social media and digital technology generally provides much greater agency and opportunities to develop a brand with limited resources, which is unconnected to a product and, by implication, unconnected to a broader arrangement made on behalf of the athlete's team or club.

While the sports authorities appeal to the need to maintain exclusive and restrictive relationships with sponsors to deliver events and, subsequently, are required to protect those interests by also restricting athletes freedom to pursue other commercial interests, there are questions about how far an athlete can be asked to jeopardize their own livelihood by neglecting their ongoing obligations and relationships. At the heart of this debate is a question about whether these new media environments are an extension of commercial media space, or whether they are more like personal communication spaces. Twitter has (generally) no editorial structure that affects the things people say. In this sense, it is not directly analogous to a professional broadcaster, even though it is a commercial platform. Yet, it is also naïve for users to conclude that their content has no political currency, or that it can only be seen as personal expression. One complicating factor in resolving this matter is that content online now migrates from one place to another. Where previously an advertisement or form of communication existed within one space – a billboard, a radio station, a television channel – today content can be embedded into multiple locations, and this may make it difficult to ensure that no breaches of contract occur, if an athlete publishes something.

The spectator

The second category of new media innovation concerns the affect on the spectator's experience. In 1995, Hemphill imagined the possibility of 'head cams' worn by people to locate themselves within the world and how these might be utilized as part of the sport experience (Hemphill, 1995). Twenty years later, the previously large apparatus of a head camera was mistaken in one crucial aspect – size. Today's prototypes that would make possible such scenarios are focused much more on the nanoscale and altering sensory experiences by adapting our biology, rather than appending an object to ourselves. Thus, there already exists prototype technology for digitally augmented glasses, using Google's *Glass*, which could permit digital content being shown through the device, transforming the eye into a digital interface. Recent developments in augmented reality indicate how the physical world will be layered with additional digital content within our field of vision. So, as spectators watch an ice hockey match wearing the lenses, they would be able to add layers of content, from data about the athletes, zoom in close to see their faces, or be able to monitor their physical state to know if, for instance, an athlete is fatigued. Where once such possibilities were the stuff of science fiction, today they are an imminent and, in some respects, realized aspect of sports competition.

In the interim, the population of spectators is expanding as a result of digital technology, which has increased the communal space in which shared sports spectatorship takes place – perhaps no more so than the erection of giant urban screens, which become live sites during important sports events. Yet, the small screen has also become a way of creating new audiences and new spectator experiences. Industry professionals now look to leveraging the 'second screen' (Cruickshank *et al.*, 2007) within their sports broadcasting, especially as more people begin to consume sport live to mobile. Indeed, far from taking viewers from television, consumption of content via the second screen has been shown to increase the television viewing hours of sports (Edgar, 2012). Equally, experiments within broadcasting are changing the conditions of sport spectatorship. Television broadcasters provide a comprehensive feed to all content, rather than just select the most iconic moments to broadcast, while viewers choose their own event programme.

Sports producers are also changing the landscape of the playing field through new media. Digital Replacement Billboards (Sprogis *et al.*, 1996) is one example of how elements within the real world are transformed into screens within screens, allowing broadcasters to tailor what advertisements a television viewer sees. So, sports fans watching in South Korea would see different billboards within the field of play compared to someone in the United Kingdom. In this world, the physical space of the sports arena becomes literally a digital void, a blank unit populated with content only in the case of mediation.

The role of the spectator is also being altered by the rise of new media – social media in particular. Today's spectator is now a co-producer of sports news and entertainment, as status updates, tweets, video diaries, and photographs produced by spectators at events become part of the digital assets of an event. In this respect, their function also intersects with that of the professional media producers – journalists – creating a need for the media industries to both manage and marshall such content or risk jeopardizing their ability to leverage interest from their media privileges at sports events.

The implications of digital technology reconfiguring the sports arena are enormous, raising challenges for how sports are produced and managed. Consider an example from the art world, which sheds light on how experiences within sports stadia may change. In 2010, the Museum of Modern Art in New York was occupied by two rebel artists who decided to stage their own exhibition within the gallery using augmented reality. Their intervention was titled 'We AR in MoMA,' but was not commissioned by or approved by the MoMA as one of its exhibitions. Instead, their art work was overlaid onto 'MoMA's "real" galleries using augmented reality technology' (Thiel, 2010), creating a rogue exhibition within their exhibition. Their actions provoked discussion about who owns physical space when our experience of it is mediated via a digital device, which is a crucial predicament for sports, where space is currency. In the case of the MoMA, visitors would walk around the gallery, activate their AR application on their digital devices, and witness floating objects alongside the exhibits. The implications of this are immense and present questions over who owns the digital signals within a building. Presently, there are no signal scramblers within sports events, but it is conceivable that digital innovation could allow companies to ambush the space within the arena. This is increasingly important as more of the physical experience is enriched via a mobile device. Spectators at sports may spend a considerable amount of their time looking at the playing field through a device – camera or phone – and so even the stadium is not an unmediated space.

The *second screen* in sports spectating also changes the kinds of organizations that are able to co-produce content. For example, in platforms like Twitter, the use of a hashtag (essentially a key word that becomes a collective way of capturing a conversation) can be a way for audiences to organize their communal experience and curate the news content it generates. This changes the media industry hierarchy considerably, compelling sports producers to adapt to these trends or face growing redundancy. In part, this is why, at the London 2012 Paralympic Games, spectators within the arena were invited to use Twitter hashtags to share content, with some of the tweets displayed on large screens within the venue in real-time. It is also why, as of this writing, large sports federations and organizations like the IOC are building relationships with digital innovators, which provide video sharing opportunities (e.g. YouTube), broad socialized media experiences (e.g. Facebook), microblogging platforms (e.g. Twitter), and photograph-sharing opportunities (e.g. Flickr and Instagram), so as to constantly ensure a presence within the most popular sharing platforms of the day (Miah and Jones, 2010).

One may argue that these new media players are not disrupting the dominance of long-term media broadcasters, but there is evidence of how much value can be accrued by using new media to access new markets. For instance, since Beijing 2008, the IOC has established relationships with Google to livestream sports content on YouTube within territories that have no rights agreement, principally Asia and Africa. Among the places included for both Beijing 2008 and London 2012 are Afghanistan, Bangladesh, Cambodia, and the Democratic Republic of Congo. Nevertheless, the expanding costs of winning the rights may also make it challenging for public broadcasters to compete with commercial broadcasters, which may result in limiting the amount of live sports audiences see. This has particular implications for host nations, as events like the Olympic Games involve considerable public cost. As such, to locate the televisual content behind a pay wall could jeopardize public support. This concern also reminds us of the importance of establishing compatible legal agreements around the sharing and broadcasting of content that underpins the possibility of change resulting from digital innovation. Indeed, many of the issues that limit the use of new media within sports hinge on matters of intellectual property. Whether it is sharing permissions at a sports event in digital form or challenges over territories, an understanding of international media law within these discussions is paramount.

Finally, regarding the increased use of social media by spectators, one of the problems was made apparent by the London 2012 Olympic Games Opening Ceremony where, the day after, British Member of Parliament Aiden Burley tweeted that the content was 'multicultural crap,' which caused a media storm. Burley defended his right to express a personal view, but neglected the fact that followers give value to his comment in part because he is an MP. In this sense, the example exemplifies the user's own naivety about whether any kind of public voice can be simply personal. The reactions to his comment indicate that it cannot, even if the Twitter biography includes a caveat indicating as much. Thus, the key point here is that social media collapses the remaining space of personal expression into a pervasive public sphere. In short – and to refer to early debates about the Internet in academic literature – tweeting is not like going down the pub and having a chat, it is more like getting up on a soap box and making an argument. Yet, because social media occupies a place in our lives that is often outside of working hours or space, this distinction becomes blurred for users.

Another example of the challenges arising from social media is what happened after the initial diving performance of Team GB athlete Tom Daley. Very soon after, an abusive tweet from a spectator created controversy (Miah, 2012). Specifically, a 17-year-old directed a message toward Daley's account saying 'you let that your dad down i hope you know that'. Daley's father passed away the previous year and was a central part of his career development and, while this may be considered by some to be simply bad taste, it led to a police inquiry and the arrest of the teenager. However, the twist in the tale is that the notoriety and fuss surrounding the message came not from the tweet itself, but by the fact that Daley included the message and the person's username within a re-tweet which read 'After giving it my all…you get idiot's [sic] sending me this…' Had Daley just ignored the message, it is unlikely that anyone would have noticed.

Even the mainstream media cannot avoid controversy related to social media, which changes the power relationships among media providers. One good example of this during the London 2012 Olympics was also the night of London 2012's Olympic Games opening ceremony, during which the hashtag #NBCfail began to trend on Twitter due to criticisms over its coverage, a narrative that continued throughout the Olympic and Paralympic Games. NBC's perceived failing in deciding not to screen the ceremony live and cutting elements from their coverage led one British journalist to tweet the email address of the NBC Olympics President. He was subsequently suspended from Twitter (temporarily) for breaching their guidelines, which provoked a debate about whether this person's email was private. Yet, the more intriguing point is that these matters were played out entirely within a social media environment and a trending hashtag within Twitter can be an influential force within the news agenda. This example reveals how new media can expose gaps within the media system that allow citizens – either in their personal or public roles – to stage campaigns that call into question the operational practices of the media.

These examples speak to the challenges arising when people make public their comments about sport, which must be seen as part of a broader debate about how people negotiate their public and private lives within online environments. Yet, it also reminds us how athletes are becoming part of the spectator's entourage and the media coverage, as their comments on each others' performances become part of how the sports event is communicated and experienced. On numerous occasions during the London 2012 Games, direct quotes from commentators were lifted directly from their social media feeds, bypassing the interviewer process altogether.

The officials

A third dimension of sport that is changing through digital technology is the role of the officials. One change in this area is the introduction of artificial officiating devices, more often than not some kind of camera-based or laser technology to monitor the playing field with a view to making more accurate judgements over what is taking place. An early utilization of such technology was the Hawk-Eye surveillance system first used by the US Tennis Open in 2004. As Repanich (2010, para 2) describes:

> The system works by mounting 10 high-speed cameras around the court with five dedicated to each side of the net to capture the ball's movement from multiple angles, measuring its speed and trajectory. Then a computer processes that information, pinpointing the spot on the court within 3mm of where the ball hit the ground and calculating the ball's compression to determine the size and shape of the mark that represents where the ball touched the court.

One of the most significant changes in this regard – and one of the more longstanding debates – is the inclusion of goal-line technology within football. Over the years, there has been resistance to using such technology for two principal reasons. The first is a concern over interrupting the flow of the game, while the second is on the financial cost. Yet, goal-line technology is a relatively simple system compared to the number of other ways that digital innovation could increasingly regulate what happens within sports competitions. Even the use of microphones for athletes during competition demonstrates how relatively primitive digital technology can change the conditions of a playing field, for athletes and spectators.

Yet, technological advances are no guarantee of a better sport experience or even a more accurate measurement of what took place. For example, one of the controversies of the London 2012 Olympic Games was an incident in fencing whereby a failure for a countdown clock to function effectively meant that one competitor proceeded to a gold medal match, while another did not. In this case, it was a combination of human and technological error that led to the mistake. The example highlights a problem around digitalization within sports that is broader than the debate about deciding whether a human is more effective at officiating than a technological device. Rather, most technology of this kind implies a human–computer interaction, and the synergy of this relationship is crucial in ensuring that the right kinds of interests are promoted. It cannot be assumed that better digital technology implies better results. Furthermore, it cannot be assumed that automation removes the role of human judgement, since there is often a human somewhere in the loop interpreting what the technology says.

Many sports continue to resist the implementation of digital officials and other forms of innovation that may change the experience of a sport. In some cases, there may be legitimate ethical reasons why an athlete would seek to ensure that microphones are not required during competition. Sports are, after all, arenas of cultural endeavor where certain expectations of behavior that would otherwise be required of people are absent. Athletes can interact physically with others in a way that is not permissible in wider society. By implication, one might argue that the conduct of athletes within the playing field in terms of what they say should also be free from conditioning via digital surveillance. Yet, to the extent that athletes enjoy a life that is partly predicated on their being role models – on and off the field – then this view seems a relatively weak basis on which to maintain the sports field as a different kind of social space. Indeed, when athletes do transgress rules dramatically, wider civil or criminal laws may become a means of punishment, even if they took place within the playing field – one thinks of racial abuse, physical assault as primary examples.

Furthermore, the digital solution to an official's limited capacity need not be solved by digital innovation. For instance, football has also considered adding additional officials whose role is specifically to watch the goal line to see whether a ball has crossed or not. Thus, there may be human solutions to sport's problems that are less rooted in digital solutions. Yet, the digital imperative may often obscure other such solutions, perhaps in part due to its being a more economically desirable solution.

Besides camera and laser technology, smart phones may also prove to be another innovation that changes the way officials work. For instance, in 2012, the Mexican Indoor Football League utilized a new form of carding system, whereby the referee used a device to display red and yellow cards, rather than actual cards. This mobile app called RefereePro had the additional functionality of replacing pencil and paper as a way of tracking fouls and other statistics (Laird 2012).

Conclusion

As sports become further constituted by digital technologies and the user culture that surrounds them, their values and the experience change as well. These changes are presenting challenging implications for how sport is organized, commercialized and experienced. For instance, there may be a strong social argument to relocate some sports within solely virtual arenas, rather than physical worlds. The travel required of sports competitions is incompatible with the depleting resources in the world and the carbon emissions deriving from such travel. Sports that are dependent on natural resources, like golf, may not be possible without some kind of technological solution. At the same time, the high stakes of sport demands that technology improves the reliability of decisions that affect the outcome – who wins. In large part, this is why line surveillance technology have become such important aspects of the officiating process. In these cases, it is the inability of humans to ascertain what is happening in the field of play that leads humanity towards a digital era.

This chapter has considered ways in which new media in a very broad sense presents challenges for the production and practice of sports. It demarcated three territories as distinct categories – athletes, spectators and officials. Within these three categories, I have also considered aspects of the sports industries, such as sponsors and broadcasters and how their work may be challenged or enriched by some of the new processes within the media.

What made the London 2012 Games worthy of being called the first social media Olympics was the way that the sports reporting was driven by social media content. From the latest athlete's tweet, to Twitter audience polls on breakfast television coverage, social media became pervasive not just in terms of the volume of people using it, but how content within social media drove the news cycle. When considering directions of new media within sport, recent years indicate a capacity within professional media to adapt to and appropriate new media environments and platforms, coupled with a migration to other spaces of consumption. Yet, control over the content remains a challenging issue for sports administrators and there remains resistance to completely opening channels of communication. This is most apparent within Twitter accounts where corporations may be reluctant to share someone else's content in case it is seen as an endorsement, and where there is still a culture of following only those who are considered part of the sports family.

Nevertheless, perhaps the single most important issue in this aspect of sport's digital future is how the increased management of social communication will take place. For instance, if Tom Daley had been advised by his manager to ignore the abusive tweet, rather than re-tweet it himself, there might not have been the same kind of public outcry and distraction from his competition. Yet, a situation where all public communication requires approval in advance may be a world that is more impoverished and devoid of meaningful human interactions, both good and bad. This is also why the rules that govern public communication do not map neatly on to social media. It is the playing out of one's ideas in public and the capacity to redefine these without catastrophic judgement that allows a society to progress and flourish, rather than the excessive stifling of thoughts, even if they are ill-informed and misguided.

Note

1. The term *exergaming* applies to any digital game experience that involves strenuous gross motor activity, often within the sports genre. Exergames may be played within computer game arcades, home consoles, or may be more like a pervasive game, where the experience is defined by navigating a real physical world, using a mobile navigation device, as for geocaching.

References

Anderson, C., Gentile, D. and Buckley, K. (2007) *Violent Video Game Effects on Children and Adolescents: Theory, Research, and Public Policy*. Oxford: Oxford University Press.

Andrews, G. (2006) Land of a couple of dances: Global and local influences on freestyle play in dance dance revolution. *Fiber Culture*, 8. Retrieved 5 November, 2012, from http://eight.fibreculture.org/fcj-048-land-of-a-couple-of-dances-global-and-local-influences-on-freestyle-play-in-dance-dance-revolution

Bideau, B., Multon, F., Kulpa, R., Fradet, L. and Arnaldi, B. (2004) *Virtual Reality Applied to Sports: Do Handball Goalkeepers React Realistically to Simulated Synthetic Opponents?* In VRCAI '04 Proceedings of the 2004 ACM SIGGRAPH international conference on Virtual Reality continuum and its applications in industry (pp. 210–216). New York: ACM.

Byron, T. (2008) *Safer Children in a Digital World: The Report of the Byron Review*. Nottingham: DCSF Publications.

Comstock, G. and Scharrer, E. (2007) *Media and the American Child*. San Diego, CA: Academic Press.

Cruickshank, L., Tsekleves, E., Whitham, R., Hill, A. and Kondo, K. (2007) Making interactive TV easier to use: Interface design for a second screen approach. *The Design Journal*, 10(3), 41–53.

Edgar, A. (2012) *The Olympic Games: Meeting New Global Challenges*. The Olympic Media, conference, Oxford University, 13 August, 2012.

Finkelstein, E.A. and Kosa, K.M. (2003) Use of incentives to motivate healthy behaviors among employees. *Gender Issues*, 21(3), 50–59.

Hemphill, D.A. (1995) Revisioning sport spectatorism. *Journal of the Philosophy of Sport*, XXII, 48–60.

Huffman, R.K. and Hubbard, M. (1996) A motion based virtual reality training simulator for bobsled drivers. In S. Haake (ed.), *The Engineering of Sport* (pp. 195–203). Rotterdam, The Netherlands: Balkema Publishing.

Laird, S. (2012, November 15) Smartphone replaces red cards in pro soccer match. *Mashable.com*. Retrieved 10 March 2013 from http://mashable.com/2012/11/15/smartphone-soccer-referee

Levy, R.M. and Katz, L. (2007) *Virtual Reality Simulation: Bobsled and Luge, IACSS International Symposium Computer Science in Sport, 2007*. Retrieved 15 October 2012 from http://people.ucalgary.ca/~rmlevy/Publications/Levy_Katz_IACSS2007.pdf

Marshall, S. J., Biddle, S. J. H., Gorely, T., Cameron, N. and Murdy, I. (2004) Relationships between media use, body fatness and physical activity in children and youth: A meta-analysis. *International Journal of Obesity*, 28, 1238–1246.

Miah, A. (2012, August 10) London 2012: A social media Olympics to remember. *BBC Online*, Retrieved from http://www.bbc.co.uk/news/technology-19191785

Miah, A. and Jones, J. (2012) The olympic movement's new media revolution: Monetization, open media and intellectual property. In S. Wagg and H. Lenskyj (eds), *Handbook of Olympic Studies* (pp. 274–288). Basingstoke: Palgrave.

Millington, B. (2012) Amusing ourselves to life: Fitness consumerism and the birth of bio-games. *Journal of Sport and Social Issues*. doi: 10.1177/0193723512458932

Mitchell, W. (1995) *City of Bits: Space, Place, and the Infobahn*. Cambridge MA: MIT Press.

Ott, M. and Pozzi, F. (2011) Digital games as creativity enablers for children. *Behaviour and Information Technology*, 31(10), 1011–1019.

Repanich, J. (2010) Can cameras and software replace referees? *Popular Mechanics*. Retrieved April 1, 2013, from http://www.popularmechanics.com/outdoors/sports/technology/cameras-fouls-and-referees

Rogers, K. (2012, July 31) Olympic athletes take to Twitter to rally against strict sponsorship rules. *The Guardian* [online]. Retrieved April 5, 2013, from http://www.guardian.co.uk/sport/2012/jul/31/olympic-athletes-twitter-sponsorship-rules

Smith, J. (2004) I can see tomorrow in your dance: A study of Dance Dance Revolution and music video games. *Journal of Popular Music Studies* 16(1), 58–84.

Sprogis, P., Wilf, I., Tamir, M. and Sharir, A. (1996) Electronic Billboard Replacement Switching System [United States Patent No, US 6,191,825 B1, Date of Patent: Feb 20, 2001].

Theil, T. (2010) *ARt Critics Face Matrix*. Retrieved 31 October 2012 from http://www.mission-base.com/tamiko/We-AR-in-MoMA/index.html

Walls, J., Bertrand, L., Gate, T. and Saunders, N. (1998) Assessment of upwind dinghy sailing performance using a virtual reality dinghy sailing simulator. *Journal of Science and Medicine in Sport*, 1(2), 61–72.

PART II

Sports/media producers

8

THE EVOLUTION FROM PRINT TO ONLINE PLATFORMS FOR SPORTS JOURNALISM

Pamela C. Laucella

INDIANA UNIVERSITY

Technology has influenced sports journalism's development and growth in American society, and has transformed how journalists and organizations work and report the news. The symbiotic relationships between sport, media, technology, and culture have evolved, and their impact on information gathering, processing, and dissemination have been crucial in journalism's longstanding practice, profession, and public service. The purpose of this chapter is to discuss sports journalism's rise from its roots in an agricultural, agrarian society to its current status in today's fast-paced, fragmented, 24/7 digital media environment, where information is instantaneous, interactive, and powerful.

Bryant and Holt (2006) divided sport media's developments into three epochs: The Agricultural Age, The Industrial Age, and The Information Age. In all three, sport has been a "conduit or medium through which feelings, values, and priorities are communicated" (Wenner, 1998: xiii).

The Agricultural Age

The Agricultural Age of the late eighteenth and nineteenth centuries featured reports on horse racing, boxing, baseball, and rowing, which first appeared in newspapers, and then sport magazines like *American Turf Register and Sporting Magazine, Spirit of the Times*, and *New York Clipper*. Sport gained further interest after the Civil War, due in great part to the popularity of baseball (Fountain, 1993). The *New York Herald's* Henry Chadwick is viewed as the first full-time newspaper sports journalist, and he specialized in baseball coverage (Boyle, 2006). He created the first rulebook and invented the box score, and earned a place in the Baseball Hall of Fame (Bryant and Holt, 2006; Chadwick, 2012).

The penny press was vital during this period of growth since it expanded newspaper circulation, content, and advertising. It made news accessible, readable, and valuable for the masses, and not just the colonial newspapers' small, elite group of readers (Bryant and Holt, 2006). Advertisers recognized papers' expansive reach, and revenue enabled editors and publishers to try advanced printing equipment and novel news-gathering techniques. Distribution methods changed as vendors purchased papers from publishers (100 copies for 67 cents) and sold them on the streets for a penny. The content also shifted as editors focused more on straight news over partisanship (Emery and Emery, 1988).

The Industrial Age

The second era of sport media growth is The Industrial Age. The steam engine propelled the Industrial Revolution in late eighteenth-century Britain, and within fifty years, it reached the United States. American life changed as industrialization, urbanization, and modernization impacted individuals' relationships (Lowery and DeFleur, 1995). The factory system and corporations brought about a bureaucratized society where individuals felt less connected to others, and more connected to efficiency and organization. As society became more mechanized, individuals left rural areas for towns and cities, which united disparate people. Not only were people from rural communities moving to cities, but immigrants from Europe, Asia, and Africa also settled in urban areas. They used sport and communication as means for assimilation and social cohesion. They played for neighborhood teams, sports and jockey clubs, and leagues, and coverage increased to satiate interest. Sport overcame ethnic, racial, and class differences by uniting identities and evoking pride. Cities and residents were a central focus, and the interrelationships between cities' elements helped create sport's historical narratives (Hardy, 1997; Riess, 1990). These groups diversified sports and fan bases, and their interests led to increased newspaper coverage and a varied "sports-media profile" in America (Bryant and Holt, 2006: 25). According to Oriard (1991: 11), "Sport accommodated participants' desire to play, while at the same time enabling the advocates of sport to harness the play impulse to the new industrial order."

At the end of the nineteenth century the US gained global industrial power, and innovations and communication technologies such as the telegraph, telephone, radio, television, and printing advancements helped propel mass media and sport's further development. Other influences included states' compulsory-education movement and the increase in literacy rates, which led to higher readership. Additionally, technological developments led to a decreased workweek from 60 hours to 48 hours in the 1920s, and as standard of living increased and Sunday blue laws dissolved, Americans had more money and time to enjoy sport (Inabinett, 1994).

Modernization expanded consumption of products and individuals' uses of print, film, and broadcast media (Lowery and DeFleur, 1995). Sports reporting became a regular part of America's daily newspapers, and sports writers became as famous as the athletes and coaches they covered (Bryant and Holt, 2006: 26–27). The press valued regular and innovative sports reporting, and the *New York Sun's* Charles A. Dana, the *New York World's* Joseph Pulitzer, and the *New York Journal's* William Randolph Hearst received praise for creating the first daily sports sections (Betts, 1953; Fountain, 1993; Garrison and Sabljak, 1993; Pedersen, Miloch and Laucella, 2007). Separate sports sections, departments, and editors also appeared, which reinforced sport's importance in journalism and American life. As sports journalism expanded, publications outside of New York City arose in the 1880s, including *Sporting Life* and *The Sporting News* in Philadelphia and St. Louis, respectively. At the time, these trade papers mainly covered the facts in brief stories about games and athletes (Bryant and Holt, 2006; Halberstam and Stout, 1999; Pedersen, Miloch and Laucella, 2007).

From 1900 to 1920, the US developed as a military and world power (Noverr and Ziewacz, 1983). Sport prepared individuals and countries for individual and world events, and journalism bolstered its legitimacy (Dyreson, 1989). After World War I, sport represented an escape for a war-weary public and gained status, popularity, and prestige in American society. During the

1920s "Golden Age of Sport," sports pages became a vital part of the nation's newspapers and were the "medium of place and community" (Shaw, Hamm and Knott, 2000: 64). Journalists like Grantland Rice, Paul Gallico, Ring Lardner, and Damon Runyon became celebrities like the athletes they covered. These included Babe Ruth, Bobby Jones, Helen Wills Moody, Bill Tilden, Babe Didrikson, Ty Cobb, Red Grange, and others, and coverage analyzed strategy, illuminated background, and descriptively characterized these celebrity athletes. In this decade, one out of four readers bought a newspaper solely for the sports section (Evensen, 1993; Inabinett, 1994; McChesney, 1989).

In addition to newspapers, film developed as a mass medium in the late-nineteenth and early-twentieth centuries. Sports reels highlighted heroes and cemented their status in society. Radio also was suited to sports coverage. KDKA in Pittsburgh broadcast the first major league baseball game on August 5, 1921, and fans could hear the crack of bats and fans' reactions. The NBC and CBS radio networks were part of the first national medium by the 1930s, where listeners could hear and share messages concurrently (Shaw *et al.*, 2000).

While radio was popular and added intimacy and drama to sports experiences, television was the biggest technological development during the Industrial Age. It offered immediacy, action, drama, and state-of-the art technological developments in large part to Roone Arledge's pioneering production techniques like microphones on the field, multiple cameras, instant replay, and graphics. He and the late NFL Commissioner Pete Rozelle developed *Monday Night Football* (and later the Super Bowl), which extended football weekends with its progressive technology, game coverage, and commentators' personalities. Television was America's national medium, and its production values and technology catapulted the NFL into a national sport. The big three networks – National Broadcasting Company (NBC), Columbia Broadcasting System (CBS), and American Broadcasting Company (ABC) – all featured sport programs during this age (Bryant and Holt, 2006). Television broadcast sport globally and transported audiences to live events instantly (Rader, 2004).

The sports magazine also evolved during the Industrial Age. *Sport* magazine was published in 1946 and featured full-page pictures, and Henry Luce created *Sports Illustrated* (*SI*) in 1954 (Bryant and Holt, 2006). Magazines had inventive photography, printing technologies and methods, and fit a market niche better than other media (Shaw *et al.*, 2000). *Sport* focused more on personalities, and *SI* published compelling stories and photos (Pedersen, Miloch and Laucella, 2007).

Cable television, specifically ESPN's inception on September 7, 1979, was vital in sport's technological progression as well. When ESPN founder Bill Rasmussen and his son Scott proposed broadcasting sports 24 hours a day on cable television by satellite, networks and newspapers downplayed its impact, not realizing fans' fervor with the 24/7 sport cycle. Rasmussen's decision to buy a transponder on the satellite before others recognized its potential was the first step in ESPN's rise to world dominance, according to Miller and Shales (2011). It reinforced the importance of distribution technology early in cable television's use, and ESPN is now the "worldwide leader in sports" (Smith and Hollihan, 2009: xiv). ESPN's seminal "SportsCenter" broadcast its 50,000th show on September 13, 2012 (Fay, 2012). ESPN is worth more than the National Football League (NFL), and more than the National Basketball Association (NBA), Major League Baseball (MLB), and National Hockey League (NHL) combined (Miller and Shales, 2011). It owns the rights to the NFL, MLB, NBA, major football conferences, Major League Soccer (MLS), tennis Grand Slams, National Association for Stock Car Auto Racing (NASCAR), and golf's majors including the US and British Opens, and the Masters. ESPN sells these properties and programs in multiple formats and platforms, which include mobile applications – ESPN's fastest-growing platform (Greenfeld, 2012).

As multiple platforms expanded, newspapers added more sports coverage. In fact, sports at one time constituted 25 percent of *USA Today* (Bryant and Holt, 2006). Newspapers also featured in-depth coverage of games, athletes, and coaches (Reed, 2011). This included more work on sport's economic, legal, political, and social aspects (Garrison and Salwen, 1989). By the end of the Industrial Age, newspapers, magazines, television, and radio all covered sports (Bryant and Holt, 2006). The growth of sports journalism over time has been characterized by an increase in editorializing, as commentary, opinion, and speculation have gained more importance and boundaries have been blurred (Boyle, 2006).

As new technologies emerge and rival old ones, innovations influence journalism's norms and practices, and groups maximize opportunities to stress agendas (Lasorsa, 2012; Shaw *et al.*, 2000). Walter Lippmann's seminal work, *Public Opinion,* said the power of the media lies in transmission of second-hand pseudo-events, where individuals' realities are formulated through others' interpretations of those events (1997: xiii). The media are spotlights, or searchlights, that draw attention to certain events and individuals, and impact our perceptions of reality (p. xiv).

The 1947 report of the Commission on Freedom of the Press, written by Robert Maynard Hutchins and other intellectuals, laid out the need for a "truthful, comprehensive, and intelligent account of the day's events in a context which gives them meaning" (Hutchins *et al.*, 1947: 21). This includes the need for accuracy and the differentiation between facts and opinions. Other requirements include a "forum for the exchange of comment and criticism" (p. 23). A marketplace of ideas and free discussion are vital, and in their words, the "identification of source is necessary to a free society" (p. 25). Other societal imperatives include an active and engaged citizenry – participatory democracy has been inherent in American political philosophical ideals of Thomas Jefferson, Alexis de Tocqueville, John Stuart Mill and John Dewey – and "the projection of a representative picture of the constituent groups in society" (Hutchins *et al.*, 1947: 26; Putnam, 2000). The press also needs to represent and clarify societal values and goals, and the public needs open and total access to the "day's intelligence" (Hutchins *et al.*, 1947: 28).

The ideals presented in the Hutchins Report are still relevant many decades later despite differing technology and communication media. As Downie Jr. and Kaiser said in *The News About the News: American Journalism in Peril*, "Good journalism does not often topple a president [as in Woodward and Bernstein's stories about President Richard Nixon], but it frequently changes the lives of citizens, both grand and ordinary" (2002: 3). It holds communities together and promotes shared experiences, providing useful information and affording a sense of participation in society (pp. 4 and 6). Journalists maintain a unique role in preserving America's "culture of accountability" in checking power and satiating individuals' curiosity for knowledge (pp. 7 and 9).

Technology has potential to unite, divide, or segment audiences in America (Dizard, 2000). Individuals' options are more individualized and commoditized as communication and information sharing has become prevalent (Lievrouw and Livingstone, 2006). Technology enables consumers to tailor entertainment and news preferences in private, which promotes individual choices, yet potentially fosters solitary rather than community engagement (Putnam, 2000). As a result, the last era has seen economic, technological, demographic, and social changes as traditional media have matured, and new and emerging media continue to evolve.

The Information/Digital Age

The Information Age started in the 1990s and has morphed into a Digital Age as technology and media affect individuals' and journalists' experiences, interactions, and global worldviews.

According to Real (1998), "the world of sports in the age of mass media has been transformed from nineteenth-century amateur recreational participation to late-twentieth-century specta-tor-centered technology and business" (p. 18). In large part this is due to television, and more recently, the Internet. The Internet's "accessibility, interactivity, speed, and multimedia content are triggering a fundamental change in the delivery of mediated sports, a change for which no one can yet predict the outcome" (Real, 2006: 171).

The Information Age has focused on interactive media with an increasing rate of change. According to Pew Research Center's Project for Excellence in Journalism's (PEJ's) *State of the News Media 2012*, digital media has transferred power toward emerging technologies, yet the written word remains important in this era of "continuity and change" (Boyle, 2007: 12). Journalism's enduring function continues to be the transmission of information and the impor-tance of storytelling (Oates and Pauly, 2007), yet evolution, progress, and change characterize social, economic, and technological shifts (McQuail, 2010). The distinction between personal and mass communication has blurred since the same technologies are used for both. The lines between publisher, producer, distributor, and consumer have blurred as well, since gate-keeping is no longer reserved just for media organizations and the ascent of new media creates vast changes (McQuail, 2010). According to McQuail (2010), communication has moved from a "one-way, one-directional and undifferentiated flow to an undifferentiated mass," where inter-activity and network connectivity abound (pp. 136 and 141).

Specialized programs meet a fragmented audience and environment where convergence, digitization, and consolidation thrive (Bernstein and Blain, 2003; Bryant and Holt, 2006). Postman wrote in *Amusing Ourselves to Death* (1985: 8), "The news of the day is a figment of our technological imagination. It is, quite precisely, a media event. We attend to fragments of events from all over the world because we have multiple media whose forms are well suited to fragmented conversation." In today's "mass media world," the quantity and speed of informa-tion are infinite and the major media are seemingly unavoidable (Bagdikian, 2004: xii–xiii). The transitory digital world has a landscape where new media, especially the Internet, digital tele-vision, and mobile phones, have created new distribution channels and platforms for transmitting and delivering sports content to a rabid audience (Bernstein and Blain, 2003). Fans supplement traditional media with digital content that blurs the lines between journalism, marketing, and entertainment (Coakley, 2009). Fans' participation and consumption, and expanding sports journalists' job responsibilities all affect content and opportunities for inter-activity. According to Bernstein and Blain (2003: 96), "the global availability of sports information and analysis via digital networks is transforming the way in which breaking news about sport is gathered, selected, and disseminated." Further, there has been a huge increase in outlets for sports news, which promotes competition and impacts the news cycle (Andrews, 2011). At the root of much content, however, is still the news organization.

According to PEJ's *State of the News Media 2012*, news organizations must keep pace of new mobile platforms and social media channels in order to narrow the gap between news and technology industries (p. 3). As technology giants like Apple, Google, Amazon, and Facebook consolidate and permeate every aspect of our digital worlds, the news industry as a late adapter must catch up and follow, rather than lead, in the digital era (p. 3). Online audiences grew, yet print circulation numbers and advertising revenues still decreased. Newspapers must adapt to the migration of readers from print to online in order to survive. Even with these two combined revenues, the newspaper industry still has decreased 43 percent since 2000 (p. 4). Over the past five years, an average of 15 papers have disappeared annually. More than 150 newspapers have adopted some type of digital subscription model, including *The New York Times*, which has close to 400,000 subscribers (PEJ *State of the Media*, 2012). They have also acquired digital sites to boost their presence. For instance, Gannett's *USA Today* Sports Media Group acquired Big Lead Sports for $30 million in 2012. The sports blog consistently scores high in comScore's monthly top 10 most trafficked sports sites (Fisher, 2012a, 2012c). *USA Today* Sports Media Group also partnered with digital media firm Perform, which provides video highlights to local Gannett outlets (Fisher, 2012b). And it announced a syndicated content module called *USA Today* Sports Pulse, which will aggregate sports content from Gannett's local media brands, Sports on Earth, sites within *USA Today*'s Sports Digital Properties, and others ("*USA Today* Sports introduces," 2012). These examples show outlets' commitments to digital efforts.

Raymond Boyle (2007) defined characteristics of sports journalism's Digital Age. These include the fast pace of information transference across platforms, the increasing synergies across disparate media entities and the impact on news values, and elite sports and their reliance on media organizations (Boyle, 2007). Sports departments and newsrooms now need to break and report news, as well as blog, tweet, and give live game updates (Andrews, 2011). News organizations must still remember their civic mission as "providers of information and defenders of democracy" (Fry, 2011). However, printing and publishing information and distributing quickly are also vital since now anyone can publish, including teams, leagues, organizations, agents, athletes, coaches, fans, and others (Fry, 2011). Routines are being redefined in accordance with social and technological issues (Price, Farrington and Hall, 2012).

There are challenges, yet increasingly more opportunities to publish, as newspaper websites produce new content. At *The Indianapolis Star*, reporters provide expert "takes" from games that offer insider analysis and insight as well as game recaps, and must be comfortable in print and digital, tweeting, shooting video, taking pictures, and interacting with readers (Lefko, personal communication, October 10, 2012).

Journalists build the brand, drive traffic, and captivate readers (Kindred, 2010: 53). In the digital era, there is pressure to break news first, and with this potentially comes misinformation. One example was the premature story that appeared on Joe Paterno's death. More than 12 hours before he died in January 2012, Penn State's *Onward State* incorrectly tweeted and published a story that the university's legendary football coach had died. Other outlets, including CBS Sports followed suit, and the hoax was shared to hundreds online (Ramos, 2012a). Sites like *Deadspin* have further complicated coverage and evoked controversy, especially in the Manti Te'o "catfishing" story (Myerberg, 2013). *Deadspin*, without speaking to the college football star, his family, or his school, quoted an unnamed (later revealed) source who said he was "80 percent sure" that Te'o was involved in the hoax concerning a relationship with a nonexistent girlfriend who died of leukemia (Burke and Dickey, 2013). Te'o denied involvement, and Ronaiah Tuiasosopo confessed to creating her persona. In an interview with Manny Randhawa for the National Sports Journalism Center's website, *Deadspin* Editor-In-Chief Tommy Craggs defended the usage of the quote even though the site criticizes other media outlets for their reporting practices (Randhawa, 2013).

Organizations like Poynter Institute stress the importance of ethics, professionalism, and accuracy. Journalists' perceptions about ethics impact media content (Shoemaker and Reese, 1996: 95). According to Poynter Institute's Kelly McBride, "Today's sport media corporations that dominate content are more enmeshed in the entertainment business than in promoting the public interest" (personal communication, September 25, 2012). Media conglomerates like General Electric, News Corporation, Disney, Viacom, Time Warner, and CBS run newspapers, broadcast outlets, motion picture studios, and other information outlets, and control 90 percent of what 277 million Americans read, watch, or listen to daily (Captain, 2012). Media critic Ben Bagdikian warned against the power of the oligopolies that control the media market. "A handful of powerful, monopolistic corporations inundate the population day and night with news, images, publications, and sounds," he wrote. Questions remain about whether mergers are good for journalism, especially as sports journalists are expected to be multi-faceted across platforms (Huang *et al.*, 2006).

As media convergence continues, job functions reflect consolidation. Content convergence occurs when media outlets share content from other competing outlets. Form, or technological convergence, refers to use of all mediated communications to tell stories on the web. Corporate convergence centers on media mergers and synergy that come about due to vertical and horizontal integration. According to Turow, "synergy means the coordination of parts of a company so that the whole actually turns out to be worth more than the sum of its parts acting alone" (1997: 265). Disney can promote ESPN, which in turn can cross-promote its many entities on all platforms. Role convergence is when journalists perform different roles in different media (Huang *et al.*, 2006). Organizations have partnerships with people they cover, and that also impacts journalistic responsibilities, values, and roles for journalists (McBride, personal communication, September 25, 2012).

While certain trends and challenges transcend sports, the pressures on sports journalists are much greater than they are on news journalists today (Armstrong, 2012; McBride, 2012). According to Whiteside, Yu and Hardin, "sports journalism is at a crossroads" as new media producers and bloggers have challenged traditional journalistic norms and news values (2012: 24). Pressures come from within the organization, as well as outside the organization, and social media have accelerated the process. The interdependent parts all have specific and standardized functions and roles. Outside the organization, information sources, revenue sources, social institutions, economic environment, and technology all impact content (Shoemaker and Reese, 1996: 175). Gatekeepers include owners and publishers, editors, reporters, photographers, and others. Like outside influences, these occur at individual, media, organization, extramedia, and ideological levels (pp. 141 and 176). As Lowes (1999) found, work norms, routines, and organizations' expectations impacted sports journalism content, especially in regard to negative stories and potential sourcing and access problems. It is important to bring context to rumors; there must be a similar standard of news judgment and professionalism where a story is confirmed (McBride, personal communication, September 25, 2012). Online journalists believe in delivering credible and accurate information, yet it is shaped by individuals and is highly variable (Reed, 2011: 46). One example of this is micro-blogging.

Micro-blogging

Twitter was introduced in 2006 and was initially intended to be a cell phone application. It has expanded, however, into a global news and information network used across platforms (Lasorsa *et al.*, 2012). Twitter is a micro-blogging tool where users create 140-character tweets and share information online that can be accessed via computer, smart phones, or readers like Tweetdeck (Price *et al.*, 2012). Sports media and leagues have acknowledged Twitter as a "potentially powerful and revolutionary tool" (Schultz and Sheffer, 2010: 231). Twitter helps in news gathering and production processes, and can be used to break news, publicize journalists' work on multiple platforms, and provide avenues for conversations in real-time (Schultz and Sheffer, 2010). As Wann found (2006), mediated sports are vital for fan identification. Journalists use Twitter as a crowd-sourcing tool where they can find information and sources on their own or through their media organization, and can connect to a worldwide network (Price *et al.*, 2012).

Lasorsa *et al.* (2012) found that micro-blogs influence journalistic norms through communicating opinions and conveying information from others, as well as offering hyperlinks

(p. 402). The first two deal with objectivity and gatekeeping, or adhering to the facts in a non-biased way and creating and sustaining a flow of relevant and credible information. Hyperlinking deals with transparency, or the need for being clear about sources and other parts of the news process (p. 403). Attribution is key in order for journalists and organizations to maintain professionalism and legitimacy. Overall, journalists use Twitter effectively for exposure and interactions, and its speed in breaking stories is a strength. There have been instances of reckless and irresponsible use, however, such as when *The Washington Post*'s Mike Wise falsely claimed that the NFL would decrease quarterback Ben Roethlisberger's suspension – a claim he allegedly made to show eroding standards and credibility of sport media outlets and sourcing ("*Washington Post* suspends Mike Wise," 2010).

Ronnie Ramos, the *Indianapolis Star*'s sports director, said problems arise when journalists apply different standards on Twitter rather than viewing it as a platform for their work like a newspaper or website. "The blurring of the line between good, respectable news sources and those that are not respectable happened way before Twitter arrived on the scene," he wrote (Ramos, 2012b). ESPN's senior vice president, editorial, print and digital media, Rob King said, "Social media is a red herring… This is all an IQ test to see whether, when left to their own devices, journalists are willing to adhere to the core principles of any professional news organization: accuracy, professionalism, fairness, etc." (personal communication, October 19, 2012).

Sports reporters now break stories by reading and extracting athletes' quotes on Facebook and Twitter. Many athletes and coaches use Twitter to directly reach fans and manage information. In the past, fans could only learn about their favorite sports personalities through intermediary sports journalists. Social media has changed that. (Kassing and Sanderson, 2010: 113). Para-social interaction (PSI) signifies media users' relationships and rapport with media figures and the ensuing bonds that develop over time (Auter and Palmgreen, 2000; Horton and Wohl, 1956; Kassing and Sanderson, 2009, 2010). Whereas previously, journalists provided expert insight and information and were gatekeepers, now fans can maintain their own para-social and social relationships (Kassing and Sanderson, 2010).

Conclusion

As journalism changes and evolves, journalists navigate through social media and content decisions based on audience and other factors (Reed, 2011: 57). Some organizations like ESPN have social networking policies that include Twitter. Personal sites and blogs with sports content are prohibited, and employees need supervisor approval before participating in social networking. Newsrooms are still coming to terms with social media. Organizations must enact policies that present clear guidelines, yet give journalists freedom to possess a personal brand and personality.

In addition to organizational and job challenges, leagues, owners, teams, and athletes no longer rely on the journalist to communicate with fans and set agendas. According to Ted Leonsis (owner of Washington Capitals, Wizards and Mystics), "I have a direct, unfiltered way to reach our audience now, and I think that harnessing that is what you have to do as ownership, because we are media brands… I don't want *The Washington Post* to get the most clicks. I want the most clicks" (Steinberg, 2011). Jason Fry (2011) noted this trend toward elimination of an intermediary, disintermediation, and suggested that journalists find their niche in statistical analysis, investigative reporting, scouting opponents, minor-league reports, and historical perspective, among others.

A fundamental aspect to technological change in communication is a shift toward more user control (Shaw *et al.*, 2000). According to the PEJ's *State of the News Media 2012*, 133 million

Americans (54 percent of online US population) spend an average of seven hours monthly on Facebook. Facebook has 1 billion visitors per month (Hof, 2012). There are 24 million Twitter users in the United States (p. 5). And more people are using mobile devices for information as 27 percent of Americans get their news from mobile devices (Pew Research Center's Project for Excellence in Journalism, 2012). Organizations want good content that is delivered efficiently and effectively through mobile devices, engagement marketing, and social media (Sutton, 2011).

The media are "platforms that reflect competing social agendas" (Shaw *et al.*, 2000: 74). The web's opportunities afford more space for a range of sports coverage that traditional media do not highlight (Boyle, 2006: 158). According to WomenTalkSports' co-founder, Ann Gaffigan (2012), digital efforts have "served as a testing pool" where bloggers and journalists wrote about women's sports on sites. The strong response proved there is a market if women's sports are adequately promoted (personal communication, October 16, 2012). It is one example of how technology has expanded opportunities and agendas.

As the image of sports journalism changes, journalists must cover a wide array of political, legal, economic, social, and journalistic issues. Even in a transitory and technologically rich media environment, journalists remain cultural storytellers who inform and serve a public good in fostering innovation and progress through the exchange of diverse ideas and information. According to ESPN's Rob King, "In the end, the roles, responsibilities and norms embraced by sports journalists remain unchanged. Quality, accuracy, creativity and fairness become even more precious" (personal communication, October 19, 2012). The new media world is interactive, vibrant, and autonomous with much potential for freedom and equality. Journalists must continue to embrace change and maximize exposure to satiate consumers' fervent passion for sport. As technology evolves so must sports journalists, and as a result, everyone benefits in today's information-rich, digital-first environment.

References

Andrews, J. (2011, April) *Tackling the Digital Future of Sports Journalism: A Look at Sports Journalism in the United Kingdom and United States* [A report for the Robert Bell Travelling Scholarship]. Retrieved from http://www.saps.canterbury.ac.nz/docs/robert_bell_report_april11.pdf

Armstrong, K. (2012, September 20) [Personal communication]. Guest lecture in J-460 class at IU School of Journalism-Indianapolis.

Auter, P.J. and Palmgreen, P. (2000) Development and validation of a parasocial interaction measure: The Audience-Persona Interaction Scale. *Communication Research Reports*, 17(1), 45–56.

Bagdikian, B.H. (2004) *The New Media Monopoly*. Boston, MA: Beacon Press.

Bernstein, A. and Blain, N. (eds) (2003) *Sport, Media, Culture: Global and Local Dimensions*. London: Frank Cass.

Betts, J.R. (1953) Sporting journalism in nineteenth-century America. *American Quarterly*, 5, 39–56.

Boyle, R. (2006) *Sports Journalism: Context and Issues*. London: Sage Publications.

Boyle, R. (2007) Sports journalism and communication: Challenges and opportunities in the digital media age. In *Asia Communication and Media Forum*. 14–16 September 2007, Beijing, China.

Bryant, J. and Holt, A.M. (2006) A historical overview of sports and media in the United States. In A.A. Raney and J. Bryant (eds), *Handbook of Sports and Media* (pp. 21–43). Mahwah, NJ: Lawrence Erlbaum Associates.

Burke, T. and Dickey, J. (2013, January 16) Manti Te'o's dead girlfriend, the most heartbreaking and inspirational story of the college football season, is a hoax. *Deadspin.com*. Retrieved March 3, 2013 from http://deadspin.com/5976517/manti-teos-dead-girlfriend-the-most-heartbreaking-and-inspirational-story-of-the-college-football-season-is-a-hoax

Captain, S. (2012, June 14) 6 media companies tell you most everything you know. *Tech News Daily*. Retrieved October 6, 2012 from http://www.technewsdaily.com/4423-6-companies-control-90-percent-media.html

Chadwick, H. (2012) *National Baseball Hall of Fame and Museum*. Retrieved September 19, 2012, from http://baseballhall.org/hof/chadwick-henry

Coakley, J. (2009) *Sports in Society: Issues and Controversies* (10th edn.). Boston, MA: McGraw Hill.

Dizard, W. Jr. (2000) *Old Media, New Media: Mass Communications in the Information Age* (3rd edn.). New York: Longman.

Downie, L. Jr. and Kaiser, R.B. (2002) *The News About the News: American Journalism in Peril.* New York: Alfred A. Knopf.

Dyreson, M. (1989) The emergence of consumer culture and the transformation of physical culture: American sport in the 1920s. *Journal of Sport History,* 16(3), 261–281.

Emery, M. and Emery, E. (1988) *The Press and American: An Interpretive History of the Mass Media* (6th edn.). Englewood Cliffs, NJ: Prentice Hall.

Evensen, B.J. (1993) Jazz age journalism's battle over professionalism, circulation, and the sports page. *Journal of Sport History,* 20, 229–246.

Fay, J. (2012) ESPN's Scott Van Pelt looks back as "SportsCenter" set to air 50,000th episode. *SportsBusiness Daily.* Retrieved October 1, 2012, from http://www.sportsbusinessdaily.com/Daily/Issues/2012/09/13/Media/SportsCenter.aspx

Fisher, E. (2012a, January 24) USA Today Sports Media Group acquire Big Lead Sports for about $30 million. *Sports Business Daily.* Retrieved October, 12, 2012, from http://www.sportsbusinessdaily.com/Daily/Issues/2012/01/24/Media/Big-Lead-Sports.aspx?hl=Eric%20Fisher&sc=0

Fisher, E. (2012b, October 4) Local Gannett outlets gain access to video highlights via new content deal. *Sports Business Daily.* Retrieved October 12, 2012, from http://www.sportsbusinessdaily.com/Daily/Issues/2012/10/04/Media/USA-Today.aspx

Fisher, E. (2012c, October 9) ESPN.com tops monthly ComScore sports rankings for second time since '08. *Sports Business Daily.* Retrieved October 12, 2012, from http://www.sportsbusinessdaily.com/Daily/Issues/2012/10/09/Media/comscore.aspx

Fountain, C. (1993) *Sportswriter: The Life and Times of Grantland Rice.* Bridgewater, NJ: Replica.

Fry, J. (2011, September 15) Rules of the game change as sports journalists compete against teams they cover. *Poynter Institute website.* Retrieved September 10, 2012, from http://www.poynter.org/latest-news/top-stories/146069/rules-of-the-game-change-as-sports-journalists-compete-against-teams-they-cover/

Garrison, B., with Sabljak, M. (1993) *Sports reporting* (2nd edn.). Ames, IA: Iowa State University.

Garrison, B. and Salwen, M. (1989) Newspaper sports journalists: A profile of the "profession." *Journal of Sport and Social Issues,* 13(2) 57–68.

Greenfeld, K.T. (2012, August 30) ESPN: Everywhere Sports Profit Network. *Businessweek.* Retrieved from http://www.businessweek.com/articles/2012-08-30/espn-everywhere-sports-profit-network

Halberstam, D. and Stout, G. (eds) (1999) *The Best American Sports Writing of the Century.* Boston, MA: Houghton Mifflin.

Hardy, S. (1997) Sport in urbanizing America: A historical review. *Journal of Urban History,* 23(6), 675–708.

Hof, R. (2012, October 4) Congrats, Facebook, You've hit 1 billion users. Now what? *Forbes.com.* Retrieved October 13, 2012, from http://www.forbes.com/sites/roberthof/2012/10/04/congrats-facebook-youve-hit-1-billion-users-now-what/

Horton, D. and Wohl, R.R. (1956) Mass communication and para-social interaction. *Psychiatry,* 19, 215–229.

Huang, E., Davison, K., Shreve, S., Davis, T., Bettendorf, E. and Nair, A. (2006) Bridging newsrooms and class-rooms: Preparing the next generation of journalists for converged media. *Journalism and Communication Monographs,* 8(3), 221–262.

Hutchins, R.M., Chafee, Jr., Z., *et al.* (1947) The Commission on Freedom of the Press. Retrieved from http://journalism-education.org/wp-content/uploads/2012/04/1-1-Tweeting-with-the-Enemy.pdf

Inabinett, M. (1994) *Grantland Rice and his Heroes: The Sportswriter as Mythmaker in the 1920s.* Knoxville, TN: University of Tennessee.

Kassing, J.W. and Sanderson, J. (2009) "You're the kind of guy that we all want for a drinking buddy": Expressions of parasocial interaction on floydlandis.com. *Western Journal of Communication,* 73, 182–203.

Kassing, J.W. and Sanderson, J. (2010) Fan-athlete interaction and Twitter tweeting through Giro: A case study. *International Journal of Sport Communication,* 3, 113–128.

Kindred, D. (2010) The sports beat: A digital reporting mix – with exhaustion built in. *Nieman Reports,* 64(4), 51–53.

Lasorsa, D. (2012) Transparency and other journalistic norms on Twitter. *Journalism Studies,* 13(3), 402–417.

Lasorsa, D., Lewis, S.C. and Holton, A.E. (2012) Normalizing Twitter. *Journalism Studies,* 3(1), 19–36.

Lievrouw, L.A. and Livingstone, S. (eds) (2006) *Handbook of New Media: Social Shaping and Social Consequences of ICTs* (updated student edn.). London: Sage.

Lippmann, W. (1997) *Public Opinion* (Free Press Paperbacks edn.). New York: Free Press Paperbacks.

Lowery, S.A. and DeFleur, M.L. (1995) *Milestones in Mass Communication Research: Media Effects* (3rd edn.). White Plains, NY: Longman Publishers.

Lowes, M.D. (1999) *Inside the Sports Pages: Work Routines, Professional Ideologies, and the Manufacture of Sports News.* Toronto, Canada: University of Toronto Press.

McBride, K. (2012, September 25) [Personal communication]. Guest lecture in J-660 class at IU School of Journalism-Indianapolis.

McChesney, R.W. (1989) Media made sport: A history of sports coverage in the United States. In L.A. Wenner (ed.), *Media, Sports, and Society* (pp. 49–69). Newbury Park, CA: Sage.

McQuail, D. (2010) *McQuail's Mass Communication Theory* (6th edn.). Los Angeles, CA: Sage.

Miller, J.A. and Shales, T. (2011) *ESPN: Those Guys Have all the Fun, Inside the World of ESPN.* New York: Little, Brown & Company.

Myerberg, P. (2013, January 18) The nine craziest things about the Manti Te'o hoax story. *USA Today.* Retrieved March 1, 2013, from http://www.usatoday.com/story/gameon/2013/01/16/teo-deadspin-story-eight-crazy-things/1840729/

Noverr, D.A. and Ziewacz, L.E. (1983) *The Games they Played: Sports in American History, 1865–1980.* Chicago, IL: Nelson-Hall.

Oates, T.P. and Pauly, J. (2007) Sports journalism as moral and ethical discourse. *Journal of Mass Media Ethics,* 22(4), 332–347.

Oriard, M. (1991) *Sporting with the Gods: The Rhetoric of Play and Game in American Culture.* New York: Cambridge University.

Pedersen, P.M., Miloch, S. and Laucella, P.C. (2007) *Strategic Sport Communication.* Champaign, IL: Human Kinetics.

Pew Research Center's Project for Excellence in Journalism. (2012, March 19) *The State of the News Media 2012: An Annual Report on American Journalism.* Retrieved September 24, 2012, from http://stateofthemedia.org/files/2012/08/2012_sotm_annual_report.pdf

Postman, N. (1985) *Amusing Ourselves to Death: Public Discourse in the Age of Show Business.* New York: Penguin Books.

Price, J., Farrington, N. and Hall, L. (2012) Tweeting with the enemy? The impacts of new social media on sports journalism and the education of sports journalism students. *Journalism Education,* 1(1), 9–20. Retrieved from http://journalism-education.org/wp-content/uploads/2012/04/1-1-Tweeting-with-the-Enemy.pdf

Putnam, R.D. (2000) *Bowling Alone.* New York: Simon & Schuster.

Rader, B.G. (2004) *American Sports: From the Age of Folk Games to the Age of Televised Sport* (5th edn.). Upper Saddle River, NJ: Prentice Hall.

Ramos, R. (2012a, February 29) Four ways social media has deteriorated traditional journalism. *National Sports Journalism Center.* Retrieved from http://sportsjournalism.org/sports-media-news/four-ways-social-media-has-deteriorated-traditional-journalism/

Ramos, R. (2012b, September 26) Twitter power: NFL, local broadcaster fell backlash amid highly publicized mishaps. *National Sports Journalism Center.* Retrieved October 1, 2012, from http://sportsjournalism.org/sports-media-news/twitter-power-nfl-local-broadcaster-feel-backlash-amid-highly-publicized-mishaps/

Randhawa, M. (2013, February 26) *Journalistic standards in reporting of the Te'o hoax: Q&A with Deadspin's Tommy Craggs.* Retrieved from http://sportsjournalism.org/uncategorized/journalistic-standards-in-reporting-of-the-teo-hoax-qa-with-deadspins-tommy-craggs/

Real, M. (2006) Sports online: The newest player in mediasport. In A.A. Raney and J.Bryant (eds), *Handbook of Sports and Media* (pp. 171–184). Mahwah, NJ: Lawrence Erlbaum Associates.

Real, M.R. (1998) MediaSport: Technology and the commodification of postmodern sport. In L.A. Wenner (ed.), *MediaSport* (pp. 14–26). London: Routledge.

Reed, S. (2011) Sports journalists' use of social media and its effects on professionalism. *Journal of Sports Media,* 6(2), 43–64.

Riess, S.A. (1990) The new sport history. *Reviews in American History,* 18, 311–325.

Schultz, B. and Sheffer, M.L. (2010) An exploratory study of how Twitter is affecting sports journalism. *International Journal of Sport Communication,* 3, 226–239.

Shaw, D., Hamm, B.J. and Knott, D.L. (2000) Technological change, agenda challenge and social melding: Mass media studies and the four ages of place, class, mass and space. *Journalism Studies,* 1(1), 57–79.

Shoemaker, P.J. and Reese, S.D. (1996) *Mediating the Message: Theories of Influences of Mass Media Content* (2nd edn.). White Plains, NY: Longman Publishers.

Smith, A.F. and Hollihan, K. (2009) *ESPN the Company: The Story and Lessons Behind the Most Fanatical Brand in Sports*. Hoboken, NJ: John Wiley & Sons, Inc.

Steinberg, D. (2011, January 11) Snyder and Leonis on the media. *The Washington Post*. Retrieved October 8, 2012, from http://voices.washingtonpost.com/dcsportsbog/2011/01/snyder_and_leonsis_on_the_medi.html

Sutton, B. (2011, March 14) Social media at the heart of strategy to achieve fan connectivity. *Sports Business Journal*, p. 12.

Turow, J. (1997) *Media Systems in Society: Understanding Industries, Strategies, and Power* (2nd edn.). New York: Longman Publishers.

USA Today Sports introduces new syndicated content module "USA Today Sports Pulse". *Yahoo! Finance*. Retrieved October 15, 2012, from http://finance.yahoo.com/news/usa-today-sports-introduces-syndicated-140000423.html

Wann, D.L. (2006) The causes and consequences of sport team identification. In A.A. Raney and J. Bryant (eds), *Handbook of Sports and Media* (pp. 331–352). Mahwah, NJ: Lawrence Erlbaum.

Washington Post suspends Mike Wise one month after Twitter hoax. (2010, August 31) *Sports Business Daily*. Retrieved September 26, 2012, from http://www.sportsbusinessdaily.com/Daily/Issues/2010/08/Issue-242/Sports-Media/Washington-Post-Suspends-Mike-Wise-One-Month-After-Twitter-Hoax.aspx

Wenner, L.A. (ed.) (1998) *MediaSport*. London: Routledge.

Whiteside, E.A., Yu, N. and Hardin, M. (2012, Spring) The new "toy department": A case study on differences in sports coverage between traditional and new media. *Journal of Sports Media*, 7(1), 23–38.

9

THE CHANGING ROLE OF SPORTS MEDIA PRODUCERS

Paul M. Pedersen

INDIANA UNIVERSITY

Over the past couple of decades, newspapers – and their affiliated sports desks, sections, and staffs – have witnessed monumental turmoil brought on by several often interrelated factors, including the new digital shift. In terms of sportswriting, print sports reporters are still expected to be good writers, skilled reporters, and knowledgeable professionals (Murray, McGuire, Ketterer and Sowell, 2011). But in the digital media era, sportswriters – in addition to their continued embracing of traditional journalistic practices and principles – are expected to use new media technologies and adjust their newsgathering, dissemination, and readership and source interaction activities accordingly. New media influences, digital interactivity and partic- ipatory elements, and the overall technological impact have significantly shifted the landscape in newspaper sports reporting and the surviving print sportswriters have embraced – or been forced into – their new role as digital sports journalists. This chapter – which begins with a quick overview of the current state of newspapers – covers the challenges and opportunities for sportswriters in the digital era as well as predictions for print sports journalism.

Newspaper upheaval and convergence

The arrival of the Internet and the emergence of Web 2.0 have had a significant effect on newspapers and print sports journalism. In its infancy as it applies to the sports print media, the Internet was just a platform where sports content was provided on newspaper websites with limited or no opportunities for reader input and interactivity. Newspapers increasingly felt web 1.0 influences as more and more sports media consumers began getting their sports informa- tion online. Sports sections and newspaper sports personnel were then significantly impacted with the emergence of Web 2.0, with its emphasis on user interconnection, participation, and collaboration through social media usage, interactions, and platforms. While the new and social media influences are often blamed for the upheaval encountered by newspapers, the digital media revolution is not the only reason for the usage and overall viability questions that have faced the print media. In fact, a host of issues (Edmonds, Guskin and Rosenstiel, 2011; Kian and Zimmerman) have brought about the perfect storm that newspapers – and in turn their affiliated sports sections – have faced: increased media competition (e.g. proliferation of broad- cast channels, cable television networks, satellite radio stations, tablet and mobile devices, and a host of other digital media options) and consumer fragmentation (e.g. empowerment of the media consumers), declining newspaper readership rates and circulation numbers, decreased revenues overall, declines in advertising revenues, broad economic disturbances, and an overall outdated business model with inherent inefficiencies and rising labor and production costs.

This perfect storm has permanently changed the print media landscape. During the first decade of this century, hundreds of newspapers were impacted with a downsizing of thousands of newspaper personnel. The significant budget cutbacks and reductions in newspapers and the workforce have been staggering, and that downward trend is predicted to continue. For instance, the director of the USC Annenberg Center for the Digital Future stated, "Most print newspapers will be gone in five years" (Cole, 2011). Because of the dramatic economic, business, and technological challenges since the turn of the century, newspapers and sports sections have increasingly been forced to integrate or adopt new models in order to survive the advertising shifts, business downsizing, readership changes, and a host of challenges – and opportunities – presented with the new digital sport communication marketplace. For surviving newspapers, the convergence expectations have been so swift and stressful that some argue that newspapers might be engaged in too much innovation too quickly (Pexton, 2012). Regardless, multimedia convergence is now the norm for newspaper operations, sports sections, sports editors, and sports reporters. Because this is the norm, many sportswriters have left their print media positions because of job cuts, layoffs, and personal decisions. Some have moved into full-time digital sports journalism positions while others have become entrepreneurs. For instance, Steve Rudman and Art Thiel were sports columnists for the *Seattle Post-Intelligencer*, and after the paper's move to online-only they founded the sports website, *Sportspress Northwest*. Thiel (n.d.) notes that his publication includes credentialed sports journalists, "who enjoy journalism's standards, technology's opportunities and users' passion. We enjoy good writing and clear thinking... there are decent livings to be made on the web providing quality commentary, reporting and research." Thus, displaced newspaper sports journalists have either ventured into online sports reporting, taken on freelance roles and projects, gone back to school for retraining in areas such as digital journalism, migrated over to other media professions (e.g. public relations), or exited the field altogether. Those print media professionals still on board have had to quickly adapt in the areas of convergence, new skill development, and timeliness in reporting or they are increasingly left behind by the digital revolution.

Cutting-edge sports reporting

Multimedia convergence by today's newspaper sports reporters involves the integration of their words, photos, videos, audio recordings, and interactions across legacy and digital media platforms. Traditional writing and reporting duties for the print edition of newspapers have been the norm for decades. However, sports journalists have participated in convergence activities for quite some time, going back to Grantland Rice's activities across the print, radio, television, and film platforms. Over the years, sportswriters engaged in multimedia convergence as they worked for the newspaper but were also involved in hosting radio shows and participating in television broadcasts ranging from local sports shows to nationally syndicated programs such as *Sportswriters on TV*. Since the turn of the century there has been an increase in sportswriters as hosts or prominent fixtures on national shows such as *Pardon the Interruption*. Thus, sportswriters have for nearly a century participated in varying degrees of multimedia convergence, but only recently have they been engaged in digital media convergence. While some have been forced into this era of convergence, others are early adopters and have embraced it. For instance, former *ESPN The Magazine* columnist Bill Simmons founded *Grantland.com*, a popular website that includes longer stories, opinion pieces, a sports blog (*The Triangle*), and other features. Simmons, in addition to being a bestselling author, is an influential podcaster and social media user with a Twitter account that has nearly two million followers and a Facebook account with over 400 subscribers. Whether a sportswriter has embraced or been forced to engage in this convergence, the influences of the digital media have dramatically affected all sportswriters. In order to be more competitive and timely in the 24/7 sports news cycle, more responsive to changing media consumption demands, and more relevant in the crowded digital marketplace, most surviving print sports journalists now participate in online interactivity, social media engagement, and overall digital media convergence. As noted by Sherwood and Nicholson (2013: 13) in their study of sports journalists, "Using Web 2.0 platforms has simply become part of the newsgathering, sourcing and reporting routine." This digital media shift has brought about numerous challenges and opportunities for sportswriters.

Challenges

There are significant challenges for print media professionals in the new digital sports media environment. Because newspaper sportswriters have in varying degrees entered the dynamic field of online sports journalism, they are expected to be tech-savvy. While technical proficiency in publishing online stories and working with audio and video files is not necessarily a requirement (except of course for those sports reporters working as backpack journalists), at a product level, cutting-edge sportswriters use some combination of the latest technological reporting devices or software for writing, interviewing (e.g. a digital voice recorder and software or Internet-based services), recording and uploading video, navigating the mobile web and interacting with readers. Having the latest technology provides speedy access to online resources, helps reporters discover and post instant updates and breaking news, and allows them to engage in immediate interaction with sources, readers, and editors. Overall, generally, the most effective sportswriters have technological proficiency and can communicate with their audience across various media channels and multimedia platforms. Just keeping up with all the digital innovations, new media products, content distribution outlets, and social media offerings can be quite difficult as technology keeps evolving with the addition in terms of products, sites, software packages, service platforms, applications, and interaction opportunities. Even sites that have been around for a few years (e.g. Facebook) regularly update their offerings to increase their appeal and interactive elements or periodically release new social networking platforms (e.g. Google+). Niche social networks have also surged, allowing updates and connectivity with specific groups instead of a wide audience. With the active social media involvement of sport stakeholders and sport media audiences, sportswriters are expected to be proficient in the digital media usage, reporting, and interactive opportunities presented through Web 2.0. Even tech-savvy sports journalists can find it hard to keep up with and be early adopters of the latest social networking services and websites.

Similarly, sportswriters can often be overwhelmed with the amount of sports information produced from content distribution digital outlets. Sportswriters are increasingly expected to keep abreast of news and rumors related to the stakeholders affiliated with their assigned beats, other sport media personnel, fan postings on blogs and message boards, and a plethora of social media accounts. Keeping up with all the online gossip in the sport industry and using a variety of means to separate fact from fiction in the digital media era make for significant challenges for sportswriters. Unconfirmed reports come from a variety of sources. The online rumors – which come from any number of outlets and many times are false but still must be investigated – are often erroneous in terms of timing, as in the premature and unconfirmed reports about the death of IndyCar driver Dan Wheldon in 2011.

In addition to information overload and increased demands regarding keeping up with stories and rumors, another related challenge involves the difficulties of breaking news in the increasingly competitive and 24/7 sports news cycle. Sports reporters are expected to maintain professional and often time-consuming standards and practices even when many amateur and untrained competitors may not be holding themselves to the same high expectations (Whiteside, Yu and Hardin, 2012). Amateur reporters – often called citizen journalists – produce user-generated sports content and engage in what some have referred to as occasional and random "acts of journalism." Independent producers of sports content (e.g. independent bloggers) are increasingly prevalent (Holton, 2012) and often – because of different standards – break news before the professional journalist can do so (Whiteside *et al.*, 2012). Often, the work by the untrained is done unaided, sometimes with input from others and referred to along the lines of open-source journalism, and sometimes in the assistance of the work of a professional journalist or others (referred to as participatory or networked journalism). In the past, sports stories were linear, and audiences simply received the information. But in today's environment sports reporting is often more participatory (e.g. non-linear), with audience interaction. Such participatory reporting or its variations – such as ambient journalism, citizen journalism, coffee shop journalism, community news labs, etc. – have increased as individuals not connected with traditional media in either training or affiliation engage in reporting, collaborate to produce content for blogs, websites, and social media outlets.

With the increase of sports content brought about at least in part because of the rise of user-generated content and amateur sports reporters, the abundance of information has reduced some of the influence and gatekeeping function of professional sportswriters. In the past, sports media professionals held significant power in terms of information as they often acted as gatekeepers. That old model is no longer as valid as sport industry stakeholders (e.g. audiences, athletes, team personnel) many times are the providers of sports content. The consumers (e.g. athletes, sports personnel, readers, fans) are no longer simply receivers of the mediated sports messages; they are empowered in the digital era as they actively engage in sports reporting, post their own sports information through podcasts, opinion blogs, personal website commentaries and videos, and bypass the media in various ways. Sport organizations can now control their own message, break their stories to the public on their own terms, release proprietary information as they wish, and circumvent sports reporters. Non-media sport stakeholders (e.g. athletes, boosters, fans, general managers, owners) become their own media outlets and disseminate information on their own terms when they want, where they want, through whatever platform they want, and to whichever audience they want. They do this – and become the new gatekeepers – through new media and social media. An example is the announcement by Shaquille O'Neal about his retirement by posting a video on his Twitter account in 2011. Therefore, not only is it difficult for sportswriters when they are bypassed, but keeping up with technological advancement and with all the information provided through sports websites, social networking accounts, and other online distribution outlets can be exhausting. Thus, sportswriters face significant stressors and challenges in their attempts to stay viable and competitive, engage in innovative digital sports reporting, and strive to serve the sports consumers belonging to their print and digital readership audiences. Despite the challenges and expectations brought on by the demands of the digital sports media marketplace, those reporters still employed take advantage of the opportunities presented by the technological changes in their field.

Opportunities

Tech-savvy sportswriters take advantage of the opportunities offered through digital convergence technologies and multimedia platforms. At a most basic level, sports reporters engage in multimedia convergence for pragmatic reasons, such as using cross-promotion strategies to reach and expand their readership. They can use social media, such as through microblogging, to promote content that has been published in the print or online editions. In addition to such promotional endeavors, skilled sportswriters also take advantage of the unique opportunities presented through the new media for innovative writing. For the most part, talented and successful sportswriters have typically been good storytellers. Storytelling is still important in this digital sports media era, even if there are differences in terms of the content a sportswriter may provide for the print and online editions. While there can be more in-depth reporting and more linear writing for print editions and more precise and interactive writing for online editions, there are unique digital media opportunities for storytelling and reporting, such as the long-form sportswriting in ESPN's online sports magazine *Grantland.com*, launched in 2011, and on other sites. Regardless, storytelling now typically involves using text along with audio, video, data, photos, links, and other multimedia packages to tell their sports stories. Tech-savvy reporters still engage in many of the aspects of traditional print media sports reporting, but in addition to their writing for print and online editions they integrate various aspects of multimedia convergence in their newsgathering, information dissemination, and interactive sports reporting, each of which is examined below.

Hutchins (2011: 251) noted that the "growth in digital media communication systems is transforming sports production and consumption." Sports newsgathering is now a 24/7 activity that demands the attention and adaptation of reporters. Sportswriters are still engaged in traditional newsgathering activities, but they must now follow myriad multimedia outlets. While inaccuracies in sports reporting can come about through reliance – without fact checking and substantiation – on new media outlets and social media sites, information published online can often help sports reporters in newsgathering and sourcing. Many of these websites have no affiliation with newspapers or other media. Sports reporters must keep up with the online postings of individual athletes, sports leagues, and teams who often post information and breaking news on their own websites. In addition to content on athlete or organization-affiliated websites, information is also found through the work of sports content aggregators, who collect and redistribute content produced by professional journalists and non-affiliated sports bloggers. While content aggregators compete with sportswriters for the sports audience, and news aggregation sites sometimes borrow content and simply repackage content, they can provide timely information of which professional sportswriters must be aware. Similarly, rumors and breaking news can often be found on sports websites that publish the articles and commentaries of amateur writers and citizen reporters and "community-powered" sports websites. For example, *BleacherReport.com* (acquired by Time Warner in 2012) has been an open-source content distribution outlet where mainly independent and amateur bloggers provide opinions and analyses related to sports. Sports information is published on sports websites that are not affiliated with a legacy publication. Some of these sites have been quite successful in breaking news, providing commentary, developing a large readership base and have been purchased by conglomerates, such as the 2012 acquisition of *TheBigLead.com* by the *USA TODAY* Sports Media Group. Sports reporters must also keep up with information on network-affiliated websites such as CBSSports.com and other online distribution outlets of broadcast and print media, such as those affiliated with *Sports Illustrated* and *The Sporting News*.

Social media sites and interactive user-generated outlets are also increasingly used by sports-writers in newsgathering activities and as information sources (Reed, 2011). Sports reporters are expected to keep up with content provided through blogs, social networking sites, message boards and a host of other interactive media sources. Microblogs are increasingly used by sports-writers as sources of information. Twitter is the most obvious – and, arguably the most studied (e.g. Hutchins, 2011; Sanderson and Hambrick, 2012; Sherwood and Nicholson, 2013) – as most print sports journalists have an account and are expected to follow the accounts of sports personnel, other sports journalists and beat writers, independent amateur reporters, athletes, as well as Twitter trends and hashtags. In addition to the popular microblogging and social networking sites noted above, location-based social networks are used in sports reporting. In sports, for example, fans can take photos, check-in, and track their attendance at sporting events and venues. Journalists can keep up with such postings. Snow and Lavrusik (2010) pointed out that digital journalists can use location-sharing apps for locating targeted contacts, breaking news, sourcing information, learning about subjects, discovering and monitoring trends, publishing and distributing content, and crowdsourcing news. All of these can be applied to sports journalism, as tech-savvy sports journalists can use the apps by, for example, finding a real sports fan in attendance at a football game, sending instant notifications with updates to follow-ers, discovering "tips" posted by users which may be used as background material for a story, using them as sources to learn about an athlete's habits and communication, discovering emerg-ing activities or patterns at a sports facility, offering comments and links to info they have produced, and so forth. In addition to following the social networking accounts and website updates of various sports stakeholders, sportswriters can leverage the new media and Web 2.0 outlets to find contact information, secure source and interaction opportunities, and other newsgathering and reporting activities.

The print edition is no longer the only outlet for a sportswriter to publish a gamer, sidebar, column, or other content. In this digital era, tech-savvy print sports reporters are now expected to deliver their sports content to (and through) a variety of media platforms and channels rang-ing from tablet devices to smartphones. Beyond the material provided for the print editions, the digital delivery of sports content created by sportswriters is done through new media and social media outlets. Thus, digital content involves both the standard online content (e.g. stories) as well as the more advanced and interactive digital media elements. Sportswriters use various digital content distribution such as those in the form of online videos (webcasts), audio content (podcasts), visual stills (photo galleries or uploads of photos at a sporting event or press confer-ence), social networking sites, blogging, and microblogging. The last two in particular are time-consuming and increasingly important online activities used by sportswriters. Blogging as it relates to sports journalism has recently received attention by scholars (e.g. Hardin and Ash, 2011; Holton, 2012; Kian, Burden and Shaw, 2011; Schultz and Sheffer, 2010; Whiteside *et al.*, 2012) who have examined the work of citizen reporters and professional sportswriters in this area. Often, sports reporters are active in their use of weblogs created by the newspaper or through online publishing tools. This activity ranges from general blogging and live-game blog-ging to post-game reaction blogging and mobile blogging. Sportswriters contribute to newspaper-affiliated blogs by covering everything from high school athletics to professional sports.

In addition to traditional blogging, the phenomenon of microblogging has captured the attention of sport communication researchers (e.g. Hutchins, 2011; Reed, 2011; Sheffer and Schultz, 2010) and significantly assisted sportswriters in their content delivery. While services such as Tumblr, Sina Weibo and Yammer are popular, it would be hard to deny that Twitter is the microblogging platform most used by reporters. Sanderson and Hambrick (2012) found in their case study that sportswriters used Twitter to offer commentary, break news, and link to content as well as for interactivity and cross promotion. In the past, newspaper reporters would often break news to readers when the paper was delivered in the morning. With the 24/7 sports news cycle, print reporters with a scoop regarding sourced material or proprietary information often break their news on their newspaper website or through their social networking site (e.g. a reporter's or a newspaper's Facebook account). While a newspaper may have a policy against reporters breaking news on their own without the information being vetted through editors or against reporters breaking news through a platform such as Twitter instead of through print or online editions first, often sports reporters provide their scoops through digital means first as opposed to waiting for the publication of the print edition. Thus, for instance, a sportswriter can instantly inform an audience through microblogging.

However, because journalistic standards (e.g. fact checking, sourcing, confirming) are not adopted by everyone who participates in online sports information, it is increasingly difficult for professional sports reporters to break news. For instance, there were inaccurate and uncon-firmed reports in the last hours of coach Joe Paterno's life in January 2012. During the premature reports of his death by others, the sports editors for the *Atlanta Journal-Constitution* tweeted, "Folks, if/when we can CONFIRM a #Paterno death, we will tweet it. But we want to be accurate, not just fast. Please stand by." Professionalism in reporting activities such as that helps build trust with readers and is often what separates the trained reporter from many of the amateur sports bloggers and message board enthusiasts. "Not lifting us up compared to others in the media, but we walk the fine line of how news is reported and we do have higher stan-dards than most when it comes to sourcing," said one sportswriter (Wilson, 2012). Thus, it is not surprising that Sherwood and Nicholson (2013) found that Australian sportswriters used Twitter for research and monitoring purposes, but the "sports journalists were divided in whether or not to use it as a platform to break new" (p. 12).

The future

Despite the already dramatic shifts, overwhelming challenges, and unique opportunities that newspaper sports journalists have encountered over the past couple decades, those involved in print media reporting will continue to face an even more dynamic future. Because of the evolving digital media marketplace, it is impossible to predict what innovations will next impact sportswriters in particular and newspapers overall. With the competitive environment and readership demands in sport communication, newspaper sports departments and personnel will certainly need to make adjustments. Technological, economic, and audience changes in the print sports media have come quickly throughout this new millennium and they will no doubt continue to do so in this second decade of the twenty-first century. While sports journalism faces an uncertain future, many of the predicted changes in the field will have a negative effect on print sports media professionals. For instance, there will most likely be a rise in sports content aggregators (although legal decisions may curtail some of this). It can be predicted that sports organizations and personnel will increasingly bypass the traditional media and commu-nicate directly with their stakeholders. Untrained sports enthusiasts will mostly likely get even more involved in covering, delivering, and contributing to the sports content consumed by other fans and the media. Newspaper print editions will continue to move online due to many of the factors noted in this chapter. Such transitions and other emerging technological innova-tions and new products and software will continue to affect sportswriters. Just as the merging and usage of digital media technologies have had a significant influence, down the road advancements into Web 3.0 and artificial intelligence may begin to affect sports journalists. For instance, robots and software programs are being developed now that can create content on their own without the need of a sportswriter. An example of this is "Stats Monkey", in which an AP formatted game story and headline can be generated by simply inputting various information (e.g. box score) into a computer system ("Projects," 2010).

While the impact of Web 3.0 still might be a few years away, the innovations in and usages of Web 2.0 alone will require sportswriters to continue to embrace technological evolvement in terms of products, usage, and interactions. Such expectations are similar to what they have faced over the past couple of decades. For a variety of reasons (e.g. economic downturn, newspaper business model inefficiencies, multimedia convergence expectations, readership changes), sports reporters for daily newspapers have encountered significant challenges and opportunities in this digital media era. Despite the upheaval, the professional journalistic standards and expectations of print sports journalists have remained constant. Innovative and professional sports journalists are not headed for extinction as they will continue to be called upon to produce quality and credible print and online content. Because of the professionalism, training, skills, principles, practices, and standards of most print sports reporters, sports sections in particular and newspapers overall are still valued and trusted in most communities and will remain in some format. However, just as has happened over the past few years, tech-savvy sportswriters will only remain viable by making stylistic and performance adaptations while embracing opportunities that come through their engagement in multimedia convergence.

References

Cole, J.I. (2011, December 14) Is America at a digital turning point? *USC Annenberg News.* Retrieved January 18, 2012, from http://annenberg.usc.edu/News%20and%20Events/News/111214CDF.aspx

Edmonds, R., Guskin, E. and Rosenstiel, T. (2011, March 14) Newspapers: Missed the 2010 media rally. *The State of the News Media 2011.* Retrieved December 17, 2012, from http://stateofthemedia.org/2011/newspapers-essay/

Hardin, M. and Ash, E. (2011, Spring) Journalists provide social context missing from sports blogs. *Newspaper Research Journal,* 32(2), 20–35.

Holton, A. (2012) Baseball's digital disconnect: Trust, media credentialing, and the independent blogger. *Journal of Sports Media,* 7(1), 39–58.

Hutchins, B. (2011) The acceleration of media sport culture. *Information, Communication and Society,* 14(2), 237–257.

Kian, E.M. and Zimmerman, M.H. (2012) The medium of the future: Top sports writers discuss transitioning from newspapers to online journalism. *International Journal of Sport Communication,* 5, 285–302.

Kian, E.M., Burden, Jr., J.W. and Shaw, S.D. (2011) Internet sport bloggers: Who are these people and where do they come from? *Journal of Sport Administration and Supervision,* 3(1), 30–43.

Murray, R., McGuire, J., Ketterer, S. and Sowell, M. (2011) Flipping the field: The next generation of newspaper sports journalists. *Journal of Sports Media,* 6(2), 65–88.

Pexton, P.B. (2012, January 6) Is The Post innovating too fast? *The Washington Post.* Retrieved January 10, 2012, from http://www.washingtonpost.com/opinions/is-the-post-innovating-too-fast/2012/01/06/gIQAji5pfP_story.html

Projects > Stats Monkey. (2010) *Intelligent Information Laboratory.* Retrieved January 16, 2012, from http://infolab.northwestern.edu/projects/stats-monkey/

Reed, S. (2011, Fall) Sports journalists' use of social media and its effects on professionalism. *Journal of Sports Media,* 6(2), 43–64.

Sanderson, J. and Hambrick, M. E. (2012) Covering the scandal in 140 characters: A case study of Twitter's role in coverage of the Penn State saga. *International Journal of Sport Communication,* 5, 384–402.

Schultz, B. and Sheffer, M.L. (2010) Sports journalists who blog cling to traditional values. *Newspaper Research Journal,* 28(4), 62–76.

Sheffer, M.L. and Schultz, B. (2010) Paradigm shift or passing fad? Twitter and sports journalism. *International Journal of Sport Communication,* 3, 472–484.

Sherwood, M. and Nicholson, M. (2013) Web 2.0 platforms and the work of newspaper sport journalists. *Journalism, 14*(7), 942–959. doi: 10.1177/1464884912458662

Snow, S. and Lavrusik, V. (2010, May 14) 7 ways journalists can use Foursquare. *Mashable.* Retrieved January 15, 2012, from http://mashable.com/2010/05/14/journalists-foursquare/

Thiel, A. (n.d.) About. *Sportspress Northwest.* Retrieved December 17, 2012, from http://sportspressnw.com/about/

Whiteside, E.A., Yu, N. and Hardin, M. (2012) The new "toy department"?: A case study on differences in sports coverage between traditional and new media. *Journal of Sports Media, 7*(1), 23–38.

Wilson, P.B. (2012, January 17) Why Caldwell firing threw us for a loop. *Indystar.com.* Retrieved December 18, 2012, from http://blogs.indystar.com/philb/2012/01/17/why-caldwell-firing-threw-us-for-a-loop/

10

LOCAL TV SPORTS AND THE INTERNET

Brad Schultz

UNIVERSITY OF MISSISSIPPI

Mary Lou Sheffer

UNIVERSITY OF SOUTHERN MISSISSIPPI

In a very short time, Ashley Russell made quite a name for herself in sportscasting. In 2012, Russell hosted *Yahoo! Sports Minute*, a program that received 22 million page hits per month; an unrelated fan web page dedicated in her honor received nearly half a million views. Another sportscaster, Ines Sainz (a sports broadcaster who made news in 2010 after she was harassed by players for the New York Jets) had more than 300,000 followers on Twitter in 2012, and Seattle-based sportscaster Brad Adam had such popularity that even his hair had its own Twitter page ("Top 11," 2010).

Russell, Sainz and Adam all show how the Internet has impacted local television sports. Before the web, local sportscasters could expect to reach only those audiences within range of their station's signal. Today, the Internet has opened up new global opportunities, and in many senses, the local sports is not so "local" anymore. But this same shift toward wider audiences also negatively impacted the local sports segment, and in some ways threatened its survival. This chapter addresses the issues related to local television sports and the Internet, and what affect those issues had in the sports media environment.

Background

From a television perspective, sports have been a constant source of programming almost from the beginning of local news. WNBT television in New York signed on the air in July 1941 and its very first telecast was a professional baseball game ("NBC history," 2003). In developing local newscasts to suit their audiences, stations usually included sports and weather. In 1961, for example, WKMG started the first full-time news department in Orlando, Florida, and its newscast included a sports report by Frank Vaught ("The history of," 2003).

Sports became an important part of local television, especially in those early days. "Television got off the ground because of sports," said pioneering television sports director Harry Coyle. "Today, maybe, sports need television to survive, but it was just the opposite when it first started" ("Sports and television," 2012). Local television news grew into a ratings power-house in the 1970s, at which point it became the favored source of news for most Americans and was frequently producing 60 percent of a station's overall profit (Hallin, 1990). According to Brady (2003: 8), "For the audience, local TV news is a habitual thing. Sitting at home each evening, we tune in in search of the familiar."

But the familiar began to change in the 1980s with the growth of cable, the rise of ESPN and the gradual fragmentation of the local sports audience. As cable and satellite penetration increased dramatically, the multiplicity of channels gave sports audiences real choice for the first time. When it began in 1979, ESPN had a modest 1.3 million subscribers, but by 2012 that number had grown to more than 100 million (Amin, 2012). Local sports broadcasters, often limited to a few minutes of content in a newscast, found it hard to compete with outfits like ESPN that offered sports 24 hours per day. As a result, "There is little doubt that broadcasters and mainstream outlets have seen their audiences erode in favor of newer alternatives" (Webster and Ksiazek, 2012: 39).

As that erosion cut dramatically into local newsroom profitability, television executives began reassessing the role of sports within the newscast, especially in light of research that suggested sports actually ranked near the bottom of reasons as to why people watched local news ("Journalism and," 1998). According to Paul Conti, who spent several years as a local news director, "The people that process money say, 'Why are we putting this much energy and money to sports coverage if only 30 percent of the audience cares?' That's been a bad thing for local sports" (Dougherty, 2012). In many television markets, time for local sports was substantially reduced or the segment was dropped entirely.

Local sports TV and blogging

The emergence of the Internet as a newsroom tool in the late 1990s came at a time when local television sports were going through a difficult period. At that time, the local sportscast had been static for several years, with little or no change in style, presentation and content (Schultz and Sheffer, 2004). Such rigidity belied what was going on in television as a whole. The development of digital technology created a media environment defined by more channels and options, high speed communication, and above all, consumer choice and empowerment (Poindexter and McCombs, 2001). "Moving from broadcast TV to broadband TV changes the whole industry," said Moshe Lichtman of IPTV (Levy, 2005).

Rather than trying to change the sports segment to meet modern demands, many local television executives found it easier, and more cost efficient, to simply get rid of it. In 2005, WTEN in Albany, New York, eliminated the traditional anchored sports segment at the end of the newscast and instead mixed sports stories into the body of the news (McGuire, 2005). That same year, WDSU in New Orleans did the same thing with its sports segment in the aftermath of Hurricane Katrina. At KPNX in Phoenix, the time for sports was reduced and the station began to use sports talent to cover general news stories (Buch and Dupont, 2003). In other cities, including large markets such as Las Vegas, Tampa and Virginia Beach, the sports segment was dropped entirely.

During this winnowing process, other stations turned to the Internet as a possible lifeline for struggling sports segments. The Internet seemingly offered bigger audiences and a way of interacting with sports consumers, who often use the mediated experience to build strong attachments to their favorite players and teams (Wann, 1997). One of the earliest interactive Internet opportunities was the web log, or blog, in which local sports journalists could offer information and opinions several times a day. It also allowed for viewers to respond to postings and engage in real-time interactive conversations with the local sports journalist. In effect, blogging is essentially a technological extension of sports talk radio, which has succeeded because of its ability to create a social community through discussion and engagement (Tremblay and Tremblay, 2001; Haag, 1996). Most bloggers seem to be very similar demographically to the sports audience as a whole (Lenhart and Fox, 2006).

But early research into blogging (Schultz and Sheffer, 2007) suggested that, at least initially, the introduction of blogging to local sports journalism met with resistance and negativity. Additionally, such studies indicated that that little, if any, change was taking place and the impact of such change was minimal. This was attributed to journalists' perceptions that blogging had little value in terms of contribution to the media outlet or personal development. It could also have been related to age, professional experience, and entrenched work roles that evolved over a period of decades (Deuze, 2003; Sigal, 1973).

Part of the resistance was based on the fact that blogging was an additional layer of work for sports journalists at no extra pay. There was also a sense among sports journalists that their outlet managers required the additional work without providing any training or direction in terms of how to implement it. In 2007, one sports journalist observed, "Our management has a seemingly unique take on blogging. Do it, but don't expect us to check it, read it or even edit it very closely. That has been very frustrating" (Schultz and Sheffer, 2007: 71). By nature, blogs are intended to be personal, subjective and opinionated (Trammell and Keshelashvili, 2005; Bowman and Willis, 2003), which further puts them at odds with traditional journalistic values. "Blogging as it has evolved has been very different from conventional reporting," said media ethics professor Jane Kirtley. "Blogs are not intended to be objective. They are supposed to be opinionated, snarky and in your face – and that's not the way the mainstream media usually goes about reporting" (Hull, 2006/2007).

Many television managers ignored these distinctions, causing more friction for sports journalists. According to one television news director, "Blogging allows the ability to write without the fear of affiliation and concern for objectivity. With traditional journalists, it challenges them to actually form an opinion where usually it might just be a few thoughts here or there on an event. We want opinions" (Sheffer and Schultz, 2009: 14). This same research indicated that many managers were rigid and unwilling to listen to negative feedback from their own journalists.

Just as internal forces reduced the impact of local sports blogging, so too did external forces, as many fans began blogging on their own. The growth of digital technologies allowed anyone to create and maintain a blog, which proliferated rapidly (Stern, 2010). Technorati, a website that measures blog use, estimated that in 2012 there were at least 122 million blogs on the Internet, many of which were sports-oriented blogs created by fans.

The power of fan-based blogs was demonstrated by *SB Nation*, which in 2012 described itself as "a collection of more than 300 individual communities, each offering high quality year-round coverage and conversation led by fans who are passionate about their favorite teams, leagues or sports. By empowering fans, SB Nation has become the largest and fastest growing grassroots sports network" ("SB Nation," 2012). The site became so popular that it boasted an audience of more than 20 million unique visitors per month and received $10.5 million in funding from a group of media investors (Ingram, 2010). Its success confirmed the work of Burton (1999), who noted that while the media use new technologies as a means of increasing audience, these same technologies might cause audiences to abandon the local media. Thus, blogging became a double-edged sword for local sports broadcasters. It allowed them to reach and interact with larger audiences, but many of these same audiences then ignored the local sportscast and created their own rival content.

The rise of social media

Not long after blogging became popular, local sportscasters had to deal with a new wave of Internet applications. Social media – Facebook, Twitter and other similar services – exploded in the cultural consciousness and once again forced local television sports to adapt. "I thought the social networking sites were strictly a phenomenon of teenagers and young kids," said television news director Bob Jordan, "(but) it's now the primary way a lot of people communicate, share and obtain information. Not to be in that space would be just the dumbest thing anyone could do, if you're in the communications business" (Petner, 2009, para. 5, 6).

Social media refers to the interactive media technologies that allow consumers to create and disseminate their own content, connect with media outlets and other networked users, and voice their opinions on any number of topics, often in real time. Roughly 2.4 billion people, more than one out of every three on the planet, use the Internet, and social media usage has exploded (Internet usage statistics, 2013). In 2012, Facebook passed one billion users while Twitter, the social-networking site that lets people share 140-character messages, was used by 13 percent of all online adults in the US (Moire, 2012). Use of Twitter by people in the 25–34 age group doubled in just two years (Womack and Pulley, 2010). According to Solis (2009), Twitter and social media are powerful platforms to broadcast news, crowd-source stories, and expand the media's role and relevance.

Social media seem especially relevant in the sports world, where Gregory (2009) noted that Twitter and other such technologies have the potential to permanently alter the athlete–fan interaction. In 2012, there were 3.8 million people following the NBA Twitter site, while 3.4 million were following the Real Madrid soccer team. The NFL had 2.8 million followers ("Top 100," 2012). In 2012, the largest athlete following belonged to soccer stars Cristiano Ronaldo (14.2.million), Kaka (13.4 million followers), and NBA player LeBron James (6.6 million) ("Top 10," 2012). "We're hitting (Twitter) hard," said NBA player Chris Bosh. "You can put up what you're doing. Or if you have a question, you'd be surprised how much people know. You can be, like, 'I need directions to this spot. People will tell you'" (quoted in Feschuk, 2009, para. 5).

As with blogging, the growth of social media presented opportunities and challenges for local television sports. Interactive technologies made it easier to communicate with audiences, but they also made it easier for athletes to bypass the mainstream media. When former baseball star Barry Bonds was under federal investigation related to possible steroid use, he never talked to sports reporters, and communicated to fans only through his blog. Former NBA star Shaquille O'Neal was especially proactive in the social media, managing his image through the help of advisor Amy Jo Martin. When O'Neal announced his retirement from the NBA in 2011, social media allowed him to break the news without going through traditional media channels. "He had full control of when, where and how he wanted to make that announcement," said Martin. "No press releases needed. It was about him using this influence he had built to communicate directly with his fans" (quoted by Ortiz, 2011, para. 20).

O'Neal's announcement showed how social media had assumed the role traditionally held by local broadcasters. Social media reduced the sports/news cycle from days and hours to minutes and seconds. As a result, stories no longer wait for the 6 o'clock news; they funnel immediately through Twitter and Facebook. "When I first started in the '90s, you waited until the 6 and 11 o'clock news to get the scores and highlights," said former sportscaster Brian Sinkoff. "You were pretty much planted by your TV at 6:20 and 11:20. With the boom of the Internet and 24-hour cable outlets, now everyone is able to get their scores virtually instantly" (Dougherty, 2012).

Much like the attitudes toward blogging, some sports journalists resisted social media, especially older journalists (Schultz and Sheffer, 2010). However, others began to incorporate social media in various ways. Obviously, Twitter is an ideal platform for breaking stories and almost all local sports outlets used it for that purpose. But compared to their print counterparts, local broadcast sports journalists saw the value of Twitter as a stand-alone tool and used it in newer ways. (Schultz and Sheffer, 2010). They recognized the ability of Twitter to more closely connect to fans and make sports journalism more direct and interactive. Broadcasters also used Twitter and Facebook to promote the journalists' work on other platforms. In other words, they announced upcoming stories through social media as a means to drive traffic to the local sportscasts.

While many sports journalists said they used social media primarily for breaking news and promotion, a look at their actual social media use showed something different. An investigation (Sheffer and Schultz, 2010) into Twitter use showed that while only 33 percent of sports journalists admitted to using the platform for opinion and commentary, in actuality 58 percent of analyzed posts were considered to be some form of opinion. Some comments had nothing to do with sports, such as the television sports reporter who tweeted, "It literally took me 3-and-a-half hours to mount a clock to the wall. Living room wall is riddled with holes like we just got drive-by'd" (Sheffer and Schultz, 2010: 480).

This type of opinion and commentary could be dismissed as inconsequential, but it may also reflect how technologies like Twitter began to reshape sports communication. Given that it is primarily a social networking tool, Twitter embodies the concepts of personal conversation and dialogue (even if the conversation involves millions of people). Conversation often includes rumor, gossip, innuendo and other techniques that are typically discouraged by the professional journalistic community. The advent of radio and television did not necessarily threaten journalistic standards because they were seen simply as new ways of distributing traditional information. But in the case of Twitter, McLuhan (1964) may be correct in saying that the medium is the message: a new way of communicating rather than just a new distribution system. According to Johnson (2009), Twitter adds ". . . a second layer of discussion and [brings] a wider audience into what would [be a] private exchange. We're having a genuine, public conversation that extends far beyond our family and our next-door neighbors" (paras 10 and 12).

The challenge for local sports television

Historically, change in television sports has been incremental. It took years for such transitions as black-and-white pictures to color, film to videotape, and analog transmission to digital. The transition to digital took decades, and even with all that time to prepare, television broadcasters had difficulty adjusting to the new environment. Local news and sports broadcasters dealt with a similarly monumental change in the Internet, although the change seemed to happen overnight. Thus, many in the television industry struggled with issues related to the Internet and how to best use the technology and its assorted applications within the context of local sports television.

One huge issue was that of cost and monetization. National sports media outlets such as ESPN and *Sports Illustrated* quickly leveraged their massive audiences into Internet millions. By 2012, ESPN received 18 million unique page hits per month during football season and its NFL site doubled that ("Ahead of," 2010). But that windfall did not necessarily trickle down to the local level. Internet advertising was only a small part of revenue at many television stations, which still view the newscast as the main economic engine. WFAA-TV in Dallas,

Texas, traditionally had some of the highest-rated news programming in the country, but as of 2012 still derived 96 percent of its revenue from television advertising and re-transmission agreements, while only 4 percent came from the Internet. "We don't make a dime on social media such as Facebook," WFAA general manager Mike Devlin said at the time. "We have to figure out how to monetize it; we may not be able to. Our newsroom costs $15–16 million in salaries and equipment. How are you going to pay for that with 4 percent?" (M. Devlin, personal communication, July 11, 2011).

While television managers worried about the financial implications of the Internet, sports journalists tried to figure out how to incorporate the new medium into their traditional work roles. The job of the local sports reporter changed drastically in the Internet era. Much of the reporter's success depends on access to athletes, coaches and organizations, and the ability to turn such access into exclusive, compelling content for audiences. The Internet shifted control of access from reporter to the newsmaker, who could then circumvent the local television station and newspaper in any number of ways. Sports reporters must now include Twitter, Facebook and other similar sites into their daily reporting routines. Graham Watson, who blogged football for ESPN, admitted, "You wake up at 7 a.m. and put your face into the computer until 10 p.m. It's a grueling, demanding job and burnout is a real danger" ("Ahead of," 2010).

The new environment also required speed, which has created some concerns related to ethics and credibility. The need to get information out quickly to a demanding audience, especially via social media, put a tremendous strain on the traditional journalistic tenets of accuracy, fact-checking and deliberation. "We're losing the vetting process and a degree of journalistic integrity," said sportscaster Reggie Rivers in 2010. "There's no time to consider or edit anything" ("Ahead of," 2010). That same year, in an attempt to "test the accuracy of social media reporting," *Washington Post* sports columnist Mike Wise purposely tweeted false information about NFL quarterback Ben Roethlisberger. The tweet quickly circulated through the social media, and many reporters passed it on to audiences without bothering to verify it. The result was a major embarrassment for the *Post*, which suspended Wise for a month. In regard to his suspension, Wise tweeted: 'Probably not the best way to go about the experiment. But in the end, it proved two things: I was right about nobody checking facts or sourcing, and I'm an idiot. Apologies to all involved' (quoted in Benoit, 2010).

Sports reporters also had to learn to interact with fans and audiences, which was a significant change from the "we write, you read" dogma of traditional journalism (Deuze, 2003). In the Internet age, the sports media consumer is interested in taking part in the process, either by creating and distributing content or voicing an opinion to a larger audience. The number of people creating and distributing their own content, a concept widely known as citizen journalism, grew dramatically. Gillmor (2004: xv) called it:

> ...a global conversation that is growing in strength, complexity and power. When people can express themselves, they will. When they can do so with powerful, yet inexpensive tools, they take to the new-media realm quickly. When they can reach a potentially global audience, they can literally change the world.

In a sports context, dozens of independent companies emerged as distributors of audience content. Bleacher Report began in 2008 to provide a platform for bloggers and amateur sports writers to offer their news and opinions. By 2011, the company had 1,000 featured columnists, 7,000 contributors and had secured $22 million in funding (Kelly, 2011). In the Washington, DC, area DigitalSports used parents, coaches, fans and even former journalists to shoot and post content of sporting events. The site claimed more than a quarter million unique visitors in any given month, using what company executives called the "media entrepreneurial model," (Goldfarb, 2007: D1). Such companies obviously presented an enormous challenge to local television sports, which previously had exclusive distribution capabilities. As a result, many stations made a greater effort to include audience content on their sportscasts and websites.

Conclusions

According to Groothuis:

> Major technological innovations don't just add something new to the environment, but change the whole environment. The printing press just didn't add more books. It transformed how people acquired knowledge, how they thought, and so on.
>
> *(in Kellner, 1997: 55)*

It appears the emergence of the Internet, and specifically the social media, fundamentally transformed the local sports television industry and created a new environmental reality.

Local stations made halting efforts to address these new realities, but in many cases the speed and uncertainty of the transition made meaningful change difficult. Several stations seem to have reacted in a knee-jerk fashion by phasing out, reducing or eliminating their local sports presence. "Whether it's medical or education or crime or government or Michael Vick, all news has to earn its way into the newscast," said Shane Moreland of WTKR-TV in Hampton, Virginia, which dropped its local sports segment in 2007. "There's no longer going to be a segment where you just give someone three minutes" (Holtzclaw, 2007, para. 3). In 2011, the Poynter Institute observed that at a time when local television news was rebounding from several down years and more television journalists were being hired, "local TV sports time is shrinking" (Potter, 2011, para. 5).

Local stations concluded that "it's fruitless to try to compete with networks and Web sites that are devoted to sports all the time," said former journalist Malcolm Moran. Moran also predicted that stations around the country would drop sports news altogether by the year 2015 (Farhi, 2011, para. 7). To avoid that scenario, local television executives must come up with more imaginative solutions. The Internet could be a lifeline for a local television sports industry that appears to be slowly going under. However, the present course suggests that it may not be long before the Internet, Facebook and Twitter sink the industry for good.

References

"Ahead of the curve: Multimedia and the future of sports journalism." (2010, August 5) Panel presentation at the national convention of the Association for Education in Journalism and Mass Communication, Denver, CO.

Amin, V. (2012, April 5) ESPN founder talks about investing in ideas, dreams. *Daily Kansan*. Retrieved November 27, 2012, from http://kansan.com/archives/2012/04/05/espn-founder-talks-about-investing-in-ideas-dreams/

Benoit, A. (2010, August 30) Mike Wise admits Roethlisberger lie. *CBSSports.com*. Retrieved February 13, 2012, from http://www.cbssports.com/mcc/blogs/entry/22475988/24211952

Bowman, S. and Willis, C. (2003) We media: How audiences are shaping the future of news and information. *The Media Center at the American Press Institute*. Retrieved September 18, 2008, from http://www.hypergene.net/wemedia/download/we_media.pdf

Brady, J. (2003, September 8) When local TV news came from faces you could trust. *Crain's New York Business*, 19(36), 8.

Buch, A. and Dupont, N. (2003, September 8) Guest commentary: Sports no longer rules newscasts. *TV Week*. Retrieved September 20, 2005, from http://www.tvweek.com/article.com?articleId=20460

Burton, R. (1999) A world wide web of sports. *Advertising Age*, 70(46), 66.

Deuze, M. (2003) The web and its journalisms: Considering the consequences of different types of media online. *New Media and Society*, 5, 203–230.

Dougherty, P. (2012, September 29) Sports loses in news game. *Albany Times-Union*. Retrieved November 27, 2012, from http://www.timesunion.com/sports/article/Sports-loses-in-news-game-3905628.php

Farhi, P. (2011, August 1) Brett Haber, Emmy-winning sports anchor, resigns from WUSA. *Washington Post*. Retrieved February 17, 2012, from http://www.washingtonpost.com/lifestyle/style/brett-haber-emmy-winning-sports-anchor-resigns-fromwusa/2011/08/01/gIQAJ9FUoI_story.html

Feschuk, D. (2009, February 17) Bosh, NBA all a-Twitter over latest blogging fad. *Toronto Star*. Retrieved February 22, 2009, from http://www.thestar.com/Sports/NBA/article/588483

Gillmor, D. (2004) *We the Media: Grassroots Journalism by the People for the People*. New York: O'Reilly Media.

Goldfarb, Z. (2007, December 3) Can youth sports coverage pay off online? *Washington Post*, D1.

Gregory, S. (2009, June 5) Twitter craze is rapidly changing the face of sports. *Sports Illustrated*. Retrieved June 5, 2009, from sportsillustrated.cnn.com/2009/writers/the_bonus/06/05/twitter.sports/index.html?eref=sihpT1

Haag, P. (1996) The 50,000-watt sports bar: Talk radio and the ethic of the fan. *The South Atlantic Quarterly*, 9(2), 453–470.

Hallin, D. (1990) Whatever happened to the news? *Media and Values*, Issue 50. Retrieved from http://www.medialit.org/reading-room/whatever-happened-news

Holtzclaw, M. (2007, August 29) Channel 3 dropping nightly sports news. *Hampton (VA) Daily Press*. Retrieved September 15, 2007, from http://www.dailypress.com/news/dp-13341sy0aug29,0,5677004.story?coll=hr_tab01_layout

Hull, D. (2006/2007, December-January) Blogging between the lines. *American Journalism Review*. Retrieved February 13, 2007, from http://www.ajr.org/article.asp?id=4230

Ingram, M. (2010, November 8) What hyper-local news sites can learn from SB Nation. *Gigaom*. Retrieved February 16, 2012, from http://gigaom.com/2010/11/08/what-hyper-local-news-sites-can-learn-from-sb-nation/

Internet usage statistics. (2013) *World Internet Users and Population Stats*. Retrieved September 5, 2013, from http://www.internetworldstats.com/stats.htm

Johnson, S. (2009, June 5) How Twitter will change the way we live. *Time*. Retrieved July 23, 2009, from http//www.time.com/time/business/article/0,8599,1902604,00.html

Journalism and ethics integrity project. (1998) *Radio and Television News Directors Foundation*. Retrieved January 13, 1999, from http://www.rtnda.org/research/judg.shtml

Kellner, M.A. (1997, September 1) Losing our souls in cyberspace: Douglas Groothuis on the virtues and vices of virtual reality. *Christianity Today*, 41(10). Retrieved from http://www.christianitytoday.com/ct/1997/september1/7ta054.html

Kelly, M. (2011, August 25) Bleacher Report isn't playing fantasy funding, scores $22M. *Venture Beat*. Retrieved January 31, 2012, from http://venturebeat.com/2011/08/25/bleacher-report-isnt-playing-fantasy-funding-scores-22m/

Lenhart, A. and Fox, S. (2006, July 19) Bloggers: A portrait of the Internet's new storytellers. *Pew Internet and American Life Project*. Retrieved August 18, 2006, from http://www.pewinternet.org/pdfs/PIP%20Bloggers%20Report%20July%2019 %202006.pdf

Levy, S. (2005, May 30) Television reloaded. *Newsweek*, p. 52.

McGuire, M. (2005, March 23) WTEN to alter nightly sports. *Albany Times-Union*. Retrieved April 22, 2005, from http://timesunion.comaspstories/storyprint.asp?StoryID=344447

McLuhan, M. (1964) *Understanding Media: The Extensions of Man*. New York: New American Library.

Moire, J. (2012, February 7) Facebook's 845 million members may not all visit the site. *All Facebook*. Retrieved February 13, 2012, from http://www.allfacebook.com/facebook-users-2012-02

NBC history. (2003) *WNBC Television*. Retrieved January 9, 2003, from http://www.wnbc.com/wnbc/1169359/detail.html

Ortiz, M.B. (2011) Amy Jo Martin blazes trials with Shaq. *ESPN*. Retrieved June 27, 2011, from http://sports.espn.go.com/espn/page2/story?page=burnsortiz-110627_amy_jo_martin&sportCat=nba

Petner, T. (2009, September 2) Twitter alights in TV newsrooms. *TVNewsCheck*. Retrieved September 2, 2009, from http://www.tvnewscheck.com/articles/2009/09/02/daily.1/?promo

Potter, D. (2011, August 1) More signs of change in local TV news. *Poynter Institute*. Retrieved February 17,

2012, from http://www.newslab.org/2011/08/01/more-signs-of-change-in-local-tv-news/

Poindexter, P. and McCombs, M. (2001) Revisiting the civic duty to keep informed in the new media environment. *Journalism and Mass Communication Quarterly*, 78(1), 113–126.

SB Nation. (2012) *Technorati*. Retrieved February 16, 2012, from http://technorati.com/blogs/www.sbnation.com

Sigal, L.V. (1973) *Reporters and Officials: The Organization and Politics of Newsmaking*. Lexington, MA: DC Heath.

Schultz, B. and Sheffer, M.L. (2007) Sports journalists who blog cling to traditional values. *Newspaper Research Journal*, 28(4), 62–76.

Schultz, B. and Sheffer, M.L. (2004, August 6) *Band-aids for a Compound Fracture*. Paper presented at the national convention of the Association for Education in Journalism and Mass Communication, Toronto, ON.

Schultz, B. and Sheffer, M.L. (2010) An exploratory study of how Twitter is impacting sports journalism. *International Journal of Sport Communication*, 3(2), 226–239.

Sheffer, M.L. and Schultz, B. (2009) Blogging from the management perspective: A follow up study. *International Journal on Media Management*, 11(1), 9–17.

Sheffer, M.L. and Schultz, B. (2010) Paradigm shift or passing fad? Twitter and sports journalism [Special issue on Social Media and Sports Communication]. *International Journal of Sport Communication*, 3(4), 472–484.

Solis, B. (2009, June 17) Is Twitter the CNN of the new generation? *TechCrunch*. Retrieved June 20, 2009, from http://www.techcrunch.com/2009/06/17/is-twitter-the-cnn-of-the-new-media-generation/

Sports and television. (2012) *The Museum of Broadcast Communications*. Retrieved February 14, 2012, from http://www.museum.tv/eotvsection.php?entrycode=sportsandte

Stern, G. (2010, February 15) Keeping track of the ever-proliferating number of blogs. *Information Today*. Retrieved February 16, 2012, from http://www.infotoday.com/linkup/lud021510-stern.shtml

The history of WKMG-TV. (2003) *WKMG Television*. Retrieved January 9, 2003, from http://www.local6.com/orlpn/insidewkmg/stories/insidewkmg-20000911-122225.html

Top 10 Twitter athletes (2012, January 31) *Tweeting-athletes.com*. Retrieved January 31, 2012, from http://www.tweeting-athletes.com/TopAthletes.cfm

Top 100 Twitaholics based on followers. (2012, January 31) *Twitaholic.com*. Retrieved January 31, 2012, from http://twitaholic.com/

Top 11: Best local TV sportscasters. (2010, July 29) *Seattle Sportsnet*. Retrieved February 15, 2012, from http://seattlesportsnet.com/2010/07/29/top-11-best-local-tv-sportscasters/

Trammell, K. and Keshelashvili, A. (2005) Examining the new influencers: A self-presentation study of A-list blogs. *Journalism and Mass Communication Quarterly*, 82(4), 968–982.

Tremblay, S. and Tremblay, W. (2001) Mediated masculinity at the millennium: The Jim Rome Show as a male bonding speech community. *Journal of Radio Studies*, 8(2), 271–291.

Wann, D.L. (1997) Aggression among highly identified spectators as a function of their need to maintain positive social identity. *Journal of Sport and Social Issues*, 17, 134–142.

Webster, J.G. and Ksiazek, T.B. (2012) The dynamics of audience fragmentation: Public attention in an age of digital media. *Journal of Communication*, 62(1), 39–56.

Womback, B. and Pulley, B. (2011, June 1) Twitter use climbs to 13% of US adults online boosted by older Americans. *Bloomberg*. Retrieved June 7, 2011, from http://www.bloomberg.com/news/2011-06-01/twitter-use-increases-to-13-of-adults-online-as-mobile-tweets-lead-growth.html

11
TEXTING AND TWEETING
How social media has changed news gathering

Jed Novick and Rob Steen

UNIVERSITY OF BRIGHTON

> You put out the paper, you do the best you can and you know that no matter what you do, you're not going to be breaking the exclusive. This isn't where people are going to get that news first.
>
> *(Neil Robinson, Sports Editor,* The Independent*)*

Once upon a time it was all so simple. Journalist finds news and writes it up. Reader buys newspaper and finds out news. It was a very straightforward recipe. But nothing stands still, and after centuries of monopoly, newspapers find themselves under threat as never before. No one can say it has not been coming.

First radio and then television stole the thunder and muted the thunderers of the written press. By the 1980s, the sale of live broadcast rights together with the emergence of television "pages" such as Ceefax and Teletext had ensured that newspaper journalists were seldom first to break the news, especially when it came to sport. The final nail in the ink-and-paper coffin, it seemed, was the advent of the web, a medium unencumbered by time zones, geographical borders, conventional deadlines and space. It was less concerned with exclusive material than information, and almost instantly updateable. Then, just when we imagined that the world could not possibly whirr any faster, along bounced social media and, in particular, the two Ts: Texting and Tweeting. Written by practicing journalists each with 30 years' experience of the colony formerly known as Fleet Street, this chapter addresses these profoundly twenty-first-century phenomena.

Jack Dorsey, creator of the microblog service Twitter, described it:

> We came across the word "twitter", and it was just perfect. The definition was "a short burst of inconsequential information", and "chirps from birds". And that's exactly what the product was.
>
> *(Sarno, 2009, para 21)*

Social media. Citizen journalism. Both help the journalist and the wider public by widening the area that journalists can cover. We often bemoan cutbacks and tightening of belts with the attendant complaint that investigative journalism is not what it was. Newspapers, it is rightly but sadly pointed out, simply do not have the resources to allow journalists to investigate a story for months on end.

While the Internet allows us to access the world without ever having to leave the comfort of our desks, it has also controlled the way that information is disseminated. For example, through their websites, the sports clubs and governing bodies have, with some success, controlled information. This has helped journalists but made them content with reporting bland news instead of digging for more searching insights. At the same time, the myriad websites and blogs seldom offered exclusive information worthy of being re-tweeted – as the saying now goes – by newspapers. It has taken social media, which has given both players and fans a voice they had never had before, to shake things up.

Lack of resources led to a kind of groupthink. Maybe it is no surprise that the collective noun for the press is "pack." We talk of the press pack in the way we'd talk about a gang or a group. As Zeynep Tufekci, a fellow at the Center for Information Technology Policy at Princeton University, said:

> Journalists won't admit this often, but they tend to be pack animals. . . . Staying in the same hotel. Hanging out in the same bar. Attending the same press conference. Going to the same event. Taking the same picture from a near-identical angle. Packs often made their decisions collectively as well.
>
> *(Zeynep, 2011, para. 1, 2)*

Journalists confer after a press conference. Critics will be given the same press information at a film screening; cricket reporters receive the same service before a match or tournament. The same press release is sent out to all journalists working in the same field (so long as the PR company has done its homework). Time is tight. And money is tight. And so, as Zeynep says, "Packs often made their decisions collectively as well" (2011, para. 3).

The tightening of belts, the pack mentality and the reliance on spoon-fed information has led to the rise of "churnalism" (regurgitated press releases). Increasingly it seems that Twitter is now where stories break and where we learn the news.

Social media has allowed a freedom of thought and freedom of expression in an unprecedented way, creating a world where we are all journalists, where journalism fits more into George Orwell's dictum – "Journalism is printing what someone else does not want printed: everything else is public relations" – and less into Rupert Murdoch's.

Punk journalism reborn

Print journalists have always been a flexible breed. In the face of rapid and graphic alternatives, we have had to be. Social media has been around for a while – albeit in different forms with different names. Freesheets are not new. Gossip sheets are not new. The magazine world was turned upside down in July 1976 when *Sniffin Glue*, the first punk fanzine, was published by Mark Perry after he had seen *The Ramones*, the prototype American three-chord thrashers, in London. Perry saw the show, loved it, wrote about it, then distributed his review. Forget the technology and means of delivery, that Perry used a photocopier and a stapler to produce it, and that the distribution network comprised Perry and his girlfriend. It was social media in action. It was reporting from the action, as it happened, by someone who was not, in the traditional sense of the word, a "journalist." Perry was simply a fan with a view. He had no expertise. No one gave him permission to express himself. No one commissioned him, edited him or published him. He simply grabbed the means of communication and communicated.

Twitter is but the latest next stage and is, in many ways, the embodiment of punk journalism. In a sense, this is not new and it is not anything to do with Twitter. Newspapers have long been facing a threat to their position as breakers of news. While America had embraced the idea of sports news on the radio for quite some time, in Britain things moved slower, and despite niche programming such as midweek football and boxing on Radio 2, the game-changer did not come until March 1994. Before that, if you wanted a report of last night's match, you had to buy the next day's newspaper. The launch of Radio 5 Live changed that for British sports lovers. Suddenly, by the time the next day's newspaper came out, the sports fan could have already heard the match report and seemingly endless debate.

In our accelerated culture, Twitter has stepped on the gas. "You put out the paper, you do the best you can and you know that no matter what you do, you are not going to be breaking the exclusive, this is not where people are going to get that news first," said Neil Robinson, who at the turn of 2013 offered a uniquely broad viewpoint as sports editor of *The Independent* and *The Independent on Sunday* as well as *The I* and the *London Evening Standard*. He added:

> If there's a press conference with, for example, Arsène Wenger, who says something interesting, immediately there's a video of him up somewhere saying the same things. I can't think of one managerial change where the exclusive was revealed by a news-paper. It's very difficult to know what judgements you should make because if you're only telling someone what they already know, is there any purpose to it?
>
> *(Robinson, 2013)*

This has caused a number of problems for the profession. Stories are what journalists live and die by. We spend our time chasing stories, nurturing contacts, feeding the ground. But if the stories are out there on Twitter for anyone to see, where does that leave the journalist? Will this force newspapers to become more like magazines? To use a phrase coined by one of *The Independent*'s former editors Simon Kelner, will they become "viewspapers" rather than news-papers?

"Yes, increasingly that's where it's going," said Robinson, adding:

> The value of a newspaper is in its judgement and in someone's assessment of some-thing. The news that Arsène Wenger has quit or whatever will be out on millions of websites immediately it happens, so you cannot hope to get that as an exclusive. But people will continue to buy newspapers because they'll want to know our writers' take on Wenger quitting or whatever. There's so much wild speculation and rumour on the web that if you can turn to the newspaper and feel that you can read some-thing approximating to the truth then there's a real value in that.
>
> It does make you increasingly question what's the point of running that story as straight news because people know it already. It takes you to a very difficult place and it's not a question that's been entirely resolved.
>
> *(Robinson, 2013)*

Twitter's impact remains difficult to quantify. On the one hand, journalists' job in the digital era, further aided by the accessibility via the Internet of a vast web of news sources as well as the proliferation of club websites (often if not always the first for news), is distinctly easier. Rather than going to matches or training grounds and actually watching or meeting their subjects, it is now eminently feasible to be an efficient and effective reporter without leaving the office, or even home.

One way of looking at Twitter is as a twenty-first-century news wire. In the old days, the news wire clattered away in the corner, churning out news and stories. Now we've got our

Twitter accounts. "Twitter has become crucial," says Robinson. "So many people use it to pull out what's happening, reactions to events. It's there to alert you to something. For me, that's the most important thing" (Robinson, 2013).

If Twitter is acting as a news wire, it is a news wire that everyone has access to. We do not need a newspaper to subscribe to the service; we do not need a newspaper to make the wire stories more reader-friendly. The other major difference is the people feeding that service – this new wire service – are the newspapers' own journalists. They are the ones Tweeting the "exclusive." And whoever is Tweeting, is Tweeting under their own name rather than that of the newspaper. Where does that leave newspapers?

The problem for newspapers is that on the one hand they actively encourage their journalists to Tweet. "Yes, it's part of their brief now," confirms Robinson. "If they do not do it they are not dismissed, but they are encouraged to do it. It's seen as a means of promoting both the paper and themselves" (Robinson, 2013). By doing so, they are, in a sense, putting themselves in competition with their writers. And so far the evidence is showing that readers have loyalty to the writer rather than the paper.

"Yes, that may be the case now," says Robinson. "It's quite interesting to see our football writers have much higher followings than we do as a department. Every story that comes in will go on our Twitter feed as well as his, but his following is much higher" (Robinson, 2013). In March 2013, Sam Wallace, the chief football correspondent of *The Independent*, had 79,769 followers, while his department's Twitter feed – @TheIndyFootball – had 3,716. (The sports department's feed – @TheIndySport – had 3,430 followers, while the newspaper – @TheIndependent – had 193,038).

Journalists have thus found themselves in a position where they can have a direct line to the reader. The reader ceases to be a reader of, for example, *The Daily Planet,* who likes a particular writer. Now the reader follows the writer who happens to be a writer for *The Daily Planet.* It is subtle difference, but an important one. Twitter effectively turns the writer – be it a journalist or a member of the public – into the publisher. Whereas before people might go a buy a newspaper, now they can follow a journalist. The journalist becomes the product. But while journalists post links to their articles and drive readers to the newspaper website, are they becoming more concerned with how many followers they have, fuelling a cult of the personality, thus weakening the position of the newspaper and perhaps, ultimately, making them redundant?

Journalists, as Robinson rightly stresses, get their credibility from their newspapers. Would Wallace have his following – effectively a fan base – if he was not chief football correspondent of a national newspaper? But could we get to a stage where Wallace does not need *The Independent*? "Yes," says Robinson. "But it's difficult to know where they would get their credibility from without some organisation helping them" (Robinson, 2013).

There are instances of where this has already happened. The obvious example is Paul Staines (Guido Fawkes) in the political sphere, where he has established himself as a breaker of stories with a reputation, and that has been done entirely off his own bat as, effectively, a blogger. There is, at present, no sporting equivalent of a Guido Fawkes at all – but that does not mean there will never be. And that is a scenario that threatens the very existence of newspapers as we know them.

Credibility is the key here. Newspapers have had to adapt. They have to interpret the story, comment on it, contextualize it. In the same way that the Monday report had to differ from the Sunday report, so this has to become the norm. Analysis, comment, reflection, reaction, consequences... these are what is now required. Not just reporting the news, but making sense of it (Price, Farrington and Hall, 2012). In a world where, in the public eye, journalists occupy the same moral ground as politicians and estate agents, the reporters and feature writers (as well as the omnipresent columnists) found themselves positioned, ludicrously to some, as the voice of reason. The post-Internet world is a place where anyone can say anything, where anyone can break a story, report the news and disseminate information, but only trained or experienced journalists can do this with authority. They alone have the power of the masthead and logo to back up what they say and be aware of the consequences. At a time when the law regarding social media is still in its infancy – not really knowing the boundaries – this is increasingly important.

Taking information from non-journalists carries with it certain risks, and the brave new world has claimed its share of victims. The unshakeable thirst for instant information – and for ever more quotes that could be expanded into a story worthy of a provocative headline – has led to a lazy, sometimes desperate reliance on unsubstantiated stories from dubious sources, on blogs composed by non-journalists and on that mine of ill-founded "information."

The growth of social media has taken journalism outside the "pack" and has meant that the number of voices has exploded, as has the number of different viewpoints expressed. Allowing more voices into the mix gives a voice to the people on the ground. More often than not, this is a good thing. "One of the biggest weaknesses in foreign-news journalism," declared Zeynep, "[is] that journalists are not part of the story they are writing and are, almost by definition, lacking in understanding of the context" (2011, para. 26). The other side is that non-attached traditional journalists who are not part of the story they are writing are in a position to better see the story from different – non-partisan – points of view, and are thus more likely to verify their facts and sources. In other words, proper journalism.

The consequences for veracity, insight and credibility, however, could be grave, as was highlighted in January 2011 by the anonymous author of They All Count, "nearly a football blog" and a site we last encountered more than 18 months later, in September 2012, by which time it was dominated by photos of famous players' wives and partners in various states of undress.

Jack Wilshere, Arsenal's promising young midfielder, the author lamented, had become a Twitter addict. "Bring Becks to Arsenal" exhorted one such missive. "What a great example he would be for all of us! His professional attitude, ability and experience! Love 2 work with him!" (Sign up Becks, 2011). On those 140 characters alone were based scores of headlines, such as the *Daily Mail*'s classic attempt to turn a pint into a quart: "Sign up Becks, Arsene! Arsenal youngster Wilshere urges Wenger to snap up former Manchester United star." They All Count was not amused.

"Is this what sports journalism has come to?" the blogger wondered under the headline "How Twitter is destroying football journalism." The blogger added:

> Journalists sitting patiently by their twitter feeds, just in case any footballers happen to divulge 140 characters worth of 'news' which can be beefed up into an article, just to keep their site's constant flow of sub-standard and mind-numbing content rolling along.
>
> *("How Twitter", 2011)*

Hoaxers have thrived. In the latter half of 2008, a still-unidentified perpetrator created a fictional soccer player named Masal Bugduv. Initially the subject of forum posts by a mischievously creative blogger, Bugduv quickly clambered up the feeding chain of European football media by going from an insertion on a Wikipedia page to comments in forums, blog posts and then – after penetrating the mainstream media – to a football magazine and finally to the "Football's Top 50 Rising Stars" list of 2009 in *The Times*:

30. Masal Bugduv (Olimpia Balti)
Moldova's finest, the 16-year-old attacker has been strongly linked with a move to
Arsenal, work permit permitting. And he's been linked with plenty of other top clubs
as well.

(Burnton, 2009, para. 4)

Not that *The Times* was alone in being duped. "The problem was the identity of those who
had been doing the linking," said Simon Burnton, who related the well-spun yarn for readers
of *The Guardian*. He added:

> Their story started unravelling when the website theoffside.com alerted readers to the
> list, and a blogger posted a message suggesting that Bugduv did not exist at all. On his
> own blog the author, known as Makki, had already detailed, in Russian, his failure to
> find any evidence of the player on any Moldovan website, including that of his
> supposed club. Searches in English had found stories apparently written by the
> Associated Press (although not in a style regular AP readers would recognize) linking
> the 'midfielder' with Arsenal and Zenit St Petersburg and boasting about international
> appearances that simply never happened.

(Burnton, 2009, para. 5)

Mark Stephens, a social media lawyer at Finers Stephens Innocent, said he did not think special
laws were needed for Twitter, "though we do need to take account of the way people are now
getting their information and distributing it" (Rudd, 2012). The mere existence of social media
lawyers underlines how rapid the legal response has had to be.[1]

Cairns v. Modi

A landmark case was required to apply a vestige of order, and legal and media history was duly
made in May 2012 when the cricketer Chris Cairns won £90,000 in damages for a tweet made
on in January 2010 by Lalit Modi, then commissioner and cheerleader-in-chief for the Indian
Premier League, accusing the former New Zealand captain of match-fixing. It was the sporting equivalent of removing the pin from a grenade, timed for maximum impact: Cairns had
just been omitted from the list of candidates for the IPL auction. The offending message read:
"Chris Cairns removed from the IPL auction list due to his past record in match fixing. This
was done by the Governing Council today" (Royal Courts of Justice, 2012). As a case study,
this ruling reflects cricket's surging profile in the first decade of the century and its concurrent
troubles with corruption, as well as the astonishingly rapid rise of social media.

Cairns, a belligerent, multi-talented player, was hired to lead Chandigarh Lions in the Indian
Cricket League, the first Twenty20 league outside England and soon to be terminated with
extreme prejudice by Modi and the IPL. The official line was that Cairns had breached the terms
of his contract, having failed to disclose an ankle injury. Modi alleged that Cairns had not only
sought to fix matches, but involved teammates in the scam. Cairns sued Modi. The Cairns–Modi
libel trial lasted nine days at London's High Court, during which three of Cairns' teammates
testified that he had sought to bribe them. To be thus accused, he insisted, was "one of if not *the*
most serious and damaging of all allegations that could possibly be levelled against a professional
sportsman. Uncorrected it will destroy all that I have achieved over a successful 20-year sporting career." He also claimed that his media work had "dried up" since Modi's tweet, that he had
not played professional cricket since and that his achievements had been turned to "dust."

Justice Bean ruled in Cairns' favour and awarded £400,000 in interim costs in addition to the £90,000 damages. Modi, he pronounced, had "singularly failed" to provide any reliable evidence that Cairns was involved in match-fixing or spot-fixing, or even strong grounds for suspicion of cheating. "It is obvious," he elaborated:

> that an allegation that a professional cricketer is a match-fixer goes to the core attributes of his personality and, if true, entirely destroys his reputation for integrity. The allegation is not as serious as one of involvement in terrorism or sexual offences. But it is otherwise as serious an allegation as anyone could make against a professional sportsman.
>
> ("Setback for Lalit Modi," 2012, para. 12)

In October 2012, the Court of Appeal rejected Modi's appeal. What is interesting is not so much what Modi said, but how he said it. While it is possible to say he could have made his remarks at any time through any media – he was, after all a Big Fish who could command an audience – the story illustrates two things. First, the individual can now publish anything without any checks or balances. Had Modi expressed his opinion through, for example, a newspaper article, the journalist would have checked. The sub-editor, the section editor, the paper's lawyer – it would never have gotten through. Second he did not check himself. It could have been as simple as 1) think, 2) write, 3) send. And then, in a flash, the Tweet had gone round the world. No going back. Never before has an individual had this power.

Bonfire of the inanities?

The other problem with social media is possibly more problematic. Once upon a time, in the sepia-toned days before George Best, footballers travelled to matches with fans on the Number 27. That world has long since given way to one where agents, personal managers, media trainers and the PR machine shield players from fans. The players have been smoothed and planed and smoothed again; they have been media-trained to the point where there is nothing individual left save a famous name and face. In the process, their very individualism has been eroded; to reach the public they still needed to go through a journalist.

If only they could cut out the journalist. Why allow them to depict you in an unflattering light? Why let them control how the public sees you? Why risk quotes being used out of context?

Twitter has allowed fans to get to know players in an unprecedented way. It is public intimate, a twenty-first-century version where contact is at once direct and personal and at the same time distant and detached. Fans – consumers – glean insights into the lives of the rich and famous and can even obtain a direct answer to a direct question through the simple expedient of the @ sign. But no one actually meets; no one actually makes contact.

We can write to our favourite stars, they can write back to us. We know what they had for dinner last night, what they thought of the latest BBC drama. We get a glimpse through the window into their lives, and it feels very much like a direct communication, a communication that has not been put through the PR mincer, that has not been media-managed.

As Rob Steen (2013: 218) wrote in the *Cambridge Companion to Football*:

> Freed from the tyrannical leash of mundane cliché and PR-speak, media-trained footballers use the new medium to cut out the middleman, bypassing print and television and communicating directly with anyone who has the vaguest interest in their

utterances. Journalists, as a consequence, are on perpetual Twitter-watch. This cuts both ways. While what ensues is largely a bonfire of the inanities, exceptions, refreshingly, are on the rise.

Take Javi Poves, a defender with Sporting Gijon in Spain's La Liga, who in tweeting his retirement described his profession as "putrid" and "corrupt." To continue in this "circus" would offend his principles: "Footballers are valued too much by our society compared to others who should be the true heroes. The system is based on being sheep and the best way to control them is to have a population without culture" (Marcotti, 2011: 15).

Amid the riots that panicked England in the summer of 2011 – to the delight of many and the fury of more – high-profile players such as Manchester United's Rio Ferdinand even dared to defy the chief law of the modern sporting jungle, adopting a stance that could easily be construed as political. Inevitably, clubs imposed fines. It was an indication of the arrogance of those that run football, not to say different priorities, that in September 2011, Steve Elworthy, head of marketing at the England and Wales Cricket Board, asserted that "the general awareness" of the national cricket team had never been higher, attributing this in good measure to "digital media such as Facebook and Twitter allowing followers to get closer to their heroes" (Gillespie and Wilde, 2011).

In a sense, Twitter has taken us back to those sepia-tinged days. The stars most prepared to play ball are rewarded with a new status, the most blatant case in point being the footballer Joey Barton. In the land BT (Before Twitter), the man now known as @Joey7Barton was a professional footballer who made a good living. But what he was really known for was being a thug. In December 2004, he stubbed out a lit cigar in the eye of a youth player, Jamie Tandy. In May 2005 he broke a 35-year-old pedestrian's leg while driving his car in Liverpool. In a pre-season tour of Thailand, he assaulted a 15-year-old Everton fan. In May 2007, he assaulted another teammate, Ousmane Dabo, and carried on hitting him even after he fell unconscious. By the time the court case came around, Barton was already in prison, this time for attacking a teenager in Liverpool city centre.

Yet for all that he is, at the same time, smart and articulate and can, as Daniel Taylor has written in *The Guardian*, be "charming and eloquent and can hold his own in any company" (2012, para. 2). Whatever we may feel about him, he has used Twitter better than most, and has seemingly spent as much time Tweeting as he has on the playing field. More, some might say, as it is yet impossible to be sent off Twitter. Barton was, seemingly, always on Twitter, quoting Smiths lyrics and Nietzsche. He seemed so terribly reasonable. "Why do people always want to solve any conflict with a fight?" he asked on Twitter. "As a pacifist, I find it incredible" (Taylor, 2012, para. 11). As a pacifist. Barton loved Twitter. And Twitter loved Barton back.

But it was not only Twitter that loved him. Everyone loved him. He was invited into *The Guardian* and allowed into the morning conference. He was invited to appear on *Newsnight*. A book deal followed. It is easy to see why. Twitter showed Barton was smart: joshing with all the important journalists, on first-name terms with everyone who could write an opinion piece about him, playfully drawing people in with small yet human devices such as suggesting a song for the day. This last example might sound ridiculously inconsequential, but in a world where "star" footballers spoke like robots and uttered cartoon clichés about "the lads" and "the boss", he was a revelation.

"Everyone is so pathetically grateful to see a footballer with a bit of personality," wrote Taylor. "Barton was embraced as some kind of class experiment and broadsheet pin-up... Football is littered with people who are as colourless as water. It is the way they are media trained: to see little and say even less. So thank heavens there will always be the odd rogue" (Taylor, 2012, para. 11).

More pertinently, Barton knew that if he gave a conventional interview, the questions would all be about his violent conduct and stabs at anger management. Through Twitter, Barton could control what was said about him and by extension control his image in a way hitherto impossible.

The curtain came down on The Barton Show on May 13, 2012, the last day of the season. Barton was sent off for violent misconduct after elbowing Manchester City's Carlos Tevez in the face. He kicked Sergio Aguero and tried to head-butt Vincent Kompany. As he attempted to take on Mario Balotelli, he was dragged off the pitch by Micah Richards.

Barton's next stop was Marseilles. Would he have been offered that loan deal had he not had such a high profile, if he had just been Joey the thug? As he has shown, Twitter has offered the opportunity to become more than just a footballer, more than just a star. He can become that most modern creation, a "personality." For Sam Wallace read Rio Ferdinand. As the former *News of the World* editor Phil Hall has observed: "Twitter turns you into a franchise. Instead of someone like Rio Ferdinand being part of the Manchester United franchise he is effectively creating his own" (Gibson, 2012).

For clubs that traditionally have been run along disciplinarian, almost feudal lines, this can present a problem. If a player is, for whatever reason, unhappy, the temptation now is to exercise that twitchy Twitter finger. In February 2012, Aston Villa winger Charles N'Zogbia was substituted in a match against Newcastle at St James' Park. Almost immediately he tweeted: "For the first time in my life I'm not happy playing football" (Moxley, 2012). The story went around, the level of discontent at the club grew, and in the summer McLeish was sacked. N'Zogbia's Tweet did not sack McLeish. But it contributed to the white noise of discontent.

Little wonder some clubs, such as Leeds United, have banned their players from using Twitter; when Steve Cotterill took over at Nottingham Forest he said he would impose fines at £1,000 a word if the Tweets slated the club or the fans. He said, "I have a rule that anyone using Twitter or Facebook is not allowed to talk about the football club, their team-mates or the supporters" (Hill, 2011).

The KP saga

Perhaps the most high-profile sporting casualty to this writing has been Kevin Pietersen, one of many South African economic migrants who came to England and cast themselves as victims of the post-Apartheid quota system that had supposedly – although not actually – reduced opportunities at national level for whites. By 2005 he had established himself as his adopted country's premier batsman, one of the game's top box-office draws and its most flamboyant and incautious self-promoter. Come the summer of 2012, the ego had not only landed, nested and earned millions but was busy thrusting its beak into a brand new form of media-stoked maelstrom. Pietersen, in short, became the Twitter Twit. If only the fallout had been half as light-hearted as that irresistible play on words.

In 2011, Pietersen reacted to his omission from the team by informing his tens of thousands of Twitter followers before it was officially announced. Other outbursts followed, as did sundry punishments. Overruling his colleague Steve Elworthy, Hugh Morris, the managing director of the national team, decried Twitter as "a complete and utter nightmare for those of us trying to manage and lead teams" and comparing it to "giving a machine-gun to a monkey" (Hill, 2011).

Cats joined pigeons when Richard Bailey, an acquantaince of Stuart Broad, an England regular, set up a fake Twitter account, @KevPietersen24, and began dispensing witty tweets, purportedly from Pietersen himself but plainly parody. Much mirth ensued as his image – brash, naïve, childishly sensitive, far too selfish for a team game – was firmly upheld.

Then, in August, in the middle of a test match against South Africa, Pietersen texted a couple of friends in the opposing team, allegedly sniping at colleagues, in particular his captain, Andrew Strauss, and – or so ran the conjecture – perhaps even leaking strategies. Even as we write, the complete picture of what would descend into a PR disaster has yet to emerge, but for Pietersen it proved, at least temporarily, a *faux pas* too far.

Despite playing one of the finest innings of his career in that Headingley Test, Pietersen was dropped for the next test – a brave decision given that victory was imperative if England were to stop the touring side from displacing it at the top of the world rankings. The home team lost both the match and its long-time captain, Strauss, who resigned, eventually conceding, with characteristic understatement and loyalty, that the Pietersen fiasco had made his final days tricky. Before the winter tour to India, the ECB announced that agreement had been reached for Pietersen's "re-integration."

It was difficult to stifle the sense that this was a dressing room spat of the sort that has always gone on, but one that in the past would have been played out behind doors. Social media took it out of dressing room and put it into the public arena. The Pietersen story generated enough inches of print – inky and virtual – to reach the moon but would not have arisen without the deceptive freedoms afforded by social media. Maybe that is what Twitter has become – an information access-all-areas pass where the lines between private and public are not so much blurred as eradicated.

The pendulum is swinging with customary force. A generation of sports folk to whom honesty had become a luxury now have a voice. It may be too loud for their purported masters, but as the serfs have grown wealthier and more powerful, so another dilemma surfaces.

Note

1. A useful exercise is to try this test, a working hyperlink in spring, 2013: http://accidentaloutlaw.knowthenet.org.uk. It does not matter how long you've been a journalist, how long you have been a writer, it will still trip you up.

References

Burnton, S. (2009, January 15) Masul Bugduv: The 16-year-old Moldovan prodigy who doesn't exist. *The Guardian*. Retrieved from http://www.guardian.co.uk/sport/blog/2009/jan/15/masal-bugduv-moldova-hoax-player

Gibson, O. (2012, September 19) There's Trouble @ Twitter. *The Observer*. Retrieved from http://www.guardian.co.uk/sport/2010/sep/12/twitter-owen-gibson

Gillespie, J. and Wilde, S. (2011, September 18) Cricket's big hitters cross £1m boundary. *Sunday Times*. Retrieved from http://www.thesundaytimes.co.uk/sto/news/uk_news/People/article778310.ece.

Hill, G. (2011, October 18) Steve Cotterill will fine Nottingham Forest players for using Twitter. *The Sun*. Retrieved from http://www.thesun.co.uk/sol/homepage/sport/football/3877950/steve-cotterill-will-fine-nottingham-forest-players-for-using-twitter.html.

How Twitter is destroying football journalism (2011, January 6) *Theyallcount.com*. Retrieved from http://www.theyallcount.com/2011/01/how-english-football-press-got-lazy-and.html.

Marcotti, G. (2011, August 15) Footballers and ideology combine for curious mix. *The Times*. [The Game supplement], p. 15. Retrieved from http://www.thetimes.co.uk/tto/sport/columnists/gabrielemarcotti/article3134229.ece

Moxley, N. (2012, February 5) N'Zogbia in Twitter blast: For the first time in my life I'm not happy playing football. *Daily Mail*. Retrieved from http://www.dailymail.co.uk/sport/football/article-2096843/charles-nzogbia-twitter-blast-aston-villa-substitution.html

Price, J., Farrington, N. and Hall, L. (2012, April) Tweeting with the enemy? The impacts of new social media on sports journalism and the education of sports journalism students. *The Journal of the Association for*

Journalism Education, 1(1), 9–20. Retrieved from http://journalism-education.org/wp-content/uploads/2012/04/1-1-Tweeting-with-the-Enemy.pdf

Robinson, N. (2013, February 26) [Interview with author.]

Royal Courts of Justice (2012, March 26) Judgment. Retrieved from http://www.judiciary.gov.uk/Resources/JCO/Documents/Judgments/cairns-v-modi-judgment.pdf

Rudd, M. (2012, April 29) Tweet and Be Damned. *Sunday Times*. Retrieved from http://www.thesundaytimes.co.uk/sto/news/focus/article1027239.ece

Sarno, D. (2009, February 18) Twitter creator Jack Dorsey illuminates the site's founding document. *Los Angeles Times*. Retrieved from http://latimesblogs.latimes.com/technology/2009/02/twitter-creator.html

Setback for Lalit Modi, loses libel case against Chris Cairns. (2012, March 26) *Times of India*. Retrieved from http://timesofindia.indiatimes.com/sports/cricket/top-stories/Setback-for-Lalit-Modi-loses-libel-case-against-Chris-Cairns/articleshow/12414248.cms

Sign up Becks, Arsene! Arsenal youngster Wilshere urges Wenger to snap up former Manchester United star. (2011, January 4) *Daily Mail*. Retrieved from http://www.dailymail.co.uk/sport/football/article-1344037/Arsenal-boss-Arsene-Wenger-urged-sign-David-Beckham-Jack-Wilshere.html

Steen, R. (2013) Sheepskin coats and nannygoats: The view from the press box. In R. Steen, J. Novick and H. Richards (eds), *The Cambridge companion to football*. Cambridge: Cambridge University Press.

Taylor, D. (2012, May 19) Joey Barton's latest act of violence proves he is no renaissance man. *The Guardian*. Retrieved from http://www.guardian.co.uk/football/blog/2012/may/19/joey-barton-qpr-violence-renaissance-man

Zeynep, T. (2011, November 30) Journalism, social media and packs and cascades: Lessons from an error. *Technosociology: Our tools, ourselves*. Retrieved from http://technosociology.org/?p=638.

PART III

The message:
Shaping, marketing, branding

12

SPORT, PUBLIC RELATIONS AND SOCIAL MEDIA

Raymond Boyle

UNIVERSITY OF GLASGOW

Richard Haynes

UNIVERSITY OF STIRLING

Sport is simultaneously a global phenomenon and a local and personal one. It is simultaneously a gigantic commercial business and a gigantic voluntary enterprise. Sport fulfils all of these conflicting roles in global society through a multi-layered and mutually dependent relationship with the media and other commercial interests. There is no simple definition of what modern sport stands for and therefore no simple solutions to its many problems.

(Bose, 2012: 570)

Sport has long been a medium through which marketing communications have sought to capture an audience for commercial services and goods, and for participation in a sport itself. Nineteenth-century sports newspapers and pamphlets carried advertising for the latest tonic for a healthy body, or the latest innovation in lawnmower technology to enable the suburban upper middle classes to have pristine lawns for tennis and croquet. Victorian and Edwardian sports administrators took to using pseudonyms as they engaged in early forms of sports journalism, in an effort to both inform and persuade their public about the wonders of their sport or to lobby for changes in the organisation or rules of the game (Vamplew, 2004). Media relations have therefore always formed an aspect of sport, and the historical connection between sport, communications and what we now understand as the promotional industries of advertising, marketing and public relations is both long and strongly interlocked with the operational activities of most sports administrators, teams, leagues, governing bodies, athletes and associated agencies.

Unpacking the complexity of these interrelationships is no easy matter. The nexus around which sport engages with media and communications has gained even more complexity since the development of the Internet and what Brett Hutchins and David Rowe have labelled 'networked media sport' – 'the movement away from broadcast and print media towards digitized content distributed via networked communications technologies' (Hutchins and Rowe, 2012: 5). More recently, the evolution of mobile social networked media has given a more direct public voice to athletes who are cosseted from mainstream media outlets by agents and communications managers, but at the same stroke, are given a new freedom of expression through sites and applications such as Facebook and Twitter to engage with their fans. The variegated nature of the relations between athletes, sponsors, the media, and fans means that communications strategies of sports organisations are more differentiated than ever before, and understanding the flows of communication between the different stakeholders is a challenge. The plenitude of content created by networked media sport is so expansive that it is increasingly difficult to fully comprehend the multitude of ways in which sport relates to new communications technologies. This is not only an issue for academic researchers of the sport–media nexus, but also for the sports industries, the media industries and consumers of sport alike.

Historically, and for nearly half a century, television has dominated the sports media landscape, maturing to a state where the political economy of elite professional sport ticked over to its every whim. But with networked media sport, the screens on which sport is produced, distributed and consumed are multiple, delivered in an array of formats and consumed in differential and mobile spaces. This is not to argue that television has become less important. It remains one of the key platforms through which supporters and fans engage with sport, and crucially, remains a key platform in allowing key sports events to resonate with an audience beyond the dedicated sports fan. The television audiences for the London 2012 Olympics and Paralympics in the UK on free-to-air (FTA) television were impressive and indicative of the enduring appeal of watching sport on this particular screen. However, networked media sport will arguably change the nature of the TV–sport relationship, and the demands of television executives and advertisers are inflected with quite different business models and economic imperatives, which are no longer directly in their control. One obvious example here is the rise of television piracy (so called), which in terms of sports content is a virulent global phenomenon, that potentially undermines the media rights models of exclusive contracts, national markets, pay-walls and a rights regime that has given some sports untold riches. Meanwhile, other online companies such as Dailymotion and YouTube spent much of 2012 acquiring the online streaming rights to various forms of sports content from the Wimbledon tennis championship (Dailymotion) to French Ligue 1 football (Dailymotion, YouTube).

In such a volatile and evolving media environment there is a need to know how sport has responded to such challenges. To what extent is sport a key driver of new media technologies and their uptake, and alternatively, in what ways is its symbiotic relationship with television a conservative force blocking new modes of communication. Do the various actors and agencies in media sport use social networked media in the same way, and if not, how are they differentiated? Finally, what strategies, guidelines and regulations have been introduced to manage networked media sport and its stakeholders, and how do they impact on the media relations of athletes, teams and governing bodies of sport? We first outline the approach of corporate sponsors of sport to public relations and networked media sport. We then map out the ways in which sports organisations and athletes have responded to networked media, and then invert the question to ask what media organisations, particularly the press and television, have done to adapt their practices to the demands of networked media.

Sport sponsorship, public relations and social media

In the context of sports public relations and communications management, network media sport has introduced opportunities and challenges for both sports industries and the media. As Lewis and Kitchin (2011: 208) have noted, the 'social web' has enabled corporate sport to break down barriers between the organisation and its consumers by creating 'more tangible and vibrant relationships.' Sport has always helped drive the uptake of new communications technologies; the practices of journalists, broadcasters and public relations professionals has often had to fit with the culture of sport in quite distinct and unique ways. With the rise of social networked media we might want to ask if this remains the case. Has the evolution of the Internet and the digital cultures that have been inspired and created from it, transformed the ways in which sport now engages with the media? Or, are there continuities in what sport delivers to networked media sport, in terms of its cultural and economic value?

One way in which it is possible to approach such questions is to explore the market-driven discourse of professional sport and look at some of the recent market research and intelligence available and circulated among those who work in the sports industries and the associated cultural industries that gravitate around it. Again, as Hutchins and Rowe (2012) have argued, much of the rhetoric that surrounds the discourse of sports and media industries is mere boosterism, an attempt to inflate 'the new' in new media, and promote a sense of radical change when incremental developments occur. The language of sport in this context is one of branding, sponsorship, event management, public relations, and television rights and, most crucially in the context of digital communications, social media activity.

It is useful to draw on the data produced by this industry when examining the impact of socially networked media on sport because it tells us something about the strategic goals of both major sports organisations and the commercial partners they connect with. Both have turned to social media as a public relations and marketing tool. Both have arguably a long way to go before analysis of what is happening in this domain of communications provides any tangible understanding for the social and cultural engagement with sport via the Internet. Advertisers demand consistency in appraising the economic value of investment in sport. The greatest risk for advertising in sport is the uncertainty of return from expenditure, and there is a need to know how effective a campaign has been (Gratton *et al.*, 2012). Sponsorship, which is a function of both the advertising and the wider public relations activity of a company, presents further risks, not least because of the multiplicity of objectives that any one sponsor might have for its investment in sport (for, example, building brand image and visibility, corporate hospitality, launching new products, and so on). When combined with the complex social relations of networked media sport, how the sports industries and their sponsors evaluate social media activity remains a murky science. One thing we might want to investigate, therefore, is how global sports organisations and their sponsors approach media research in this context, and what kinds of questions are being asked.

For example, early market data from the London 2012 Olympic Games, heralded in some quarters as the 'Social Olympics,' revealed that a number of the International Olympic Committee's blue-chip Olympic Partner (TOP) sponsors gained what they perceived to be huge traction from viral social marketing campaigns via sites such as Twitter, Facebook and YouTube. In the lead-up to London 2012, between April 18 and June 29, the global consumer product corporation Proctor and Gamble created what was termed a 'social media buzz' with more than 17,000 posts mentioning their brands in connection to the Games. This far outstripped the 'buzz' generated by other TOP sponsors such as Samsung, Visa, Coca-Cola, Acer, Dow Chemical, General Electric, Omega, McDonald's and Atos by some considerable margin (*Sport Business International*, August 2012, No.181, p.4). While the need for major sports sponsors to measure the effectiveness of social media campaigns is merely an extension of a long-established model of market research around sport, the reporting of Proctor and Gamble's 'success' in this field suggests a shift in priorities in the commercial strategies of global corporations and sport. The scale of the 'buzz' was equated with an improved 'sentiment' by consumers towards their leading brands, which is arguably highly subjective, but nevertheless taken as a serious indicator to justify the £1.4 billion invested by the company in London 2012 (*The Independent*, 2012).

Critical approaches to social networked media (Boyd and Ellison, 2007) have noted that the 'bean counting' approach to 'followers' on the microblog Twitter or 'likes' of videos uploaded on YouTube only tells a partial story of engagement with such media texts, and indeed, tells us absolutely nothing about the qualitative experience of clicking through and reading or watching such material online, which is further complicated by the technologies being used to access social media which ranges from mobile phones, personal computers and tablet devices. Social media have moved to accommodate such criticism. For instance, in October 2011 social-networking platform Facebook introduced a new metrics system called 'Talking about this,' which measures unique users who make a story, on top of which another metric measures the 'engagement ratio' to account for the depth of any encounter with stories and threads.

Although marketing companies may have introduced more subtle and nuanced metrics to interpret what is going on in the world of social media, there is a sense to which the presence of corporate logos and official social media sites of global corporations is both unwelcome and indeed, largely ignored by the majority of users of such technologies. Take for example, this reaction in a reader comment to *The Independent* newspaper in July 2012, by no means isolated, to the news that sponsors were clamping down on ambush marketing around London 2012:

> How is it possible that the words 'gold, silver and bronze' can be appropriated by corporate sponsors, let alone 'summer'? Will the London Metal Exchange be shut down for the duration? And the Met Office? At least the article obligingly provides me with a list of companies to boycott.
>
> *(Posted on* www.independent.co.uk*, 16 July 2012)*

Such reactionary commentary, now archived on newspaper websites, social media threads and assorted social media including blogs, provide both qualitative and sustained criticism of the inroads of corporate sponsors in sport, and a staunch rebuke to the 'sentiment' that such corporations are the true 'gamesmakers' of major sporting events. The idea that sponsorship is a benevolent force in sport is both problematic and increasingly critiqued by a range of competing stakeholders in sport including its consumers (Horne, 2006).

Global sports organisations and social media

The media has been central to the evolution and economic development of professional sport throughout its history (Holt, 1989; Bose, 2012). In the latter half of the twentieth century the link between global sports organisations such as the IOC, FIFA and North American mega-brands such as the NBA, has been commercially tied to the economics of the media – particularly television – which has thereby had a strong influence on the economics of sport (Gratton and Solberg, 2007). Hutchins and Rowe (2012: 47) illustrate a sense of complacency in the 'media sports content economy,' which is born of cultural as well as economic dependency and conservatism.

The rise of social networks, and the kinds of production and distribution practices it has fostered, is now transforming the communications strategies of those sports organisations willing to explore and experiment with developing new forms of media relations that exploit the communication power (Castells, 2009) of digital media. This process has been ongoing for more than a decade (Boyle and Haynes, 2004), but is now rapidly advancing with rapacious intent. A decade ago the barrier to online and mobile sports development proved to be a broadband infrastructure that was not robust enough or extensive in its reach. The rise of fast broadband connections and 3G and 4G has helped to erode this barrier. Examples of the fusion of television and the Internet include the Indian Premier League's contract with Google to transmit live coverage of every match in the 2010 season on its social media site YouTube, and Total College Sports run by global sports media company Perform Group, whose corporate website claims 20 million unique viewers per month to its ePlayer – embedded in more than 250 national and regional news outlets in the United States.

These developments are not only significant commercial partnerships, but also provide differentiated social media experiences for fans and consumers. Many sports clubs and franchises have developed branded YouTube channels, tapping in to a realisation that fans are willing to download both live and recorded streamed video to keep in touch with their favourite teams. The innovation of sports branded applications (apps) for mobile technologies such as 3G and 4G smartphones and networked tablet technologies have spurred the development of online sports. For example, Fanatix.com is a sports app that launched in 2011, initially as a messaging vehicle to connect fans at events and at home during the game or match. By 2012 it had evolved from a messaging app, to one that was also a sports news aggregator and attempting to engage with fans beyond the confines of the event itself, be it a football or tennis match, as the rise of the smart phone gave 24/7 mobile global access to dedicated sports fans. These types of technologies have been welcomed by sport because they offer far more control over the networked media experience than technologically open platforms such as the Web. Apps effectively offer a 'walled garden' approach to networked media sport, and ensure clarity of copyright control and user interface. They also enable micropayments, advertising and online gaming, creating new revenue streams and business opportunities.

Where social media presents a challenge to global sports organisations is with the less regulated technologies of blogs and micro-blogs. A number of previous studies have illustrated the challenges faced by sports organisations in the management of 'information accidents' (Hutchins and Rowe, 2012), where scandals and public criticism may harm the sport, individual athletes and teams, sponsors and associated commercial partners (Boyle and Haynes, 2012). Most crucially, issues can arise from both within and outside the areas of control of a sport. Understanding multiple publics and stakeholders, and how to manage their expectations, attitudes and behaviour is now a full-time occupation of communications managers. Indeed this trend is prevalent across the public relations industry, with reputation management and online social media profile identified by the sector as the contemporary challenges for PR professionals in 2012. The tensions between freedom and control in networked media sport are redolent here. The global sports industries propound the virtues of the widening choice for sports fans, and at the same stroke, nervously look over their shoulders to ensure that the integrity of their sport and their commercial partners are not compromised in any way. Of course these are not uncontested areas. The US Olympic athletes in particular seemed unhappy about not being able to namecheck their sponsors on platforms such as Twitter and Facebook. They organised Twitter hashtags #WeDemandChange and #Rule40 to pressure the IOC. Policing this type of regulation is also a challenge for organisations, and indeed violations of the code did take place, and went largely unpunished. However, expect a new modified set of regulations for athletes in Rio 2016, as these emerging battle lines continue to get drawn.

As a matter of course, and now standard governance practice, most global sports organisations have introduced guidelines and regulations on social media activity associated with their events and of the athletes and teams competing in their competitions. Analysis of blogging during the 2008 Beijing Olympics by Hutchins and Mikosza (2010) suggested that while the threat of a major scandal never materialised, the overbearing information management and control of the IOC introduced a new level of surveillance to the media activities of athletes and teams. This policy carried through to London 2012, where confusion reigned as to what athletes were allowed to do and the kinds of engagement they could have with the public. The IOC guidelines (IOC, 2012) encouraged 'participants and other accredited persons to post comments on social media platforms or websites and tweet during the Olympic Games' but forbade video, taken on a smartphone for instance, being broadcast on any social media platform. In the Olympic village, athletes could post photographs, but to do so required full permission of anyone in the frame and images, could not be exploited for commercial purposes. The word Olympic could be used as a point of reference, but no association could be made with third parties, and the logos and emblems of the IOC and LOCOG could not appear in photographs. These and more restraints represent an attempt to micro-manage the use of social media by athletes and ensure compliance with the commercial security of the Games and its commercial partners.

Not all sports competitions have so stringent approach to managing social media. The sport of cricket has followed an 'empowered approach' that understands the opportunities for personal communication in social networks, but also flags up the responsibilities and risks that are associated with it. Unfortunately, the sport has been drawn in to a number of controversies primarily based on the behavior of international players and their comments and criticisms of the sport, fellow cricketers and management via networked media technologies. In 2012 the star England cricketer Kevin Pietersen found himself at the centre of a storm over Blackberry messages he had sent to opposition players in the South African team that purportedly criticised the then-England captain Andrew Strauss in defamatory language. The player was withdrawn from the English Test squad and his international career placed in serious doubt. The player missed the World T20 finals in Sri Lanka, and was obliged to make a public apology over the affair in order to be reinstated to the England squad. Pietersen had also been the target of a parody Twitter account 'KP Genius' set up by Richard Bailey, an acquaintance of a number of high-profile England and Nottinghamshire players, including Stuart Broad and Graham Swann. Pietersen claimed the spoof account had been fed stories by fellow England cricketers, which poked fun at Pietersen's aloofness in the dressing room. There was no evidence to suggest this had been the case, but the fact that a number of England players were followers of the spoof account was an indicator of continued isolation of Pietersen in the England dressing room. The series of events undermined attempts by the ECB to pursue a more enlightened approach to social media, ultimately damaging public confidence in its management and structures of governance.

Episodes of this nature provide evidence of major sports organisations struggling to maintain control over networked media, which ultimately have the potential to damage relations with sponsors and media partners. Similar controversies have occurred in football (Boyle, 2012), tennis (Boyle and Haynes, 2013), golf (Boyle and Haynes, 2012) and during the London Olympics when Swiss footballer Michael Morganella was dismissed and sent home from the Games after making a racist comment about a South Korean competitor. In so many of these cases, including the Pietersen story, it is the instantaneous velocity of communications, from the banal and ephemeral moment of thumbing a text or 'tweet' to its wider public reception and re-distribution into mainstream media, that networked social media has introduced something quite different into the sport–media nexus.

As the culture and volume of social media messages by athletes shows no signs of abating, it is the interface with established media, journalists, broadcasters and online publishers that presents a challenge to orthodox media relations. Increasingly sports organisations have taken a proactive approach to social media, not only encouraging use of Facebook and Twitter, but also developing communications policies that foster positive public relations through networked media sport. In the lead-up to London 2012, the English Football Association's Women's Super League developed a digital ambassador programme to provide insight into the lives of leading players and encourage more girls and women in to engage in the sport. More proactive communications policies, utilising the power of social networks, can help some sports, particularly those trying to build their profile with various publics.

Sports journalism, media relations, and social media

Another way to understand the impact of networked media sport is to look at the practices of sports journalism, both in the everyday work of journalists and the narratives and forms of content they produce. Digitisation has impacted journalism at a range of levels. Structurally journalism organisations are struggling to find viable business models to sustain their work, in an era in which news content appears ubiquitous and often free at the point of consumption.

Professionally the impact of this structural change and the manner in which technology has reshaped practice for journalists has been documented elsewhere (Boyle, 2006). Social media has quickly become an increasingly important element of the day-to-day life of journalists, both those working in sports and also other journalistic arenas (Boyle, 2012). Sports journalists use social media as a news feed to follow players, journalists and supporters. They use it to promote their own profile and that of the organisation they are working for, as well as to engage in real-time conversations with readers and other sporting stakeholders.

Again these changes need to be viewed as part of longer process that has seen sports journalists – particularly those in the print sector – and their unique access to a 'ringside seat' at sporting events alter and erode over the years (Koppet, 2003). Initially this occurred through the advent of radio, then the arrival of television and subsequent dedicated sports channels and more recently the rise of the Internet from the mid 1990s and now social media. As football journalist Kevin McCarra from *The Guardian* has reflected:

> I believe that it is in football that the relationship between writer and reader has most changed, particularly since those roles are no longer fixed. Access to the Internet, I am glad to say, has done away entirely with the silly assumption that journalists have access to a higher knowledge. Countless websites cover all aspects of football in virtually every nation. If any player at a World Cup is an unknown quantity it will be purely because the research has not been carried out with sufficient thoroughness. Websites, whether statistical, solemn, esoteric or comic, disseminate limitless quantities of information about even the most obscure footballers and managers. The press fool themselves if they suppose for an instant that they can be a priesthood who own a sacred knowledge.
>
> (McCarra, 2010, para. 8)

Thus the challenges to sports journalists to deliver something distinctive are increased, as they are in other areas of journalism. However, it would be wrong also to view sports journalism as past its sell-by date. Despite some of the hyperbole that surrounds the new age of citizen journalism, we are not all journalists yet (Tunney and Monaghan, 2010).

It is often only when mainstream journalists pick up and run with stories that they gain mainstream traction in public profile, even if the origins of these stories may lie among the plethora of bloggers and online commentators that can be found around online sporting discourse. Social media has shortened the timescale in which a 'scoop' can retain its exclusive value to a journalist. The issue of the pace of information flow has resulted in the always-on journalist and, as we've noted above, raised issues for professional communicators working in the sports arena.

Two examples highlight some of these issues and the intertwining of journalism, PR and sports. When Liverpool FC's Luis Suarez refused to shake the hand of Manchester United's Patrice Evra at the league match between the clubs in February 2012, it was the latest instalment in a very public falling out of the players that resulted in the FA finding Suarez guilty of making racist comments at the Manchester United player. However, what happened next signalled how digital media had changed the environment within which sporting events and their participants now operated. For the then-Liverpool manager Kenny Dalglish, it was an example of how he had simply failed to adapt to a media culture that had evolved since his previous time at the club twenty years earlier.

As live television coverage of the non-handshake at the start of the match was broadcast, so social networking sites reported and commented on this event. Yet when Dalglish was interviewed after the match, live on television, he not only indicated that he was unaware that Suarez had refused to shake hands with Evra, but accused the media of inflaming the situation. This performance from Dalglish drew strong criticism from journalists and further damaged the reputation of the club. Both Dalglish and Liverpool later apologised for the behaviour of Suarez that day, but by then the racism story that should have ended that day had been given fresh impetus. Liverpool launched an internal enquiry, presumably asking how Dalglish could be allowed to carry out a live post-match interview seemingly unaware that the incident (which he claimed he knew nothing about) had been seen around the world, had gone viral on social networks and was being extensively commented on by fans online. A PR professional with a smartphone would have been aware of the damage being done to the club's reputation even 10 minutes after the incident. The fact that Ian Cotton, the club's Director of Communication left Liverpool (having been there for 16 years), just three months later also suggested that Dalglish was not someone who felt he needed a communications expert to tell him how to deal with the media, yet that is precisely what is needed in the digital sports age.

The rise of real-time social media has also forced sports bodies to re-think their strategies regarding media relations. The English Premier League (EPL) doubled its communications team in early 2012 by hiring a four-strong social media team as it became increasingly concerned that the voice of the EPL was not being heard though its digital media platforms (*PR Week*, 17, February, 2012). Meanwhile, within the English FA the internal debate was about the location of the social media element of its communications and whether this should be located within the Marketing arm of the organisation or within the PR/Comms part of the institution. Both organisations have recognised that social media allow them to spread news in real-time to stakeholders, give them a space to address crisis situations quickly and in so doing help protect their brand identity while ensuring that people are getting accurate information about the organisation. In this sense we would argue that viewing social media solely through a marketing lens misses the broader communicative role that these media platforms are now helping to facilitate.

Conclusion

As we write late in 2013, the media profile of sport in the UK over the past two years has never been higher. The summer of 2012 saw the success of Team GB at the London Olympics displace other news coverage across media outlets across the UK, while the BBC, using its digital capacity, carried every event online. The subsequent Paralympics allowed Channel 4 (a UK FTA terrestrial TV network) to record some of its largest audience figures for a decade, while British wins for Bradley Wiggins (2012) and Chris Froome (2013) in the Tour de France, Andy Murray at the US Tennis Open (2012) and Wimbledon (2013), and the success of the European Ryder Cup golf team in October 2012 have all resulted in extensive and sustained media and public profile being given to sport and sporting achievement.

At the core of these collective experiences has been television (both FTA and Pay-TV) complemented by social and online media and a print media that has often been able to focus on the back story that the live mediated event has framed. All this suggests that sports' intrinsic appeal remains undiminished despite the corporate edifice that now accompanies elite sports events and its culture. This makes sports an extremely appealing cultural vehicle for the continued exploitation by a range of commercial and other stakeholders with a host of agendas from revenue generation to social inclusion projects. To this end the role of PR and its linkage with sports media coverage will continue to evolve and develop.

The synergies between the sports and entertainment industries discussed elsewhere (Boyle, 2006) are clear in 2012. When F1 driver Lewis Hamilton announced he would be leaving McLaren for Mercedes at the end of the season, Simon Fuller of XIX Entertainment, whose stable of talent spans the music, entertainment and sports arenas, carried out the deal. Andy Murray's first Grand Slam tennis victory just a few weeks earlier meant that Fuller had enjoyed an extremely lucrative couple of months with Murray also part of the XIX Entertainment team. For some commentators the deal breaker for McLaren was its refusal to allow drivers to retain their image rights. Mercedes was happy to sign away Hamilton's image rights, thought to be worth in the region of £10 million a year. This arrangement is also indicative of how issues around rights, copyright and policing the digital environment are all part of an emerging research agenda for those examining the media sports relationship in the digital age.

This will present a new set of challenges to sports stakeholders and its custodians. In an age of screens and mobile media, do you attempt to police media usage in stadiums to protect rights holders (the IOC position), or be more relaxed about this, as in the case of the San Francisco 49ers' owner Jed York, who said that

> his new stadium has to be equipped for the modern fan who doesn't just want to watch the game but also to share, comment, monitor their fantasy team, make bets or even just keep their kid calm with a video.
>
> *(Shortt, 2012, Executive Summary)*

Rather than lock down a stadium, Yorks wants to drive a younger audience to the event, who will not enter an environment that is not digitally robust. The social media genie is out of the bottle. Rather than displace television, it will work with this platform as sports remain at the forefront of the emerging media milieu for the foreseeable future.

References

Boyd, D. and Ellison, N. (2007) Social network sites: Definition, history, and scholarship. *Journal of Computer-Mediated Communication*, 13(1), 210–230.

Bose, M. (2012) *The Spirit of the Game: How Sport Made the Modern World*. London: Constable.

Boyle, R. (2012) Social media sport? Journalism, public relations and sport. In R. Krøvel and T. Roksvold (eds), *We Love to Hate Each Other: Mediated Football Fan Culture*. Gothenburg, Sweden: Nordicom.

Boyle, R. and Haynes, R. (2004) *Football in the New Media Age*. London: Routledge.

Boyle, R. (2006) *Sports Journalism: Context and Issues*. London: Sage.

Boyle, R. and Haynes, R. (2012) Sport, the media and strategic communications management. In L. Trenberth and D. Hassan (eds), *Managing Sport Business: An Introduction* (pp. 318–337) London: Routledge.

Boyle, R. and Haynes, R. (2013) Sports journalism and social media: A new conversation? In B. Hutchins and D. Rowe (eds), *Digital Media Sport*. New York: Routledge.

Castells, M. (2009) *Communication Power*. Oxford: Oxford University Press.

Gratton, C., Liu, D., Ramchandani, G. and Wilson, D. (2012) *The Global Economics of Sport*. London: Routledge.

Gratton, C. and Solberg, H. A. (2007) *The Economics of Sports Broadcasting*. London: Routledge.

Holt, R. (1989) *Sport and the British: A Modern History*. Cambridge: Clarendon Press.

Horne, J. (2006) *Sport in Consumer Culture*. London: Palgrave.

Hutchins, B. and Mikosza, J. (2010) The Web 2.0 Olympics: Athlete blogging, social networking and policy contradictions at the 2008 Beijing Games. *Convergence: The International Journal of Research into New Media Technologies*, 16(3), 279–297.

Hutchins, B. and Rowe, D. (2012) *Sport Beyond Television: The Internet, Digital Media and the Rise of Networked Media Sport*. New York: Routledge.

IOC (2012) *IOC Social Media, Blogging and Internet Guidelines for Participants and Other Accredited Persons at the London 2012 Olympic Games*. Retrieved 19 September, 2012, from http://www.olympic.org/Documents/Games_London_2012/IOC_Social_Media_Blogging_and_Internet_Guidelines-London.pdf

Koppett, L. (2003) *The Rise and Fall of the Press Box*. Toronto, Canada: Sport Classic Books.

Lewis, R. and Kitchin, P. (2011) New communications media for sport. In M. Hopwood, P. Kitchin and J. Skinner (eds), *Sport Public Relations and Communication* (pp. 187–214). London: Routledge.

McCarra, K. (2010, 28 June) Open Door, *The Guardian*. Retrieved May 27, 2013, from http://www.guardian.co.uk/commentisfree/2010/jun/28/world-cup-reporting-technology.

Shortt, A. (2012) *Social Media in Sport*. London: Sportsbusiness.

Tunney, S. and Monaghan, G. (eds) (2010) *Web Journalism: A New Form of Citizenship?* London: Sussex Academic Press.

Vamplew, W. (2004) *Pay Up and Play the Game: Professional Sport in Britain, 1875–1914*. Cambridge: Cambridge University Press.

13

NEW MEDIA AND THE CHANGING ROLE OF SPORTS INFORMATION

Erin A. Whiteside

UNIVERSITY OF TENNESSEE

In 2010, sports information directors from around the United States and Canada gathered in San Francisco for the industry's annual convention. The organization had secured Ari Fleischer as its keynote speaker, an event that had been heavily promoted among the membership. Although Fleischer is best known for his political expertise, the former White House press secretary is the chief executive of a sports communication firm that consults athletes and coaches on crisis communication and media strategy. Following his speech, Fleischer participated on a panel related to strategic messaging at the conference, which provided just one of several opportunities for the attending sports information directors to learn about effective communication strategy. The keynote event that year and the related conference programming reflected what has become a pointed shift in the direction of sports information's organizing body, called College Sports Information Directors of America (CoSIDA) and its member SIDs. Once known as information specialists, SIDs face a changing set of responsibilities, many of which stem from changes in media technology (Stoldt and Humenik, 2008).

Front and center in this shift in responsibilities is a focus on strategic messaging; the profession is responding to new opportunities in which SIDs play a fundamental role in both selling the athletic brand to media – as well as fans. In doing so, SIDs have transitioned from solely assisting sports journalists to becoming a version of sports journalists themselves. Indeed, SIDs are at the forefront of a growing trend in which teams and leagues produce content that is intended to compete with traditional media outlets while also using such content strategically to enhance the athletic department's brand equity. A large part of the rise in league- and team-produced fan content is a function of changing media technology and its related low barriers to entry (Hutchins and Rowe, 2009). In light of these issues, this chapter reviews the role sports information directors play in the media production process, addresses the changes and challenges confronting those within it, and reviews questions for future research.

Introduction to the field

In general, sports information directors promote a university's sports teams to the media and community. They have traditionally occupied what the public relations industry often refers to as a "technician" role, in which they complete such tasks as coordinating interviews, writing and distributing material to assist sports journalists (often called "game notes), producing media guides, and promoting teams through the athletic department's various media outlets. In addition, SIDs have traditionally been responsible for keeping and managing statistics, as well as completing other operational duties (Connors, 2007; Mullin, Hardy and Sutton, 2007; Stoldt, Miller and Comfort, 2001). SIDs are typically assigned to work with specific sports; those with higher profile teams often travel with those teams on the road and attend major events like conference championships. Within their office, SIDs are part of an internal hierarchy that includes the sports information director (often the head of the department), followed by associate, assistant and graduate assistant levels (Stoldt, 2000). Within the overall athletic department, SIDs have reported perceptions of low institutional value; their historical jobs as behind-the-scene technicians may be one reason the profession's members have not garnered the respect of their colleagues, and have even "seen their influence diminish in the last 20 years" (Moore, 2012: 47).

A 2010 survey provides the most recent demographic data; consistent with the makeup of many sports-related professions, SIDs are overwhelmingly white and male (Whiteside and Hardin, 2010). Demographic data from that survey also showed that the majority (61 percent) had worked in sports information for fewer than 10 years; in general, the profession is comprised of relatively young professionals, and has a high turnover ratio, especially among women (Stoldt *et al.*, 2001; Whiteside and Hardin). According to Whiteside and Hardin, SIDs are most likely to be assigned to football, men's basketball or women's basketball, which reflects a wider trend of where athletic departments are currently prioritizing their resources (Clotfelter, 2011).

Strategic communication directors

In 2008 CoSIDA unveiled a strategic plan that highlighted a new vision for the organization. Front and center in the plan was an effort to showcase the critical function of strategic messaging, and the plan specifically urges its members to re-brand themselves as "communication directors" vs. "information directors" to reflect these new priorities (CoSIDA Strategic Plan, 2008: 15). Many individual offices have heeded this suggestion; although historically referred to as "sports information," many have recently undergone name changes, now operating under the titles of "athletics media relations" or "athletics communications" offices. These changes, according to John Humenik, CoSIDA's executive director, "project a person who has broader, more global duties and who is viewed more in a strategic and visionary capacity" (Stoldt, 2008: 460). The vision of a proactive, strategic role played by SIDs is also a response to perceptions that they lacked influence and prestige within the athletic department (Moore, 2012). Demonstrating their worth to an organization is one way in which such professionals may regain status and, under Humenik, it appears CoSIDA has made that a priority. Among the most visible changes was the launch of a new logo with a new tagline reading *Strategic Communication Directors* (Moore, 2012).

The change in strategic vision for the profession has developed in tandem with the rise of new media technology, and indeed, sports organizations regularly provide content across myriad social and multi-media platforms (Moore and Carlson, 2013.) The adoption of new media technology among SIDs has not been quick, however, and the profession has been "remarkably slow in embracing and accepting" new media platforms (Clavio, 2011: 309). Even for the most conservative of media strategists, it is hard to ignore the potential such technology offers to athletic departments as a venue through which to enhance the fan experience – and in turn cultivate strong relationships between fans and the larger athletic brand. Perhaps nowhere are such opportunities more evident via an online presence than athletic department websites. What was once considered an "afterthought" has now become the most visible face of the athletic department (Smith, 2009a, para 4). As part of this shift, SIDs are now responsible for creating and maintaining an online space that fans seek out as a primary source of sports information that is simultaneously engaging and credible.

Producing their own web content is just one part of a fundamental shift in sports media generation and distribution processes, which has seen teams and leagues also launch their own networks, the Big Ten Network among the most successful (Weaver, 2011). In doing so, teams and leagues are now directly competing with traditional media outlets. Although such content often resembles that produced by sports journalists and broadcasters, the ultimate goals are more complex in that teams and leagues look to go beyond simply amassing an audience by also looking for ways to use their messages in ways that strengthen connections between that audience and the athletic brand.

Building a brand through online content

Although collegiate athletics are technically amateur, the industry itself is a lucrative one, and athletic departments are critically aware of the importance of building their respective brand equity – what Cunningham and Sagas (2002) define as fan awareness and perceived value in relation to the brand. Effective brand management is "vital" to collegiate athletic departments from a revenue point of view (Boyle and Magnusson, 2007); successful brand management has been shown to protect the brand against fan attrition during losing seasons (Gladden, Milne and Sutton, 1998) as well as negative associations during times of crisis (Dewar and Pillutla, 2000). Fans with a strong brand association also demonstrate stronger purchase intentions, a valuable component to an athletic department's revenue stream (Cobb-Walgren, Ruble and Donthu, 1995).

Athletics websites represent an important venue for building the kind of valuable brand equity that is imperative in today's saturated sports marketplace (Cooper and Pierce, 2011). The website management is often outsourced to companies like CBS College Sports, and such relationships have proven to be especially lucrative; the University of Nebraska, for instance, signed a 13-year, $112.5 million contract in 2009 with website specialty company IMG College (Smith, 2009b).

Balancing credibility and organization goals

Although the websites are outsourced to various management companies, SIDs are largely responsible for providing the content (Cooper and Weight, 2011; Smith, 2009b). In doing so, SIDs must create content that will generate consistent page views, which requires them to go beyond simply re-posting press releases and overt marketing material and instead move toward generating content that competes with what is produced in traditional sports journalism venues (Cooper and Weight). That shift has begun to manifest, and "schools and conferences are starting to look at their sites as more entertainment-based . . . They're looking at how they keep the viewer there longer, in part, to satisfy advertisers. If you can do that, it can become very powerful" (Smith, 2009b, para 13).

Research has begun to address questions regarding website content from a business point of view. A study modeling audience behavior on collegiate athletics websites found that loyalty among fans on such sites follows a "sequential process"; more specifically, a "high quality sport website increases fan satisfaction; likewise, heightened levels of satisfaction improve consumer loyalty to the website" (Hur, Ko and Valacich, 2011: 468). The formula for a 'high quality' website, however, is still unsettled. Among public relations scholars, effective website management includes four central tenets:

1. include useful information on the site;
2. frequently update sites and generate new content to engage publics and encourage return visits;
3. make the sites easy to use and navigate; and
4. strive to keep publics on the site.

(Briones, Kuch, Liu and Jin, 2011: 38)

Research evaluating organizational goals and strategy related to website content has pointed to the heavy emphasis of multi-media components on websites. In his survey of Division I athletic departments, Cooper (2010) found that participants rated video broadcasts as most critical in building an athletic department's brand image, followed by audio broadcasts and social networking links. A content analysis of 120 collegiate websites confirmed that video and audio are the most frequently used multi-media components available to fans (Moore and Carlson, 2013).

Regardless of message delivery platform, the overall website must still be deemed credible by fans as a legitimate sports news site. Along with avoiding an overt public relations and marketing feel, achieving credibility may be stem from acknowledging so-called 'negative' news. Professional leagues provide one model; MLB.com famously conducted the first interview with Alex Rodriguez following his steroids scandal, posting the story on the front page of its website. Major League Baseball also aired the first interview with Mark McGwire following his admission to using steroids on its MLB Network (Garfield and Franklin, 2010). In an interview, Tim Franklin, Director of the National Sports Journalism Center at Indiana University, called the McGwire story a "watershed moment" in the evolution of sports media, adding that it symbolized "a paradigm shift from traditional legacy news organizations to new media."

When team- and league-produced website content is deemed credible by fans, it can effectively compete in even the most saturated media markets (Garfield and Hammond, 2009). In addition, such processes provide athletic institutions with the ability to control the message, something that is especially useful in an unflattering situation (Garfield and Franklin, 2010). Still, much more research is needed evaluating the practices of SID- and athletic-department-generated content in its effectiveness in both attracting viewership and meeting its goals in the brand management process.

New media technologies, old sport hierarchies

The relative new 'priority status' bestowed on collegiate athletic websites has raised questions related to how resources in the way of SID time and technical expertise are allocated and to what effect. Within each athletic department, a kind of hierarchy exists, in which certain sports are deemed more worthy, or valuable than others (Suggs, 2005). These hierarchies often pit men's and women's sports against each other, especially when it comes to the distribution of resources (Messner and Solomon, 2007). Scholars have lamented the growing trend by athletic departments in emphasizing profit maximization when making decisions, a practice that is especially pronounced at the Division I level (Cooper and Southall, 2010). For instance, in using capitalistic incentives as a sole guiding compass, many athletic departments have sacrificed non-revenue-producing men's sports in favor of shifting more resources in to football. Advocates for non-revenue sports have raised concerns with this practice and urged athletic departments to re-imagine the priorities governing collegiate athletics (Clotfelter, 2011). Similar questions should be addressed in relation to the adoption and implementation of new media technology, and several scholars have begun exploring how the distribution of these resources may contribute to the maintenance of traditional sports hierarchies.

In general, content analyses of athletic department websites show that SIDs and others who exert control over the website direct much of their resources toward the sports with the highest return on investment, especially major men's sports (Cooper and Cooper, 2009). However, the disparities go beyond simple gender lines; in a 2011 content analysis of athletic department websites, the authors found that gender disparities in quantity of content were most pronounced at the Division I level; in contrast, websites at the Division III level, where the commercialization of sport is more muted, featured a more equitable distribution of content by team gender. The results "support the notion that Division I athletic departments focus on the mainstream media sports that offer the greatest potential for a strong return on investment" (Cooper and Pierce, 2011: 78). This assertion echoes a study by Cunningham and Sagas (2002), which found that athletic departments bestow equal amounts of resources online to women's basketball in comparison to men's teams only when the women's brand equity reflects that of men's teams (Cunningham and Sagas).

Along with women's sports, so-called "Olympic sports" – a moniker often given to all sports excluding football and basketball – may feel the brunt of the relationship between commercialization and new media technology. As athletic departments continue to funnel resources toward football and men's basketball, "it seems inevitable that nonrevenue teams will have to use the Internet effectively in future years to remain sustainable" (Cooper and Southall, 2010: 8). Yet, content analyses suggest that athletic department websites may not be serving Olympic sports in a way that sustains their respective fan base. In their work on collegiate wrestling, Cooper and Southall (2010) have urged coaches to bypass sports information and marketing offices in favor of creating the content themselves via social media.

Although institutional resources seem to be allocated based on a cost-benefit analysis only, SIDs themselves may not adhere to that logic; a survey of Division I SIDs showed that the majority believe too many resources are directed toward football, which may suggest that SIDs support a more equitable distribution of resources, including those related to new media (Whiteside, Hardin and Ash, 2011). It is unclear, however, how much influence SIDs have in the website content production process. Such individuals already work 70- to 80-hour work weeks and providing more content on, say, a men's tennis match may only happen if a particular SID creates such content after finishing his or her duties in relation to revenue producing sports. It is a tall order, and researchers should continue to address the types of resources allocated to websites, and their respective distribution.

Social media as a strategic tool

Shifts in SIDs' responsibilities have occurred in tandem with shifts in how sports fans access information on their favorite teams. Like many organizations looking to connect with various publics, athletic departments have begun experimenting with myriad social media platforms. Research suggests that embracing effective social media strategy will be critical for athletic departments interested in widening their fan base; for instance, an analysis of one large Football Bowl Subdivision (FBS) school's fan base showed that fans in the 18- to 29-year-old age group were more likely than any other age groups to regularly access team information via Facebook. Those in the 18- to 29-year-old age group and the 30- to 39-year-old age group were also more likely than any other age demographics to regularly access team information on Twitter (Clavio, 2011).

Engagement

Regardless of the communication platform, building connections with various audiences is a function of sound public relations practice; in general, public relations theorists argue that facilitating a two-way, or dialogic communication stream is imperative in building an effective relationship with a given public (Briones *et al.*, 2011). Communication strategists have pointed to social media as a useful platform in creating a space in which users feel like they belong and are some way connected to the organization/brand (Yan, 2011). In sports, creating a social identity with a team – defined as group affiliation – has been shown to result in higher perceived quality of the athletic program (Boyle and Magnusson, 2007). Social media is uniquely situated to enhance that feeling of belonging because of its interactive nature, and successful social media strategy is often described as one that encourages audience participation and dialogue (Yan, 2011). Indeed, the concept of "engagement" is central to effective social media implementation. For example, The Big Ten has made game footage available to fans, so they can edit and ultimately create their own mash-ups to share with other fans; this practice has positioned the Big Ten as a leader in creating a fan-centric experience (Steinbach, 2009, para 7). Ultimately, such tactics allow fans to talk and share information about the team with each other, something Yan (2011) argues is indicative of a successful exploitation of social media, a platform that is built to facilitate such multi-directional interaction. Other types of engagement range from asking for feedback, posting polls, responding to fan comments and providing unique and fresh content to reinforce connections with the team (Germann, 2010).

Making social media a visible part of the athletic department's strategy may help those organizations better compete within the broader sports marketplace. A 2012 survey showed that sports fans are increasingly accessing sports information on their favorite teams via social media websites (Broughton, 2012). Fifty-eight percent of those surveyed said they used Facebook to discuss college football and 53 percent said they used the site to discuss college basketball. As a point of comparison, 71 percent of respondents said they used Facebook to discuss the NFL, followed by Major League Baseball (64 percent) and the NBA (62 percent). A higher percentage of college basketball fans said they had "liked" their team's Facebook page (82 percent of college basketball fans) or "followed" their team's Twitter feed (42 percent) compared to any other sport. Again, as a point of comparison, 78 percent of NFL fans had liked their team's Facebook page and 22 percent had followed their team's Twitter feed. The survey also showed that fans were most likely to engage in social media related to their team following wins, a finding that points to the importance of exploiting that desire to engage at strategic times (Broughton, 2012).

SIDs and social media

Athletic departments are using social media to varying degrees of success, at least in terms of fan engagement. In their content analysis of Big XII athletic program Facebook pages, for example, Wallace, Wilson and Miloch (2011) saw great disparities; at the time of their study, the University of Texas had 608,007 fans on Facebook, followed by the University of Oklahoma (257,748) and the University of Nebraska (162,591). This compared to the University of

Colorado, which had just 5,318 fans. The study also looked at the number of fans on NCAA-sponsored sport-specific pages and found wrestling had amassed more fans than any sport (128,243), including football (118,524). Consistent with existing trends on the allocation of resources around athletic department websites, research suggests SIDs may also be directing more attention to men's sports on social media sites; a content analysis of four athletic conference Twitter feeds showed that men received 66 percent of the links to video while just 12 percent of such links directed fans to women's sports content (Reichert-Smith, 2011). The analysis also showed that male athletes and teams garnered 70 percent of the overall tweets and that 50 percent of all tweets focused on football and men's basketball alone, leading the author to suggest that social media may be facilitating a "move toward further gender disparity" (p. 157). It will be important for researchers to continue to assess how the deployment of social media may stabilize – or challenge – existing sports hierarchies, either along gender lines, or those related to a sport's commercial potential.

Athletic departments are also experimenting with how to mobilize its resources around social media. The University of Washington was among the industry's early leaders, as it established a position in the sports information department specifically geared toward overseeing the athletic department's social media strategy in 2009 (Ramos, 2013). Washington's director of new media/recruiting has sought to expand the university's brand awareness through a variety of outlets, especially Facebook, Twitter, Pinterest, Tumblr and Instagram (Ramos). Conversely, the University of Oregon launched its "QuackCave" in 2012, which handed off some of the social media responsibilities to students. These efforts are part of the athletic department's strategic communication efforts, and will help the athletic department "monitor" what it calls "one of the top brands in college athletics" ("Ducks Launch," n.d., para 6). These two examples converge at the point of focusing on social media, but diverge in the management of those tools. As sports information offices continue to develop their social media presence, it will be important for researchers to assess the success of such efforts from various points of view. Wallace *et al.* (2011) provide a starting point; in their content analysis of Big XII and NCAA Facebook pages, the authors found that the most frequent type of status update were those that included links, which ultimately direct users away from Facebook and its interactive platform. In evaluating this practice, the authors concluded that the platform's tools were "underused" in terms of facilitating fan interactivity and suggest that future research explore fans' uses and gratifications when it comes to social media use. Future research may also want to evaluate how and why athletic departments are using certain social media sites. Pinterest, for instance, has a predominantly female fan base, something sports organizations have taken notice of, including the University of Washington athletic department and various collegiate women's basketball teams (Laird, 2012).

Changing media landscape

When the University of Arizona hired Rich Rodriguez to be its football coach, the news broke not through the *Arizona Republic* or one of Tucson's local media outlets, but via the athletic director's Twitter page. Although the deployment of effective communication strategy via social media and institutional websites may be a function of athletic departments' overall brand management goals, the byproduct has been a fundamental shift in the media production process. SIDs are still responsible for media relations duties, but they often do so now while simultaneously creating content that directly competes with those they are also helping.

A survey conducted by the Curley Center for Sports Journalism at Penn State in 2010 showed that SIDs are aware of their role in producing new forms of content (see Table 13.1).[1]

Table 13.1 Percentage distribution of SID responses to new media related questions

	Strongly disagree	Disagree	Neutral	Agree	Strongly agree
We use new media, such as Facebook, Twitter, and blog posts to communicate with the public regarding our teams	1.5	4.8	4.4	45.6	43.8
Social media allows the institution to better connect with media covering our teams	3.3	21.7	16.5	45.6	12.9
I effectively use the Internet and social media in my capacities as an SID	1.8	4.8	17.0	47.2	29.2
Reporters generally follow the storylines we push through our new media messages	1.8	4.8	16.9	47.1	29.0

Note: SID = sports information director

The vast majority reported using new media tools to connect with various publics, although a smaller percentage reported feeling comfortable with using the Internet and social media in their capacities as an SID. Not surprisingly, younger SIDs reported feeling more comfortable with such tools.[2] The findings were less overwhelming when SIDs were asked to evaluate the value of such content; a quarter disagreed or strongly disagreed that the deployment of such technology helps SIDs better connect with the media. These SIDs may be reacting to the changing media landscape in that the type of content sports information offices are providing is not always geared necessarily toward meeting media needs, but competing with those media. Still, more than three quarters of those surveyed felt that reporters generally follow the story-lines their respective institutions push through their new media channels.

Perhaps the biggest advantage athletic departments hold in this regard is their access to "insider" content that is not readily accessible to traditional sports journalists. Even a casual glance at major athletic department websites reveals a bevy of "insider" content, ranging from videos featuring players on the bus, eating at training table or engaged in any number of light-hearted activities. Such content is not earth shattering, of course, but does help attract fans looking for information on their teams.

At the same time, when much off-the-field news breaks it is unclear what role SIDs play in this process. During the Duke Lacrosse scandal, for instance, university public relations officials handled the crisis communication duties, and the university established a website in which individuals could access pertinent information about the case (Fortunato, 2008). Similarly, little news about the Jerry Sandusky scandal at Penn State was posted on that institution's athletic website during the events that unfolded in 2012. Scholars interested in the relationship between brand equity and team- and league-produced content should evaluate how athletic department media may shape perceptions of credibility among fans. On the other hand, the success of these emerging sports sources deserves critical reflection, as well. Team- and league-produced media provide fans with more options than ever before in terms of seeking out sports content on their favorite teams (Garfield and Franklin, 2010). However, if the goal is to use that content to facil-itate fan connections to the brand, the blurring of public relations and entertainment ultimately leaves lingering questions about the social cost of such increase in content for fans. The Mark McGwire steroids story provides an example; although renowned sports journalist Bob Costas conducted the famous interview which aired on MLB Networks, there was an unavoidable business interest at stake, which functioned as a constraint on the production of content (Garfield and Franklin, 2010). SIDs are thus at a similar critical intersection, and fans must ultimately be aware of how business interests and the focus on strategic messaging shape the final product.

Notes

1. Data collected from a 2010 phone survey of Division I FBS SIDs ($n = 272$). Respondents were chosen from a random sample of 450 SIDs, yielding a response rate of 60.4%. Respondents included SIDs at all levels, from graduate assistant to department heads and reflected the industry demographics reflected in earlier studies on sports information.
2. Younger SIDs reported a higher mean answer to the question "I effectively use the Internet and social media in my capacities as an SID" as indicated by a moderate, negative Spearman's Rank Order correlation, $rs (261) = -.239, p < .01$.

References

Boyle, B. A. and Magnusson, P. (2007) Social identity and brand equity formation: A comparative study of collegiate sports fans. *Journal of Sport Management*, 21, 497–520.

Briones, R. L., Kuch, B., Liu, B. F. and Jin, Y. (2011) Keeping up with the digital age: How the American Red Cross uses social media to build relationships. *Public Relations Review*, 37(1), 37–43.

Broughton, D. (2010, July 16) Survey: Social-media continues to fuel fans. *Sports Business Journal*. Retrieved from http://m.sportsbusinessdaily.com/Journal/Issues/2012/07/16/In-Depth/Catalyst-Survey.aspx

Clavio, G. (2011) Social media and the college football audience. *Journal of Issues in Intercollegiate Athletics*, 4, 309–325.

Clotfelter, C. T. (2011) *Big-time Sports in American Universities.* Cambridge, MA: University Press.

Cobb-Walgren, C. J., Ruble, C. A. and Donthu, N. (1995) Brand equity, brand preference, and purchase intent. *Journal of Advertising*, 24(3), 25–40.

Connors, K. (2007) Sports information functions at the University of Massachusetts. In B. J. Mullin, S. Hardy and W. A Sutton (eds), *Sport Marketing* (3rd edn.). Champaign, IL: Human Kinetics.

Cooper, C. G. (2010) New media marketing: The innovative use of technology in athletic department e-branding initiatives. *Journal of Marketing Development and Competitiveness*, 5(1), 23–32.

Cooper, C. G. and Cooper, B. D. (2009) NCAA website coverage: Do athletic departments provide equitable gender coverage on their athletic home web pages? *The Sport Journal*, 12(2). Retrieved from http://www.thesportjournal.org/article/ncaa-website-coverage-do-athletic-departments-provide-equitable-gender-coverage-their-athlet

Cooper, C. G. and Pierce, D. (2011) The role of divisional affiliation in athletic department web site coverage. *International Journal of Sport Communication*, 4, 70–81.

Cooper, C. G. and Southall, R. M. (2010) The pursuit of sustainability: Examining the motivational consumption preferences of online consumers of nonrevenue sport teams. *International Journal of Sport Communication*, 3(10), 1–11.

Cooper, G. C. and Weight, E. A. (2011) Participation rates and gross revenue vs. promotion and exposure: Advertisement and multimedia coverage of 18 sports within NCAA Division I athletic department websites. *Sport Management Review*, 14(4), 399–408. doi: 10.1016/j.smr.2010.12.005

CoSIDA Strategic Plan (2008) *CoSIDA.com.* Retrieved from http://cosida.com/CoSIDAStrategicPlan/csp_index.aspx

Cunningham, G. B. and Sagas, M. (2002) Utilizing a different perspective: Brand equity and media coverage of intercollegiate athletics. *International Sports Journal*, 6, 134–145.

Dewar, N. and Pillutla, M. M. (2000) Impact of product-harm crises on brand equity: The moderating role of consumer expectations. *Journal of Marketing Research*, 37, 215–226.

Ducks Launch the Quack Cave (2012, August 8) *Goducks.com.* Retrieved from http://www.goducks.com/ViewArticle.dbml?DB_OEM_ID=500&ATCLID=205572436

Fortunato, J. (2008) Restoring a reputation: The Duke University lacrosse scandal. *Public Relations Review*, 34, 116–123.

Garfield, B. (Interviewer) and Hammond, R. (Interviewee) (2009) Making the team. [Interview Audio File]. *On the Media*. Retrieved from http://www.onthemedia.org/2009/oct/09/making-the-team/

Garfield, B. (Interviewer) and Tim Franklin (Interviewee) (2010) A network of their won [Interview Audio File]. *On the Media*. Retrieved from http://www.onthemedia.org/2010/feb/05/a-network-of-their-own/

Germann, M. (2010, August 17) Effectively interacting with fans through social media. *New Media Expo Blog*. Retrieved from http://www.blogworld.com/2010/08/17/effectively-interacting-with-fans-through-social-media/

Gladden, J. M., Milne, G. R. and Sutton, W. A. (1998) A conceptual framework for assessing brand equity in Division I college athletics. *Journal of Sport Management*, 12(1), 1–19.

Hur, Y., Ko, Y. J. and Valacich, J. (2011) A structural model of the relationships between sport website quality, e-satisfaction, and e-loyalty. *Journal of Sport Management*, 25, 458–473.

Hutchins, B. and Rowe, D. (2009) From broadcast scarcity to digital plenitude: The changing dynamics of the media sport content economy. *Television and New Media*, 10(4), 354–370.

Laird, S. (2012, February 24) Pinsanity: How sports teams are winning on Pinterest. *Mashable*. Retrieved from http://mashable.com/2012/02/24/pinterest-sports/

Messner, M. A. and Solomon, N. (2007) Social justice and men's interests. *Journal of Sport and Social Issues*, 31(2), 162–178.

Moore, J. (2012) Strategic influence in college sports public relations. *CoSIDA e-Digest*, December, 47–54. Retrieved from http://www.cosida.com/digest/index.aspx

Moore, J. H. and Carlson, A. (2013) Reaching the audience: New communication technology practices in college sports public relations. *Journal of Global Scholars of Marketing Science: Bridging Asia and the World*, 23(1), 109–126. doi: 10.1080/21639159.2012.744515

Mullin, B. J., Hardy, S. and Sutton, W. (2007) *Sport marketing* (3rd edn.). Champaign, IL: Human Kinetics.

Ramos, R. (2013) Q&A with University of Washington's new media manager Daniel Hour. *CoSIDA E-Digest*, January, 35–36. Retrieved from http://www.cosida.com/digest/index.aspx

Reichert-Smith, L. (2011) The less you say: An initial study of gender coverage in sports of twitter. In A. C. Billings (ed.), *Sports Media: Transformation, Integration, Consumption*. New York: Routledge.

Smith, M. (2009a, June 15) Schools finding new ways to cash in on Web. *SportsBusiness Journal*. Retrieved from http://www.sportsbusinessdaily.com/Journal/Issues/2009/06/20090615/SBJ-In-Depth/Schools-Finding-New-Ways-To-Cash-In-On-Web.aspx?hl=%2522sports%20information%2522&sc=0

Smith, M. (2009b, January 5) Schools seek better ways to leverage Web. *SportsBusiness Journal*. Retrieved from http://www.sportsbusinessdaily.com/Journal/Issues/2009/01/20090105/SBJ-In-Depth/Schools-Seek-Better-Ways-To-Leverage-Web-Content.aspx?hl=%2522sports%20information%2522&sc=0

Stoldt, G. C. (Interviewer) and Humenik, J. (Interviewee) (2008) Interview with John Humenik, executive director of the College Sports Information Directors of America. *International Journal of Sport Communication*, 1, 458–464.

Stoldt, G. (2000) Current and ideal roles of NCAA Division I-A sports information practitioners. *Cyber-Journal of Sport Marketing*, 4(1). Retrieved http://fulltext.ausport.gov.au/fulltext/2000/cjsm/v4n1/stoldt41.htm.

Stoldt, G. C., Miller, L. K. and Comfort, P. G. (2001) Through the eyes of athletic directors: Perceptions of sports information directors and other public relations issues. *Sport Marketing Quarterly*, 10(3), 164–178.

Steinbach, P. (2009) Social media revolutionizing how sports are consumed. *Athletic Business*, October [online]. Retrieved from http://www.athleticbusiness.com/articles/article.aspx?articleid=2716&zoneid=40

Suggs, W. (2005) *A Place on the Team: The Triumph and Tragedy of Title IX*. Princeton, NJ: Princeton University Press.

Wallace, L., Wilson, J. and Miloch, K. (2011) Sporting Facebook: A content analysis of NCAA organizational sport pages and Big 12 Conference athletic department pages. *International Journal of Sport Communication*, 4, 422–444.

Weaver, K. (2011) A game change: Paying for big-time college sports. Change: *The Magazine of Higher Learning*, 43(1), 14–21.

Whiteside, E.A. and Hardin, M. (2010) Public relations and sports: Work force demographics in the intersection of two gendered industries. *Journal of Sports Media*, 5(1), 21–52.

Whiteside, E.A., Hardin, M. and Ash, E. (2011) Good for society or good for business? Division I sports information directors' attitudes toward the commercialization of sports. *International Journal of Sport Communication*, 4(4), 473–491.

Yan, J. (2011) Social media in branding: Fulfilling a need. *Journal of Brand Management*, 18(9), 688–696.

14

SOCIAL MEDIA IN THE OLYMPIC GAMES

Actors, management and participation

Emilio Fernández Peña, Natividad Ramajo, and María Arauz

CENTRE D'ESTUDIS OLÍMPICS (CEO–UAB), UNIVERSITAT AUTÒNOMA DE BARCELONA

The Olympic Games and the Olympic movement are, by their very nature, open to public participation. It is this inclination to involve the public in general, and young people in particular, that is at the essence of the Olympic movement, rendering new social media, and particularly social networks, devices that have a large strategic ability to connect audiences and allow them to share the Olympic values and ideals, as acknowledged by the president of the International Olympic Committee, Jacques Rogge (Koop, 2011). One of the key issues associated with social media is that they are able to turn every fan into an advocate of the cause (Fernández Peña and Arauz, 2011) – the users have a main role in disseminating messages.

The Beijing 2008 Olympic Games witnessed the emergence of social media. The International Olympic Committee (IOC) reached an agreement with YouTube to re-broadcast the Games via this Internet platform and create an official channel of the 2008 Beijing Games (Fernández Peña, 2009a). The IOC and the organising committee of the Games started on the social networks Facebook and Twitter, as independent initiatives during the Vancouver Games (Basich, 2010). The London 2012 Games, classified by the media as the first "social Olympics" (Rooney, 2012), saw the spread of the Olympic presence to other new social platforms, blogs, photo-sharing applications and ad filters (e.g. Instagram), as well as to new local members seeking global expansion to those markets with specific language requirements and political characteristics such as China.

Towards a definition of the term social media

To discuss social media is to discuss a generic concept within what are known as new media, that is, those media that are based on the Internet and that allow any user to produce and disseminate messages on the net. In social media, therefore, what is known as user generated content has a notable role (Jenkins, 2006). Following this concept are the social media platforms such as blogs or YouTube. The social networks Facebook and Twitter are also social media, although these have specific features: they directly connect people with each other and with organisations by means of public or semi-public profiles (Boyd and Ellison, 2007). For

Musial and Kazienko (2012) two key elements define a social network: "the finite set of nodes (actors) and edges (ties) that link these nodes" (Musial and Kazienko, 2012). Other specific characteristics of social networking websites are their ability to incorporate elements from other social media (YouTube videos, photos, maps), to allow opinions on contents to be expressed by means of comments or votes (Kim, Jeong and Lee, 2010) and their ability to combine previous Internet communication devices such as chat, instant messaging and electronic mail (Musial and Kazienko, 2012).

The system of actors in the Olympic Movement

Contemporary realities such as the Olympic Games are complex. A variety of actors contribute to organising, spreading and financing them, converting them into a system in which the interaction of different elements reaches greater potential and effectiveness than if they were operating separately, in such a way that some influence and condition others. For example, the communication policy in social networks will be partly conditioned by the obligations contracted by the IOC with the broadcasters who acquire the audio-visual rights to broadcast the televised images of the Games in the different countries, and represent the main source of funding for the Games.

The IOC is, according to the Olympic Charter, "the supreme authority" and leader of what is known as the Olympic Movement, the "three main constituents" of which are, together with the IOC, the International Sports Federations (IFs) and the National Olympic Committees (NOCs) (IOC, 2011). As far as the IOC is concerned in the purpose of this article, it is the owner of the Olympic Games and all the aspects concerning its organisation. It entrusts a candidate city with representing, disseminating, recording and reproducing the Games using all existing and future communication media (IOC, 2011). This part of the Olympic Charter implicitly acknowledges the systemic and interrelated nature of all the ways of disseminating the Games. Alongside this above mentioned main actor is the Organising Committee of the Olympic Games, to which the IOC entrusts, under its control and supervision, the organisation of the Games.

The key actors in dissemination are the television channels, which buy the audio-visual rights to rebroadcast on the basis of two criteria: "sales territory and exclusivity" (Fernández Peña, 2009a). The television turns a local event such as the Olympic Games global. There is an element of symbiosis about the alliance between the Olympic Games and television. For the Olympic Games, television has been a dissemination tool of athletes' images of effort, success or failures and Olympic values, as well as being a main source of funding for the Olympics. For television channels, the Games are a formula that guarantee large audiences and, in the case of private television channels, guarantee returns on the investment made through advertising (Fernández Peña, 2009a, 2011). In the period 2009–2012, television income derived from the Olympic Games reached $3.9 billion (IOC, 2012a), thereby becoming the main source of income. This income is closely related to the television's ability to generate global audiences. Moreover, the London Olympic Games reached a potential audience of 4.8 billion spectators worldwide (IOC, 2012a).

In turn, the TOP sponsorship programme, inaugurated in the mid-1980s (Payne, 2006), is composed of 12 global companies which, for being associated with the image of the Olympic Games, spent $957 million in the period 2009–2012 (IOC, 2012a). The TOP sponsorship programme is closely linked to the sale of television rights, since it is the global image mainly created by television that makes investment in Olympic sponsorship attractive and profitable for these large international brands.

Social media have a cross-cutting nature, since all the actors in the Olympic family and their members participate in this type of communication, unlike what occurs with traditional media: the IOC and the Organising Committee for the Olympics Games (OCOG) disseminate the event, its symbols, educational elements and positive values; television supports the main activity and ways of involving the audience and getting them to participate; sponsors reinforce the image of the brand and directly or indirectly that of the sponsors and audiences of the Games.

Logic of communication in social networks

The presence of the Olympic organisations IOC and OCOG, the sponsors and the athletes follow a different logic to that of traditional media, the main aim of which is to obtain large audiences. There are two key terms when discussing communication in social networks. One refers to what occurs within the social networks and is known as engagement. The other concept is external and is oriented towards the whole, systemic, i.e. it refers to the relations, collaborations and feedback between the different presences of the institution on the Internet: web page, YouTube channel, presence on Facebook and Twitter and other social networks. We could call this process cross-pollination (Fernández Peña and Arauz, 2011).

Engagement refers to how the public becomes involved and participates with the presence on social networks. The first phase of this engagement is measured by the total number of friends or followers, but this method can be deceptive because engagement needs to be constantly renewed on every publication, comment and photograph on social networks. To measure the engagement of a publication there are various criteria, all of which refer to active behaviour by followers or friends: one is the number of "likes", but of the participative behaviour it is the most passive type. Another is the adding of comments or questions to the publication. A third level is based on sharing published contents, opening them up to the social network of the person who published them (Fernández Peña and Arauz, 2011). While this shows engagement it also produces spreadability (Jenkins *et al.*, 2008) between people who are not fans of the page that originally published the content. In the case of Twitter, re-tweeting or adding comments reveal the level of engagement.

In the case of Facebook, the act of sharing means that the user's engagement, as in the case of re-tweeting, extends beyond the social network of those who voluntarily added themselves as fans or followers of a page. This is related with the three degrees of influence rule (Christakis and Fowler, 2009), which refers to that possibility: what is communicated on a page can be influential via friends of our friends, that is, contacts who are not directly in our social network. This is made possible by systems of social recommendation, which are based on the tendency so typical of humans to imitate the social behaviour of others (Christakis and Fowler, 2009).

In the external and systemic concept of cross-pollination, social networking sites must form part of the organisation's Internet communication strategy as a whole. This integral, all-embracing strategy seeks cross-pollination between and among all the institution's presences on the Internet. Communication on social networks should become yet another element of interaction with the website and provide information in a close-up way, through the friend-to-friend mode of communication that social networking sites facilitate, and develop into an essential component of permanent institutional communication.

Traditional websites currently represent static content that is nonetheless accessible via the Internet anytime, anywhere. While they are a repository or store for the institution's whole virtual presence, they remain a static element that internauts generally only visit when they are interested in an organisation's content. This is where social networking sites like Facebook and Twitter can help them become more dynamic (Fernández Peña and Arauz, 2011).

The arrival of the Olympic Games to social media

The 2008 Beijing Olympic Games were the Web 2.0 Olympic Games (Hutchins and Mikosza, 2010) marked by the abundance of information from Internet media, blogs of digital journalists and athletes (Miah, García and Zhihui, 2008). They were also the beginning of the alliance between IOC and social media (Fernández Peña, 2009b). Before the London Games the IOC created the YouTube Olympic Channel for 77 countries in Asia, Africa and the Middle East, where the Olympic Games' Internet rights had not been sold. The Google service was only accessible from those parts of the world and, consequently, only YouTube users in those geographical areas could access images of the Olympics Games (Fernández Peña and Lallana del Rio, 2011). As this channel was being created, the alliance between both organisations aimed to ensure the exclusivity of the television rights acquired by the rights-holding broadcasters, eliminating from YouTube any video published by a YouTube user that could prove detrimental to the exclusivity of the broadcasters (Fernández Peña, 2009a). For the London Olympic Games, the experience initiated in Beijing was fully consolidated through the Olympic Games Channel on YouTube. This channel provided live as well as summarised coverage of the Olympic ceremonies and competitions in 64 countries in Asia and Africa, where no television channel had acquired the right to broadcast the event. Olympic Games YouTube provided 11 simultaneous signals in high definition to follow the competition live. In total the IOC provided approximately 2,200 hours of television on the Olympic Games via YouTube (IOC, 2012b).

However, the big leap to social networking websites took place weeks before the 2010 Vancouver Olympic Games with IOC and the 2010 Vancouver Olympic Games Organising Committee (VANOC) launching its presence on Facebook and Twitter (Huot, 2010). Up to that point, social networks were a territory unexplored by organisations governing large global sports events. The IOC was a pioneer in the use and management of these social networks, inaugurating models that have since been followed by other similar organisations. The main presences of the Olympic Movement on Facebook, The Olympic Games (IOC) and VANOC obtained more than one million Facebook users in less than one month, during the weeks prior to the Games and the days on which they were held. This fact shows that social networks are fed by the capacity to build the current situation and to focus the audience's attention on a specific topic (Fernández Peña and Arauz, 2011).

Nevertheless, for VANOC, social networks did not play a notable role in the online communication of the event, the main element being the organising committee's webpage. According to Graeme Menzies, director of online communications, publications and editorial services in the 2010 Vancouver Olympic Games, "Everything we do in our approach to social media is in the context and with the knowledge that the website is the mother lode and the mother ship" (Silverman, 2010). This explains why, during these games, Facebook and Twitter were used to rebroadcast information that had already been published on the webpage, without the social networks being used to have live interaction with the public, encourage conversation and respond directly to questions from the public, all of which are key and differential elements for communication on social networks (Fernández Peña and Arauz, 2011).

IOC social media rules

The communication situation of the Olympic Games has changed remarkably with the advent of social media. In old media, organisations, producers and broadcasters controlled the communication flow. On social networks each user is a communication broadcaster. The dissemination of messages created in this way depends on the number of followers a message has (Facebook) or its ability to become a trend (Twitter). In this case the contents of social media such as Twitter are linked to the ability to build large television audiences. In October 2012 Lebron James was at the top of the list of leading Olympic athletes with 18.5 million followers, and some 6 other athletes had more than 10 million fans each, according to data from the Olympic Athletes' Hub (IOC, 2012d). Usain Bolt's performance in the 200 metre final provoked more than 80,000 tweets per minute and the 100 metre final gave rise to 74,000 (Rooney, 2012). With the aim of moderating the abundant new streams of communication created during the Games by the different actors – athletes, coaches and other members of the official teams in the Games, in the Beijing Games (Hutchins and Mikosza, 2010), the Vancouver Games and the London Games – the IOC published the document IOC Social Media and Blogging Guidelines (IOC, 2012c).

The last of the versions dedicated to the London Olympic Games encourages athletes and official staff to publish their experiences by "posting, blog or tweet" (IOC, 2012c) as long as they do it in first person and it does not concern aspects related to the competition and they do not reveal confidential information. Consequently, they must always be in keeping with the Olympic spirit. Comments that interfere "with the competitions or the ceremonies of the Olympic Games or with the role and responsibilities of the IOC or the Organizing Committee of the Olympic Games" are forbidden (IOC, 2012c). In order to protect the exclusivity of the audio-visual rights of the rights-holding broadcasters and the sponsors, the publication of audio or video material made during the competition is prohibited. On the other hand, the athletes and official staff cannot "promote any brand, product or service" (IOC, 2012c) using social media during the duration of the Games, in line with the guidelines of Rule 40 of the Olympic Charter (IOC, 2011), which also protects the interests of the TOP Sponsors and official sponsors of the Olympic Games. The Social Media Guidelines also protect the Olympic brands and symbols, prohibiting their appearance in publications.

Thus, the IOC considers that such rules are justifiable on two grounds: ethical, seeking to ensure that respect and fairplay reign supreme inside and outside competition among athletes and their support staff (coaches, physicians, managers, etc.); and financial, protecting official sponsors, television rights holders and the Olympic brands.

These measures were criticised for restricting the freedom to communicate because "it was brutally evident that the IOC had no understanding of the role social media platforms have played in shaping the way the world, and more specifically the Millennial generation, communicates today" (Lopez, 2012). These onerous communication rules reveal to what degree new media, which turn every Olympic actor into a communication broadcaster, can affect freedom of expression and communication and rules of coexistence. New rules for new social uses. The first consequence of these norms occurred before the start of the London Games. On 22 July 2012 the triple jump athlete Voula Papachristou was expelled from the Greek Olympic Games team for making a scornful or supposedly racist comment on her Twitter page concerning African immigrants in Greece.

Olympic family social media environment

London 2012 carried out a communication campaign on the Internet focused on the official website that, according to Alex Balfour, head of New Media London2012, sought to provide dynamism and live publication by being continuously updated and by launching two mobile applications fed by constantly updated information, which led more than 52% of the traffic (Balfour, 2012) to the official web page of the Games. To achieve this, the web page acquired a type of social participation, for which it provided buttons to support and promote the event.

At the same time, the official page generated a special feed so that the results could be directly transferred to the Facebook pages of the athletes, thereby using the synergies between the real protagonists of the event and the page of the organising committee, and strengthening the role of Facebook as a conductor of traffic towards the webpage. The presence on Twitter was divided across 46 accounts, the majority of which were dedicated to live sports commentaries, and also with the presence of mascots. The cross social media strategy combines the social networks with the highest number of subscribers with a Foursquare account and live blogs that discuss the backstage of the opening and closing ceremonies (Balfour, 2012).

Faced with a fragmented strategy that did not adequately exploit the feedback from social media in the 2010 Vancouver Games, the London Games represented a growth strategy in the number of social media in which they were present, and at the same time, a commitment to the concentration of contents through the creation of what is known as the Olympic Hub. As well as the Facebook and Twitter accounts, the IOC signed up to blogs, through an alliance with the microblogging platform and social networking website Tumblr, reached an agreement with Instagram for the social sharing of photographs, and with the location-based social networking website for mobile devices Foursquare. Its new alliance with the social networking website Google+ is also notable. In China, where the rest of the social networks in which the IOC is present are not established for political and linguistic reasons, collaboration agreements were signed with the social networks of this country, Sina Weibo and Youku (Lunden, 2012a, 2012b).

Weeks prior to the Games, the International Olympic Committee created The Olympic Athletes' Hub, a platform that brought together the activity of the athletes scattered up to that point throughout Facebook and Twitter. The platform was connected to the rest of the institution's presences, to the IOC webpage and to that of the organising committee of the London Games. The entire stream of publications from all the Olympic athletes who wanted to voluntarily sign up to the project was concentrated in the hub. To promote public engagement, competitions were held and prizes were given. Another element included in the Olympic Athletes' Hub was Inside the Olympic Village, through which live chat with the athletes was provided. The aim of the Olympic Athletes' Hub was that Olympic followers would see the different athletes' participation in Facebook and Twitter that was appearing in individual publications grouped together in one platform under the umbrella of the Olympic brand. The Olympic Athletes' hub clearly reveals that the kings of tracking on social networks are the athletes.

In turn, Facebook, Twitter and Google+ launched similar platforms. In the case of Facebook, it launched Explore London 2012, a hub uniting the athletes present on the platform and providing a view of all the updates of the athletes present on the social network as well as information about competitions, medals and photos of the history of the Olympic Games (Lunden, 2012a). The Twitter hub on the Games was the result of a collaboration with the channel broadcasting the Games exclusively for the North-American market, NBC Universal. This provided a space where the athletes' tweets were concentrated, along with participation by the public who were following the Olympic Games on television (Kelly, 2012). This collaboration between the social networking websites and the television channels, which also spread to Facebook, aimed to play with the synergies between television and social networks within the current culture of multitasking and to promote public participation by means of incorporating what is known as the Facebook Talk Meter into the screen of the television set in the rebroadcasting of NBC for the North-American audience.

The wide variety of new media channels, the consequent dispersion of messages and the resulting increase in participation rendered the experience of hubs necessary. They followed two philosophies: to bring together what had been dispersed, make it the main subject and position it under the powerful brand of the Olympic Games.

Facebook participation and contents

The participation of the public and their interaction with contents are, as we have outlined, differential elements of communication on social networks. Figure 14.1 shows a comparison between the participation levels on the Facebook pages of the Olympic Games and of the Olympic Games organising committees during the 2010 Vancouver Games and the 2012 London Games. There are three participation options for Facebook fans: press the "Like" button, write a comment on a publication or share it with friends. In the Vancouver Games the Facebook page did not provide data on the publications being shared; this novelty was introduced for London 2012. It can be observed that the main interaction users made with the official publications on Facebook was "Like". In all cases, this exceeded 80% of the total participation behaviour, with sharing contents being second. A large majority of the contents published on Facebook appear with a photograph and in no case were Facebook videos posted, which were published on the respective webpages and on the official YouTube channel. Figure 14.1 also shows how the level of participation via comments in London 2012 decreases compared to the data from Vancouver. The increase in shares does not balance this decrease in commenting, which is the most active form of involvement. This could be due to the concept of non-interactive unidirectional communication proposed on Facebook by both institutions, which have a similar consideration of social networks to that of traditional media (mass communication by the institution) without encouraging more active public participation in the form of comments or opinions.

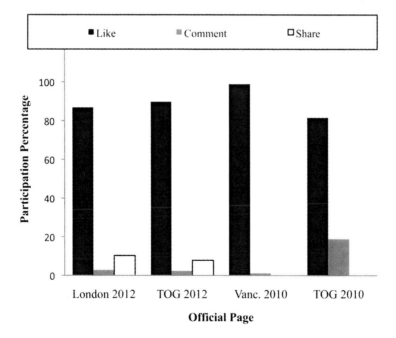

Figure 14.1 Percentages of participation in the official pages of London 2012, The Olympic Games (TOG), and Vancouver 2010, on Facebook

Source: Compiled by the authors using data taken from the Facebook page

Tables 14.1 and 14.2 provide a detailed summary of the participation figures on the previously mentioned Facebook pages.

The sample taken is of 29 days, one week prior to the Games and another week after the Games, to observe how the current situation of the competition and the global mega-event created by the television affected the growth patterns of the number of fans on Facebook and their participation. The section "Evolution of Likes Page" shows the figures of growth in the number of new fans in the 30 days prior to the Games. It can be observed that the number of "Likes" by fans the day before the start of the Games had multiplied seven-fold and remained in six figure numbers for three days. The closing ceremony of the Games also reveals a high percentage of participation, measured in Likes. These data are consistent with those of Vancouver 2010 in which, like in London 2012, participation in the form of Likes increased on the days on which the successful sports performances of athletes were held, through dedications on Facebook (Fernández Peña and Arauz, 2011).

Table 14.1 Participation in London 2012 page on Facebook

Day	Evolution of Like Page	Posts	Likes	Comments	Shares
Jul-18	190,873	3	19,652	3,150	4,775
Jul-19	204,761	3	18,650	593	3,090
Jul-20	231,717	2	28,155	647	6,098
Jul-21	245,969	2	7,951	319	888
Jul-22	265,541	3	19,567	662	3,977
Jul-23	282,886	2	20,702	541	4,918
Jul-24	301,755	3	10,060	301	1,827
Jul-25	323,285	5	35,941	1,079	6,490
Jul-26	367,942	2	8,195	410	1,610
Jul-27	663,952	2	26,365	467	6,467
Jul-28	872,966	5	107,715	4,780	14,117
Jul-29	976,925	6	136,851	2,287	14,272
Jul-30	1,066,131	5	79,311	2,448	11,813
Jul-31	1,127,596	4	27,002	904	3,105
Aug-1	1,158,267	5	94,694	7,930	10,482
Aug-2	1,163,405	4	37,316	856	5,430
Aug-3	923,148	5	67,550	1,125	5,275
Aug-4	789,874	5	119,999	3,326	16,414
Aug-5	768,646	5	101,560	4,239	12,399
Aug-6	707,499	3	31,506	575	3,570
Aug-7	665,049	5	70,667	1,560	4,076
Aug-8	627,249	3	16,711	668	1,453
Aug-9	645,345	7	106,041	3,980	14,391
Aug-10	660,602	5	72,349	1,100	4,799
Aug-11	636,951	5	95,534	2,240	10,217
Aug-12	818,614	7	225,297	5,242	24,787
Aug-13	876,843				
Aug-14	852,176				
Aug-15	829,993				
Aug-16	752,001				
Aug-17	631,561				
Aug-18	521,689	1	4,701	114	557

Source: Compiled by the authors using data taken from the Facebook page

Table 14.2 Participation in The Olympic Games page on Facebook

Day	Evolution of Like Page	Posts	Likes	Comments	Shares
Jul-18	534,298				
Jul-19	565,601				
Jul-20	742,324	4	42,342	668	1,717
Jul-21	765,990	3	15,838	555	1,976
Jul-22	834,916	4	26,281	432	3,726
Jul-23	860,952	3	31,855	537	3,118
Jul-24	1,267,027	8	31,003	900	2,942
Jul-25	1,799,463	4	29,951	767	1,637
Jul-26	1,959.430	4	35,854	906	4,449
Jul-27	2,420,369	8	219,25	3,912	19,005
Jul-28	2,674,323	12	241,534	8,404	35,060
Jul-29	2,801,536	14	184,816	5,854	10,439
Jul-30	2,120,320	13	90,732	1,903	9,000
Jul-31	1,903,546	6	88,643	2,637	4,754
Aug-01	1,725,891	9	190,206	3,445	10,770
Aug-02	1,454,804	2	71,686	1,892	5,378
Aug-03	1,356,976	6	114,468	1,956	5,871
Aug-04	1,186,305	9	172,206	5,091	13,509
Aug-05	1,235,875	10	103,951	5,846	8,527
Aug-06	1,354,870	4	37,566	1,069	2,119
Aug-07	1,098,361	5	87,345	3,111	14,463
Aug-08	932,564	3	30,927	412	2,107
Aug-09	1,013,914	10	112,043	2,510	6,230
Aug-10	1,208,533	7	112,366	2,763	12,827
Aug-11	1,637,931	7	81,567	2,030	5,851
Aug-12	2,129,402	8	168,436	4,329	16,484
Aug-13	2,285,661	4	134,319	3,340	15,855
Aug-14	1,278,326				
Aug-15	769,308				
Aug-16	541,913				
Aug-17	420,921	2	38,806	438	2,084
Aug-18	293,876				

Source: Compiled by the authors using data taken from the Facebook page

Table 14.3 shows the content of the posts of the two main presences of the Olympic movement on Facebook, specifically the pages of the London Organising Committee for the Olympic Games (London 2012) and the IOC (The Olympic Games, TOG).

Tributes to the different sports (Olympic Sport) received the highest number of posts on The Olympic Games page (33), and recognition of the athletes became a topic of great interest for both pages on the social networks (53 in total). In the case of London 2012 there was a higher number of contents dedicated to information on the sports venues (Event venue info, 18), Final results info (7), promotion of the city through iconic photos (Host city, 18 posts), and there is no reference to the sale of tickets as occurred in the case of Vancouver (Fernández Peña and Arauz, 2011). For the Olympic Games, the presence of the IOC on Facebook, the portrayal of The Olympic atmosphere (27), the promotion of the Hub of Athletes, a new IOC initiative

Table 14.3 Type of contents on the official pages of London 2012 and The Olympic Games (TOG) on Facebook

Content	London 2012	TOG
Final results info	7	–
Event venue info	18	6
Ticket sales	–	–
Athletes' recognition	23	29
Olympic sport	13	33
Volunteers	1	2
Sponsors	1	–
Olympic symbols	9	8
Mascots	1	1
Ceremonies	8	17
Host city	18	9
Olympic atmosphere	3	27
Questions	5	22
Contests	–	1
Live chats	–	5
Link to hub	–	9
Total posts	107	169

Source: Compiled by the authors using data taken from the Facebook page.

linking to athletes' comments and tweets (Link to Hub, 9), as well as motifs on the opening and closing ceremony (Ceremonies, 17) comprised the majority of the contents.

To sum up, the Olympic Games Facebook page concentrated on global aspects of the Olympic Summer Games as a four-yearly event, such as its symbols, opening and closing ceremonies, the dissemination of Olympic sports and the role of athletes. In contrast, the London 2012 Facebook page had a more local perspective, focusing on the event and the city in particular, and paying special attention to up-to-date information about the sporting events and the promotion of London. Both pages – the Olympic Games and London 2012 – expressed their recognition of the athletes and volunteers.

Assessment and future challenges

In barely four years since the first alliance of the Olympic Games with a social media to create the official Olympic Games channel on YouTube, and two and a half years since the inauguration of the presence on Facebook and Twitter, the role of communication on social networks in the communication strategies of the Olympic family has developed in various aspects. Unlike the approach used in Vancouver 2010 in which the Twitter and Facebook presences operated independently, London 2012 saw a more systemic and combined approach with presences on different platforms and an attempt to have the different presences and Olympic actors integrating and collaborating. While in Vancouver 2010 many of the so-called Top Sponsors were not present on the social networks as such, in London a lot of them created specific pages and played with interaction with the athletes, leaders in the tracking of these networks, and made the most of the social networks to promote their presence in the Olympic brand.

Despite the cross-pollination between social networks and web platforms being better exploited, participation has a notable unidirectional nature, very similar to that of traditional media, with a low percentage of contributions based on commentaries. However, spreadability is increasing, as demonstrated by the fact that many users now share Olympic Family member's publications with their friends. By doing so, content is reaching a higher number of people, including those who have not previously shown any interest in the Olympic Games.

The participation promoted in the public is merely emotional. The aim is not that people following the social networks of the Olympic movement and its members contribute to the progress and improvement of the Olympic movement. This is particularly important during the Olympiad, the period between Games, a period in which contributions from the public should be promoted by means of a more sincere and direct communication, counting elements that are usually not counted, including followers or fans of the new future challenges, converting them into missionaries who spread the philosophy and values of the Olympic movement. The publication rules for social media established by the IOC comprise an essential response to the challenge of the changes brought about in the forms of communication with the advent of social networks. The need to put order into the athletes' freedom of expression has too many limitations, particularly on the two previously mentioned grounds: ethical, which could be considered acceptable if we believe that, at a mega-event like the Olympic Games, the Olympic values of friendship, excellence and fairplay should reign supreme, and that the sole protagonist should be sport; and financial, if we believe that protecting television rights holders and sponsors should be adapted to the new, diverse social media reality where everyone is a broadcaster with enormous potential to gain a following, which is particularly the case for certain athletes. It is also important to remember the secular spiritual aspect of individual participation and improvement that lies in the foundations of the Olympic movement. If we limit participation in social networks to a mere marketing tool expressing empty emotion, lacking transcendence and soul, with no capacity to build and improve, we are not using the role of sport and the Olympic movement as a tool for change and human excellence. Social media seem to be a suitable instrument for this noble proposal.

References

Balfour, A. (2012, August 13) London Olympic and Paralympic Games: Time Digital Report. *Slideshare*. Retrieved from www.slideshare.net

Basich, T. (2010, February 26) Social Media Analysis: The 2010 Winter Olympics. *Mashable*. Retrieved from www.mashable.com

Boyd, D.M. and Ellison, N.B. (2007) Social network sites: Definition, history, and scholarship. *Journal of Computer Mediated Communication,* 13(1), 210–230.

Christakis, N.A. and Fowler, J.H. (2009) *Connected: The Surprising Power of Our Social Networks and How They Shape Our Lives.* New York: Little, Brown and Company.

Fernández Peña, E. (2009a) Olympic Summer Games and Broadcast Rights. Evolution and Challenges in the New Media Environment. *Revista Latina de Comunicación Social,* 64, 1.000–1.010. La Laguna, Tenerife: Universidad de La Laguna. doi: 10.4185/RLCS-64-2009-876-1.000-1.010-Eng

Fernández Peña, E. (2009b) Beijing Olympic Games: Mass media and the role of the internet. [Lecture in the 49th Session for Young Participants]. *International Olympic Academy.* Ancient Olympia, Greece.

Fernández Peña, E. and Arauz, M. (2011) Social Networking and the Olympic Movement: Social media analysis, opportunities and trends. *Centre d'Estudis Olímpics.* Universitat Autònoma de Barcelona, p. 333 [Report commissioned by the International Olympic Committee].

Fernández Peña, E. and Lallana del Río, I. (2011) Television and the Olympic Games: Symbiosis, globality and the construction of meaning. In Fernández Peña, E., Cerezuela, B., Gómez, M., Kennet, C. and de Moragas Spà, M. (ed.), *An Olympic Mosaic: Multidisciplinary Research and Dissemination of Olympic Studies, CEO-UAB: 20 Years* (1st edn.). Barcelona: CEO-UAB and Ajuntament de Barcelona, pp. 133–42.

Fernández Peña, E. (2011) New Media and the Olympic Games: The Olympic Movement and the Social Web in the dissemination of messages. In E. Fernández Peña, B. Cerezuela, Gómez, M., Kennet, C. and de Moragas Spà, M. (ed.), *An Olympic Mosaic: Multidisciplinary Research and Dissemination of Olympic Studies, CEO-UAB: 20 Years* (1st edn.). Barcelona: CEO-UAB and Ajuntament de Barcelona, pp. 143–52.

Huot, A. (2010) *Sharing the Olympic magic with fans* [Facebook blog]. Retrieved from http://www.facebook.com/blog/blog.php?post=298571017130

Hutchins, B. and Mikosza, J. (2010) The Web 2.0 Olympics: Athlete blogging, social networking and policy contradictions at the 2008 Beijing Games. *Convergence: The International Journal of Research into New Media Technologies*, 16(3), 279–297

International Olympic Committee (IOC) (2011) *The Olympic Charter: In Force as from 8 July, 2011.* Lausanne, Switzerland: IOC. Retrieved from http://www.olympic.org/Documents/olympic_charter_en.pdf

International Olympic Committee (IOC) (2012a) *London Olympic Games Marketing: Media Guide.* Lausanne, Switzerland: IOC.

International Olympic Committee (IOC) (2012b) *IOC to Live Stream London 2012 in 64 Territories on its YouTube Channel.* Lausanne, Switzerland: IOC.

International Olympic Committee (IOC) (2012c) *IOC Social Media, Blogging and Internet Guidelines for Participants and Other Accredited Persons at the London 2012 Olympic Games.* Lausanne: IOC. Retrieved from http://www.olympic.org

International Olympic Committe (IOC) (2012d) *Olympic Athletes Hub.* Retrieved from http://hub.olympic.org/

Jenkins, H. (2006) *Convergence Culture* (1st American edn.). New York: New York University Press.

Jenkins, H., Li, X., Korpf, K. and Green, J. (2008) *If it Doesn't Spread It's Dead: Treating Value in a Spreadable Market.* Cambridge, MA: Convergence Culture Consortium. Retrieved from www.educat.dsm.usb.ve

Kelly, A.M. (2012, July 24) How tweet is Twitter's Olympics hub plan? *Forbes.* Retrieved from http://www.forbes.com/sites/annemariekelly/2012/07/24/how-tweet-is-twitters-olympics-hub-plan/

Kim, W., Jeong, O. R. and Lee, S.W. (2010) On Social Websites. *Information Systems*, 35(2), 215–236.

Koop, N. (2011) International Olympic Committee President Jacques Rogge Video chats via chinese social media Weibo. *NESN.* Retrieved from www.nesn.com

Lopez, A. (2012, March, 3) A new social media strategy for the Olympics, Future sporting events can adopt today. *Forbes.* Retrieved from http://www.forbes.com/sites/adrianalopez/2012/08/03/a-new-social-media-strategy-the-olympics-future-sporting-events-can-adopt-today/

Lunden, I. (2012, July 19) IOC gets social with new Olympics hub integrating Instagram, Facebook, Google +, Twitter, Tumblr, Foursquare. *Techcrunch.* Retrieved from www.techcrunch.com

Lunden, I. (2012, June 18) Facebook's Social Olympic Ambition, Explore London 2012: A dedicated Athlete Portal, But No Ads. *Techcrunch.* Retrieved from www.techcrunch.com

Miah, A., García, B. and Zhihui, T. (2008) We are the media: Non-accredited media and citizen journalist at the Olympic Games. In M.E Price and D. Dayan (eds). *Owning the Olympics: Narratives of the New China* (pp. 320–345). Ann Arbor, MI: The University of Michigan Press.

Musial, K. and Kazienko, P. (2012) Social networks on the Internet (pp. 3– 27) *World Wide Web*, 16(1), 31–72. doi:10.1007/s11280-011-0155-z

Payne, M. (2006) *Olympic Turnaround.* Westport, CT: Praeger Publishers

Rooney, B. (2012, August 16) Social media proves gold for promoting athletes. *Wall Street Journal.* Retrieved from http://blogs.wsj.com/tech-europe/2012/08/16/social-media-proves-gold-for-promoting-athletes/

Silverman, C. (2010) Inside the social media strategy of the Winter Olympic Games. *Mediashift.* Retrieved from www.pbs.org

15

SPORTS MARKETING AND NEW MEDIA

Stephen W. Dittmore and Shannon T. McCarthy

UNIVERSITY OF ARKANSAS

The world of marketing is an ever-changing landscape. At the dawn of the marketing era, marketers reached consumers through traditional channels such as print media, radio spots, and elaborate television commercials. Today, consumers are bombarded with messages through traditional channels, but also myriad new, and more specifically directed vehicles such as text messaging, email, social media and customized Internet advertising. The landscape is saturated with media messages from every conceivable angle. From television commercials to in-show and stadium advertising to billboards and signs, media marketing is impossible to avoid. The simple act of tuning into network television guarantees the presence of advertisements. Sport marketers have increasingly looked to a relationship marketing approach to their job to identify ways to make their product stand out in the mind of the consumer and new media enhances the consumers' ability to build an association in their mind (Bee and Kahle, 2006).

New media defined

Historically, the term *media* referred to television and radio (electronic); magazines, newspapers, and books (print) (Baym *et al.*, 2012). Traditional media focuses on a user's exposure to a given media and the delivered content. As times and technology have changed, so has the definition of media. Today, media encompasses traditional forms, but has expanded to include avenues like blogs, social networks, and video games.

Previously, organizations competed against one another for the attention of traditional media with the hope of utilizing these communication channels to freely distribute information about the organization to large audiences; a process defined as publicity, or free media (Stoldt, Dittmore and Branvold, 2012). As the definition of media has expanded, organizations have more options for connecting with target consumers.

New media is the merging of traditional media forms with interactive digital technology, with a focus on interactivity with the customer. This content can and should be personalized for each individual consumer (Dittmore, Clavio and Miloch, 2012).

Social media or user generated media are other frames for viewing new media. Each definition incorporates interactivity and technology. Social media encompasses online information created, initiated, circulated and used by consumers intent on educating each other about products, brands, services, personalities, and issues (Blackshaw and Nazzaro, 2004, as cited in

Mangold and Faulds, 2009). User generated media is content "produce[d], design[ed], publish[ed], or edit[ed]" by the consumer (Krishnamurthy and Dou, 2008: 1). It is divided into two categories: rational and emotional. Rational content includes knowledge-sharing and advocacy, whereas emotional content focuses on social connections and self-expression.

Without question, new media thrives on social or interactive components. Dittmore *et al.* (2012) explained the importance of this "metapersonal connection," – in that "sports fans are increasingly interested in electronically mediated personal engagement from their sources of sports entertainment, in addition to (or as opposed to) face-to-face personal engagement" (p. 185). The authors elaborate, suggesting:

> Fans want to feel special and appreciated by the athletes and teams that they follow, and they look upon new media as a vehicle for such interaction. While such a relationship would have been impractical from both the fan perspective and the sport figure's perspective prior to the arrival of the new media age, the capabilities of digital, interactive technology have made such connections possible.
>
> *(Dittmore et al., 2012: 185)*

The task of providing interactive personalized messages to consumers is where new media has had the greatest impact in marketing. Organizations are no longer forced to rely on traditional media to deliver publicity as tools exist for organizations to bypass those systems. It is with this in mind that former *Financial Times* writer Tom Foremski is often credited with developing the notion that in today's digital climate, every company is a media company, or EC=MC.

> Every company is a media company because every company publishes to its customers, its staff, its neighbors, its communities. It doesn't matter if a company makes diapers or steel girders, it must also be a media company and know how to use all the media technologies at its disposal. While this has always been true to some extent, it is even more important today, because our media technologies have become so much more powerful.
>
> *(Foremski, 2010, paras 3–5)*

Foremski argues the norm in marketing is now a two-way communication process. Whereas traditional one-way communication focused on providing accurate and favorable information to relevant stakeholders, two-way communication emphasizes interaction and dialogue (Stoldt *et al.*, 2012). The challenge for marketers is having this two-way communication messaging stick with customers and other stakeholder groups, a process which will be discussed later in this chapter.

Relationship marketing

First coined in 1983, relationship marketing is attracting, maintaining, and enhancing customer relationships (Berry, 1983). Simply, it is about using an exchange, or relationship, with stakeholders to cultivate and grow customer-organizational bonds and strengthen brand loyalty, leading to increased sales. As Milne and McDonald (1999: 143) presciently noted, "marketers who want to be successful in the future must constantly be listening to their customers, gathering information on the types of products they want and services they desire." Brand loyalty is essential in sport because the quality of the product changes year to year. Sport marketers should focus on building strong relationships with their customers.

While the Internet in its current form did not exist in the 1980s or 1990s when Berry and Milne and McDonald initially studied relationship marketing, as marketing has shifted toward social media and building customer relationships, it has become more relevant.

Bee and Kahle (2006) proposed a model of relationship marketing in sport which is useful to apply when considering new media tools. These authors applied three levels of social influence to relationship marketing in sport: compliance, identification, and internalization. The identification level is most applicable here. Identification is maintained if the relationship is viewed as relevant and attractive. The sport organization must continually provide the consumer with the desired self-esteem functions, reinforcement or enhancement, and be attractive to the consumer.

According to Berry (2002), relationship marketing is most relevant when several factors are in play: (a) an ongoing and periodic desire for the service by the customer; (b) the ability for the customer to control the selection of the supplier; and (c) the existence of alternative suppliers creating frequent customer switching. Further, Berry states that these factors exist in most service firms as very few services are single-use services and the customer has several service providers from which to choose.

As sport is not a one-time buy for spectators, but can be viewed as a continual service, relationship marketing is exceptionally relevant for sport marketers. Sports provide unique challenges, due to the nature of the business and the changing quality of the product. The core services that sport marketers sell are fandom, an intangible asset, and the game day experience, a limited and perishable product. Berry (2002) considers the ideal core service to be the service that actually "attracts new customers through its need-meeting character, cements the business through its quality, multiple parts, and long-term nature, and provides a base for the selling of additional services over time" (p. 63).

From the time the tickets are purchased to the arrival at the stadium on game day to the in-game experience, marketers aim to provide the best fan experience to help grow the relationship. Fullerton (2007: 385) argues "this loyalty may result in a fan's insistence to attend a specific sporting event, even when alternative entertainment options are available." However, as not all fans are able to attend games on a regular basis, building strong relationships helps grow the desire for the service in ways aside from traditional game day attendance.

Brand loyalty is a fundamental element of relationship marketing. According to Fullerton (2007), longer fan–team relationships lead to a stronger bond. Fans are more likely to take negative occurrences in stride, as they are keen to protect the long-standing fandom relationship. That emotional bond is echoed in fan loyalty. The more highly committed the fan is to the team, the stronger the emotional bond. Relationship marketing understands success involves attracting and maintaining customers over an extended period of time and the cost of maintaining relationships is smaller than the cost of attracting new fans (Fullerton, 2007).

Using new media in concert with sport fan motives

Research on fan identification suggests individuals who identify with a successful team or player exhibit high levels of self-esteem. This concept, known as Basking in Reflected Glory, or BIRGing, and its counterpart, Cutting Off Reflected Failure, or CORFing, present simultaneous challenges and opportunities for sport marketers (Campbell, Aiken and Kent, 2004). Wann, Melnick, Russell and Pease (2001) identified eight primary motives why spectators claim their fandom, or motivation to consume sport. These motives include escape, economic, eustress, self-esteem, group affiliation, entertainment, family, and aesthetics. Please see Chapter 2 of this volume for a more thorough discussion of sport fandom.

Sport fan motivation factors that influence BIRGing behavior appear to be determinants of conative (behavioral intentions) loyalty (Trail, Anderson and Fink, 2005). Because the sport fan decides through what avenues to pursue their fandom, understanding which motives are most common is an easy way for marketers to develop plans which will increase revenue. In fact, Mahony, Howard and Madrigal (2000) showed BIRGing behavior leads to increased merchandise and media consumption, along with increased attendance.

New media tools can be utilized to enhance spectator interaction with the brand, hopefully creating improved loyalty and desired purchase behaviors. Some popular examples of these tools include free ticket giveaways and social media days.

Many organizations have given away free game tickets through Twitter, sometimes referred to as "TwitTix", to fans replying to an organizational Twitter account or physically meeting up with an organizational representative at a location announced via the organization's Twitter account. Shaquille O'Neal was one of the pioneers in this in 2009 when he Tweeted "I'm at the fashion sq mall, any1touches me gets 2 tickets, tag me and say yur twit u hv 20 min" (SHAQ, 2009). Other sport organizations have adopted similar giveaways (D'Andrea, 2008; Peck, 2009).

Similarly, McNeese State University engaged its fans base in new media interactivity when it hosted a Social Media Day in advance of a women's basketball game against rival Nicholls State on January 23, 2012. The athletic department blacked out its website and directed users to social media in an attempt to increase the number of "likes" and followers on McNeese social media sites. News and information was posted only on Facebook and Twitter for that day. As incentive, fans interacting via social media were given the opportunity to win a number of prizes including season tickets for sporting events and gift cards to area restaurants (Ivey, 2012). The results of this new media-only approach was an 11.6% increase in "likes" on the athletic department's Facebook page and a 3.5% increase in the number of followers to its Twitter account. The effort also generated 50 new database entries (Ivey, 2012).

Major League Baseball has also employed social media nights as a way to increase fan interaction. While no two social media nights are exactly the same, there are commonalities like specially priced tickets for online fans, specific hashtags to market the event, and contests to win prizes (Associated Press, 2012b). The Kansas City Royals recently added a social media night to their lineup of promotions, which included a social hour with pitcher Danny Duffy, an exclusive @Royals t-shirt, and $10 in concessions or merchandise credit (Kansas City Royals Publicity Department, 2012). For teams struggling for attendance growth, connecting with fans in ways that appeal to younger demographics may be a way to hold the short attention span of today's ADHD population.

The Cubs utilized a similar approach by dedicating specific seat blocks at games and promoting special giveaways for those attending the event. After the immense success of the Cubs' first Social Media night, the Cubs opted for a second Social Media night, which included a free t-shirt chosen by fans, access to a special pre-game event with media which included the chance to win the opportunity to throw out the first pitch, a hashtagged specialty hot dog selected by social media followers, and a Pinterest contest leading up to the event (Bleacher Nation, 2012).

While each sport league's season is different, one commonality among all sports is the fans' desire to attend games. As sport marketers, the job is to create a product unlike the competition and make each and every game a special experience, regardless of the team's quality. Owners and coaches are responsible for the year-to-year quality and marketers have no control over a team's record. Building a strong relationship based on sport fan motivations can stem the loss in ticket sales among fair weather fans. However, ticket sales do not tell the whole story of the sports team–fan relationship. In sport, the definition of service includes anything from in-person game attendance to television viewership to purchasing and wearing team-branded gear as a way to gain social acceptance to actively engaging in social media through Facebook likes and Twitter posts.

Historically, the Chicago Cubs have been a heartbreaking team for fans, starting each season optimistically, before spiraling into a perennial Major League footnote. Oddly, they still manage to sell out games, are regularly in the top 10 for Major League Baseball season attendance, and have only failed to crack 3 million in attendance twice between 2003 and 2012 (ESPN, 2012). The Cubs build strong fan identity and attendance desire regardless of the product quality, due to the longstanding relationships they have built with their fans. To help grow and strengthen the desire to view games, the Cubs have maintained an active and positive presence in Chicago, which has helped stem some of the drop off from disappointed fans. Cubs' pitcher Kerry Wood started the Wood Family Foundation to shepherd grassroots giving initiatives in the city of Chicago (Wood, 2012). A longtime Cub, Wood recognizes the value the city places on giving and athletes making a positive difference in the city.

Using multiple new media platforms to engage the brand

As mentioned previously, fans tend to exhibit periods of BIRGing or CORFing, based on the fortunes of their associated team or player. Since product quality fluctuates, marketers also need to compete against alternative suppliers of entertainment for the attention of spectators. While competition exists in the form of television broadcasts, radio play-by-play, Internet broadcasts, and social media newsfeeds, sport marketers often focus their efforts on increasing or main-taining ticket sales. Due to the availability of tickets and attendance costs, it is common for customers to change their usage patterns, depending on the supply of the good and varying demand. Sport marketers should focus on creating an environment for customers to access content wherever they are located, or risk losing customers.

For example, organizations should consider developing portable interactivity with a fan regardless of if the fan is watching in the stadium, in a bar with 40 of their closest friends, or watching the game at home on their couch. New media is a strong avenue to build this rela-tionship wherever the fan is located. The MLB PrePlay app allows fans to predict outcomes of plays and games in real time, score points for correct predictions, and tracks points and stand-ings to allow users to challenge their friends at the game (Major League Baseball, 2012). Fans feel connected to the game, regardless of their location. They can connect with like-minded fans and grow the discussion and relationship. For teams looking to grow their fan base, new media can support active growth outside of the geographical area, increasing demand for addi-tional supply outlets.

The University of Oregon spent the better part of the past two decades working to build the national presence of the Ducks. Though not a traditional powerhouse, Oregon built itself into an appealing brand, partially due to strong connections with Nike. Nike regularly makes sizable donations to the University's athletic department and consistently redesigns the Ducks' uniforms with innovative designs, functional elements, and flash that recruits want on their jerseys. Phil Knight's money helped build and elevate the Oregon brand to the national stage and ESPN's Colin Cowherd has reported the Oregon Ducks are second in brand popu-larity to only the University of Florida Gators (Duin, 2011). The Ducks have gone so far to embrace social media as to create the "Quack Cave," an on-campus social media hub designed to monitor and grow the social media brand of Oregon (Stites, 2012). The visibil-ity of the department was made clear on January 2, 2012, when the term "Oregon helmet" was the number one worldwide trending topic on Twitter (Stites, 2012). Celebrities are often seen wearing Duck gear, including LeBron James, Jack Black, and Snoop Dogg, with James calling the uniforms the "best in all of college football" (Stites, 2012). Most of these celebrities are not alumni; they simply choose to be fans. Celebrity brand endorsements have been used for decades, but social media allows celebrities to put their stamp of approval on brands and reach millions of fans with the quick typing of 140 characters, irrespective of whether they are paid spokespeople.

A final example of creating ongoing engagement with the brand is the successful "Summer Social" cross-platform new media marketing initiative run by the University of Louisville in 2012. The campaign used the school's mascot, Louie the Cardinal, to engage fans on a different social media site, including Pinterest, YouTube, Facebook, Twitter, and Instagram, on each day of the week. Louisville boasted it had "one of the 30 largest social media followings among NCAA Division I schools" and offered "exclusive insights and interactive contests . . . to connect with the Cardinals" (Louie the Cardinal, 2012).

The school's director of social media, Nick Stover, deemed the Summer Social campaign a success, as "it kept fans entertained. It helped direct people to these different sites they may not have otherwise used. It gave them something to talk about during the slow time of the summer" (Stover, as quoted in Ramos, 2012).

Louisville was so pleased with results of the summer campaign, it began a similar campaign in Fall 2012 titled "Collect the Cards" which focused on driving fans to the Facebook and Twitter pages of all the Louisville sport teams. The school identified three goals for the Collect the Cards campaign: improve content on the athletic department's web site, work on overall branding, and provide social media support to all teams (Ramos, 2012).

Blending concepts

As established previously, demand for the sport product fluctuates and fans of a particular organization have the ability to choose alternate suppliers for their entertainment dollars. One way for marketers to mitigate this churn and maintain long-term relationships with their stakeholders is by creating unique messages, which stand out amid an ocean of marketing images.

Baym *et al.* (2012) argued that the hallmark characteristics of new media are portability, interactivity, and ubiquity. These mirror the relationship marketing factors discussed above, which were ongoing desire for the product (ubiquity), customer controls (interactivity), and alternative suppliers (portability). Table 15.1 illustrates this relationship between the research from Berry and Baym *et al.*

Today's sports fans want access to desirable content on their schedule and not just during the 11:00 local news broadcast or the next morning's newspaper. The ability of marketers to generate fresh messages and content can cement relationships with consumers. In addition, the ability to deliver those messages across multiple platforms speaks to the portability and ubiquity characteristics of new media.

Major League Baseball took notice of the utility of this new form of media and began incorporating it into their games and marketing programming. During the 2012 All-Star game, MLB Public Relations (@MLB_PR) tweeted that "through 1st inning, 290K+ social media comments related to #ASG, already surpassing total from entire 2011 #ASG" (MLB_PR, 2012). The clear rise in social media engagement from 2011 to 2012 showcases the general public's embracing of the media, as well as MLB's successful marketing integration.

Table 15.1 The relationship between the research from Berry and Baym *et al.*

Berry's (2002) relevant relationship marketing factors	Baym et al.'s (2012) characteristics of new media	Interpretation	Sport marketing example
Ongoing desire for the service	Ubiquity	Marketers need to make content available across a broad range of platforms	University of Louisville's Summer Social
Customer controls selection of the supplier	Interactivity	Marketers should focus on brand building through engagement with fans	Social media days
Alternative suppliers exist and switching is common	Portability	Customers want to be able to engage with brands wherever they are. Failure to create this may result in churn	MLB PrePlay app

Using new media to create brand ambassadors

Hogshead (2010) emphasized the importance of interactivity for marketers, stating "the more people want to engage with, play with, learn from, talk about, and, above all, connect with something or someone, the greater its social currency" (p. 42). A key component to increasing social currency, according to Hogshead, is to create messages that fascinate and inspire others to market your organization for you. "For marketers, it's not about marketing a message – it's about getting the market to create messages about you" (p. 44).

The notion of using new media to create brand ambassadors has proven particularly effective for several sport organizations. Prior to the 2010 season, the Cleveland Indians, working with Digital Royalty, created a "one-of-a-kind social media experience providing attendees both stunning views of the on-field action and the ability to network in their own private, Wi-Fi enabled suite" (Indians Social Suite Application, n.d.). To apply, fans are required to describe their social media use, and on which new media sites they actively post. Additionally, applicants are asked to describe, in 140 characters or less, why they should attend a game in the Indians' Social Suite and their favorite Indians memory.

As Fisher (2010) noted, during the game fans are encouraged to share their experiences on their social media networks, within parameters set forth by the Indians and MLB. In explaining the objective for this social media area, Indians Director of Communications and Creative Services, Curtis Danburg, said the club was doing it, in part, to sway public opinion. "Our target audience right now is pretty negative [on the club], and we need to do everything we can to engage them. We need to be very active in this space, and part of that conversation that is happening" (Danburg, as quoted in Fisher, 2010).

By creating this social suite and allowing fans to attend and discuss their experience via social media, the Indians have effectively used new media to develop relationships with some of their most highly identified fans while simultaneously empowering them to share their positive experiences about the Indians.

The NBA's Oklahoma City Thunder has employed a different approach to using new media to create its brand ambassadors, a group known as the Blue Alliance. The Thunder identifies the

Blue Alliance as "an organization of fans who have committed themselves to spreading the Thunder spirit throughout the state" (Blue Alliance, n.d.). Fans starting a local chapter of the Blue Alliance in their hometown are known as Blue Alliance Captains and receive benefits including a game ticket and Thunder yard flag. In exchange, Captains organize community Thunder watch parties, monitor a community fan Facebook page, and assist with promotional initiatives in their community (Blue Alliance, n.d.).

The brand ambassador concept can even expand to individual athletes. One Major League Baseball athlete who was quick to embrace Twitter was Logan Morrison, a left-fielder for the Miami Marlins. In 2011, just halfway through his first major league season, he had more than 26,000 Twitter followers, which often eclipsed the Marlins actual in-stadium attendance numbers (ESPN News Service, 2011). By September 2012, @LoMoMarlins had accumulated more than 123,000 followers (https://twitter.com/LoMoMarlins).

An increasingly popular approach to creating brand ambassadors in college athletics has been the growing trend of placing a university-specific Twitter hashtag on the field, to encourage fans and viewers of that particular team to utilize the hashtag when tweeting. This evolution began during the 2011 college football season and has expanded throughout college athletics.

Mississippi State's athletic director Scott Stricklin is an active user of Twitter to engage fans and generate support for the university. In anticipation of its annual rivalry game with Ole Miss, Mississippi State aimed to become a trending topic on Twitter, by becoming the first college football team to put a hash tag, #HAILSTATE, on its field (Laird, 2011).

While it may have seemed faddish during fall 2011 to hashtag a field, once spring football games rolled around, many major college football teams were hashtagging their field, in an attempt to promote their team on Twitter. Teams utilizing hashtags at their spring games included Michigan (#GOBLUE), Arkansas (#GOHOGS), and North Carolina State (#gopack) (Associated Press, 2012a; Kirk, 2012; Sallee, 2012).

University of Arkansas Athletic Director Jeff Long, a major proponent of social media, said in a statement regarding the 2012 spring game on-field hashtag,

> The hashtag on the field is just another example of our commitment to engaging our fans with the Razorbacks through social media. It is a simple way for our fans to show their support for our team and the student-athletes representing the University of Arkansas. We have one of the largest social media followings in the country among intercollegiate athletic programs. We will continue to work on building our fan followings on Twitter, Facebook and other outlets as a way to further connect with our fans.
>
> *(University of Arkansas Athletic Media Relations, 2012)*

Like an increasing number of athletic directors, Long recognizes the value of new media and its utility in strengthening a connection with fans.

In early 2013, Hendon FC, a 7th Division soccer club in the United Kingdom, donated the shirt sponsorship on its home jersey to a soccer charity, Street League. The Hendon shirt began featuring the charity's hashtag, #ChangeLivesThroughFootball a program designed to help unemployed 16–25 year olds in the United Kingdom. Hendon's chairman Simon Lawrence noted the arrangement helps develop a relationship with the charity and with fans as well. "We applaud the hard work being done at Street League and want to be a part of it" ("Hendon FC donate," 2013, para. 7).

Ambushing the competition: Guerilla marketing at work

Guerilla warfare involves smaller militia-type gangs doing battle with larger, stronger, better-maintained fighting forces. Because they are not as well armed, militias must innovate to play to their strengths and translate their opponent's strengths into weaknesses. Smaller groups tend to be faster, more adaptable, and more willing to fight dirty. Marketers utilize these same tactics when going up against larger organizations. Guerrilla, or ambush, marketing is "the planned effort (campaign) by an organization to associate themselves indirectly with an event in order to gain at least some of the recognition and benefits that are associated with being an official sponsor" (Sandler and Shani, 1989: 11). Organizations attempt to piggyback their marketing campaigns off of larger events without paying a licensing or advertising fee to the larger organization. While an organization cannot claim to be a sponsor of an event if they are not, they can attempt to associate their product or services through the careful use of imagery, sponsorship of related athletes, or thematic similarity in events.

A prime example of ambush marketing in media is Subway's airing of commercials leading up to and during the Olympics. Subway is a notable sponsor of Olympian Michael Phelps. While Subway does not officially sponsor the Olympics, prior to the Vancouver Games, Subway produced ads showing Phelps swimming towards Vancouver, subliminally aligning themselves with the Games. "Rule 40," as it is known, precludes athletes, coaches, trainers, and officials who are participating in an Olympic Games from publically endorsing any brand or product that is not an official sponsor of the Games during the period immediately before, during, and after the Games (London Organising Committee of the Olympic Games and Paralympic Games Limited, 2011). Subway does not use currently competing athletes during their respective Games, which is how they skirt Olympic sponsorship rules. Michael Phelps appears in advertisements surrounding the Winter Olympics, while athletes like Robert Griffin III and Shaun White are used during summer Games.

Recently, teams have begun ambush marketing using Twitter. During the 2012 NBA play-offs, the NBA heavily promoted the #NBAPlayoffs hashtag in all of their broadcast and marketing materials (Scibetti, 2012). However, Edge Shave Zone and Degree Men both utilized Promoted Tweets (tweets advertisers pay to reach a broader audience) that appeared in searches for #NBAPlayoffs. As Degree is not the official deodorant of the NBA, this presents a problem for the NBA and the sponsors paying for the privilege of being the "official" product of the NBA. While no one can own a hashtag, it raises questions as to who is responsible for protecting marketing efforts and advertising contracts within the social media realm.

As social media has gained popularity over the past several years, marketers have come to see it as a viable avenue to gain market share and grow brand awareness. For one, social media is either free or relatively inexpensive when compared to the cost of commercial airtime. For small organizations, this is crucial, as most teams cannot sink millions of dollars into marketing. According to Awareness, Inc., 57% of marketers surveyed do not actually specifically allocate financial resources for social media; they simply rely on their "people resources" (Awareness, Inc., 2012). Additionally, regardless of size, most companies (74%) utilize one to three people for their social media efforts.

A second reason for social media's popularity among marketers is the ability to connect with millions of fans with ease. While an increasing number of companies see social media as a way to generate new sales, the top three measures of return on investment for marketers are still the number of fans and followers, traffic to the organization's website, and mentions across different social media platforms (Awareness, Inc., 2012). While generating sales is important in a more retail driven business, sport is different. Not every sport fan is able to go to games on a regular basis, due to the location, distance, and game time; and sporting events can still be viewed on television, streamed online, or followed through real-time event updates.

Conclusion

Relationship marketing has shown itself to be one of the best routes to build long-standing customers for organizations (Berry, 2002). Due to the growth and prevalence of new media, sport marketers are expected to find ways to connect with fans and consumers in new and innovative ways. From smartphone apps to exclusive content through social networks to the incorporation of social media into actual events, organizations both large and small are working to connect with their targeted customer base to build and strengthen those relationships.

Successful sport marketers are achieving these results by creating dynamic messages that stand out in a crowded marketplace and by encouraging its fan base to interact with the organization. The results indicate sport marketers have been successful at engaging fans to become brand ambassadors for their favorite organizations.

References

Associated Press (2012, April 13) Michigan putting hashtag on field. *ESPN College Football.* Retrieved from http://espn.go.com/college-football/story/_/id/7806192/michigan-wolverines-add-

Associated Press (2012, May 19) Social networking comes to the ballpark. *The New York Times.* Retrieved from http://www.nytimes.com/2012/05/20/sports/baseball/major-league-baseball-embracing-twitter-and-facebook.html?_r=4&pagewanted=all

Awareness, Inc. (2012) *State of Social Media Marketing Annual Survey Report.* Retrieved from http://info.awarenessnetworks.com/The-State-Of-Social-Media-Marketing.html

Baym, N., Campbell, S. W., Horst, H., Kalyanaraman, S., Oliver, M., Rothenbuhler, E. and Miller, K. (2012) Communication theory and research in the age of new media: A conversation from the CM Café. *Communication Monographs,* 79(2), 256–267. doi:10.1080/03637751.2012.673753

Bee, C. C. and Kahle, L. R. (2006) Relationship marketing in sports: A functional approach. *Sport Marketing Quarterly,* 15, 102–110.

Berry, L. L. (1983) Relationship marketing. In L. L.Berry, G. L. Shostack and G. Upah (eds), *Emerging Perspectives on Services Marketing* (pp. 25–28). Chicago, IL: American Marketing Association.

Berry, L. L. (2002) Relationship marketing of services: Perspectives from 1983 and 2000. *Journal of Relationship Marketing,* 1(1), 59–77.

Bleacher Nation (2012, September 14) Cubs hosting second social media night on Monday, September 17, 2012. Retrieved from http://www.bleachernation.com/2012/09/14/cubs-hosting-second-social-media-night-on-monday-september-17-2012/

Blue Alliance: A Thunder state of mind (n.d.) Retrieved from http://thunder-nba.com/promotions/bluealliance/

Campbell, R. M., Aiken, D. and Kent, A. (2004) Beyond BIRGing and CORFing: Continuing the exploration of fan behavior. *Sport Marketing Quarterly,* 13, 151–157.

D'Andrea, N. (2008, Nov 21) Shaq and the Suns give game tickets away on Twitter. *Phoenix New Times.* Retrieved from http://blogs.phoenixnewtimes.com/valleyfever/2008/11/shaq_and_the_suns_give_game_ti.php

Dittmore, S. W., Clavio, G. and Miloch, K. S. (2012) Promotional mix, public relations, and emerging technologies. In B. L. Parkhouse, B. A. Turner and K. S. Miloch (eds), *Marketing for Sport Business Success* (pp. 173–192). Dubuqe, IA: Kendall Hunt Publishing Company.

Duin, S. (2011, Sept 24) Showing the University of Oregon some love. *Oregon Live.* Retrieved from http://www.oregonlive.com/news/oregonian/steve_duin/index.ssf/2011/09/showing_the_university_of_oreg.html?mobRedir=false

ESPN (2012) *MLB Attendance Report- 2012* [data file]. Available from http://espn.go.com/mlb/attendance

ESPN News Service (2011, June 2) *Logan Morrison a Hit on Twitter.* Retrieved from http://sports.espn.go.com/mlb/news/story?id=6611550

Fisher, E. (2010, April 19) A true bleacher nation: Indians unveil new social media effort. *Sports Business Daily.*

Retrieved May 4, 2010, from http://www.sportsbusinessdaily.com/Daily/Issues/2010/04/Issue-150/Franchises/Atrue-Bleacher-Nation-Indians-Unveil-New-Social-Media-Effort.aspx

Foremski, T. (2010, March 30) *Welcome – when every company is a media company*. Retrieved September 25, 2012 from http://www.everycompanyisamediacompany.com/every-company-is-a-media-/2010/03/welcome-when-every-company-is-a-media-company.html

Fullerton, S. (2007) *Sports Marketing*. New York: McGraw-Hill/Irwin.

Hendon FC donate home shirt sponsorship to football charity Street League until the end of the season (2013, February 21) Retrieved from http://www.times-series.co.uk/sport/10240512. Hendon_donate_shirt_ sponsorship_to_football_charity/

Hogshead, S. (2010) *Fascinate: Your 7 Triggers to Persuasion and Captivation*. New York: Harper Collins.

Indians Social Suite Application (n.d.) Retrieved September 25, 2012, from http://cleveland.indians.mlb.com/cle/fan_forum/social_suite.jsp

Ivey, R. (2012, Feb. 7) *Social Media Day*. Retrieved Feb. 15, 2012, from http://www.nacmaonlinelibrary.com/best-practices/social-media-day

Kansas City Royals Publicity Department (2012) *Royals host Social Media Night on August 1* [Press release]. Retrieved from http://mlb.mlb.com/news/article.jsp?ymd=20120720&content_id=35245502&vkey=pr_kc&c_id=kc

Kirk, J. (2012, April 21) *Photo: N.C. State's Field Hashtag the Most Prominent Yet This Year*. Retrieved from http://www.sbnation.com/ncaa-football/2012/4/21/2965022/photo-n-c-states-field-hashtag-the-most-prominent-yet-this-year

Krishnamurthy, S. and Dou, W. (2008) Advertising with user-generated content: A framework and research agenda [Note from special issue editors]. *Journal of Interactive Advertising*, 8(2), 1–4.

Laird, S. (2011, November 22) *First Football Endzone Hashtag Touches Down in Mississippi*. Retrieved from http://mashable.com/2011/11/22/football-twitter-hashtag/

London Organising Committee of the Olympic Games and Paralympic Games Limited (2011) Rule 40 Guidelines. Retrieved from http://www.london2012.com/mm/Document/Publications/General/01/25/29/32/rule-40-guidelines_Neutral.pdf

Louie the Cardinal (2012, June 14) *Louie the Cardinal Announces Summer Social Media Plan*. Retrieved from http://www.gocards.com/genrel/061412aad.html

Mahony, D. F., Howard, D. R. and Madrigal, R. (2000) BIRGing and CORFing behaviors by sport spectators: High self-monitors versus low self-monitors. *International Sports Journal*, 4, 87–106.

Major League Baseball (2012) *MLB PrePlay*. Retrieved from http://mlb.mlb.com/mlb/fantasy/preplay/index.jsp?partnerId=aw-8555600837734882690-107.

Mangold, W. G. and Faulds, D. J. (2009) Social media: The new hybrid element of the promotion mix. *Business Horizons*, 52(4), 357–365.

Milne, G. R. and McDonald, M. A. (1999) *Sport Marketing: Managing the Exchange Process*. Sudbury, MA: Jones and Bartlett.

MLB_PR (2012, July 10) Through 1st inning, 290K+ social media comments related to #ASG, already surpassing total from entire 2011 #ASG. @MLBONFOX [Twitter post]. Retrieved from https://twitter.com/MLB_PR/status/222857816388538369

Peck, J. (2009, Feb 26) *Timberwolves using Twitter for Ticket Giveaway* [Blog post]. Retrieved from http://www.jasonfpeck.com/2009/02/26/timberwolves-using-twitter-for-ticket-giveaway/

Ramos, R. (2012, Sept. 6) *Louisville Implements Inventive Strategies to Engage Year-round*. Retrieved from http://sportsjournalism.org/sports-media-news/louisville-implements-inventive-strategies-to-engage-year-round/

Sallee, B. (2012, April 19) *Arkansas Football: Razorbacks to Paint Twitter Hashtag on Field for Spring Game*. Retrieved from http://bleacherreport.com/articles/1152521-arkansas-football-razorbacks-to-paint-twitter-hashtag-on-field-for-spring-game

Sandler, D.M. and Shani, D. (1989) Olympic sponsorship vs. "ambush" marketing: Who gets the gold? *Journal of Advertising Research*, 29(4), 9–14.

Scibetti, R. (2012) Guerrilla marketing by hashtag. Retrieved from http://www.thebusinessofsports.com/2012/05/02/guerrilla-marketing-by-hashtag/?utm_source=feedburner&utm_medium=feed&utm_campaign=Feed%3A+thebusinessofsports2+%28The+Business+of+Sports%29

SHAQ (2009, Feb 24) I'm at the fashion sq mall, any1 touches me gets 2 tickets, tag me and say yur twit u hv 20 min [Twitter post]. Retrieved from https://twitter.com/SHAQ/status/1245950406

Stites, S. (2012, Oct 1) *How the University of Oregon became a #NationalBrand*. Retrieved from http://dailyemerald.com/2012/10/01/how-the-university-of-oregon-became-a-national-brand/

Stoldt, G. C., Dittmore, S. W. and Branvold, S. E. (2012) *Sport Public Relations: Managing Stakeholder Communication* (2nd edn.). Champaign, IL: Human Kinetics.

Trail, G. T., Anderson, D. F. and Fink, J. S. (2005) Consumer satisfaction and identity theory: A model for sport spectator conative loyalty. *Sport Marketing Quarterly*, 14, 98–111.

University of Arkansas Athletic Media Relations (2012) *UA to add Hashtag on Field for Red-White Game* [Press release]. Retrieved from http://www.arkansasrazorbacks.com/ViewArticle.dbml?DB_OEM_ID=6100&ATCLID=205416374

Wann, D. L., Melnick, M. J., Russell, G. W. and Pease, D. G. (2001) *Sport Fans: The Psychology and Social Impact of Spectators*. New York: Routledge Press.

Wood, K. (2012, Nov 23) Kerry Wood prepares for a season of charity. *Chicago Sun Times*. Retrieved from http://www.suntimes.com/lifestyles/splash/16541412-418/winding-up.html

16

WHEN CRISIS STRIKES THE FIELD

The evolution of sports crisis communication research in an era of new media

Natalie A. Brown and Kenon A. Brown

UNIVERSITY OF ALABAMA

Joshua Dickhaus

BRADLEY UNIVERSITY

Newspaper and website headlines, sports radio talk shows, and television sports news segments, are constantly updating sports fans about player lockouts, National Collegiate Athletic Association (NCAA) investigations, the arrests of star players, and other crises that face both collegiate and professional sports organizations. Coombs (2012: 4) states that a crisis "disrupts or affects the entire organization or has the potential to do so." Recent cases such as the Penn State University sex abuse scandal and the New Orleans Saints bounty scandal that offered monetary incentive for inflicting injuries upon opposing players show the far-reaching negative consequences that can result from such crisis situations, affecting both game performance and a sporting organization's overall reputation. When a crisis strikes, a sports organization must immediately employ carefully orchestrated crisis response strategies in order to minimize the impact on the organizational reputation. However, recent trends in communication technology, namely the rise of social media websites, alter the delivery and content of the traditional organizational crisis response.

In the new era of social media, sports organizations have, in many ways, lost some of the control they once possessed over the crisis narrative. In many instances, organizations no longer control the dissemination of their own messages by planning news releases around broadcast and print news deadlines. Rather, one simple Tweet, Facebook post, Instagram photo, or YouTube video can propel an event or story to become "viral" in minutes. Coombs (2012) acknowledges that social media is driven by user-generated content, placing much control and power in the hands of average stakeholders. No longer can organizations simply feed their key stakeholders information; rather, active stakeholders desire more interaction and connectivity, especially during times of crisis. Audiences are no longer passive recipients of messages designed by organizations; rather, they are now active, and sometimes aggressive, information-seekers who desire instant information (Stephens and Malone, 2009). This new environment makes it crucial for organizations to ensure that their stakeholders will be advocates and spokespersons on behalf of the organization on their social media accounts.

Perhaps no organization has more engaged and active stakeholders than sports-affiliated organizations and athletes. Sports fans are driven by their sense of connection to their team (Wann, 2006), leading them to utilize the power afforded to them by social media to drive the conversation. Several studies have examined organizational crisis response (e.g. K. Brown and White, 2011; Coombs and Holladay, 2008; Fortunato, 2008), but few have considered how social media outlets have allowed fans to adopt and implement similar response strategies on behalf of the organization or sports figure with which they identify.

This chapter will begin by examining the role of crisis response in the crisis communication process, and explore two predominant crisis response theories: Benoit's Image Repair Theory (IRT) and Coombs' Situational Crisis Communication Theory (SCCT). After we provide the theoretical background, we will discuss the evolution of the study of crisis response in sports and social media's role in sports crisis response. Finally, we will examine how the rise of social media should serve as a catalyst for an expansion of crisis response literature, providing a new theoretical lens through which scholars can better examine sports crises.

Crisis response

A major component of crisis communication management is the actual crisis response – how a sports organization or athlete reacts to a crisis through statements and behaviors. Once a crisis hits, the crisis manager and his or her team must work to prevent the crisis from further affecting internal and external stakeholders, as well as mitigating the crisis as soon as possible to prevent further damage (Mitroff, 1994). For example, when Greek Olympian Voula Papachristou tweeted a racially insensitive comment, the Greek Olympic Committee expelled her from their roster. In response to this crisis, Papachristou deleted the tweet and immediately posted an apology to prevent further damage. Mismanagement of organizational crisis response can cause major problems for an organization or athlete's financial success, image, reputation and survival (Fearn-Banks, 2007).

The content of crisis response has been divided into a sequential order of three categories: (1) instructing information, (2) adjusting information and (3) reputation management (Coombs, 2007a; Sturges, 1994). Instructing information tells people affected by the crisis how to protect themselves physically and financially from the crisis (Barton, 2001). Adjusting information is information that helps the people affected by a crisis cope psychologically (Coombs, 2007a). The final stage of crisis response content, reputation management, is the most investigated component of crisis response content, although instructing and adjusting information must be provided before the organization can begin providing responses designed to repair its reputation (Coombs, 2007a).

Crisis response strategies

The crisis response strategy typologies from Benoit's Image Repair Theory (IRT) and Coombs' Situational Crisis Communication Theory (SCCT) have been the predominant typologies used in reputation management research. Two key assumptions guide Benoit's (1995) IRT: (1) communication is a goal-directed activity, and (2) maintaining a favorable image is one of those goals. Based on a synthesis of previous literature rooted in apologia theory, self-defense rhetoric and rhetorical response to guilt, Benoit (1995) gives 14 image restoration strategies, organized into five categories: denial, evading responsibility, reducing offensiveness, corrective action, and mortification. Table 16.1 gives a detailed list of these strategies. The denial strategies

Table 16.1 Benoit's (1995) Crisis Response Strategies based on Image Repair Theory

Categories	Strategies and explanations
Denial	• Simple denial
	Stating that the organization or individual did not perform the act in question
	• Shifting the blame
Evading responsibility	• Provocation
	Scapegoating, claiming the actions were provoked by the actions of another person or organization
	• Defeasibility
	Claiming the action was provoked by lack of information or misinformation
	• Accident
	• Good intentions
Reducing offensiveness	• Bolstering
	Stressing the positive traits of the organization or individual
	• Minimization
	Claiming the crisis is not as serious as the public or media perceives
	• Differentiation
	Making the act seem less offensive than the public perceives
	• Transcendence
	Places the crisis in a more favorable context
	• Attack the accuser
	• Compensation
Corrective action	• Corrective action
	Promising to correct the problem
Mortification	• Mortification
	Admitting the crisis was the organization's or individual's fault and asking for forgiveness

include the *simple denial*, which can evolve into *shifting the blame* onto another person or organization. When an organization cannot deny the actions, evading responsibility strategies help the organization avoid or reduce blame. Four strategies are present in this category: *provocation*, *defeasibility* or claiming the act was an *accident* or done with *good intentions*.

The organization can also try to reduce negative perception caused by the crisis. Benoit (1995) gave six strategies for reducing offensiveness: *bolstering, minimization, differentiation, transcendence, attacking the accuser* or *compensation*.

The final two categories have no variants. *Corrective action* involves the organization promising to correct the problem. Benoit (1995) stated that there are two forms of corrective action: restoring the situation to its state before the crisis or promising to prevent the recurrence of the crisis. *Mortification* involves the organization admitting the crisis was its fault and asking for forgiveness. These two strategies are often used together by apologizing for the crisis and vowing to fix the existing problem and preventing it from happening again.

Coombs' (2007a) reputation repair typology stems from the development of his Situational Crisis Communication Theory (SCCT). According to SCCT, in order to choose the correct response to a crisis situation, a crisis manager must first assess the initial degree of crisis responsibility placed on the organization. Then, based on the state of the organization's crisis history and relationship with its stakeholders, the degree of responsibility may increase. After the crisis and relationship history is determined, the crisis manager chooses the response based on the refined level of responsibility (Coombs, 2007b). SCCT reputation repair strategy typology was created through a synthesis of previous response typologies, including Benoit's (1995) IRT typology. Table 16.2 provides Coombs' (2007a) ten reputation repair strategies, which are clustered into four postures. The denial posture strives to remove any connections an organization has with a crisis. These include *attacking the accuser, simple denial* and *scapegoating*. The diminishment posture attempts to reduce attributions of organizational control and reduce negative effects of the crisis. These include *excusing* and *justification*. The rebuilding posture attempts to improve the organization's reputation. These include *compensation* and *apology*. Bolstering strategies seek to build a positive connection between an organization and its publics. These include *reminding, ingratiation* and *victimage*. It is recommended that the bolstering strategies should be used only in conjunction with other strategies to avoid a superficial perception placed on the organization because of the strategies' focus on the organization (Coombs, 2007a).

The rise of social media demanded its inclusion in crisis response. Coombs (2012) suggested three main rules when using online crisis communication channels: "(1) Be present; (2) Be where the action is; (3) Be there before the crisis" (p. 27). These rules suggest that organizations must commit to establishing a strong social media presence before a crisis strikes, ensuring the organization's ability to use these channels to filter selected crisis response strategies to stakeholders during the crisis response phase.

Crisis response in sports

The study of the use of response strategies in sport began with the rhetorical analysis of image repair strategies used in athletes' public statements for past incidents (Meyer, 2008). Kruse's (1981) initial analysis of sports image repair concluded that focusing on the topic was not important because fans were more interested in the success or failure of the team rather than character issues of their athletes. However, sports image repair has taken on greater importance because of the globalization of sports, increased news coverage of troubled athletes through

Table 16.2 Coombs' (2007) Crisis Response Strategies based on Situational Crisis Communication Theory

Crisis response postures and explanations	Crisis response strategies
Denial posture: Strives to remove any connections an organization had with a crisis	• Attacking the accuser • Simple denial • Scapegoating
Diminishment posture: Attempts to reduce attributions of organizational control and reduce negative effects of the crisis	• Excusing • Justification
Rebuilding posture: Attempts to improve the organization's reputation	• Compensation • Apology
Bolstering posture: Seeks to build a positive connection between an organization and its publics	• Reminding • Ingratiation • Victimage

traditional, new media and social media outlets, and also increased activism of sports fans (Meyer, 2008). These reasons stress a need for an athlete's image to be created, nurtured and defended to sustain a positive reputation with his/her stakeholders and fans (Brazeal, 2008).

Most rhetorical studies of the response to transgressions are analyzed using IRT; however, the majority of those cases examine an athlete's (individual) response to transgressions, rather than organizational response. The initial study was Benoit and Hanczor's (1994) analysis of Tonya Harding's defense of her image after people close to her attacked her teammate and rival, Nancy Kerrigan. During an interview, Harding used several bolstering strategies (including stressing her family values and her intent to contribute to the Special Olympics), denial of her participation, and attacking her primary accuser, ex-husband Jeff Gillooly. The researchers argued that these attempts were ineffective to repair her image with the public, however, primarily because Harding lied about her knowledge of the attack initially and the overwhelming amount of evidence against her.

Brazeal (2008) examined strategies used by Terrell Owens during his contract negotiations with and eventual suspension from the Philadelphia Eagles. Owens used mortification and bolstering strategies successfully during the negotiations. Once he was suspended, Owens unsuccessfully used shifting the blame strategies by attempting to make him look like a victim during the negotiations, which contradicted his earlier apology. This made Owens look like a hypocrite in the public eye, which provides an example of how choosing the wrong strategy can further damage an athlete's image.

K. Brown, Dickhaus and Long (2012) used Brazeal's (2008) study as context for an experiment to determine which strategy would be most effective in repairing LeBron James' image after he announced his future team during an hour-long ESPN special titled "The Decision." The image repair of LeBron James was studied not because of a legal issue or scandal, but because of a hit to his credibility due to his actions during his free agency and the negative public outcry that resulted. Results showed that mortification was the only strategy that improved James' image after the announcement, while the use of shifting the blame and bolstering strategies hurt his image. These strategies were chosen based on strategies used by Terrell Owens during his contract negotiations because it was a similar situation (Brazeal, 2008). James actually did utilize the mortification strategy when he apologized to Cleveland fans for leaving to join the Miami Heat (Klopman, 2011). Public disapproval of how James handled "The Decision" followed him through the 2012 NBA Playoffs, which resulted in the James's Miami Heat winning the NBA Championship. James, normally an avid social media user went silent on Twitter from April 27 until after the Heat's victory in June to concentrate on the playoffs. After claiming the championship, James broke his social media silence by tweeting, "OMFG I think it just hit me, I'm a CHAMPION!! I AM a CHAMPION!!"

Although the majority of cases examined athlete response to transgression, there are a few cases devoted to organizational response to crises in the sports arena. These cases have also been primarily rhetorical studies that have used IRT as the theoretical framework. For example, Fortunato (2008) examined internal communication used during the Duke Lacrosse scandal in an attempt to frame the story. Initially, the university used corrective action and mortification in an attempt to restore Duke's reputation after the arrests of lacrosse players on charges of sexual assault. The university then switched to a strategy of attacking the accuser once the certainty of evidence and victim's accounts, as well as the credibility of Durham District Attorney Mike Nifong was called into question.

Len Rios (2010) conducted a content analysis of news articles and internal documents from Duke University during the lacrosse scandal to determine which response strategies were used most frequently. Results were consistent with Fortunato's (2008) findings: the university initially relied on simple denial and mortification strategies, then engaged in bolstering, corrective action and attacking-the-accuser strategies to defend the university's image once credibility issues were discovered for the suspect and Nifong. The content analysis also showed that the attacking the accuser strategy resulted in the most positive media coverage.

The only study found that used Coombs' early theoretical development of the symbolic approach, which is the predecessor to SCCT (Coombs, 1995), was a study conducted by Williams and Olaniran (2002). The researchers used rhetorical analysis to examine the crisis response strategies used by Texas Tech University and the city of Lubbock, TX, after three members of the Hampton University women's basketball team were arrested and falsely accused of attempting a parking lot scam the day before a game between Hampton and Texas Tech. The study used Coombs' research on organizational crises to analyze the strategy used by Texas Tech to separate the university from the racially-charged scandal plaguing the city of Lubbock after the false accusations.

Bruce (2008) performed a textual analysis of news articles related to an Australasian men's rugby league scandal in which the Canterbury Bulldogs were accused of a salary cap breach of nearly $1 million. In the article, Bruce (2008) noted that a new crisis response strategy of *diversion* might be particularly useful for sports organizations involved in a crisis. Diversion allows sports organizations to capitalize on the intense, existing connection between fans and their favorite athletes when management's failures cause a crisis, as fans believe that athletes and management operate independently of one another. In the case of the Canterbury Bulldogs, the organization responded to allegations of gross financial mismanagement by consistently offering up the Bulldogs' players as innocent victims, thereby, minimizing the overall damage to the team. Thus, by protecting the source of fans' identification with a team, the players and coaches, "the organization ensured that the relationship with at least one key stakeholder group would continue" (Bruce, 2008: 113). This case provides a strong example of the importance of fans in sport-related crises, an importance that has only grown with the rise of social media.

Sport, crises, and social media

While it is well documented that crises can have a strong, negative impact on both athletes and sports organizations (Williams and Olaniran, 2002; Brazeal, 2008), the rise of new/social media has altered the manner in which crises develop and the practice of crisis response. Coombs (2012) noted that the Internet has seemingly increased the pressure felt by organizations in crisis, as the definition of what constitutes a "quick" crisis response has been altered to require a nearly instantaneous crisis response. Pew Internet and American Life (2006) found that during a crisis, the public's social media use actually increases, as they seek out additional information. As such, social media allows for a quick dispersal of information, especially during crises. Yet, Coombs (2012) warns this process can also perpetuate rumors through social networks in such a way that can develop crises or prolong existing crises. Yet, social media can aid crisis managers by providing tools that allow for immediate feedback from stakeholders, as well as efficient dispersal of follow-up information. Through the use of social media, organizations possess a direct link to stakeholders who have self-selected to receive information from the organization, ensuring that they care about the organization's message. For instance, the Ultimate Fighting Championship (UFC) President Dana White commented:

> Before [social media] if I was going to make an appearance somewhere, I would have to buy radio, online, newspaper, whatever, and you still wouldn't know if you were reaching the people that really care. But, 1.4 million people on Twitter opt in to

follow me. They go out of their way to say, 'I want to follow this guy. I want to know what is happening.' That's huge.

(Ortiz, 2011a: 1)

Since the rise of social media and its growing prominence in sports (Sanderson, 2011), several examples of both individual and organizational crises have been both created and managed online.

For professional and collegiate athletes, the rise of social networks provides additional opportunities to foster relationships with their fans. For example, Portuguese soccer star Cristiano Ronaldo uses social media to request photos and videos from his 54.9 million Facebook fans and 16.5 million Twitter followers, and also refutes any media falsehoods about him in order to alleviate potential crises. John Halpin (2012) comments that due to social media's prominence in sport, athletes with a large number of social media followers are no longer required to "court the media as much as [they] used to. [They] can just talk to fans [themselves], and that's a powerful shift in the communication paradigm" (p. 77). While this ability to directly address fans has certainly helped increase fan/athlete engagement (Sanderson, 2011), the unfiltered messages have also created crisis situations for both athletes and sport organizations.

In 2012, the Football Association (FA) banned and fined former England captain and Chelsea player, John Terry for a "racially-aggravated public order offense" (*The Telegraph*, 2012). The FA's decision followed the Westminster Magistrates Court's ruling that cleared Terry, largely in part to Terry's teammate, Ashley Cole's testimony regarding the incident. Yet, the FA felt that discrepancies in Cole's testimony warranted Terry's punishment. The ruling led Cole to lash out against the FA on Twitter by posting, "Hahahahaa, well done #fa I lied did I, #BUNCHOFTWATS." Cole quickly deleted the tweet; however, due to the large number of "retweets," the message quickly circulated online. The FA, then, cited improper conduct as it fined Cole £90,000, or the equivalent to $145,000, for his comments (*The Telegraph*, 2012). This incident prompted the FA to develop a new code of conduct that states that players "must not publish (on Twitter or Facebook) anything that may cause or embarrass a member of the FA, the England squad and management" (Witherington, 2012: 1). In addition to forbidding Tweets or Facebook posts involving any type of criticism, players were also forbidden from posting on social media the day before or the day of a match (Witherington, 2012).

The rise of similar crises that originate online led some sporting organizations to develop policies meant to regulate athlete social media use by fining athletes for tweets that violate the policies. The National Football League, National Basketball League, and National Hockey League all forbid athletes from posting to social media websites beginning in the hours leading up to games and ending after final media interviews conclude. Athletes from these leagues have also been fined for violations of social media policies. For example, Chad 'OchoCinco' Johnson was fined $25,000 for tweeting 77 minutes before his team, the Cincinnati Bengals, played the Philadelphia Eagles in a pre-season game (Ortiz, 2011b). In direct contrast, the Ultimate Fighting Championship, the leading promoter of Mixed-Martial Arts, supports a social media policy that, not only encourages, but actually pays fighters to engage their fans through social media by establishing a $240,000 social media incentive program (Ortiz, 2011a). UFC President Dana White uses social media during every UFC event for more than just fan engagement; he also uses social media for effective crisis prevention by constantly monitoring fan feedback. White scans Twitter during each event to confirm that UFC fans are not experiencing any pay-per-view outages or ticket problems (Ortiz, 2011a). Thus, when problems do arise, they are handled.

While sports crisis communication research has primarily focused on teams and players affected by a crisis situation (Len Rios, 2010; Brazeal, 2008), the rise of social media has increased the importance of a group of specialized, active stakeholders: sports fans. Coombs (2012) asserted that the audience-driven nature of social media allows stakeholders to create content that will be shared with their social networks, perhaps increasing the power of the average person. In the case of sports, social media has shifted a great deal of power to fans, who have a larger opportunity to interact with their favorite teams and athletes while, also, commenting on developing crises. This shift in power also places additional pressure on sports organizations in times of crisis, as fans now demand a nearly constant flow of information that updates them on any developing questions or concerns (Coombs, 2012).

N. Brown and Billings (2013) discovered a new area of crisis communication research, coining the term fan-enacted crisis communication. Essentially, sports fans possess a unique connection to their respective sports organization. Wann (2006) noted that fans have a unique psychological connection to their favorite sports teams and athletes that is directly connected to their own self-worth. When a crisis strikes a fan's preferred sports team, the resulting stress can cause them to search for a resolution to the situation, leading many fans to social media use.

Sanderson (2011: 72) asserted that "social media is a viable mechanism for people to display their fandom." Sports' inherent social nature has moved online, as many sports fans utilize social media websites to interact with other sports fans, athletes, and sports journalists, especially during times of crisis. Such websites have become the outlet to which fans flock to express their fandom. Since heavily identified sports fans are so connected to their teams and athletes, it should come as no surprise that these stakeholders possess a vested interest in protecting a team's reputation by using the tools at their disposal, primarily social media websites. Therefore, as an active stakeholder, a fan decides to speak out publicly about the crisis facing an organization, making the community an integral part of crisis response as they turn to social media websites to help shape the story.

Very few corporations or other organizations are so closely tied to a person's own personal sense of identity; therefore, he/she will not be prompted to act out on behalf of most organizations when they are attacked. For example, a sports fan's unique connection to a team makes them more likely to speak out on behalf of that team during times of crisis than a BP consumer would following the Gulf oil spill. Coombs (2012) stated that the rise of social media use has not created a revolution within crisis communication tactics, but has, instead, hastened the evolution of crisis response. While this might be true in corporate crisis response, the concept of fan identification clearly shows that fans have harnessed power afforded to them by social media to garner some control of an organizational crisis response (N. Brown and Billings, 2013).

Sanderson (2010) explored how Tiger Woods's fans harnessed the power social media afforded them following the disclosure of Woods's ongoing extramarital affairs that involved several mistresses. As the story continued to grow and develop, fans flocked to Woods's Facebook page to speak on his behalf. Sanderson (2010) purported that this practice of intervening on an athlete's behalf can, perhaps, heighten a fan's feelings of parasocial interaction toward a specific athlete. Sanderson (2010) also suggested that sports figures with a large social media following can benefit as fans "voluntarily perform public relations work" on their behalf, thus providing them with an "unprecedented means to generate support and promulgate favorable public representations (p. 449).

Social media has allowed active stakeholders to serve as unofficial spokespersons on an organization's behalf during times of crisis in which organizational response might be limited. For instance, policy states that NCAA member institutions will not formally comment on ongoing infractions cases (Katz, 2011). In 2011, the University of Miami faced egregious NCAA allegations, including providing thousands of dollars in impermissible benefits to players, illegal parties that included the use of illegal drugs and prostitution, and the funding of an abortion. While the university's official comments were limited, fans' comments were not. N. Brown and Billings (2013) performed a content analysis of University of Miami fan tweets and found that fans engaged in traditional crisis communication response strategies as defined by Coombs (2007a), primarily the attack the accuser, reminder, and ingratiation strategies. Thus, sports fans became an unofficial arm of the university's crisis response. Coombs (2012) stated that viral messages likely originate from average people. This was certainly seen in Miami's case, where fans were able to insert their own positive message among the negative headlines being circulated about the University of Miami. Through a fan-generated effort, thousands of fans tweeted one uniting message, the Twitter hashtag "#IStandWithTheU," causing it to trend nationwide.

N. Brown, Billings and Brown (2013) further explored the concept of fan-enacted crisis communication through an examination of Penn State fan tweets following the Penn State sex abuse scandal in which former assistant coach Jerry Sandusky was found guilty of 45 counts of child abuse. This study attempted to determine which existing crisis response typology, Benoit (1995) or Coombs (2007a), was better suited to examine fan-enacted crisis response. While neither typology was able to encompass all fan response strategies, Coombs' (2007a) was selected due to its ability to encompass a large majority of fan responses. Analysis of Penn State fan tweets showed that they, also, engaged in traditional crisis response strategies, namely the reminder, ingratiation, and scapegoat strategies. However, it is interesting to note that instead of acting on behalf of the university, Penn State fans scapegoated the Penn State administration, even more often than Jerry Sandusky, himself. Fans seemed to be more highly identified with their legendary coach, Joe Paterno, which prompted them to defend him, even at the cost of their university.

While it is apparent that fans have harnessed much power from social media's rise in popularity, it is imperative that organizations understand that this power-shift has occurred. In 2012, the social media manager for the NFL's Kansas City Chiefs sent a direct message on Twitter to Travis Wright, a disgruntled fan who had previously tweeted disparaging comments about Kansas City's owner, Clark Hunt. Wright tweeted, "I'm not much of a @kcchiefs fan anymore. Clark Hunt's yearly 30m under the cap [expletive] is unethical. Greedy bastard owners can F.O. cc @nfl." Kansas City responded by tweeting, "Would help if you had your facts straight. Your choice to be a fan. Cc: get a clue." Unfortunately, Kansas City's social media manager vastly underestimated the power of sports fans, as Wright, himself is a social media manager for a Silicon Valley company and had more Twitter followers than the Kansas City Chiefs account (Laird, 2012). Thus, Wright screen-captured Kansas City's response and posted it on Reddit, the self-proclaimed "front page of the Internet," causing the message to go viral and forcing Kansas City's account to issue Wright an apology (Laird, 2012). This case provides one example of how sports fans' increase in power due to the availability of social media can create crises for sports organizations if ignored.

Overall, the Tiger Woods, Miami, Penn State, and Kansas City Chiefs cases showed that fans grasp the power provided to them by social media to engage in crisis response. Yet, this concept shows the importance of fan identification when determining the manner in which sports fans will engage in crisis response. In the case of Miami, the institution drew the fan's loyalty along with their crisis response strategies; however, in the case of Penn State, fans were more highly identified with Joe Paterno than the institution itself, leading them to turn on the institution in favor of Paterno. Yet, in both cases, fans utilized similar strategies found in Coombs (2007a).

The reminder and ingratiation strategies were used to unite the fan bases and remind them of the schools' accomplishments. Both fan bases also utilized an "attack" strategy. In Miami's case, they "attacked the accuser," Nevin Shapiro; whereas, Penn State fans searched for a scapegoat, blaming the sports media, university administration, and Jerry Sandusky. Since both studies have clearly shown that fans are utilizing social media websites to engage in crisis response, it is important to determine the effectiveness of fan-enacted crisis communication. Further research should explore the power that fan-enacted crisis communication possesses to impact the public perception of a sports organization or individual facing a crisis.

Expanded Sports Crisis Communication Theory

Studies have shown that traditional crisis communication theories such as Benoit's IRT and Coombs' SCCT can be applied in the realm of sports (e.g. Brazeal, 2008; N. Brown and Billings, 2013; K. Brown, Dickhaus and Long, 2012; Fortunato, 2008). Although the majority of rhetorical research used IRT as a theoretical lens – and N. Brown, Billings and Brown (2013) noted that SCCT's reputation repair strategies seemed to fit better than IRT strategies to analyze fan response – neither crisis theory provided an ideal theoretical lens to examine sports crises. It is clear that sports organizations and corporations face very different challenges during times of crisis, eliciting different response strategies. Also, the rise of social media has given prominence to sports fans that have claimed their role as active stakeholders, engaging, themselves, in crisis response.

As sports crises occur more frequently because of the immediacy of new media and social media outlets, as well as the ease and willingness for these outlets to report stories that were non-crises 20 years ago, both sports and crisis communication scholars should more closely examine them through a crisis communication theoretical framework that is tailored to sports-related events. Scholars must recognize that sports crises are quite different from corporate and organizational crises, which served as the foundation for SCCT and individual and political crises, which were the foundation for IRT. Ideally, the theoretical framework should be modeled after Coombs' SCCT theory, as it encompasses a list of crisis types, a typology of crisis response strategies, and a theoretical linkage between the two. In order establish a sports-specific theory, a new typology of crisis type should be created. Coombs' (2007a) list of crisis types is clearly geared toward corporations and business and is not applicable to classify sports crises. For example, Coombs' (2007a) list includes events such as product tampering and defective products, which are not necessarily crises that an athlete or sports team would face. After creating a new typology of crisis type, existing crisis response strategies such as Benoit (1995) and Coombs (2007a) should be synthesized through case studies and content analyses, including only response strategies that are relevant to resolving sports-related crises. Finally, studies using experimental and survey design should test the theoretical linkages between the two typologies.

The creation of sports-specific crisis communication theoretical framework would both improve and increase the validity of sport crisis communication research. Coombs (2012) recognized that each crisis situation is unique and should be examined as such. Thus, it is no longer prudent for scholars to assume that corporate-focused crisis communication theories can be adequately applied to very different crisis situations.

Given the recent growth of social media, a sports-specific crisis communication theoretical framework would give scholars a tool to analyze this new form of fan involvement. The concept of fan identification in sports allows key stakeholders to become involved in the crisis response, a phenomenon that is not as likely to enter into the corporate environment. In fact,

Coombs (2012) noted that the rise of social media might lead to more crises for corporations due to opportunities for increased surveillance. Yet, the trend in sports seems to involve active stakeholders becoming an unofficial arm of organizational crisis response (N. Brown and Billings, 2013). While studies have determined that fans do engage in traditional crisis communication response strategies, a sports-specific crisis communication theoretical framework would help to better understand the response strategies that they are most likely to use, helping both scholars and practitioners better understand this new type of involvement.

References

Barton, L. (2001) *Crisis in Organizations II*. Cincinnati, OH: College Divisions South-Western.

Benoit, W. (1995) *Accounts, Excuses, and Apologies: A Theory of Image Restoration Strategies*. Albany, NY: State University of New York Press.

Benoit, W. and Hanczor, R. (1994) The Tonya Harding controversy: An analysis of image restoration strategies. *Communication Quarterly*, 42, 416–433.

Brazeal, L. (2008) The image repair strategies of Terrell Owens. *Public Relations Review*, 34, 145–150.

Brown, K., Dickhaus, J. and Long, M. (2012) "The Decision" and LeBron James: An empirical examination of image repair in sports. *Journal of Sports Media*, 7, 149–167.

Brown, K. and White, C. (2011) Organization-public relationships and crisis response strategies: Impact on attribution of responsibility. *Journal of Public Relations Research*, 23, 75–92.

Brown, N. A. and Billings, A. C. (2013) Sports fans as crisis communicators on social media web sites. *Public Relations Review*, 39(1), 74–81.

Brown, N., Billings, A.C. and Brown, K. (2013, April) 'May no act of ours bring shame': Fan enacted crisis communication surrounding the Penn State sex abuse scandal. Paper presented at the conference for Broadcast Education Association, Sports Division, Las Vegas, NV.

Bruce, T. (2008) Unique crisis response strategies in sports public relations: Rugby league and the case for diversion. *Public Relations Review*, 34(1), 108–115.

Coombs, W. (1995) Choosing the right words: The development of guidelines for the selection of the appropriate crisis response strategies. *Management Communication Quarterly*, 8, 447–476.

Coombs, W. (2007a) *Ongoing crisis communication: Planning, managing and responding*. Thousand Oaks, CA: Sage.

Coombs, W. (2007b) Protecting organization reputations during a crisis: The development and application of situational crisis communication theory. *Corporate Reputation Review*, 10, 163–176.

Coombs, W. (2012) *Ongoing crisis communication: Planning, managing and responding* (3rd edn.). Thousand Oaks, CA: Sage.

Coombs, W. and Holladay, S. (2008) Comparing apology to equivalent crisis response strategies: Clarifying apology's role and value in crisis communication. *Public Relations Review*, 34, 252–257.

Fearn-Banks, K. (2007) *Crisis Communications: A Casebook Approach*. Mahwah, NJ: Lawrence Erlbaum Associates.

Fortunato, J. A. (2008) Restoring a reputation: The Duke University lacrosse scandal. *Public Relations Review*, 34(2), 116–123.

Halpin, J. (2012) Using social media to reach stakeholders. In G. C. Stoldt, S. W. Dittmore and S. E. Branvold, *Sport Public Relations: Managing Stakeholder Communication* (2nd edn.). Champaign, IL: Human Kinetics, pp. 77–8.

Katz, A. (2011, Aug. 23) Ex-Miami coaches in limbo at new schools. *ESPN.com*. Retrieved from http://espn.go.com/mens-college-basketball/blog/_/name/katz_andy/id/6888175.

Klopman, M. (2011) LeBron apologizes to Cleveland, explains "The Decision." *Huffington Post*. Retrieved from http://www.huffingtonpost.com/2011/05/12/lebron-james-apologizes-decision_n_861073.html.

Kruse (1981) Apologia in team sport. *Quarterly Journal of Speech*, 67, 270–283.

Laird, S. (2012) Dissed fan teaches NFL Team a social media lesson on Twitter. *Mashable*. Retrieved from http://mashable.com/2012/09/12/nfl-fan-chiefs/.

Len-Rios, M. (2010) Image repair strategies, local news portrayals and crisis stage: A case study of Duke University's lacrosse team crisis. *International Journal of Strategic Communication*, 4, 267–287.

Meyer, K. (2008) An examination of Michael Vick's speech of apologia: Implications for the study of sports apologia and image repair. *Conference Papers – National Communication Association*, 1. Retrieved from http://www.ebscohost.com

Mitroff, I. (1994) Crisis management and environmentalism: A natural fit. *California Management Review*, 36, 101–111.

Ortiz, M. B. (2011a) Dana White leads UFC into social realm. *ESPN.com*. Retrieved from http://sports.espn.go.com/espn/page2/story?page=burnsortiz/110606_ufc_dana_white.

Ortiz, M. B. (2011b) Guide to leagues' social media policies. *ESPN.com* Retrieved from http://espn.go.com/espn/page2/story/_/id/7026246/examining-sports-leagues-social-media-policies-offenders.

Pew Internet and American Life (2006) *Blogger callback survey*. Retrieved from www.pewinternet.org.

Sanderson, J. (2010) "The nation stands behind you": Mobilizing social support on 38pitches.com. *Communication Quarterly*, 58(2), 188–206.

Sanderson, J. (2011) *How Social Media is Changing Sports: It's a Whole New Ballgame*. New York: Hampton Press.

Stephens, K. K. and Malone, P. C. (2009) If the organizations won't give us information…: The use of multiple new media for crisis technical translation and dialogue. *Journal of Public Relations Research*, 21(2), 229–239.

Sturges, D. (1994) Communicating through crisis: A strategy for organizational survival. *Management Communication Quarterly*, 7, 297–316.

The Telegraph. (2012) Ashley Cole brands the FA as a 'bunch of t – – ' in Twitter rant after written reasons for John Terry ban revealed. *The Telegraph*. Retrieved from http://www.telegraph.co.uk/sport/football/teams/chelsea/9589621/Ashley-Cole-brands-the-FA-a-bunch-of-t – in-Twitter-rant-after-written-reasons-for-John-Terry-ban-revealed.html

Wann, D. L. (2006) The causes and consequences of sport team identification. In A. A. Raney and J. Bryant (eds), *Handbook of sport and media* (pp. 331–352). Mahwah, NJ: Lawrence Erlbaum Associates.

Williams, D. and Olaniran, B. (2002) Crisis communication in racial issues. *Journal of Applied Communication Research*, 30, 293–313.

Witherington, L. (2012) England's FA gives players new rules on social media. *The Wall Street Journal*. Retrieved from http://online.wsj.com/article/SB10000872396390444734804578062641765330554.html

17

COMMUNICATING CORPORATE SOCIAL RESPONSIBILITY IN SPORT ORGANIZATIONS

Incorporating new media

Melanie Formentin

PENNSYLVANIA STATE UNIVERSITY

Kathy Babiak

UNIVERSITY OF MICHIGAN

Beyond the win and loss columns, sports provide a venue for encouraging fandom and a sense of community. Sports can provide space for rallying communities in crisis – such as in the aftermath of Hurricanes Katrina and Sandy (Freeman, 2013; McDonnell, 2012) – and for creating traditions that bind fans as friends and family (Branscombe and Wann, 1991). Recently, sport organizations have started embracing their role as central members of the communities in which they operate. Through philanthropic and charitable endeavors, sports leagues and teams are increasingly being positioned as organizations that contribute more than the pleasure of athletic competition. Statements by the National Football League's (NFL) Roger Goodell reveal that his league provides annually $10 million in grants, runs a $150 million NFL Youth Football Fund, and has encouraged "the NFL, its teams, players, and fans" to donate millions of dollars in emergency relief support (National Football League, 2011). Similarly, David Stern of the National Basketball Association (NBA) stated that "there is a fundamental belief throughout our organization and our teams that we have an obligation to be leaders in social responsibility. In some ways, the government agencies don't do the same job they used to do. So sports has an opportunity to lead by calling attention to certain issues, whether we're building houses or working hard to develop places where kids can learn and play" (Leaders Magazine, 2012, para. 12). It is apparent that corporate social responsibility (CSR) has become integral to sport organization operations.

The central idea behind CSR is that corporations have an obligation to work for social betterment (Frederick, 2006). The *Corporate Social Responsibility Initiative* at Harvard University defines CSR as "encompass(ing) not only what companies do with their profits, but also how they make them. It goes beyond philanthropy and compliance and addresses how companies manage their economic, social, and environmental impacts, as well as their relationships in all key spheres of influence: the workplace, the marketplace, the supply chain, the community, and the public policy

189

realm" (Harvard Kennedy School, 2013, para 1). Research on CSR has started examining the discrete benefits that activities such as philanthropy, community outreach, cause-related marketing, employee volunteer programs and other socially beneficial activities have on an organization and its constituents. Benefits range from customer loyalty and other positive post-purchase behaviors (Bhattacharya and Sen, 2003), to increased employee loyalty and retention (De Schutter, 2008), to benefits for nonprofit partners of the firm (Noble, Cantrell, Kyriazis and Algie, 2008).

In recent years CSR has extended beyond philanthropic efforts to use as a strategic management practice. CSR is being defined by its "underlying strategic purpose (e.g. legitimacy, responsibility for social externality, competitive advantage), by its drivers (e.g. market, social regulation, soft government regulation), and by its manifestations (economic, legal, ethical, discretionary)" (Chapple and Moon, 2005: 416). Porter and Kramer (2006) advocate a strategic approach to managing CSR by mapping the social impact of its various value chain activities to identify opportunities for the firm to reduce the negative ones and find positive openings to achieve social and strategic distinction. This strategic dimension of CSR has gained increasing relevance (Hess and Warren, 2008; Pohle and Hittner, 2008; Porter and Kramer, 2006) to leverage the most value for the business and to serve as a platform for sustainable growth and differentiation while serving as "insurance" for future misdeeds (Gardberg and Fombrun, 2006; Godfrey, 2005). A key strategy for reaping the benefits of CSR is to communicate and articulate the socially responsible efforts of the firm. Indeed CSR is used as a tool for marketing, branding and identity building. Bonini, Mendonca and Oppenheim (2006) suggest that CSR awareness and communication tactics should be incorporated into core strategic decision-making processes to avert long-term financial and reputation risks, to find opportunities for development of products or marketing strategies, and to allow the firm to gain stability by anticipating change in unstable environments.

The sports industry in particular is one that engages with CSR on all these levels. Over the past decade, CSR has become a central function for sport organizations (Babiak and Wolfe, 2009; Breitbarth and Harris, 2008; Breitbarth, Hovemann and Walzel, 2011; Inoue, Kent and Lee, 2011; Sheth and Babiak, 2010; Walker and Kent, 2009; Walters, 2009; Walters and Anagnostopoulos, 2012; Walters and Tacon, 2010). Sport businesses engage in CSR by investing and allocating organizational resources in key areas including labor relations, community relations, philanthropy, diversity and equity, sustainability, and governance (Babiak and Wolfe, in press). Walker, Kent and Vincent (2010) argued that a balanced approach to communicating and articulating sport businesses' CSR efforts is central to attaining the desired potential relational (e.g. reputation) and transactional (e.g. patronage) business outcomes. Given this shifting role to a more central business function, and considering the intended benefits organizations aim to receive, the communication and articulation of CSR efforts becomes critical. In general, the reporting of CSR has as its target audience society at large, but also targeted stakeholders such as investors, actual and potential employees, partners, sponsors, non-governmental organizations (NGOs), local governments, and customers (Esrock and Leichty, 1998). In this chapter, we identify key new media outlets used to disseminate information about CSR, discuss approaches and challenges in how sport organizations communicate CSR to their stakeholders, and examine the digital media channels of this communication. We conclude with key recommendations for practice and further research.

CSR in sport

Similar to trends in other industries, sport businesses such as professional teams are increasingly focusing on CSR as a vehicle both to impact positively the communities in which they operate and to leverage strategic advantages for themselves. Babiak and Wolfe (2009, in press) discussed the distinct facets that make sport unique with respect to CSR, and thus merit making CSR worthy of investigation. These unique aspects include: passion, economics, transparency, and stakeholder management. Babiak and Wolfe (2009) argue that CSR may impact or be impacted by these factors. A number of these factors lend themselves to strategic opportunities – particularly in communicating around team and league activities. For example, passion is a formative attribute differentiating sport from other industries and includes the emotion, devotion and passion that the product (the athlete, team, game) generates among fans/consumers (Cashman, 2004). Given the strong emotions generated by sport, there may be a more attentive audience than among businesses or employees from other industries that could benefit communities as a whole – by encouraging and strengthening community integration (Wakefield and Wann, 2006; Wilkerson and Dodder, 1987) – and sport businesses themselves.

Another related facet that makes sport unique – particularly within the context of communications – is the transparency and symbiotic relationship that sport organizations have with the media. Almost everything achieved by the leadership of a sport team (e.g. player signings, player salaries, who plays, who sits, trades, changes in strategies), as well as team outcomes (i.e. wins/losses) and contributions to good causes, is open (Armey, 2004). Organizations in other industries typically do not face the same type of scrutiny of their business practices or employees' behaviors. Finally, success in the sport industry necessitates the ability to work with a complex set of stakeholders (e.g. various levels of government, sponsors, fans, local communities, minor leagues, media, and players). Strong relations with stakeholders can benefit from CSR activities (Wallace, 2004), and stakeholders also put pressures on sport organizations to behave responsibly. Along the same lines, Smith and Westerbeek (2007) argued that the popularity and global reach of sport can ensure that CSR has mass mediated distribution and communication power. The prominence of sport within the media helps to promote and communicate CSR activities (Paramio-Salcines, Babiak and Walters, in press). Recognizing these unique elements of professional sport and how each is related to CSR provides the rationale for addressing CSR in sport as a phenomenon different from CSR in other domains – though there certainly are areas of overlap. From a more applied perspective, addressing these differentiating factors allows practitioners to strategically position CSR initiatives and increase its impact.

Communicating CSR practices

Communication around CSR needs to be carried out properly and carefully to "counteract the growing skepticism [of] corporate communication, particularly companies that overstate their social behaviors" (Birth, Illia, Lurati and Zamparini, 2008: 183). Esrock and Leichty (1998) suggest the importance of effectively communicating CSR efforts as public opinion is the corporate gatekeeper of organizational CSR. Given the importance of image and public opinion for organizations, CSR communication aims to provide information legitimizing an organization's behavior by influencing stakeholders' and society's image of the company (Birth *et al.*, 2008). The more transparent and the greater the extent of reporting, the likelier the company is engaged and takes its CSR responsibilities seriously (Chapple and Moon, 2005). Arguably, these strategic communication strategies can be enacted by using interactive communication channels available to organizations, particularly websites and social media.

CSR communication channels

> Companies use a wide range of channels for CSR communication, including social reports, thematic reports, codes of conduct, web sites, stakeholder consultations, internal channels, prizes and events, cause-related marketing, product packaging, interventions in the press and on TV, and points of sale. However, three channels in particular – social reports, web sites, and advertising – seem to play the prominent role.
>
> *(Birth* et al., *2008: 185)*

We discuss the articulation of CSR by highlighting opportunities that three different channels offer, discussing the downsides of using such types of communication outlets, and offering examples of their use in the professional sport industry.

CSR and websites

Websites are now ubiquitous and a standard means of presenting the image and identity of a business (Wanderley, Lucian, Farache and de Sousa Filho, 2008). Presenting the activities and efforts around social responsibility on websites is an important function of an organization's communication strategy. Studies about web-based CSR communication focus primarily on the use of corporate websites to disseminate information about CSR positions and activities (Du, Bhattacharya and Sen, 2010).

The early 2000s were a time of web-based growth for many organizations (Antal, Dierkies, MacMillan and Marz, 2002; Esrock and Leichty, 2000; Snider, Hill and Martin, 2003). Research explored how businesses were using websites to communicate with stakeholders, and the interactive possibilities were considered one of the greatest advantages against traditional media (Esrock and Leichty, 2000). The "growth of the Internet" was considered a "key development" (Antal *et al.*, 2002: 34) for communicating CSR, and early studies revealed how the Web was used to report CSR efforts. Esrock and Leichty's (1998) landmark study revealed that 80 percent of corporate websites addressed social responsibility. However, additional studies showed that even though companies were communicating about CSR via the web, they were not displaying CSR messages prominently on their sites (Esrock and Leichty, 2000). Mid-decade surveys of web-communicated CSR showed reluctant growth in this area (Coope, 2004). While companies were growing more likely to talk about CSR efforts on organizational websites, the majority of information was contained in extensive reports and press releases, and few tools were available for stakeholders to interact with companies (Coope, 2004; Esrock and Leichty, 1998). The one-way messages were most likely to reinforce organizational ethical codes through value and mission statements and to provide information about environmental policies and philanthropic activities (Pollach, 2003; Snider *et al.*, 2003). However, significant shifts occurred within the next five years, establishing the web as "an essential space through which to diffuse information about corporate responsibility" (Capriotti and Moreno, 2007: 87).

Internationally, conflicting reports about web-based CSR communication emerged. Chaudri and Wang (2007) discovered that Indian information technology companies were not likely to communicate CSR via their corporate websites, finding that only 30 of the 100 examined websites "had a dedicated CSR section" (p. 238) and made CSR statements. Within these sections, almost half of the sample ($n = 13$) had only one page dedicated to CSR, only six of the sites offered news clips or press releases about their CSR efforts, and only one company had an official CSR report. These findings were countered by work examining the websites for

Spanish Stock Exchange (IBEX-35) companies and the top 50 revenue-generating Japanese companies. Capriotti and Moreno (2007) found nearly 70 percent of IBEX-35 companies had dedicated CSR pages. Unfortunately, page content was not interactive, instead functioning as a source of one-way, descriptive information about CSR. Japanese organizations seemed to be at the forefront of CSR communication, with 90 percent of organizations offering CSR reports that primarily focused on environmental responsibility (Fukukawa and Moon, 2004). However, despite the greater likelihood of Japanese companies to communicate CSR, they were less likely than companies in other countries to discuss ethical codes.

More recently, research has shown that companies embracing the web's potential for presenting CSR communication and that online communication can enhance stakeholder trust and perceptions about organizational CSR (Gomez and Chalmeta, 2011; Hong and Rim, 2010; Moreno and Capriotti, 2009). An examination of the top-50 Fortune 500 companies showed "80 percent had fully functioning CSR websites" (Gomez and Chalmeta, 2011: 94). Annual reports were easy to find, and almost all companies stated CSR goals and objectives. However, the depth of information provided is still lacking. Tools for direct interaction are still hard to find or are unavailable via the web, and few sites offer social media. These findings are disappointing considering Hong and Rim's (2010) research, which suggests consumer engagement with company websites positively impacts perceptions about a company's socially responsibility efforts and leads to stronger trust and a greater willingness to "engage in positive word-of-mouth communication" (p. 390).

In the professional sport setting, websites are a vital communication channel for CSR reporting. Each professional sport team in the four main North American leagues typically has a dedicated location on their webpages to describe and communicate their efforts in the community and their social responsibility in other key areas (such as diversity and equity and the environment). For example, the Detroit Lions of the NFL have a Community tab where the team highlights its efforts to support league-wide CSR initiatives (such as *Play 60*), as well as customized initiatives to address issues facing the community (in Detroit's case, the Lions' *Living for the City* initiative which is "a reflection of the Detroit Lions' commitment to Detroit's resurgence and our focus on areas of critical need. [This program] supports innovative citizen philanthropy and promotes personal and community wellbeing" [Detroit Lions, 2013]). Communication about social responsibility efforts can also be woven throughout a website, where for instance, the environmental initiatives of a team might be communicated in various sections. The advantages of CSR communication via website for sport organizations are customization, opportunities for brand identity and image development, and ease of searching. Disadvantages are that website communication is one-way; interacting and connecting with the organization directly to ask questions or seek more information is difficult. Important information may also be lost in the scope of initiatives – it is difficult to tell which initiatives are of strategic priority (such as Detroit's 'Living in the City') or peripheral (such as a clothing drive for Thanksgiving). Some of these challenges may be overcome with social media platforms, which are increasingly being adopted by businesses to communicate about CSR.

CSR and social media

In their synthesis of CSR literature, Du *et al.* (2010) explore CSR communication strategies and channels but barely address social media as a tool for reaching key stakeholders. Lumping social media sites with other social networking tools such as blogs and chat rooms, the authors point to sites such as Facebook as an opportunity to enhance word-of-mouth communication among active stakeholders. Even so, website-focused research has offered a strong foundation for research exploring social media-based CSR communication.

Given the perceived flaws in current web-based communication strategies, social media presents opportunities for companies to deliver messages about CSR efforts. Generally speaking, the web is considered an "essential instrument" for CSR communication (Moreno and Capriotti, 2009: 169). Web-based communications lends itself to interactivity, which is considered a hallmark of effective CSR communication (Dawkins, 2004). Even so, many companies fail to generate stakeholder awareness about socially responsible efforts (Du *et al.*, 2010). However, social media presents an opportunity for bridging the interactive gaps that corporate websites seem to leave open. Korschun and Du (2012) suggest social media-based CSR is different from traditional CSR communication because social media creates a space for information exchange. Additionally, it engages diverse stakeholder segments by presenting corporate information (Korschun and Du, 2012). Although social media is a popular and growing communication tool for businesses and organizations to communicate with stakeholders (Korschun and Du, 2012; Mangold and Faulds, 2009), little research has explored how social networking sites are used to communicate CSR.

One of the benefits of social media is the ability to create more interactive, dialogic communication with stakeholders (Korschun and Du, 2012; Bortree and Seltzer, 2009; Mangold and Faulds, 2009; Seltzer and Mitrook, 2007). As a communication tool, it can open the door for companies to promote causes (Mangold and Faulds, 2009). Unfortunately, few organizations seem to be harnessing the potential to communicate directly with stakeholders in a conversational, responsive fashion. Both blogs (Seltzer and Mitrook, 2007) and Facebook pages (Bortree and Seltzer, 2009) for environmental organizations have been examined for dialogic principles and potential for stakeholder involvement. Seltzer and Mitrook (2007) found that blogs – more than websites – afforded environmental watchdog organizations opportunities to create two-way communication channels. Likewise, the social networking platform Facebook has been used for the same purpose, but many organizations seem to fall short of creating dialogue because of the perception that "the mere creation of an interactive space via a social networking profile is sufficient for facilitating dialogue" (Bortree and Seltzer, 2009: 318).

Although benefits of using social media are apparent, companies do not seem to be embracing social media to disseminate information about CSR activities. McCorkindale (2010) provides one of the earliest studies of Facebook-based CSR strategies, analyzing Facebook pages for the top 50 Fortune 500 companies. Using a coding scheme that identified "social responsibility… as the presence of community-based or volunteer activities outside the scope of the corporation itself" (McCorkindale, 2010: 9), analysis revealed that less than a quarter of the companies referred to CSR activities via social media. In general, companies were failing to share the same information on Facebook as they were on their primary websites, something McCorkindale considered a "missed opportunity" (2010: 10). Du and Vieira (2012) found oil companies posted CSR messages via social media, but use of these sites was mixed. Some companies failed to link to their social media sites via the corporate websites, used the sites as means for one-way communication, or had inactive pages. However, those who maintained more interactive, updated pages did so effectively. For example, ConocoPhillips, Chevron, and BP actively maintained and linked to Facebook, Twitter, YouTube, Flickr and LinkedIn pages via their corporate websites. They opened opportunities for two-way communication by encouraging stakeholder feedback via polls and interactive features. They also encouraged stakeholders to share stories and testimonials, all activities that can "foster favorable CSR perceptions and build connections with stakeholders" (Du and Vieira, 2012: 421).

The potential reach for sports organizations is evident when examining Facebook and

Twitter for both leagues and teams. The National Football League (NFL) – which boasts an estimated $9.5 billion in annual revenue, far surpassing other major professional US leagues (Gaines, 2012) – has garnered more than 6.7 million likes and 4.3 million Twitter followers (NFL, 2013). The most profitable NFL team, the Dallas Cowboys, rise as the most popular NFL team with more than 5.3 million Facebook likes (Berkman, 2013; Ozanian, 2012). By the end of the 2012 season, more than half of the NFL's teams (18) had more than 1 million page likes. However, the NFL's followings pale in comparison to the social media following enjoyed by the National Basketball Association (NBA). The NBA has accumulated more than 15.5 million likes on Facebook and nearly 6.6 million Twitter followers (Fan Page List, 2012a), with the most popular sports team being the Los Angeles Lakers with nearly 15.9 million Facebook likes and more than 2.9 million Twitter followers (Fan Page List, 2012b).

However, the number of "likes" and Twitter followers should be viewed cautiously as a measure of fan interaction. Although fans do not appear to be completely passive social media users, the number of overtly active fans is low. The Pittsburgh Steelers led the NFL by generating 351,380 comments during the season (Berkman, 2013), but this is a relatively small number considering the team has more than 4.8 million Facebook likes (Pittsburgh Steelers, 2013). Additionally, many teams have to contend with the rise of fake Twitter followers. By the end of the 2012 season, a reported 38 percent of New York Jets Twitter followers were fake accounts (Walder, 2012). Although this percentage far surpasses those of other NFL teams, it points to a greater flaw when determining the effectiveness of social media. Teams and leagues may be reaching fans, but it is hard to determine how interactive fans truly are, a distinct challenge when communicating about CSR. However, communication that is personally relevant, factually based, and interactive is the best way to reach stakeholders and disseminate organizational messages, and with millions of fans connecting to team and league pages, opportunities to communicate about CSR in an effective manner are readily available in sport.

In this sense, sports organizations appear to be using social media to their advantage when communicating CSR messages, seamlessly incorporating CSR messages into their social media streams. In doing so, they are arguably normalizing the presence and practice of social responsibility in sport. The NBA, for example, reaches fans with Facebook posts related to its healthy living initiative NBA Fit. Using videos and photos featuring star players and league partners such as ESPN, the NBA engages fans on both Facebook and Twitter by highlighting key partnerships and program-related events while promoting messages about maintaining healthier lifestyles. For example, one Facebook post included a video of the Miami Heat's Dwayne Wade working out: "See how Dwayne Wade keeps NBA FIT in the off-season! http://www.nba.com/nbafit/." Like similar Facebook posts, the league provides a link to the league-maintained NBA Fit website, which offers pages highlighting the NBA Fit mission, programs associated with the initiative, fitness and nutrition tips for readers, and lists of corporate partners (NBA.com, 2013). Not only are connections made by highlighting a star player, but readers are also pointed in the direction of more program-related information.

As of 2012, NBA Fit is part of the larger NBA Cares program. Messages about the initiative are also promoted on a Facebook page and Twitter feed dedicated specifically to NBA Cares. In both of these cases, league-maintained accounts focus solely on the "NBA's global community outreach initiative." This allows the league to share and disseminate even more information about responsible efforts. On its primary pages, the league can share posts made by the NBA Cares Facebook page and Twitter account. On Twitter the league also uses hashtags and @replies to promote specific topics, such as #nbafit, and enhance connections with the main league Twitter stream, individual team sites, and individual players involved in promoting initiatives such as the NBA Fit program.

This all-encompassing approach to promoting a specific league-wide program – NBA Cares – as well as a particular initiative – NBA Fit – shows the strength of social media when communicating CSR. For a league that has more than 20 million followers via Facebook and Twitter combined, this is an immense strategic communication opportunity. In addition to promoting specific causes such as health awareness, leagues and teams are able to promote socially responsible initiatives in such a way that fans see social responsibility as a normal part of the sports experience. Links to both the Facebook and Twitter feeds are readily available and easily accessible on the NBA Cares site. However, the true effectiveness of these strategies, as of this writing, is still debatable. Although the NBA has more Facebook followers than any other league – 15.5 million – the sister NBA Cares page has less than 40,000 "likes." The NBA Cares Twitter feed has a little more than 43,000 followers. Additionally, the league does not share all of the updates from the NBA Cares page on its main page. A visit to the NBA Cares Facebook page reveals that there are numerous videos and photo albums highlighting player and team work within communities that are not shared with the millions of followers on the primary league Facebook page. Messages are also distinctly one-way forms of communication. For example, on the main NBA Facebook page messages about NBA Fit are more likely to tell viewers to "see how" a player is doing something as opposed to encouraging active participation – something that is more likely to happen on the NBA Cares Facebook page. And although the NBA Cares website is highly developed and well-maintained, links to the NBA Cares site and sister social media pages are not readily available via any of the primary league sites. Links to NBA Cares and its related initiatives are buried at the bottom of NBA.com, and none of the six website links provided on the NBA's Facebook "About" page direct readers to CSR pages. As such, one has to question whether the league is effectively using its reach or whether it is falling into the noted trap of believing that simply creating a social media page is enough to constitute interactive communication (Bortree and Seltzer, 2009).

Other forms of new media are gaining prominence as well in the communication of CSR. Vehicles such as e-newsletters, cell/text communications, advertising, web-based articles, emerging social-media platforms and mobile apps are all growth areas in CSR communication and merit further consideration and academic investigation.

Conclusions and recommendations

More organizations are using forms of new media to talk about social responsibility – and teams, leagues and organizations in the professional sport industry are also communicating their CSR efforts. Social media has changed the way companies engage – with examples such as Pepsi's Refresh Project and GE's Ecomagination Challenge – and businesses see the opportunity for their good deeds to go viral. The rise of new media as a communication vehicle for professional sport organizations' CSR efforts has paralleled the growth and expansion of these initiatives (Babiak and Wolfe, 2009).

Embracing new media can allow sport professionals to share information, keep abreast of information and industry trends, engage with consumers, and build networks in an open and transparent way (Babiak and Wolfe, 2009). It has fundamentally altered the nature of CSR reporting from an annual event to a constant stream that is embedded in the minds of consumers.

Despite the potential afforded by social media, an acknowledgement of the greatest limitations of social media-based research should be offered: These sites change so dramatically and quickly that it is difficult to truly track how effectively companies are using these pages (McCorkindale, 2010). So while this chapter offered insights into how new media is becoming integrated into the CSR function, it is still not evident that a greater impact on society is being made. Having a Facebook page or Twitter ID does not guarantee that followers will connect or have interest in what the team or league is doing. It is essential that a business determines the goals for social interaction and then chooses the most relevant technological tools to achieve them (Meranus, 2010). So while new media can be a powerful tool for advocacy, and businesses can use it to better understand the concerns and expectations of their communities (and direct their CSR efforts to address those concerns), efforts should be made to understand the most effective approaches to the communication and positioning of CSR in the professional sport setting.

New media tools are not a replacement for essential documents such as annual CSR reports, but they do open a channel for stakeholders to interact directly with a professional sport team's CSR program. As Mohin (2012) states, "these tools are still very new, and no company has perfected their use, but it is clear that social media is a game you cannot afford sit out" (para 9).

References

Antal, B. A., Dierkes, M., MacMillan, K. and Marz, L. (2002) Corporate social reporting revisited. *Journal of General Management*, 28(2), 22–42.

Armey, C. (2004) Inside and outside: Corporate America vs. the sports industry. In M. Falls (ed.), *Inside the Minds: The Business of Sports* (pp. 65–80). Boston, MA: Aspatore, Inc.

Babiak, K. and Wolfe, R. (2009) Determinants of corporate social responsibility in professional sport: Internal and external factors. *Journal of Sport Management*, 23(6), 717–742.

Babiak, K. and Wolfe, R. (in press) Perspectives on CSR in sport. In J. L. Paramio-Salcines, K. Babiak and G. Walters (ed.), *Routledge Handbook of Sport and Corporate Social Responsibility*. London: Routledge.

Berkman, F. (2013, January 31) Super Bowl teams are losers on Facebook likes. *Mashable.com*. Retrieved from http://mashable.com/2013/01/31/nfl-super-bowl-facebook/.

Bhattacharya, C. B. and Sen, S. (2003) Consumer-company identification: A framework for understanding consumers' relationships with companies. *Journal of Marketing*, 67(2), 76–88.

Birth, G., Illia, L., Lurati, F. and Zamparini, G. (2008) Communicating CSR: Practices among Switzerland's top 300 companies. *Corporate Communications: An International Journal*, 13(2), 182–196.

Bonini, S. M., Mendonca, L. T. and Oppenheim, M. J. (2006) When social issues become strategy. *McKinsey Quarterly* Retrieved from https://www.mckinseyquarterly.com/When_social_issues_become_strategic_1763

Bortree, D. S. and Seltzer, T. (2009) Dialogic strategies and outcomes: An analysis of environmental advocacy groups' Facebook profiles. *Public Relations Review*, 35, 317–319. doi:10.1016/j.pubrev.2009.05.002.

Branscombe, N. R. and Wann, D. L. (1991) The positive social and self concept consequences of sports team identification. *Journal of Sport and Social Issues*, 15(2), 115–127.

Breitbarth, T. and Harris, P. (2008) The role of corporate social responsibility in the football business: Towards the development of a conceptual model. *European Sport Management Quarterly*, 8(2), 179–206.

Breitbarth, T., Hovemann, G. and Walzel, S. (2011) Scoring strategy goals: Measuring corporate social responsibility in professional European football. *Thunderbird International Business Review*, 53(6), 721–737. Retrieved from http://onlinelibrary.wiley.com/doi/10.1002/tie.20448/abstract

Capriotti, P. and Moreno, A. (2007) Corporate citizenship and public relations: The importance and interactivity of social responsibility issues on corporate websites. *Public Relations Review*, 33(1), 84–91.

Cashman, B. (2004) Winning on and off the field. In M. Falls (ed.), *Inside the Minds: The Business of Sports*. Boston, MA: Aspatore, Inc.

Chapple, W. and Moon, J. (2005) Corporate Social Responsibility (CSR) in Asia: A seven-country study of CSR web site reporting. *Business and Society*, 44(4), 415–441.

Chaudri, V. and Wang, J. (2007) Communication corporate social responsibility on the internet: A case study of the top 100 information technology companies in India. *Management Communication Quarterly*, 21(2), 232–247. doi: 10.1177/0893318907308746.

Coope, R. (2004) Seeing the "Net potential" of online CR communications. *Corporate Responsibility Management*, 1(2), 20–25.

Dawkins, J. (2004) Corporate responsibility: The communication challenge. *Journal of Communication Management*, 9(2), 108–119.

De Schutter, O. (2008) Corporate social responsibility European style. *European Law Journal*, 14, 203–236.

Detroit Lions (2013) Retrieved from http://www.detroitlions.com/news/article-1/The-Detroit-Lions%E2%80%99-New-Living-for-the-City-Supports-Community-Wellness-Workforce-Development/e748def0-92c4-4f73-b70a-2fa61be00073

Du, S., Bhattacharya, C. B. and Sen, S. (2010) Maximizing business returns to corporate social responsibility (CSR): The role of CSR communication. *International Journal of Management Review*, 12(1), 8–19. doi: 10.1111/j.1468-2370.2009.00275.x.

Du, S. and Vieira, E. T. (2012) Striving for legitimacy through corporate social responsibility: Insights from oil companies. *Journal of Business Ethics*, 110(4), 413–427. doi: 10.1007/s10551-012-1490-4.

Esrock, S. L. and Leichty, G. B. (1998) Social responsibility and corporate web pages: Self-presentation or agenda-setting? *Public Relations Review*, 24(3), 305–319.

Esrock, S. L. and Leichty, G. B. (2000) Organization of corporate web pages: Publics and functions. *Public Relations Review*, 26(3), 327–344.

Fan Page List (2012a) US Sports Brands on Facebook. Retrieved from http://fanpagelist.com/category/brands/sports/

Fan Page List (2012b) US Sports Brands on Facebook. Retrieved from http://fanpagelist.com/category/sports-teams/usa/

Frederick, W. C. (2006) *Corporation, be Good! The Story of Corporate Social Responsibility*. Indianapolis, IN: Dogear Publishing.

Freeman, M. (2013) Tagliabue's hand in saving Saints aided New Orleans' Katrina rally. *CBS sports*. Retrieved from http://www.cbssports.com/nfl/story/21619371/tagliabue-didnt-save-new-orleans-by-himself-but-was-major-player

Fukukawa, K. and Moon, J. (2004) A Japanese model of corporate social responsibility? *Journal of Corporate Citizenship*, 16, 45–59.

Gaines, C. (2012, Oct. 9) Sports chart of the day: NFL revenue is nearly 25% more than MLB. *Business Insider*. Retrieved from http://www.businessinsider.com/sports-chart-of-the-day-nfl-revenue-still-dwarfs-other-major-sports-2012-10.

Gardberg, N. and Fombrun, C. F. (2006) Corporate citizenship: Creating intangible assets across institutional environments. *Academy of Management Review*, 31(2), 329–346.

Godfrey, P. C. (2005) The relationship between corporate philanthropy and shareholder wealth: A risk management perspective. *Academy of Management Review*, 30(4), 777–798.

Gomez, L. M. and Chalmeta, R. (2011) Corporate responsibility in US corporate websites: A pilot study. *Public Relations Review*, 37, 93–95. doi:10.1016/j.pubrev.2010.12.005.

Harvard Kennedy School (2013) *Corporate Social Responsibility Initiative*. Retrieved from http://www.hks.harvard.edu/m-rcbg/CSRI/prog_bid.html

Hess, D. and Warren, D. E. (2008) The meaning and meaningfulness of corporate social initiatives. *Business and Society Review*, 113(2), 163–197.

Hong, S.Y. and Rim, H. (2010) The influence of customer use of corporate websites: Corporate social responsibility, trust, and word-of-mouth communication. *Public Relations Review*, 36, 389–391. doi:10.1016/j.pubrev.2010.08.002.

Inoue, Y., Kent, A. and Lee, S. (2011) CSR and the bottom line: Analyzing the link between CSR and financial performance for professional teams. *Journal of Sport Management*, 25(6), 531–549.

Korschun, D. and Du, S. (2012) How virtual corporate social responsibility dialogs generate value: A framework and propositions. *Journal of Business Research*. Retrieved from http://dx.doi.org/10.1016/j.jbusres.2012.09.011.

Leaders Magazine (2012) Making an impact. An interview with David J. Stern, Commissioner, National Basketball Association. Retrieved from http://www.leadersmag.com/issues/2012.4_Oct/PDFs/LEADERS-David-Stern-National-Basketball-Association.pdf

Mangold, W. G. and Faulds, D. J. (2009) Social media: The new hybrid element of the promotion mix. *Business Horizons*, 52, 357–365. doi: 10.1016/j.bushor.2009.03.002.

McCorkindale, T. (2010) Can you see the writing on my wall? A content analysis of Fortune 500's Facebook social networking sites. *Public Relations Journal*, 4(3), 1–13.

McDonnell, W. G. (2012) Healing the wounds of Hurricane Sandy through the generosity of sport. *Forbes*. Retrieved from http://www.forbes.com/sites/waynemcdonnell/2012/11/12/healing-the-wounds-of-hurricane-sandy-through-the-generosity-of-sports/

Meranus, R. (2010) Spotlighting your social responsibility. Strategies to keep people from thinking you're only in it for the money. *Entrepreneur.com*. Retrieved from http://www.entrepreneur.com/article/206850

Mohin, T. (2012) The Top 10 trends in CSR for 2012. *Forbes*. Retrieved from http://www.forbes.com/sites/forbesleadershipforum/2012/01/18/the-top-10-trends-in-csr-for-2012/.

Moreno, A. and Capriotti, P. (2009) Communicating CSR, citizenship and sustainability on the web. *Journal of Communication Management, 13*(2), 157–175. doi: 10.1108/13632540910951768.

National Football League (2011, June 15) A letter from the Commissioner. Retrieved from http://www.nfl.com/news/story/09000d5d82054f96/article/a-letter-from-the-commissioner.

NBA.com (2013) *NBA/WNBA FIT*. Retrieved from http://www.nba.com/nbafit/.

NFL (2013) [Facebook homepage.] http://www.facebook.com/NFL.

Noble, G. I., Cantrell, J., Kyriazis, E. and Algie, J. (2008) Motivations and forms of corporate giving behaviour: Insights from Australia. *International Journal of Nonprofit and Voluntary Sector Marketing, 13*(4), 315–325.

Ozanian, M. (2012, Sept. 5) Dallas Cowboys lead NFL with $2.1 billion valuation. *Forbes*. Retrieved from http://www.forbes.com/sites/mikeozanian/2012/09/05/dallas-cowboys-lead-nfl-with-2-1-billion-valuation/.

Paramio-Salcines, J. L., Babiak, K. and Walters, G. (eds) (in press) Introduction. In *Routledge Handbook of Sport and Corporate Social Responsibility*. London: Routledge.

Pittsburgh Steelers. (2013) [Facebook homepage.] Retrieved from https://www.facebook.com/steelers

Pohle, G. and Hittner, J. (2008) Attaining sustainable growth through corporate social responsibility. *IBM Institute for Business Value*. Retrieved from http://www-935.ibm.com/services/us/gbs/bus/pdf/gbe03019-usen-02.pdf

Pollach, I. (2003) Communicating corporate ethics on the World Wide Web: A discourse analysis of selected Web sites. *Business Society, 42*(2), 277–287.

Porter, M. E. and Kramer, M. R. (2006) Strategy and society: The link between competitive advantage and corporate social responsibility. *Harvard Business Review, 84*(12), 78–92.

Seltzer, T. and Mitrook, M. A. (2007) The dialogic potential of weblogs in relationship building. *Public Relations Review, 33*, 227–229. doi:10.1016/j.pubrev.2007.02.011

Sheth, H. and Babiak, K. (2010) Beyond the game: Perceptions and priorities of corporate social responsibility in the sport industry. *Journal of Business Ethics, 91*(3), 433–450.

Smith, A. and Westerbeek. H. (2007) Sport as a vehicle for developing corporate social responsibility. *Journal of Corporate Citizenship, 25*(7), 43–54.

Snider, J., Hill, R. P. and Martin, D. (2003) Corporate social responsibility in the 21st century: A view from the world's most successful firms. *Journal of Business Ethics, 48*(2), 175–187.

Wakefield, K. L. and Wann, D. L. (2006) An examination of dysfunctional sport fans: Method of classification and relationships with problem behaviors. *Journal of Leisure Research, 38*(2), 168–186.

Walder, S. (2012, December 13) NY Jets lead league in fake Twitter followers, according to report. *New York Daily News*. Retrieved from http://www.nydailynews.com/sports/football/jets/jets-tweet-sour-article-1.1219963.

Walker, M. and Kent, A. (2009) Do fans care? Assessing the influence of corporate social responsibility on consumer attitudes in the sport industry. *Journal of Sport Management, 23*, 743–769.

Walker, M., Kent, A. and Vincent, J. (2010) Communicating socially responsible initiatives: An analysis of US professional teams. *Sport Marketing Quarterly, 19*, 125–131.

Wallace, C. (2004), An insider's look at – and love for – pro basketball. In M. Falls (ed.), *Inside the Minds: The Business of Sports*. Boston, MA: Aspatore, Inc.

Walters, G. (2009) Corporate social responsibility through sport. The community sports trust model as a CSR delivery agency. *Journal of Corporate Citizenship, 35*, 81–94.

Walters, G. and Tacon, R. (2010) Corporate social responsibility in sport: Stakeholder management in the UK football industry. *Journal of Management and Organization, 16*(4), 566–586.

Walters, G. and Anagnostopoulos, C. (2012) Implementing corporate social responsibility through social partnerships. *Business Ethics: A European Review, 21*(4), 417–433.

Wanderley, L. S. O, Lucian, R., Farache, F. and de Sousa Filho, J. M. (2008) CSR information disclosure on the web: A context-based approach analysing the influence of country of origin and industry sector. *Journal of Business Ethics, 82*(2), 369–378.

Wilkerson, M. and Dodder, R. A. (1987) Collective conscience and sport in modem society: An empirical test of a model. *Journal of Leisure Research, 19*, 35–40.

18

SOCIAL IDENTIFICATION AND SOCIAL MEDIA IN SPORTS

Implications for sport brands

Brandi A. Watkins

UNIVERSITY OF ALABAMA

For many, being a sports fan transcends the on-field competition where fandom becomes an integral aspect of one's identity. Fans create value for the sport brand through shared experiences with the team and its connection to their social identity (Arvidsson, 2006). Sports have become a major player in the recreation and entertainment industry (Mason, 1999), and thus the importance of developing a team's brand has increased. Sports teams depend on fans for a large part of their financial well-being; providing revenue through ticket sales, television viewing, and purchasing team-licensed memorabilia (Fisher and Wakefield, 1998). Therefore, an effective sport brand is one that turns fans into paying customers (Richelieu and Pons, 2006).

Previous research on sports branding has produced several models that attempt to measure a team's brand equity. Gladden, Milne and Sutton (1998) conceptualized a framework for assessing brand equity in collegiate sports based on team-related antecedents and marketplace consequences. Ross (2006) developed the spectator-based brand equity model (SBBE) for the understanding of experience-induced antecedents that lead to an increase in spectator-based brand equity. Underwood, Bond and Baer (2001) presented a third model of sport brand equity called the social identity-brand equity (SIBE) model, which assumes that the more one identifies with a sport team, the more the team's brand equity increases. Sport marketers can manipulate certain characteristics of the service marketplace to increase identification with the team.

This chapter focuses on social identification and its implications for sport brands. Through the distinctive characteristics of sports and sport fans, social identity theory provides a useful framework for studying fan behavior (Donavan, Carlson and Zimmerman, 2005). Social identification is proposed to facilitate the use of social media among sport fans and lead to increased positive perceptions of customer-based brand equity for a team.

In the following sections, social identification is defined as it relates to sports. Social identification is discussed in terms of predicting social media use and perceptions of brand equity. Results are reported from a survey of NBA fans finding support for social identification predicting social media use and brand equity. The chapter concludes with a practical explanation of the benefits of social identification for sport brands.

Social identity theory

Social identity is the knowledge that a person is a member of a social group, which is a collection of individuals who share a common bond and pronounce themselves as members of the same social category (Tajfel, 1982; Ashforth and Mael, 1989; Tajfel and Turner, 2004). Membership in an organization allows one to create a positive social identity (Bergami and Bagozzi, 2000). Social identity theory assumes that (1) one socially identifies with a group when they perceive feelings of belonging with the group; (2) social identification occurs through categorization of other groups (in-group vs. out-group); and (3) as one identifies with a group, one tends to take on the attitudes and actions of the group (Ashforth and Mael, 1989). The following sections explain this theory and its relation to sports.

Social identification: Feelings of belonging to a group

One achieves social identification through affiliation with a group (Bergami and Bagozzi, 2000). Feeling a sense of belonging with an organization leads one to form a perception of "psychological ownership" in the organization (Donavan *et al.*, 2005). A person need only perceive oneness with the group to attain membership status with the group. As an individual becomes more identified with the group, the self-concept becomes depersonalized where in a sense, "I becomes we" (Brewer, 1991: 476). People form strong connections with other sport fans through shared symbols, rituals, and traditions associated with the team, thus making sports a likely target of social identification (Heere and James, 2007).

Social identification: In-group/out-group comparisons

According to social identity theory individuals categorize themselves and others in terms of group membership (Ashforth and Mael, 1989) allowing them to make sense of the world (Carlson and Donavan, 2008). Individuals who identify with a team are more likely to make positive judgments toward other fans and are more critical of rival team fans (Fink, Parker, Brett and Higgins, 2009). Sports fans make obvious in-group/out-group comparisons through rivalries occurring between teams. For instance, fans of the Boston Celtics define themselves in terms of their shared connection as Celtics fans, but also in relation to their rival out-group, Los Angeles Lakers fans (Donavan *et al.*, 2005). Fans use the rival (e.g. the out-group) as a reference to reinforce their identity and differentiate themselves from other groups.

Social identification: Behavior assimilation

For socially identified group members, the values and emotions of the group are internalized creating a sense of shared identity (Phua, 2010). Highly identified group members tend to adopt beliefs and behaviors of the group and are motivated to maintain these actions to ensure group membership (Christian, Bagozzi, Abrams and Rosenthal, 2012). For professional sport teams, high levels of identification between the team and fans engender the same type of emotional connection and brand loyalty experienced through brand communities (Parker and Stuart, 1997). An individual is likely to choose to identify with a team when identification leads to positive social identity and self-enhancement (Donavan *et al.*, 2005). The more a person is involved with the group, the more salient the group identification becomes (Christian *et al.*, 2012) and the more likely they are to replicate behaviors and attitudes of the group. Even in the face of a losing season, a sports fan is likely to remain committed to their team through the emotional connection they share with other fans and the organization itself (Wann and Branscombe, 1993).

Social identification and sports

Sports teams are likely targets of social identification (Heere and James, 2007). Involvement with sports brings people together and provides a common bond for that group through shared symbols, rituals, and traditions (Sutton, McDonald, Milne and Cimperman, 1997). Since most sports teams are linked to cities and communities, fan identification is typically higher and more persistent (Phua, 2010) and provides a symbolic representation of social identification with community life (Heere and James, 2007). Team identification brings together individuals to form a cohesive group who seek out to protect the image of the group (i.e. the sports team) (Phua, 2010).

Sports fans range from casual spectators to highly involved fans, from watching or attending a game every now and then to being a season ticket holder and attending or watching as many games as possible (Funk and James, 2001). Fan identification is a manifestation of social identity theory in the sports context (Underwood *et al.*, 2001). Sutton *et al.* (1997) define fan identification as the commitment and involvement sport consumers have with the organization. This definition emphasizes the connection between the fan and the sports organization and the value that connection holds for the fan. For highly identified fans, one's identification with a team is a defining characteristic of their self-concept to the point that team success and failure impacts their self-esteem (Wann and Dolan, 1994).

Individuals who identify themselves as a fan of a sports team are likely to demonstrate their team allegiance through actions. As the individual grows more attached to the team, the fan's commitment to the team develops into a form of brand loyalty, which is a manifestation of the psychological and emotional commitment a fan makes to the team (Bauer, Stokburger-Sauer and Exler, 2008). Identified fans are more likely to be more knowledgeable about the team and their history, participate in discussions about the team with other fans, and purchase licensed team merchandise (Donavan *et al.*, 2005). Team loyalty can be translated into behavior by attending games live, watching the team on television, wearing the team logo and recruiting others to be a fan of the team (Bauer *et al.*, 2008). These outward actions by fans increase the brand equity of the team by making it look more desirable to outsiders.

The more identified a sports fan is, then the more likely they are to find ways to publicly demonstrate their fandom (Wann and Branscombe, 1993); thus increasing the brand awareness and brand associations for the team to less identified consumers and making group affiliation appear more desirable. As a result, sports marketers should create opportunities for interaction between fans and the team to strengthen the existing emotional connection a fan has with the team (Apostolopoulou and Biggers, 2010). Social media provides one such tool for sports brand managers to develop opportunities for fan interaction with the team.

Social identification and social media

Social media and mobile apps are changing the way marketers approach their branding strategies (Simmons, 2007). Through built-in, motivated fan bases, sports teams are positioned to use social media to encourage interaction among fans and the team (Wallace, Wilson and Miloch, 2011). Brand managers for sports teams are developing online branding strategies to convert casual fans to highly identified fans (Ioakimidis, 2010). Social networks, specifically designed for sports teams, allow for increased levels of fan engagement and loyalty, which is necessary to meet relationship-marketing goals.

Social media provides brands with a platform for promoting two-way communication with consumers (Igenhoff and Koelling, 2009) and allows brands to communicate with consumers in a timely, cost-effective, and efficient manner (Kaplan and Haenlein, 2010). Sports organizations have used the capabilities of social media to connect with fans, provide information about the team, sell tickets, promote the team, and increase overall brand awareness (Hambrick, Simmons, Greenhalgh and Greenwell, 2010). Brands that have a strong social media presence are better equipped to garner consumer attention, increase brand awareness, and maintain communication with consumers (Kwon and Sung, 2011).

Through social media, sports organizations have an unprecedented opportunity to establish and nurture a relationship with their fans and create online fan communities. Online activities reinforce the fan experience and serves as a socializing agent, bringing together fans from all over the world (Phua, 2010). Social media allows identified fans to affirm their in-group status and maintain positive identification with the team (Phua, 2010). Interacting with sports fans through social media can create desirable outcomes for sport organizations (Hambrick *et al.*, 2010), including reaching fans who live outside of the team's immediate area and providing emotional and financial support for the team (Kerr and Gladden, 2008).

In the social identity-brand equity (SIBE) model for sports branding developed by Underwood *et al.* (2001), social identification is the catalyst that allows fans to connect with a sports team on an emotional level and provides a direct influence on customer-based brand equity. Building on this proposition of the SIBE model, social identification is hypothesized to not only predict brand equity, but also predict the likelihood that a fan will use social media to follow the team.

Branding and social media

Brand equity is the value of the brand in the mind of the consumer (Bauer *et al.*, 2008). Involvement with a sports team provides a different set of experiences for fans, which create unique brand associations for the consumer that strengthens the brand equity for the team. Bauer *et al.* (2008) suggests that brands have high customer-based brand equity when the consumer has developed "favorable, strong, and unique brand associations" with the brand (p. 209). Therefore, the use of social media to interact with the brand should result in increased brand associations with the team.

For sports, communication technology such as social media and mobile apps have provided fans unprecedented access to sport organizations (Kerr and Gladden, 2008). Simmons (2007) suggests that by using the Internet as part of the overall marketing strategy, brands can reach the same audience as mass media but in a more personalized manner. Social media provide sports fans with a platform to talk about their favorite team and express their opinion (Seo and Green, 2008). Professional sport teams are developing online brand strategies to increase their fan base and to convert casual fans to highly identified fans (Ioakimidis, 2010). Teams like the Phoenix Suns and Seattle Seahawks have created social networking sites for fans to engage with one another and with the team (Williams and Chinn, 2010). Interacting with the team and other fans on these types of websites allow the sports fan to feel more connected to the team, which increases fan loyalty. Thus, research investigating how sport fans interact with teams through social media can have practical implications for sport brand managers.

Many sport teams have integrated social media into their marketing strategies. For example, in April 2010 the NBA's New Jersey Nets (now Brooklyn Nets) sponsored a promotion to give away five hundred tickets for a Monday night game against the Charlotte Bobcats. Consumers could receive a free ticket to the game by checking in at various locations around New York and New Jersey. The promotion was considered a success as fifteen percent of people who found a ticket attended the game (Kaplan, 2012). Many teams use Twitter to promote the team to followers. The San Antonio Spurs will often ask followers a trivia question to win tickets for an upcoming game. The Miami Heat offered a special pre-sale for playoff tickets exclusively for Twitter followers. Twitter followers of the brand can use their mobile devices to access Twitter and participate in these types of promotions. These activities not only enhance the relationship between the fan and the team but also enrich the fan's experience with the team.

This chapter focuses on two social media outlets – Twitter and mobile apps – and their influence on customer-based brand equity. The interactive features of Twitter allow for two-way communication between Twitter users (Kwon and Sung, 2011). Brands, especially sport brands, have taken to Twitter as part of their overall marketing strategy to build and maintain consumer relationships (Clavio and Kian, 2010). Mobile social media are available on various applications (mobile apps) accessible through smart phones and tablet devices. Many sport teams have developed apps for fans to use on mobile phones. NBA teams that have developed mobile apps include the Miami Heat, Dallas Mavericks, and New York Knicks. The current study proposes that use of social media (Twitter and mobile apps) will have a direct, positive influence on a team's brand equity.

Hypotheses

Individuals who are identified with a team will be more motivated to seek out ways to publicly demonstrate their affiliation with the team including using social media to follow the team and connect with other fans (Wann and Branscombe, 1993). The current study proposes social identification has a positive influence on the use of social media and customer-based brand equity for the team.

H1a: Social identification will have a positive influence on Twitter use related to the sports team.

H1b: Social identification will have a positive influence on use of mobile apps associated with the team.

H1c: Social identification will have a positive influence on consumer's perceptions of the team's brand equity.

One of the defining characteristics of customer-based brand equity is that brand value is created in the mind of the consumer through brand associations created by lived and mediated experiences with the brand (Underwood *et al.*, 2001). Therefore, social media use is hypothesized to have a positive influence on the brand equity of the sports team.

H2a: Twitter use will have a positive influence on consumer's perceptions of the team's brand equity.

H2b: Mobile apps use will have a positive influence on consumer's perceptions of the team's brand equity.

Method

Data collection

Data was collected among fans of three NBA teams – the Dallas Mavericks, Miami Heat, and New York Knicks using social media to recruit participants. Data-collection took place during the 2012–2013-basketball season. Respondents completed a 10-minute online survey, specific to each team under investigation, which assessed their opinions and experiences about their favorite team (i.e. Dallas, Miami, and New York). The survey measures included (1) social media use (2) fan identification, and (3) customer-based brand equity. Data analysis was conducted using structural equation modeling using AMOS version 20.0.

Scale Reliability

The scales used in this study were all adopted from existing literature and are accepted as reliable. Reliability for each scale was calculated using Cronbach's alpha scores. All scales were above the acceptable level between .80 and .90. Reliability scores are as follows: fan identification/social identification = .89, twitter involvement = .94, mobile apps involvement = .95, and brand equity = .88.

SEM: Goodness-of-Fit

SEM provides several indications of model fit that must be examined before analyzing hypotheses. Data can be considered a good fit for the model when the GFI (.922), AGI (.852), and TLI (.935) values are close to 1.00, which in this case they are; additionally, a NFI (.915) value greater than .8 and CFI (.935) value greater than .9 indicate a good fit (Reinard, 2006). Marsh and Hocevar (1985) suggest a chi square ratio less than five is acceptable; therefore, the Chi-square analysis indicated a good fit for the data $\chi^2/df = 3.875$. Therefore, the overall goodness-of-fit indices provide support for the model and the modification index did not reveal any method for improving the model.

Sample

A total of 240 surveys were completed. The mean age of respondents was 22 years old ($SD = 5.266$ years), with a reported range from 19 to 59 years old. The gender of respondents was nearly even with 50.4 percent of respondents was male ($n = 121$) and 49.6 percent were female ($n = 119$). The race of respondents was as follows: Asian ($n = 12$, 5 percent), African American ($n = 30$, 12.5 percent), Hispanic ($n = 13$, 5.4 percent), Native American ($n = 1$, .4 percent), White/Caucasian ($n = 181$, 75.4 percent), and 1.3 percent of the sample indicated a race other than listed ($n = 3$).

Results

Social identification and social media

This study provides an empirical assessment of the influence of social identification on the use of social media and a team's brand equity. Social identification is hypothesized to have a positive influence on social media use, specifically Twitter (H1a) and team sponsored mobile apps (H1b). Findings from this analysis support these hypotheses with social identification having a positive influence on Twitter ($\beta = .40, p < .001$) and mobile apps use ($\beta = .27, p < .001$). Social identification is hypothesized to have a direct, positive influence on a team's brand equity (H1c). Results of the SEM analysis indicate strong support for H1c ($\beta = .67, p < .001$) on brand equity.

Figure 18.1 reveals the results of the SEM analysis on the model under investigation. Social identification is proposed to be the catalyst that drives sports fans to seek out ways to identify

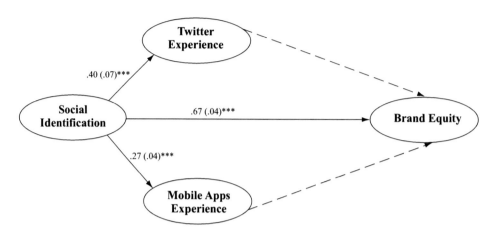

Figure 18.1   Results of SEM

Note. Results of Structural Equation Model. Dotted lines indicate nonsignificant paths. The numbers in parentheses indicate standardized error. ★★★*p* < .001.

with the team, which in this setting is operationalized as using social media. The data supported these hypotheses; social identification had a significant, positive influence of use of Twitter and mobile apps. Therefore, this study provides support that identified fans will likely use social media to follow the team. Of interest to note is the difference in the strength of influence – social identification had a stronger influence on use of Twitter (β = .40) than mobile apps (β = .27). This could be attributed to the difference in adoption and usage rates of the different technologies. Mobile apps represent a new technology; trends and preferences for the use of mobile apps in branding are still developing.

As previously suggested by Underwood *et al.* (2001), social identification should have a direct positive influence on a team's brand equity. As evidenced in Figure 18.1, social identification had a significant and strong influence on brand equity (β = .67). Of all variables under investigation, social identification had the strongest influence on brand equity (followed by use of Twitter (β = .40) and mobile apps (β = .27). This provides support for the importance of social identification in sports branding. The brand equity of the team is likely to increase as one sees oneself as connected to the team (Underwood *et al.*, 2001). The emotional connection between the team and fan is an important component for relationship marketing.

Social media and brand equity

Additionally this study sought to evaluate the direct influence of social media use on customer-based brand equity. Specifically, Twitter (H2a), and mobile apps (H2b) are hypothesized to have a positive influence on brand equity. Support was not found for Twitter (H2a) or mobile apps (H2b) to have a significant influence on brand equity. Based on current understanding of brand equity, using social media to interact with the team should provide a unique experience that generates brand associations that lead to increased brand equity, this was not found in the model. More research on the connection between brand equity and social media use can provide more insight into why this connection was not made.

Use of social media was proposed to have a positive influence on a team's brand equity. Brand equity increases as fans have unique experiences with the brand, such as use of social media.

However, as Figure 18.1 shows, the analysis did not find a significant, positive influence of social media use on brand equity. Brand equity is developed in terms of unique brand associations one has with a brand (i.e. through their experiences and interactions). Therefore, the findings of the current study are contrary to basic understanding of brand equity. In light of this, these findings should at best be considered inconclusive but highlight an important consideration for the further development of branding theory. Given the differences of service-sector brands from consumer brands, the lack of support is likely attributable to inadequacy of consumer brand equity scales in a service-sector context. In order to advance theory on brand equity, new scales relevant to service-sector brands should be developed and used to further explore the influence of social media on brand equity.

Discussion

Studying social media use among sports fans is a burgeoning area of research. The interactive capabilities of new media allow sports fans unprecedented access to their favorite teams, players, and other fans around the world. For the sport brand, social media is a tool for establishing and maintaining relationships with sport fans. Social identification is key to creating an emotional connection between the fan and team, which is an important first step to developing strong consumer–brand relationships (Underwood *et al.*, 2001). Building on previous research in sports branding, the study reported in this chapter proposed that social identification with a team leads to the use of social media to follow the team and will have a positive influence on the team's brand equity. The study also explored the direct influence of social media use on a team's brand equity.

As suggested in the SIBE model, social identification is assumed to have a positive influence on the customer-based brand equity of the team (Underwood *et al.*, 2001). The study reported in this chapter furthered this work by suggesting that social identification with a team will have a positive influence on the use of social media to follow the team. Results of the study reported in this chapter provide empirical support for each of these propositions; social identification was found to have a significant, positive influence on a team's brand equity and the use of social media to follow the team. The study reported here also examined the direct influence of social media use on customer-based brand equity; however results of the analysis did not indicate support for this influence.

Future research should investigate the brand-related consequences of using social media. Researchers have cited that social media can be an effective tool for developing consumer-brand relationships and increasing customer-based brand equity, but to date no published studies have posited specific brand outcomes of social media use. Results of the study reported here did not find support for a direct influence on brand equity but this does not preclude it from having an influence on other brand consequences. Social media has potential to bring consumers and brands together on an interpersonal level. Brand relationships may be a more appropriate venue for studying how brands use social media.

The current research project focused exclusively on Twitter and mobile apps. Future research should consider the impacts of other forms of social media, such as Facebook, Vine, Foursquare, and YouTube, on brand-related consequences. Each form of social media has distinguishing characteristics that could result in different brand outcomes. More research is needed to better understand how new technologies contributes to branding efforts.

The data revealed a lack of support for a direct influence of social media on brand equity, which raises an important implication for future research. Brand equity for sports teams includes intangible experiences of being a sports fan – attending games, supporting the team and interacting with other fans. However, the scales used to measure brand equity in this study were adopted from consumer research and may not reflect the attributes that make sports unique. Service-sector brands, such as professional sports, may require separate scales from consumer goods. Future research should take into consideration the distinctiveness of sports brands and work to develop scales that measure brand outcomes specific to sports.

Practical applications

Branscombe and Wann (1991) suggest fan identification provides an individual with a sense of belonging with the team and other fans. Teams can use social media to facilitate these feelings of group belonging among fans. The Dallas Mavericks host their own social networking page for fans of the team (www.friends.mavs.com) where fans must answer a series of questions about the team before being granted a profile on the site. Once a fan gains admission to the site, they are able to discuss the team or upcoming games with other fans (or MFFLs as they call themselves). Carlson and Donavan (2008) suggest that identifying with an athlete on the team leads to increased social identification with a team. Using social media, a sports team can host a special Twitter chat with one of their star players for fans to engage with the player. Social media provides sports teams with limitless opportunities for connecting fans and engaging them with the team and players. As the current study demonstrates, this can have a positive influence on social identification and ultimately the customer-based brand equity of the team.

Results of this study demonstrated that social media use is more likely among socially iden-tified fans of the team. Teams should also consider using social media to enhance fan experience by creating apps that allow for fan identification or providing outlets for fans to meet online to chat during games. Providing fans with outlets to connect with other fans, such as hosting watch parties for away games or hosting pre-game meet and greet sessions with players and coaches can enhance a fan's experience of going to the game and allow them to socialize with other fans increasing their identification with other fans.

Conclusion

Sports branding represents a relatively new area of research and currently there are few models of sports branding available in the literature (see Gladden *et al.*, 1998; Underwood *et al.*, 2001; Ross, 2006). Based on the findings of the current research project, the next step for sports brand-ing research should build around social identification. The more one identifies with a sports team, the more the team is integrated into their identity thus enhancing the emotional connec-tion between the fan and team (Underwood *et al.*, 2001). In terms of relationship marketing, establishing an emotional connection between the consumer and the brand is an integral part of the relationship building process (Berry, 2000). Survey results indicated social identification to have a positive influence on use of social media and a direct influence on brand equity. Thus, social identification should be a key component of future sports branding theory development.

References

Apostolopoulou, A. and Biggers, M. (2010) Positioning the New Orleans Hornets in the 'Who Dat' city. *Sports Marketing Quarterly*, 19, 229–234.
Arvidsson, A. (2006) *Brands: Meaning and Value in Culture*. London: Routledge.

Ashforth, B. E. and Mael, F. (1989) Social identity theory and the organization. *The Academy of Management Review, 14*(1), 20–39. Retrieved from http://www.jstor.org/stable/258189

Bauer, H. H., Stokburger-Sauer, N. E. and Exler, S. (2008) Brand image and fan loyalty in professional team sport: A refined model and empirical assessment. *Journal of Sport Management, 22,* 205–226.

Bergami, M. and Bagozzi, R. P. (2000) Self-categorization, affective commitment and group self-esteem as distinct aspects of social identity in the organization. *British Journal of Social Psychology, 39,* 555–577.

Berry, L. L. (2000) Cultivating service brand equity. *Journal of the Academy of Marketing Science, 28*(1), 128–137.

Branscombe, N. R. and Wann, D. L. (1991) The positive social and self-concept consequences of sports team identification. *Journal of Sport and Social Issues, 15*(2), 115–127.

Brewer, M. (1991) The social self: On being the same and different at the same time. *Personality and Social Psychology Bulletin, 17,* 457–482. Retrieved from http://psp.sagepub.com/content/17/5/475

Carlson, B. D. and Donavan, D. T. (2008) Concerning the effect of athlete endorsements on brand and team-related intentions. *Sports Marketing Quarterly, 17,* 154–162.

Christian, J., Bagozzi, R., Abrams, D. and Rosenthal, H. (2012) Social influence in newly formed groups: The roles of personal and social intentions, group norms, and social identity. *Personality and Individual Differences, 52,* 255–260. doi: 10.1016/j.paid.2011.10.004.

Clavio, G. and Kian, T. M. (2010) Uses and gratifications of a retired female athlete's Twitter followers. *International Journal of Sport Communication, 3,* 485–500.

Donavan, D. T., Carlson, B. D. and Zimmerman, M. (2005) The influence of personality traits on sports fan identification. *Sports Marketing Quarterly, 14,* 31–42.

Fink, J. S., Parker, H. M., Brett, M. and Higgins, J. (2009) Off-field behavior of athletes and team identification: Using social identity theory and balance theory to explain fan reactions. *Journal of Sport Management, 23,* 142–155.

Fisher, R. J. and Wakefield, K. (1998) Factors leading to group identification: A field study of winners and losers. *Psychology and Marketing, 15*(1), 23–40.

Funk, D. C. and James, J. (2001) The psychological continuum model: A conceptual framework for understanding an individual's psychological connection to sport. *Sport Management Review, 4,* 119–150.

Gladden, J. M., Milne, G. R. and Sutton, W. A. (1998) A conceptual framework for assessing brand equity in Division I college athletics. *Journal of Sport Management, 12*(1), 1–19.

Hambrick, M. E., Simmons, J. M., Greenhalgh, G. P. and Greenwell, T. C. (2010) Understanding professional athletes' use of Twitter: A content analysis of athlete tweets. *International Journal of Sport Communication, 3,* 454–471.

Heere, B. and James, J. D. (2007) Sport teams and their communities: Examining the influence of external group identities on team identity. *Journal of Sport Management, 21,* 319–337.

Igenhoff, D. and Koelling, A. M. (2009) The potential of websites as relationship building tool for charitable fundraising NPOs, *Public Relations Review, 35,* 66–73. doi: 10.1016/j.pubrev.2008.09.023.

Ioakimidis, M. (2010) Online marketing of professional sport clubs: Engaging fans on a new playing field. *International Journal of Sports Marketing and Sponsorship, 11*(4), 271–282. Retrieved from http://www.imrpublications.com/JSMS/

Kaplan, A. M. (2012) If you love something, let it go mobile: Mobile marketing and mobile social media 4x4. *Business Horizons, 55,* 129–139. doi: 10.1016/j.bushor.2011.10.009

Kaplan, A. M. and Haenlein, M. (2010) Users of the world, unite! The challenges and opportunities of social media. *Business Horizons, 53,* 59–68. doi: 10.1016/j.bushor.2009.09.003

Kerr, A. K. and Gladden, J. M. (2008) Extending the understanding of professional team brand equity to the global marketplace. *International Journal of Sport Management and Marketing, 3*(1/2), 58–77.

Kwon, E. S. and Sung, Y. (2011) Follow me! Global marketers' Twitter use. *Journal of Interactive Advertising, 12*(1), 4–16.

Mason, D. S. (1999) What is the sports product and who buys it? The marketing of professional sports leagues. *European Journal of Marketing, 33*(3/4), 402–418.

Marsh, H. and Hocevar, D. (1985) Application of confirmatory factor analysis to the study of self-concept: First and higher order factor models and their invariance across groups. *Psychological Bulletin, 97,* 562–582.

Parker, K. and Stuart, T. (1997) The west ham syndrome. *Market Research Society, 39*(3), 509–517.

Phua, J. J. (2010) Sports fans and media use: Influence on sports fan identification and collective self-esteem. *International Journal of Sport Communication, 3,* 190–206.

Reinard, J. C. (2006) *Communication research statistics.* Thousand Oaks, CA: Sage Publications.

Richelieu, A. and Pons, F. (2006) Toronto Maple Leafs vs. Football Club Barcelona: How two legendary sport teams built their brand equity. *International Journal of Sports Marketing and Sponsorship, 7*(3), 231–250.

Ross, S. D. (2006) A conceptual framework for understanding spectator-based brand equity. *Journal of Sport Management, 20, 22–38.*

Seo, W. J. and Green, B. C. (2008) Development of the motivation scale for sport online consumption. *Journal of Sport Management, 22, 82–109.*

Simmons, G. J. (2007) "i-Branding": Developing the Internet as a branding tool. *Marketing Intelligence and Planning, 25*(6), 544–562. doi: 10.1108/02634500710819932

Sutton, W. A., McDonald, M. A., Milne, G. R. and Cimperman, J. (1997) Creating and fostering fan identification in professional sports. *Sports Marketing Quarterly,* 6(1), 15–22.

Tajfel, H. (1982) Social psychology of intergroup relations. *Annual Review of Psychology, 33,* 1–39. doi: 10.1146/annurev.ps.33.020182.000245

Tajfel, H. and Turner, J. C. (2004) The social identity theory of intergroup behavior. In J. T. Jost and J. Sidanius (eds), *Political Psychology: Key Readings* (pp. 276–293) New York NY: Psychology Press.

Underwood, R., Bond, E. and Baer, R. (2001) Building service brands via social identity: Lessons from the sports marketplace. *Journal of Marketing Theory and Practice,* 9(1), 1–13.

Wallace, L., Wilson, J. and Miloch, K. (2011) Sporting Facebook: A content analysis of NCAA organizational sport pages and Big 12 conference athletic department pages. *International Journal of Sport Communication,* 4, 422–444.

Wann, D. L. and Branscombe, N. R. (1993) Sports fans: Measuring degree of identification with their team. *International Journal of Sport Psychology,* 24, 1–17.

Wann, D. L. and Dolan, T. J. (1994) Attributions of highly identified sports spectators. *The Journal of Social Psychology,* 134(6), 783–792.

Williams, J. and Chinn, S. J. (2010) Meeting relationship marketing goals through social media: A conceptual model for sport marketers. *International Journal of Sport Communication,* 3, 422–437.

PART IV

Audiences: Fanship, consumption

19

SOCIALMEDIASPORT

The fan as a (mediated) participant in spectator sports

Nicholas David Bowman and Gregory A. Cranmer

WEST VIRGINIA UNIVERSITY

In 1998, sport communication scholar Lawrence Wenner coined *MediaSport* as the "cultural fusing of sport with communication" (p. xiii). The concept – and the associated volume of the same name – attempted to explain the increased political, social, economic and cultural influence of spectator sports on society, as well as the fusing of sports as both performance and mediated entertainment. The specific focus on spectator sports is no happenstance: after all, the role of spectator is by definition one relegated to being an audience member – one watching action from a relative distance, whether in the stands or through a mediated lens. Likewise, the role of media in spectator sports has always been to bring spectators as close to on-field action as possible – in many cases closer than can be done through in-person attendance (cf. Bowman, 2013). March 5, 1733 saw the first sports-related story printed in a US newspaper when the *Boston Gazette* ran a reprinted story about a prize fight copied from a London newspaper, providing the primarily English-born colonials a glimpse of sporting life back home (Enriquez, 2002). KDKA Pittsburgh transmitted the first live sports radio broadcast when junior lightweights Johnny Dundee and Johnny Ray met at Motor Square Garden on April 21, 1921, and less than four months later they began broadcasting professional baseball. In these examples, we see media playing an important interlocutory role in removing space-time barriers between sports fans and on-field action, placing the non-collocated spectator into the sports arena through the use of the technologies of the time.

It is our contention that social media platforms represent a continuation of this trend of media technologies substantially reducing the space-time barrier between spectators and sports. Indeed, we argue that the "create and collaborate" nature of social media as a Web 2.0 technology (O'Reilly, 2005) has transformed the modern sports spectator from a passive audience member to an active contributor to the "sports/media production complex" (Wenner, 1998: 9). Social media have rendered obsolete the physical and semantic divides between fan and sport (Bowman, 2013) and ushered in an era of fan/sports/media production complex – an era of *SocialMediaSport* in which sports fans actively seek and create meaningful connections with their favorite athletes, organizations, media, and each other through the co-production and dissemination of a larger sport narrative. In turn, these athletes, organizations and media groups have responded by reaching out to fans on an increasingly intimate and social level – engaging them not only as customers but as co-producers of their respective messages, brands and identities.

In the following chapter, we analyze emerging usage patterns of social media by the shareholders of the SocialMediaSport complex – the fans, athletes, organizations, and legacy (or "old") media identified as the key "communities of sport" by Billings, Butterworth and Turman (2012: 22). After demonstrating the increased usage of social media by these sports shareholders, we suggest ways in which social media usage influences each by extending relevant theories and perspectives to the study of (social) mediated communication. Finally, we conclude by discussing the importance of SocialMediaSport as more than just a felicitous application of Wenner's concepts but rather a meaningful extension of the same to an emergent new media ecology. Notably for this chapter, we have adopted a definition of social media suggested by Kaplan and Haenlein (2010: 61) as "a group of Internet-based applications . . . that allow the creation and exchange of user-generated content." In this way, we include the more exemplar platforms such as Facebook (a network of persistent individual user profiles and organizational pages that are created, maintained and whose content is shared publicly) and Twitter (a micro-blogging service that provides individual users – both private and public citizens and organizations – with a public space for discourse) as well as platforms such as YouTube (a video sharing service that features user-generated content, be it professional media organizations or private individuals, that is open for commentary and redistribution among users). Across these platforms, the most critical aspect of social media is realized: the lessening of the distinction and the possibility of increased interaction between media producer and media consumer.

Adoption and usage of social media platforms

Mirroring the growth of the platforms themselves, there has been rapid adoption of social media platforms amongst all shareholders of the SocialMediaSport complex. In part, this rapid adoption can be primarily explained by the novelty of social media technology. Most social media platforms such as Facebook (launched in 2004) and Twitter (launched in 2006) are new and as such, sharp adoption curves would be expected as the platforms continue to diffuse through society (cf. Rogers, 1962). Associated with this rapid diffusion and adoption is the generativity of the platforms; their ability to be co-opted by individual users to satisfy any number of end goals (cf. Zittrain, 2008). Particularly as they become more transparent and easy-to-use for individuals, the nature of their usage becomes more complex as users adopt the platforms to satisfy a wider range of personal objectives (cf. Bowman, Westerman and Claus, 2012). Importantly for this chapter, this increased adoption, generativity, and complexity has been observed for all members of the SocialMediaSport complex.

Fans' use of social media

The number of sports fans using social media continues to grow. Social media sites such as Facebook, YouTube, and Twitter are all increasing in popularity amongst sports fans, with one in five fans using social media in 2011 and one in four using as of 2012 (Laird (2012b). In May 2012, the National Basketball Association (NBA) became the first professional sports league with over five million Twitter followers, and other major US professional sports leagues have seen similar growth (Laird, 2012a). Beyond following sports leagues, fans have also begun to follow individual athletes via social media, with stars such as Portuguese soccer player Cristiano Ronaldo gaining staggering numbers of social media followers – in fact, it is often the case that individual athletes have far more followers than the teams or leagues they play for (Ronaldo having nearly 12 times as many followers as the Fédération Internationale de Football Association, or FIFA; Laird, 2012a.)

In addition to merely following sports media, fans create their own sports-related content. In 2010, the most viewed sports video on YouTube at the time – a user-created video on NBA star Lebron James' dramatic departure from his hometown Cleveland Cavaliers that same year ("Cleveland Smacks Lebron") – had just over seven million unique views (Chase, 2010). The next year, a user-created video involving a mountain biker being attacked by a wild buck during a race in South Africa (appropriately labeled "Mountain Biker gets taken out by BUCK – CRAZY footage – Only in Africa") landed 12.6 million views (Inbar, 2011); moreover, both videos and countless similar others remain popular even today.

Similar to the sport-talk radio show format, fans have taken to the social media 'airwaves' to voice their opinions about any number of sports-related topics, bypassing the call-in switch-board and speaking frankly about their favorite and hated sports entities. One way they are able to do this is by utilizing Twitter's hashtag folksonomy to organize and search for sports-related content (e.g. #11in11 for St. Louis Cardinals fans following that team's run to the 2011 MLB World Series title). In fact, of the 15 most-used Twitter hashtags as of 2012, nearly half were related to live sports events that occurred in the previous year (Hernandez, 2012). More popular sporting events such as the NFL's Super Bowl and international soccer tournaments (e.g. FIFA's European Cup) have already begun to push the limits of Twitter's servers. For example, over 15,000 tweets per second were sent during early rounds of the 2012 EuroCup, representing a five-fold increase over the "normal" Twitter workload of 3,000 tweets per second (Graham, 2012; Widrich, 2012). Overall, trends in fan usage of social media suggest fans are creating, viewing, and discussing more content in addition to following more athletes, teams, and organizations.

Athletes' use of social media

In the three years from 2009 to 2012, there was a ten-fold increase in the number of professional athletes using Twitter – growing from 700 to nearly 7,000 (Tweeting Athletes, 2012). There are various explanations for this growth, including overt rewards by sports leagues and owners for Twitter engagement and covert rewards like increased market value for socially engaged (and engaging) athletes. For example, in an effort to increase the visibility and popularity of mixed-martial arts competitions, Dana White, the president of the Ultimate Fighting Championship, requires all of his athletes to have Twitter accounts and offers financial incentive to fighters for gaining followers and posting the most creative content (Ortiz, 2011). Some of White's UFC fighters have taken to using social media channels to engage in trash-talking in preparation for major fights, which Manfred (2012) argues can drive up fan interest – a particularly effective strategy for combative sports. For example, former UFC title contender Chael Sonnen launched numerous tirades about champion Anderson Silva's heritage, family, and athletic ability for months leading up to their two title fights. The rematch drew over 1.6 million pay-per-view buys in the US alone, shattering pay-per-view records for UFC by nearly 600,000 buys "in no small part" to the ongoing social media feud between Silva and Sonnen (Obi, 2012, para. 2).

While other sports organizations may not require their athletes to use social media, the benefits associated with social media exposure – such as the increased promotional and publicity opportunities, more intimate connections with fans, and enhanced public image – are enough to encourage athletes to use them. For instance, former Cincinnati Bengals receiver Chad Johnson (@ochocinco) has been recognized for his prowess in using Twitter to interact with fans and the media, including organizing numerous informal 'meet and greets' with local fans and even launching his own news network (OCNNReport.com) to cover sports-related news. The receiver once expressed interest in tweeting live from NFL games he was playing in before receiving a $25,000 fine from the league for tweeting during a pre-season contest against the Philadelphia Eagles (La Canfora, 2010). Other athletes accomplish self-promotion by posting advertisements for products, books, or television and radio appearances via their social media accounts. Doster (2012) argues that Olympic hurdler and bobsledder Lolo Jones was able to rise from relative obscurity to being featured in ESPN's *The Body Issue* in part by engaging her social media followers on more personal topics such as her overcoming a debilitating back surgery and her sexual chastity. In general, a major usage of social media by athletes is for promotional purposes – be it event-related, sports-related or even personal promotion.

Sports organizations' use of social media

Professional sports organizations – teams, leagues and franchises – are adopting new social media platforms and incorporating unique aspects of those platforms into their business models in efforts increase the size of their digital footprint. For example, both the MLB and NBA have created Pinterest and Tumblr accounts – two social bookmarking platforms that allow users to link and share team-branded content such as photos of popular or most-wanted player jerseys or stories from NBA.com and other internal sources. Other teams have begun to incorporate social media features into the actual game environment. For example, Mississippi State University was the first college football team to utilize a hashtag end zone (#HAILSTATE) during the 2011 Egg Bowl against Ole Miss, with the University of Arkansas and University of Michigan following suit by incorporating "#GOHOGS" and "#GOBLUE" (respectively) in the following season. The Philadelphia Wings – a professional lacrosse team in the National Lacrosse League (NLL) – promoted individual athletes' social media presence by replacing players' last names on the back of in-game jerseys with their Twitter handles during one game in 2011, and both the Washington Nationals and some LPGA broadcasts show athletes' Twitter names along with their other on-screen information.

In addition to using social media to increase a team or organization's online footprint and connect with fans, several sports organizations use social media to get fans more actively engaged with the sport and with each other. For example, the NBA and MLS both accept all-star ballots via social media and the NHL encourages fans to share their all-star votes on personal Facebook and Twitter accounts. Some leagues have even allowed fans to influence game-related outcomes, as fans' Twitter votes helped decide the winner of the 2012 NBA all-star dunk contest and music-sharing social media service Spotify was used by fans to determine the entrance music of some UFC fighters. When not bringing fans closer to game action, organizations are utilizing social media to bring fans closer to each other, such as MLB's "Fan Cave" – a social media-based platform sponsored by the league which is specifically structured to foster discussions between fans during MLB games (Sirabian, 2012).

Legacy media social media usage

Similar to fans, athletes, and organizations, sports journalists are also increasingly using social media. The preferred social media platform for these reporters appears to be Twitter likely due to that platform's live nature, with the most popular reporters both representing television networks such as ESPN's Adam Schefter (1.6 million followers as of 2012) and Fox Sports' Erin Andrews (1.3 million followers; Tweeting Athletes, 2012). Nearly all of the legacy sports media have created social media accounts for a variety of applications – ESPN for example maintains separate Twitter accounts for each of the major NCAA Football Championship Series conferences (i.e. @ESPN_BigTen and @ESPN_Big12 for the Big Ten and Big 12 conferences, respectively) and most major daily newspapers have created similar accounts for their more popular beat writers (*Denver Post* columnist Woody Paige @woodypaige and former *Chicago Sun-Times* reporter Jay Mariotti @MariottiJ as two more prominent examples). Even smaller-market daily and weekly newspapers such as the *Willoughby* (OH) *News-Herald* (@NHPreps) and the *Asheville* (NC) *Citizen-Times* (@acthshuddle) have begun using social media platforms to cover high school and regional sports.

Reed (2011) writes about reporters and columnists using social media platforms to identify and verify stories. Similar to larger trends in journalism, legacy sports media have begun to rely on crowdsourcing techniques to solicit information from eye-witnesses to any number of events happening worldwide. Crowdsourced sports stories have shown to be particularly useful for identifying novel perspectives on various sports issues, including the creation of a documentary collection of stories told by Detroit Lions fans via social media (tentatively called "The Season of Your Life," Laird, 2012c) and Canadian Broadcasting Company's CBCSports featuring of NHL fan's "Comment of the Day" in which they have highlighted fan's Facebook and Twitter comments regarding the league's labor disputes that resulted in a greatly abbreviated 2012–2013 season. Unfortunately, such crowdsourcing techniques can backfire as social media sources can be difficult to verify – as was the case when CNBC's Darren Rovell solicited stories from 'real people' about the partial cancellation of the 2011–2012 NBA season due to a labor dispute. In sifting through story ideas, he came across and told the false story of a man "Tim" who claimed a nearly 30 percent revenue decrease for his escort service as a result of the cancelled games (Deggans, 2012). Reed (2011) suggests pessimistically that professionals' reliance on social media for fact-checking will continue to increase, leading to decreased professional identification and possibly causing the quality of sports journalism to suffer. However, in an effort to combat these concerns many organizations from the Poynter Institute to the American Journalism Review to even Twitter itself (@TwitterForNews) have offered best practice guidelines to help sports and other news professionals accurately and ethically implement social media technologies into their practices.

The influence of SocialMediaSport on the shareholders

Shifting from a focus on usage patterns, the prominence of social media can be expected to influence the many identified shareholders in the SocialMediaSport complex in a variety of ways. While much of the extant research and theory tends to focus on sports fans and legacy media, the following section suggests research areas of theoretical and practical significance to better understand how these groups as well as the sports organizations and entities themselves are using and being influenced by social media.

Effects on sports fans

It is not a stretch to suggest that one of the most prominent influences of social media technology is the ability of these platforms to bring individuals semantically closer together and create digital places of discourse (Christakis and Fowler, 2009; Shirkey, 2008). In this digitally connected world, connections between friends and strangers are facilitated through construction of social networks in which users share their thoughts and opinions with few encumbrances. Of course, discussions of connectedness in virtual spaces often beg the question as to whether or not these virtual connections are indeed important social actors in one's life, and vice versa.

Para-(?) social interactions

On this point, we can draw parallels – as did Sanderson (2011) – to Horton and Wohl's (1956) notion of the para-social interaction, or the "seemingly face-to-face relationship between spectator and performer" that entertainment media consumers have been known to report having with their favorite actors, musicians, and athletes. In defining said interactions as "para-" we implicitly (and perhaps, explicitly) recognize that they are false – as explained by Horton and Wohl (1956), said relations are often considered far more real and important to the spectator than the performer. However, emerging research suggests these social interactions to be two-way dialogues rather than one-way directives. Hambrick, Simmons, Greenhalgh and Greenwell (2010) found that over one-third of tweets from a sample of 510 professional athletes could be classified as interactive. Pegoraro (2010) and Shockley (2010) similarly found that athletes appear to be actively engaging their fan bases – reaching out, touching and making more real the relationship between spectator and performer (Bowman, 2013). Sports entities such as owners and journalists have also been known to engage both each other and their fan bases, as is represented by a July 2012 exchange between Dallas Mavericks owner Mark Cuban (@mcuban) and Grantland.com editor Bill Simmons (@sportsguy33) ferociously debated Cuban's off-seasons roster moves –a discussion that eventually involved an anonymous fan (@CmackChase). During the debate, Cleveland Cavaliers owner Dan Gilbert (@cavsdan) retweeted much of Cuban's scathing response to Simmons, thereby expanding the audience of this once-personal and private debate through the SocialMediaSport audience.

In fact, this increasingly reified relationship between athletes and their fans appears to be extending to non-sports; each of the studies cited above also finds that athletes and fans express their opinions on myriad topics ranging from the topical to the mundane. Recent examples of this include a letter pinned by Minnesota Vikings punter Chris Kluwe (@ChrisWarcraft) in September 2012 to express his support of gay rights issues that has enjoyed widespread circulation amongst sports fans and political activists alike; fellow NFL player Brendon Ayanbadejo (@brendon310) also joined on this debate which eventually made it to National Public Radio (2012). Such personal sharing might be considered in terms of narrative bits, or "narbs" (Mitra, 2010), by which social media users create and share stories with one another. Indeed it is this "narb"ing that represents one of the unique dimensions of SocialMediaSport in that it brings the many creators of sports content together, providing each a "behind the scenes" look at the other (Bowman, 2013).

At the base level, we might expect increased feelings of connectedness with sports professionals to drive game attendance, merchandise sales and other markers of fan involvement – such as the fan avidity markers of on-field participation (playing or working for teams, passive engagement (following teams through media), purchasing (buying merchandise) or social engagement (attending games, tailgates, and other events; DeSarbo and Madrigal, 2011). Beyond this, emerging research suggests that our perceptions of athletes – in particular, their indiscretions – can be shaped by our perceived relationship with them (Earnheardt, 2010). As well, increased feelings of connectedness with athletes might also foster enhanced feelings of identification with athletes and organizations (cf. Sanderson, 2011). One such study by Kassing and Sanderson (2010) found that fans of the Giro d'Italia felt a greater sense of immediacy and intimacy between themselves and a select group of cyclists who were active on Twitter during the event.

Intra-audience effects

Hocking (1982) presented the notion of the intra-audience effect when describing the appeal of attendance at live sporting events. His discussion centered around the increased enjoyment spectators often report when attending sporting events in person as opposed to watching the games from home – even though it is often the case that the home viewer has a much better view of the game action. From this, Hocking argued that not only can being part of a live audience increase enjoyment of an event, but the disposition of fellow audience members can moderate this relationship. Of course, Hocking's contention can be interpreted to suggest that while these technologies are making the fan experience increasingly vivid and interactive, they do not foster the sense of sports community and social connectedness that comes with attending live events, similar to Putnam's (1995) challenged views on media entertainment as a decidedly solitary pursuit. On this point, we might see how the social media breaks from other media advancements in that it embraces rather than discourages social interactions.

Such increased interactions between fans in particular, and sports shareholders in general, might be combined with logic from Hocking to suggest that SocialMediaSport consumers are at least ambiently aware of each other (Thompson, 2008) vis-à-vis their passive involvement on social media or active engagement with each other as social actors with thoughts and feelings about the sport being spectated. On this latter point, concepts from research on social presence – the awareness of others in online interactions combined with some appreciation for the interpersonal dynamics of the interactions (Short, Williams and Christie, 1976) – might be beneficial. For example, if Hocking's arguments about intra-audience effects are rooted in the notion that the presence of social actors (fellow fans and spectators) is providing the witnessed influence on enjoyment, increased social presence in a social network of fans, press and sports institutions should also benefit enjoyment. Such a perspective – as well as potential beneficial or deleterious effects on the fan experience – has yet to be researched, although major sports media organizations such as NBC Sports have worked to increasingly integrate social media more centrally into the overall diet of events such as the 2012 London Summer Olympics (Miah, 2012).

Motivations for media consumption

Broadly, we tend to assume that the driving motivation for fans to consume sports media is because they are fans – that is, they watch because, often, sports media is the lone conduit between the fan and the sport they love. However, fan motivations are a bit more nuanced than this. Raney (2006a) has identified cognitive, emotional and social dimensions of sports viewership that explain how we are able to use sports media to distract ourselves and get excited about (for better or worse) our favorite performances and share these experiences with other fans. Similarly, Wann (1995) explains sports fan motivation more granularly in terms of needs associated with eustress, self-esteem, escape, entertainment, economic, aesthetic, group affiliation and family needs (some of which are subsumed by Raney's dimensions). Across these conceptualizations we see a common notion of socialization akin to that alluded to by Hocking (1982). Stories of Super Bowl parties, fantasy football draft gatherings and heated water-cooler debates about 'last night's game' are often cited as anecdotal evidence of sport media's socializing force – fans watch sports because it brings them together with like-minded individuals. Indeed, studies on SocialMediaSport would be well-served to consider social media as a particularly well-suited media form at fostering socialization between fans as the technologies exists outside the boundaries of space-time and thus, might be even more efficient in providing places of discourse for fans.

Effects on press coverage

Earlier in this chapter we discussed several novel ways by which legacy media have incorporated social media into their operations. Focusing more specifically on media research, we might consider how social media has altered the manner in which stories are produced, both in terms of the manner in which content is framed as well as the source of content.

Disintermediation and framing effects

Prior to social media, news cycles – at least when considering written stories – were much slower as reporters attended contests, events, recorded what they saw, wrote game stories, and submitted them for editing by senior staff members before the stories were approved for publication either in print or online. However, this editorial process is being challenged by social media platforms that allow reporters of all types to immediately post live from events, effectively converting print reporters to live commentators as fast as they can post to Twitter. In this way, social media channels have introduced a process of disintermediation – removing barriers to publication – that traditionally served as quality controls for the editorial process, and some fear that the renewed focus on being first might come at the expense of being accurate (such as the aforementioned Rovell's coverage of the fictitious "Tim" struggles during the NBA labor disputes).

Beyond story accuracy, a particular area of concern for this increased disintermediation is that such shortened news cycles might lead way to an increased prevalence of racialized and sexualized frames already present in coverage (cf. Billings, 2004; Mecurio and Filak, 2010). The line of argumentation invoked here suggests that increased disintermediation allows for more of an opportunity for journalists to (sub)consciously invoke these frames similar to what has been observed regarding broadcast media such as television commentary (Bruce, 2004; Rada and Wulfemeyer, 2005). Already, evidence suggests social media to be encouraging the use of said frames. In one particularly vulgar example, the career-high 38-point performance by previously-unheralded Asian-American New York Knicks point guard Jeremy Lin was both celebrated and chided by Fox Sports' columnist Jason Whitlock (@WhitlockJason) who commented on Twitter that "Some lucky lady in NYC is gonna [sic] feel a couple inches of pain tonight" (referencing Asian-American genitalia stereotypes; Langford, 2012). Content analysis research by Sanderson and Hambrick (2012) further suggests that social media platforms are dissolving professional and personal lines for many sports reporters. Their analysis of nearly 2,000 Tweets sent by 151 different sports writers regarding the child molestation conviction of former college football coach Jerry Sandusky found much of the coverage to be strongly biased – including frequent comments attacking Sandusky and verbally sparring with sports fans and other reporters. Reporters also defended each others' usage of personal frames and referenced each others' columns as further commentary in support of their own beliefs. Here, we see the implicit and explicit invocation of frames to tell larger stories beyond the witnessed on-field action.

Increased competition and media niches

Sanderson (2011) suggests that social media platforms have allowed audiences access to a wide variety of new outlets for sports-related news as "the leveling of the sports media hierarchy is one of the most evident changes that the Internet has generated in sports media" (p. 18). Highlighting the rise of niche sports companies such as profootballtalk.com (now an affiliate of NBC Sports) and Deadspin.com, Sanderson notes that smaller outlets traditionally marginalized in the legacy media ecology have been able to enjoy sustained commercial and critical success. These are examples of what O'Reilly (2005) considered the long tail of information distribution: niche websites with specific and quality information that make up the large majority of online information. Indeed, such a media environment provides a unique test of Dimmick's (2003) theory of media niche, arguing that older and new media forms often coexist rather than compete for audience members as users sample from a growing menu of highly-focused niche publications – including those written completely by fans such as the Facebook group ChatBlues (devoted to fan chatter about the NHL's St. Louis Blues) – rather than a few broad ones. Moving further, identifying niche media audiences as discrete gratifications sets (Katz, Blumler and Gurevitch, 1974) might further our understanding of how audiences' sports media tastes are both driving and being shaped by sports media.

Not only do legacy media face increased competition niche publications, the co-production of media content by other shareholders also threatens to steal audience share. Bowman and Willis (2003) discuss the general rise of citizen journalists' "active role in the process of collecting, reporting, analyzing, and disseminating news and information" (p. 7). On the one hand, this may be viewed as a positive as sports fans are able to take a more interactive role – partially in conjunction with legacy media – to co-create elements of the SocialMediaSport complex such as has been seen in traditional reporters' crowdsourcing information from these highly-engaged fans. However, the sports' fans ability to network and express themselves may come at the expense of the journalists' ability to hold an audience as they (fans) turn to each other for news and information about the very sports they are watching. While Reed (2011) argues partly that the credibility that comes with being a professional journalist is an advantage fans do not possess, others might contest that the unadulterated views of fans might be more appealing to audiences.

Effects on sports organizations and athletes

Social media has arguably most affected the relationship between fans and organizations or athletes within the SocialMediaSport complex. The traditional journalism model utilizes the legacy journalist as the mediator between athletes or organizations and sports fans. However, social media circumvents journalists and (potentially) marginalizes them. This occurrence is meaningful from the lens of the fourth wall perspective (cf. Stevenson, 1995), which argues that mediated entertainment is performed behind a metaphorical demarcation line between spectator and performer so that both spaces can be reified separately and neither interferes with the other. Bowman (2013) writes that this line serves to potentially enhance entertainment of mediated sports because it allows us to focus on the athletic competitions separately from the real-world actions and behaviors of the athletes themselves; in this way, sports serves as an escape from reality where we can focus on cheering for our heroes and booing our villains in an effort to restore justice (cf. Raney, 2006b). Utilizing this metaphor in conjunction with the SocialMediaSport perspective changes the audiences' desired destination as a result of using social media: no longer is the sole goal of media to bring the audience closer to the action of game play, but rather to bring the audience closer to the actors themselves (in this case, the athletes or organization). In essence, the goal of social media is not to break down the fourth wall but rather bring the audience back stage. Additionally, it is no longer the legacy journalist who ushers the audience to their desired destination but rather the athletes and organizations themselves. For example, without social media, fans interactions with UFC president Dana White would be mediated by journalists in a decidedly traditional and one-sided fashion;

however, through social media platforms nearly 2.1 million fans follow and regularly interact with White (Hatamoto, 2012). In here, we might suggest research aimed at understanding the influence of such audience immersion both on sports fandom as well as the athletes or organizations themselves.

Conclusion

While conclusions that social media usage is increasing in sports journalism might be considered moot when considering the general widespread adoption of social media in various aspects of journalism and human communication in general, our chapter suggests specific areas of research aimed understanding the impacts of this usage. Primarily, we suggest that the emergence of social media has placed the sports fan in an increasingly active role in the co-production of mediated sports content; as equal players in the MediaSport complex proposed by Wenner nearly two decades ago. Social media platforms have removed layers of mediation from sports content for fans, athletes, organizations and even the traditional press – and the transactional communication processes encouraged by social media have given rise to a SocialMediaSport complex representing each stakeholder's role in the cultural fusing of sport and communication.

References

Billings, A. C. (2004) Depicting the quarterback in black and white: A content analysis of college and professional football broadcast commentary. *Howard Journal of Communications,* 15, 201–210. doi:10.1080/106461704905211580

Billings, A. C., Butterworth, M. L. and Turman, P. D. (2012) *Communication and Sport: Surveying the Field.* Thousand Oaks, CA: Sage.

Bowman, N. D. (2013) Social media, spaghetti westerns, and modern spectators sports. In D. Coombs and B. Batchelor (eds), *American History through American Sports* (pp. 31–48). Santa Barbara, CA: Praeger.

Bowman, N. D., Westerman, D. K., Claus, C. J. (2012) How demanding is social media: Understanding social media diets as a function of perceived costs and benefits – A rational actor perspective. *Computers in Human Behavior, 28*(6). doi:10.1016/j.chb.2012.06.037

Bowman, S. and Willis, C. (2003) *We Media: How Audiences are Shaping the Future of News and Information.* Reston, VA: American Press Institute.

Bruce, T. (2004) Marking the boundaries of the 'normal' in televised sports: The play-by-play or race. *Media Culture Society,* 26, 861–879. doi:10.1177/0163443704047030

Chase, C. (2010, December 18) The top 10 viral sports videos of 2010. *Yahoo Sports.* Retrieved from http://sports.yahoo.com/blogs/post/The-top-10-viral-sports-videos-of-2010?urn=top-297468

Christakis, N. A. and Fowler, J. H. (2009) *Connected: The Surprising Power of Our Social Networks and How they Shape Our Lives.* New York: Little, Brown & Company.

Deggans, E. (2012, June 7) *Rovell's Mistake Provides Crucial Lessons for Crowdsourcing.* [National Sports Journalism Center.] Retrieved October 1, 2012, from http://sportsjournalism.org/sports-media-news/rovells-mistake-provides-crucial-lessons-for-crowdsourcing/

DeSarbo, W. and Madrigal, R. (2011) Examining the behavioral manifestations of fan avidity in sports marketing. *Journal of Modelling and Management,* 6(1), 79–99.

Dimmick, J. (2002) *Media Competition and Coexistence: The Theory of the Niche.* Mahwah, NJ: Lawrence Erlbaum Associates.

Doster, R. (2012, August 8) Lolo Jones outclasses her critics. *NationalReview.com.* Retrieved from http://www.nationalreview.com/right-field/313403/lolo-jones-outclasses-her-critics-rob-doster

Earnheardt, A. (2010) Exploring sports television viewers' judgments of athletes' antisocial behavior. *International Journal of Sport Communication,* 3(2), 167–189.

Enriquez, J. (2002) Coverage of sports. In W. D. Sloan and L. M. Parcell (eds), *American Journalism: History, Principles, Practices* (pp. 198–208). Jefferson, NC: McFarland.

Graham, J. (2012, June, 6) Twitter teams with NASCAR to corral fan tweets. *USA Today.* Retrieved from http://www.usatoday.com/tech/columinst/talkingtech/story/2012-06-06/nascar-twitter/55430444/1

Hambrick, M. E., Simmons, J. M., Greenhalgh, G. P. and Greenwell, T. C. (2010) Understanding professional athletes' use of Twitter: A content analysis of athlete tweets. *International Journal of Sport Communication,* 3, 454–471.

Hatamoto, M. (2012) UFC: The ultimate fighter live's social media efforts greatly help Spotify. *Bleacher Report.com.* Retrieved from http://bleacherreport.com/articles/1217232-ufc-tuf-live-social-media-efforts-greatly-help-spotify

Hernandez, B. A. (2012, February 6) The top 15 tweets-per-second records. *Mashable.com.* Retrieved from http://mashable.com/2012/02/06/tweets_per_second_records_twitter/#4711914-NBA-Finals_Lebron-Tweet

Hocking, J. E. (1982) Sports and spectators: Intra-audience effects. *Journal of Communication,* 32(1), 100–108.

Horton, D. and Wohl, R. (1956) Mass communication and para-social interaction: Observations on intimacy at a distance. *Psychiatry,* 19(3), 215–229.

Inbar, M. (2011, October 17) Mountain biker attacked by antelope: 'It was scary'. *USA Today.* Retrieved from http://www.today.com/id/44928583/ns/today-today_pets/t/mountain-biker-attacked-antelope-it-was-scary/#.UiyTLsakpTI

Kaplan, A. M. and Haenlein, M. (2010) Users of the world, Unite! The challenges and opportunities of social media. *Business Horizons,* 53, 59–68. doi: 10.1016/j.bushor.2009.003

Kassing, J. W. and Sanderson, J. (2010) Fan-athlete interaction and twitter tweeting through the Giro: A case study. *International Journal of Sport Communication,* 3(1), 113–128.

Katz, E., Blumler, J. G. and Gurevitch, M. (1974) Utilization of mass communication by the individual. In J. G. Blumler and E. Katz (eds), *Uses of mass communications,* 3: 19–32. Beverly Hills, CA: Sage Publications.

La Canfora, J. (2010, August 24) In-game tweeting costs Bengals' Ochocinco $25,000. *NFL.com.* Retrieved October 1, 2012, from http://www.nfl.com/news/story/09000d5d819fb95a/article/ingame-tweeting-costs-bengals-ochocinco-25000

Laird, S. (2012a, May 14) NBA is first league to get 5 million Twitter followers. *Mashable.com.* Retrieved from http://mashable.com/2012/05/14/nba-twitter-5-million

Laird, S. (2012b, June 11) 1 in 4 American fans follows sports via social media [study]. *Mashable.com.* Retrieved from http://mashable.com/2012/06/11/1-in-4-american-fans-follow-sports-via-social-media-study/

Laird, S. (2012c, September 9) Crowd-sourced documentary to tell story of NFL fans' season. *Mashable.com.* Retrieved October 1, 2012, from http://mashable.com/2012/09/09/nfl-crowd-sourced-documentary/

Langford, R. (2012, February 14) Jason Whitlock shows true colors on Twitter with lame Jeremy Lin Tweet. *Bleacher Report.com.* Retrieved September 12, 2012, from http://bleacherreport.com/articles/1066390-jason-whitlock-shows-true-colors-on-twitter-with-lame-jeremy-lin-tweet

Manfred, T. (2012, July 12) Meet Ronda Rousey, the trash talk MMA fighter who just landed on the cover of ESPN's body issue. *BusinessInsider.com.* Retrieved from http://www.businessinsider.com/mma-fighter-ronda-rousey-life-story-2012-7?op=1

Mecurio, E. and Filak V. F. (2010) Roughing the passer: The framing of black and white quarterbacks prior to the NFL draft. *Howard Journal of Communications,* 21, 56–71. doi:10.1080/1063443707084348

Miah, A. (2012, August 10) Viewpoint: London 2012, a social media Olympics to remember. *BBC.co.uk.* Retrieved September 13, 2012, from http://www.bbc.co.uk/news/technology-19191785

Mitra, A. (2010) Creating a presence on social networks via narbs. *Global Media Journal,* 9(16). Retrieved November 4, 2011, from http://lass.calumet.purdue.edu/cca/gmj/PDF_archive/amer_edition/spring2010/GMJ-SP10-article7-mitra.pdf

National Public Radio (Producer) (2012, September 12) Same-sex marriage finds new support in NFL [Podcast transcript]. Retrieved October 1, 2012, from http://www.npr.org/2012/09/12/161025947/same-sex-marriage-finds-new-support-in-nfl

Obi, N. (2012, July 10) UFC 148: Anderson Silva vs. Chael Sonnen draws 19 million viewers in Brazil. *Bleacher Report.com.* Retrieved from http://bleacherreport.com/articles/1254211-ufc-148-anderson-silva-vs-chael-sonnen-draws-19-million-viewers-in-brazil

O'Reilly, T. (2005) What is Web 2.0? *O'Reilly Media.* Retrieved August 1, 2012, from http://oreilly.com/web2/archive/what-is-web-20.html

Ortiz, M. B. (2011, June 6) Dana White leads UFC into social realm. *ESPN.com.* Retrieved September 12, 2012, from http://sports.espn.go.com/espn/page2/story?page=burnsortiz/110606_ufc_dana_white

Pegoraro, A. (2010) Look who's talking – Athletes on Twitter: A case study. *International Journal of Sport Communication,* 3(4), 501–514.

Putnam, R. D. (1995) Bowling alone: America's declining social capital. *Journal of Democracy,* 6(1), 65–78.

Raney, A. A. (2006a) Why we watch and enjoy mediated sports. In A. A. Raney and J. Bryant (eds), *Handbook of Sports and Media* (pp. 313–330). Mahwah, NJ: Lawrence Erlbaum Associates.

Raney, A. A. (2006b) The psychology of disposition-based theories of media enjoyment. In J. Bryant and P. Vorderer (eds), *Psychology of Entertainment* (pp. 56–68). Mahwah, NJ: Lawrence Erlbaum Associates.

Rada, J. A. and Wulfemeyer. K. T. (2005) Color coded: Racial descriptors in television coverage of intercollegiate sports. *Journal of Broadcasting and Electronic Media*, 49, 65–85. doi:10.1207/s15506878jobem4901_5

Reed, S. (2011) Sports journalists' use of social media and its effects on professionalism. *Journal of Sports Media*, 6, 43–64.

Rogers, E. (1962) *Diffusion of innovations.* Glencoe, NY: Free Press.

Sanderson, J. (2011) *It's a Whole New Ballgame: How Social Media is Changing Sports.* New York: Hampton Press.

Sanderson, J. and Hambrick, M. E. (2012) Covering the scandal in 140 characters: A case study of Twitter's role in coverage of the Penn State Saga. *International Journal of Sport Communication*, 5, 384–402.

Shirkey, C. (2008) *Here Comes Everybody: The Power of Organizing Without Organizations.* New York: Penguin.

Shockley, J. A. (2010) *Unfiltered? A Content Analysis of Pro Athletes' Twitter Use.* Unpublished thesis. East Tennessee Sate University, Johnson City, TN.

Short, J., Williams, E. and Christie, B. (1976) *The Social Psychology of Telecommunications.* London: John Wiley.

Sirabian, C. (2012, June 20) Sport and social media: 3 innovative examples. *Business to Community.com*. Retrieved from http://www.business2community.com/social-media/sports-and-social-media-3-innovative-examples-0200907

Stevenson, J. (1995) *The Fourth Wall and the Third Space.* New Paltz, NY: Centre for Playback Theatre.

Thompson, C. (2008, September 8) Brave new world of digital intimacy. *New York Times*. Retrieved September 13, 2012, from: www.nytimes.com/2008/09/07/magazine/07awareness-t.html?pagewanted=all.

Tweeting Athletes. (2012, September 23) Retrieved from http://www.tweeting-athletes.com/

Wann, D. L. (1995) Preliminary validation of sport fan motivation scale. *Journal of Sport and Social Issues*, 19(4), 377–396.

Wenner, L. (1998) *MediaSport.* New York: Routledge.

Widrich, L. (2012, February 27) Every 60 seconds 175,000 tweets are sent. *Buffer.com*. Retrieved from http://blog.bufferapp.com/every-60-seconds-175000-tweets-are-sent-infographic.

Zittrain, J. (2008) *The Future of the Internet: And How to Stop It.* New Haven, CT: Yale University Press.

20

THE NEW GAME DAY

Fan engagement and the marriage of mediated and mobile

Vincent L. Benigni

COLLEGE OF CHARLESTON

Lance V. Porter

LOUISIANA STATE UNIVERSITY

Chris Wood

JWA COMMUNICATIONS

The apparent need for continual consumption is evident in the sports fan's appetite for mediated and live sporting events, as well as the now prevalent technologies and digital innovations – from social to mobile media – that afford the marriage of the two. Fan involvement in the new mediated sports experience goes beyond the nature of fan consumption of and contributions to Fan-Based Internet Sports Communities (FBISCs) and beyond the casual attention to television coverage's "in-game" features. As Porter, Wood and Benigni (2011) noted, FBISCs are an ideal means for fans to come together with common, often rabid interests in favorite teams and players, to engage in what researchers have referred to as Basking in Reflected Glory (BIRGing; Cialdini *et al.*, 1976) or Cutting Off Reflected Failure (CORFing; Wann and Branscombe, 1990) after a loss, or even Cutting Off Future Failure (COFFing; Wann *et al.*, 1995), and to form their own communities as a result of these emotional, cognitive, and/or behavioral intentions. However, these Web-based "communities" have until recently lacked a means for real-time fellowship during the games that provide the ultimate stimuli for their focus and camaraderie. Instead, FBISCs tend to be places where *uber* fans gather online either before or after the game, and preferably after a win (Porter *et al.*, 2011). Today, rather than waiting until they get home from a game to connect to their favorite FBISC from a personal computer, fans can commiserate and celebrate in real time while at the live sporting event.

With their "always-on" and expanding social capabilities, mobile devices offer increasing numbers of both casual and intense fans a way to stay connected before, *during*, and after a game, whether fans are in the stadium or on the couch. A recent Pew study found that more than 50% of adults use their phones while watching television (Smith and Boyles, 2012).

Among tablet and smartphone owners, those numbers are even higher, with Nielsen reporting that 86% of tablet owners and 84% of smartphone owners in the United States use the "second screen" while watching television within the past 30 days (NielsenWire, 2012). However, the effects of the phone as the primary screen at the stadium on game day have yet to be studied. The connected fan has graduated from the enjoyment of linear FBISC participation to an ultimate level of fan involvement made possible by the increasingly mediated game day.

The idea of the "second screen" is not new. In 2007, prior to the rise of the smartphone and tablet, Cruickshank *et al.* showed how the development of an improved user interface or "second screen' might improve interaction and navigation with interactive television. Now we are starting to see the smartphone usher in that reality in sport. For fans previously consumed with preparations for a sporting event and analysis afterward, traditional print, broadcast, cable and Web content – including that provided on FBISCs – would suffice. However, the growth of digital, mobile, and social media platforms have afforded that fan the ability to extend the game-day experience, with mediated in-game content offering the additional value of being commoditized because of the traditional and new audiences it can engage. We are undergoing the fastest and most significant technological and business change in history. The Internet and its digital, mobile and social platforms present new opportunities for fans to unite by offering unprecedented opportunities to interact in real time with each other and their favorite teams, while teams and universities are able to showcase their product like never before.

Today's game day: Connecting the stadium and the couch

On a fall Saturday or Sunday, fans invest the majority of the day in bonding measures (Porter *et al.*, 2011), with the game being the centerpiece. Game day has long been a mediated experience for fans, with their continual, collective media consumption culminating on the day of the event. Their game-day experience is undergoing tremendous change.

With traditional and new media featuring at least branded extensions or platforms in digital, social, and/or mobile form, sports audiences can constantly access, share, and even create sports media. Media is becoming more personalized, customizable, bite-sized, time-shifted, and fragmented. However, sports programming remains one type of content that audiences prefer to watch live and in a synchronous stream. Therefore, sports programming may be one of the last bastions of the old model of interruptive advertising. Even so, audiences are moving beyond the television model to a post-PC and device-centric universe that allows them to access sports content on the go. While the fan stadium experience and the traditional mediated event experiences have been separated by time and distance, digital media are bringing those two encounters into the same realm. In the park or stadium, as Levinson (2013) notes, we can be liberated through smartphones and mobile media, and advances in 3D-technology/augmented reality, as mobile phones provide fans at home with unprecedented access and with that, more expectations.

Fans can text, tweet, Facebook, Instagram, and Vine their live celebrations and laments to each other during the game. Loudmouths can take to their own news feeds to shout electronically to the world, while more reticent fans can choose to merely "lurk" on newsfeeds. Whether separated by stadium sections or by thousands of miles, fans can access real-time sports content through a merged and mediated platform, as an even more "refreshing" and live game experience is possible via their mobile devices.

Uses and gratifications, selective exposure, and the enjoyment of sports entertainment

The uses and gratifications perspective presumes that we must first understand audience needs and motives (Maslow 1970) for media behavior before we can explain the effects of the media. Uses and gratifications has been described as an overriding theory that encompasses several models (Blumler, 1979; Windahl, 1981), with those primary components of the uses and gratifications perspective being further identified in several studies, most notably those of Katz, Blumler and Gurevitch (1974) and Rosengren (1974). More specifically, Rubin (1983) examined the interrelationships of media use motives and how they facilitate attitudes and behaviors.

While considering the potential enjoyment and entertaining qualities of sports media, Zillmann and Bryant (1986: 281) first noted how "an understanding of audience consumption patterns enhances an explanation of media effects ... the overriding belief (is) that individuals differentially select and use communication vehicles to gratify or satisfy felt needs." Thus, the appeal of digital/mobile media to sports fans wanting to "stay connected" even during the games in which they experience in person or watch live on television or via other new/digital technologies.

Zillmann and Bryant (1986) also note that *selective exposure* to entertainment includes the notion that "the program that holds the greatest appeal at a given time and under given circumstances, for whatever particular reasons, is likely to be picked" (p. 306).

The entertaining, dramatic nature of sports contests is influenced by a number of variables, including a fan's disposition toward teams and players (Zillmann *et al.*, 1989; Bryant and Raney, 2000; Raney, 2006), the nature of the contest and degree of fan involvement (Gantz *et al.*, 2006), and the thrills and suspense of the games (Bryant *et al.*, 1994; Su-Lin, *et al.*, 1997; Peterson and Raney, 2008). Raney (2006) asserts there are three major reasons for, or categories of, sports media consumption – emotional, cognitive, and behavioral/social.

The disposition theory of sports spectatorship has contributed to a better understanding of enjoyment regarding the sports fan's consumption of mediated content (Zillmann *et al.*, 1989; Bryant and Raney, 2000; Raney, 2006). Media consumption and subsequent enjoyment is determined at least in part by "the disposition held toward the competitors" in the game (Raney, 2006: 306).

Applied further, disposition theory may help explain or at least identify two inverse motives for the consumption of digital, mobile mediated sports content, especially in-game. If there is strong liking for a team and disdain for an opponent, viewers are likely to be more involved and emotionally engaged in the media-viewing – or in the case of applied digital technologies, the media-generating – experience. To the contrary, less involved "patrons," as opposed to "fans," may manifest their disinterest through consumption of digital, mobile media content, which may not even be sports-related, in turn creating an entirely new non-traditional game-day audience – such as women and children – to be commoditized and reached through expanded (digital/mobile) mediated content. As Wann *et al.* (2004) contend, sports fans may seek traditional or alternative media as a means for escape or release from over-stimulation or under-stimulation, such as boredom, possibly even created by disinterest in the game unfolding right before them.

Infrastructure and opportunity: Cultivating connectedness

In the 1990s, more than $16 billion was spent on US stadiums and arenas (Miller and Washington, 2011), in some part because of the tepid or even harsh fan response to the antiseptic cookie-cutter, multi-purpose structures of the previous two decades (Bellamy, 2010). In the 2000s, *SportsBusiness* Journal reports that of the $32.3 billion spent on stadium/arena construction, $23 billion was earmarked for professional teams, with just $9 billion for collegiate structures, and less than $4 billion for stadiums (Sports Marketing, 2012).

Howard and Crompton (2003) analyzed the honeymoon effect of new stadiums, noting that while the novelty quickly fades, teams are better off with newer facilities. The authors also address the aura of "stadiums as destinations," inferring that fan "bucket lists" are more likely to include pilgrimages to nostalgic edifices. College and pro stadium expansions and reconstruction are being accompanied by the proposed expansion of the mediated in-game experience. It's as if the powers that be – whether athletic departments at major colleges or owners of pro sports franchises – are pursuing not just more (seats and suites), but more *to do* (Wi-Fi capability and capacity) at event sites. Ericsson announced in late 2012 (Essers, 2012) that it had developed a Wi-Fi access point that would allow users to switch easily from clogged cellular networks to local Wi-Fi networks at crowded sporting events in Europe. Mobile users are actively sharing images in Australian cricket (along with AFL football and Open tennis), with few repercussions in relation to the "draconian (photo-sharing) rules" toward larger/zoom cameras in an attempt to protect broadcast media partners (Bhatt, 2012).

In 2012, National Football League (NFL) commissioner Roger Goodell noted that the fan experience at home is outstanding and the league must create the same kind of environment inside stadiums (Iyer, 2012). Recent developments in professional sports to enhance the fan experience include a safety policy – promoted through outlets such as scoreboards, game programs and public-address announcements – in which fans can anonymously text stadium security to deal with unruly spectators. In 2012, Goodell established a pilot group of Wi-Fi-enabled NFL stadiums, while announcing that all venues should be connected to popular NFL platforms, such as Red Zone Channel, and seek to attract fantasy football followers. While the NFL was wary to sign with a telecommunications partner because of the speed in tech development (Katzowitz, 2012), the league continues to pursue innovations such as synch apps for the Super Bowl (Winslow, 2012).

While the digital media (especially mobile) infrastructure gap between pro and college teams may seem striking, it may not be just financially driven, but market and sociologically based. The NFL features 31 of 32 teams within the top 50 American markets, the exception being the iconic Green Bay Packers. Of the Top 25 college football teams as of October 2012, fewer than half fit within the top 50 markets. While fans flock to these bucolic stadiums, this passion may not translate to the digital media landscape. If universities improve Internet infrastructure, they still may not have the "market" to inspire a new tradition of interconnectedness that complements the close-knit interpersonal nature of college game day.

The game-day experience doesn't start inside the stadium. James *et al.* (2001) established six constructs (friends, family, part of the game, fun, don't remember, miscellaneous) for reasons to start to tailgate and seven constructs (social interaction, drinking, food, being outside, game atmosphere, fun, miscellaneous) for reasons why fans continue to tailgate.[1] Given the social, mobile and digital advances in connecting friends – current and future – the notion of virtual tailgating seems obvious. Through platforms such as Facebook and Twitter, FourSquare and Pinterest, or evolving social network or mobile applications, any of these will be able to connect host institutions with fan constituents.

With escalating costs to field high-level teams, organizations seek new revenue streams. In the late 1980s, seven of 10 spectators noticed and correctly identified ads and locations that were "part of the game" and were more effective than scoreboard ads (Stotlar and Johnson, 1989). Today, newer stadiums utilize games and "fan cams" between plays or during timeouts on video display boards to attract eyes (Jarvis and Coleman, 2003) to sponsored areas. In a sport like football (or even baseball), there is significant downtime between plays in which a large, captive audience can be reached by sponsors.

Hitting the fan: Stimulus or suffocation?

Drawing from theories on environmental psychology, Uhrich and Benkenstein (2010) identified four dimensions of sport stadium atmosphere, such as what can be experienced during a Euro professional soccer match: stimuli emanating from spectators in their behavior, stimuli relating to the architecture of the stadium, stimuli elicited by the organizers, and stimuli caused by the action of the game (the architectural stimulus is especially critical when analyzing the limitations of non-smart stadiums). The study also established 16 reflective indicators of the affective fan states, six of which – constant fan chanting, songs and club anthem played frequently, fans performing set choreography, fans on grandstands shouting at each other, stadium announcer encouraging spectators, and active/loud participation by many spectators – are direct prompts by organizers (teams) to illustrate active fandom.

The European tradition of chanting and singing is clearly a part of venue atmosphere, whether in a soccer match or the "Ole Ole" chants in a stirring Ryder Cup victory. Across the pond, American fans also engage in chants, such as New Yorkers pronouncing "J-E-T-S, Jets, Jets, Jets," or more tribal assertions accompanying the "Tomahawk Chop" at home games of the Florida State Seminoles. Crowd participation is often sparked by "prompts" (PA announcer, scoreboard), but mobile technology may allow for more spontaneous or creative activity.

Digital technology through social and mobile outlets can enhance this stimulation, while allowing for multiple gatekeepers and organic interconnectedness. Fans are increasingly seen as stakeholders, and communication strategies can include tactics such as stadium microsites (Walters, 2011), or specialized pages within a defined site. Gunston (2006) notes that "competitions have become sense-bombarding experiences" (p. 135) and suppliers are satiating fan demand through a litany of sports sponsorships to an increase of 10,000 percent of the past score. Sports media companies interact directly with consumers without the filter (through fan-driven content sites such as Deadspin.com) of traditional media, resulting in increased bartering, cost-sharing and integrated multi-platform distribution strategies (Rein *et al.*, 2007).

The proliferation of social media outlets in sport led to what Schultz and Sheffer (2011) referred to as a complexity of consumption. The authors found that social media may be the key to empowering previously ignored audiences such as women (especially Millennials), African-Americans, and older respondents. According to Smith (2011), the notion of profitability should be examined in terms of targeting female audiences through potentially antiquated content-delivery models. However noble the intent for new media to engage new audiences, including those underserved or trivialized in the past, mediated content on digital, social, and mobile platforms also has the potential to expand an already significant information and media literacy gap. Mobile media have the potential to invite the previously disinterested to the in-game experience, but these innovations also can enhance the game-day experiences of highly active and involved audiences.

The culture of digital communication has accelerated sports media through a sociology of modernity (Redhead, 2007). Stadium access and fan mobility are greatly dictated by what Hagemann (2010) calls "the urbanization of the event" that has prompted host cities to create fan zones and the "eventization of the city" (p. 726). Reysen *et al.* (2012) cite the social identity perspective and an implied notion that the corporatization of sport can elicit negative emotional responses that cause a "threat to distinctiveness" and long-held traditions (p. 355).

Leyner (2000) laments that "the live event – the game itself – will become, at best, a point-of-purchase display... stadiums and arenas will simply turn into malls and food courts" (p. 92).

We are seeing developments that support Leyner's fears. In Allen, Texas, where "Friday Night Lights" and "bigger is better" are proud stereotypes, a high school's $60 million stadium features high-definition video and free Wi-Fi for 18,000 spectators. It should be noted that Allen's students benefit from this lab experience that could serve as a prototype to future college edifices/infrastructures (ABCNews.com, 2012).

Today's marketplace burgeons with revenue opportunities ranging from sponsorship exclusivity to premium/insider content options. The London Olympics featured 500,000 Wi-Fi hotspots controlled by BT, which charged €5.99 for 90 minutes or €10/day for fans to utilize smart technology in venues such as Olympic Stadium, the Aquatics Centre, and the Velodrome, with no free Wi-Fi in Olympic Park (Espiner, 2012). Through Cisco Connected Stadium Solution, iconic brands, such as Real Madrid soccer and the Pan American/Parapan Games, will plan on utilizing incentives to display exclusive material for those in attendance (Riggins, 2011).

Universities are slowly "dotting the connects," as Stanford became the first Wi-Fi equipped college football stadium in 2011, with rival California also providing mobile access at AT&T Park (pro stadium) at home games (Kunnath, 2012). Penn State, rocked with scandal in 2012, has launched Wi-Fi as part of its rebranding efforts (Mink, 2012).

These developments only scratch the surface. Fans are hungry for more digital, social and mobile experiences. In the past few years, they have already turned to fan-based Internet sports communities (FBISCs) to supplement the information they receive from traditional media outlets who cannot keep pace with the insatiable demand for sports news (Porter *et al.*, 2011). Of particular interest are the overarching trends that will feed this fan frenzy.

Mobile revolutionizes access

Mobile devices are becoming the main way fans interact with their teams. By 2013, mobile phones will overtake PCs as the most common way for people to access information on the Web (Gartner, 2012). As of February 2012, smartphones, which combine the functions of a personal digital assistant (PDA) with a mobile phone, exceeded feature phones as the dominant phone owned in the United States (Hardawar, 2012). This monumental change is important in the context of the sports industry as it places information literally in the hands of the fan. Mobilization also has the potential to mediate all sports experiences, connecting fans and providing direct access to the game-day experience for those outside of the stadium.

Fans no longer have to wait until after the game to log onto FBISCs. Fans watching through traditional broadcasts can exchange information to others inside the stadium. Knowing this, ownership and organizers of FBISCs are providing real-time chats and posts on their sites to correspond directly with engaged fans during featured events, from game day to signing day. As more fans become connected via mobile devices, stadiums likewise will move toward becoming entirely mediated, with fans being able to interact with each other, see scores/stats, and even interact with the players (likely at the pro level). At the same time, the second screen has been shown to provide an interactive television environment, whereby fans can control, enrich, share and transfer television content (Cesar *et al.*, 2008). Fans watching on television will be jacked into the experience through 3D-television/augmented reality and their mobile device of choice, while being connected with others in the crowd. Simultaneously, fans in the stadium will be connected to numerous games/experiences taking place all over the world. Soon, media and market interest in network and cable television ratings and shares of sporting events will be secondary compared to their interest in the smartphone and second-screen app use and data/media plans of subscribers to various mobile phone providers.

Mobile devices also serve to democratize coverage of sports at all levels. Smartphones come equipped with high-definition video cameras and Internet connectivity. Before long, media companies will deputize remote correspondents to provide live video and audio commentary on everything from high-school track and field to middle-school tennis. Live stats can also be uploaded and accessed from fans (and athletes) at any location.

But what can connect can also divide. As event managers discover that digital streams equal revenue streams, tiered access models may disenfranchise fans already paying for personal seat licenses, on-site parking and university or club booster fees.

Sports apps kill the direct web

Mobile applications are changing the way fans get on the Web. The seeds of this trend can be traced most recently to the proliferation of FBISCs (Porter *et al.*, 2011), where fans have book-marked favorites or pre-loaded FBISCs to the home screen of their smartphones and tablets. If mobile devices become the dominant means by which fans access sports information, applications or "apps" (rather than Web searches) will become the primary way that fans interact with information accessible via the Internet. Smartphone users spend two-thirds of their time on apps versus using mobile versions of browsers (NewMediaTrend, 2012). In June of 2011, mobile users were utilizing custom applications 81 minutes per day vs. 74 minutes of Web use (Wasserman, 2011). Mobile apps are now direct taps to online sports data. As this trend continues, another apparent irony accompanies it. With the proliferation of mobile apps, which in a sense provide a gatekeeping function for users, fans may be giving up some of their independence and autonomy that are inherent in Web searches and Internet content consumption, for the sake of the ease and convenience of apps. This may run counter to the stereotypical profile of the sports fanatic, who has typically conformed to no form of predetermined content.

Using Applied Programming Interfaces or "APIs," apps can pull information from other sources such as Google or Facebook to provide fans with a constantly updated sports data stream. For example, one app might integrate APIs from ESPN and Twitter to provide a screen that shows the latest scores and stats from your favorite teams and players as well as comments and "smack talk" from your friends.

The most frequently used API at this point is the Facebook Open Graph. The Open Graph allows application developers to build apps that can access nearly 1 billion users on the Facebook platform. This new mobile app ecosystem transforms the Web from an open search-based system to a more closed system where fans access information through branded applications rather than through open searches through a Web browser. This closed system could serve to separate fans even more into their own balkanized camps, increasing bonding and reducing bridging. For example, if fans choose to only access information through their university's own branded application, they would be less likely to access information from fans outside that ecosphere. Rather than tuning into ESPN or another team-agnostic source, the app-enabled college fan is likely to go directly to the school's app to access scores, news and fan-based information, as it is aggregated by that university/team. In this way, the institutions themselves become the gatekeeper. FBISCs had already begun this process (Porter *et al.*, 2011), but apps will tend to accelerate this increase in bonding over bridging.

Gameday content rises to the fore

As regular media content shifts to the cloud, live programming will increase in prominence. Sports contests will serve as programming that audiences prefer to access synchronously. The increased use of digital video recorders (DVRs) has the media industry in a state of panic. Fox recently sued Dish Network over Dish's PrimeTime Anytime and AutoHop service, which records eight days worth of prime-time network television content, claiming that the service would result in a massive reduction in network commercial viewers as consumers opted to skip advertisements (Schneider, 2012; LA Times, 2012).

As audiences shift their consumption patterns to mobile, and media outlets eventually adjust distribution accordingly, cloud technology will bridge the gap in both storage and processing power. Live or synchronous content such as sports will increase in importance for advertisers as asynchronous media content with a longer shelf life such as books, films, music, etc. moves more toward a "rent" versus "own" revenue model. Audiences will no longer own much of their asynchronous media content, instead paying subscription fees to access this type of content from the cloud at their convenience. Therefore, sports programming will increase in prominence, as viewers will prefer to view this type of programming live. Traditional media planners will find sports as one of the few types of programming left that offer an effective use of an interruptive 30-second spot.

Sports brands become everything in a crowded marketplace

The move away from traditional 30-second spots will open numerous new marketing options. As fans become more connected with their team, branding opportunities will proliferate, with universities/teams eventually embracing these connections, empowering them, and monetizing them. Teams can reach out to fans on game day, including pre-game/tailgate and in-game, with everything from contests to social media to score/video updates, etc. on smartphones in generally old and unwired stadiums that have more than 100,000 fans in the area for most of the day – creating potential sponsorship/income for a captive, but not necessarily captivated group.

This linked yet anonymous group constitutes a challenging dynamic. As Chadwick (2006) notes, marketplaces are crowded and communication is vital, so marketing builds a differential advantage, while maximizing revenues in selling products in methods that – while exploitative – are increasingly receptive to the power of the customer. In a study of social media promotion of television stations, Ferguson and Greer (2013) note that innovations such as Pinterest provide a subtle branding via association by attracting a specific type of audience member who develops loyalty based on content related only tangentially to the organization. Affinity to a site revolves around lifestyle content/boards and interactivity, with more effective promotion likely stemming from less overt tactics.

From links to likes to verbs: Sports become socialized

While some research has shown that social media only exacerbates the status quo around issues like unequal gender coverage on Twitter (Smith, 2011), others have pointed out the possibilities for social media to radically alter the fan, media and athlete dynamic. Sanderson and Kassing (2011) pointed out that social media (blogs and Twitter in particular) have the power to be transformative, adversarial and integrative in sports media. Social media is transforming the dynamic between reporters, fans, and sports teams, in that athletes can now take a more active role in shaping their images online by breaking their own stories, which are then reported by traditional media. This same shift has allowed sports media to become more adversarial as athletes can now confront reporters and even their own teams directly in times of conflict. Finally, social media are integrating the collective perspectives of athletes, fans and sports organizations into sports media content.

Recent changes in the Facebook platform have resulted in users sharing the activities of their lives (in Mark Zuckerberg's word) "frictionlessly." The Facebook platform has moved beyond the "like" to the "verb," with Facebook users sharing the music they listen to and the television they watch through applications plugging into the Facebook API. For instance, users of the music service Spotify share their listening activities to their Facebook ticker/timeline without having to post updates. Similarly, the Nike Fuelband shares users' athletic achievements and vital signs to their Facebook and/or Twitter feeds. Soon, athletes will be hooked into the same type of feed, sharing individual achievements along with aggregated team efforts to social media live. Fans can follow along while inside or outside the stadium.

The "MASF" future of sport connectedness

Sports events already offer highly personal, synchronous, interconnected and shared experiences. Today's mobile and social fan (MASF) expects a multitude of stimuli that stadiums and outside grounds must provide to complement game action. As more objects and observations become "mediated," the sports experience will only become more digitized. Consider the future when all sports objects contain microchips that are networked with fans. The ball will contain a chip measuring velocity. Wearable technology allows uniforms and helmets to contain chips that measure speed and force, not to mention specialized cameras offering fans their own selected points of view on the field. The field itself will be outfitted with chips that help simulate the game experience for viewers outside of the stadium. Three-dimensional experiences will become the norm as television technology advances. As all mobile devices offer ubiquitous high-definition cameras, all sporting events will become broadcast. When sports become mediated, they become monetized on some level through advertising and subscriptions. As fans are more connected to their teams (and each other), more sports will find audiences. When all sports become mediated, all sports become profitable on some level.

Tiered access and premium subscriptions may become the price of doing game-day business, as cable and phone companies battle to negate net neutrality. With escalating team budgets, will the freight be passed on to the MASFs? Or can teams provide fast and free content through the use of interstitials or other interruptive advertising, as is the norm to watch our favorite shows on Hulu or Netflix? The seven-fold increase of Hulu political advertising (Blumenthal, 2012) evidences potential revenue shifts. While most home entertainment programs must adapt in the skipping/DVR culture, sports fans often just zap to another game or fix a snack. At the stadium, fans – especially in baseball and football where there is significant downtime – are captive; thus, teams could promote their products on mobile devices during measurements, player substitutions, and of course . . . "TV timeouts."

For generations of sports enthusiasts, nostalgia and even naiveté have been a welcome distraction or void-filler. We still pour into coliseums and bowls and cheer a scoreboard update or public-address announcement that a heated rival trails, or when your player breaks a school record. But will that satiate the MASFs who are used to constant access on mobile and digital platforms? The Monday Morning Quarterback is now a game-day signal-caller, one who can be engaged and enraged. And most importantly, with the right stimuli and signals . . . he or she can be bought.

Note

1. "Tailgating" is the practice of hosting picnics and parties from the tailgate of a vehicle, often on the parking lot of a sports stadium, which originated in America.

References

ABCNews.com (2012) $60 Million High School Football Stadium. Retrieved October 8, 2012, from http://abcnews.go.com/blogs/business/2012/08/60-million-high-school-football-stadium/

Bellamy, R. (2010) [Keynote address.] Fourth Summit on Communication and Sport, Cleveland, OH.

Bhatt, N. (2012) Exclusive: Cricket Australia's Poor Twitter Form. *Technology Spectator*. Retrieved February 23, 2013, from http://www.technologyspectator.com.au/emerging-tech/social-media/cricket-australias-poor-twitter-form

Blumenthal, P. (2012) Hulu political advertising jumped 700 percent in 2012. *The Huffington Post*. Retrieved October 8, 2012, from http://www.huffingtonpost.com/2012/10/05/hulu-political-advertising_n_1943111.html?utm_hp_ref=elections-2012

Blumler, J.G. (1979) The role of theory in uses and gratifications studies. *Communications Research*, 6, 9–36.

Bryant, J. and Raney, A.A. (2000) "Sports on the screen." In D. Zillmann and P. Vorderer (eds), *Media entertainment: The psychology of its appeal* (pp. 153–74). Mahwah, NJ: Lawrence Erlbaum.

Bryant, J., Rockwell, S. and Owens, J. (1994) "Buzzer beaters" and "barn burners": The effects of enjoyment of watching the game go down to the wire. *Journal of Sport and Social Issues*, 18(4), 326–339.

Cesar, P., Bulterman, D.C. and Jansen, A.J. (2008) Usages of the Secondary Screen in an interactive television environment: Control, enrich, share, and transfer television content. In M. Tscheligi, M. Obrist and A. Lugmayr (eds), *EuroITV* (pp. 168–177). Berlin, Germany: Springer-Verlag.

Chadwick, S. (2006) Dispelling sports marketing myths. *International Journal of Sports Marketing and Sponsorship*, 7(2), 95.

Cialdini, R.B., Borden, R.J., Thorne, A., Walker, M.R., Freeman, S. and Sloan, L.R. (1976) Basking in reflected glory: Three (football) field studies. *Journal of Personality and Social Psychology*, 34, 366–375.

Cruickshank, L., Tsekleves, E., Whitham, R., Hill, A. and Kondo K. (2007) Making interactive TV easier to use: Interface design for a second screen approach. *The Design Journal*, 10(3), 41–53.

Espiner, T. (2012) London becomes a Wi-Fi wonderland for the Olympics. *ZDNet.com*. Retrieved October 8, 2012, from http://www.zdnet.com/uk/london-becomes-a-wi-fi-wonderland-for-the-olympics-7000002046/

Essers, L. (2012) Ericsson readies Wi-fi system optimized for sports stadiums. *CIO.com*. Retrieved February 15, 2012, from http://www.cio.com/article/718861/Ericsson_Readies_Wi_fi_System_Optimized_for_Sports_Stadiums?source=rss_all&utm_source=feedburner&utm_medium=feed&utm_campaign=Feed%3A+cio%2Ffeed%2Farticles+%28CIO.com+Feed+-+Articles%29/

Ferguson, D.A. and Greer, C.F. (2013) Pinning and promotion: How local television stations are using Pinterest for branding and audience connectivity. Paper submitted to the Broadcast Education Annual Convention.

Gantz, W., Wang, Z., Bryant, P. and Potter, R.F. (2006) Sports versus all comers: Comparing TV sports fans with fans of other programming genres. *Journal of Broadcasting and Electronic Media*, 50(1), 95–118.

Gartner. (2010, January) *Gartner Newsroom*. Retrieved September 4, 2012, from http://www.gartner.com/it/products/newsroom/index.jsp

Gunston, R. (2006) The Future of Sports. In *Sports Marketing* (pp. 134–143). Loganville, GA: Richard K. Miller and Associates.

Hagemann, A. (2010) From the stadium to the fan zone: Host cities in a state of emergency. *Soccer and Society*, 11(6), 723–736.

Hardawar, D. (2012, March 29) The magic moment: Smartphones now half of all US mobiles. *Venture Beat.com*. Retrieved October 8, 2012, from http://venturebeat.com/2012/03/29/the-magic-moment-smartphones-now-half-of-all-u-s-mobiles/

Howard, D.R. and Crompton, J.L. (2003) An empirical review of the stadium novelty effect. *Sport Marketing Quarterly*, 12(2), 111–116.

Iyer, V. (2012) Better connection: NFL improves in-game experience with technological perks. *The Sporting News*. Retrieved October 8, 2012, from http://aol.sportingnews.com/nfl/story/2012-07-12/nfl-roger-goodell-wireless-connection-wi-fi-under-the-hood-smartphones-game-rewi

James, J., Breezeel, G.S. and S. Ross (2001) A two-stage study of the reasons to begin and continue tailgating. *Sport Marketing Quarterly*, 10(4), 212–222.

Jarvis, R.M. and Coleman, P. (2003) Fireworks, fan cams, and lawsuits: A guide to stadium scoreboards. *Seton Hall Journal of Sport Law,* 13(2), 177–202.

Katz, E., Blumler, J.G. and Gurevitch, M. (1974) Utilization of mass communication by the individual. In J.G. Blumler and E. Katz (eds), *The Uses of Mass Communications: Current Perspectives on Gratifications Research* (pp. 19–32). Beverly Hills, CA: Sage.

Katzowitz, J. (2012) "Not all NFL stadiums will get Wi-Fi in 2012." CBSSports.com. Retrieved on Oct. 8, 2012 from: http://www.cbssports.com/nfl/blog/eye-on-football/19598102/not-all-nfl-stadiums-will-get-wi-fi-in-2012

Kunnath, A. (2012) Stanford Stadium first in college football with Wi-Fi. *SB National Bay Area.* Retrieved on Oct. 8, 2012 from: http://bayarea.sbnation.com/stanford-cardinal/2011/8/19/2373153/stanford-stadium-wi-fi-att-wireless

L.A. Times (2012, May 13) NBC Broadcasting head no fan of Dish's commercial skipping device. Retrieved on October 2, 2012, from http://latimesblogs.latimes.com/entertainmentnewsbuzz/2012/05/nbc-broadcasting-chief-dish-commercial-skipping-device.html

Levinson, P. (2013) *New New Media* (2nd edn.). Boston, MA: Pearson.

Leyner, M. (2000) Will we still go out to the game? *Time,* 155(7), 92.

Maslow, A.H. (1970) *Motivation and Personality* (2nd edn.). New York: Harper and Row.

Miller, R.K. and Washington, K. (2011) Stadiums and arenas. *Sports Marketing,* 79–86.

Mink, N. (2012) Football eve event marks debut of Beaver Stadium upgrades, including Wi-Fi. *Statecollege.com.* Retrieved October 8, 2012, from http://www.statecollege.com/news/local-news/football-eve-event-marks-debut-of-beaver-stadium-upgrades-including-wifi-1123610/

NewMediaTrendWatch (2012) Mobile devices: New Media Trend Watch USA. Retrieved October 8, 2012, from http://www.newmediatrendwatch.com/markets-by-country/17-usa/855-mobile-devices

NielsenWire (2012) DoubleVision: Global trends in tablet and smartphone use while watching TV. [Q4 2011 Nielsen survey.] Retrieved on October 2, 2012, from http://blog.nielsen.com/nielsenwire/online_mobile/double-vision-global-trends-in-tablet-and-smartphone-use-while-watching-tv/

Peterson, E.M. and Raney, A.A. (2008) Reconceptualizing and reexamining suspense as a predictor of mediated sports enjoyment. *Journal of Broadcasting and Electronic Media,* 52(4), 544–562.

Porter, L.V., Wood, J.C. and Benigni, V.L. (2011) From analysis to aggression: The nature of fan emotion, cognition and behavior in Internet sports communities. In A.C. Billings (ed.), *Sports Media: Transformation, Integration, Consumption* (pp. 128–145). London: Routledge.

Raney, A.A. (2006) Why we watch and enjoy mediated sports. In A.A. Raney and J. Bryant (eds), *Handbook of Sports and Media.* Mahwah, NJ: Lawrence Erlbaum.

Redhead, S. (2007) Those absent from the stadium are always right: Accelerated culture, sport media, and theory at the speed of light. *Journal of Sport and Social Issues,* 31(3), 226–241.

Rein, I., Kotler, P. and Shields, B. (2007) The future of sports media. *The Futurist,* 41(1), 40–43.

Reysen, S., Snider, J.S. and Branscombe, N.R. (2012) Corporate renaming of stadiums, team identification, and threat to distinctiveness. *Journal of Sport Management: Human Kinetics,* 26, 350–356.

Riggins, J. (2011) Real Madrid to have Europe's highest-tech stadium. *Smartplanet.com.* Retrieved October 8, 2012, from http://jkriggins.wordpress.com/2011/11/17/real-madrid-to-have-europes-highest-tech-stadium-smartplanet-nov-17-2011/

Rosengren, K.E. (1974) Uses and gratifications a paradigm outlined. In J.G. Blumler and E. Katz (eds), *The Uses of Mass Communications: Current Perspectives on Gratifications Research* (pp. 269–286). Beverly Hills, CA: Sage.

Rubin, A.M. (1983) Television uses and gratifications: The interactions of viewing patterns and motivations. *Journal of Broadcasting,* 27, 37–51.

Sanderson, J. and Kassing, J.W. (2011) Tweets and blogs: Transformative, adversarial, and integrative developments in sports media. In A.C. Billings (ed.), *Sports Media: Transformation, Integration, Consumption* (pp. 146–161). London: Routledge.

Schultz, B. and Sheffer, M.L. (2011) Factors influencing sports consumption in the era of new media. *Web Journal of Mass Communication Research,* 37(October).

Schneider, J. (2012) Fox seeks ban on Dish's ad skip feature pending US trial. *Bloomberg.com.* Retrieved October 2, 2012, from http://www.bloomberg.com/news/2012-08-27/fox-seeks-ban-on-dish-s-ad-skip-feature-pending-u-s-trial.html

Smith, A. and Boyles, J. L. (2012, July 7) The rise of the "connected viewer." *Pew Internet and American Life Project.* Retrieved on October 2, 2012, from http://pewinternet.org/~/media//Files/Reports/2012/PIP_Connected_Viewers.pdf

Smith, L.R. (2011) The less you say: An initial study of gender coverage in sports on Twitter. In A.C. Billings (ed.), *Sports Media: Transformation, Integration, Consumption* (pp. 114–127). London: Routledge.

Sports Marketing. (2012) Stadiums and arenas. In *Sports Marketing* (pp. 126–134). Loganville, GA: Richard K. Miller and Associates.

Stotlar, D.K. and Johnson, D.A. (1989) Assessing the impact and effectiveness of stadium advertising on sport spectators at Division I institutions. *Journal of Sport Management,* 3(2), 90–102.

Su-lin, G., Tuggle, C.A., Mitrook, M.A., Coussement, S.H. and Zillmann, D. (1997) The thrills of a close game: Who enjoys it and who doesn't? *Journal of Sport and Social Issues,* 21(1), 53–64.

Uhrich, S. and Benkenstein, M. (2010) Sport stadium atmosphere: Formative and reflective indicators for operationalizing the construct. *Journal of Sport Management, Human Kinetics,* 24, 211–237.

Walters, G. (2011) The implementation of a stakeholder management strategy during stadium development: A case study of Arsenal football club and the Emirates Stadium. *Managing Leisure,* 16, 49–64.

Wann, D.L., Allen, B. and Rochelle, A.R. (2004) Using sport fandom as an escape: Searching for relief from under-stimulation and over-stimulation. *International Sports Journal,* 8(1), 104–113.

Wann, D.L. and Branscombe, N.R. (1990) Die-hard and fair-weather fans: Effects of identification on BIRGing and CORFing tendencies. *Journal of Sport and Social Issues* 14(2), 103–117.

Wann, D.L., Hamlet, M.A., Wilson, T.M. and Hodges, J.A. (1995) Basking in reflected glory, cutting off reflected failure, and cutting off future failure: The importance of group identification. *Social Behavior and Personality,* 23(4), 377–388.

Wasserman, T. (2011, June 20) Consumers now spending more time on mobile apps than the Web. *Mashable.com.* Retrieved on September 4, 2012, from http://mashable.com/2011/06/20/app-use-over-takes-web-use/

Windahl, S. (1981) Uses and gratifications at the crossroads. In G.C. Wilhoit and H. deBock (eds), *Mass Communication Review Yearbook* 2: 174–85. Beverly Hills, CA: Sage.

Winslow, G. (2012, February 3) SecondScreen to power synch apps for Super Bowl. Retrieved on October 2, 2012, from http://www.broadcastingcable.com/article/480088-SecondScreen_to_Power_Synch_Apps_for_Super_Bowl.php?rssid=20068&utm_source=twitterfeed&utm_medium=twitter

Zillmann, D. and Bryant, J. (1986) Exploring the entertainment experience. In J. Bryant and D. Zillmann (eds), *Perspectives on media effects* (pp. 303–321). Hillsdale, NJ: Lawrence Erlbaum.

Zillmann, D., Bryant, J. and Sapolsky, B. (1989) Enjoyment from sports spectatorship. In J.H. Goldstein (ed.), *Sports, Games, and Play: Social and Psychological Viewpoints* (2nd edn.). Hillsdale, NJ: Lawrence Erlbaum, pp. 241–78.

21

FANTASY SPORT

More than a game

Brody J. Ruihley

UNIVERSITY OF CINCINNATI

Robin L. Hardin

UNIVERSITY OF TENNESSEE

Culture is considered a shared way of life and shared understandings of people who interact with one another (Coakley, 2009). Included in culture are the ideas, beliefs, and attitudes used to give meaning to experiences, people, and events (Coakley, 2009). Many subcultures can exist within a particular culture, and this is certainly the case in sport, as subcultures abound from the outdoor enthusiasts to the armchair quarterbacks to the parents involved in youth soccer. Sport cultures can be broken into two main groups. The first is a culture created as sport participants begin to form together and develop a set of shared ideas and beliefs. The second group can be classified as fans. Sport fans represent the creation of culture in the nonparticipation aspects of sport. It has been well-documented that social reasons and affiliation are primary motivating actors for attending sporting events, and this has been evident in research examining attendance at a variety of sporting events (Koo, Andrew, Hardin and Greenwell, 2009; Koo and Hardin, 2008; James and Ridinger, 2002; Trail, Fink and Anderson, 2003). Research examining culture is also available in activities surrounding events such as tailgating[1] (Drenton, Peters, Leigh and Hollenbeck, 2009) and watching the broadcast of a sporting event (Raney and Depalma, 2006; Sargent, Zillman and Weaver, 1998).

One sport culture, hosted through a traditional form of mass media, is the area of sports talk radio. Many sports talk radio shows have loyal followings, and on the local level, some of the more consistent callers develop a following of their own. Sports talk radio opens a public space to allow for the sharing of ideas and beliefs (Nylund, 2004; Zagacki and Grano, 2005). Nylund (2005) highlights a commercial proclaiming, "it's not just sports talk, it's culture" (p. 136). The advent of the new media machine, the Internet, and the increase in its adoption, has provided an accessible platform for the creation of even further segmented cultures within sport fandom. Utilizing online sport consumption research and conceptual frameworks set forth by Hur, Ko and Valacich (2007) and Seo and Green (2008), researchers have examined many online sport areas including purchasing decisions (Hur *et al.*, 2007), website use (Carlson, Rosenberger and Muthaly, 2003; Seo and Hong, 2001), message board use (Hardin, Koo, Ruihley, Dittmore and McGreevey, 2012; Ruihley and Hardin, 2011b), and fantasy sport participation (Billings and Ruihley, 2013; Dwyer and Drayer, 2010; Ruihley and Hardin, 2011a). In addition, social networks such as Twitter, have allowed the spread of ideas and information that ultimately creates communities among strangers and friends alike. Sport consumers can now follow particular athletes and events on Twitter where there is a common interest in the person or the sporting event itself (Hambrick, 2012). The focus of this chapter, however, is the subculture of fantasy sport.

Growth of fantasy sport

From its humble beginnings in 1960 to the early 1990s, fantasy sport saw marginal growth to 500,000 participants (Vichot, 2009). From the early 1990s to the current day, the activity has seen tremendous advancement. Growth from 1990 to 2003, thanks in large part to the Internet and other forms of new media, went from 500,000 to 15 million participants ("Fantasy Sports Industry Grows," 2009; Vichot, 2009). In this time frame, the Internet provided a platform for fantasy sport organizations to expand operations beyond pencil and paper. As a result of the expanded reach of fantasy providers via the Internet, in 2012, participation was estimated at 35 million in North America (Fantasy Sport Trade Association, 2012a). These participants have taken this, once-considered-niche hobby, and turned it into a powerful sport industry and a dominant sport subculture creating and utilizing new sport media. Billings and Ruihley (2013) found the average amount of time per week devoted to fantasy sport is 4.3 hours, and this time is devoted to researching, analyzing, and following fantasy players. In addition, Billings and Ruihley (2013) discovered a near 60% increase in overall media consumption from those *not participating* in fantasy sport to those *that do participate*.

Fantasy sport is an interactive team management activity based on statistics accrued by athletes of real-life professional sport organizations or college athletics. Fantasy sport users (FSUs) create or join leagues with a pre-determined amount of participants or team owners. These participants then form their own team by selecting athletes from the sport league of focus, either college or professional sport athletes, to represent their fantasy team. A Pew Internet and American Life Project report, simply states, "the 'team' is an artificial assembly of players from a variety of real teams" or a collection of athletes in individual sports (Pew Internet and American Life Project, 2005, ¶ 3). Selecting athletes to be a part of a team is traditionally accomplished in a draft format, with participants selecting athletes by taking ordered turns, or by means of an auction style format, where participants acquire athletes through a bidding procedure with other league participants. Once teams are formed and the season begins, teams compete against each other using statistics generated by real athletes as points for their fantasy team. "The basic statistics of those players are then aggregated after each real-world game to determine how well the team is doing" (Pew Internet and American Life Project, 2005, ¶ 3). During the season and amidst competition, participants have the ability to start or reserve athletes on their team, trade athletes with other teams in their league, drop athletes from their roster, or add athletes found on a list of available participants not already chosen by a team. The pre-season, season, and post-season actions and decisions are similar to those made by real-life general managers, coaches, or sport management professionals (Davis and Duncan, 2006; Roy and Goss, 2007). These decisions require surveillance of sport-related information through sport media outlets and expert opinion, analysis of that information, and implementation.

A common idea is that FSUs are just average sport fans and can be grouped in with the entire sport culture. After all, consumers of this activity are quite homogenous and match the stereotypical North American sport fan. These characteristics primarily include being White (Billings and Ruihley, 2013; Coakley, 2007; Levy, 2009; Roy and Goss, 2007; Smith, 2009), male (Billings and Ruihley, 2013; Farquhar and Meeds, 2007; Levy, 2009; Randle and Nyland, 2008; Roy and Goss, 2007; Spinda and Haridakis, 2008), college educated (Global Fantasy Leaders,

2009; Levy, 2009), and one with discretionary time (Farquhar and Meeds, 2007). While FSUs, as a group are diversely narrow, there is reason to consider this group a unique and important aspect to the sporting landscape.

The purpose of this chapter is to highlight ways fantasy sport is creating a subculture that is changing the way sport fans view and consume sport media. The subculture of fantasy sport can be added to the list of other subcultures – mainly sport message board users, sports talk radio listeners, and Twitter communities. The chapter also argues that fantasy sport is becoming a powerful new outlet for sport consumers, a new sport subculture, and a new sport media in and of itself. The specific reasons supporting these claims revolve around areas of fantasy sport organizational structure, media consumption, and content development. The "organizational structure" portion of this chapter addresses culture development through the emphasis placed on industry, league, and team management. The "media consumption" section highlights how and to what extent media companies are devoting air time, energy, personnel, and resources towards fantasy sport. Finally, when discussing content development, attention will be given to the way in which fantasy sport is creating a new information lens and outlet for enhanced knowledge, as well as adding words to the lexicon.

Fantasy sport organizational structure

Fantasy Sport Trade Association

The fantasy sport industry has expanded from the traditional sports of football, golf, basketball and baseball, to hockey, auto racing, cycling, college athletics, and even bass fishing. If it is a sport, then it is likely that a fantasy league has been created to cover it. Access to multiple outlets, information sources, and technology have allowed for this type of expansion. Many fantasy sport leagues and participants began fantasy participation with pen and paper, reading of box scores, and calculations by hand. With the type of technological reach the Internet offered in the late 1990s, the industry grew exponentially and the Fantasy Sport Trade Association (FSTA) formed in 1999 as a result. One of the stated goals for the FSTA is to "provide a forum for interaction between hundreds of existing and emerging companies in a unique and growing fantasy sports industry" (Fantasy Sport Trade Association, 2012b, ¶ 1). Its primary mission statement reads:

> We serve the small, the large, the entrepreneurs, and the corporations. We serve the pioneers that invested in and grew the industry in the 1980s and 1990s. And we serve the visionaries, innovators, investors, advertisers, and sponsors that would like to network and learn more about the exciting fantasy sports industry.
>
> *(Fantasy Sport Trade Association, 2012b, ¶ 1)*

The actions of the FSTA mirror its mission. In addition to providing information on the association website and Twitter, face-to-face conference meetings are held twice per year and include presentations focusing on consumption research, trend analysis, technology, and other time-sensitive information. Presentations are designed to inform the fantasy media giants like ESPN, Yahoo!, and CBS Sports and also the up-and-coming organizations like Daily Joust and Dynasty Field. Information-delivering organizations (i.e. Rotoworld.com and Rotowire.com) are also in attendance to learn, interact, and share industry insight. One of the most interesting opportunities at the FSTA conference is a segment called Elevator Pitch. In this portion of the conference program, new fantasy sport ideas are brought to the forefront.

This association, conference meetings, and activities like the Elevator Pitch are important to fantasy sport because it is here, where ideas come to the forefront about this relatively new sport media powerhouse. It is here that this industry can seek out new ideas to create and utilize new sport media. In the January 2013 conference, new sport media topics abounded with panels focused on building for mobile, switching from online to mobile, and leveraging "second screens." In addition to the industry panels focusing on maximizing new sport media, the Elevator Pitch ideas offered new and innovative ideas to enhance the fantasy sport experience. These ideas ranged from expanding Twitter use and creating online fantasy activity (accessed through a smart phone) specific to in-person sporting contests.

League and team options

Another unique aspect about fantasy sport is the further subdivision of leagues and teams. FSUs will have an opportunity to manage their team, compete, and test their skills against others by creating or joining leagues (usually 8–12 teams). It is important to point out that fantasy sport has no physical boundaries. The global nature of the Internet means that league access is not restricted geographically, and leagues are formed with all types of participant division across the world (e.g. coworkers, family, friends, or complete strangers). The technology that is now available has made this a much easier task and thus encouraged participants to take on league managerial positions and also allows FSUs to participate in multiple leagues. The information, now available through new media, allows FSUs to make more informed decisions, increased competition level, and has raised intensity. Division occurs with these characteristics in mind and creates choice as to which type of league offered best suits the participant. The following are considerations to take into account when FSUs join a league:

- **Free vs. Pay** – Certain sport media organizations charge a type of administrative fee for hosting league play, offering live statistic updates, providing news, keeping track of league history, and providing access to other organizational media (e.g. CBS Sports' fantasy participants have access to Major League Baseball game audio). A significant amount of revenue is obtained through these types of league fees. Other organizations choose to offer a similar fantasy product at no charge to the consumer. The hope is to create routine and habit in searching for information through the fantasy sport site; if a participant is participating on the site, then it is likely their information search will start and stay on the same host site (Ruihley and Hardin, 2013). Advertising revenue also plays a role in the offering of free leagues. The more attention and devoted time on a fantasy site or smart phone/tablet app, the more awareness an advertisement may receive.
- **Social vs. Competitive** – Recreational leagues in participation sports (e.g. basketball, bowling, golf, soccer, softball, etc.) have competitive participants wanting to win and those participating to have a good time, socialize, and escape the daily routine. FSUs are no different. There are leagues, across North America, filled with those that take their participation seriously and those that let the draft, lineup changes, and trades just pass them by. Choosing a league with this criterion in mind is important because being an activity primarily hosted online, experiencing others' loafing and simply forgetting about the league is a common occurrence for social league participants. Each of these two groups (i.e. competitive and social) utilized new sport media in unique ways. Those in competitive leagues will diligently use the Internet or mobile applications for information regarding their fantasy roster and matchups or to follow live game action. In addition, competitive and social participants alike

utilized social media applications (e.g. Twitter, chat rooms, or message boards) to communi-cation about fantasy-related items.

- **Snake Draft vs. Auction** – Drafting is one of the areas most impacted by the advent of the Internet. In the early days of fantasy sport, groups of people would have to be physically present in order to draft their fantasy roster. The league commissioner and other participants would have to mark down picks with pen and paper. With Internet technology removing that physical requirement, drafting can take place in many different ways. Most fantasy leagues draft by either a "snake draft" or auction-style format. Simply stated, a snake draft format is drafting players to a roster in a pre-determined order and reversing the order in each of the next rounds. Each team will select a player when it is their turn to draft. In this type of drafting situation, preparation is important, but a participant auto-drafting (i.e. auto-pilot) or just selecting by viewing expert rankings, can draft some high-quality players. The other option is an auction-style format. ESPN.com writer, Cockcroft (2012, ¶ 7), argues for and defines an auction style draft appropriately:

> Gone are the frustrations of knowing that only one person in the room, one purely lucky individual, will even have a crack at Arian Foster [NFL running back]. Gone is the internal struggle over how early you should select your quarterback, or your tight end. Gone is the annoyance that is losing the player that you *oh-so-wanted*, vultured by the very team with the pick right in front of you. In an auction, it's no-holds-barred. If Foster is your object, you've got a can't-miss way to get him: Just open up your wallet and pay the extra buck. Want three first-round draft talents at the expense of having to fill the cracks with late-round, sleeper-caliber material? You can do that too. Have you always wanted to spread your risk, sacri-ficing top-shelf talent for the effective equivalent of populating your roster with every fifth-rounder in a draft? Again, that's a can-do.

When discussing the opening of a wallet, this can mean artificial money or real. In some leagues, with a prize fund, you are given a certain amount to spend. For example, a participant may buy into the league for $100.00 and have $100,000 to use for drafting and picking up play-ers. Or a participant may join a league with no prize fund or buy-in and be granted a set amount of money for player acquisitions.

Media consumption and content development

The participants or league administrators control the draft, style of play, and management aspect of fantasy sport. These people are making their management decisions based on information concerning fantasy sport and the messages being disseminated. Fantasy sport has also impacted the culture and content of messages from the communications industry itself. The increase in fantasy sport participation and the demand for information about fantasy sport has created new patterns of media consumption, new positions with the sport communication profession, and communication messages directly covering fantasy sport. The following section will highlight these areas.

Media consumption

FSUs are seeking basically any insight they can when trying to predict player or team perform-ance. This can be anything from knowing the batting average of a Major League Baseball player in afternoon games versus night games, knowing how well a quarterback performs when the top wide receiver on a team is not playing due to an injury, or how well an auto racing driver performs on specific tracks. This type of situation causes a search for information so participants will have the knowledge to better determine who to play and who not to play. It also leads to the actual formation of a roster for a FSU. An example of this type of information search comes from the 2012–2013 NFL season. The New York Giants' wide receiver, Ramses Barden, had 16 *career* catches as he was in his fourth year in the league. Giants' starting wide receiver Hakeem Nicks was out for that week's game with an injury, forcing Barden into the starting lineup. He responded with nine catches for 138 yards, which means points in the world of fantasy sport. With that performance, FSUs, needing a wide receiver, could easily pick him up as a free agent, but would have to be leery of playing him because consideration must be made on how his playing time will be impacted when Nicks recovers from his injury. The same is true for a soccer player, basketball player, or any other athlete who would be competing because of an injury to another player. These are the decisions that fill the minds of FSUs. Finding more information to assist in solving that problem led to a scouring of information regarding players, injuries, and lineups.

Several research studies have examined the motivations of online sport consumers and found surveillance of information to be significantly important (Hur *et al.*, 2007; Seo and Green, 2008). Applying this factor to fantasy sport has also created affirmation of its importance to the activity (Billings and Ruihley, 2013; Davis and Duncan, 2006; Dwyer and Drayer, 2010; Farquhar and Meeds, 2007; Ruihley and Billings, 2013; Ruihley and Hardin, 2011a). As evidence of the importance of surveillance to the FSU, please consider the following statistic. ESPN's Department of Integrated Media Research (2010) claims the average ESPN consumer (aged 12 to 64) spends more than seven hours per week consuming ESPN media. Tripling that amount, the FSU consumes 22 hours and 40 minutes (Billings and Ruihley, 2013; ESPN Integrated Media Research, 2010). This one statistic stands alone when trying to justify the need for fantasy sport information and coverage.

Ruihley and Hardin (2013) examined how FSUs use the media in their fantasy sport experience and how that created a niche form of the information that is desired by the fantasy sport culture. Their research showed 78.3% of FSUs using television as part of the fantasy sport experience, but it also revealed a heavy use of the Web, with 65.5% of FSUs using the Internet (aside from their hosting a fantasy sport website). Other media use in fantasy sport showed 19.9% use radio, 41% use magazines, and 24.8% use newspapers as part of their participation in fantasy sport. This indicates that there is certainly a need for communication outlets to be aware of the informational needs of their consumers and that fantasy sport information needs to be disseminated.

Media professionals

This fantasy sport culture has created a new type of media content relating to sport. Fantasy sport experts, created by the demand for information, also led to this new type of content. Not only is there analysis of players' past, current, and future performance but also there are game stories written solely on fantasy performance. Articles or media broadcasts are not necessarily about a team winning or losing or how well someone finished in an individual sport but how well they performed from a fantasy sport perspective. This area is specialized just as for other experts involved in golf, soccer, football, baseball, hockey, or any other sport. There are experts who provide commentary for sports, and there are also experts who provide information about sports from a fantasy sport perspective. Newspapers, magazines, radio, television, and websites have fantasy experts offering advice on the activity. This advice includes what players should comprise your team, who should be starting, and other insight that may give someone an edge in fantasy competition. For instance, a golfer may not have overwhelming statistics when playing on certain types of golf courses. The fantasy expert studies and refines statistics like this to give FSUs advice on which athletes will be most productive each week.

These aforementioned stories are examples of how new media are being developed based on this subculture of sport fans. Networks like ESPN, CBS Sports, and Yahoo! are hiring analysts and writers to chiefly provide information and commentary on fantasy sport. Many experts and writers have columns, blogs, podcasts, or Twitter presence to share information pertaining to fantasy performance. Websites such as ESPN's Fantasy and Games and CBS' Fantasy News offer breakdowns and analysis of players through professional sports. The analysis offers performance predictions and other relevant information to the FSU. SiriusXM satellite radio also has a channel devoted to fantasy sport that features programming from fantasy experts. To highlight one media giant's effort, ESPN primarily promotes two fantasy-focused individuals, Matthew Berry and Eric Karabell. Both are inductees into the Fantasy Sports Writers Association Hall of Fame, and each brings a unique perspective to print and visual media. Between Karabell's podcasts and stories and Berry's witty on-air personality and commentary (not to mention 560,000 Twitter followers), ESPN has invested in these knowledgeable experts, as well as their fantasy sport coverage.

Media development

Having first fought the fantasy sport movement, professional leagues are now embracing the once considered "niche hobby" (Spinda and Haridakis, 2008: 187). In the midst of professional leagues creating and maintaining their own fantasy sport leagues, the NFL recognized that fans desired fantasy sport information, and to that end, mandated all NFL teams to develop and display real-time fantasy statistics in their stadiums. This policy began with the 2011 season, and was implemented to make attending a game more attractive and more conducive to the information-seeking fan. NFL spokesman, Brian McCarthy, said the league recognizes it must do more to keep people attending games and wants to replicate the at-home experience at the stadium (McCarthy, 2011). DirecTV, the creator and provider of the NFL Sunday Ticket, allows viewers to watch any NFL game of their choosing; or even eight at one time! Fantasy sport enters the equation as viewers have the ability to closely monitor their fantasy sport team. One even has the option to create an application or display with their fantasy football team roster displayed right on the television screen. This allows for real-time statistical updates of their fantasy players and television channel information for their fantasy players.

Other content and programming changes include information pertaining to fantasy sport during pregame and postgame television shows, as well as, news shows. Preview shows offer advice as to what players could have an impact in fantasy competition, while postgame highlight shows feature fantasy statistics as part of the game recap. The sport, that is perhaps the standard for gathering statistical information, is baseball. Baseball highlight shows share an abundance of statistical information about the outcome of the game, and also in regards to what players stood out from a statistical and fantasy perspective. Traditionally, highlight shows would provide the score, winning and losing pitchers, and top performers. In today's media climate, baseball highlight programs will feature stat lines for each pitcher, and the box score for all players in the lineup. In addition, fantasy sport has created a demand that more information be made available while viewing a broadcast. This is changing the message, as statistics are being altered to meet the surveillance needs of a FSU. The rolling scroll bar, prevalent during football and baseball broadcasts, is a prime example. Fantasy sport administrators demand certain statistical information be present on the scroll. They know what type of information is needed to keep fantasy consumers from looking elsewhere and understand that this type of information can keep viewers on that station for longer periods of time.

A final way new media is being used in the fantasy sport experience is through the creation and development of mobile applications for smart phone, tablet, or computer-based operating systems. Not only do these applications make fantasy sport more accessible, but it also allows for the user to actively consume more than one screen. For a FSU, the television may be tuned into the live-action of the fantasy athletes and the tablet set on the fantasy scoreboard. This is a major issue for fantasy organizations because the second screen grants creative and innovative developers an opportunity to be a part of the industry, share more information, and provide more access to participants; participants that are proven to be a group that enjoys surveying the sport media landscape (Billings and Ruihley, 2013; Ruihley and Hardin, 2011a). This is all done in a way that avoids recreating the wheel. There is endless opportunity to explore, create, and enhance the sport and fantasy sport experience.

Conclusion

The expansive and quick growth in fantasy sport has created a unique and powerful subculture within sport media consumption and sport fandom. Fantasy sport participation has increased from 500,000 people in 1990 (Vichot, 2009) to more than 35 million (Fantasy Sport Trade Association, 2012a); taking it from a (once thought of) hobby, to a powerful industry captivating the lives of many sport fans. The industry is becoming a new sport media, in and of itself, and relies heavily on other forms of sport media. Fantasy sport would not have the popularity in the sport communication landscape without the assistance of three major items: technology growth, increased user friendliness of technology, and media attention.

Technological growth in the way of Internet invention, introduction of tablets, video game integration, and amazing smart phone capabilities are all areas that have changed the world forever. Fantasy sport is an industry that owes a lot of gratitude to those technologies. The Internet explosion of the 1990s took this hobby and gave it the proper platform to be visible, accessible, and user friendly. The Internet also gave this activity the technological facelift it desperately needed; taking it away from pen and paper calculations, searching for newspaper box scores, and keeping track of player moves by hand. Digital information instantly delivered to your computer screen, tablet, or smart phone has changed the way FSUs can go about their participation.

Media giants like ESPN, CBS Sports, and Yahoo!, as well as professional leagues (e.g. MLB, NFL, NBA, and NHL) have taken fantasy sport and created websites and software to assist with the abundance of player moves (e.g. drafting, trading, adding, and dropping), numerical calculations, and standings. This makes the user experience accessible and easy to navigate. With a few simple mouse clicks, drafting and setting lineups is made easy. Another point of ease for FSUs is searching for news and information. Many of the providers have in-house experts who deliver their input right on the player profile page; some even provide video highlights on the lineup screen.

Media companies are utilizing traditional (i.e. magazines and television) and new media (e.g. Internet, smart phones, tablet, social networking, and podcasts) to host fantasy sport on their network, their broadcast, or their website. These companies are aware of the amount of surveillance and information scouring FSUs partake in. This type of consumption has created a demand for a new type of media professional – the fantasy sport expert. Changes in programming have put emphasis on supplying the statistics that are important in fantasy play.

With the information provided, it should be apparent that fantasy sport has become an industry itself, with the sheer number of participants devoting time, energy, and money. None of the growth and consumption could have been possible without new media and emerging technology. Fantasy sport exists as a virtual culture with no physical limits based on location or geography. All physical barriers for participation in this type of culture are eliminated; as the only thing needed to be a participant is Internet access and a device of some sort to access the Web. Technology is what ties this culture together and allows it to exist, grow, and thrive.

Note

1. "Tailgating" is the practice of hosting picnics and parties from the tailgate of a vehicle, often on the parking lot of a sports stadium, which originated in America.

References

Billings, A. C. and Ruihley, B. J. (2013) Why we watch, why we play: The relationship between fantasy sport and fanship motivations. *Mass Communication and Society,* 16(1), 5–25.

Carlson, J., Rosenberger, P. J., III and Muthaly, S. (2003) Nothing but net! A study of the information content in Australian professional basketball websites. *Sport Marketing Quarterly,* 12(3), 184–189.

Coakley, J. (2007) *Sports in Society: Issues and Controversies* (9th edn.). Boston, MA: McGraw Hill.

Coakley, J. (2009) *Sports in Society.* New York: McGraw-Hill.

Cockcroft, T. H. (2012) Fantasy football auction strategy. Retrieved from http://sports.espn.go.com/fantasy/football/ffl/story?page=nfldk2k12auctionstrategy.

Davis, N. W. and Duncan, M. C. (2006) Sport knowledge is power: Reinforcing masculine privilege through fantasy sport league participation. *Journal of Sport and Social Issues,* 30(3), 244–264.

Drenton, J., Peters, C. O, Leigh T. and Hollenbeck, C. R. (2009) Not just a party in the parking lot: An exploratory investigation of the motives underlying the ritual commitment of football tailgaters. *Sport Marketing Quarterly,* 18(2), 92–106.

Dwyer, B. and Drayer, J. (2010) Fantasy sport consumer segmentation: An investigation into the differing consumption modes of fantasy football participants. *Sport Marketing Quarterly,* 19(4), 207–216.

ESPN Department of Integrated Media Research. (2010, April 15) ESPN top ten list for sport research. Broadcast Education Association Research Symposium, Las Vegas, NV.

Fantasy Sports Industry Grows. (2009) Fantasy sports industry grows to a $800 million industry with 29.9 million players. Retrieved from http://www.emediawire.com/releases/2008/7/emw1084994.htm

Fantasy Sport Trade Association (2012a) [Home page.] Retrieved from http://www.fsta.org/

Fantasy Sport Trade Association (2012b) *What is the FSTA?* Retrieved from http://www.fsta.org/what_is_the_fsta

Farquhar, L. K. and Meeds, R. (2007) Types of fantasy sports users and their motivations, *Journal of Computer-Mediated Communication,* 12(4), 1208–1228.

Global Fantasy Leaders (2009) *Fantasy Sport Demographics.* Retrieved on August 5, 2009, from http://www.worldfantasygames.com/site_flash/index-3.html.

Hambrick, M. E. (2012) Six degrees of information: Using social network analysis to explore the spread of information within sport social networks. *International Journal of Sport Communication,* 5(1), 16–34.

Hardin, R. Koo, G, Ruihley, B. J., Dittmore, S. and McGreevey M. (2012) Motivation for consumption of collegiate athletics subscription web sites. *International Journal of Sport Communication,* 5(3), 368–383.

Hur, Y., Ko, Y. J. and Valacich, J. (2007) Motivation and concerns for online sport consumption. *Journal of Sport Management,* 21(4), 521–539.

James, J. D. and Ridinger, L. L. (2002) Female and male sport fans: A comparison of sport consumption motives. *Journal of Sport Behavior,* 25(3), 260–278.

Koo, G. and Hardin, R. (2008) Difference in interrelationship between spectators' motives and behavioral intentions based upon emotional attachment. *Sport Marketing Quarterly,* 17(1), 30–43.

Koo, G., Andrew, D. P. S., Hardin, R. and Greenwell, T. C. (2009) Classification of sports consumers on the basis of emotional attachment: A study of minor league ice hockey fans and spectators. *International Journal of Sport Management,* 10(3), 1–23.

Levy, D. P. (2009) Fanship habitus: The consumption of sport in the US. In K. Robson and C. Sanders (eds), *Quantifying Theory: Pierre Bourdieu* (pp. 187–199). New York: Springer.

McCarthy, M. (2011, September 9) NFL orders clubs: Show fantasy stats at stadiums this year. *USA Today*. Retrieved from http://content.usatoday.com/communities/gameon/post/2011/09/nfl-fantasy-football-stadiums-green-bay-packers-new-orleans-saints/1.

Nylund, D. (2004) When in Rome: Heterosexism, homophobia, and sports talk radio. *Journal of Sport and Social Issues,* 28(2), 136–168.

Pew Internet and the American Life Project. (2005) *Online Sports Fantasy Leagues*. Washington, DC: L. Rainie. Retrieved from http://www.pewinternet.org/Reports/2005/Online-sports-fantasy-leagues.aspx.

Randle, Q. and Nyland, R. (2008) Participation in internet fantasy sports leagues and mass media use. *Journal of Website Promotion*, 3(3/4), 143–152.

Raney, A. A. and Depalma, A. (2006) The effect of viewing varying levels of aggressive sports programming on enjoyment, mood, and perceived violence. *Mass Communication and Society*, 9(3), 321–338.

Roy, D. P. and Goss, B. D. (2007) A conceptual framework of influences on fantasy sports consumption. *Marketing Management Journal*, 17(2), 96–108.

Ruihley, B. J. and Billings, A. C. (2013) Infiltrating the boys club: Motivations for women's fantasy sport participation. *International Review for the Sociology of Sport*, 48(4), 435–452.

Ruihley, B. J. and Hardin, R. (2011a) Beyond touchdowns, homeruns, and 3-pointers: An examination of fantasy sport participation motivation. *International Journal of Sport Management and Marketing*, 10(3/4), 232–256.

Ruihley, B. J. and Hardin, R. (2011b) Message board use and the fantasy sport experience. *International Journal of Sport Communication*, 4(2), 233–252.

Ruihley, B. J. and Hardin, R. (2013) Meeting the informational needs of the fantasy sport user. *Journal of Sports Media*, 8(2), 53–80.

Sargent, S. L., Zillmann, D. and Weaver, J. B., III (1998) The gender gap in the enjoyment of televised sports. *Journal of Sports and Social Issues*, 22(1), 46–64.

Seo, W. J. and Green, B. C. (2008) Development of the motivation scale for sport online consumption. *Journal of Sport Management*, 22(1), 82–109.

Seo, W. J. and Hong, K. H. (2001) Contents marketing strategy for Korean professional soccer teams' website. *Korean Journal of Physical Education*, 40, 433–449.

Smith, S. A. (2009) Up front: To heck with fantasy. I'm about what's real. *ESPN Sports*. Retrieved from http://sports.espn.go.com/espnmag/story?id=3556641.

Spinda, J. S. and Haridakis, P. M. (2008) Exploring the motives of fantasy sport: A uses-and gratifications approach. In L. W. Hugenberg, P. M. Haridakis and A. C. Earnheardt (eds), *Sport Mania: Essays on Fandom and the Media in the 21st Century* (pp. 187–202). Jefferson, NC: McFarland.

Trail, G. T., Fink, J. S. and Anderson, D. F. (2003) Sport spectator consumption behavior. *Sport Marketing Quarterly*, 12(1), 8–17.

Vichot, R. (2009) History of fantasy sports and its adoption by sports journalists. *News Games: Research on the Relationship between Journalism and Videogames at Georgia Tech*. Retrieved from http://jag.lcc.gatech.edu/blog/2009/01/history-of-fantasy-sports-and-its-adoption-by-sports-journalists.html.

Zagacki, K. S. and Grano, D. (2005) Sports talk radio and the fantasies of sport. *Critical Studies in Media Communication*, 22(1), 45–63.

22

NEW MEDIA AND THE EVOLUTION OF FAN–ATHLETE INTERACTION

Jimmy Sanderson

CLEMSON UNIVERSITY

Jeffrey W. Kassing

ARIZONA STATE UNIVERSITY

New media have amplified fan–athlete interaction significantly and irrevocably. Social media tools like Facebook and Twitter have facilitated quicker and more instantaneous exchanges between fans and athletes, but fan–athlete relationships have incubated for some time due to a host of other Internet-enabled technologies like listservs, chat rooms, community forums, and web logs ("blogs") (Hambrick, Simmons, Greenhalgh and Greenwell, 2010). Online sports fans or those who use the Internet to engage in a broad range of sport-related activity regularly visit sport websites, check on and confirm the game results for their favorite teams, purchase team apparel and related merchandise, seek and enjoy interaction with other fans through discussion forums, and participate in online fantasy sport leagues (Hur, Ko and Valacich, 2011).

Thus, there is no doubt that new media have a sizeable foothold in the world of sports. Consider that every franchise in the NBA, MLB, NHL and NFL has a Twitter presence and that roughly half of all pro athletes do too. The pace of new media in sports continues to grow exponentially. As an example, Twitter reported that during Super Bowl XLVII (and the halftime performance by Beyoncé) there were 24.1 million tweets. This Super Bowl also included a power outage that halted game play that resulted in 231,500 tweets per minute as people discussed this unprecedented event (Farber, 2013). Additionally, the National Basketball Association reported that approximately 386 million fans followed the league's 2013 All-Star festivities (Jessop, 2013).

In this chapter we consider the impact new media are having on fan–athlete interaction. Historically sports media have been a focal point for facilitating fan–athlete interaction. Through interviews, press conferences, news reports and the like, fans have come to know and bond with their sporting heroes. With the advent of new media, fan–athlete interaction has accelerated and intensified in many respects (Hutchins, 2012; Kassing and Sanderson, 2012; Sanderson, 2011a). In the pages that follow we take a closer look at how new media are contributing to, changing, and detracting from fan–athlete interaction.

Parasocial interaction (PSI) provides a particularly heuristic lens through which to interpret and understand the fan–athlete relationship in general and the way in which new media are (re)shaping these relationships. In this chapter we discuss the existing and ever-evolving connection between fan–athlete interaction and new media, paying particular attention to PSI as a fundamental component of these relationships. PSI concerns how media users relate to and develop relationships with media personae. For example, a television viewer may feel he or she has bonded with a fictional character from a popular drama – thinking about the character when not watching the show, anxiously awaiting the next episode, and wondering what will happen to the character as the show's plotline develops. Horton and Wohl (1956) suggested that over time and due to repeated exposure viewers develop bonds of intimacy with media personalities. These relationships resemble interpersonal social interaction, but differ in that they remain one-sided and mediated. The study of PSI has paralleled the development of different media forms, beginning with early examinations of newscasters and television personalities (Rubin, Perse and Powell, 1985; Rubin, Haridakis and Eyal, 2003), then radio talk show hosts (Rubin, 2000), and eventually online resources (Hyuhn-Suhck and Lee, 2004).

As the locations for studying PSI evolved, so too did conceptualizations of the concept. Gleich (1997) recognized the potential active aspects of PSI, describing emphatic interaction as that which entails some degree of behavioral or affective response from viewers. Such thinking indicated that PSI was not merely passive in nature and certainly could entail behavioral responses (e.g. speaking to the character, feeling bad for him/her) that resembled those exercised in actual social relationships. Giles (2002) argued for understanding the differences in PSI between truly fictional characters and actual celebrities, suggesting that an authenticity-realism continuum underpins the construct and that PSI would manifest differently for those engaging real celebrities versus fictionalized characters. Additionally, Auter and Palmgreen (2000) explored the dimensionality of PSI and found that it involved taking an interest in the media personality, as well as identifying with that person and appreciating how he or she dealt with adversity.

Scholars have examined PSI in relation to high-profile media cases that showed athletes like Magic Johnson, O. J. Simpson, and Mark McGwire dealing with public relations crises (Brown and Basil, 1995; Brown, Basil and Bocarnea, 2003; Brown, Duane and Fraser, 1997). Researchers also have considered how athletes use new media, particularly blogs as a mechanism to enhance PSI with fans (Kassing and Sanderson, 2009; Sanderson, 2008a, 2008b). For example, Kassing and Sanderson (2009) examined fan postings that appeared on American cyclist Floyd Landis' website and discovered that fans tended in many cases to communicate in ways that resembled social rather than parasocial interaction. Similarly, Sanderson (2008a) discovered that fans offered advice but also criticized Boston Red Sox pitcher Curt Schilling while posting comments to his blog. Via their convenience and accessibility, new media have escalated fan–athlete interaction.

Fan–athlete interaction and new media

New media are having a considerable impact on sport and we contend that this can be seen unequivocally within fan–athlete interaction (Sanderson, 2011a). The properties of new media enhance the sports experience for fans in a multiplicity of ways. Indeed, "local information becomes global information at the same time that the general is made specific" and this information "can be circulated quickly and widely" (McCarthy, 2011: 266). As a result, sports fans can enjoy an integrated media experience of sports like never before. The advances that new media introduce into the fan–athlete relationship are not limited simply to information sharing and convergence of interests. There are more nuanced attributes of new media that enrich fan–athlete interaction as well. The capacity of Twitter to foster PSI was captured by Hutchins (2012) who suggested that Twitter messages "hint at the 'real person' behind the celebrity persona, promising intimate and immediate insight into the backstage dimensions of a sports star's social life" (p. 242). He added that tweets "build a sense of 'common experience' between athletes and their followers, be they fans, observers or dedicated tweeters. In other words, the cultural distance between the elite athlete and fan is erased momentarily through a repetitive communicative act" (p. 242). The ability of new media to help acquire, organize and distill information coupled with its facility to draw people closer together across time and distance makes it a powerful medium for enabling PSI.

The directness and connectivity afforded by new media that in turn foster PSI are not lost on journalists reporting about sport. In 2011, the founder of *Deadspin* (a sports news website) Will Leitch wrote:

> When I founded *Deadspin* in 2005, I wanted to help promote fans' voices, but they didn't need my help. Thanks to Twitter and team blogs and players taking control of the narrative, fans have a greater understanding of all issues, from officiating to athlete 'discipline' to press-athlete interaction. In the past, sports issues were filtered through the eyes of elderly white men in mustard-stained ties . . . Now I am the filter; fans are the filter.
>
> *(Leitch, 2011: 27)*

Leitch's comments touch on several aspects of new media that contribute to greater opportunities for the emergence of PSI in fan–athlete relationships: interactivity, opinion sharing, and insider perspectives (Sanderson and Kassing, 2011; Sanderson, 2011a). Similarly, sports writer Jon Wertheim (2011) likens receiving tweet acknowledgements from athletes as the modern day equivalent of an autograph.

Interestingly, while new media clearly are changing the way in which PSI occurs and/or how it is experienced it does not necessarily seem to be reconstituting the traditional sporting fan base. There is some evidence to suggest that online and new-media sports fans tend to be male, white, highly educated, and comparatively affluent (Clavio, 2008; Clavio and Kian, 2010). So, while new media reshapes the experience of fandom it may not be reconfiguring in any fundamental way the sporting fan base. Like other contexts, sports may be a place where the democratizing promise of new media has yet to be realized (Postmes, Spears and Lea, 1998).

PSI, identification, and new media

Identification is an important component of PSI (Auter and Palmgreen, 2000). New media facilitate identification not just with athletes but also with particular sports, fellow fans, clubs and franchises, and the personnel that run those clubs and franchises. For example, Lewis (2001) examined fan conversations occurring online with regard to the relocation of professional sports franchises and found that people displayed tendencies to either remain highly identified, loyal, and supportive of the team even in the new city or to sever ties to the team as the result of one's fractured sense of identification with the relocated franchise. In an interesting case study, McCarthy (2011) traced the impact that new media have had on sports that historically receive less media coverage, particularly by considering gymnastics. She illustrated how fans used new media to connect with one another to share information about the sport, create new content, and archive disparate artifacts – all of which contributed to collective intelligences about the sport and identification with it. She concluded that fans of gymnastics using new media were able to meet specific information functions that mainstream media had been unable to provide and recognized that new media platforms served to build identification for sports fans with niche interests.

Other work has revealed how new media can be used as a tool to cultivate identification with professional teams and club personnel (Coombs and Osborne, 2012; Gibbons and Dixon, 2010). In Philadelphia, for example, an avid and determined group of fans called the Sons of Ben engaged one another, Major League Soccer, and the various entities orchestrating the awarding of a franchise to the city through new media. Identification largely coordinated and realized through new media focused in this case not on specific athletes as they had yet to arrive, but rather on the vision of a franchise in the future (Gibbons and Dixon). In a related case, an already well established English football club (Aston Villa Football Club) successfully used new media to cultivate a supportive fan culture while undergoing a significant change in club ownership and management when American Randy Lerner (owner of the Cleveland Browns) bought AVFC in August 2006 (Coombs and Osborne).

As part of a wholesale effort to ensure that the American-based owner's group would respect and uphold club traditions and usher in new ones with the consent and approval of fans, the club introduced a new club crest – but not before presenting choices at the club's website for fans who were encouraged to provide feedback and vote on their favorites. Additionally, a designated high ranking official in the club (General Charles Krulak) began posting on four AVFC fan websites. "Through this medium, General Krulak became a recognizable and accessible figure for AVFC supporters" (p. 214). Circumventing traditional boundaries that prevented all but the wealthiest supporters from direct communication with executive personnel at the club, the General's posts provided unusual access to upper management for common fans and an outlet for them to share their feedback directly.

Several recent studies have attempted to track fans' and athletes' patterns of new media use. For example, Clavio and Kian (2010) found that fans used Twitter for three reasons: organic fandom (i.e. following to receive direct information about the athlete, to enjoy what the athlete says, to track the athlete's career, and to be entertained), functional fandom (buying the athlete's products, keeping up with the athlete for one's own business purposes), and interactive (following to see the athlete's interaction with fans and other athletes). In other work, Pegoraro (2010) discovered that athletes used Twitter for a variety of reasons, but predominantly for responding directly to fan inquiries and disclosing personal information about their lives. In fact, for some high-profile athletes (e.g. Kerry Rhodes, Larry Fitzgerald and Shaquille O'Neal) direct responses to fans accounted for three-quarters or more of their tweets. Findings indicate that fans in turn use Twitter to connect and communicate with other fans about their favorite sports, teams, and athletes thereby creating "personalized spaces where they can express support for their favorites and discuss sports" (Hambrick *et al.*, 2010: 455).

Thus, new media afford unprecedented opportunities for fans and athletes to interact, but the assurance of new opportunities does not guarantee their civility. To the contrary, there is mounting evidence that new media can foster maladaptive PSI or communication that is laced with inappropriate, hypermasculine, and negative commentary about athletes or opposing fans (Kassing and Sanderson, 2012) – a theme we pick up and discuss later in this chapter. For example, Millward (2007) looked at e-zine messageboards from two English football clubs (Liverpool FC and Oldham Athletic) and found that they were fertile ground for xenophobic comments about foreign, non-European players whom users criticized more heavily than native born and European players. Likewise fans from rival clubs Glasgow Celtic FC and Glasgow Rangers FC in the Scottish Premier League have used online sites to hurl insults at one another (McMenemy, Poulter and O'Loan, 2005). These exemplars reflect the diverse range of PSI that occurs via new media, a topic we expand on in the following section.

The enactment of PSI via new media

There are several ways in which fans and athletes have begun to use new media to enact PSI. We touch briefly on those practices in this section before moving to a discussion of how new media have led to the evolution of PSI. In particular we consider how PSI manifests in relation to self presentation, self defense, and emphatic interaction.

Self presentation

Athletes, both professional and amateur, have used new media to broadcast aspects of their personality – disclosures that are likely to induce fans to reciprocate with PSI (Sanderson, 2011a, 2013). Sanderson (2013) explored how rookie athletes in the NBA, NFL, NHL, and MLB used Twitter to build their identity after entering the professional ranks. Many of these tweets, by their nature, were designed to cultivate PSI. For example, athletes described their popular culture preferences (e.g. favorite musician), requested assistance from fans (e.g. recommending a restaurant), and shared insights into their personal life. Such messages expand avenues for fans to find connections with athletes, similarities that are the building blocks for PSI.

Self defense

Cultivating PSI can be a tremendous benefit for athletes, particularly when they experience adversity. For example, in March, 2010, professional golfer John Daly asked his Twitter followers to telephone and harass sports journalist Gary Smits after Smits wrote an article disclosing disciplinary issues from Daly's PGA Tour file. Although most callers hung up, Smits reported that approximately 25% of callers left messages, some of which were quite abusive (Gola, 2010). By sharing the reporter's telephone number via new media, Daly was able to quickly (apparently calls began shortly after Daly's tweet) and directly rally support from his fans.

Former Boston Red Sox pitcher Curt Schilling provides another vivid example. In 2007, during a game between the Red Sox and Baltimore Orioles, Orioles play-by-play commentator Gary Thorne alleged that Schilling had faked an injury during the 2004 post-season playoffs. Schilling underwent an experimental ankle procedure so he could pitch during the 2004 American League Championship Series (ALCS) and as he was pitching the ankle began bleeding through his sock. Schilling pitched a masterful game and the "Bloody Sock" became a signifier of the Red Sox's tenacity in their run to the World Series championship (Sanderson, 2008a). In response to Thorne's allegation, Schilling took to his blog to attack the commentator and to defend himself against these allegations, which prompted an overwhelming response from fans.

New media enable athletes to disclose information that fosters PSI with fans, and serves as a venue to directly or indirectly encourage fans to take action on athletes' behalf. Moreover, new media allows fans to potentially "return and report" their efforts in support of athletes, which can then be acknowledged, thereby reinforcing fans' PSI. If more athletes mimic John Daly's example and request fans to take action, it seems plausible that fans will gladly comply and report back.

Emphatic interaction

The fact that fans mobilize in support of idolized sports figures suggests that new media capitalize on the emphatic interaction possibilities of PSI. This is apparent in several of the subsequent themes discussed but can be seen directly in Kassing and Sanderson's (2009) study of American cyclist Floyd Landis before he was stripped of his titles and confessed to doping. At that time fans had every reason to believe his amazing comeback win during the Tour de France was legitimate and clearly found it to be riveting as it unfolded. Fan postings to Landis' blog indicated that while some fans disclosed traditional PSI displays (e.g. expressing admiration) others shared the intense physical reactions they were experiencing as they watched Landis compete. For instance, one fan noted that after watching Landis that s/he needed to "take the rest of the day off to recover" (p. 192).

In a more recent cycling case now disgraced American cycling icon Lance Armstrong tweeted a photo of himself laying on his couch at his home in Austin, Texas surrounded by all seven of his yellow jerseys with the caption, "Back in Austin and just layin' around..." The tweet, sent before he confessed but after he had been stripped of his victories, drew widespread news coverage and a firestorm of responses from fans. These ranged from emphatic support (e.g. "LOVE THIS!!!" No matter what they say YOU STILL WON THOSE!!" and "Love the subtle defiance Lance. They were wrong to go after you after all this time"), to questioning his intelligence (e.g. "That attitude is exactly why the USADA and The Feds went after you"), character ("Lance, you're making yourself into a joke. The longer you deny the truth, the weaker and weaker you look. Everyone else has had the courage to come clean, but you're still hiding in the basement"), and even his motives (e.g. "you obviously posted this to gauge public sentiment"). In the same set of responses fans emphatically supported or questioned Armstrong and when necessary defended or attacked him when engaging with one another.

Emphatic interaction manifests behaviorally but also becomes apparent in affective responses (Gleich, 1997), which gets fashioned both constructively and destructively. Constructively, fans offer advice to athletes, but this advice can be critical at times which offers a glimpse into how quickly and easily PSI can become aggressive and offensive (i.e. maladaptive) when exhibited via new media.

Advice giving

New media have prompted fans to engage in what might be termed a PSI role reversal, as fans give advice rather than seek it (Kassing and Sanderson, 2009; Sanderson 2008a, 2008b). In the aforementioned study, Kassing and Sanderson (2009) found that fans offered Landis advice regarding how best to ride the remaining stages of the race and to protect his lead. Similar supportive advice giving patterns were evident in Sanderson's (2008b) examination of Dallas Mavericks owner Mark Cuban as he participated on American Broadcasting Corporation's (ABC) hit television show *Dancing With the Stars*. Specifically, people posted advice on Cuban's blog that in their estimation would prolong his tenure on the show. Examples included, "do ★not★ sing along! i know it's hard esp. – if you have a good song... but it's distracting and doesn't come across well on TV;" and "...you really need to work on being precise in your movements... The crispness is still lacking from your performance" (p. 162).

The feedback provided in these cases was favorable, but it also can slip into something much more critical at times (Sanderson, 2008a). Sanderson observed that fans critically counseled Curt Schilling in several ways. Some implored Schilling to curtail his public comments, saying things like "Sorry Curt but you need to do a little less playing into the drama and get yourself into shape... mentally, physically, and emotionally" (p. 348) while others admonished him for being inconsistent with regard to his espoused Christianity questioning his use of God in certain circumstances (e.g. after the bloody sock performance) but not in others (e.g. while blogging) and criticizing him for "using the Holy Scriptures like bullets, out of context, and out of control" (p. 349). The fact that advice giving can be both helpful and critical illustrates the span of emphatic interaction and invites the possibility that PSI in general and emphatic interaction in particular can become ugly and hurtful.

Maladaptive interaction

The shift from advice-seeking to advice-giving suggests that via new media, fans are more brazen in their PSI with athletes and sports figures. Accordingly, researchers have noted the presence of *maladaptive PSI* that is represented by critical and in many cases, hateful language (Kassing and Sanderson, 2012). Sanderson (2008a) observed critical PSI on Curt Schilling's blog as fans condemned him for his candor, overt religiosity, and support for the Republican Party and (at the time) President George W. Bush. Fans declared that Schilling was "nothing but a media whore;" and one individual asked him "What would Jesus do? I believe in Him too, and I seriously doubt he would act like you. You are so self righteous and holier than thou" (p. 351). Another person suggested that Schilling was implicitly accountable for the consequences of the Iraq War stating, "You've got the blood of 3373 (and counting) decent, dead American soldiers on your hands through your shilling for George Bush and Dick Cheney and their useless war" (p. 351).

It is evident that, fundamentally, PSI may be changing with the advent of new media. New media now present unprecedented access to athletes, access that is less filtered and more spontaneous. As a result we are witnessing a new set of interaction possibilities evolving alongside fans and athletes use and continued adoption of new media.

The evolution of PSI via new media

New media clearly have expanded PSI between fans and sports figures. However, as new media have evolved into a more social-oriented process, so too has PSI. The days of posting to an athlete's website have been replaced by the use of social media (e.g. Twitter, Facebook) that afford more direct, interactive, and sustained connections between fans and athletes. For example, athletes will randomly tweet that they have a given time period to answer questions and invite fans to submit inquiries. Or they may reach out to fans with or for social invitations to meet in person.

Consider the following story involving NBA star Kevin Durant. Durant, of the Oklahoma City Thunder, connected via Twitter with an undergraduate student from Oklahoma State University named George Overbey (Mayberry, 2011). As a result of their day-long interaction, Durant ended up spending Halloween night 2011 in Stillwater, OK, playing in an intramural flag football game. Earlier that day Durant tweeted: "This lockout is really boring [referring to the NBA lockout that was underway at the time]... anybody playing flag football in Okc." Overbey responded directly, saying: "Got a game tonight in Stillwater!! I need a deep threat!!" In the hours that followed the two exchanged additional tweets, text messages, and eventually met in person at Overbey's house before proceeding to the intramural game. Interestingly, the events were publicized via another new media technology, YouTube, in a video that captured highlights from the game and an interview with Overbey describing the chain of events that culminated in Durant's appearance at the game. Here, a combination of new media was essential for connecting fan and athlete socially. Twitter allowed for the initial contact to be made, text messaging for the follow-up virtual conversation to take place, and YouTube for documenting the seemingly implausible unfolding of events.

As a result of the increased social connections, Kassing and Sanderson (2012) introduced the concept of circum-social (fan–athlete) interaction (see Figure 22.1). This term denotes how new media facilitate orbital or spherical patterns of fan–athlete interaction that move between and capitalize on relational attributes that are more or less parasocial/social in nature. Fan–athlete interaction is understood to span along a continuum that ranges from interaction that is parasocial (mediated, one-to-many, and in virtual space) to interaction that is social (occurring face-to-face, one-to-one, and in real time). In between lies interaction that is (para)social in nature as it mixes elements of the two. That is, one-to-one interaction that remains virtual, mediated, and public – for instance when a fan uses new media to disparage an athlete and in turn draws a direct response from the athlete via new media. Something akin to actual social interaction transpires in these instances yet it remains mediated, occurs in virtual space, and is observable to a larger audience.

Accordingly, different and evolving uses of new media pull users closer to one another in relational space, moving them away from interactions that are historically seen as parasocial and toward those that are more social in nature. Certain behaviors, like *invitational uses* (i.e. inviting social interaction from the other) and *bridging functions* (i.e. using new media to coordinate and schedule social interaction) of new media allow for interaction to cross over from parasocial to legitimate social interaction. In these instances fans and athletes meet and socialize in person. While this is not occurring on a large scale, there is anecdotal evidence to suggest that is it

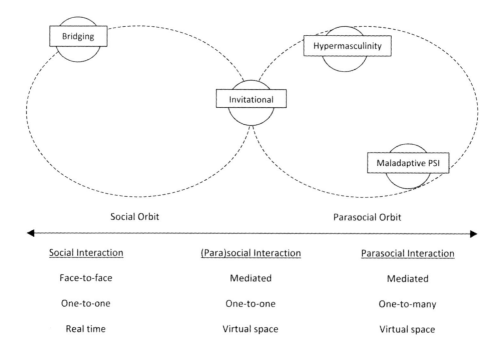

Figure 22.1 Circum–Social Fan–Athlete interaction
Source: Kassing and Sanderson, 2012

happening with increasing frequency (Kassing and Sanderson, 2012). Furthermore, once enacted social interaction could easily retreat back to PSI. The concept of circum-social interaction shows how fan–athlete interaction ebbs and flows between parasocial and social interaction via new media in a cyclical and repetitive fashion.

Circum-social (fan–athlete) interaction represents just one direction for future PSI research in sport. It is worth mentioning that as new media have evolved and become more "social" in nature, PSI has progressed as well. Researchers must ensure that scholarship is capturing how PSI is changing along with the technology that affords these behaviors to be displayed. As this chapter has illustrated, new media have played a significant role in fan–athlete PSI. We conclude this chapter by discussing several implications arising from the PSI/new media connection.

Implications of/for PSI and new media

In the final section we discuss two particularly pressing issues related to the implications of new media: governance and education. The first concerns how new media will be monitored and controlled in the sports context. Historically, it appears that athletes' use of new media is threatening for sports organizations as they struggle to catch up with new media, particularly social media channels such as Twitter and Facebook (Sanderson, 2011a). Indeed, many sports organizations take a negative view towards new media restricting athletes from using these communicative tools (Sanderson, 2011b), while freely using them for organizational purposes (e.g. marketing and promotion). For example, during training camp prior to the 2012 NFL season the Cincinnati Bengals head coach banned his players from using Twitter (Associated Press, 2012). Similar policies have been enacted at the collegiate level where head coaches at various Division I schools have restricted their players from using Twitter during the sports season. In perhaps the most restrictive case, Old Dominion University head football coach Bobby Wilder banned his football players from using Twitter during the entire time they are enrolled at the university (Minium, 2012).

It appears that sports organizations are taking a reactive, rather than proactive approach to new media (Sanderson, 2011b). For instance, many sports organizations prohibit their players from using new media, in the misguided view that such action will prohibit incidents. Unfortunately, this often occurs at the collegiate level – as educational institutions restrict collegiate athletes from using new media, an ironic stance, as the goal of these institutions is to educate. Other sports organizations turn to monitoring and surveillance of athletes' new media, which enables them to increase surveillance of athletes. New media are here to stay – they are not a temporary fad. Accordingly, sports organizations that ignore, prohibit, and utilize intrusive surveillance measures are simply reacting to concerns about new media use rather than proactively educating users and capitalizing on the potential of new media to connect fans and athletes.

Thus, education – of both users and consumers – stands as another important implication of new media. One of the more alarming new media trends has been the increasing propensity for hostile messages to be directed at athletes, including student-athletes. In these cases, the maladaptive uses of new media discussed and illustrated in this chapter can be overpowering and unforgiving. For instance, Pennsylvania State University (PSU) kicker Sam Ficken received a host of off-color tweets after missing multiple field goal attempts in a 2012 early season loss to the University of Virginia. The emotionally charged tweets included: "@sficken1 You fucking suck!!!! You piece of shit!!! Fuck you from all of penn state . . . you fuck piece of shit;" and "@sficekn1 you're probably kicking yourself right now . . . Well nevermind you're probably missing." Fan outbursts such as these are unfortunate, especially at the collegiate level where education is meant to be paramount. Education is necessary in these instances to help athletes deal effectively with this seemingly personal affront, understanding it as an artifact of the technology that allows for insults and criticism to be exaggerated and immediate (Browning and Sanderson, 2012). Teaching athletes to ignore or absorb such criticism in healthy and non-reactionary ways would prove beneficial, as repeated exposure and the need to defend oneself could move athletes to respond in an equally insulting manner. Additionally, using these tweets to teach athletes how to deal with criticism, which will follow them throughout their athletic career, is another important educational endeavor.

Which brings into relief a second focus of new media education – the public nature of the forum. Users need to be made aware that their comments while seemingly appealing to some are an affront to others. When highly identified fans slip into emphatic interaction and resort to maladaptive PSI, athletes as well as the larger audience end up subjected to insensitive emotional rants that if not for new media would likely fail to reach the intended athletic target or the larger audience. Thus, there is a need for fostering sensitivity among new media users – fans and athletes alike – that addresses both the appropriateness of virtually accosting athletes and the fact that new media texts are accessible and potentially insulting to countless others (Kassing and Sanderson, 2012).

Given that digital literacy efforts have been called for (Kassing and Sanderson, 2012), it may be more practical to focus these efforts on athletes in order to help them understand PSI behavior so they can learn how to respond to it proactively. Athletes are clearly aware of their accessibility to fans via new media (Browning and Sanderson, 2012). Thus undertaking literacy efforts with professional and amateur athletes represents a vital next step in curbing maladaptive PSI practices. This, however, will involve a shift from current training programs that tend to be grounded in prohibitions and restrictions (Sanderson, 2011b). For instance, athletes, sports figures, and sports organizations can work together to invite participation from fans, create community among fans, and maintain civil dialogue with them. Such training would involve devising how inflammatory and insensitive remarks should be handled and the appropriate sanctions put in place to deter these occurrences.

Conclusion

New media are now an integral part of the sporting experience (Sanderson, 2011; Sanderson and Kassing, 2011). PSI between fans and athletes across a host of digital platforms is one of the contributing factors to this fundamental change. New media have created accessible avenues for fans to express their PSI directly to athletes and other sports figures, who in turn can cultivate PSI through their message content. Whereas this behavior has been largely positive, it also has promoted maladaptive PSI – behavior that clearly warrants continued attention from scholars as well as sports practitioners (Kassing and Sanderson, 2012). New media, especially social media, is not going away. Platforms and channels may change, but opportunities for PSI will continue to evolve across digital media. What form these take will continue to demand the attention of scholars. For example, in April 2012, German pole vaulter Ariane Friedrich received a sexually explicit message and photograph from a fan over Facebook. Friedrich publicly "outed" the offender by posting the man's name and information on her Facebook page (Ryan, 2012). Whether this kind of response becomes the exception or a trend remains to be seen. One thing is certain, new media are now one of, if not *the*, primary driving force behind PSI between fans and athletes – a driving force that is gaining momentum and attention as it envelopes the community of sport.

References

Associated Press. (2012, July 28) Bengals barred from using Twitter. *ESPN*. Retrieved from http://espn.go.com/nfl/trainingcamp12/story/_/id/8209416/cincinnati-bengals-marvin-lewis-bans-twitter-training-camp

Auter, P. J. and Palmgreen, P. (2000) Development and validation of a parasocial interaction measure: The audience-persona interaction scale. *Communication Research Reports*, 17, 79–89.

Brown, W. J. and Basil, M. D. (1995) Media celebrities and public health: Responses to "Magic" Johnson's HIV disclosure and its impact on AIDS risk and high-risk behaviors. *Health Communication*, 7, 345–370.

Brown, W. J., Basil, M. D. and Bocarnea, M. C. (2003) The influence of famous athletes on health beliefs and practices: Mark McGwire, child abuse prevention, and androstenedione. *Journal of Health Communication*, 8, 41–57.

Brown, W. J., Duane, J. J. and Fraser, B. P. (1997) Media coverage and public opinion of the O.J. Simpson trial: Implications for the criminal justice system. *Communication Law and Policy*, 2, 261–287.

Browning, B. and Sanderson, J. (2012) The positives and negatives of Twitter: Exploring how student-athletes use Twitter and respond to critical tweets. *International Journal of Sport Communication*, 5, 503–521.

Clavio, G. (2008) Demographics and usage profiles of users of college sport message boards. *International Journal of Sport Communication*, 1, 434–443.

Clavio, G. and Kian, T. M. (2010) Uses and gratifications of a retired female athlete's Twitter followers. *International Journal of Sport Communication*, 3, 485–500.

Coombs, S. R. and Osborne, A. (2012) A case study of Aston Villa Football Club. *Journal of Public Relations Research*, 24, 201–221.

Farber, D. (2013, February 3) Twitter users spawn 24.1 million Super Bowl game tweets. *CNET News*. Retrieved from http://news.cnet.com/8301-1023_3-57567363-93/twitter-users-spawn-24.1-million-super-bowl-game-tweets/

Gibbons, T. and Dixon, K. (2010) 'Surf's up!': A call to take English soccer fan interactions on the Internet more seriously. *Soccer and Society*, 11, 599–613.

Giles, D. C. (2002) Parasocial interaction: A review of the literature and a model for future research. *Media Psychology*, 4, 279–305.

Gleich, U. (1997) Parasocial interaction with people on the screen. In P. Winterhoff-Spurk and T. H. A. Van der Voort (eds), *New Horizons in Media Psychology: Research Co-operation and Projects in Europe* (pp. 35–55). Opladen, Germany: Westduetscher Verlag.

Gola, H. (2010, March 4) Daly's tweet revenge. In snit, puts writer's cell number on the web. *New York Daily News*. Retrieved from the Lexis-Nexis Academic Database.

Hambrick, M. E., Simmons, J. M., Greenhalgh, G. P. and Greenwell, T. C. (2010) Understanding professional athletes' use of Twitter: A content analysis of athlete tweets. *International Journal of Sport Communication*, 3, 454–471.

Horton, D. and Wohl, R. R. (1956) Mass communication and para-social interaction. *Psychiatry*, 19, 215–229.

Hur, Y., Ko, Y. J. and Valacich, J. (2011) A structural model of the relationships between sport website quality, e-satisfaction, and e-loyalty. *Journal of Sport Management*, 25, 458–473.

Hutchins, B. (2012) The acceleration of media sport culture. *Information, Communication and Society*, 14, 237–257.

Hyuhn-Suhck, B. and Lee, B. (2004) Audience involvement and its antecedents: An analysis of the electronic bulletin board messages about an entertainment-education drama on divorce in Korea. *Asian Journal of Communication*, 14, 6–21.

Jessop, A. (2013, February 17) All-star weekend highlights the NBA's international brand growth. *Forbes.com*. Retrieved from http://www.forbes.com/sites/aliciajessop/2013/02/17/all-star-weekend-highlights-the-nbas-international-brand-growth/

Kassing, J. W. and Sanderson, J. (2009) "You're the kind of guy that we all want for a drinking buddy": Expressions of parasocial interaction on floydlandis.com. *Western Journal of Communication*, 73, 182–203.

Kassing, J. W. and Sanderson, J. (2012, September 13) Playing in the new media game or riding the virtual bench: Confirming and disconfirming membership in the community of sport. *Journal of Sport and Social Issues*. Advance online publication. doi: 10.1177/0193723512458931.

Leitch, W. (2011) The wired world of sports. *The Nation* (August 15–22 issue), 26–27.

Lewis, M. (2001) Franchise relocation and fan allegiance. *Journal of Sport and Social Issues*, 25, 6–19.

Mayberry, D. (2011, November 1) Kevin Durant plays intramural flag football with Oklahoma State students. *NewsOK.com*. Retrieved from http://blog.newsok.com/thunderrumblings/2011/11/01/kevin-durant-plays-intramural-flag-football-with-oklahoma-state-students/

McCarthy, B. (2011) From Shanfan to Gymnastike: How online fan texts are affecting access to gymnastics media coverage. *International Journal of Sport Communication, 4,* 265–283.

McMenemy, D., Poulter, A. and O'Loan, S. (2005) A robust methodology for investigating old firm related sectarianism online. *International Journal of Web Based Communities, 1,* 488–503.

Millward, P. (2007) True cosmopolitanism or notional acceptance of non-national players in English football: Or why 'bloody foreigners' get blamed when 'things go wrong.' *Sport in Society, 4,* 601–622.

Minium, H. (2012, September 15) ODU football Twitter ban among most restricted in US *HamptonRoads.com.* Retrieved from http://hamptonroads.com/2012/09/odu-football-twitter-ban-among-most- restrictive-us

Pegoraro, L. (2010) Look who's talking: Athletes on Twitter: A case study. *International Journal of Sport Communication, 3,* 501–514.

Postmes, T., Spears, R. and Lea, M. (1998) Breaching or building social boundaries? Side- effects of computer-mediated communication. *Communication Research, 25,* 689–715.

Rubin, A. M. (2000) Impact of motivation, attraction, and parasocial interaction on talk radio listening. *Journal of Broadcasting and Electronic Media, 44,* 635–654.

Rubin, A. M., Haridakis, P. M. and Eyal, K. (2003) Viewer aggression and attraction to television talk shows. *Media Psychology, 5,* 331–362.

Rubin, A. M., Perse, E. M. and Powell, R. A. (1985) Loneliness, parasocial interaction and local television viewing. *Human Communication Research, 12,* 155–180.

Ryan, E. G. (2012, April 25) Badass athlete unleashes vigilante justice against her Facebook stalker. *Jezebel.com.* Retrieved from http://jezebel.com/5905188/badass-athlete-unleashes-vigilante-justice-against-her-facebook-stalker

Sanderson, J. (2008a) "You are the type of person that children should look up to as a hero": Parasocial interaction on 38pitches.com. *International Journal of Sport Communication, 1,* 337–360.

Sanderson, J. (2008b) Spreading the word: Emphatic interaction displays on BlogMaverick.com. *Journal of Media Psychology: Theories, Methods, and Applications, 20,* 157–168.

Sanderson, J. (2011a) *It's a Whole New Ball Game: How Social Media is Changing Sports.* New York: Hampton Press.

Sanderson, J. (2011b) To tweet or not to tweet…: Exploring Division I athletic departments social media policies. *International Journal of Sport Communication, 4,* 492–513.

Sanderson, J. (2013) Stepping into the (social media) game: Building athlete identity via Twitter. In R. Luppicini (ed.), *Handbook of Research on Technoself: Identity in a Technological Society* (pp. 419–438). New York: Idea Group Global.

Sanderson, J. and Kassing, J. W. (2011) Tweets and blogs: Transformative, adversarial, and integrative developments in sports media. In A. C. Billings (ed.), *Sports Media: Transformation, Integration, Consumption* (pp. 114–127). New York: Routledge.

Wertheim, L. J. (July, 2011) Tweet smell of #success. *Sports Illustrated, 115*(1), 20–21.

23

THE ENJOYMENT AND POSSIBLE EFFECTS OF SPORTS VIOLENCE IN NEW (AND OLD) MEDIA

Arthur A. Raney and Andrew Ellis

FLORIDA STATE UNIVERSITY

Sports and violence are inextricably connected. The sport-as-war metaphors used by coaches, players, reporters, broadcasters, marketers, and fans all tacitly acknowledge the inherent violence: "Battle lines have been drawn." "The team is loaded with weapons." "Their aerial attack cannot be stopped." "The battle was won in the trenches." At one time, the Arena Football League even promoted itself as "The 50-Yard Indoor War." The relationship between sports and violence can be plotted on a line of succession from Milo of Croton, the Roman gladiators and charioteers to Mike Tyson, James Harrison, Todd Bertuzzi, and (at least for one incomprehensible headbutt) Zinedine Zidane. In this chapter, we will examine sports violence in our current media environment.

At the outset, some boundaries should be drawn. Sports violence scholarship generally focuses on two key phenomena: on-the-field violence by athletes and off-the-field violence by fans. For the past four decades, media scholars[1] have examined the relationship between these behaviors and media exposure, with research on in-game violence by far the more plentiful. Therefore, this chapter will focus primarily on the enjoyment of violence occurring in the rink and ring and on the court, field, and pitch. We will also briefly discuss the potential role of media in fan violence. In the course of doing so within this specific anthology, we must confront the challenge presented by the dearth of scholarship on sports violence and new media. The reader should be aware that at some points we will be left to speculate on the applicability of research conducted on traditional – or old – media audiences with users of various new media technologies and platforms. We hope that our speculation may, in part, serve to extend the scholarly conversation in the area.

Operationalizing sports violence

Finding consensus on what qualifies as sports violence – at least the in-game variety – is a difficult task. Some argue that acts during the run of play are to be considered *violent* only when they violate the rules of the game; others assert that even sanctioned acts (e.g. a tackle in football, a punch in boxing, a foul in basketball) can be labeled as *violent*. Unfortunately, the scholarly record does not provide the desired operational clarity. Like the laity, sports media scholars often use the generic term *violence* to describe on-the-field play that is both sanctioned and unsanctioned by the rules (e.g. Bryant, 1989; Coakley, 2001; Goldstein, 1983; Messner, 1990; Young, 2002). Other researchers have used more benign terms like *roughness* (Zillmann, Bryant and Sapolsky, 1989), *rough-and-tumble play* (Bryant, Comisky and Zillmann, 1981), *aggressiveness* (DeNeui and Sachau, 1996), and *hostility* (Bryant, Brown, Comisky and Zillmann, 1982; Sullivan, 1991) to describe the actions in question.

In truth, many sports behaviors would be considered violent in our society if not sanctioned by the rules of engagement. Nevertheless, not all sports behaviors are sanctioned; some do break the rules. Referees must judge the difference, as must viewers. Sports media scholars have come to acknowledge this reality, avoiding pre-ordaining some sports acts as violent in favor of measuring viewers' *perceptions of sports violence* (e.g. Bryant, 1989; Raney and Depalma, 2006; Raney and Kinnally, 2009). In other words, media scholars have come to understand that, to some extent, sports violence is in the eye of the beholder.

Explaining the enjoyment of in-game sports violence

Over the past several decades, media scholars have identified numerous factors that shape perceptions of in-game violence, which in turn impact our enjoyment of mediated sports (Bryant, 1989; Bryant, Zillmann and Raney, 1998; Raney, 2006). Generally speaking, these factors are associated with one of four categories: the contests themselves, the combatants involved, the nature of the coverage, and the media consumers.

The contests

No matter how you look at them, some sports are more violent than others. It stands to reason that the nature of the games themselves influence perceptions of violence and, in turn, enjoyment. Sargent, Zillmann and Weaver (1998) asked participants to evaluate 25 televised sports on a variety of dimensions, including violence and danger. As expected, combative team (i.e. football, ice hockey) and individual (i.e. boxing, karate) sports were rated significantly more violent and dangerous than all others. Furthermore, the violent team sports were rated as most enjoyable. Similarly, DeNeui and Sachau (1996) examined spectator reactions to 16 amateur hockey games to determine which factors best predicted enjoyment. Only those indicating aggressive or violent play – the number of penalties committed and penalty minutes assessed – reliably predicted enjoyment. In fact, *violent* has been found to be the sports characteristic – from a set including risk, artistry, and speed, among others – most associated with enjoyment (Zillmann, 1995).

Surprisingly, few studies have directly compared the appeal of aggressive and nonaggressive play. In the seminal work, Bryant and his colleagues (1981) found that participants rated NFL plays high in roughness as significantly more enjoyable than those categorized as low or intermediate. Raney and Depalma (2006) also found violent sports to be rated as more enjoyable than a nonviolent one. Thus, it appears that violent and combative sports are generally enjoyed more than their nonviolent counterparts and that viewers do indeed like them *because of* the violence.

The combatants

The participants involved in the contests also influence perceptions of in-game violence. Some teams and athletes simply play with a more physical style than others; most ardent fans can readily name those with such a reputation in a given sport. Additionally, scholars have recently increased their interest in sports rivalries (e.g. Dalakas and Melancon, 2012; Luellen and Wann, 2010). One study demonstrated how the contentiousness of these games can impact perceptions of violence and also shed light on how game outcome might affect those perceptions. Raney and Kinnally (2009) examined four televised college football games featuring the same hometown team: two against heated rivals, two against nonrivals. The hometown team won one of the rivalry games, while losing the other; the same was the case for the nonrivalry games. The researchers found that viewers rated the rivalry games to be more violent than the nonrivalry games, regardless of the outcome (or regardless of many in-game features such as penalties, turnovers, and injuries). Moreover, the games won were perceived to be more violent than those lost; in fact, perceptions of violence were associated with greater enjoyment across all the games. Finally, only fanship – per disposition theory of sports spectatorship (Zillmann, Bryant and Sapolsky, 1989; Zillmann and Paulus, 1993) predictions – was a stronger predictor of enjoyment than perceived violence in a rivalry game won by the hometeam. Thus, as viewers perceive more rivalry between the combatants, they also perceive more violence in the play with meaningful impacts on enjoyment, especially if the team they favor wins.

Fans perceive violence and animosity between rival teams for a variety of reasons: years of vying for the same crowns and trophies, close geographic proximity between teams and clubs, national pride, old grudges, and presumed cosmic injustices, to name a few. Real hostility between players might also contribute to these perceptions. In our persistently connected world, players routinely make public comments or post material online that derogate an upcoming opponent; typically these comments end up as de facto motivational "locker room material" for the other team. One recent phenomenon is the "Twitter War," in which players use the popular social media site as a forum for posting insulting comments about opponents. For example, in 2012, NFL players Osi Umenyiora and Lesean McCoy played out an ongoing feud in the Twitterverse, with the former tweeting "Happy Mothers Day Lesean Mccoy! Enjoy your special day!!," and the latter calling Umenyiora a "ballerina in a Giants uniform" (Youngmisuk, 2012). As one might imagine, the insults often turn more aggressive. In 2010, another NFL player – Chad (Ochocinco) Johnson – tweeted to an upcoming opponent that "even though you play offense i will whoop yo [butt]" and "this shh done got personal, when i see you on the field i am going straight to the jaw, i will take the fine 4 beatin u up" ("Bengals and Ravens . . . ," 2010). American football is not the only sport prone to Twitter wars; in recent years, the international cricket scene has experienced similar incidents, with the most noted being big-hitter Chris Gayles' repeated tweet-based rows with members of the Australian national team ("West Indies batsman . . . ," 2013). It is reasonable to expect that such verbal skirmishes impact the way fans view the contests themselves. But precisely how such fights on Twitter and other social media actually impact a viewer's perception of rivalries or aggression between opponents or enjoyment of the actual game is still up for evaluation.

The coverage

Perceptions of violence are also shaped by the way that sports are covered in the media. Historically, scholars have focused their attention on how the commentary that accompanies live televised sports impacts such perceptions. In one classic study, participants viewed clips of a hockey match containing either normal or unusually rough play (Comisky, Bryant and Zillmann, 1977). Some viewers saw the clips without commentary; others viewed them with the commentary from the original broadcast. The viewers of the normal play with commentary perceived the action to be more intense and violent than identical action without commentary. Moreover, normal play, accompanied by aggression-embellishing commentary, was rated as rougher than actual, physical play. Similar findings emerged in an experimental study of televised basketball (Sullivan, 1991), as well as an examination of children's reactions to soccer fouls (Beentjes, Van Oordt and Van Der Voort, 2002). Bryant and his colleagues also demonstrated how commentary can influence perceptions of violence with *noncontact* sports (Bryant *et al.*, 1982). The researchers created three versions of a tennis match differing in one respect: the reported relationship between the two players as best friends, bitter enemies, or nonexistent. Viewers of the participants-as-enemies version perceived the players to be more hostile, tense, and competitive than participants viewing the other two versions; they also reported enjoying the match significantly more than viewers in the other two groups.

Another coverage-related influence on perceptions of violence and enjoyment is the sense of "being there" promoted through the visual clarity and vividness in emerging television technology. Beginning with HDTV, televisions have increasingly provided images that facilitate immersive viewing. Generally speaking, image quality is positively associated with a viewers' sense of immersion (Bracken, 2006). Studies also consistently demonstrate that immersion leads viewers to experience more social and physical presence with the content, which is further associated with greater enjoyment (Kim and Biocca, 1997). Still newer technologies, such as stereoscopic 3-dimensional television (3DTV) and Ultra HD formats, promise to unlock even greater levels of viewer enjoyment by further blurring the boundaries between mediated content and reality.

In the case of 3DTV, the potential for an enhanced sports viewing experience is being explored by several major content producers. ESPN is investing confidently in the belief that 3DTV, with its added dimension of visual depth, will lead to more immersive experiences. The network pioneered 3D production techniques and launched television's first full-time 3D network in June 2010. Since its launch, ESPN3D has offered hundreds of live sporting events, including Wimbledon, the Masters, and the UEFA Champions League to millions of households in the US, Australia, and Brazil. Though the network airs a wide variety of sport, ESPN3D's marketing and production efforts most centrally feature American football action, typically relying upon brutal hits to highlight the added visual dimension.

To our knowledge, no studies have examined perceptions of violence with 3DTV; however, early research suggests that 3D sports viewers do experience greater levels of enjoyment, feelings of engagement, and sense of presence as compared to 2D viewers of the same content (ESPN Media Zone, 2010). Our own study comparing 2D and 3D clips of various sporting events yielded similar results with significantly greater attention, feelings of presence, and enjoyment observed in 3D viewers (Raney, Ellis and Janicke, 2012). Also, sporting events shot in 3D require new (or nontraditional) camera angles, which may impact viewer perceptions. For instance, the use of a "subjective" camera angle in sports coverage – that is, a shot that provides the viewer with a first-person visual perspective of the action – can lead to an increased sense of spatial presence and engagement (Cummings, 2009); we might assume that this effect would be enhanced by the added depth-of-field with 3DTV. Further, digital-games research identifies a consistent relationship between the experience of presence and perceptions of violence and hostile thoughts (e.g. Nowak, Krcmar and Farrar, 2008; Tamborini *et al.*, 2004), with some indication that gaming experience – perhaps analogous to sports fandom for our purpose – strengthens this relationship. Given all this, it seems reasonable to assume that as 3DTV encourages immersive viewing and feelings of presence, it might also heighten audience perceptions of sports violence.

3DTV is not the only emerging technology likely to influence perceptions of sports violence. With at least four times the resolution of current HD sets, Ultra HD technology promises to challenge 3DTV in the marketplace by further enhancing the realism of on-screen action. By using super high-resolution technology, Ultra HD televisions are designed to offer unprecedented clarity on wall-filling displays, allowing consumers to enjoy much larger screens without sacrificing picture quality. Although no studies yet exist on the influence of Ultra HD on perceptions of violence, numerous studies have examined the influence of screen size on variables likely to influence perceptions of sports content. Generally, studies report that increased screen size can influence responses critical to the viewing experience, including arousal, feelings of presence, and enjoyment (Lombard, Ditton, Grabe and Reich, 1997; Reeves, Lang, Kim and Tatar, 1999). We might assume that the same would be the case – with resulting impacts on perceptions of violence – with Ultra HD sets.

Technology aside, the "coverage" of sports violence involves much more than the rough action during the officially, copyrighted broadcast of the live event. Sports media makers routinely celebrate violent play as a part of their marketing efforts, from up-coming game promotions to newscast lead-ins. For several years ESPN ran a segment during its NFL coverage titled *Jacked Up!*, highlighting the "biggest, baddest, bone-rattling hits" from the previous week (Bryant, 2010). Brutal collisions take center stage in the BBC and ITV promotions of and introductions to rugby matches, as well. In general, broadcasters openly celebrate acts of sports violence as displays of peak athleticism and game play, and athletes themselves take notice. Players report that hard-hitting replays are frequently used in team meetings to stir "pride and intimidation" in the players and coaches (Bryant, 2010). In one study, 83% of the athletes surveyed agreed that the media's condoning of sports violence leads to its perpetuation on the field (Lance and Ross, 2000). It is reasonable to expect that at-home viewers experience similar effects as well.

But broadcasters are not the only ones celebrating violent plays on the field. User-generated content, social media, and video-sharing sites like YouTube, Facebook, Tumblr, and Twitter have also become forums on which fans discuss, distribute, and pay homage to sports violence. For example, many Twitter users immediately comment on violent collisions and hard fouls seen on television, often with language that praises the violence (e.g. #HugeHit, #LitHimUp). Similarly, smartphone pictures and videos documenting sports violence and its aftermath fly out of stadiums at an alarming pace.

Users also create and distribute via social media sites their own sports violence "greatest hits" videos – from knockout punches to motocross wrecks – often accompanied by an aggressive, head-thumping soundtrack. These videos occasionally contain amateur-shot footage from local events, like high school or even Pee Wee football games. More often, though, footage from network broadcasts are edited together in a celebration of pain; a quick search on YouTube for "football hits" returned links to more than 250,000 videos; "MMA" (for mixed martial arts) returned more than 1 million hits. Perhaps even more disturbing is the increasing number of fights or other forms of violence between fans that are being caught on smartphone cameras and distributed for the pleasure of others; a search for "fan fight" yielded more than 360,000 YouTube videos.

The consumers

Finally (and unsurprisingly), the appeal of sports violence varies across the population. Similar to the literature on media violence in general, studies repeatedly demonstrate that, for instance, males enjoy sports violence more than females (Bryant *et al.*, 1981; Raney and Depalma, 2006; Sargent *et al.*, 1998; Zillmann, 1995). This is not to say that females *dislike* violent sports. In fact, females report viewing more violent team sports than any other and enjoying them at a very high rate (Sargent *et al.*, 1998); Zillmann (1995) found that males and females alike named *violent* as the sports characteristic most associated with enjoyment. The point here is that males may enjoy aggressive play more than females, but all generally report finding it more enjoyable than most other types of play.

Scholars have also examined how perceptions of violence might be moderated by general sports fandom. But, to date, this picture is still somewhat incomplete due to a paucity of studies. Sullivan (1991) found no differences between sports fans and nonfans in perceptions of violence across different versions of a basketball game, but Raney and Depalma (2006) reported that fans enjoyed a boxing match more than nonfans. The picture is similarly unclear about the influence of numerous personality variables on the appeal of mediated sports violence, as again the research is quite limited (and unsystematic). Individuals scoring high on the Sensing (S-N) dimension of the Myers-Briggs Type Indicator have shown a preference for sports programming in general, though not sports violence in particular (Nolan and Patterson, 1990). Bryant found that viewers scoring high on the Buss-Durkee Hostility Inventory were "particularly fond of sports violence" (Bryant, 1989: 287), while another study found that the surface trait Curiosity About Morbid Events (CAME) was somewhat related to attitudes toward advertisements containing violent sports action (McDaniel, Lim and Mahan, 2007). Clearly, more research is needed in this area.

Another viewer-related phenomenon that warrants more scrutiny is verbal aggression. In many sports contexts, such chatter is often dismissed as mere "trash talk." Pregame, chest-thumping predictions are common among sports fans, as is gloating about wins and angrily bemoaning losses. Of course, much taunting occurs during the games themselves, at the arenas, sports bars, and other public viewings. Expanding our scope a bit, we also note that some forms of verbal aggression show up in the media as letters to the editor, calls to sports talk radio programs, and posts on fanboards. Over the past decade, new media technologies have offered more and farther-reaching opportunities for fans to join in trash-talking conversations. During the 2012 Super Bowl, fans averaged more than 12,000 tweets per second (Olivarez-Giles, 2012); one can only imagine how many 140-character taunts and insults were exchanged! For the most part, the talk is good-natured and fairly harmless. However, occasionally the language turns mean-spirited and outright aggressive, especially when opposing teams, players, and coaches are the targets. For example, after missing a potential game-winning shot in the 2012 NBA playoffs, Los Angeles Laker guard Steve Blake and his family received numerous profanity-filled death threats via his wife's Twitter account (Medina, 2012). The same was true for San Francisco 49er Kyle Williams after his two turnovers helped contribute to his team's defeat in the 2012 NFC Championship Game (Padilla, 2012). But the threats and abuse do not just travel in one direction. When a soccer fan tweeted to Wayne Rooney that he would "smash ya head in with a pitchin wedge an bury ya with a ballast fork," the Manchester United player quickly responded "I will put u asleep within 10 seconds hope u turn up if u don't gonna tell everyone ur scared u little nit. I'll be waiting" ("Rooney mixed up...", 2011).

Another way fans communicate their vitriol toward the enemy is the creation of *I Hate* (insert team, athlete, or coach name) websites and fan pages on Facebook and other social media outlets. No doubt, most of these forums are unserious and light-hearted fun. But, as Tertullian wrote, "Where there is rivalry, there also are madness, bile, anger and pain, with all the things that flow from them." This is surely the case on some of these sites, like *IHateLeBronJames.com*, where the NBA star is described as "a complete monstrosity" and a "pompous jerk." The creator writes, "Why does this site exist? Simple: because I hate LeBron James. I hate him for many reasons... I hate LeBron James with the white-hot intensity of a thousand suns" ("Why Hate?," n.d.). But the NBA superstar is not alone. Multiple *I Hate* pages can be found on Facebook for athletes in nearly every sport: Michael Vick (football), Tiger Woods (golf), Raffi Torres (hockey), Kurt Busch (racing), Cristiano Ronaldo (men's soccer), Floyd Mayweather (boxing), even Hope Solo (women's soccer).

Some fans even turn the anger and aggression inwardly. In 2002, before newly hired football coach Ron Zook had called a single play, a few University of Florida fans launched the website *FireRonZook.com*. "In a sense, it was funny and original – a grassroots attempt to disseminate a message about a coach that two University of Florida alumni couldn't stand. But it was also cruel, and it took the nasty and personal nature of the ubiquitous Internet-driven rants against coaches to a new level" ("Site to stay...", 2004). Copycat versions of the site sprang up across the sports world calling for the coaching axe to fall in numerous situations; one such site was the *FireRonZook: Illinois Edition*, where the coach landed after indeed being fired by Florida. Sites like these can, and often do, push well beyond good-natured trash talking among fans to personal attacks involving mean-spirited, aggressive, and hateful speech.

To be clear: No direct, causal relationship has been found – or necessarily is being suggested – between on-the-field aggressive play and verbal aggression among fans. However, verbally aggressive exchanges between sports fans are undeniably commonplace. Further, aggressive sports talk within our current digital media environment demands more scholarly attention. Accessing the technology is simple. Global distribution is assured; global redistribution is likely if you have enough followers, friends, or subscribers. And perhaps, most importantly, nearly anything can be communicated with a certain degree of (at least temporary) anonymity. These factors create a situation that might promote more frequent and extreme forms of verbal sports aggression, including, as noted above, threats of actual violence toward opposing fans, coaches, and athletes.

Media coverage and fan violence

Much has been written from a sociological perspective about how contemporary sport generally contributes to a growing, hypermasculine culture of violence (e.g. Messner, Dunbar and Hunt, 2000). Moreover, researchers have examined how sports fanship and spectatorship might contribute directly to real-world violence in the stands, in the streets, and at home (for an excellent overview, see Wann *et al.*, 2001). However, for psychologists, identifying and disentangling the unique contribution of sports media to these complex phenomena is nearly impossible. No doubt: Sports content can lead to an increase in hostile thoughts and negative emotional responses (e.g. Arms, Russell and Sandilands, 1979; Goldstein and Arms, 1971; Raney and Depalma, 2006). But drawing a causal connection between sports media consumption and specific violent behavior is extremely difficult. As a result, the literature attempting to do so is quite limited.

Anecdotes tie watching a beloved team win a championship to spontaneous "celebrations" often resulting in vandalism, looting, and other violent behavior; for example, riots (again) erupted in Los Angeles in June 2005 after the Lakers defeated the Orlando Magic for the NBA title... in Orlando (Rose, 2009). In a few cases, social media networks have been credited with (or blamed for) facilitating sports-related riots. In 2011, after the Vancouver Canucks lost Game 7 of the Stanley Cup Finals, a small number of people set an automobile afire outside the arena. Soon dozens, and then hundreds, of onlookers gathered to document the escalating event on various social media sites. Some fans took "tourist-type" pictures in front of the burning car and riot police; others turned their smartphone cameras toward the police themselves, seemingly taunting them to act in a manner that might serve as fodder for a viral video. In the aftermath, some argued that it was the energy of the crowd – rallied and stoked by social media

– that transformed a few people burning a car into a full-scale riot resulting in significant damage to downtown Vancouver (Brooks, 2011).

Similarly, University of Kentucky fans celebrated their 2012 NCAA Men's Basketball Tournament Championship win by rioting at several locations near the campus in Lexington, in what was later described as the "perfect storm of celebration, violence, and voyeurism" (Laird, 2012). During the course of the events, some fans used smartphones to monitor the local police scanner, tweeting the most shocking moments and gruesome details around the world. The Lexington riot tweets swiftly ranked among the most popular on the site, as "a mesmerized Twitterverse followed the riots in real time" (Laird, 2012). YouTube, Twitter, and other social media sites also played a vital role in the global distribution of images and accounts of the horrific violence that saw 74 soccer fans killed and more than 1,000 injured in Port Said, Egypt in 2012 (Mackey, 2012).

Scholars have also searched for a connection between televised sports and a set of specific violent crimes. First, correlational studies find a consistent and systematic – though complex and at times somewhat weak – link between sports viewing and domestic violence. In the most comprehensive study to date, Gantz and his colleagues analyzed more than 26,000 domestic violence reports from 15 NFL cites following more than 1,150 games played between 1996 and 2002 (Gantz, Bradley and Wang, 2006). Among their many findings, they reported a football–domestic violence link that was consistent across cities and years, an increase in violence as the games became more important during the season, and a spike in domestic violence with the Super Bowl. These findings are similar to those reported by others (Sachs and Chu, 2000; White, Katz and Scarborough, 1992). An attempt to find an analogous link between sports viewing and child abuse (thankfully) revealed no such pattern (Drake and Pandey, 1996).

However, Phillips (1986) reported a delayed link between broadcast coverage of heavyweight championship boxing matches and an increase in national homicide rates; White (1989) found similar – though more delayed – results in a study of homicides in cities with and without participating NFL playoff teams. Several scholars call these findings into question (e.g. Baron and Reiss, 1985; Miller, Heath, Molcan and Dugoni, 1990), and additional studies have failed to replicate the results (e.g. Phillips, 1983). As noted above, attempts to isolate the unique contribution of sports media to complex phenomena like fan violence is extremely difficult, but this is no reason why we should stop trying.

Concluding thoughts

The lines differentiating new and old media are certainly blurring; however, those lines – especially when it comes to live mediated sports – still exist and are distinct. Fans must still use different media to engage one form or the other. They must watch the game on television and tweet about it on their smartphone or computer. Blogs do not broadcast live events, and network coverage cannot be retweeted (at least not yet). But, as technologies evolve, the distinctions between media forms will surely fade away, leaving fans with just *media*. For example, many new televisions are "connected," offering users the same features found on their smartphones. Facebook, YouTube, and Twitter functions are built directly into the user interface on these sets. Furthermore, YouTube has a 3D channel that can be played directly through these televisions, ensuring the most immersive environment possible for viewers.

Also, we previously discussed the reasons why in-game sports violence is enjoyable, but most of those factors occur or can primarily be found within the context of a competition. The types of comments, photos, and videos that are shared across new media are primarily devoid of any such context. They are typically just isolated, celebrated incidents of violence. As media scholars (and humans), we must question the appeal of this material. Why are we compelled to share and consume violence? Why and how do we find it entertaining? And, moreover, we must try to understand how the popularity of sharing these contents might perpetuate social problems, leading some to acts of violence *for the purpose* of filming and distributing them (cf. the "happy slapping" phenomenon). In one high-profile case, a University of Alabama fan was indicted on sexual battery charges for assaulting an intoxicated and unconscious LSU fan after the 2012 BCS Championship game (Watson, 2012); the fan's actions were recorded on a companion's cell phone, posted online, and the video went viral soon thereafter. While quite distant from our earlier focus on in-game aggressiveness, these actions surely fall under the broad heading of "sports-related violence" (Young, 2008). Sports media scholars are encouraged to examine the role of new media technologies as new avenues for the celebration of all types of sports-related violence.

In closing, our approach herein has been to examine previous work on sports media violence for insight into what the future might hold. In retrospect, empirical investigations of mediated sports violence have seemingly stalled, despite the perpetually shifting winds of content and technological innovation. We hope that this overview can (re)spark interest in this socially significant field.

Note

1. Although violence and sport have been examined from many perspectives within communication studies, the lens that we apply is empirical in nature. Our perspective is associated with the "media effects" tradition, informed by social, cognitive, and behavioral psychology, and typically relying on an experimental methodology in the field or the laboratory. Our work differs from that of many sports psychologists in that ours focuses on *mediated* sports, which we argue are constructed versions of reality shaped by the delivery system, commentary, advertising, camera-angle selection, technological enhancements, and a host of viewer factors.

References

Arms, R. L., Russell, G. W. and Sandilands, M. L. (1979) Effects of viewing aggressive sports on the hostility of spectators. *Social Psychology Quarterly, 42,* 275–279.

Baron, J. N. and Reiss, P. C. (1985) Reply to Philips and Bollen. *American Sociological Review,* 50, 372–376.

Beentjes, J. W., Van Oordt, M. and Van Der Voort, T. H. A. (2002) How television commentary affects children's judgments of soccer fouls. *Communication Research,* 29, 31–45.

"Bengals and Ravens begin Twitter war" (2010, September 15) *FootballNewsNow.com.* Retrieved on November 2, 2012 from http://www.footballnewsnow.com/2010/ bengals-and-ravens-begin-twitter-war/

Bracken, C. C. (2006) Perceived Source Credibility of Local Television News: The Impact of Television Form and Presence. *Journal of Broadcasting and Electronic Media,* 50(4), 723–741. doi:10.1207/s15506878jobem5004_9

Brooks, B. (2011, July 17) Vancouver riot: Social media's dominating role in the violence. *Bleacher Report.* Retrieved February 15, 2013, from http://bleacherreport.com/articles/738456-vancouver-riot-social-medias-dominating-role-in-the-violence.

Bryant, H. (2010, October 27) Football, credibility and the game's future. *ESPN.com.* Retrieved November 2, 2012 from http://sports.espn.go.com/espn/commentary/news/ story?page=bryant/101027.

Bryant, J. (1989) Viewers' enjoyment of televised sports violence. In L. A. Wenner (ed.), *Media, Sports, and Society* (pp. 270–289). Newbury Park, CA: Sage.

Bryant, J., Brown, D., Comisky. P. W. and Zillmann, D. (1982) Sports and spectators: Commentary and appreciation. *Journal of Communication,* 32, 109–119.

Bryant, J., Comisky. P. W. and Zillmann, D. (1981) The appeal of rough-and-tumble play in televised professional football. *Communication Quarterly,* 29, 256–262.

Bryant, J., Zillmann, D. and Raney, A. A. (1998) Violence and the enjoyment of mediated sport. In L. A. Wenner (ed.), *MediaSport* (pp. 252–265). London: Routledge.

Coakley, J. J. (2001) *Sport in Society: Issues and Controversies* (7th edn.). New York: McGraw-Hill.

Comisky, P., Bryant, J. and Zillmann, D. (1977) Commentary as a substitute for action. *Journal of Communication*, 27, 150–153.

Cummins, R. G. (2009) The effects of subjective camera and fanship on viewers' experience of presence and perception of play in sports telecasts. *Journal of Applied Communication Research*, 37(4), 374–396.

Dalakas, V. and Melancon, J. P. (2012) Fan identification, *Schadenfreude* toward hated rivals, and the mediating effects of Importance of Winning Index (IWIN). *Journal of Services Marketing*, 26, 51–59.

DeNeui, D. L. and Sachau, D. A. (1996) Spectator enjoyment of aggression in intercollegiate hockey games. *Journal of Sport and Social Issues*, 20, 69–77.

Drake, B. and Pandey, S. (1996) Do child abuse rates increase on those days on which professional sporting events are held? *Journal of Family Violence*, 11, 205–218.

ESPN Media Zone (2010, November 4) *ESPN announces results of comprehensive 3D study*. Retrieved January 15, 2012, from http://www.espnmediazone3.com/us/2010/11/ 04/3d-study/.

Gantz, W., Bradley, S. D. and Wang, Z. (2006) Televised NFL games, the family, and domestic violence. In A. A. Raney and J. Bryant (eds), *Handbook of Sports and Media* (pp. 365–381). Mahwah, NJ: Lawrence Erlbaum Associates.

Goldstein, J. H. (ed.) (1983) *Sports Violence*. New York: Springer-Verlag.

Goldstein, J. H. and Arms, R. L. (1971) Effects of observing athletic contests on hostility. *Sociometry*, 35, 83–90.

Kim, T. and Biocca, F. (1997) Telepresence via television: Two dimensions of telepresence may have different connections to memory and persuasion. *Journal of Computer Mediated Communication*, 3(2). doi: 10.1111/j.1083-6101.1997.tb00073.x

Laird, S. (2012, April 3) #LexingtonPoliceScanner: Twitter listens, reacts to Kentucky riots. *Mashable.com*. Retrieved February 15, 2013, from http://mashable.com/2012/04/03/lexingtonpolicescanner-twitter-listens-reacts-to-kentucky-riots-pics/.

Lance, L. M. and Ross, C. E. (2000) Views of violence in American sports: A study of college students. *College Student Journal*, 34, 191–199.

Lombard, M., Ditton, T. B., Grabe, M. E. and Reich, R. D. (1997) The role of screen size in viewer responses to television fare. *Communication Reports*, 10(1), 95–106.

Luellen, T. B. and Wann, D. L. (2010) Rival salience and sport team identification. *Sport Marketing Quarterly*, 19, 97–106.

Mackey, R. (2012, February 1) Egyptians see poltical overtones in deadly soccer riots. *New York Times*. Retrieved on February 18, 2013, from http://thelede.blogs.nytimes.com/2012/02/01/dozens-killed-in-egyptian-soccer-riot/

McDaniel, S. R., Lim, C. and Mahan III, J. E. (2007) The role of gender and personality traits in response to ads using violent images to promote consumption of sports entertainment. *Journal of Business Research*, 60, 606–612.

Medina, M. (2012, May 17) "Steve Blake upset about fans' threatening messages." *Los Angeles Times*. Retrieved on February 22, 2013, from http://articles.latimes.com/2012/may/17/ sports/la-sp-ln-la-steve-blake-upset-about-fans-threatening-messages-20120517.

Messner, M. A. (1990) When bodies are weapons: Masculinity and violence in sport. *International Review for the Sociology of Sport*, 25, 203–220.

Messner, M. A., Dunbar, M. and Hunt, D. (2000) Televised sports manhood formula. *Journal of Sport and Social Issues*, 24, 380–394.

Miller, T. Q., Heath, L., Molcan, J. R. and Dugoni, B. L. (1990) Imitative violence in the real world: A reanalysis of homicide rates following championship prize fights. *Aggressive Behavior*, 17, 121–134.

Nolan, L. L. and Patterson, S. J. (1990) The active audience: Personality type as an indicator of TV program preference. *Journal of Social Behavior and Personality*, 5, 697–710.

Nowak, K. L., Krcmar, M. and Farrar, K. M. (2008) The causes and consequences of presence: Considering the influence of violent video games on presence and aggression. *Presence: Teleoperators and Virtual Environments*, 17, 256–268.

Olivarez-Giles, N. (2012, February 6) Super Bowl XLVI sets new tweet-per-second record. *Los Angeles Times*. Retrieved February 18, 2013, from http://www.latimes.com/business/technology/la-twitter-super-bowl-46-new-york-giants-new-england-patriots-eli-manning-tom-brady-madonna-20120206,0,1184572.story

Padilla, D. (2012, January 23) Kyle Williams threatened after game. *ESPN.com*. Retrieved on February 22, 2013, from http://espn.go.com/nfl/playoffs/2011/story/_/id/7493708/2012-nfl-playoffs-san-francisco-49ers-kyle-williams-received-death-threats

Philips, D. P. (1983) The impact of mass media violence on US homicides. *American Sociological Review*, 48, 560–568.

Philips, D. P. (1986) Natural experiments on the effects of mass media violence on fatal aggression: Strengths and weaknesses of a new approach. In L. Berkowitz (ed.), *Advances in Experimental Social Psychology*, 19, 207–50. New York: Academic Press.

Raney, A. A. (2006) Why we watch and enjoy mediated sports. In A. A. Raney and J. Bryant (eds), *Handbook of Sports and Media* (pp. 313–329). Mahwah, NJ: Lawrence Erlbaum.

Raney, A. A. and Depalma, A. (2006) The effect of viewing varying levels of aggressive sports programming on enjoyment, mood, and perceived violence. *Mass Communication and Society*, 9, 321–338.

Raney, A. A., Ellis, A. J. and Janicke, S. H. (2012) The future of sports television? 3DTV and the sports reception experience. *Journal of Chengdu Sport University*, 38, 26–33.

Raney, A. A. and Kinnally, W. (2009) Examining perceived violence in and enjoyment of televised rivalry sports contests. *Mass Communication and Society*, 12, 311–331.

Reeves, B., Lang, A., Kim, E. Y. and Tatar, D. (1999) The effects of screen size and message content on attention and arousal. *Media Psychology*, 1(1), 49–67.

"Rooney mixed up in Twitter row" (2011, May 19) *ESPN.com*. Retrieved on February 22, 2013, from http://espnfc.com/news/story/_/id/921341/wayne-rooney-mixed-up-in-twitter-row?cc=5901.

Rose, A. (2009, June 15) Lakers riot: Walking through downtown Los Angeles after the NBA championship. *Los Angeles Times*. Retrieved on November 2, 2012, from http://latimesblogs.latimes.com/sports_blog/2009/06/lakers-celebrations.html.

Sachs, C. J. and Chu, L. D. (2000) The association between professional football games and domestic violence in Los Angeles County. *Journal of International Violence*, 15, 1192–1201.

Sargent, S. L., Zillmann, D. and Weaver, J. B. (1998) The gender gap in the enjoyment of televised sports. *Journal of Sports and Social Issues*, 22, 46–64.

Site to stay up for rest of season (2004, October 25) *ESPN.com*. Retrieved on November 2, 2012, from http://sports.espn.go.com/ncf/news/story?id=1909339.

Sullivan, D. B. (1991) Commentary and viewer perception of player hostility: Adding punch to televised sport. *Journal of Broadcasting and Electronic Media*, 35, 487–504.

Tamborini, R., Eastin, M. S., Lachlan, K., Skalski, P., Fediuk, T. A. and Brady, R. (2004) Violent virtual video games and hostile thoughts. *Journal of Broadcasting and Electronic Media*, 48, 335–357.

Wann, D. L., Melnick, M. J., Russell, G. W. and Pease, D. G. (2001) *Sports Fans: The Psychology and Social Impact of Spectators*. New York: Routledge.

Watson, G. (2012, May 18) Alabama fan indicted for sexual assault against passed out LSU fan. *Yahoo!Sports.com*. Retrieved on November 2, 2012, from http://sports.yahoo.com/blogs/ncaaf-dr-saturday/alabama-fan-indicted-sexual-assault-against-passed-lsu-164146641.html

"West Indies batsman Chris Gayle in another Twitter war with Australia's cricket team" (2013, February 7) *FoxSports.com.au*. Retrieved on February 18, 2013, from http://www.foxsports.com.au/cricket/west-indies-batsman-chris-gayle-in-another-twitter-war-with-australias-cricket-team/story-e6frf3g3-1226573037867#.USKuIvLAVIo.

White, G. F. (1989) Media and violence: The case of professional championship games. *Aggressive Behavior*, 15, 423–433.

White, G. F., Katz, J. and Scarborough, K. E. (1992) The impact of professional football games on battering. *Violence and Victims*, 7, 157– 171.

Why Hate? (n.d.) *IHateLeBronJames.com*. Retrieved on February 20, 2013, from http://ihatelebronjames.com/?page_id=10.

Young, K. M. (2002) From "sports violence" to "sports crime": Aspects of violence, law, and gender in the sports process. In M. Gatz, M. A. Messner and S. J. Ball-Rokeach (eds), *Paradoxes of Youth and Sport* (pp. 207–224). Albany, NY: State University of New York Press.

Young, K. (2008) From violence in sports to sports-related violence. In B. Houlihan (ed.), *Sport and Society* (2nd edn.). London: Sage, pp. 174–204.

Youngmisuk, O. (2012, September 26) McCoy: Osi Umenyiora 'a ballerina.' *ESPN.com.* Retrieved on November 2, 2012, from http://espn.go.com/new-york/nfl/story/_/id/8423893/lesean-mccoy-takes-feud-osi-umenyiora-ballerina-level.

Zillmann, D. (1995) Sports and the media. In J. Mester (ed.), *Images of Sport in the World* (pp. 423–444). Cologne, Germany: German Sports University.

Zillmann, D., Bryant, J. and Sapolsky, B. (1989) Enjoyment from sports spectatorship. In J. H. Goldstein (ed.), *Sports, Games, and Play: Social and Psychological Viewpoints* (2nd edn.). Hillsdale, NJ: Lawrence Erlbaum Associates, pp. 241–78.

Zillmann, D. and Paulus, P. B. (1993) Spectators: Reactions to sports events and effects on athletic perform-ance. In R. N. Singer, M. Murphey and L. K. Tennant (eds), *Handbook of Research on Sports Psychology* (pp. 600–619). New York: Macmillan.

24

EYE TRACKING AND VIEWER ATTENTION TO SPORTS IN NEW MEDIA

R. Glenn Cummins

TEXAS TECH UNIVERSITY

As sports fans seek out content in heavier doses across screens both big and small, researchers have adopted an increasingly diverse number of tools to develop an understanding of their viewing habits, motivations, and associated viewing outcomes. One burgeoning technique for studying mediated sport spectatorship is eye tracking. As this chapter will argue, new media portals for consuming sports – such as smart phones, tablet and desktop computers, smart or Internet-connected TVs, game consoles, and other devices – present viewers with increasingly complex interfaces where viewers can selectively attend to any number of onscreen elements. Moreover, sports fans are supplementing traditional viewing with second- and third-screen media devices, likewise presenting multiple elements that continuously compete for their attention. Eye tracking can provide highly granular insights into exactly where sports viewers choose to focus their attention, both within and across screens.

Visual complexity in sports and new media interfaces

When the Fox network first introduced its "Fox Box" in 1994 in order to continuously allow viewers to monitor a game's score and time clock (Quindt, 2001), producers of the telecast likely had no idea of the wave of technological embellishments (or, depending on one's perspective, intrusions) that would follow. Today's "traditional" sports telecasts are populated with myriad features – game clocks, score tickers, digitally inserted sponsor logos, "k-boxes" – all competing for viewer attention. The increased use of such graphics has drawn both praise and condemnation (Lemke, 2006). To wit, Sandomir (2004) asserted in his assessment of the 2004 Sugar Bowl telecast that such technology "has created broadcasts that are more cluttered than a spring break motel room" (p. 2).

As fans' appetites for sports has grown, content providers have developed visually rich new media portals such as online sites, subscription-based apps, smart-TV widgets and more, which allow unprecedented control over the viewing experience while also introducing a bevy of visual elements onscreen. Case in point – Major League Baseball annually offers its "MLB at Bat" app for smartphones and tablets, which can inundate the baseball fanatic with a wealth of information to supplement game play such as in-game or player statistics, on-deck information, graphical display of pitch location, and more (Figure 24.1).

A second approach to satiating this appetite for content has been through mosaic-style presentations that either present single events from different perspectives or multiple events at once (Manly, 2006). Despite their tremendous visual complexity, such presentations have become increasingly common as a novel way to present sports via traditional and new media interfaces (Grant, 2005). For example, satellite television provider Dish Network conducted an early test of this format that allowed viewers to interactively select among various camera angles for telecasts of college football (Dish Network, 2005). Mosaic-style presentations that allow fans to monitor or select among multiple perspectives or games are now common components of subscription-based online or cable-television packages for the National Football League's GameMix Channel, NASCAR's HotPass, and others (e.g. Grotticelli, 2010; Hiestand, 2007, 2008). Again returning to the example of Major League Baseball, its MLB.TV service allows mosaic-style presentations of sports for those viewing on computers or via Internet-connected game consoles or smart-TV devices (Figure 24.2). Likewise, ESPN's online portal ESPN3 allows site visitors tremendous agency as they can choose to watch one or multiple events (live or pre-recorded), alter the relative size of each in the viewing window, inform Facebook friends about what they're watching, all the while chatting with other site visitors (Figure 24.3).

Figure 24.1   "MLB at Bat" presentation of game play enhanced with in-game statistics, pitch information, and more. Major League Baseball trademarks and copyrights are used with permission of MLB Advanced Media, LP. All rights reserved

Figure 24.2   MLB.TV mosaic-style presentation of multiple games. Major League Baseball trademarks and copyrights are used with permission of MLB Advanced Media, LP. All rights reserved

Figure 24.3   ESPN3's mosaic user interface depicting multiple games, social media activity, and programming information. Screen shots courtesy of ESPN Enterprises, Inc.

These new media portals clearly stand in stark contrast to early television broadcasts of sports and also illustrate two key aspects of viewing sports via new media. First, they demonstrate the interactivity afforded to sports fans thanks to contemporary technology. Viewers are afforded tremendous agency, as they can often create media interfaces tailor-made for their own tastes and preferences by selecting onscreen channels of information that suit their own liking. Moreover, fans can interact with each other online, bringing social motivations for sport consumption into the twenty-first century (e.g. Eastman and Land, 1997; Gantz, 1981). Second, these new media portals are an extreme example of the visual complexity that has become part and parcel of modern sports telecasts, where viewers are faced with a multitude of visual elements continuously competing for their attention.

Although public reception of these viewing experiences is not always pleasant (e.g. Sandomir, 2010; Stewart, 2006), content providers are eager to employ them as a means of reaching hard-core fans willing to pay for immersive, engaging viewing experiences (Armour, 2006). In an era when technological evolution has rendered twentieth-century notions of scarcity irrelevant, over-the-top video services like these represent an opportunity to woo and monetize such viewers. However, traditional methods of gauging sports consumption are problematic, as attention can rapidly shift among visual elements. Within this technological milieu, an increasingly popular means of studying these viewing experiences is eye tracking.

Eye tracking and new media interfaces

Eye tracking provides an illuminating means of examining how sports fans use and interact with these new media offerings by continuously documenting attention allocation within an information-rich viewing context. Empirically gauging visual attention to television messages has long been of interest to media scholars, although past studies often relied on relatively crude measures such as "eyes on screen" to assess visual attention (e.g. Wartella and Ettema, 1974). In light of the abundance of information presented in interfaces like the aforementioned examples (e.g. actual athletic competition, in-game stats, scores from other games), such gross measures fail to pinpoint exactly which screen element is attracting attention. Moreover, the example of multiscreen viewing illustrates how simply recording viewership fails to document attention paid to competing media platforms. As such, the benefit of eye tracking is its ability to gauge, moment by moment, attention to specific message elements or technologies. In the example of an interface like MLB at Bat (Figure 24.1), eye tracking provides a precise index of which piece of information is attracting attention at a given moment. Furthermore, researchers can also examine how attention allocation varies based on a number of factors like individual characteristics (i.e. gender, degree of team identification), formal characteristics (i.e. onscreen arrangement of elements), or content elements (i.e. what is actually happening during competition).

Eye-tracking research rests on a number of assumptions linking eye movement, attention, and cognitive processing, and a brief review of key terms and concepts is useful in understanding these assumptions. Josephson (2000) noted that the eye is in constant motion, taking in elements within one's visual field. This motion is characterized by a series of brief (200 to 600 milliseconds) pauses or *fixations*. During these pauses, objects within one's visual field fall within the eye's foveal vision where visual acuity is greatest (Jacob, 1995). Based on the greater acuity of the fovea, eye tracking rests on the assumption that redirection of the eye to place an element within one's fovea represents the overt, observable act of attention allocation (Duchowski, 2007; Josephson, 2000).

One common analytical technique within eye tracking is to define and often aggregate these fixations within a researcher-defined *area of interest* (AOI). To illustrate, Figure 24.4 depicts the home page for TexasTech.com with a number of hypothetical areas of interest imposed, such as navigation elements, headlines, images, etc. Thus, a researcher may not be interested in one specific fixation, but instead how many of these fixations fell within one of these regions (i.e. *fixation frequency*) and how much time is spent fixating with a particular AOI (i.e. *gaze duration*).

Although fixation frequency and duration are two popular metrics indicating visual attention, additional measures are also common. For example, many eye-tracking systems can also monitor pupil dilation as a continuous, online index of autonomic arousal in response to a stimulus (Bradley, Miccoli, Escrig and Lang, 2008). Rather than rely on self-report measures after viewing, measuring arousal through pupil dilation can pinpoint specific arousal responses throughout the viewing experience and also note differences in attention allocation that relate to these responses. For example, two people could view identical content yet exhibit differing responses purely as a function of selective attention to different screen elements (e.g. game play versus ancillary information). Furthermore, a growing body of research seeks to examine *scanpaths*, or the sequence of eye movements across a stimulus (Noton and Stark, 1971). To return to the example of the Texas Tech athletics homepage, eye tracking could reveal not only which page elements attracted attention, but also where visitors look first, second, and so forth.

Figure 24.4 Examples of potential areas of interest (AOIs) within a sample webpage

Finally, it also bears noting that eye tracking is not a method, per se, much like a questionnaire itself does not constitute a survey. Instead, eye tracking can be employed in various research designs as an operational indicator of attention. For example, eye tracking could be employed to provide descriptive data on attention allocation and shifts in attention in a dual-screen environment where viewers watch a sporting event on television and supplement this by monitoring game statistics on a secondary device (e.g. Holmes, Josephson and Carney, 2012). In this context, eye tracking could be employed to generate observational data, such as which message elements receive greatest attention in a visually complex interface, in what order they view constituent elements, and more. Alternately, an experimental design could employ eye tracking to gauge differences in visual attention between stimuli (i.e. two versions of a team's website), participants in various groups sharing some common property (i.e. differences in attention allocation by fans versus nonfans), or message elements (i.e. the use of varying types of onscreen information elements).

Industry applications of eye tracking in new media

Given the breadth of applications where eye tracking may be used, it is no wonder that the technique is growing in use both in applied and scholarly research settings. For obvious reasons, much applied industry research employing eye tracking remains proprietary (Duchowski, 2007; McClellan, 2009). Although specific research findings are largely unavailable, ESPN has repeatedly disclosed the nature and results of some of its studies employing eye tracking, as well as the network's general commitment to innovative audience research. Evidence of this commitment is exemplified in the Disney Media Lab located in Austin, TX. The space houses a number of research labs – including eye tracking and other biometric measurement tools – designed to examine viewing of new and traditional media across all parts of the Disney media empire, including ESPN (Barnes, 2009).

Given that advertising is the lifeblood of most content providers, it is of little surprise that eye tracking has been employed to examine attention to advertising elements in sports programming, as well as how to attract attention to these elements. Indeed, the lab's executive director Duane Varan notes that often, "there is a commercial imperative that is driving the study. There is some question that we are trying to resolve" (personal communication, September 25, 2012). For example, one widely reported study conducted for ESPN at the lab used eye tracking to examine attention to the scrolling ticker found at the bottom of the screen on ESPN networks during both program and commercial content (Barnes, 2009). The obvious motivation of the study was to allay advertiser fears that the visual element would distract viewer attention to paid commercial content and undermine their effectiveness. To address this question, the lab performed an experiment where viewers were randomly assigned to one of two viewing conditions where the ticker was either present during commercial breaks or absent. Although data revealed that viewers did allocate some attention to that element during the break – 12.6% of commercial time – it did not influence memory for or attitude toward the advertisements (Barnes, 2009; Hiestand, 2009).

The design foreshadowed similar investigations that would follow. Innerscope Research, a company that produces integrated hardware and software for measuring biometric response to media content, investigated a novel form of co-presentation of television and commercial content, a split-screen presentation of NASCAR racing alongside a commercial. Fox, along with cable networks ESPN and TNT, have employed the technique as a means of both providing continuous coverage of the competition as well as prevent channel changing, or "zapping," during commercial breaks (Hiestand, 2012; Figure 24.5). Although specific findings remain

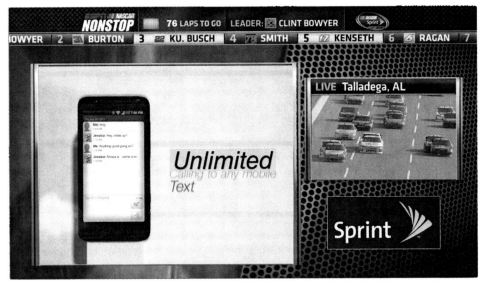

Figure 24.5 Split-screen presentation of commercial content alongside NASCAR race coverage. Screen shot courtesy of ESPN Enterprises, Inc. and NASCAR

proprietary, Innerscope reported that "Ads seen in that format 'delivered much higher engagement levels' to the broadcast as 'eye tracking' measurements found viewers' eyes 'darting' back and forth between the racing and the ads" (p. 3C). Moreover, the Fox network announced plans to integrate the format across its sports presentations (Consoli, 2013).

The Disney lab has now performed numerous studies for ESPN examining viewer response to both traditional television viewing, such as the previously mentioned "ticker" study, as well as new media portals such as viewing on mobile devices (Barnes, 2009) or online sites (McClellan, 2009). Perhaps the most widely heralded example of these studies was the network's large-scale investigation of viewer response to one new format for presenting sports, in 3D. The project employed coverage of the 2010 World Cup soccer games covered by the family of ESPN networks, and it encompassed more than 2,700 hours of lab testing across 1,000 experimental sessions (Phillips, 2010).

Again, specific results of the investigation remain proprietary. However, some publicly released findings indicate different gaze patterns in 3D versus traditional 2D viewing, with viewers who watched in 3D exhibiting more focused viewing in terms of movement patterns (Cohen, 2010). In addition, traditional self-report measures of memory and subjective response seem to privilege the 3D presentation of content in terms of advertising recall and program liking (Phillips, 2010).

As sports content increasingly migrates to online portals and new media applications like tablet-based apps, eye tracking serves as a useful aid to examining attention and how it relates to viewer response. For example, eye tracking can be deployed simultaneously with other psychophysiological measures, such as skin conductance to measure viewer arousal response. The benefit of such triangulation is that eye tracking allows researchers to make more specific connections between attention and viewer response. For example, without the aid of eye tracking to pinpoint a viewer's point of gaze, arousal responses to sports viewed in an online-mosaic-style presentation would fail to reveal the specific source of arousal (i.e. which screen element). As such, the study of sports consumption on new media platforms would benefit from such granular, moment-by-moment assessment of precisely what media users are focusing on.

Scholarly applications of eye tracking

The line of demarcation between scholarly and applied research is not an absolute, as some scholarly research endeavors tend to have more applied use, and some industry research is conducted with theoretical implications in mind, using sound empirical methods. Nonetheless, published studies of mediated sports spectatorship that employ eye tracking are quite rare. To date, they have been generally limited to controlled studies of pre-recorded examples of novel presentations of sports content. Cummins and his associates (Cummins, Tirumala and Lellis, 2011; Cummins, Lellis and Meeds, 2011; Cummins, Youngblood and Milford, 2011; Cummins, Matthews and Wise, 2012) have conducted a series of studies using both eye tracking, self report, and secondary task reaction time measures to examine viewer attention to and subjective evaluation of one mosaic presentation of mediated sports, EPSN's Full Circle Presentation of the October 14, 2006 telecast of the Auburn University versus University of Florida college football game. The network's Full Circle initiative represented a series of broadcasts where a single event was presented in various formats across ESPN properties (Cossar, 2006; Stewart, 2006). For example, for the September 4, 2006 competition between Florida State University and University of Miami, the network featured a traditional telecast on its flagship network, a mosaic-style presentation of the game on ESPN2, a continuous presentation of the game from the overhead or skycam on ESPN-U, as well as additional coverage of the event on ESPN Deportes, ESPN Radio, ESPN News, and more. The network took a similar approach for telecasts of both college and professional basketball, as well as NASCAR racing (Cossar, 2006). Although the telecasts were on a "traditional" medium, its relation to similar mosaic-style presentations via new media are obvious.

The element of the Full Circle coverage examined in this programmatic series of studies was the mosaic-style telecast of the game (Figure 24.6). The largest screen element consisted of the traditional broadcast – including onscreen graphics, while tiles around the screen's left and bottom contained various isolation shots of players and coaches for the teams, as well as the scrolling ticker along the bottom and game clock and score along the top. The utility of eye tracking as a means of studying selective attention to these multiple screen elements is obvious. Thus, the first in this series of studies used eye tracking to examine the distribution of attention across these screen elements, as well as whether visual attention varied as a function of the nature of game play, repeated exposure to the format, personal relevance of the content, and viewer interest in sports.

In their study, Cummins, Tirumala and Lellis (2011) acknowledged that selective exposure to specific message elements is a function of both top-down (i.e. the result of a viewer's deliberate choice) or bottom-up processes (i.e. the result of structural design elements or content properties) (e.g. Bucher and Schumacher, 2006). For example, studies of advertising or webpage layout have espoused a number of design conventions employed to strategically direct the reader's attention to select ad execution elements like brand or product imagery (Cooke, 2005). Thus, viewers of ESPN's mosaic interface could exercise agency in attending to specific elements within the message.

To examine the allocation of attention to these screen elements, the researchers had viewers watch a series of excerpts from game play that systematically varied in the exciting or dull nature of the competition. Gaze data were recorded throughout the presentation, and quantitative measures of fixation frequency and gaze duration were collected and examined as a

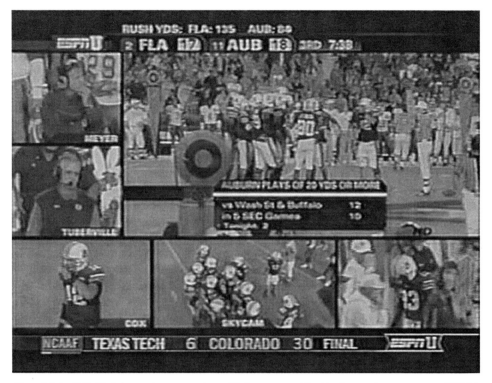

Figure 24.6   Full Circle's mosaic presentation of Auburn versus Florida. Screen shots courtesy of ESPN
Enterprises, Inc.

function of four defined AOIs: the primary screen element, isolation cameras of the head
coaches, isolation cameras of game play, and graphic elements. Unsurprisingly, viewers allocated
greatest attention to the largest screen element containing the traditional presentation of game
play. Additional data revealed deliberate selective attention. For example, during exciting game
play, viewer attention remained on the largest element, whereas during dull play, viewers
engaged in greater visual exploration of the ancillary screen elements that surrounded the traditional telecast. The authors also noted that even though remaining screen elements were
roughly equal in size, viewers exercised control over attention to those elements, paying greater
attention to isolation cameras of game play relative to cameras depicting head coaches. As
further evidence of selective attention, viewers allocated greater attention to information that
was motivationally relevant to them. Specifically, viewers took note when the scrolling ticker
contained information about their home team and paid greater attention when it displayed the
score from a Texas Tech football game (see Figure 24.6).

Visual complexity and co-presentation of advertising

In a follow-up study, Cummins, Lellis and Meeds (2011) observed that the mosaic format was
uniquely suited to the co-presentation of advertising elements along with program content.
Indeed, mediated sports has long been acknowledged as a vehicle for effective presentation of
paid commercial content given the live nature of consumption, frequent pauses in competition,
and ability to digitally insert brand elements into competition (Bellamy, 2006; Billings, 2006).

The validity of their design is corroborated by novel attempts at co-presentation, such as the aforementioned split-screen presentation of NASCAR competition (Hiestand, 2012). Moreover, other scholars have examined the co-presentation of advertising content employing mediated sports as the genre accompanying ad content. Chowdhury, Finn and Olsen (2007) tested the effectiveness of a split-screen format where advertising was embedded in the telecast of a volleyball match either in a traditional sequential fashion or simultaneously using a split screen. Their results demonstrated that although the split screen was effective at dissuading channel-changing behavior, or zapping, the simultaneous presentation could undermine advertising objectives and harm brand evaluations. As previously noted, proprietary industry research has also employed eye tracking in similar scenarios (Hiestand, 2012).

Given the opportunity to use the mosaic interface as a commercial vehicle, Cummins, Lellis and Meeds (2011) employed eye tracking to examine allocation of attention to unfamiliar brand elements digitally inserted into a series of segments from the game. In a series of studies, the authors inserted unfamiliar brand logos in one of two positions within the screen, either the top- or bottom-left video elements. Moreover, they varied the timing of the brand onset to occur either in the lull prior to game play or during play. Once again, viewers watched a series of excerpts of game play with these brand elements inserted while their gaze behavior was continuously recorded. Their results indicated the utility of this novel form of co-presentation, as viewers paid greater attention to regions of the screen when advertiser logos were inserted compared to when those regions contained their original content (i.e. either a head coach or isolation shot of game play). Furthermore, viewers spent more time looking at the inserted logos when they appeared prior to play compared to during play.

Subjective evaluations of the mosaic format

Although eye tracking provides a unique index of attention to these screen elements, it is best used in conjunction with other measures to develop a more complete understanding of viewer response. For example, Cummins, Tirumala and Lellis's (2011) initial study of the format also employed self-report questionnaires to gauge viewers' subjective evaluations of the format. Their results indicated that viewers with greater interest in sports liked the novel format significantly more than those with less enthusiasm for the genre. In subsequent research, Cummins, Youngblood and Milford (2011) explored the impact of identification with the team on evaluation of the mosaic format. Indeed, a wealth of research has documented how team identification influences a number of behavioral, affective, and cognitive responses to game play (Wann, 2006). To assess responses from viewers who did and did not identify with one of the teams depicted in the games, the authors collected self-report data at two locations – Texas Tech and Auburn University. They reported that in comparison to the more traditional presentation, viewers generally disapproved of the mosaic format; this was particularly true for the sample of students from Auburn University who participated in the study.

Cognitive processing of the mosaic format

Finally, Cummins, Matthews and Wise (2012) employed an alternate measure of attention – secondary task response time (STRT) – to study whether viewing the mosaic format represented an overly challenging cognitive task relative to the more traditional broadcast. In short, STRT measures ask a research participant to engage in a primary task, here watching a series of game excerpts, while also performing a secondary task, in this case monitoring for brief audio tones embedded in the video clips (e.g. Lang, Bradley, Park, Shin and Chung, 2006). In this study, participants viewed game segments taken from either a traditional version of the telecast or the visually complex mosaic-style presentation. Meanwhile, they were instructed to press the spacebar on a computer as quickly as possible after hearing the tones inserted into game excerpts. The logic behind the measure is that greater attention to and effort required by the primary task should result in a longer reaction time to the secondary task (barring cognitive overload), whereas viewers watching less cognitively demanding fare are able to press the spacebar more quickly. Their findings suggested that the mosaic presentation was no more cognitively demanding than the traditional broadcast, despite the added visual complexity characteristic of the mosaic-style presentation.

Although that study did not employ eye tracking, data from a previous study offers a parsimonious explanation for that somewhat counterintuitive finding. Recall that initial study of the distribution of visual attention across myriad components of the mosaic screen revealed that viewers largely concentrated their gaze on a single element, the largest video tile, and only selectively sampled from other elements (Cummins, Tirumala and Lellis, 2011). Thus, perhaps due to the potential for cognitive overload, viewers exercised selective attention to screen elements (e.g. Bucher and Schumacher, 2006). Although this post-hoc explanation needs further validation via simultaneous collection of eye tracking alongside additional measures of attention such as STRT, it resonates with the assertion that eye tracking is a useful tool for empirically assessing user inputs that are often implicitly assumed in theories of media effects (D. Varan, personal communication, 2012).

Together, these studies illustrate the utility of eye tracking as a measure of attention in a variety of applications, first to explore how attention varies dependent upon design elements as well as individual preference and exposure, and second to test the use of this interface for the co-presentation of advertising content. Furthermore, the combined use of eye tracking with more traditional self-report measures provides a more holistic picture of viewer response to and evaluation of this particular form of visual complexity in mediated sports.

Eye tracking and future sports media interfaces

Although these studies represent a sound start to this line of inquiry, the dearth of research using eye tracking to examine how sports fans use and interact with new media interfaces suggests a wealth of opportunities for continued study. As previously noted, media interfaces continue to escalate in their complexity. Moreover, sports consumers are using new media in novel ways to supplement traditional viewing. Both scholars and practitioners alike would benefit from a richer understanding of how attention is allocated across these myriad streams of information elements.

Although research using eye tracking to examine sports viewing in a new media environment may take numerous forms, three examples illustrate its potential utility. First, descriptive studies could employ eye tracking to provide a granular understanding of attention allocation to screen elements and the determinants of viewer attention. For example, the technique could be used to examine how viewers use new media portals that present multiple streams of information in a single interface. For example, satellite television provider DirecTV offers subscribers of its "NFL Sunday Pass" access to a Fantasy Football app that presents game play accompanied by player statistics. Researchers could employ eye tracking to continuously monitor visual attention during viewing to examine attention allocation across screen elements. Moreover, eye tracking could be combined with quantitative or qualitative assessment of motivations associated with these shifts in attention.

A second useful application of eye tracking is to examine attention in a multiscreen viewing context. NBC's coverage of the 2012 Olympic Games in London spanned numerous platforms including traditional television broadcasts, mobile devices, and web portals (Comcast, 2012). Moreover, sports leagues and content providers have recognized the opportunity to foster greater audience involvement through proprietary apps that compliment traditional coverage (Pardee, 2012). Although traditional measures of audience exposure (i.e. program ratings, site traffic) could provide information on audience size, they fail to indicate precisely how viewers consume sports content across these platforms simultaneously. Eye-tracking data could be coded to identify associations between events that elicit shifts in visual attention (e.g. Holmes, Josephson and Carney, 2012). Indeed, television networks have begun to employ eye tracking to denote shifts in gaze during second-screen media consumption (Russell, 2012).

Finally, eye tracking could be an integral component of understanding the interactivity characteristic of new media sports spectatorship. As previously noted, ESPN's online viewing portal, ESPN3 is an excellent example of both visual complexity and the increased control afforded the contemporary sports fan over his or her own viewing experience. Although this interactivity and customization is both a boon to the sports fan and characteristic of contemporary entertainment technology (e.g. Bryant and Love, 1996), it serves as a challenge to the systematic study of these interfaces due to the highly idiosyncratic nature of each person's viewing experience. For example, each viewer can select among a multitude of competitions, as well as customize the spatial arrangement of these events. Whereas permitting such freedom in customization of the viewing experience is essential to the ecological validity of the viewing context, it is the antithesis of the control often needed for the systematic study of a phenomenon in a research environment.

If the goal of both social scientists and content providers is to develop general principles of how viewers attend to and interact with these interfaces, then the aforementioned challenges call for a research agenda that requires eye tracking to be combined with a variety of measures. Clearly, the granular detail afforded by this technique provides new insight for the continued study of how sports fans view content on screens big and small.

References

Armour, N. (2006, December 16) Advances in technology changing way fans see the game. *AP Newswire*, p. 1. Retrieved June 9, 2007 from LexisNexis Academic database.

Barnes, B. (2009, July 27) Watching you watching ads. *The New York Times*, p. B1.

Bellamy, R.V., Jr. (2006) Sports media: A modern institution. In A.A. Raney and J. Bryant (eds), *Handbook of Sports and Media* (pp. 63–76) Mahwah, NJ: Lawrence Erlbaum.

Billings, A.C. (2006) Using televised sport to benefit prime-time lineups: Examining the effectiveness of sports promotion. In A.A. Raney and J. Bryant (eds), *Handbook of Sports and Media* (pp. 253–264). Mahwah, NJ: Lawrence Erlbaum.

Bradley, M.M., Miccoli, L., Escrig, M.A. and Lang, P.J. (2008) The pupil as a measure of emotional arousal and autonomic activation. *Psychophysiology*, 45, 602–607.

Bryant, J. and Love, C. (1996) Entertainment as the driver of new information technologies. In R.R. Dholakia, N. Mundorf and N. Dholakia (eds), *New Infotainment Technologies in the Home* (pp. 91–114). Hillsdale, NJ: Lawrence Erlbaum.

Bucher, H.-J. and Schumacher, P. (2006) The relevance of attention for selecting news content. An eye-tracking study of attention patterns in the reception of print and online media. *Communications*, 31, 347–368.

Chowdhury, R.M.M.I., Finn, A. and Olsen, G.D. (2007) Investigating the simultaneous presentation of advertising and television programming. *Journal of Advertising*, 36(3), 85–96.

Cohen, D.S. (2010, November 10) ESPN research lab uses hard science to bust stereo myths. *Daily Variety*, 309(28), 12.

Comcast. (2012, July 23) Comcast's Xfinity TV brings customers NBCUniversal's coverage of 2012 London Summer Olympic Games July 25–August 12. *Comcast* [Press release]. Retrieved from http://corporate.comcast.com/news-information/news-feed

Consoli, J. (2013, January 9) Fox aims to roll out split-screen commercial format in all sports telecasts. *Broadcasting and Cable*. Retrieved from http://www.broadcastingandcable.com

Cooke, L. (2005) Eye tracking: How it works and how it relates to usability. *Technical Communication*, 52(4), 456–463.

Cossar, H. (2006) ESPN "Full Circle" and media convergence. *Flow*, 5(4). Retrieved from http://flowtv.org/2006/12/espns-full-circle-and-media-convergence/

Cummins, R.G., Lellis, J.M. and Meeds, R.M. (2011, August) *Brand Placement in the Mosaic Screen: How Placement and Animation Impact Viewer Attention*. Paper presented at the annual meeting of the Association for Education in Journalism and Mass Communication, St. Louis, MO.

Cummins, R.G., Matthews, C.B. and Wise, W.T. (2012, May) *Inter- versus Intra-Channel Selective Attention: Viewer Response to the Mosaic Screen*. Paper presented at the annual meeting of the International Communication Association, Phoenix, AZ.

Cummins, R.G., Tirumala, L.N. and Mulieri-Lellis, J. (2011) Viewer attention to ESPN's mosaic screen: An eye-tracking investigation. *Journal of Sports Media*, 6, 23–54.

Cummins, R.G., Youngblood, N.E. and Milford, M. (2011) Can visual complexity impact appreciation of mediated Sports? Team identification and viewer response to a complex presentation of college football. *International Journal of Sport Communication*, 4, 454–472.

Dish Network. (2005, September 6) Dish Network first to broadcast sports event via interactive TV mosaic [Press release]. *Business Wire*. Retrieved from LexisNexis Academic database.

Duchowski, A. (2007) *Eye Tracking Methodology: Theory and Practice* (2nd edn.). London: Springer-Verlag.

Eastman, S.T. and Land, A.M. (1997) The best of both worlds: Sports fans find good seats at the bar. *Journal of Sport and Social Issues*, 21, 156–178.

Gantz, W. (1981) An exploration of viewing motives and behaviors associated with television sports. *Journal of Broadcasting*, 25, 263–275.

Grant, P. (2005, August 30) New on TV: The multiple-channel screen. *The Wall Street Journal,* p. B1.

Groticelli, M. (2010, October 22) AT&T Multiview wins the hearts of sports fans. *Broadcast Engineering*. Retrieved from http://broadcastengineering.com

Hiestand, M. (2007, February 16) Pick a driver, channel in and watch him run. *USA Today*, p. 3C.

Hiestand, M. (2008, September 4) NFL viewers calling shots, as of tonight. *USA Today*, p. 3C.

Hiestand, M. (2009, July 31) 'Sports Center' goes Pavlovian. *USA Today*, p. 3C.

Hiestand, M. (2012, July 6) Split screen makes total sense; Coverage can satisfy viewers, advertisers. *USA Today*, p. C3.

Holmes, M.E., Josephson, S. and Carney, R.E. (2012) Visual attention to television programs with a second-screen application. *Proceedings of the Symposium on Eye Tracking Research and Applications* (pp. 397–400). Retrieved from http://dl.acm.org/

Jacob, R.J.K. (1995) Eye tracking in advanced interface design. In W. Barfield and T.A. Furness (eds), *Virtual Environments and Advanced Interface Design* (pp. 258–288). New York: Oxford University Press.

Josephson, S. (2000) Eye tracking methodology and the Internet. In K.L. Smith, S. Moriarty, G. Barbatsis and K. Kenney (eds), *Handbook of Visual Communication: Theory, Methods, and Media* (pp. 63–80). Mahwah, NJ: Lawrence Erlbaum.

Lang, A., Bradley, S.D., Park, B., Shin, M., Chung, Y. (2006) Parsing the resource pie: Using STRTs to measure attention to mediated messages. *Media Psychology*, 8, 369–394.

Lemke, T. (2006, December 7) Sports TV's biggest turnoffs: Some of networks' best-laid plans have bombed out in a hurry. *Washington Times*, p. C1.

Manly, L. (2006, November 19) Your TV would like a word with you. *The New York Times.* Retrieved from http://www.nytimes.com/2006/11/19/arts/television/19manl.html?pagewanted=all&_r=0

McClellan, S. (2009, July 29) Disney preps ad lab. *AdWeek*. Retrieved from http://www.adweek.com/news/television/disney-preps-ad-lab-99974

Noton, D. and Stark, L. (1971) Scanpaths in saccadic eye movements while viewing and recognizing patterns. *Vision Research*, 11, 929–942.

Pardee, T. (2012, May 14) Sports leagues look for ways to maximize social interaction. *Advertising Age*, 83(20), 8–9.

Phillips, A. (2010, November 4) ESPN announces results of comprehensive 3D study. *ESPNMediaZone.com* [Press release].

Quindt, F. (2001) The evolution of the Fox Box. *Sporting News, 224*(40), 6.

Russell, M. (2012, July 3) Social TV keeps viewers engaged when minds might wander, study says. *Advertising Age*. Retrieved from http://adage.com/article/media/social-tv-viewers-engaged/235739/

Sandomir, R. (2004, January 7) By the numbers, the college bowl games have less action. *The New York Times*, p. D2.

Sandomir, R. (2010, October 30) Online World Series is no stand-in for broadcast. *The New York Times*, p. D3.

Stewart, L. (2006, September 6) ESPN 'Full Circle' doesn't square with viewers. *Los Angeles Times*. Retrieved from http://articles.latimes.com/2006/sep/06/sports/sp-espn6

Wann, D.L. (2006) The causes and consequences of sport team identification. In A.A. Raney and J. Bryant (eds), *Handbook of Sports and Media* (pp. 331–352). Mahwah, NJ: Lawrence Erlbaum.

Wartella, E. and Ettema, J.S. (1974) A cognitive developmental study of children's attention to television commercials. *Communication Research*, 1(1), 69–88.

25

CHILDREN, MEDIA, AND SPORT

The role of new media and exergames in engaging children in sport and exercise

Kimberly L. Bissell and Scott Morton

UNIVERSITY OF ALABAMA

Younger children spend approximately 25 percent of their waking time watching television and are consequently exposed to television programming that may de-emphasize the importance of exercise for health (Harrison and Marske, 2005) and participation in sport for competition or recreation. It is during this important developmental stage that children are said to form many of their attitudes, beliefs, and perceptions about their health and the factors related to living a healthy lifestyle (Signorielli and Staples, 1997). Given the sedentary nature of television viewing and other types of media consumption, it is quite possible that children today are choosing to not play a sport or engage in exercise in lieu of engaging with some form of media. However, over an individual's lifespan, babies, toddlers, children, teens, and adults spend much of their time doing two key activities: consuming media and playing some form of sport or game (Wen, Kite, Merom and Rissel, 2009), even if the time spent with the media trumps participation in sport. From infancy on, babies are exposed to different forms of media via television, movies, music, hand-held devices, books, and video games. These key variables become agents of socialization as children learn about themselves and the world around them from either their consumption of media or their involvement or activity in a sport. However, decades ago, these two activities were separate. With changes in new media technologies and with the evolution of media, an intersection of media and sport has been reached, especially when it comes to children. The present chapter will synthesize the literature as it relates to children's use of new media as a means of becoming more physically active, playing sports or games, and exercising. Along these lines, the use of exergames to engage children in sport and physical activity will also be discussed.

It is important to address two key factors that are relevant to a discussion of children, media, and sport – media and health literacy. Media literacy, in its simplest definition, is one's ability to access, analyze, and evaluate mediated messages (Center for Media Literacy, 2013). The US Department of Health and Human Services defines health literacy as the "degree to which individuals have the capacity to obtain, process and understand basic health information needed to make appropriate health decisions and services needed to prevent or treat illness" (US Department of Health and Human Services, 2011). Health literacy is crucial in addressing childhood obesity. Yet, the population at the greatest risk of becoming overweight or obese is least likely to recognize risk factors associated with weight gain. Both of these factors are key in understanding the intersectionality between children, media, and sport because a child's ability to process mediated messages, regardless of the form they are received, will largely influence that child's knowledge, thoughts, and feelings about the subject.

Children and media use

Children are exposed to many types of media: traditional media (television, books, music, magazines), "new" media (the Internet, cell phones, hand-held devices such as iPods), social media (which encompasses use of the Internet but includes use of Internet websites that allow children to engage in social activities with live people or with avatars, and then integrated new media (video games, hand-held gaming devices, or Internet-based video games).

Traditional media use includes exposure to books, magazines, radio (both music and talk) as well as television and DVDs, Blu-Rays, VHS, etc. A recent survey by Nielsen found that adolescents between the ages of 6 to 11 spend more than 28 viewing hours per week watching television (McDonough, 2009). Furthermore, according to a recent survey by the Pew Foundation, adolescents age 8 to 11 spend over 7 hours a day using media (e.g. television, music, video, video games etc.). This time spent in mainly sedentary activities significantly outweighs the time available for activities that are less passive and sedentary.

New media use includes exposure to recently established or emerging technologies such as the Internet, social media, smart phones, tablets, and hand-held music players such as the iPod. All of these devices and technologies are highly interactive, constantly growing and capable of absorbing hours of use per day (Gutnick, Robb, Takeuchi and Kotler, 2010). And as these technologies become increasingly user friendly, younger children are learning to use them. For example, Kessler (2011) reported that at least 80% of children age 5 and under who have learned to use the Internet do so on a weekly basis. Furthermore, children between the ages of 8 and 18 consume almost 20% of their video watching online, most often with a portable hand-held device such as a cell phone or tablet.

Monthly use of digital/new media devices has been steadily on the rise in recent years (www.frankwbaker.com/mediause.htm). According to this site, the average American spends up to 5 hours a month watching video content on a cellular phone, 28.5 hours per month watching video content on the Internet from a home computer, and 11.5 hours a month watching content from time-shifted TV (DVRs). The growing trend toward new media usage is rising steadily. For example, the same site reports that in 2006, the average American spent approximately 6.3 hours a month watching TV online. By 2011, this figure rose to slightly over 23 hours per month. Sites such as Netflix, Hulu, and YouTube are streaming high quality (often high definition) content online. The access of faster, more affordable broadband connections coupled with an almost ubiquitous network of wireless connections has fostered this growth along with the mass adoption of smart phones and tablets with HD screens and Blu-Ray players with online streaming capability.

As of 2012, 190 million households were projected to use gaming consoles of one form or another (www.grabstats.com), and approximately 97% of today's youth play video games in one form or another (Irvine, 2008). Today's gamers not only use home consoles but 35% of gamers play via smart phones and tablets (www.gamergirltay.com). The main issue with traditional video game use is gameplay requires little energy expenditure and physical activity. While many video games are sedentary in nature, video game manufacturers introduced newer gaming devices (e.g. Wii, Kinect) that offer players opportunities to be more active through game play. A good body of research suggests that video game usage has a negative effect on players with regard to violence, weight, and social isolation, but limited research includes exergames as a game under analysis with potential pro-social effects. Video gaming in one form or another has been around since the early 1970s, existing as both arcade machines in gaming halls and in homes with the earliest Atari consoles (telegames, as it was often called then). According to a report by The Kaiser Family Foundation, examples of various gaming platforms over the past several decades include such devices as television sets, consoles, computers including desktops, laptops, tablets, cell phones as well as legacy systems like coin operated arcade stations (Kaiser Family Foundation, 2002). With every new form of interactive technology that comes along, a game has been produced for it. With the new gaming devices that have been developed in the last decade, children and adults now have greater opportunity for media cross-over by being able to watch specific shows on television and then play along with television characters in a video game setting. New video game platforms have enabled users to bring television and movie characters such as Winnie the Pooh or Harry Potter into the household via a gaming unit designed for Nintendo's Wii, the Xbox, or more recently, Kinects. And, as the waistline of children and adults continues to expand, game producers have realized they might be able to capitalize on combining gaming with exercise in the form of an exergame. However, with the new gaming devices in place, what isn't known is how many kids are using them. Data on media consumption patterns only reveal the amount of time spent with different media – television, video games, hand-held devices, etc. – rather than time spent with specific types of media content. While these new gaming technologies seem to offer parents and educators new way to introduce children to exercise, very little empirical evidence exists documenting the effectiveness of exergames.

Correlates of obesity

Childhood weight problems remain one of the greatest health challenges facing the nation. One in three children in the United States is overweight or obese, and no race, ethnicity, or income group emerged unaffected (National Initiative for Children's Healthcare Quality, 2008; Obesity Society, 2009). The problem carries serious consequences for the physical and mental health of children. Children are developing physical health problems once witnessed only in adults, such as Type 2 diabetes, and weight problems may lead youths to suffer emotionally because of society's bias against fat (Centers for Disease Control and Prevention, 2007).

As noted above, the changes in media consumption patterns have led to a variety of physical and social outcomes with some of the most important being the expanding waistlines of American children. The changes in media consumption and the decrease in physical activity also coincide with societal changes and changes in the households. These changes in media consumption are just one of the many factors blamed for the increased number of children who are classified as overweight or obese. Clinicians cite the 1980s as the time when significant increases in obesity were observed (Anderson and Butcher, 2006). It was during this time when many other factors in children's lives began to change. Fast food establishments became more prevalent and popular, convenience foods and soft drinks become more readily available to children at home and at school, both fast foods and convenience foods were advertised to children in greater number, and the familial structure at home began to change significantly with increased numbers of parents working outside of the home. Environmental changes that were directly linked to decreases in physical activities also became more evident between the mid 1980s and mid 1990s – fewer children walked to school, physical education and recess time began to be replaced by more time in the classroom, and the explosion of media-related products and services – video games, music players, increased cable offerings, and movies on VHS –

also resulted in children becoming more sedentary (Malecka-Tendera and Mazur, 2006; Anderson and Butcher, 2006). The increases in childhood obesity are multi-dimensional and can not be blamed on any one factor – genetic or environmental. However, these same multi-factorial variables may also be related to a child's expanding waistline or general decline in health. No empirical study to date has pinpointed the most prevalent or dominant cause of childhood obesity as the issue is very individualized. Research from empirical studies of the issue have noted that a parent's role in the child's food consumption, media consumption, and general behavior observed at home are instrumental in shaping a child's eating and activity.

Media use and obesity

Even though parents are responsible for the food children consume at home, Donkin, Neale and Tilston (1993), Jeffrey, McLellarn and Fox (1982) and many others suggest the media, especially advertising, influence children's purchasing behavior and food purchase requests. As studies over the last decade have illustrated, food ads targeted toward children have often emphasized unhealthy versus healthy options (Signorielli and Staples, 1997; Signorielli, 1998; Strasburger, 2001). They further report that in the ads targeted toward children, few health-related messages were found, but of the ones with some mention of health, the message was related to the food containing natural ingredients or that the food was low in calories.

As it relates to exercise, while television viewing displaces chances for more stringent exercise, it cannot be said that children who watch large quantities of television are necessarily inactive. Several studies have documented correlations between heavy television viewing and obesity in children. The question, however, remains, does an overweight child choose to spend more time with television because he or she is uncomfortable participating in physical activities or does the media use drive the sedentary behavior, which may lead to a child becoming overweight or obese? For example, data collected during the National Health and Nutritional Examination Survey between 1988 and 1994 showed that obesity was least prevalent among children who watched an hour or less of television a day. The highest prevalence was documented among children who watched four or more hours of television a day (Crespo, Smit, Troiano, Bartlett, Macera and Andersen, 2001). A longitudinal study examining similar variables found that participants who watched the most television during childhood showed the largest gain in body fat between preschool and early adolescence (Proctor, Moore, Gao, Cupples, Bradlee, Hood and Ellison, 2003). Obesity, in turn, may affect the amount of exercise a child gets. Studies have found that obese children are less likely to regularly exercise, less likely to express confidence in their ability to perform well in physical activities, and less likely to take part in organizations focused on physical activities such as team sports (Trost, Morgan, Saunders, Felton, Ward and Pate, 2000). Researchers recommend that any intervention program targeting childhood obesity teach children about the importance of physical activity, and show overweight and obese children that they, too, can succeed (Trost *et al.*, 2000).

Linking obesity to sport participation

While blaming the media for the obesity epidemic in this country may seem to be the simplest thing to do, children's participation in sport has not decreased, so the question arises, if more children are getting involved in sport, why are more children overweight? The answer to the question or the blame for the problem lies in many areas – media consumption, changes in parental employment outside of the home, and food intake. As the second parent moved out of the household and into the workforce, the reliance on quick foods or convenience foods led to poorer nutrition and greater consumption of sugary foods and drinks (Chang and Nayga, 2010; Elbel, Gyamfi and Kersh, 2011). The move also resulted in fewer children having the opportunity to free play outside after school, which had been one of many forms of exercise children received decades ago. Furthermore, as research suggests, the consumption of the food poor in nutritional quality is often occurring along with the consumption of media. Whether it be watching television, watching on a hand-held device, or playing video games, users are largely inactive. However, if time spent playing video games shifted from being a sedentary activity to a more active or engaged activity, it is possible children's time spent moving during the day could increase.

Children, physical activity, and sport

Physical activity has been noted as being an important tool for the prevention of obesity and other chronic diseases, such as heart disease, hypertension, and type II diabetes (Grundy, Blackburn, Higgins, Lauer, Perri and Ryan, 1999). However, despite the health benefits of physical activity, only 29% of high school students engaged in physical activity for at least 60 minutes a day (Centers for Disease Control and Prevention, 2010). A 2009 survey noted that fewer than 20% of high school students engaged in physical activity requirements at the recommended level: 60 minutes per day (Centers for Disease Control and Prevention, 2010). And, given recent reports about physical education time being decreased in elementary and middle schools to focus more attention on academics, one has to wonder if children are getting much opportunity at all to participate in physical activity, exercise, or sport. With increased interest in video games and the development of new exergames for all video gaming platforms, it is possible the exergame could help some children incorporate some physical activity into their daily routine.

Enter the exergame

While much of the empirical literature examining the effectiveness or use of exergames to engage users in physical activity have been studies conducted with older adults, limited literature exists looking at the use of games such as the Wii to engage children in physical activity. Exergames are considered a special mode of gaming, one that incorporates not only hand/eye coordination but also complex body movements to heighten the entertainment value of the game and, as an added benefit, to raise the heart rate and burn calories during gameplay. According to Staiano and Calvert (2011), exergames are defined as "the combination of exercise and digital gaming, involving the player in exertion to develop motor abilities during gameplay, focusing on large muscle groups rather than manual dexterity or fine motor skills" (p. 17). Given the evolution of video games, it could be argued that this relatively new form of gaming could be categorized as sport. Exercise games aside, many video games designed for the Wii, Xbox, or Kinects allow users to play the sport of their choice and require users to go through the motions of the game. While standing in a room swinging a fake tennis racquet might not equate to playing on the court, for the new generation of gamers, these types of games may be the only exposure they have to sport at all. Exergames especially have a vital value-added benefit, especially considering how sedentary lifestyles coupled with a ubiquitous culture of fast food has aided this obesity epidemic. Of those two variables (exercise levels and diet), exergaming alone will not account for all of a young person's exercising needs, but it is possible it might be one way for children to get some physical activity throughout the day or become involved in a sport, albeit in a mediated way.

It wasn't until Nintendo released the Wii Fit console in 2006 that the video game industry entered the world of exercise and fitness (boingboing.net). Quickly selling over a million units, the Wii Fit consisted of Nintendo-developed training software and a Wii Balance Board that was designed to measure the user's balance and resistance. The system promised to offer gamers a fun way to exercise (boingboing.net). Competing systems quickly followed. Soon, brands like Wii and Kinects for Xbox360 have transformed the home gaming industry. Now, instead of gaming being a non-motion experience, young people and adults could enjoy gaming yet still have some caloric burn and elevated periods of heart rate. With the proliferation of games being released annually, the consumer appeal of exergaming seems to show staying power.

Exergames as a tool to promote involvement in sport and exercise

To date, only a few studies have examined the relationship between new generation video game consoles in increasing active behavior. For example, Graves, Stratton, Ridgers and Cable (2007) examined the effect of Wii games (e.g. Nintendo Wii bowling, tennis, and boxing) on overall energy expenditure. Results from the study demonstrated that exergames elicited 51% higher energy expenditure than comparative sedentary games, indicating that playing active Wii games used more energy than playing sedentary video games. White, Kilding and Schofield (2009) compared active video game (Nintendo Wii Bowling, Boxing, Tennis, Skiing and Step Aerobics) playing, sedentary activities, and physical activities, with the children's heart rate, oxygen uptake and energy expenditure and also found that playing active video games elicited higher energy expenditure than sedentary activities. In addition, children rated the active video games as the most enjoyable among the three forms of activities. Furthermore, prior research has found that exergames were enjoyable and engaging, regardless of the required level of physical activity (Peng, Lin and Crouse, 2011). For example, participants in Finkelstein and colleagues' (2011) study indicated that playing the exergame did not seem to be difficult or challenging because they were having so much fun doing it.

Perron *et al.* (2011) examined whether participation in exergaming allowed children to achieve the levels of activity recommended by national fitness guidelines. The study used two exergame consoles, the Wii Fit™ and EA Sports Active™ (p. 259) to measure use of these devices in relation to the recommended guidelines for daily physical activity as identified by the CDC. The study involved 30 children and sessions lasting between 60 to 75 minutes and concluded that the consoles used in the study were capable of producing heart-rate activities reaching intensity levels of physical activity as proposed in CDC guidelines. Furthermore, the authors found that exergame play yielded moderate levels of exercise intensity.

One of the challenges with assessing exergame effectiveness in terms of calorie expenditure or heart-rate increase is developing a measure that allows for accurate reads of participant heart rate or calorie burn. Staiano and Calvert (2011) reviewed the current measurements of physical health while playing an exergame and reported on the way built-in exergame measures could give feedback to the user to reinforce game play in a positive way (p. 17). The data produced by these measuring devices can be utilized in future studies to access the health benefits and caloric burn of prolonged periods of exergaming. Examples of built-in devices include Nintendo's WiiMote, which is an accelerometer that estimates caloric expenditure during gameplay based data entered by the user on weight, height, and age.

Grieser, Gao, Ransdell and Simonson (2012) also examined the calorie expenditure of exergames during a study of intensity levels of gaming with the Nintendo Wii Fit using indirect calorimetry tests. One of the main research objectives posed was to find out how much more intense were MET (metabolic intensity) levels during gameplay as opposed to resting periods.

The study defined a MET as more or less equal to the amount of energy a body expends during a period of rest and also as a numeric value "equivalent to the number of times above resting energy expenditure that an activity requires" (p. 137). Using six Wii Fit games in the study, the results indicated that MET levels for all six of the games during game play were significantly higher than MET levels for resting. In other words, the caloric expenditures required to actively play the six selected games far exceeded those of just watching TV or playing conventional games. These results are encouraging for those interested in curbing childhood obesity via the use of exergames. In a study designed to test the effectiveness of exergames on a population of children overweight or obese, Bissell, Zhang and Meadows (2012) examined participants' perceived enjoyment and perceived exertion of four exergames designed for the Wii. The primary finding of this study was the inverse relationship between enjoyment and exertion. Exergames requiring more physical exertion were perceived as eliciting less enjoyment than those requiring only minimum amounts of physical activity. For example, participants rated the obstacle course exergame (from Wii Fit) the most enjoyable, even though it required the least amount of physical activity. Participants in this study rated the cardioboxing exergame as the least enjoyable, even though this game resulted in the highest amount of perceived exertion. The authors noted that enjoyment in any type of physical activity whether it be participation in a traditional sport, participation in traditional exercise, or participation in an exergame will be the key to continued involvement and therefore one of several factors key in maintaining good health.

Results from the studies cited above suggest that playing an exergame can give participants moderate levels of exercise, but it has further been correlated with cognitive development of fundamental learning skills and some weight loss. This finding adds to mounting evidence supporting the link between exergaming (as a form of moderate exercise) and improved academics. Lwin and Malik (2012) studied the efficacy of exergaming as it was incorporated into physical education courses in order to examine participants' attitudes about physical education and exercise in general (including mild, moderate and strenuous activity). Their findings supported the assertion that exergaming favorably improved attitudes toward physical exercise and encouraged long-term favorability toward exercise.

Other than solely comparing exergames with traditional video games in terms of energy expenditure, a recent study included psychological factors in examining the positive effect of exergames. Song, Peng and Lee (2011) investigated the interaction effect of the video game characters and body satisfaction in playing exergames among college students. They found that individuals with low body image dissatisfaction rated the exergame as more enjoyable and subsequently reported a more positive mood after exercise when the video game characters resembled their real-life appearance. The key to involving children in exergames for more positive effects such as elevated heart rates or physical activity lies in participant enjoyment, and as demonstrated in the study above, a positive mood following engaging in an exergame was found. Like engaging in traditional forms of exercise, if a participant is unhappy or does not enjoy the activity, it is quite unlikely involvement in the activity will continue. However, another important component of this picture is educating users to the positive benefits of game play. Although participating in exergames does not equal real-world physical activity and should never be perceived as a substitute to outside activity, the complex motions and moderate levels of energy expenditure inherent in vigorous gameplay do provide quantifiable health benefits. If a child is faced with the choice of doing no exercise or physical activity at all or playing an exergame, results from empirical studies suggest that exergaming may be more beneficial to a child's overall health than no activity at all.

Using new media to improve health literacy

A challenge in educating children about the dangers of obesity is getting children to understand the link between present behavior and future consequences. If a child doesn't have the cognitive capacity to understand obesity and make links between current eating and exercise behavior and long-term health, that child may be at a higher risk for becoming overweight or obese. Children may not equate food and exercise with their short- and long-term health because they may not understand the direct relationship between weight and general health. Thus, health literacy is especially relevant for young children and children who may be at a disadvantage in knowledge, comprehension, and awareness as it relates to health. Furthermore, children may not have the cognitive capacity to link engaging in a fun activity such as an exergame with improved health outcomes. Children may select to play video games they know to be fun and enjoyable but do so without realizing that playing exergames can increase their heart rate and help them burn calories. As more video games are developed for the different gaming platforms, a child could participate in activities such as baseball, basketball, tennis, or hockey using a gaming platform and still receive some of the enjoyment often found in playing the sport for real. While obesity does not discriminate across demographic categories, minority children living in lower SES households are at a higher risk for overweight and obesity than Caucasian children living in middle-to-higher-income households (Chang and Nayga, 2010). However, Jackson, von Eye, Witt, Zhao and Fitzgerald (2011) reported that low-income children were more likely to have video game consoles in their homes and spent more time playing video games than Caucasian children. With this in mind, it is important to develop theoretical and applied models of communication that integrate these components in the context of health literacy.

As the link between media consumption, decreased levels of physical activity and psychosocial outcomes are considered, it is important to acknowledge what often happens to children emotionally when they become overweight or obese. The psychosocial effects of obesity and being overweight mean that children often become victims of bullying, children's self-esteem plummets, and their willingness to participate in group or individual sports declines (healthychildren.org). While there is limited empirical evidence documenting the effect of exergaming on these affective areas, if participating in a game or sport, even via a video game, helps a child lose weight, the positive effect of exergaming can be significant. This is where media literacy becomes all the more important. The key, however, may be getting children low in self-esteem or low in body satisfaction involved with an exergame.

Conclusion

What does the future hold for exergaming? Where will the technology evolve over the coming years? With more research being published on the effectiveness of exergames as a moderate source of exercise for young people, especially in an age where today's kids are becoming more accustomed to a sedentary way of life, designers and corporations will certainly be introducing new innovations. Innovations such as virtual realism, advanced avatar rendering, 3D incorporation and advanced ways to include and track complex motion may make for a more immersive, physically demanding gaming experience. One such game, Astrojumper, uses "immersive, stereoscopic virtual reality" along with multiple projection display (Finkelstein *et al.*, 2011: 78) and full-body motion tracking to provide for more higher expenditure of calories. Astrojumper tracks entire body motion, making it possible to track the user's head, torso, and arms in 3D space, enabling such full-body motions as jumping, reaching out and grabbing virtual figures or dodging and ducking under approaching objects. Along these lines, video games are getting closer to simulating actual games or sports whereby users have sporting equipment integrated into their game play.

As technology continues to progress, there will undoubtedly be new ways to game and consume audio/visual material. And as these ever-evolving media platforms penetrate home markets, children will continue to be exposed to them. According to Barr (2008), children under 2 years old spend approximately 1 to 2 hours daily interacting with screen media (p. 144). It is now not unusual to see a 2-year-old playing sophisticated games on devices such as tablets and cell phones. Researchers now are suggesting that media can be used in more pro-social ways and can be used to educate children about the very things that used to be considered a direct result of viewing television: high percentages of teenagers smoking, teen pregnancy, eating disorders, low self-esteem, violence, etc. As media literacy is considered in the context of health, Silverblatt (2001) expands on original definition by stating that media literacy emphasizes critical thinking, an understanding of the process of mass communication, an awareness of the possible effect media can have on society, and the development of strategies to discuss and analyze media messages. In order for children to understand messages about food, nutrition, or exercise, they should be given examples of those mediated messages in a context they are familiar with. Along these lines, children need context in order to understand why the information viewed is relevant. For example, children may be exposed to advertisements for Fruit Loops cereal or a McDonald's Happy Meal. These advertisements need to not only be seen in the context in which they are viewed but in the context of the way they might interact or engage with the items being advertised. The presentation of material in this way might lead to what Austin, Pinkleton and Hust (2005) refer to as emotional activation. As Strasburger, Wilson and Jordan (2009) state, "media literacy that includes an emotional factor seems to overcome the seductive quality of emotive advertising" (p. 528), and the researchers argued that using emotional activation might be one way to motivate individuals to engage with the information (presented via a media literacy intervention) in a more active way. If specific attention is paid to the individual factors that might aid in a child's ability to learn and might aid in a child's motivation to learn, it is possible positive changes will result. As it relates to physical activity, if children are shown ways they can become physically active in a familiar context – using a Wii gaming device, using a gaming device at home – the negative connotation often associated with exercise could be turned into something more positive.

Findings from the studies cited above have significant implications for health practitioners and parents who are seeking alternatives to physical activities among children. Although health practitioners and researchers have proposed many structured, exercise-focused interventions in the past, the mixed findings of these solutions may be attributed to one simple reason – children may think traditional activities such as running and catching are boring while watching TV and playing video games are fun. Media consumption patterns among children certainly support this conclusion. The findings from the studies of exergame effectiveness support the conclusion that playing video games coupled with moderate exercise can be entertaining and fun. Unlike previous exercise interventions, exergames have the potential to provide novel and fun ways to motivate children to engage in physical activities (Song *et al.*, 2011). Therefore, health interventions with novel technology and unique programs such as exergames should be developed and encouraged.

Other elements such as interactivity may also influence both enjoyment and engagement. The two games that were rated the highest in enjoyment in the Bissell *et al.* study (2012) – the obstacle course and canoeing – featured more interactive elements than the sports medley and cardio boxing. In the obstacle course exergame, the player encountered numerous moving elements (swinging objects, moving floors, rolling logs) compared to the sports medley that featured static elements (punching bags, stacks of bottles) or the cardio boxing (characters moving). Therefore, it is possible that exergames featuring a higher number of interactive elements increased both enjoyment and engagement. Little research has examined what media characteristics of exergames may increase enjoyment, engagement, and exertion. Future studies will need to examine the differences in game designs of exergames to determine what design elements influence theses variables.

Overall, exergames have been documented as a promising tool to promote physical activity among both adults and children (Song *et al.*, 2011). However, since little research has been done to investigate the effectiveness of exergames to promote physical activity as opposed to field exercise, future research should continue to examine this empirically. Furthermore, longitudinal studies should be conducted such that scholars have a better understanding of engagement and enjoyment of an exergame over time. In measuring a child's current physical activity level and his or her attitudes about exercise, it is important to examine media as one driving component in the development of knowledge, beliefs, and attitudes about those issues. If children are taught that exergames can be one way that they can become more physically active, they can then use that information to improve their own health. Given their limited cognitive abilities and their developmental skills, it seems crucial that information presented to children needs proper contextualization. It is argued that it is only in understanding the correlates of low health literacy that ways can be found to improve children's health literacy through devices such as exergames. Through the findings of the studies cited above, it is hoped that exergames can change children's perceptions of physical activity by providing a fun, enjoyable and engaging alternative to traditional exercise.

References

Anderson, P. M. and Butcher, K. F. (2006) Childhood obesity: Trends and potential causes. *The Future of Children*, 16(1), 19–45.
Austin, E. W., Pinkelton, B. E. and Hust, S. T. (2005) Evaluation of an American legacy foundation/Washington state department of health media literacy pilot study. *Health Communications*, 18, 75–79.
Barr, R. (2008) Attention and learning from media during infancy and early childhood. In S. Calvert and B. Wilson (ed.), *The Handbook of Children, Media, and Development* (pp. 143–165). Chichester: Blackwell Publishing.
Bissell, K., Zhang, C. and Meadows, C. (2012) *A Wii, a Mii, and a New Me: Using New Media to Increase Physical Activity in Children At-Risk for Overweight and Obesity*. Paper presented to the Entertainment Studies Division at the Annual Meeting of AEJMC, Chicago, IL.
Center for Media Literacy. (2013) [Homepage.] Retrieved August 28, 2013, from http://www.medialit.org
Centers for Disease Control and Prevention. (2007) *Youth Risk Behavior Surveillance System (YRBSS)*. Retrieved October 4, 2009, from http://www.cdc.gov/HealthyYouth/yrbs/index.htm
Centers for Disease Control and Prevention. (2010) *The Association Between School-Based Physical Activity, Including Physical Education, and Academic Performance*. Atlanta, GA: US Department of Health and Human Services;
Chang, H. H. and Nayga, R. M. (2010) Childhood obesity and unhappiness: The influence of soft drinks and fast food consumption. *Journal of Happiness Studies*, 11, 261–275.
Crespo, C. J., Smit, E., Troiano, R. P., Bartlett, S. J., Macera, C. A., Andersen, R. E. (2001) Television watching, energy intake, and obesity in us children. *Achieves of Pediatric and Adolescent Medicine*, 155, 360–436.
Donkin, A. J., Neale, R. J. and Tilston, C. (1993) Children's food purchase requests. *Appetite*, 21, 291–294.
Elbel, B., Gyamfi, J. and Kersh, R. (2011) Child and adolescent fast-food choice and the influence of calorie labeling: A natural experiment. *International Journal of Obesity*, 35, 493–500.
Finkelstein, S., Nickel, A., Lipps, Z., Barnes, T., Wartell, Z., Suma, E. (2011) Astrojumper: Motivating exercise with an immersive virtual reality exergame. *Presence*, 20(1), 78–92.
Graves, L., Stratton, G., Ridgers, N. D. and Cable, N. T. (2007) Comparison of energy expenditure in

adolescents when playing new generation and sedentary computer games: Cross sectional study. *BMJ,* 335(7633), 1282–1284.

Grieser, J. D., Gao, Y., Ransdell, L. and Simonson, S. (2012) Determining intensity levels of selected Wii Fit activities in college aged individuals. *Measurement in Physical Education and Exercise Science,* 16(2), 135–150.

Grundy, S. M., Blackburn, G., Higgins, M., Lauer, R., Perri, M. G. and Ryan, D. (1999) Physical activity in the prevention and treatment of obesity and its comorbidities. *Medical and Science in Sports Exercise,* 31, 502–508.

Gutnick, A. L., Robb, M., Takeuchi, L. and Kotler, J. (2010) *Always Connected: The New Digital Media Habits of Young Children.* New York: The Joan Ganz Cooney Center at Sesame Workshop.

Harrison, K. and Marske, A. L. (2005) Nutritional content of foods advertised during the television programs children watch most. *American Journal of Public Health,* 95(9), 1568–1574.

Jackson, L. A., von Eye, A., Witt, E. A., Zhao, Y. and Fitzgerald, H. E. (2011) A longitudinal study of the effects of Internet use and videogame playing on academic performance and the roles of gender, race, and income in these relationships. *Computers in Human Behavior,* 27, 228–239.

Jeffrey, D. B., McLellarn, R. W. and Fox, D. T. (1982) The development of children's eating habits: The role of television commercials. *Health Education Quarterly,* 9, 174–189.

Kaiser Family Foundation. (2002) *Key Facts: Children and Video Games.* Retrieved August 28, 2013, from http://kaiserfamilyfoundation.files.wordpress.com/2013/04/5959.pdf

Kessler, S. (2011, March 14) Children's consumption of digital media on the rise [STATS]. *Mashable.com.* Retrieved from http://mashable.com/2011/03/14/children-internet-stats/

Lwin, M. O. and Malik, S. (2012) The efficacy of exergames-incorporated physical education lessons in influencing drivers of physical activity: A comparison between children and pre-adolescents. *Psychology of Sport and Exercise,* 13(6), 756–780.

Malecka-Tendera, E. and Mazur, A. (2006) Childhood obesity: A pandemic of the twenty-first century. *International Journal of Obesity,* 30, S1–S3.

McDonough, P. (2009, October 26) TV viewing among kids at an eight-year high. *Newswire.* Retrieved from http://www.nielsen.com/us/en/newswire/2009/tv-viewing-among-kids-at-an-eight-year-high.html

National Initiative for Children's Healthcare Quality. (2008) Childhood obesity action network, state action network, state obesity profiles. Retrieved October 1, 2009, from http://www.nichg.org/ obesityaction-network

Obesity Society. (2009) *Childhood Overweight* [online article]. Retrieved September 28, 2012, from http://www.obesity.org.

Peng, W., Lin, J-H., & Crouse, J. (2011) Is playing exergaming really exercising? A meta-analysis of energy expenditure in active video games. *CyberPsychology, Behavior, and SocialNetworking,* 14(11), 681–688. doi:10.1089/cyber.2010.0578

Perron, R. G. (2011) Do exergames allow children to achieve physical activity intensity commensurate with national guidelines? *International Journal of Exercise Science,* 4(4), 257–264.

Proctor, M. H., Moore, L. L., Gao, D., Cupples, L. A., Bradlee, M. L., Hood, M. Y. and Ellison, R. C. (2003) Television viewing and change in body fat from preschool to early adolescence: The Framingham children's study. *International Journal of Obesity,* 27, 827–833.

Signorielli, N. (1998) Health images on television. In L. D. Jackson and B. K. Duffy (eds), *Health Communication Research: A Guide to Developments and Directions* (pp. 163–179). Westport, CT: Greenwood.

Signorielli, N. and Staples, J. (1997) Television and children's conceptions of nutrition. *Health Communication,* 9, 289–301.

Silverblatt, A. (2001) *Media Literacy: Keys to Interpreting Media Messages.* Westport, CT: Praeger.

Song, H., Peng, W. and Lee, K. M. (2011) Promoting exercise self-efficacy with an exergame. *Journal of Health Communication,* 16, 148–162. doi:10.1080/10810730.2010.535107

Staiano, A. E. and Calvert, S. L. (2011) The promise of exergames as tools to measure physical health. *Entertainment Computing,* 2(1), 17–21.

Strasburger, V. C. (2001) Children and TV advertising: Nowhere to run, nowhere to hide. *Journal of Developmental and Behavioral Pediatrics,* 22, 185.

Strasburger, V. C., Wilson, B. J. and Jordan, A. B. (2009) *Children, Adolescents, and the Media* (2nd edn.). Thousand Oaks, CA: Sage.

Trost, S. G., Morgan, A. M., Saunders, R., Felton, G., Ward, D. S., Pate, R. P. (2000) Children's understanding of the concept of physical activity. *Pediatric Exercise Science,* 12, 293–299.

US Department of Health and Human Services (USDHHS) (2011, September) *About Health Literacy.* Retrieved from http://www.hrsa.gov/publichealth/healthliteracy/healthlitabout.html

White, K., Kilding, A. E. and Schofield, G. (2009) *Energy Expenditure and Enjoyment during Nintendo Wii Active Video Games: How do they Compare to Other Sedentary and Physical Activities?* Auckland, New Zealand: Center for Physical Activity and Nutrition (CPAN), AUT University.

Wen, L. M., Kite, J., Merom, D. and Rissel, C. (2009) Time spent playing outdoors after school and its relationship with independent mobility: A cross-sectional survey of children aged 10–12 years. *International Journal of Behavioral Nutrition and Physical Activity*, 6:15. doi: 10.1186/1479-5868-6-15

PART V

Identities in the digital realm

26

SPORT, NEW MEDIA, AND NATIONAL IDENTITY

John Vincent

UNIVERSITY OF ALABAMA

Edward M. Kian

OKLAHOMA STATE UNIVERSITY

Globalization has added significant impetus to media coverage of major international sporting events such as the Olympic Games and the Fédération Internationale de Football Association (FIFA) World Cup. More than half of the world's population watches both these quadrennial international sporting events (Associated Press, 2008; FIFA, 2011). For the duration of the Olympic Games and FIFA World Cup, the symbiotic relationship between sport and the media intensifies as both traditional and new media compete to attract readers, viewers, and advertisers. This chapter provides insight into what Rowe, McKay and Miller (1998: 133) described as the "sport-nationalism-media troika," or the intersection between elite national athletes and teams, mass media, and national media audiences. The sport-nationalism-media troika is an important arena where dominant cultural ideologies about national identities are (re)produced and challenged (Crolley and Hand, 2006).

In this chapter we examine how mass media frame an overt nationalistic "us versus them" rhetoric to generate interest and excitement in the "imagined community" through the lens of English newspaper coverage of the English national soccer team competing in the World Cup and European Championship tournaments. This is then compared with the less jingoistic support of the home nation in National Broadcasting Company's (NBC) sportscasts of the United States athletes and teams competing in the Olympic Games. Finally, we provide several insights about the sport-social media-national identity nexus from the UEFA 2012 EURO tournament and the 2012 London Olympiad. These were among the first major international sporting events to feel the global diffusion and captivating, interactive influence of Twitter and Facebook.

National identity and sport

Guibernau (2007: 23) defined a nation as a "... community, sharing a common culture, attached to a clearly demarcated territory, having a common past and a common project for the future, and claiming the right to rule itself." Guibernau's definition emphasized both the territorial demarcations and the political components of a nation state while also acknowledging the importance of a shared sense of history. It also recognized the collective sense of belonging, and the distinguishing characteristics and traits that form the national culture. Von der Lippe (2002: 374) articulated how national identity is largely defined by "how a citizenry sees and thinks about themselves in relation to others." Thus, national identity itself is a multifaceted social construction of history, which is neither "...fixed and unalterable nor wholly fluid and amenable to unlimited construction," but rather "is both given and constantly reconstituted" (Parekh, 1994: 5–6).

Guibernau (2007) outlined how national identity is important because it allows citizens to "...regard as their own the accomplishments of their fellow nationals" (p.169). In this regard, of particular cultural significance are major international sporting competitions where collective identity has been (re)constructed through athletes and teams since the Greek Olympic Games (Hill, 1996). Traditionally, male athletes playing for their country are usually the representatives of popular national identity. Accordingly, a national sports team's performance at major international sporting events can reawaken the visceral emotions of national identity politics (Bairner, 2001).

While the original ethos of both the World Cup and the Olympic Games was to promote positive international relations and foster mutual understanding, in practice they can also provide nations with opportunities to demonstrate athletic superiority and, by association, political, economic, and cultural exceptionalism. As such they are often used as a forum to (re)present narratives and images of a nation and provide a stage for a country to be seen as strong and vibrant. Major international competitions provide an opportunity for a nation to publicly bask in the reflected glory of national successes (Coakley, 2009). The successes or failures of a home country's athletes or teams can be reported as a symbol of the nation's overall health and well-being (Tuck, 2003). That is one reason many nations, regardless of their political persuasion, invest significant resources in nurturing elite athletes and teams (Cashmore, 1996). As such, international sport is a site where political ideologies are contested. International sport is also an arena replete with contradictions and tensions, which enables marginal groups to potentially use it as a platform to galvanize support for symbolic forms of resistance (Coakley, 2009).

The "sport-nationalism-media troika"

Billings (2008: xi) articulated, "sports media matter because they are the way most of us consume sports." The universal appeal of major international sporting events makes them important arenas to examine various cultural identities, with collective, national identity being preeminent. In contrast to most local and regional sport, which is often viewed live at the event by supporters, the consumption of major international sporting events is done predominantly through mass media, via either television or radio broadcasts, Internet live streams, and newspaper accounts. Billings (2008: xi) noted that international "...sports bond societies and cultures in ways that nothing else can" and this is underpinned by the pivotal role of sport media in creating collective cultural memories. Guibernau (2007) articulated how nationalism is created through mediated accounts and images of shared history and culture from glorious bygone eras.

In the context of the Olympic Games, a prime example of how a moment of mediated sport became ingrained collective memory for most Americans is the "Miracle on Ice." With an inexperienced team of amateur collegians, the US ice hockey team's victory over the experienced Soviet Union in the 1980 Winter Olympic Games, became known as the "Miracle on

Ice," after commentator Al Michael's famous line, "Do you believe in miracles?" Occurring in the context of the Cold War, Butterworth (2009) noted how important a cultural form mediated international sport is because of its ability to shape public opinion about social and geopolitical issues.

Similarly, for Canadians, the fabled "shot heard around the world" resonates. In 1972, an historic ice hockey series dubbed the Summit Series took place between the Soviet Union national team and Team Canada, which consisted of the best Canadian players from the North American-based National Hockey League. This series illustrated how a hockey tournament can create ardent nationalism. The contest represented a pivotal meeting between two hockey superpowers for world hockey supremacy and comprised eight games (the first four in Canada and the last four in the Soviet Union), with many prognosticators expecting Canada to win all eight games. Heading into the eighth and final game, each team had three wins and one tie. However, because the Soviets led in goal differential, only a win in game No. 8 would deliver victory for Canada in the series. For many Canadians, one of the most famous collective memories in their nation's sport history occurred with 34 seconds left when Paul Henderson scored the winning goal, dubbed the "shot heard around the world." Earle (1995) noted how 15 million Canadians "shared in the vicarious climax" (p. 114), and how "for once, disparate notions of class, ethnicity and gender were welded into a rare Canadian moment" (p. 108). More recently when Sidney Crosby scored the winning goal for Canada in the gold medal game against arch nemesis, the United States, in the 2010 Vancouver Winter Olympic Games, sport journalist Roy MacGregor suggested Crosby's goal would become a marker of Canadianness for future generations and drew on the 'invented tradition' of Canadian hockey nostalgia by writing: "This winning goal will stand with the ones scored by Paul Hendserson, hero of the 1972 Summit Series, and Mario Lemieux, hero of the 1987 Canada Cup...He will be forever known for it..." (MacGregor, 2010: A1)

A lasting impact of the English football (soccer) team's victory over West Germany in 1966 and the ensuing patriotic celebrations was that football, and in particular the final game between England and West Germany, became an important signifier of English national identity (Weight, 2002). Kenneth Wolstenholme's famous commentary as Geoff Hurst scored England's final goal against West Germany, "Some people are on the pitch...They think it's all over...It *is*, now," has became an important part of English folklore (Weight, 2002). English media has replayed it during every subsequent tournament reminding the nation of the success of the "boys of summer" in '66. These evocative sound bites have become ingrained in the habitus or deep-set memory of the 'imagined community,' thus illustrating the profound effect mediated sporting broadcasts can have in unifying citizens around a collective national identity.

Major international sporting competitions have the power to generate interest even among casual sports observers, who can become gripped by the collective experience that is so powerful in shaping national cultural memory (Billings, 2008). Roche (2000) noted how major international sporting events have the power to transcend news and entertainment by making history (p. 167). Billings (2008) described NBC's coverage of the Olympic Games as "...the biggest show on television" (p. 1), while also noting how media coverage of the Olympic Games provides "...a global perspective by routinely introducing mass audiences to cultures they have never witnessed before" (p. 10).

"Inventing traditions" for the "imagined community"

Hobsbawm (1983) noted how historians, politicians, and journalists create the customs, myths, symbols, and rituals that form the national culture. He claimed that national identity is both reinforced and reinterpreted through the construction of an almost idealized lexicon about the nation in historical and mythological accounts, which he called "invented traditions." Hobsbawm (1983: 1) defined "invented traditions" as "[a] set of practices, normally governed by overtly or tacitly accepted rules and of a ritual of symbolic nature, which seek to inculcate certain values and norms of behavior by repetition, which automatically implies continuity with the past." The selective recollection of history plays an important role in creating and reaffirming a shared sense of national consciousness and identity. This identity is reinforced through the selective celebrations of past successes and becomes a part of the collective national consciousness that serves to differentiate the nation from other countries. This selective use of history and the shared sense of destiny it imparts serve not only to differentiate but also promote a sense of exceptionalism or superiority.

Anderson (1983) articulated that the nation is an imagined community "because the members of even the smallest nations will never know most of their fellow-members, meet them, or even hear of them, yet in the minds of each lives the image of their communion" (p. 6). Anderson concluded that a sense of national belonging can be developed through the mass consumption of mediated reports such as newspaper articles, which are read almost simultaneously by thousands of people, who are aware of each of their fellow citizens' collective existence even though they have never met each other. Anderson's theory of the imagined community illustrates the pervasive influence mediated accounts have in (re)producing the socially constructed impression that their readers have of their national identity. In the context of a major international sport, Anderson's concept about a nation being an "imagined community" becomes particularly relevant because of the interaction between media narratives and images of national teams competing in major international sporting events.

Several of these scholars (e.g. Anderson, 1983; Guibernau, 2007; Hobsbawm, 1983) noted that national identity is not fixed, but rather evolves and is re-invented to fit with contemporary culture. However, national identity is highly selective. National characteristics, drawn from "invented traditions," are often ascribed to a nation's athletes and teams. Journalists draw on "invented traditions" to generate interest, unity, and patriotism. This often manifests itself in the liberal use of personal pronouns in newspaper articles. Personal pronouns describe "our" athletes or "our" team, in comparison with the "other" nations' athletes or teams. This is often done in an "us versus them" invective, as the "imagined community" follows the fortunes of athletes who have become symbolic national warriors during international competition. The use of personal pronoun binaries can serve to create tension and conflict, which could translate into intolerance and even xenophobia (Tuck, 2003; Vincent, Kian, Pedersen, Kuntz and Hill, 2010).

We provide brief glimpses into how the sport media national identity nexus plays out in the context of newspaper coverage of the English national men's soccer (football) team competing in the World Cup and European championships, the NBC's televised coverage of the United States in the Olympic Games, and finally how social media added to the milieu in the 2012 Olympic Games and UEFA EURO tournament.

"England expects"

Forty years after England's only World Cup victory in 1966, Vincent *et al.* (2010) examined English newspaper narratives about the English national men's football team competing in the 2006 World Cup. Newspaper narratives radiated optimism at the beginning of the 2006 World Cup, buoyed by the perception that a 'golden generation' of English players could fulfill the nation's destiny to repeat the glory of the "boys of '66." At the outset of the 2006 World Cup tournament, the front page of the *Daily Mail* urged the nation to unite in support of the English team with a headline of "England expects," in reference to Admiral Horatio Nelson's inspirational signal to the fleet before the Battle of Trafalgar in 1805. Similarly, newspaper narratives elicited support for "the Eng-er-land" by drawing the invented traditions of Churchillian wartime speeches and Shakespearean lines from Henry V, from scenes from the Siege of Harfleur, and the 1415 Battle of Agincourt.

"Don't mention the war"

Contradicting the official theme of the 2006 World Cup, "a time to make friends," the English newspapers mobilized support for the English team from the "imagined community" by drawing on "us versus them" simplistic dichotomies. Although the coverage was not as egregiously xenophobic as in 1996, it was punctuated with negative German stereotypes. Several newspapers featured prominent articles about English comic John Cleese's alternative 2006 World Cup anthem, 'Don't Mention the War,' which mischievously plays on German sensitivity about World War II. It is a catchphrase made famous by Cleese's alter ego character, the notoriously bigoted Basil Fawlty in the iconic British comedy television show, *Fawlty Towers*. Vincent *et al.* (2010) suggested that these discourses, at least in part, reflected the compensatory defensive anxiety and insecurity of a nation in decline. The nation appeared to be threatened by the creeping supranational influence of the Economic European Union, Celtic devolution within the Union, and relative economic underperformance in an increasingly competitive globalized economy.

"Our finest hour"

Hobsbawm (1990) noted the emotional appeal and role of supporters in the (re)construction of national identity: "The imagined community of millions seems more real as a team. . . . The individual, even the one who only cheers, becomes a symbol of the nation himself" (p. 143). Accordingly, Vincent and Hill (2011) examined discourses about the English national team and their "army" of supporters during newspaper coverage of the 2010 World Cup by *The Sun*, England's most widely read "red top" newspaper. *The Sun* featured many photographs of English supporters' performance of Englishness in fan zones and at England games in South Africa. English supporters with painted faces and torsos or wearing 1966 replica jerseys are popular signifiers of popular English identity. English supporters were also photographed dressed in Crusader outfits or with face masks of members of the English royal family, all of which seemed to portray parodies of a historical, idealized form of English identity. However, with the 70th anniversary of the Battle of Britain about to be celebrated, a nationalistic "us versus them" tone was created in the build-up to the England versus Germany round of 16 match, where English fans were photographed posing in RAF uniforms and plastic Tommy helmets, inflatable bomber planes, and Churchill facemasks. Approaching half a century after the English men's national soccer team's only World Cup title, it still nostalgically resonates and the English versus Germany rivalry is still defined through an English frame by the nation's sporting "finest hour," winning the 1966 World Cup. Many of the pervasive narrative themes and images found in the coverage of the 1966 World Cup were still (re)produced in an almost formulaic fashion 46 years later.

Cheering for the Stars and Stripes: NBC's Olympic coverage

The potential of major international sporting events to facilitate a spirit of internationalism and peace consistent with the founder, Baron de Coubertain's original ethos of the modern Olympic Games has frequently been undermined in practice. Generally the Olympic Games "...have been a forum for fervent nationalism" rather than "peaceful competition" (Butterworth, 2007: 187). Illustrating this, Billings, Angelini and Wu (2011) noted how, in the lead-up to the 2008 Summer Olympic Games in Beijing, the Chinese declared their goal was to finish atop the collective medal standings, which would symbolize its emergence as a super-power.

Olympic television broadcasts are often replete with simplistic "us vs. them" dichotomies which serve to differentiate, for example, "...West and East, Democratic and Totalitarian, Christian and Godless, Good and Evil" (Butterworth, 2009: 137). Indeed, any notions of cosmopolitan internationalism have been frequently subverted with nationistic displays of flag-waving, and other acts of what Billig (1995) termed banal nationalism. This celebration of collective identity replete with national flag-waving and dramatic incidents and tensions created in us vs. them binary discourses and images has been captured and reflected in exhaustive media broadcasts. An examination of NBC's coverage of the Olympic Games found a profound national or home-nation bias (Billings, 2008). Between the 1996 Summer and the 2006 Winter Olympic Games, the amount of coverage the US athletes received on NBC ranged between 57% and 40.2% of the total references to all Olympic athletes, which was not merited by performance since US athletes only won approximately 11% of the medals over that span. During NBC's broadcasts of those same Olympiads from 1996–2006, Billings (2008) reported that 44 of the 60 most-mentioned athletes represented the United States. Further, the remaining athletes on the most-mentioned list were often the top rivals from other nations competing with US athletes for medals.

In an effort to generate interest from the "imagined community" of US viewers, NBC's Olympic broadcasters were also more likely to provide background information about the US athletes' hometowns or region. Billings *et al.* (2011) revealed that greater background knowledge with home nation athletes led to a deeper, more nuanced commentary, which resulted in positive, but subjective broadcasters' attributions for athletic success. In comparison to the greater depth of commentary about home nation athletes, "other" nations' athletes were described in more one-dimensional ways and portrayed almost as though they were "...emotionless cyborgs" (p. 263). Billings (2008) concluded that these examples of NBC's nationalistic bias were driven by mass media ratings and advertising rates. Broadcast rights fees have grown exponentially since NBC paid $456 million to broadcast the 1996 Summer Olympic Games. NBC paid the International Olympic Committee $1.2 billion just for the US broadcast rights to the 2012 Summer Olympic Games in London (Coakley, 2009).

The pressure on media executives to attain high prime time Neilsen ratings and advertising rates has resulted in NBC (re)packaging taped-delayed events as though they were occurring live in the evening prime-time slot over successive Olympiads. One of the most egregious examples occurred in the 1996 Centennial Olympic Games. Most viewers already knew the outcome of the women's gymnastics competition and Kerry Strug's final vault before it was (re)presented as though it were occurring live in NBC's prime-time evening coverage (Andrews, 1998). This issue was exacerbated in the era of social media and generated criticism in the two most recent summer Olympiads, Beijing 2008 and London 2012. As Tang and Cooper (2012) noted, the 2008 Beijing Olympic Games were considered the first online Olympics with NBCOlympics.com providing more than 3,500 hours of online coverage and

2,200 hours of live video coverage. By the 2012 London Olympiad, in partnership with YouTube, NBC streamed events live on its website enabling viewers to watch NBC on the Internet through their smart-phones (Taylor, 2012). Compounding this, the popularity of social media meant that most people had received instantaneous tweets or posts about Olympic events long before they aired on evening prime-time television. Nevertheless, despite angry sport fans generating acerbic tweets with a hashtag of nbcfail, NBC still reported its 2012 Olympic Games television coverage broke all previous US Neilsen ratings (Carter, 2012).

2012 London Olympics: The Twitter Games

In its infancy at the previous 2008 Beijing Olympic Games, the 2012 London Olympic Games were widely acknowledged as the first social media games. In contrast to the carefully framed and choreographed televised programming and almost formulaic coverage by the traditional print media, Twitter and Facebook provided a democratizing spontaneity, intimacy, and excitement that made it a compelling and indispensable medium during the London Olympaid. The athlete–fan interactive experience was redefined by Twitter as many Olympic athletes bypassed the traditional, meticulously scripted public relations releases and tweeted directly to their "imagined community" of followers throughout the 17-day duration of the Olympic Games. This enabled the fans to feel closer to their favorite athletes, many of whom connected with their followers through an eclectic mixture of mundane, insightful, personal, and even bizarre revelations. The very spontaneous and public nature of tweets and posts meant that many uncensored off-the-cuff comments and sometimes divisive and controversial opinions were unfurled by athletes and followers alike in this new social space. Several such examples of the sport-social media-national identity nexus are provided below.

The "plastic Brits" furor: Is she "one of us?"

In the context of the Olympic Games, British althletes representing their nation in some ways become personifications of the national identity and culture. This makes their deportment and behavior as national role models and "patriots at play" the subject of much media scrutiny (Vincent and Crossman, 2012). Guibernau (2007) noted how traditionally the image of the nation is usually told in narratives about the indigenous population and dominant racial and ethnic group. However, in the context of the 2012 Olympic Games, many of the athletes representing Britain, such as Jessica Ennis and Mo Farrah, reflected the evolving hybridity and multicultural makeup of the population.

In a quest for athletic success on home soil in 2012, British Athletics appointed Charles van Commenee, a Dutchman, as Head Athletics Coach. Under his guidance, Britain selected numerous foreign-born athletes who qualified to represent Britain through their British parents or naturalized citizenship. One such athlete, Tiffany Porter, is the embodiment of the modern diasporic athlete. She was born in the United States, the daughter of a Nigerian father and an English mother. She was eligible to compete for Britain through her London-born mother, and switched her allegiance to Britain from the United States in 2010. Several months before the London Olympiad, van Commenee controversially announced that Porter would be the British women's team captain for the World Indoor Championships. The initial controversy was compounded when journalists found that the previous summer, on American Independence day, Porter had tweeted: "It's the 4th of July!!!!!! Wishing I was in the States to celebrate this special day! I'm definitely there in spirit though : -)" (McRae, 2012). This faux pax generated discussion about the hybridity of British athletes. Much traditional tabloid and social media commentary was critical about the importation of foreign-born and, in some cases trained, athletes, dubbed in the British media discourse "plastic Brits." It was argued that the transnational "plastic Brits," who were not really "one of us," were stifling opportunities for "homegrown" British athletes. Typifying the media furor, under the inflammatory headline, "Brit skip is a Yank!", *The Sun,* known for its parochial "little Englander" ideology, reported how at a press conference, Porter, when pressed to demonstrate her British credentials by a journalist, could not recite the first few lines of the British national anthem, *God Save the Queen* (*The Sun,* 2012). Van Commenee responded to the media firestorm by reporting that he would make sure every foreign-born British athlete competing in the London Olympiad would know the words to the national anthem (Hart, 2012). Ultimately, though, it took a traditional broadsheet newspaper with a reputation for its impartial and balanced reporting to put the social and tabloid media frenzy into a more nuanced, reflexive perspective. Sport journalist Donald McRae quoted Porter:

> "I probably should have explained myself a little better. But it's hard on Twitter. That's the beauty and the curse of 140 characters. You think you're saying one thing but it can be interpreted in so many ways." Even if she had cut out the exclamation marks and the smiley face, Porter would not have been able to explain in a tweet what she says more expansively and candidly in person. "The point I was trying to make was that I am very much American. I am very much British. I am very much Nigerian. I am extremely proud to be all three. I'm not apologising for that. It's who I am. I embrace it. It's very important to be true to myself."
>
> (McRae, 2012)

Freedom of speech or political misjudgement?

A second example taken from the 2012 London Olympic Games, which illustrates how an opinionated, divisive tweet, whether intentional or not, can create controversy and elicit criticism, came from a politician's tweet. In British conservative national identity politics, multiculturalism is often pejoratively perceived to be a euphemism for the dilution of traditional Englishness. After the "plastic Brit" controversy, the multiculturalism issue surfaced again, when Aidan Burley, a British Member of Parliament, tweeted a criticism of English filmmaker Danny Boyle's Olympic Games opening ceremony. Boyle's opening ceremony extravaganza provided a kaleidoscope of British history and culture and was generally criticially acclaimed. It acknowledged the contributions of black and ethnic minority Britons with a scene artistically recreating the MV Empire Windrush ship, which brought many Jamaicans to Britain. However, during the ceremony Burley tweeted, "The most leftie opening ceremony I have ever seen – more than Beijing, the capital of a communist state! Welfare tribute next?" Burley then added a second tweet: "Thank God the athletes have arrived! Now we can move on from leftie multi-cultural crap. Bring back red arrows (sic), Shakespeare and the Stones!" (Kirkup, 2012). Burley's tweets sparked strong reactions. They were roundly criticised by leading Conservative politicians, including Boris Johnson (the Mayor of London), and David Cameron (the British Prime Minister). Cameron had previously expressed reservations about spontaneous but ill-considered ideas or thoughts expressed on Twitter by politicians and celebrities alike. A fellow Conservative MP, Gary Barwell, responded with the following twitter: "With respect, us Londoners are rather proud of the diversity of our city" at #nothingleftwingaboutit" (Watt, 2012).

The Twitter troll menace

In the lead-up to the 2012 London Olympiad, British diver Tom Daley was widely considered a genuine medal prospect. After medaling in the Commonwealth Games and the World Championships, British expectations were built up in mediated accounts and Daley was framed as a strong medal contender. The tragic premature death of his father and mentor to brain cancer in 2011 added an emotionally charged human interest angle, and an expectant nation nervously hoped Daley would perform well as a tribute to his late father. On the first Monday of the London Olympiad, Daley competed in the 10-meter men's synchronized platform diving event with his partner, Peter Waterfield. It was the first realistic opportunity of a medal for an expectant, emotionally charged home nation. Although Daley and Waterfield led after the first three dives, which prematurely raised the hopes of the "imagined community," they ultimately finished in a disappointing fourth place. In the immediate aftermath, Daley, who had an enormous following on Twitter, was subjected to abusive and menacing tweets by a Twitter troll. The troll accused Daley of letting his late father down when he failed to win a medal and even threatened to drown him. Although that particular Twitter troll was later arrested and prosecuted, this incident illustrates how Twitter provides a forum for people to publicly express their disdain for and possibly even threaten athletes.

The Twitter troll menace had been aptly illustrated a month before in the aftermath of the England men's national soccer teams exit from the EUFA EURO soccer championships. For the duration of the tournament, the English team's performances were dissected and scrutinized in the English media. Throughout the tournament, though, both the print and online versions of the English newspapers reported Twitter comments from soccer pundits, celebrities, and fans alike to faciliate a feeling of greater connection among the "imagined community." England was eliminated on a penalty shoot-out after a goal-less quarter-final match against Italy. Two of England's players, Ashley Cole and Ashley Young, both men of color, missed their penalty kicks. Illustrating the British red top newspapers' creative use of puns and gallows hunor, *The Sun*, headlined "We made an ASH of it," but in the following day's edition the front page headlined "Racist trolls target the two Ashleys" [*The Sun* (online), June 26, 2012]. Investigations editor, Brian Flynn reported two Twitter Trolls "... spewed vile abuse at England's penalty flop players" [*The Sun* (online), June 26, 2012]. These examples of the Twitter troll menace suggest that in the emotionally charged context of major international sporting tournaments, the instantaneous nature of this new medium primes divisive, racist, and even menacing tweets.

Concluding remarks

Although the relationship between sport and national identity is both complex and fluid, mass media undoubtedly play an important role in national identify formation and politics, while also serving to (re)construct, reinforce, and naturalize dominant ideologies about this area of popular culture. Media coverage of major international sport generates particular narratives or preferred readings about collective national identity at the expense of alternative, subordinated articulations. The narratives and images of major international sporting tournaments both reflect and stimulate wider cultural and political references. Boyle and Haynes (2000: 154) noted how the "... images and imaginings of a country's past, present and projections of its future, come together to underpin the mediation of sporting discourses."

Mediated coverage of major international sporting events features all components required for compelling viewing, such as partisan supporters, rituals, symbols, ceremony, pageantry, competition, and winning (Boyle and Haynes, 2000). Although coverage of global media sports events by their very nature have a global dimension, both traditional and social media coverage have a local dimension. To capture the public imagination, media coverage focuses on each nation's own athletes or team performance. Athletes become "patriots at play" in their quest to bring athletic success for their nation and the dramatic, emotional, and tension-fueled narratives and images generate compelling interest. As the examples in this chapter have shown, media coverage of megasporting events contain both overt and covert nationalist sentiment. In terms of national identity politics, traditional media discourses generally promulgate unifying ideologies and draw on shared common cultural beliefs and "invented traditions." These media discourses generally serve to subordinate any political divisions or socioeconomic inequalities that could undermine national unity (Anderson, 1983). However, in the context of the 2012 London Olympiad and the EUFA EURO 2012 tournament, the democratizing, spontaneous soundbite nature of new social media forums like Twitter produced some hyper-nationalized us-versus-them dichotomies, and tensions were heightened with acerbic, divisive, and racist tweets. Our insights suggest that the profound communal and democratizing characteristics of new social media forums provide an outlet for immediately gratifying spontaneous personal commentary. Compounding this, the 140-character limitations of Twitter also makes it an ideal medium for the expression of reductionist, nationalist "us versus them" binary rhetoric or for xenophobic lexicon to flourish. Thus, within the sport-media-nationalism nexus, some tweets may serve to exacerbate what Boyle (2006) referred to as the tabloidization of the media. Brief glimpses from the two mega sporting events from the summer of 2012 suggest this soundbite narrative genre prevails, often at the expense of more nuanaced and reflexive analysis.

The mediated accounts of the English soccer team competing at the World Cup and European Championships reveal how the team has become a signifier of popular English identity since 1966. This popular identity has been (re)produced and normalized with each successive media broadcast and newspaper narratives and images, with each drawing on the recollection of the invented traditions or favorable accounts of English history. This selective use of history has promoted a sense of English exceptionalism, and forms the basis of us-versus-them comparisons that underpin divisive, even xenophobic binary discourses. Within national identity politics, politicians from all political spectrums typically work hard to associate themselves with the feel-good dividend of national athletic success (Coakley, 2009). Reflecting this, in the aftermath of the 2012 London Olympiad, David Cameron, the British Prime Minister held a widely publicized reception at his official home, 10 Downing Street, to thank the organizers and volunteers. In his carefully prepared speech, he evoked the "invented tradition" of the halcyon summer of '66: "I think that 2012 will be like 1966, something we'll talk about with our children and grandchildren, something that will continue to delight us long after this time has passed" (Prince, 2012).

Although the partisan tone is generally less overt in television coverage, as this chapter illustrated, nationalistic framing is still present in broadcasts and livestreams of the Olympic Games. The popularity of NBC's coverage of successive Olympic games has been in large part due to the heightened, collective sense of identification, rooting, and pride in home-nation athletes and teams. Set against a contemporary background of increasingly fragmented television viewing and exponentially expensive broadcasting rights fees, NBC's coverage of successive Olympic Games had to transcend the usual sport fan demographic to show a profit. The adoption of a multiplatform approach, with television broadcasts complemented with live-streaming and social media since the 2008 Beijing Olympiad, has made NBC's coverage mesmerizing to a younger demographic, which is particularly attractive to many advertisers and sponsors (Taylor, 2012).

As the 2012 London Olympic Games and the EUFA EURO 2012 tournament were among the first major international sporting events to occur after the widespread adoption and integration of tablets and smart phones, research in the sport–social media–national identity nexus is in its infancy and should prove a productive area for future research.

References

Anderson, B. (1983) *Imagined Communities: Reflections on the Origin and the Spread of Nationalism*. London: Verso.

Andrews, D.L. (1998) Feminizing Olympic reality: Preliminary dispatches from Baudrillard's Atlanta. *International Review for the Sociology of Sport*, 33(1), 5–18.

Associated Press. (2008, September 5) Beijing TV coverage drew 4.7 billion viewers worldwide. *ESPN Inernet*. Retrieved from http://sports.espn.go.com/oly/news/story?id=3571042

Bairner, A. (2001) *Sport, Nationalism, and Globalization: European and North American Perspectives*. New York: State University of New York Press.

Billig, M. (1995) *Banal Nationalism*. London: Sage.

Billings, A.C. (2008) *Olympic Media: Inside the Biggest Show on Television*. London: Routledge.

Billings, A.C., Angelini, J.R. and Wu, D. (2011) Nationalistic notions of the superpowers: Comparative analyses of the American and Chinese telecasts in the 2008 Beijing Olympiad. *Journal of Broadcasting and Electronic Media*, 55(2), 251–266.

Boyle. R. (2006) *Sports Journalism: Context and Issues*. London: Sage.

Boyle, R. and Haynes, R. (2000) Games across frontiers: Mediated sport and national identity. In R. Boyle and R. Haynes (eds), *Power Play: Sport, the Media and Popular Culture* (pp. 143–164). London: Longman.

Butterworth, M.L. (2007) The politics of pitch: Claiming and contesting democracy through the Iraqi nationalsoccer team. *Communication and Cultural Studies*, 4(2), 184–203.

Butterworth, M.L. (2009) Do you believe in nationalism? American patriotism in Miracle. In H.L. Hundley and A.C. Billings (eds), *Examining Identity in Sport Media* (pp. 133–152). Thousand Oaks: CA: Sage.

Carter, B. (2012) NBC's coverage in London is becoming a rating success with a shot at a profit. *New York Times* [online edition]. Retrieved from http://www.nytimes.com/2012/08/06/sports/olympics/nbcs-ratings-for-london-games-improve-on-beijing.html?_r=0

Cashmore, E. (1996) *Making Sense of Sports* (2nd edn.). London: Routledge.

Coakley, J. (2009) *Sports in Society: Issues and Controversies* (10th edn.). New York: McGraw Hill.

Crolley, L. and Hand, D. (2006) *Football and European Identity: Historical Narratives through the Press*. London: Routledge.

Earle, N. (1995) Hockey as Canadian popular culture: Team Canada 1972, television and the Canadian identity. *Journal of Canadian Studies*, 30(2), 107–123.

FIFA.com (2011, July 11) *Almost half the World Tuned in at Home to Watch 2010 FIFA World Cup South Africa*. Retrieved from http://www.fifa.com/worldcup/archive/southafrica2010/organisation/media/newsid=1473143/index.html

Guibernau, M. (2007) *The Identity of Nations*. Cambridge: Polity.

Hart, S. (2012, June 5) London 2012 Olympics: Charles van Commenee will make Team GB's 'foreign' recruits learn national anthem. *The Telegraph* [online edition]. Retrieved from http://www.telegraph.co.uk/sport/olympics/athletics/9312543/London-2012-Olympics-Charles-van-Commenee-will-make-Team-GBs-foreign-recruits-learn-national-anthem.html

Hill, C.R. (1996) *Olympic Politics: Athens to Atlanta, 1896–1996*. Manchester: Manchester University Press.

Hobsbawm, E.J. (1983) Introduction: Inventing traditions' and mass producing traditions: Europe 1870–1914. In E.J. Hobsbawm and T.O. Ranger (eds), *The Invention of Tradition* (pp. 1–14 and 263–307). Cambridge: Cambridge University Press.

Hobsbawm, E.J. (1990) *Nations and Nationalism since 1780: Programme, Myth, Reality*. Cambridge: Cambridge University Press.

Kirkup, J. (2012, July 27) London Olympics 2012: Aidan Burley takes gold for political misjudgement. *The Telegraph* [online edition]. Retrieved from http://blogs.telegraph.co.uk/news/jameskirkup/100173000/london-olympics-2012-aidan-burley-takes-gold-for-political-misjudgement/

MacGregor, R. (2010, March 1) The kid comes through with a goal that brings Canada's dream to life. *The Globe and Mail*, p. A1.

McRae, D. (2012, May 28) Tiffany Porter: I am proud to be American, British and Nigerian. *The Guardian* [online edition]. Retrieved from http://www.guardian.co.uk/sport/2012/may/28/tiffany-porter-american-british-olympics

Parekh, B. (1994) Discourses on national identity. *Political Studies,* 42(3), 492–504.

Prince, R. (2012, Septemeber 10) David Cameron: Golden summer of sport is our generation's 1966 World Cup. *The Telegraph* [online edition]. Retrieved from http://www.telegraph.co.uk/news/politics/david-cameron/9533224/David-Cameron-golden-summer-of-sport-is-our-generations-1966-World-Cup.html

Roche, M. (2000) *Mega-events and Modernity: Olympics and Expos in the Growth of Global Culture.* London: Routledge.

Rowe, D., McKay, J. and Miller, T. (1998) Come together: Sport, nationalism, and the media image. In L.A. Wenner (ed.), *MediaSport* (pp. 119–133) London: Routledge.

Tang, T. and Cooper, R. (2012) Gender, sports, and new media: Predictors of viewing during the 2008 Beijing Olympics. *Journal of Broadcasting and Electronic Media,* 56(1), 75–91.

Taylor, C.R. (2012) The London Olympics 2012: What advertiser should watch. *International Journal of Advertising,* 31(3), 459–464.

The Sun (2012, March 9) Brit skip is Yank! Retrieved from http://www.thesun.co.uk/sol/homepage/sport/olympics/4181897/Tiffany-Porter-is-GB-athletics-skipper-and-she-is-a-Yank.html

Tuck, J. (2003) The men in white: Reflections on rugby union, the media and Englishness. *International Review for the Sociology of Sport,* 38(2), 177–199.

von der Lippe, G. (2002) Media image: Sport, gender and national identities in five European countries. *International Review for the Sociology of Sport,* 37(3/4), 371–395.

Vincent, J. and Crossman, J. (2012) Patriots at play: An analysis of the newspaper coverage of the gold medal contenders in men's and women's ice hockey at the 2010 Winter Olympic Games. *International Journal of Sport Communication,* 5, 87–108.

Vincent, J. and Hill, J.S. (2011) Flying the flag for the En-ger-land: *The Sun's* (re)construction of English identity during the 2010 World Cup. *Journal of Sport and Tourism,* 16(3), 187– 209.

Vincent, J., Kian, E.M., Pedersen, P., Kuntz, A. and Hill, J.S. (2010) England expects: English newspapers' narratives about the English football team in the 2006 World Cup. *International Review for the Sociology of Sport,* 45(2), 199–223.

Watt, N. (2012, July 27) Olympics opening ceremony was 'multicultural crap', Tory MP tweets. *The Guardian* [online edition]. Retrieved from http://www.guardian.co.uk/politics/2012/jul/28/olympics-opening-ceremony-multicultural-crap-tory-mp

Weight, R. (2002) *Patriots: National Identity in Britain 1940–2000.* Basingstoke: Macmillan.

27

RECLAIMING OUR VOICES

Sportswomen and social media

Toni Bruce

UNIVERSITY OF AUCKLAND

Marie Hardin

PENNSYLVANIA STATE UNIVERSITY

In the 50 years since second-wave feminism created significant challenges to cultural expectations of women (Gilmore and Evans, 2008), it can be argued that participation in sport is not only accepted but valued for girls and women. Yet, despite this sea change in expectations and an exponential rise in female participation, women's sporting activities are rarely seen as sufficiently culturally important to warrant media coverage. In short, the vast majority of women's sport still does not matter to mainstream media and, by implication, to those who read, view and listen to what these media produce. Overall, the message is "Go ahead and play, but don't expect us to pay attention" (Bruce, 2013: 131). Why this is the case is the focus of this chapter, focusing on the potential of social media to disrupt this discourse. Thus, a key goal of the chapter is "exposing the relations of power that exist within society at any given moment in order to consider how marginal, or subordinate groups might secure or win, however temporarily, cultural space from the dominant group" – in this case, through the vehicle of social media (Procter, 2004: 2).

Dominant discourses

We begin our exploration of the mainstream sport media's treatment of sportswomen by exposing a series of ideological articulations that combine to make it almost impossible for female athletes to break into mainstream news media on a consistent basis or become part of the taken-for-granted background of sports coverage. As the first author has argued elsewhere, we propose that "entrenched gender and journalism ideologies appear to have created an almost impenetrable barrier for those trying to highlight women's athletic excellence" (Bruce, 2011: 1), at least on a day-to-day basis.

If insanity, according to Albert Einstein, is doing the same thing repeatedly and expecting a different result, what then can be said of those advocating for more mainstream media coverage of women's sport? Despite a quarter of a century of policy-making and activism by sports organizations and women's sports fans to create a higher profile for sportswomen in the mainstream media, very little has changed. The results of more than 80 studies of newspaper coverage in over 30 countries demonstrate the persistent, global marginalization of sportswomen (e.g. Bruce, Hovden and Markula, 2010; Bruce, 2013; Horky, 2012). With little variation, routine mainstream print coverage of sportswomen hovers near 10% percent (although the proportion of photographs may reach 20 percent), with television news and highlights even lower at about 5 percent (Bruce *et al.*, 2010; Horky, 2012; Jorgensen, 2002, 2005). While coverage rises periodically for major events like tennis grand slams, the Olympic or Commonwealth Games, or world championships in netball, handball or football, these events represent passing showers over an ocean of media coverage of men. The problem – as Olympic archery trialist, media activist and actress Geena Davis has argued about the relative absence of female leads in Hollywood movies (in Ryan, 2010) – is that "We are teaching girls to be happy about watching boys" and "boys that they don't have to watch stories about girls" (i.e. that what sportsmen do matters and what sportswomen do does not).

There can be little doubt – despite recent disruptions in the business model around sports journalism – that the mainstream sports media workplace shows evidence of "structural rigidity" (Fountaine and McGregor, 1999: 124), both in its discursive frameworks and practices. Like any site of culture, sports media operates under a set of taken-for-granted understandings that frame how media workers think and act (see Chapman, 2012, for example). Sports journalism relies on a set of cultural understandings to create a site in which coverage is produced *about* men, *by* men, *for* an assumed audience of men. Drawing upon cultural studies theorizing, we are interested in how certain ideas or discourses become linked in ways that open up or close down opportunities for women's sport to gain public attention. When discourses are linked, they form an articulation, the theory of which can be described as "both a way of understanding how ideological elements come, under certain conditions, to cohere together within a discourse, and a way of asking how they do or do not become articulated, at specific conjunctures" (Hall, cited in Grossberg, 1996: 141–2). In the case of sport, the articulation of sport and masculinity is key. In sports media, the articulation of news coverage and the professional norm of "objectivity" is another. The cohering of such ideological elements into discourses creates powerful effects that, over time, underpin individual, organizational and cultural beliefs, decisions and actions. In short, such discourses function at the gut level, at the level of the taken-for-granted and the unquestioned. As a result, the articulations themselves may become invisible, and thus become "very difficult to disrupt" (Hall, in Grossberg, 1996: 142). Indeed, attempts to expose or challenge them, as many women's sport advocates have found to their cost (e.g. Bruce, in press; Burton-Nelson, 1995; Fountaine and McGregor, 1999), are often strongly resisted because they challenge the media's claims to objectivity, balance and impartiality (Knoppers and Elling, 2004).

Sports media producers may not be consciously sexist but rather they "speak through" existing discourses that provide the "means of 'making sense' of social relations and our place in them" (Hall, 1995: 19). Thus, it is the sets of practices and discourses through which they construct knowledge that lead to the patterns of gendered media coverage that exist. As Hall (1997: 55) puts it, "it is discourse, not the subjects who speak it, which produce knowledge. Subjects may produce particular texts, but they are operating within the limits of the *episteme*, the discursive formation, the *régime of truth*, of a particular period and culture." Sport's assumed articulation with masculinity reveals itself in layered, subtle and complex ways, playing "a decisive role" in producing coverage that "privileges men's sports...whilst simultaneously disenfranchising women's sports" (Chapman, 2012: 204; see also Claringbould, Knoppers and Elling, 2004; Lowes, 1999; Theberge and Cronk, 1986).

Researchers have consistently found that sports journalists see their decision-making as objective, natural and uncomplicated (Chapman, 2012; Fountaine and McGregor, 1999; Knoppers and Elling, 2004). Indeed, objectivity may be seen as the "holy grail" in western journalism, especially in the US. (Hoffman, 2008: 107). Dutch journalists, for example, "inevitably began the interviews by asserting that the criteria of selection are straightforward and simple and they themselves are 'neutral' in applying these criteria to the selection process" (Knoppers and Elling, 2004: 60).

Yet, the history of sports journalism as an enterprise – especially in the US – is not one grounded in objectivity or in neutrality, although this fact seems lost on sports journalists and media producers who tout objectivity as a professional value that must be applied to judgments about (non)coverage of women's sports. Historically, newspaper sports pages were designed as promotional vehicles for men's sports (McChesney, 1989), and publishers and journalists worked hand-in-hand with men's sports league promoters to publicize matches, turn male athletes into larger-than-life heroes, and drive fans to events. Objectivity as a value applied to sports coverage did not receive critical attention in newsrooms until much later, once men's sports as a commercial enterprise had taken off, and newspaper sports departments had earned a "toy department" reputation for failing to practice serious journalism (Bryant and Holt, 2006; McChesney, 1989; Zirin, 2009).

Under these conditions, it is perhaps not surprising that women's sport seems unimportant. Indeed, the intersection of discourses of sport and masculinity and news media and objectivity can be argued to limit journalists' abilities to recognize where gender bias exists in their decisions and practices. These overlapping articulations combine to create a discourse so powerful that, at least in routine coverage, there can be no place (or space) for sportswomen apart from being the 'Other' to the norm that is men's sport.

Social media: A space for resistant discourses?

We acknowledge, at the same time, that the exponential growth of Internet-based news delivery "has essentially changed the ways in which sport media is produced, distributed, and consumed" (Mahan and McDaniel, 2006: 409). Somewhat optimistically, Mahan and McDaniel argue that rapid advances in technology and availability mean that sports coverage is no longer constrained by having to focus on "telegenic events or athletes that would capture the largest audiences," a limitation that "also limited coverage to sports entities with the largest regional and/or national appeal" (2006: 410). While this argument has intuitive appeal it must be recognized that assumptions about appeal are also historically and culturally situated – in other words, they are generated within and are in response to the cultural moment's practices, norms, and ideologies. Social media provides greater voice and visibility for sportswomen, their advocates, and their fans, yet they too are caught in dominant discourses.

It is increasingly clear that social media promotes different forms of engagement for both fans and players. Mahan and McDaniel, for example, point out that "sports fans are transformed into producers" (2006: 420). Yet, Leonard (2009: 3) acknowledges that although new media has allowed fans and players "to assert power and agency, to become active agents," at the same time, the "structures of power, the level of inequality, and the aesthetics, values and ideologies remain unchanged." This quote points to the power of existing discourses, and suggests that social media may not so much transform as create more opportunities for circulating dominant ideologies. Digital media remains dominated by male athletes and men's sport, and individuals who blog, Tweet, or post to platforms such as Facebook are rarely critical of current discourse but instead often amplify it, as they are not limited by public decency standards like the mainstream media. As a result, commentary often further entrenches rather than challenges existing gender ideologies. Blogs about females in sport are "often belittling and sexist and . . . sometimes cruel" (Hardin, 2009, para. 6). This fact is not lost on many individuals who participate in digital chatter around sports; one survey of US sports bloggers (most of whom were male) found that four in 10 agreed that the blogosphere is "generally quite sexist" (Hardin, Zhong and Corrigan, 2012: 62).

Female athletes in the social media sphere

However, while the social media sports space continues to be dominated by men's sport and male contributors, there is no doubt that the lack of gatekeepers and the opportunities to 'publish' for millions of eyeballs with nothing more than access to the Internet has created space for (some) women's sport and female athletes to thrive. Indeed, some sportswomen have broken through to become public figures with huge followings on platforms such as Facebook and Twitter. Such followings can 'prove' interest to mainstream media gatekeepers, who are increasingly turning to new media formats as sources of news (Lowrey and Mackay, 2008). In April 2013, seventeen sportswomen appeared in the top 100 athletes in numbers of Facebook fans and/or Twitter followers (Fan Page List, 2013). Tennis player Maria Sharapova headed the Facebook list at #13 with almost 9.6 million Facebook fans and 3.1 million Twitter followers (Fan Page List, 2013). Seven women at the time of this writing had more than a million Facebook fans, and 11 had more than a million Twitter followers. So clearly it is possible for sportswomen to achieve visibility and popularity on social media. Yet, the composition of the list also indicates the importance of mainstream media coverage in order to become familiar enough to garner a following. Fan Page List (fanpagelist.com), a social media aggregator, is dominated by sportswomen who have previously gained mainstream media coverage as Olympians or professional tennis players, many of whom embody white, Western ideals of female beauty. Professional tennis players dominate the list (with 10 of the 17 spots) and hold the top two places. The other sports represented include football, badminton, track and field, figure-skating, BMX and gymnastics. Of the list we examined, most women were from or based in the United States, with the remainder representing India, the UK, South Korea, Colombia, Serbia, Belarus, Belgium and Denmark. In fact, only three of the top 17-ranked sportswomen were neither tennis players nor from the US. Given that mainstream coverage of sportswomen rises significantly during the Olympics, it is probably not surprising that when we visited the site, just months after the London Games, all but two were Olympians (10 of them gold medalists, and 11 of whom competed in the 2012 Games). The remaining athletes have been world champions or achieved world #1 rankings in their sports.

Formula for social media popularity

Certainly, sportswomen who have risen to prominence in social media are often those who embody both sporting competence and cultural norms of female physical attractiveness. Thus, to be popular, a sportswoman appears to need to be situated within somewhat contradictory discourses of sporting excellence and feminine beauty. In other words, they need to meet a "hetero-sexy" ideal (Griffin, 1998: 75). Based on a recent media analysis of world football championships for men and women, Thomas Horky (2012: 23) concluded that for sportswomen, "the usual formula is still 'success + good looks = media attention'." "Good looks" implies a heterosexual status for both the object of sexual attraction and the assumed heterosexual male audience.

However, despite the validation of sporting prowess, beauty appears to remain the defining characteristic in social media aggregators and female-athletes-to-follow lists, which highlight images of female bodies in bikinis, underwear or otherwise revealing attire. For example, a senior writer for a popular US sports blog site, *The Bleacher Report*, promoted tennis player Anna Kournikova, stating "as long as Anna remains hot she will stay on the list" (Star, 2010, para. 18). Although not *about* men, the discourses embodied in many social media descriptions and images imply that, similar to mainstream media coverage, the assumed audience is heterosexual males, although the gender of the producers is not always apparent. In one list on *The Bleacher Report*, many images show sportswomen with bare arms and shoulders, and the majority are bikini shots (Star, 2010). The accompanying descriptions make it clear that sporting prowess + beauty are the winning combination: "...*guys* dig Finch's fastball and blonde bombshell look on the softball diamond" (para. 20, emphasis added), "...can cause damage in two ways, both with her looks and her fists. She is one sexy combination of intimidation" (para.17); "...burns up the slopes with both her skis and her looks" (para. 16), "...not only wins on the court, but with her looks as well...she isn't just a model with a racket in her hand, and that makes her even hotter" (para. 14); "...a force in the water...first American woman to ever win six medals at one Olympics...and a force in the centerfolds. Swimming clearly did her body good" (para. 10), and "...belle of the WNBA. Her combination of looks and moves on the hardwood are a winning duo" (para. 4).

Similarly, a page on *TotalProSports* (2012, para 2), "Fifteen Female Athletes You Should Follow on Twitter," asserted that when elite athletes

> ...are candid and open and share their lives, they actually give sports fans a sense of what it would actually be like to play sports for a living. And of course, when these athletes happen to be attractive and female, well then that's even better.

The site then suggests that the athletes it recommends "have interesting things to say, are fairly candid, and tend to post entertaining (and occasionally sexy) photos of themselves and their friends. Follow them. You will not regret it." The descriptions of each athlete (identified by her #) again demonstrate the juxtaposition of sporting prowess and (hetero)sexual attractiveness:

> In addition to being pretty hot and a tremendously gifted athlete, also seems like a pretty cool person who's involved in a number of good causes. Plus she tweets tons of great pics. Did I mention she is gorgeous? Oh, right, I did. (#3)
>
> I find this Olympic gold medalist-turned-MMA star quite fascinating. When she's in the ring, with her hair pulled back tightly, she looks like such a badass. When she's out of the ring, she looks like your typical girly girl. There's something about that juxtaposition that is just awesome. (#7)
>
> [I]s probably the most dominant female athlete in the world today, having won 4 of the last 5 World Cup championships. But on top of that, she's also ridiculously attractive and travels to incredible places all over the globe. So there's always something good to check out on her Twitter page. (#10)

Feminist researchers have debated the rise of a form of representation of sportswomen within discourses of sexual attractiveness or sexualization, especially when women pose for men's magazines. Some argue that such images an offer "a sense of expanded possibility" (Heywood and Dworkin, 2003: 83), while others are concerned that these representations in the digital (or traditional) realm reflect a traditionally male gaze that constructs women as passive (see Markula, 2009). Heywood and Dworkin (2003) propose that sportswomen's bodies "when coded as athletic, can redeem female sexuality and make it visible as an assertion of female presence" (Thorpe, 2011: 83). Recent research, however, seems to confirm that hetero-sexy athletic bodies may draw eyeballs, but they do not draw eyeballs to women's sport (Kane, 2011).

Evidence of entrenched discourses

This is not to say that every female athlete with a following on social media platforms conforms to the hetero-sexy ideal. Perhaps the most noteworthy exception at the time of writing was Brittany Griner, a college basketball star who, after her college career was over and she was headed to a career in women's professional basketball, announced that she was lesbian. An article in *ESPN the Magazine* discussed Griner's use of social media, on which she had more than 40,000 Twitter followers[1] when the article was published. The writer, Kate Fagan (2013, paras 6–8), describes Griner picking up her phone and

> . . . scrolling through Twitter and Instagram, as she does routinely, to see what people are saying about her. The hits come quickly: *"You're disgusting."* [Scroll.] *"Ur a man."* [Scroll.] *"What are you? #man? #ape?"*
>
> "Here's one," she says, rolling her eyes. "You have a penis." Satisfied that her troll chorus still cares, Griner puts away the phone.

Female athletes who might deviate from the athletic-yet-picture-perfect ideal may also be publicly humiliated by fans – who have no gatekeeper for norms of civility – on social media sites. An example of cruelty involved criticism of the hairstyle of US gymnast, Gabby Douglas (Hill, 2012). On Twitter, "instead of basking in the fact that Douglas became the first African-American woman to win the individual all-around competition, people . . . were making jokes about how this 16-year-old phenom was in need of a perm or, at the very least, a more kempt ponytail" (Hill, 2012, para. 6). Hill and others, however, noted that fans quickly came to Douglas' digital defense.

The experiences of Griner, Douglas and other women who do not conform to traditional, idealized expectations for female athletes indicate that the ideologies and norms that drive mainstream media decision-making certainly influence the dominant discourses in the blogosphere and other social media. A survey of US fans who blogged daily about their favorite teams, leagues and sports found that their attitudes, values and beliefs about the appeal of women's sports did not differ from those of traditional journalists (Hardin *et al.*, 2012). Most – around two-thirds – asserted that women's sports would never be as culturally valued or entertaining as men's sports. Perhaps it is no surprise that bloggers who believed that women's sports were less interesting also were more likely to be critical of Title IX,[2] and less supportive of increased coverage of women's sports.

It may be overreaching to believe that the emergence of digital technology and social media alone will disrupt dominant discourses around sport. Twitter, Facebook, and other platforms cannot, in and of themselves, challenge ideologies. Instead, they may allow the volume to be amplified with uncritical voices (Bruce, in press). Even women who blog about sports and see themselves as advocates may "unconsciously comply with the dominant discourse," suggesting that uninterrogated cultural ideology often overpowers attempts to provide new perspectives (Hardin, 2011: 57).

Opening cultural spaces

These new platforms can, however, provide the space for individuals to "secure or win, however temporarily, cultural space from the dominant group" (Procter, 2004: 2). Bruce (2011: 9) suggested that social media may

> ...offer women's sports the chance to control their own content, to engage the passion of their fans, and to make the most of cheaper, easier-to-use technologies that might allow them to reach the world. In doing so, they may contribute to the slow process of disrupting the articulations that have long kept women's sport on the margins.

Certainly, there are pockets of such disruption on the Internet in spaces where women's sport fans, advocates, and athletes gather to share news, tips, gossip – and, most importantly, to build communities (Antunovic and Hardin, 2012). Sportswomen and women's sports organizations, such as the WNBA with almost 500,000 Twitter followers, have established a strong presence on platforms such as Twitter and Facebook. These spaces provide visibility or, at the very least, they play defense against the "symbolic annihilation" of sportswomen (Tuchman, 1978) in mainstream media, even if the discourses they promote may not, ultimately, resist dominant discourses.

Advocates, fans and athletes have also formed around blog collectives where female sports fans and fans of women's sports can share commentary and video in a variety of formats. The option for female fans to tell 'their own story' is particularly significant, especially as their experiences as fans of sport have generally been ignored or marginalized as less-than-authentic (Antunovic and Hardin, 2012: 309).

For fans of women's sport, one collective is *Women Talk Sports*. *WTS* is a blog network created to "raise the level of awareness of women in sport by providing comprehensive sport coverage, spotlighting outstanding achievements, and working with sporting associations on advocacy issues and empowering programs" (Women Talk Sports, 2011, para. 1). Interviews with bloggers on this network and an analysis of their profiles demonstrate that they seek a space to talk about sports on their own terms and to advocate for better media coverage of women's sports; they see the sacrifices they make in terms of the time and effort on their blogs as being part of the solution to the lack of media attention to sportswomen (Hardin, 2011).

An analysis of content on *WTS* and on other blogs written by women about sports indicates that female bloggers often broadcast a different understanding of sports and of fandom into the digital sphere. Such understandings – although they still must be considered for their grounding in the current cultural, ideological context – open a space to consider sport in alternative ways (Antunovic and Hardin, 2013). Again, what we do not know is the potential for such spaces to provide outlets where fans of sportswomen can talk about sports free from the restrictions of the gatekeeping process, and – ultimately – to impact the wider patterns in discourse. Although we may be hopeful, we are not overly optimistic, as we understand the power and resiliency in cultural ideologies around gender. Even so, scholars and advocates concerned with gender issues and equity for sportswomen should pay close attention to the growing and constantly changing arena of social media. If substantive change is to happen in this generation, it will no doubt be reflected in the discourse of fans, athletes and advocates engaged in the dynamic digital realm.

Notes

1. Although 40,000 is undoubtedly a small number when compared to other athletes (it would put Griner only in the top 900 athletes on Fan Page List), it is a respectable following if Griner is compared to many other female athletes).
2. Title IX is US legislation introduced in 1972 that bans discrimination on the basis of sex in educational institutions receiving Federal funds. Although not solely about sport, the overwhelming majority of complaints under its regulations have involved charges of gender discrimination against females in sport.

References

Antunovic, D. and Hardin, M. (2012) Activism in women's sports blogs: Fandom and feminist potential. *International Journal of Sport Communication,* 5(3), 305–322.

Antunovic, D. and Hardin, M. (2013) Women sports bloggers: Identity and the conceptualization of sports. *New Media and Society.* Advance online publication. doi 10.1177/1461444812472323.

Bruce, T. (in press) Battered in the media: The value of theorizing as a method for lessening the pain of lived experience. In R. Rinehart, K. N. Barbour and C. C. Pope (eds), *Ethnographic Worldviews: Transformations and Social Justice* [Chapter 14]. Dordrecht, The Netherlands: Springer.

Bruce, T. (2013) On women and femininities. *Communication and Sport,* 1(1–2), 125–137.

Bruce, T. (2011) *Shifting the Boundaries: Sportswomen in the Media.* Proceedings of the Australian and New Zealand Communication Association annual meeting. Hamilton, New Zealand.

Bruce, T., Hovden, J. and Markula, P. (eds) (2010) *Sportswomen at the Olympics: A Global Comparison of Newspaper Coverage.* Rotterdam, The Netherlands: Sense Publishers.

Bryant, J. and Holt, A. (2006) A historical overview of sports and media in the United States. In A. A. Raney and J. Bryant (eds), *Handbook of Sports and Media* (pp. 22–46). Mahwah, NJ: Lawrence Erlbaum Associates.

Burton-Nelson, M. (1995) *The Stronger Women Get, the More Men Love Football: Sexism and the American Culture of Sports.* New York: Avon Books.

Chapman, S. (2012) *The Gendering of Sports News: An Investigation into the Production, Content and Reception of Sports Photographs of Athletes in New Zealand Newspapers.* Thesis, University of Waikato, Hamilton, New Zealand.

Claringbould, I., Knoppers, A. and Elling, A. (2004) Exclusionary practices in sport journalism. *Sex Roles,* 51(11–12), 709–718.

Fagan, K. (2013, May 29) Owning the middle. *ESPN the Magazine* [online]. Retrieved from http://espn.go.com/espn/story/_/id/9316697/owning-middle

Fan Page List (2013) Retrieved from fanpagelist.com

Fountaine, S. and McGregor, J. (1999) The loneliness of the long distance gender researcher: Are journalists right about the coverage of women's sport? *Australian Journalism Review,* 2(3), 113–126.

Gilmore, S. and Evans, S. (2008) *Feminist Coalitions: Perspectives on Second-Wave Feminism in the United States.* Champaign, IL: University of Illinois Press.

Griffin, P. (1998) *Strong Women, Deep Closets: Lesbians and Homophobia in Sport.* Champaign, IL: Human Kinetics.

Grossberg, L. (1996) On postmodernism and articulation: An interview with Stuart Hall. In D. Morley and K-H. Chen (eds), *Stuart Hall: Critical dialogues in Cultural Studies* (pp. 131–150). London: Routledge.

Hall, S. (1995) The whites of their eyes: Racist ideologies and the media. In G. Dines and J. M. Humer (eds), *Gender, Race and Class in Media: A Text-reader* (pp. 18–22). Thousand Oaks, CA: Sage.

Hall, S. (1997) The work of representation. In S. Hall (ed.), *Representation: Cultural Representations and Signifying Practices* (pp. 13–74). London: Sage.

Hardin, M. (2009, Sept. 24) *Does 'new media' bring new attitudes toward women's sports?* Tucker Center for Research on Girls and Women in Sport. Retrieved from http://tuckercenter.wordpress.com/2009/09/24/does-%E2%80%98new-media%E2%80%99-bring-new-attitudes-oward-women%E2%80%99s-sports/

Hardin, M. (2011) The power of a fragmented collective: Radical pluralist feminism and technologies of the self in the sports blogosphere. In A.C. Billings (ed.), *Sports Media: Transformation, Integration, Consumption* (pp. 40–60). New York: Routledge.

Hardin, M., Zhong, B. and Corrigan, T. (2012) The funhouse mirror: The blogosphere's reflection of women's sports. In T. Dumova and R. Fiordo (eds), *Blogging in the Global Society: Cultural, Political, and Geographical Aspects* (pp. 55–71). Hershey, PA: Information Science Reference.

Heywood, L. and Dworkin, S. L. (2003) *Built to Win: The Female Athlete as Cultural Icon.* Minneapolis, MN: University of Minnesota Press.

Hill, J. (2012, Aug. 3) Gabby Douglas' hair draws criticism. *espnW.* Retrieved from: http://espn.go.com/espnw/olympics/8232063/espnw-gabby-douglas-hair-criticized-social-media-sites

Hoffman, J. (2008) *On their Own: Women Journalists and the American Experience in Vietnam.* Boston, MA: Da Capo Press.

Horky, T. (2012, May 11) *Facts and Figures: The International Sports Press Survey 2011.* Presentation to the UEFA and Sport and Citizenship workshop "The mediatisation of women sport in Europe: What is at stake and how to improve the coverage?" Nyon, Switzerland.

Jorgensen, S. S. (2005, October 31) The world's best advertising agency: The sports press. *Mandagmorgen [Mondaymorning],* 37, 1–7.

Jorgensen, S. S. (2002, November) Industry or independence? Survey of the Scandinavian sports press. *Mondaymorning* [Special issue], 1–8.

Kane, M. J. (2011, August) Sex sells sex, not women's sports. *The Nation Magazine,* 293(7), 28–29.

Knoppers, A. and Elling, A. (2004) 'We do not engage in promotional journalism': Discursive strategies used by sport journalists to describe the selection process. *International Review for the Sociology of Sport,* 39(1), 57–73.

Leonard, D. J. (2009) New media and global sporting cultures: Moving beyond the clichés and binaries. *Sociology of Sport Journal,* 26, 1–16.

Lowes, M. D. (1999) *Inside the Sports Pages: Work Routines, Professional Ideologies, and the Manufacture of Sports News.* Toronto, Canada: University of Toronto Press.

Lowrey, W. and Mackay, J. B. (2008) Journalism and blogging: A test of a model of occupational competition. *Journalism Practice,* 2(1), 64–81.

Mahan, J. E. III and McDaniel (2006) The new online arena: Sport, marketing, and media converge in cyberspace. In A. A. Raney and J. Bryant (eds), *Handbook of Sports and Media* (pp. 409–431). Mahwah, NJ: Lawrence Erlbaum Associates.

Markula, P. (ed.) (2009) *Olympic Women and the Media: International Perspectives.* New York: Palgrave Macmillan.

McChesney, R. (1989) Media made sport: A history of sports coverage in the United States. In L. Wenner (ed.), *Media, Sports, and Society* (pp. 49–69). Newbury Park, CA: Sage.

Procter, J. (2004) *Stuart Hall.* London: Routledge.

Ryan, K. (2010, March 12) *Nine to Noon with Kathryn Ryan.* Radio New Zealand National. Retrieved from http://podcast.radionz.co.nz/ntn/ntn-20100312-1010-Feature_guest_-_Geena_Davis-048.mp3

Star, J. (2010, March 26) The twenty hottest athletes to follow on Twitter. *Bleacher Report.* Retrieved from: http://bleacherreport.com/articles/369208-the-20-hottest-athletes-to-follow-on-twitter

Theberge, N. and Cronk, A. (1986) Work routines in newspaper sports departments and the coverage of women's sport. *Sociology of Sport Journal,* 3, 195–203.

Thorpe, H. (2011) *Snowboarding Bodies in Theory and Practice.* New York: Palgrave Macmillan.

Tuchman, G. (1978) The symbolic annihilation of women by the mass media. In G. Tuchman, A. Kaplan Daniels and J. Benet (eds), *Hearth and Home: Images of Women in the Mass Media* (pp. 3–38). New York: Oxford University Press.

Women Talk Sports (2011) About. Retrieved from http://www.womentalksports.com/p/about

Zirin, D. (2009) *People's History of Sports in the United States: 250 Years of Politics, Protest, People, and Play.* New York: New Press.

28

DIGITAL MEDIA AND WOMEN'S SPORT

An old view on 'new' media?

Nicole M. LaVoi and Austin Stair Calhoun

UNIVERSITY OF MINNESOTA

Forty years after the passage of Title IX,[1] sport participation for girls and women at all levels – youth, interscholastic, intercollegiate, professional, Olympic, and Paralympic – is at an historic high. The most recent data from the National Federation of High Schools and the National Collegiate Athletic Association indicates over 40 percent of US high school and collegiate athletes are female and many professional women's sport entities are thriving (e.g. WNBA, LPGA, WTA, National Pro Fastpitch). In addition, the number of female athletes in the 2012 London Olympic Games outnumbered that of male athletes for the first time, and female Paralympians in 2012 were twice the number from a decade earlier in the 1992 Barcelona Games.

Despite these impressive statistics, sport media scholars have employed Tuchman's (1978, 2012) theory to argue female athletes are *symbolically annihilated* by mass media through omission, trivialization, and condemnation of their accomplishments. Messner in 2002 contended female athletes and women's sport were "symbolically marginalized" (i.e. relegated or confined to a lower status or outer edge) rather than annihilated, through relegation to small cable channels, non-prime-time slots, obscure websites, and niche magazines – processes that serve to trivialize and make women's sport appear less important. Given contemporary research by Cooky, Messner and Hextrum (2013) where they reported televised sport media coverage of female athletes was at an all-time low (1.6%) – virtually non-existent – we see symbolic annihilation as an even more accurate and relevant construct, for the purpose of summarizing and critiquing traditional, as well as digital, sport media.

Traditional sport media: What do we know?

Evidence reported over nearly three decades by scholars studying traditional print and broadcast sport media is irrefutable – sportswomen receive a disproportionate amount of media coverage, and when they do receive coverage, it is in ways that minimize athletic competence and highlight femininity, (hetero)sexuality, and traditional gender stereotypes. In the infrequent instances in which sport media producers do cover women's sports, female athletes' athletic accomplishments are often minimized and trivialized, their performance is often compared to men, and female athletes are presented as sex objects or portrayed as incompetent or in a sarcastic manner (e.g. Duncan, 1990; Kane and Buysse, 2005; Kian, 2008; Cooky, Messner and Hextrum, 2013).

Duncan (1990) argued over two decades ago that representations of strong, athletic women hold inordinate transformative potential, yet today this potential is not realized. Scholars contend the symbolic annihilation of female athletes and women's sport serves to maintain existing power structures in which men control sport and male hegemonic ideology rules, limiting their ability to challenge and change men's ideological and institutional control of sport (Messner, 1988) – both of which serve to benefit men. Kane and Lenskyj (1998) argued that women's entrance into sports in the post-Title IX era in unprecedented numbers has disrupted hegemonic discourses around the meaning and practice of sport and has the potential to empower women and create alternative beliefs and practices about their legitimate role and place within sports. However, based on the current data, women have less opportunity and power to change male-dominated ideologies and power structures (LaVoi, 2009) or to be taken seriously as athletes (Kane, LaVoi and Fink, 2013).

As the landscape of media changes and digital media becomes more prominent, critical questions remain: Will annihilistic patterns pertaining to female athletes in traditional sport media be reproduced or challenged? Do digital media hold transformative potential for female athletes and women's sport? Can digital media free female athletes from the tyranny of traditional media that limit their potential and make it difficult for them and their particular sports to be respected? In the remainder of this chapter, we explore these questions through examination of existing, but limited, literature on women and digital sport media. We begin by defining our use of the term digital, rather than 'new' media.

Defining digital media

Drawing boundaries between media forms (print, radio, broadcast, Internet, electronic) and types (old vs. new) is becoming increasingly more difficult and ambiguous. For example, a 2012 Nielsen Report on US video consumption shows a decline in traditional television household penetration (from 99% to 95.8%) and for many, TV sets are being repurposed for gaming, DVRs, and Internet browsing. Despite a shift in how household TVs are used, it continues to be "a centerpiece of the viewing experience" (Nielson, 2012: 3) and considered a part of the traditional news media. Traditional news is characterized by content controlled by few and consumed by many, compared to the emergent contemporary model of media in which content is simultaneously controlled, produced, consumed, and repurposed by many for many (Mandiberg, 2012). As Rosen (2006) infamously observed, the media is now created by the people formerly known as the audience.

This paradigm shift and cross-purposing of media devices, as exemplified by TV use, illuminates the difficulty in naming media as decidedly old or new. Flew (2008) warns against the tendency to name things that have more history (i.e. television, print, or radio) as old because the "rate of change in media technologies, services, and uses is so rapid that any list of this sort will quickly become dated" (p. 9). Drawing from Flew (2008), we argue for the use of the term *digital media* rather than *new media* to frame this chapter pertaining to gender and sport in a Web 2.0 world.[2] We feel the term digital media better encompasses the differences between media types and conveys specific characteristics and expectations that frame this discussion. Therefore, for the purpose of this chapter, digital media are forms of media content that combine and integrate data, text, sound, and images of all kinds, are stored in digital formats; and are increasingly distributed through networks. Such media are manipulable, networkable, dense, compressible, and impartial (Flew, 2008).

Two additional definitional components of digital media – interactivity and ubiquity – help shape this chapter (Lievrouw and Livingstone, 2006). In the current sport media landscape, digital media is highly interactive and ubiquitous – almost all of the professional, collegiate, and national teams have websites, Twitter accounts, blogs, Facebook pages, and a presence on other digital media such as photo sharing apps or online reference works (e.g. Wikipedia) (Ioakimidis, 2010). Some professional teams and athletes are even moving into digital media content sharing services. The amount of digital content created via interactive online content-sharing and content-creating platforms is staggering. The 2012 London Olympic Games is a prime example of ubiquity and interactivity. Following the Games, in September 2012 there were 24,185 images tagged with the phrase 'Summer Olympics' on Flickr, a photo-sharing service, and 106 athletes were listed on Twitter as "Verified Olympians."

The 2001 launch of Wikipedia – which at that time was "new" – was followed shortly by the launch of Flickr and Facebook (2004), YouTube (2005), and Twitter (2006). With the advent of accessible digital media tools, journalists, fans, and athletes were afforded many tools with which to consume and create content and interact with each other and arguably provide an "alternative" or bypass to old/traditional/mainstream journalism and have given rise to citizen journalism (Jenkins, 2004). Citizen journalism is a generic term for a type of journalism and/or communication that is any of the following: networked, online, participatory, civic, the people's, public, and/or open source (Deuze, Bruns and Neuberger, 2007). Citizen journalism often depends on mainstream media content but offers an alternative perspective and critique, which keeps the media monopoly in check and creates a symbiotic but often tense relationship (Deuze *et al.*, 2007; Lenskyj, 2006). The role of citizen journalism in the (re)production of gender-sport-digital media triad follows.

Gender, sport, and digital media

The intertwined relationship between sport and media, often described as the sport/media complex (Jhally, 1989), is unparalleled, inarguable and continues to expand with emerging technologies. With this growth, Kane's (1988: 89) sentiment that "the mass media have become one of the most powerful institutional forces for shaping values and attitudes in modern culture" still rings true. The power of the media to transmit and mediate messages about sport is reflected in vast and varied scholarly endeavors from many disciplines over three decades (i.e. Billings, 2011; Gantz, 2011).

With the advent of "new" media, the opportunity for innovative avenues of scholarly inquiry followed. However, in a position paper, Wilson (2007) called for more sport sociology scholarship and research involving digital media: "these blind spots are conspicuous considering the link between the rise and success of social movements (especially transnational movements) and the widespread emergence of the Internet – a link that has been increasingly investigated in mainstream sociological work since 2000" (p. 458). In the last five years, sport sociologists and sport media scholars have begun to fill the research void with assessments of digital platforms including Twitter, Facebook, networked media, and college athletic department websites. Despite a growing body of digital media sport studies – with the exception of a few scholars featured in this chapter – the "gender" piece of the gender-sport-digital media triad lacks attention (Hardin, Zhong and Corrigan, 2012), intersectional analysis is nearly absent (Lisec and McDonald, 2012) and in many cases the antiquated "add women and stir" approach is applied.

Within extant and emerging scholarly endeavors, a critical question remains: *Do digital sport media challenge or reproduce dominant gender ideologies pertaining to female athletes?* In the following sections we summarize the limited existing research in which a critical gendered lens was applied to analyze common digital media sources – blogs, Facebook, Twitter, and websites. To our knowledge at this time, there is no existing gender-sport-digital media research on other popular digital sources.

Blogs

While some scholars contend blogs allow citizen journalists opportunity to offer perspectives that challenge traditional media conglomerates (Jenkins, 2004; Matheson, 2004), such claims are not globally supported by data – particularly in terms of representations of female athletes. Researchers analyzing sport blogs report equivocal results – some blogs challenged, while others reinforced stereotypical and sexualized depictions and ideologies about female athletes and women's sports (Clavio and Eagleman, 2011; Hardin, 2011; Hardin *et al.*, 2012; Lisec and McDonald, 2012; MacKay and Dallaire, 2013).

Equally important to the examination of sport bloggers and critique of blog content is for feminist sport scholars and advocates of women's sport to seek opportunities to engage in dialogue with individuals who typically do not write about women's sport or those who contribute to annihilistic narratives about women's sport. Such interactions can be a transgressive space in which teachable moments occur, contradictions, omissions, and inaccuracies can be discussed, and a focus on female athleticism can be encouraged. One such interaction occurred when we as feminist sport scholars attended the *Blog With Balls 2.0* conference – a sports new media event series. A majority in attendance were educated White men who had traditional perspectives on gender (Hardin *et al.*, 2012), rarely wrote about women's sport, and framed females as sexual conquests, girlfriends, wives, or cheerleaders. The first author was invited to sit on a five-person panel pertaining to ethical issues in blog writing, during which the issue of calling NFL quarterback Ben Rothlesberger "Rape-lesberger" was raised. One panelist said he felt it was a harmless and humorous nickname. When asked by the moderator to respond, the first author stated, "I don't think there is any situation that rape or using the word rape is funny. It makes light of a very serious, harmful crime that many girls and women endure, and that is no joke." Through the thick and awkward silence that ensued, one audience member began to clap in support and was immediately joined by others. At this moment, for many in the audience who had never critically thought about negative implications of perpetuating offensive language, cognitive dissonance was created that could potentially lead to change.

While a pluralistic approach can provide utility, as evidenced in the previous example, it is not uncomplicated or unproblematic. With difference – especially perspectives that are clearly anti-feminist – enters the possibility that power structures and oppressive ideologies not only remain intact but are reified and strengthened. For example, Lisec and McDonald (2012) analyzed content in three disparate blogs pertaining to women's basketball and found discussion board comments by readers often shift dialogue from women as athletes to sexualized jokes and references to physical appearance. On *Deadspin*, a popular sport blog collective, discussion boards often served as an unedited, unfiltered, unmediated source of homophobic, misogynistic, and sexist responses to women in sport, which, compared to traditional media, occurred in more blatant, profane, and stronger forms of language (Lisec and McDonald). In addition to gender-based backlash, Lisec and McDonald noted near a complete absence of intersectional dialogue about gender and race, which reinforces colorblind rhetoric. Lastly, sport blogs can be problematic because opinions, coverage, and analysis of sport bloggers/citizen journalists, who are most often not professionally trained or reflexive to ethical considerations, is often passed off and consumed as legitimate (Hardin *et al.*, 2012; Lisec and McDonald, 2012).

Based on the small number of studies available, coupled with the lack of female bloggers and male bloggers with progressive orientations towards women's sport (Hardin *et al.*, 2012), the annihilistic content in sport blogs to date does not support a hypothesis that digital technologies are challenging dominant ideologies about female athletes. While transgressive, pluralistic, and progressive niche sport blogs about female athletes exist (MacKay and Dallaire, 2013), they are the exception and without entrance of more women into sport blogosphere, change will be unlikely (Hardin *et al.*, 2012). Additional exploration of the sport blogosphere is needed (Hardin, 2011; Lisec and McDonald, 2012) as is research on popular social media platforms such as Facebook.

Facebook

Facebook's ubiquity as a free social networking website is staggering. In 2012, with one billion users who create and share content with friends, family and colleagues (Wikipedia, 2012a), it is the largest social network of its kind. Research with a sports focus on Facebook is lacking, due in part to abundant privacy issues that surround this particular digital media source (Sanderson, 2009). One recent study conducted by Wallace, Wilson and Miloch (2011) provided a starting point. They conducted a content analysis of NCAA and Big 12 athletic department Facebook pages and, while they did not go into the study with a gendered lens, gender differences emerged. For example, the number of Facebook users who "liked" pages for NCAA women's basketball pages were significantly lower (18,755) than "likes" for NCAA men's basketball (48,053) (Wallace *et al.*, 2011). On October 1, 2012, the disparate "likes" for these two NCAA basketball pages was even more pronounced – men's basketball 350,321; women's basketball, 29,910. These results unfortunately reinforce a dominant gender ideology that is uncritically taken up by many – people just aren't interested in women's sports. What is often missing from this assertion is that interest is primarily driven by opportunity and history of exposure, and if women's sports were given equal value, amount and type of coverage, and resources, they may also garner equal interest (Kane and Maxwell, 2011). Based on the results of one study, it is too early to ascertain whether Facebook reproduces or challenges symbolic annihilism of female athletes and women's sport. Next we summarize research on another popular digital media source – Twitter.

Twitter

Twitter is an online social networking and microblogging service founded in 2007 that enables its users to send and read text-based messages of up to 140 characters, known as "tweets." The growth of Twitter has been incredible – in 2012 the company had more than 500 million users and was one of the top 10 most-visited websites on the Internet (Wikipedia, 2012b). The popularity of Twitter also grew quickly among athletes and teams at all levels of competition, as it is cost effective and has limitless personal and professional utility (Durrett, 2009). By becoming active participants and primary sources (a.k.a. micro citizen journalists) of information via Twitter, users – particularly professional athletes – have the opportunity and autonomy to present their "brand," which may reinforce or challenge mainstream media norms (Sanderson and Kassing, 2011).

Sport organizations often encourage athletes to take advantage of Twitter to promote themselves and events. For example, the International Olympic Committee (@Olympics) tweeted to athletes at the 2010 Winter Olympics in Vancouver: "Athletes go ahead and Tweet as long as it is about your own personal experience at the Games" (Fried, 2010, para. 3). Given the multidimensional and complex application and potential outcomes of Twitter, scholarly inquiry has followed but struggled to keep pace with this digital media tool. A handful of researchers have teased out gender norms specific to female athletes' Twitter habits and tweet content (e.g. Pegoraro, 2010; Sanderson and Kassing, 2011; Smith, 2011). However, much of the current scholarship lacks a critical gender analysis as it relates to how dominant ideologies about female athletes and women's sports are portrayed and (re)produced on Twitter. To our knowledge, one study to date has employed this critical lens.

Smith (2011) used the theoretical construct of hegemonic masculinity in framing an examination of Twitter feeds of Division IA sport conferences (i.e. SEC, Pac-10, BIG 10, Big 12) to discern if gender differences existed. Based on the results, symbolic annihilism is evident in that tweets pertaining to men's sports far surpassed those for women's sports across all categories (i.e. number of tweets, number of tweets to links, pictures, and retweets). Based on the limited data, it is inconclusive whether Twitter provides a space for the presentation of non-traditional gender narratives in sport that challenge the status quo.

Network-affiliated media websites

Facebook, Twitter, and blogs fall into a subset of digital media that is decidedly social – meaning the technologies employed allow the user to create and exchange information. Websites, while lacking some of the interactive qualities of social media, are the original digital media form dating back to the 1990s (Winston, 1998). Research on websites has focused on the perpetuation of gender ideology through online media corporations (Kian, Mondello and Vincent, 2009; Kian, Vincent and Mondello, 2008) or athletic department websites (Sagas, Cunningham, Wigley and Asley, 2000).

Early data in this area indicated female athletes received less coverage on major sport news websites CBS SportsLine (now CBSSports), CNNSI, and ESPN, than male counterparts in golf, soccer, and tennis (Kachgal, 2001). More recently, researchers examining online coverage of the Olympics and college basketball reported equivocal results. In Jones (2004, 2006) longitudinal research of an Australian digital media source, *News Online*, women were represented more frequently than men during the 2004 Olympics, and representations of women increased from the 2000 Olympics – therefore challenging symbolic annihilation premises. However, Jones also noted that while women were more likely to be pictured than men, when women were represented, they were more likely to be depicted in a losing effort, which in turn trivialized female athleticism and reproduced symbolic annihilation.

Kian and colleagues (Kian *et al.*, 2008, 2009) explored ESPN's and CBSSports' online coverage of the men's and women's NCAA basketball tournaments. Some results challenged male hegemony – there were a statistically greater proportion of descriptors about physical appearances/attire, and family roles/personal relationships in men's basketball articles compared with women's basketball articles and a significantly higher proportion of descriptors about skill level/accomplishments and psychological/emotional strength appeared for female basketball players (Kian *et al.*, 2009). However, other online results reinforced male hegemony – an overwhelming majority of online coverage was devoted to coverage of men's basketball, and female athletes were "othered" in a variety of ways (Kian *et al.*, 2008, 2009). A lack of content, content not focused on athleticism, and outdated or repeated stories, all communicate to site visitors a comparative lack of importance, interest, and value in women's basketball compared to their male counterparts.

Endorsed media websites

Intercollegiate athletic departments have become ubiquitous digital media producers. Sports information professionals have played a large role in conveying information about their teams to a large body of people including the student body, alumni, and recruits. Unfortunately, despite the conviction that institutions of higher education are committed to social justice, scholars have found that gender ideology is perpetuated by athletic department websites, which are institutionally endorsed (Calhoun, LaVoi and Johnson, 2011; Cooper and Cooper, 2009; Sagas *et al.*, 2000). In a content analysis of intercollegiate athletic home Web pages, researchers found women's teams received more advertisements, articles, multimedia, and photographs than in previous years but less coverage in all four categories then men's teams and appeared in extremely disproportionate numbers when it came to their appearance in advertisements (15.5 percent) and multimedia (2.5 percent) (Cooper and Cooper, 2009). Similarly, in a comparison of NCAA Division I baseball and softball websites, softball players received less coverage in and out of season than baseball players, thus marginalizing female athletes (Sagas *et al.*, 2000). These results indicate that digital intercollegiate sport media has yet to close the gap caused by the historic symbolic annihilation of the female athlete in traditional media.

Not only are women in sport symbolically annihilated due to gender, but they (as well as men) can also be marginalized and erased due to sexual identity. One example is illustrated in our research, in which we employed framing theory to examine intercollegiate athletic websites (Calhoun *et al.*, 2011). In this study, 1,855 online biographies of head coaches from NCAA Division I and III websites were coded for textual representations of heteronormativity and heterosexism (e.g. presence or absence of family narratives – meaning we specifically looked for the mention of a wife, spouse, same sex partner, children, and grandchildren). Our "body count" study revealed an overwhelming presence of heteronormative frames and a near absence of explicit LGBT coaches and their families (2/1855 = .01 percent). Based on the data, we also suggested the digital content of intercollegiate athletic department websites reproduce dominant gender ideologies and are plagued with the same overt and subtle homophobia and gender ideologies found in the locker room, on playing field – and we argue, in the digital newsroom as well. In sum, online media outlets both challenge and reproduce dominant gender ideology, as well as help or hinder the advancement of individual athletes or women's sport in general.

Positive potential of digital media

Because of the dearth of positive presentations of women's sport in traditional forms of media, scholars and activists alike have argued for the potential of digital, particularly social, media to fill the gap (Hardin, 2009). That is, female athletes and women's sports organizations can use digital media to produce transformative visual and textual narratives that increase interest in and respect for women's sport, reconstruct the media landscape, resist sexist backlash, and shift the institutional and ideological control of sport away from men.

Using third-wave feminist ideologies of pluralism, intersectional identity politics, valuing diversity, and reclaiming popular culture, digital media can potentially be utilized and claimed as a site of empowerment for female athletes and as a site where women's sport is valued.

The use of digital media by female athletes (i.e. citizen journalists) also places the agency with them and reduces reliance on gatekeepers in traditional and digital sport media, most of whom are male (Hardin *et al.*, 2012; Lapchick, Moss, Russell and Scearce, 2011), to cover and promote women's sport in legitimate ways. Social media provide a platform to promote and manage one's self-image favorably (Mehdizadeh, 2010) as well as develop and maintain personal and professional relationships. Social media also deliver immediate, real-time, direct access for fans that transcends space, time, and geography (McCarthy, 2013). Finally, digital media offer a cost effective and accessible way to market and promote one's brand and create social change through viral messaging, but their use is not unproblematic.

Negative potential of digital media

While digital media holds great potential for female athletes and women's sport, it may also be wrought with negative consequences. Consuming and creating digital media requires access and resources, which creates inequalities. Digital media is an "opt in" space where consumers of women's sport purposely seek out and find the content they desire, but consumers may not know where to find it. Conversely, digital media provides a space for unmediated content and sexist, homophobic, and misogynistic backlash to flourish (Lisec and McDonald, 2012). This was evident in racist and sexist tweets about 2012 Olympic all-around gymnastics champion Gabby Douglas's "unkempt hair" (McEwen, 2012).

To use digital media effectively and to write about, market, and promote women's sport or one's self requires knowledge and skill. Recent research suggests that women are more savvy users of social media, and post more mature content then men (Madden, 2012). Notwithstanding, female athletes must explicitly be taught how to employ such skills in order to best increase respect for and interest in themselves and their sport. Ineffective use of digital media may include oversharing (Agger, 2012), and female athletes may inadvertently contribute to annihilistic practices (e.g. post or share nude or semi-nude photos, focus on femininity over athleticism) that may help them personally gain visibility, promote their brand, and secure sponsorships, but do little to advance women's sport. Such practices also communicate to young girls that physical appearance is more important than athletic performance, which can have detrimental effects (Daniels and LaVoi, 2013). Without digital media training, athletes may inadvertently produce content that causes controversy and trouble for themselves, their team, or their nation and contribute to symbolic annihilism.

For example, days before the 2012 London Olympic Games, Greek Olympic triple jumper Voula Papachristou was kicked off her team for a racist tweet about African immigrants' effect on Greece (Whiteside, 2012). A majority of female athletes, along with sport media and marketing professionals have uncritically internalized the belief that sex sells women's sport. Based on recent evidence, this approach is not only ineffective but counterproductive (Antil, Burton and Robinson, 2012; Kane, LaVoi and Fink, 2013; Kane and Maxwell, 2011). An increasing body of evidence demonstrates that diverse demographic groups prefer images of female athleticism compared to images that sexually objectify female athletes (Daniels, 2012; Daniels and Wartena, 2011; Kane and Maxwell, 2011) including female athletes themselves (Kane, LaVoi and Fink, 2013; Krane *et al.*, 2010).

Conclusion

The media landscape is increasingly reliant on digital technologies, and sport is no exception. Digital media and citizen journalists are now a ubiquitous part of the landscape. In this chapter we tried to answer some critical questions: Will annihilistic patterns pertaining to female athletes in traditional sport media be reproduced or challenged? Do digital media hold transformative potential for female athletes and women's sport? Can digital media free female athletes from the tyranny of traditional media that limit their potential and make it difficult for them and their particular sports to be respected?

Despite the hope and transformative potential digital media provides for challenging male hegemony and traditional gender ideologies in sport media, some data are limited or equivocal, while other data do not look promising (Hardin, 2009, 2011; Hardin *et al.*, 2012). The positive aspects and potential downsides of digital media for female athletes were also offered. Sport research that employs critical theory to digital media is needed. We conclude that research utilizing the gender-sport-digital media triad is scarce, but based on emerging data, old patterns of media representations that symbolically annihilate female athletes are being reproduced in "new" media.

Notes

1. Title IX, signed into law in 1972, prohibits discrimination based on sex in access to educational opportunities that are supported at least in part by federal government funding. This includes access to sports-related programs and activities.
2. We acknowledge Web 2.0 is itself a contested term, see Allen (2013).

References

Agger, B. (2012) *Oversharing: Presentations of Self in the Internet Age.* New York: Routledge.

Allen, M. (2013) What was Web 2.0? Versions as the dominant mode of internet history. *New Media Society,* 15(2), 260–275. doi: 10.1177/1461444812451567

Antil, J. H., Burton, E. and Robinson, M. (2012) Exploring the challenges facing female athletes as endorsers. *Journal of Brand Strategy,* 1(3), 292–307.

Billings, A. C. (2011) *Sports Media: Transformation, Integration, Consumption.* Hoboken, NJ: Taylor & Francis.

Calhoun, A. S., LaVoi, N. M. and Johnson, A. (2011) Framing with family: Examining online coaching biographies for heteronormative and heterosexist narratives. *International Journal of Sport Communication,* 4(3), 300–316.

Clavio, G. and Eagleman, A. N. (2011) Gender and sexually suggestive images in sports blogs. *Journal of Sport Management,* 7, 295–304.

Cooky, C., Messner, M. A. and Hextrum, R. H. (2013) Women play sports, but not on TV: A longitudinal study of televised news. *Communication and Sport.* Advance online publication. doi: 10.1177/2167479513476947

Cooper, C. G. and Cooper, B. D. (2009) NCAA website coverage: Do athletic departments provide equitable gender coverage on their athletic home Web pages? *The Sport Journal,* 12(2). Retrieved from http://www.thesportjournal.org/article/ncaa-website-coverage-do-athletic-departments-provide-equitable-gender-coverage-their-athlet

Daniels, E. A. (2012) Sexy versus strong: What girls and women think of female athletes. *Journal of Applied Developmental Psychology,* 33(2), 79–90.

Daniels, E. A. and LaVoi, N. M. (2013) Athletics as solution and problem: Sports participation for girls and the sexualization of women athletes. In E. Zurbriggen and T. Roberts (eds), *The Sexualization of Girls and Girlhood: Causes, Consequences, and Resistance* (pp. 63–83). New York: Oxford University Press.

Daniels, E. and Wartena, H. (2011) Athlete or sex symbol: What boys think of media representations of female athletes. *Sex Roles,* 65, 566–579.

Deuze, M., Bruns, A. and Neuberger, C. (2007) Preparing for an age of participatory news. *Journalism Practice,* 1(3), 322–338.

Duncan, M. C. (1990) Sports photographs and sexual difference: Images of women and men in the 1984 and 1988 Olympic Games. *Sociology of Sport Journal,* 7, 22–43.

Durrett, R. (2009, July 5) Athletes, teams, fans embrace social networking. *The Dallas Morning News.* Retrieved from http://www.5wpr.net/?p=1906

Flew, T. (2008) *New media: An introduction* (3rd edn.). South Melbourne, Australia: Oxford University Press.

Fried, I. (2010, February 5) Olympics to athletes: Go ahead and tweet. *CNET News.* Retrieved from http://news.cnet.com/8301-13860_3-10448256-56.html

Gantz, W. (2011) Keeping score: Reflections and suggestions for scholarship in sports and media. In A. C. Billings (ed.), *Sports Media: Transformation, Integration, Consumption* (pp. 7–18). Hoboken, NJ: Taylor & Francis.

Hardin, M. (2009, Sept. 24) Does "new media" bring new attitudes towards women's sports? *Tucker Center.* Retrieved from http://tuckercenter.wordpress.com/2009/09/24/does-%E2%80%98new-media%E2%80%99-bring-new-attitudes-oward-women%E2%80%99s-sports/

Hardin, M. (2011) The power of a fragmented collective: Radical pluralist feminism and technologies of the self in the sports blogosphere. In A. C. Billings (ed.), *Sports Media: Transformation, Integration, Consumption* (pp. 40–60). Hoboken, NJ: Taylor & Francis.

Hardin, M., Zhong, B. and Corrigan, T. F. (2012) The funhouse mirror: The blogosphere's reflection. In T. Dumova and R. Fiordo (eds), *Blogging in the Global Society: Cultural, Political and Geographical Aspects* (pp. 55–71). Hershey, PA: IGI Global.

Ioakimidis, M. (2010) Online marketing of professional sport clubs: Engaging fans on a new playing field. *International Journal of Sports Marketing and Sponsorship*, 12, 271–282.

Jenkins, H. (2004) The cultural logic of media convergence. *International Journal of Cultural Studies*, 7(1), 33–43.

Jhally, S. (1989) Media sports, culture and power: Critical issues in the communication of sport. In L. A. Wenner (ed.), *Media, Sports, and Society: Research on the Communication of Sport* (pp. 70–93). Thousand Oaks, CA: Sage.

Jones, D. (2006) The representation of female athletes in online images of successive Olympic Games. *Pacific Journalism Review*, 12(1), 108–129.

Jones, D. (2004) Half the story? Olympic women on ABC *News Online*. *Media International Australia*, 110, 132–146.

Kane, M. J. (1988) Media coverage of the female athlete before, during and after Title IX: Sports Illustrated revisited. *Journal of Sport Management*, 2, 87–99.

Kane, M. J. and Buysse, J. M. (2005) Intercollegiate media guides as contested terrain: A longitudinal analysis. *Sociology of Sport Journal*, 22, 214–238.

Kane, M. J., LaVoi, N. M. and Fink, J. (2013) Exploring elite female athletes' interpretations of sport media photographs: A window into the construction of social identity and 'selling sex' in women's sports, *Communication and Sports*. doi: 10.1177/2167479512473585

Kane, M. and Lenskyj, H. (1998) Media treatment of female athletes: Issues of gender and sexualities. In L. A. Wenner (ed.), *MediaSport* (pp. 187–201). London: Routledge.

Kane, M. J. and Maxwell, H. (2011) Expanding the boundaries of sport media research: Using critical theory to explore consumer responses to representations of women's sports. *Journal of Sport Management*, 25(3), 202–216.

Kachgal, T. M. (2001) *Home Court Disadvantage? Examining the Coverage of Female Athletes on Leading Sports Websites: A Pilot Study*. National Convention of the Association for Education in Journalism and Mass Communication, Washington, DC. Retrieved from http://list.msu.edu/cgi-bin/wa?A2=ind0109a&L=aejmc&T=0&m=2290&P=10851

Kian, E. M. (2008) A study of *The New York Times* and *USA Today* articles on college basketball counters the gender-specific stereotypes found in previous studies on television commentary of March Madness. *Newspaper Research Journal*, 29(3), 38–49.

Kian, E. M., Mondello, M. and Vincent, J. (2009) ESPN: The women's sports network? A content analysis of Internet coverage of March Madness. *Journal of Broadcasting and Electronic Media*, 53(3), 477–495.

Kian, E. M., Vincent, J. and Mondello, M. (2008) Masculine hegemonic hoops: An analysis of media coverage of March Madness. *Sociology of Sport Journal*, 25, 223–242.

Krane, V., Ross, S. R., Miller, M., Rowse, J. L., Ganoie, K., Andrzejczyk, J. A. and Lucas, C. B. (2010) Power and focus: Self-representation of female college athletes. *Qualitative Research in Sport and Exercise*, 2(2), 175–195.

Lapchick, R., Moss, A., Russell, C. and Scearce, R. (2011) The 2010–11 Associated Press Sports Editors Racial and Gender Report Card. *The Institute for Diversity and Ethics in Sport (TIDES)*. Retrieved on August 24, 2011 from http://www.tidesport.org/RGRC/2011/2011_APSE_RGRC_FINAL.pdf

LaVoi, N. M. (2009) Occupational sex segregation in a youth soccer organization: Females in positions of power. *Women in Sport and Physical Activity Journal*, 18(2), 25–37.

Lisec, J. and McDonald M. (2012) Gender inequality in the new millennium: An analysis of WNBA representations in sport blogs. *Journal of Sports Media*, 7(2), 153–178.

Lenskyj, H. J. (2006) Alternative media versus the Olympic industry. In A. A. Raney and J. Bryant (eds), *Handbook of Sports and Media* (pp. 205–230). Mahwah, NJ: Lawrence Erlbaum Associates.

Lievrouw, L. A. and Livingstone, S. (2006) Introduction to the updated student edition. In L. A. Lievrouw and S. Livingstone (eds), *Handbook of New Media: Social Shaping and Social Consequences of ICTs* (pp. 1–14). London: Sage.

McCarthy, B. (2012) A sport journalism of their own: An investigation into the motivations, behaviors, and media attitudes of fan sports bloggers. *Communication and Sport*. doi: 10.1177/2167479512469943

MacKay, S. and Dallaire, C. (2013) Skirtboarder net-a-narratives: Young women creating their own skateboarding (re)presentations. *International Review for the Sociology of Sport*, 48, 171–195.

Madden, M. (2012, February 24) Privacy management on social media sites. *Pew Research Center's Internet and American Life Project*. Retrieved from http://pewinternet.org/Reports/2012/Privacy-management-on-social-media.aspx

Mandiberg, M. (2012) *The Social Media Reader*. New York: New York University Press.

Matheson, D. (2004) Negotiating claims to journalism: Webloggers orientation to news genres. *Convergence*, 10(4), 33–54.

McEwen, L. (2012, September 6) Gabby Douglas and her ponytail: What's all the fuss about? *The Washington Post*. Retrieved from http://www.washingtonpost.com/blogs/therootdc/post/gabby-douglas-and-her-ponytail-whats-all-the-fuss-about/2012/08/02/gJQAZiFZRX_blog.html#

Mehdizadeh, S. (2010) Self-presentation 2.0: Narcissism and self-esteem on Facebook. *Cyberpsychology, Behavior, and Social Networking*, 13(4), 357–364.

Messner, M. (1988) Sports and male domination: The female athlete as contested ideological terrain. *Sociology of Sport Journal*, 5, 197–211.

Messner, M. (2002) *Taking the Field: Women, Men and Sports*. Minneapolis, MN: University of Minnesota Press.

Nielsen. (2012, September 11) *State of the Media: Cross-Platform Report Q1 2012*. Retrieved from http://www.nielsen.com/us/en/insights/reports-downloads/2012/state-of-the-media – cross-platform-report-q1-2012.html

Pegoraro, A. (2010) Look who's talking – Athletes on Twitter: A case study. *International Journal of Sport Communication*, 3, 501–514.

Rosen, J. (2006) The people formerly known as the audience. *Press Think*. Retrieved from http://archive.pressthink.org/2006/06/27/ppl_frmr.html

Sagas, M., Cunningham, G. B., Wigley, B. J. and Asley, F. B. (2000) Internet coverage of university softball and baseball websites: The inequity continues. *Sociology of Sport Journal*, 17, 198–205.

Sanderson, J. (2009) Professional athletes' shrinking privacy boundaries: Fans, information and communication technologies, and athlete monitoring. *International Journal of Sport Communication*, 2, 240–256.

Sanderson, J. (2011) *It's a Whole New Ball Game: How Social Media is Changing Sports*. New York: Hampton Press.

Sanderson, J. and Kassing, J. W. (2011) Tweets and blogs: Transformative, adversarial, and integrative developments in sports media. In A. C. Billings (ed.), *Sports Media: Transformation, Integration, Consumption* (pp. 114–127). New York: Routledge.

Smith, L (2011) The less you say: An initial study of gender coverage in sports on Twitter. In A. C. Billings (ed.), *Sports Media: Transformation, Integration, Consumption* (pp. 162–180). New York: Routledge.

Tuchman, G. (1978) Introduction: The symbolic annihilation of women by the mass media. In G. Tuchman, A. Daniels and J. Benet (eds), *Hearth and Home*. New York: Oxford University Press.

Tuchman, G. (2012) *Edging Women Out: Victorian Novelists, Publishers and Social Change*. New York: Routledge.

Wallace, L., Wilson, J. and Miloch, K. (2011) Sporting Facebook: A content analysis of NCAA organizational sport pages and Big 12 conference athletic department pages. *International Journal of Sport Communication*, 4, 422–444.

Wikipedia (2012a) *Facebook*. Retrieved http://en.wikipedia.org/wiki/Facebook

Wikipedia (2012b) *Twitter*. Retrieved from http://en.wikipedia.org/wiki/Twitter

Wilson, B. (2007) New media, social movements, and global sport studies: A revolutionary moment and the sociology of sport. *Sociology of Sport Journal*, 24, 457–477.

Whiteside, K. (2012, July 26) Athlete's Olympic dismissal provides tough Twitter lessons. *USA Today.com*. Retrieved from http://usatoday30.usatoday.com/sports/olympics/london/story/2012-07-25/voula-papachristou-twitter-controversy/56493852/1

Winston, B. (1998) *Media, Technology and Society: A History from the Telegraph to the Internet*. London: Routledge.

29

SPORT WEBSITES, EMBEDDED DISCURSIVE ACTION, AND THE GENDERED REPRODUCTION OF SPORT

Lindsey J. Meân

ARIZONA STATE UNIVERSITY

Sport is a powerful cultural site for the construction of significant fundamental identities and discourses. Amongst these, gender, sexuality and race are notable social categories and forms of knowledge and understandings that are both embedded in and arise from sport as a social and cultural site. Since sport is now predominantly consumed as media by mass audiences and dedicated fans, sport-media (or rather its producers) effectively serve as powerful gatekeepers of the meanings, understandings, and memberships of the categories of sport that have implications for wider society. Essentially sport-media has become influential in the construction and reproduction of key socio-cultural formations such as gender. It is therefore problematic that mainstream sport-media continues to produce and reproduce (re/produce) discourses that value and privilege traditional white, hypermasculine, heterosexualized male formations. Indeed the cultural familiarity and naturalization of gendered and racialized sport-media representational practices comprises a significant element of the processes through which their impact, power, and wider social significance remain invisible and deniable (Foucault, 1972). However, the recent rise of digital sport-media as a pivotal form of mass consumption has added new dimensions within which the impact of sport, sport-media, and the gendered practices embedded within these formations need to be understood and scrutinized.

Networked digital media, like websites, has changed the consumption of sport-media (Hutchins, Rowe and Ruddock, 2009; Rowe, Ruddock and Hutchins, 2010). Sport is now widely consumed as digital media, undercutting the dominance of traditional broadcast sport-media. In fact websites have themselves become naturalized as central, familiar, and routine sites of sport-media consumption, progressively influencing and guiding sport fan practices (Rowe *et al.*, 2010). This is significant because many consider websites to be more persuasive than traditional media (e.g. Graham and Hearn, 2001) and sports fans are considered especially vulnerable or subject to sport-media content (Scherer, 2007; Wenner, 1991). As such digital media are viewed as offering great potential to transform sport and its consumption, including offering greater diversity within communities of sport (e.g. Crawford, 2004), or to perpetuate existing power formations.

However most widely consumed digital sport-media is still produced by the traditional sport-media authorities, such as *ESPN*, and authoritative sport organizations and regulators, (such as the NFL, MLB, W/NBA, and socio-cultural and economic powerhouses like the Fédération Internationale de Football, FIFA (e.g. Leonard, 2009). This means that the re/production of sport as a white, heterosexual, male discourse has continued in digital sport-media and enabled the ideologically oriented, mediatized, and market-driven content and discourses of sport to be easily and directly accessed by large global audiences. In fact the multi-platform, self-referentiality of digital sport-media has been observed to have narrowed the range of discourses readily made available for consumption by audiences, further privileging traditional sporting discourses of white, heterosexual, hypermasculinity (Meân, 2010; Oates, 2009). Consequently websites and/or their producers should be understood as powerful gate-keepers of the significant identities, definitions, and understandings that permeate sport – impacting sport audiences and wider cultural formations.

In light of this, many scholars are concerned with the persuasive potential of the gendered content and representational practices that comprise sport websites. This concern is not simply because of the primacy of websites as sport-media, or the susceptibility of sports audi-ences/fans, but because of the subtle and implicit ways that meanings, identities and ideologies are embedded and reified in the production and consumption of digital sport-media given its unique characteristics. While the persuasive characteristics of websites and their consumption are generally well known, it is useful to briefly revisit these underlying features to emphasize why these are so potentially pernicious on sport websites and for sport audiences. However, the persuasiveness of sport-media, and websites in particular, needs to be understood as related to the ways in which the sporting reality they represent is convincing and naturalized.

Digital websites as persuasive, gendered sport media

Accessibility to online technologies has grown globally, shifting fan practices and patterns of consumption (Boyle and Whannel, 2010; Hutchins *et al.*, 2009; Rowe *et al.*, 2010). All media is actively rather than passively consumed, but digital media is engaged with in a different way and its actions are discursively distinct from traditional media. Essentially digital media have the ability to persuasively construct meanings because they are *social action* (Graham and Hearn, 2001; Gray, Sandvoss and Harrington, 2007). Further they have an artifice of user control; that is, consumers perceive they have control, while their consumption is in fact powerfully guided. Digital media have also blurred the boundaries between sport-media producers and audiences (Leonard, 2009), creating an illusion of participation and democratization (Graham and Hearn, 2001) that enables consumers to perform valued sporting identities despite this participation being limited and guided (Meân, 2011, 2012). The provision of easy and instant connections to other platforms or networked digital media like other websites, Twitter, Facebook, email, etc., facilitate the performance of identity and fandom in ways that are highly valued by sport fans (Rowe *et al.*, 2010).

Since sports audiences and fans are noted to be especially vulnerable to sport-media content (Scherer, 2007; Wenner, 1991), this combination of identity performance, apparent control and choice over dynamic multi-media content and participation alongside the naturalization of digital sport-media as consumption renders websites more than merely persuasive media. Consequently, the underlying definitions, identities, meanings and practices re/produced by sport websites have significant socio-political and ideological cultural action and implications. The power of sport websites to both re/produce or disrupt established discourses and practices is emphasized by many scholars (e.g. Crawford, 2004; Hutchins *et al.*, 2009; Meân, 2010; Oates,

2009; Rowe *et al.*, 2010). Similarly, research into promotional and branding opportunities confirms the persuasive potential of sport websites and other digital media (e.g. Chun, Gentry and McGinnis, 2005; Hur, Ko and Valacich, 2011; Scherer, 2007; Suh and Pedersen, 2010; Zhang and Won, 2010). But promotional content, branding, sport identities, and fandom are increasingly inextricable, as many websites and digitally mediated fan communities are built and maintained as part of international marketing strategies (Horne, 2006); marketing strategies that typically remain traditionally gendered despite increasing efforts to grow sport audiences by including women. Indeed analysis of *espnW.com* when it was launched in 2011 observed both traditional feminization and an emphasis on promotional content due to its primary focus on "brand management" and "profit maximization" for the Walt Disney Corporation (Wolter, 2012: 2). *EspnW.com* was also observed to emphasize women's bodies and lives as a project, a familiar aspect of the traditional female media genre of women's magazines.

The slippage and tension between gendered practices and women as the target of sport branding and marketing is evident in recent promotional strategies and newer sport-media. For example, the NFL's support of breast cancer awareness (a substantive amount of which was promoted via digital media) has been viewed as a strategy to promote the NFL and its merchandize to women, with a mere 5 percent of sales going to the American Cancer Society (huffingtonpost.com, 2012). Of course it is contentious to criticize the support of such worthy causes, but there are two easy points to be made. First, if the NFL really wanted to address a significant cancer health issue, raising awareness about testicular cancer and the need for young men to get screened would be a good match to its established audience. Second, women are increasingly being constructed as interested in, and marketable to, in ways that are less about charity and health and more about capturing audiences and constructing them in traditionally gendered ways. This was evident at *WNBA.com* in 2010 when breast cancer was used as the first (primary) theme provided for invited postings (Meân, 2012). This prioritizing of breast cancer over sport was one element amongst many that constructed the fans/users within traditionally feminized discourses, minimizing their sport fan identities and interests and positioning them outside the category of sport.

Posting opportunities are highly valued by many fans but provide content that guide, frame and construct users. In a September 2010 comparative analysis of *WNBA.com* and *NBA.com*, obvious asymmetry in the formalized posting opportunities was observed (Meân, 2012). The primary feminized breast cancer posting theme (noted above) of "Her Story" at *WNBA.com* did not have an equivalent topic at *NBA.com*. The second posting of "Dads And Daughters" re/produced the tradition and privilege of fathers, rather than mothers, as the sport fan initiators of children. But an equivalent Dads and Sons post was not evident at *NBA.com*, perpetuating women's sports as the site for family. On September 22, 2010, the lack of fan postings for these two opportunities (Her Story: 8 threads, 25 posts; Dads And Daughters: 7 threads, 92 posts) could be used to suggest lack of interest (either confirming women's lack of interest in sport or women basketball's lack of interest for fans). But the 1,757 threads and 32,415 posts under the fourth opportunity "All Other Discussion: Can't find a topic that fits?" suggest users/fans were looking for something different to the feminized framing of them embedded in the website topics. Instead they created their own posts to perform the sorts of traditional (male) forms of fandom female sports fans typically value (Ben-Porat, 2009; Mewett and Toffoletti, 2011).

Evidence indicates that good opportunities to post make websites enjoyable to sport fans, making their absence problematic for the success of websites and building loyalty (Hur *et al.*, 2011; Suh and Pedersen, 2010). Embedding such fundamentally gendered practices in the production of sport-media websites aimed at women or about women's sport may then make them less successful or more likely to fail (Meân, 2012), and certainly suggests they are constructed as not of interest to *real* male sports fans. This is further evident in the production of sport websites designed for women, like *espnW.com*, whose very creation reveals the default assumption that standard sport websites, like *ESPN*'s website *espn.go.com*, are for men and about men. In *espnW.com*'s claim to be "A voice for the woman who loves sport" the lack of voice for women at sites like *espn.go.com* becomes exposed by its very producers. But even more problematic is the conflation and construction of women as the only audience for women's sport (rather than sport fans) and as primarily interested in women's sport (rather than men's sport or sport generally).

For critical scholars the perpetuation of such gendered practices and understandings is especially problematic given the authoritative and influential positioning of ESPN as the most used American dedicated sport-media website and self-proclaimed "Worldwide Leader In Sports." But also as the provider of a network of integrated and highly self-referential sport-media platforms across which sport and non-sport content is shared and users guided (Meân, 2011). Of course the discursive content and self-referential marketing practices deployed on the websites of the powerful sport authorities (like ESPN, NFL, NBA and FIFA) are significant elements of the processes through which they re/produce their own authority (Dart, 2009; Meân, 2010, 2011; Oates, 2009). This in turn compounds their substantive influence of over normative, everyday understandings about gender and sexuality (Meân, 2010, 2011, 2012; Oates, 2009) as well as race, capitalism and neo-liberal discourses (Oates, 2009; Wolter, 2012).

Consequently a gendered analysis of sport websites is not simply about the comparative amount and relative positioning of male or female content, or the language choices, narratives, and visual images used to represent men's and women's sport. Equally it is not simply about availability because dedicated female sport-media websites, like *espnW.com* and *WNBA.com*, actually raise a conundrum since although they increase women's representation in sport, female sport is largely consigned to feminized websites constructed for female audiences. This continues to conflate women's sport and fandom but also constructs it as a special category, hence still peripheral in the wider category of sport.

Analysis should also emphasize the implicit and covert construction of gendered knowledge, guided interest, and audiences to observe the subtle characteristics of ideologically oriented gender constructions. Actions that are embedded in elements that reflect production values that privilege, spectacularize, and guide consumption of some content over others, such as (multi) media provision, dynamic production techniques (e.g. active, rotating images), provision of live links and "expert" content, inclusion and positioning in menu hierarchies, invitations to participate and comment (Meân, 2011).

Analyzing sport websites

The plethora of content and media formats on websites can make them appear unwieldy and overwhelming to analyze. As for traditional sport-media, the symbolic and cultural formations re/produced within the visual images and language choices of sport websites offer consistent and powerful data about category construction, dominant definitions, and prominent discourses and underlying ideological formations. Continued attention to the language choices, narratives, accounts, descriptions, details, and photographic images well evidenced in traditional sport-media forms is therefore warranted (e.g. Denham, Billings and Halone, 2002; Butterworth, 2008; Duncan and Messner, 1998), especially given the potential of digital media as a highly influential emerging form (Boyle and Whannel, 2010; Leonard, 2009). But subtle and implicit gendered constructions within the discursive action of sport websites increasingly need to be considered; this requires systematic attention to configured guiding features that effectively reveal hierarchies embedded in the text, such as menus and posting opportunities.

Size, placement and dynamism

On websites, the size/length and placement of an item construct importance and status. Whether and where the item is positioned on the homepage, in the premium position of the main "window" (on-screen) or displaced to secondary status as a "scroll down" item. That is, does the user have to scroll down to see and consume the item? Similarly, positioning and provision of a live link, or multiple live links (repetition), on the homepage function to re/produce status and newsworthiness. As such these features construct items as salient for sport consumers/fans, increasing the likelihood of consumption and the understanding of the content as news and newsworthy. Obviously content in such a premium position (notably on the homepage) is privileged as prioritized news, and the user is being guided to consume it. Typically, the home page (including scroll-down content) is dominated by men's sport and male experts (e.g. Meân, 2010, 2011). But website technology also enables both multi-media and animation, features that frame content in additional ways.

Digital technology means that websites can have multiple (rotating) headline stories, offering the appearance of substantive "news" framed as spectacular and/or newsworthy in ways that also attract readers to guide selection. Simultaneously an illusion of interaction and user control is provided as users get to select which news (if any) to consume. For example, in 2010 *espn.go.com*'s homepage was noted to enable four headline articles to share priority placement using a combination of animated production techniques to guide consumption and increase the perception of choice and control while simultaneously constructing the specific items and *espn.go.com* generally as action-packed (Meân, 2011). All four headlines were about men's sport and/or male athletes. Of course, the further from the homepage the user travels, the less central the sport or athletes, which is where most of the women's sports coverage is located. This lack of centrality and interest is further echoed in less dynamic technical production, re/producing the sport and athletes as less interesting and exciting, simultaneously framing and confirming their peripheral status within the category of sport. Similarly, an analysis of *FIFA.com* revealed that women's soccer was re/produced using far less dynamic technical production compared to men's soccer (Meân, 2010). Instead women's soccer news was represented using a narrow range of static media formats that echoed the static, unexciting images of the women's sporting news and action. In combination with content that was old and out-of-date, women's soccer was framed as uneventful and lacking in dynamic action and newsworthiness.

Consequently, the technological options deployed to put sport into action can be seen to be indicative of underlying gendered ideologies that impact production values, which in turn re/produce men's sport as dynamic, spectacular, action-oriented, eventful and newsworthy and women's sport as lacking in these. This is also evident in the greater provision of multi-media content for men's sport, content associated with higher production values even if equal space is given to men's and women's sport content. For example, Cooper and Cooper's (2009) analysis of thirty NCAA 1-A website homepages across four sport seasons measured square inches of screen but also recorded scroll versus non-scroll positioning and discriminated between multimedia, photos, and text articles. Their analysis revealed much less disproportionate gendered coverage compared to other studies with men's sport getting 60 percent of article coverage versus 40 percent for women. But attention to different formats revealed men's sport received 78.1 percent to women's 21.9 percent of the multi-media coverage associated with higher production values that frame content as more dynamic, interesting, and action-oriented compared to other media formats. This disparity, and its apparent privileging of men's sport over women's, would have been hidden if the data were collapsed or these media formats were never distinguished in the initial process of analysis. Attention to specific sports also allowed the authors to note that, in terms of their criteria, men's and women's basketball were treated equivalently.

Menus and repetition: Guiding hierarchies

Within websites, webpages exist as hierarchies of space through which users navigate in guided ways by menus and other live links to expand content to associated texts and multi-media formats. Menus are indicative of what is prioritized and privileged within a website and how the sport is being constructed for the audience. Menus are therefore key features that provide apparent choices to users, but simultaneously guide consumption, offering fans hierarchically listed categories with which to interact. The content of menus (i.e. items on the menu and their inclusion or exclusion), their order, and the placement of the menu on the webpage relative to other offerings all serve to re/produce underlying discourses and definitions held by the producers about sport and the users for whom it is being commodified.

As such inclusion and position in a menu is significant, especially in relation to where the menu itself is placed (e.g. horizontally across the top of the screen versus vertically bottom right in scroll-down space). Equally inclusion on a drop-down menu rather than as a permanently viewable menu item has relevancy. Menus as guides to consumption are very significant given that sport audiences are built and maintained by sport media rather than existing a priori (Duncan and Messner, 1998). Consequently in the 2010 comparative analysis of *NBA.com* and *WNBA.com* the high priority positioning of the *NBA* logo (placement, size, color) and priority menu positioning of the link to the *NBA* website at *WNBA.com* suggests the users of the women's site were constructed as potentially interested in the men's sport (Meân, 2012). However, the lack of similar status in the reciprocal positioning of *WNBA.com* links at *NBA.com* fails to construct *NBA.com* users as interested in women's basketball. This privileging of the male game and audience at *WNBA.com* re/produced the male game as standard, while the positioning of the link to the women's website and lack of audience building at *NBA.com* perpetuates smaller audiences for the women's game. Such gendered asymmetry in discursive action is not only discrepant but problematic, revealing the maintained peripheralization of women's sport.

There are a number of more subtle ways that production values and provisions construct webpages and the sports they represent as action-packed and news-making – or not. For example, websites can provide multiple opportunities and invitations to consume the same content in different ways in different areas of the same page, re-offering hyperlinks, menu options, and news in ways that guide users to the same content. This repetition, observed at *espn.go.com* (Meân, 2011), not only increases the likelihood of user selection but functions to construct the content as important, while the familiarity and repetition may also guide users to consume that content. Such repetition, multiple opportunities, and multiple hyperlinks also contribute to the appearance or illusion of content on a webpage, potentially making it appear more eventful and action-packed than it actually is (as the content is repetitive rather than varied). Similarly, elements such as content turnover, up-dated news, RSS-links, and opportunities to share can all be seen as ways in which perceptions of action, eventfulness, and newsworthiness are constructed, which in turn re/produce the website itself as useful and as an informative sport authority. As such the provision or absence of updating options, such as RSS links, is relevant to the construction of newsworthiness and fan interest – especially as they connect to the performance of fandom. So it is interesting to note that while the *WNBA.com* did not offer an RSS link in 2010 and *NBA.com* did (Meân, 2012), a recent check on *WNBA.com* (March, 2013) noted that an RSS link was now available.

Choice, control, and participation

Of the elements that make websites compelling and persuasive, perceptions of choice, control and participation are paramount as users appear to choose how to navigate through the website, select what content and what media formats to specifically consume, and participate in invited posts and discussions. The apparent ease with which websites can and are expected to provide up-to-date content and breaking news that users can self-select for consumption are significant elements of website usage, alongside their value as repositories of archived content. Basically websites enable users to repeat view spectacular action-packed visual and audio content previously limited to broadcast media on their own schedule. But they can also access content that offers the detail and depth of analysis typically found in print journalism. In addition many sport websites offer increased opportunities to 'personalize' homepage content (e.g. *espn.go.com*) to represent the users' sport preferences although while this may change the hierarchical order, it does not actually change content. Users can also watch or read content over and over again, as for print media, but often in multimedia formats. These things all add to the persuasive power of websites for highly identified, susceptible sports audiences. Nonetheless, it is the opportunity to comment on webpages and share or comment via media links (e.g. email, twitter, facebook) that are especially are highly valued and compelling for many sport fans; compelling because simultaneously disseminating content and interacting with others via sport talk are significant aspects of performing and constructing sport fan identities (e.g. Rowe *et al.*, 2010).

Not surprisingly then, sport websites with more of these apparent options have been found to be highly satisfying and enjoyable for sport media consumers, increasing loyalty and likelihood of future usage (Hur *et al.*, 2011; Suh and Pedersen, 2010). This suggests that sport website consumption can be powerfully guided by available options and invitations to participate, irrespective of whether they are illusory or real, making the embedded content of these opportunities potentially highly influential on communities of sports fans. Accordingly, invitations and opportunities to interact, participate and/or create content are interesting elements for analysis if researchers pay attention to what is really being offered and enacted. In an example noted earlier, starkly different posting opportunities at *WNBA.com* in 2010 guided and constructed website users/fans as outside the category of proper (i.e. male) sport fans compared to those offered at *NBA.com* (Meân, 2012). Such gendered discursive practices construct gender as a prominent aspect of the definition of sport fan and framings the practices of fandom and sport identity as male.

However, exploring the content and action within postings can reveal interesting insights into fan practices, responses and reactions (e.g. Rowe *et al.*, 2010). For example, Sanderson (2010) analyzed fan responses to commentary about race and discrimination in response to comments by a prominent African American athlete about a news story concerning the selection of a white coach over an African American coach. Findings revealed a number of strategies used by sports fans to manage the story and while there were posts that acknowledged sporting racisms, there was a strong element of overt racism, racist insults, and hostility toward those who claimed sport to be racist. The content of posts are therefore revealing about understandings, definitions, meaning making, identity work and ideological responses to threat, criticism and social issues in sport. They are also useful for exploring interactivity and interconnectivity amongst fans, irrespective of whether it is good, bad, positive, negative, or indifferent. Nonetheless what is evident is that it is the anonymity offered by website participation that is what really enables sports fans to make statements and claims that they possibly would censor in other contexts. But anonymity offers women the opportunity to participate in sport discussion and fan identity work in ways that can level the field as the problematic female categorization can be avoided, undermining gendered interpretations and responses to women's sport identity performances.

Nonetheless, the extent to which websites are really participatory, interactive, and driven by fan-produced content is a significant element for consideration. While posting might be available to everybody with adequate technology, websites' posts may be edited, managed, and even removed by site managers. But content can also be represented as fan-produced when it is not, especially given the anonymity. Websites and similar digital media offer the opportunity for sport-media producers to effectively manipulate and produce fake fan/user contributions, potentially posing as users to post controversial statements that instigate more user posting and participation. The blurring of these boundaries was evidenced in the 2006 FIFA World Cup production of fan participation blogs and stories that were actually written by professional journalists, an action that was argued to transform the democratizing potential of these blogs into a corporate platform (Dart, 2009).

Producers as consumers

Websites, like all sport-media, are produced by people. As such sport website content and practices reflect the identities, discourses, and ideologies of the people that produce them (Hardin, 2005; Hardin and Whiteside, 2006; Meân, 2010, 2011). To a large extent the continued privileging of traditional white, male sporting forms and discourses on websites is argued to arise because sport media production and sport organizations are dominated by white males (Hardin, 2005; Hardin and Whiteside, 2006; Hardin and Whiteside, 2009). But increasing the diversity of the people who produce sport media is not enough to shift these patterns because power and hegemony mean that people are subject to the discourses from which their identities arise even if they are suppressed and oppressed by the definitions, categories and understandings they themselves re/produce (van Dijk, 1993).

Many women in sport have identities that arise from the same shared masculinized sport discourses, definitions, and practices, meaning that women often manage their sporting identities in complex ways that enact male sport discourses and distance themselves from problematic feminizing categorizations (e.g. Ben-Porat, 2009; Fielding-Lloyd and Meân, 2008; Meân and Kassing, 2008; Mewitt and Toffoletti, 2011). This is in part because to resist and challenge these male sport formations and definitions is to risk losing one's membership in the sport category and potentially undermine one's own sport identity performance (Meân, 2001). This means that sport-media producers may re/produce and privilege white male sport formations, excluding and othering women from the sport category irrespective of their own race and gender. Nonetheless, who produces sport media has significant implications for how sport and its consumers are constructed in and through a number of features of sport websites suggesting stereotypical definitions of femininity are getting in the way of decent digital sport provision for female audiences and/or women's sport (given the conflation of these by sport-media producers noted earlier). Sport-media users are often sophisticated and demanding consumers, which means that sport fans generally may be turned off by feminized media-sport, especially female sport fans resisting feminizing strategies (Meân, 2012). Indeed making women's sport and women's sport fans special and separate categories from mainstream sport-media may accommodate marketing imperatives but it does not achieve the centrality, collaboration, and normalization that effective integration into mainstream sport websites could provide.

This does not necessarily mean that the producers of sport websites intentionally or consciously re/produce traditional, hegemonic discourses and practices. Rather their sporting identities mean that these versions will be constructed as accepted and normalized formations, and challenges to these are likely to be resisted. As such without acceptance and diligence to address the ways in which sport is ideologically oriented, these formations will typically get re/produced as normative and natural, while alternative understandings are ignored or undermined as challenges to established meanings. This is why simply including content, such as women's sport, is not adequate to address and redress the hypermasculine discourses of sport if it is re/produced within the traditional discourses and definitions of its boundaries. Equally, the provision of separate media-sport sites for women has not as yet been a good solution to this problem.

Shifting the emphasis of critical media literacy from consumers to producers is an element that may assist in realizing this level of re/production. Media literacy approaches suggest that consumers need to be active and critical of the media that they consume; especially of networked digital media given its unregulated and unfettered potential. (Albeit that this is also what gives it democratizing potential.) Students are consistently educated to become aware of the ideologies, motivations, and purposes underlying the media texts they consume, while the connection to the actual people that produce the texts is minimized or rendered invisible. However, it can be argued that media producers also need to be held to some notion of media literacy in the content of the media texts they produce. Analyzing underlying constructions and beliefs implicitly embedded in websites (by the text producers), how these re/produce the sport *and* the users of the text (as fans/consumers of sport), and how users understand and collaborate with (or resist) these texts as an interpretive community may contribute to the critical literacy in media production. Of course, this assumes that sport-media producers can be persuaded to attend to such societal concerns given that most are not committed to their audiences, but to their shareholders (Wolter, 2012). However, in the case of women's sport, building male audiences for women's sport and providing female sport fans with good sport-media may make good commercial and business sense. In the meantime, it is relevant to understanding sport-media as a process of both production and consumption within which identities and ideologies are powerful components.

Conclusions

Networked sport websites provide a combination of sport, vulnerable consumers, and technological features that make them highly influential as naturalized but gendered forms of sport-media consumption. The social action of sport websites makes the continued re/production of traditional gendered discourses embedded within the definitions and practices of many sport websites problematic. These include asymmetry in production values and provision that frames women as feminized and outside the main category of sport, re/producing women's sport as substantively less action-packed and newsworthy than men's sport, and women sport fans as less sophisticated than men. As such, provision aimed at female consumers of sport have further naturalized the gendered discourses effectively achieving the segregation rather than integration of women's sport into separate, feminized sport-media. However, it is in part the unique features of sport websites that facilitate a perception of control and participation amongst users while actually guiding consumption and meaning-making that renders them so powerful and persuasive, making them especially pernicious for the highly susceptible sport fans.

But the impact of the gendered sport discourses, identities and ideologies held by the people who produce sport-media websites was also noted as implicated in the representational practices and provision, suggesting that encouraging a greater diversity of people producing sport-media is not a simple solution to redress these practices. Equally, while increased critical literacy in media production might also help redress such gendered practices, the significance of sport websites for branding and marketing for producers of sport-media has to be understood as a primary aspect of their production and provision. It could be argued that the effective capturing of women sport fans and women's sport in mainstream sport-media would be the most effective, long-term marketing strategy of all.

References

Ben-Porat, A. (2009) Not just for men: Israeli women who fancy football. *Soccer and Society*, 10, 883–896.

Boyle, R. and Whannel, G. (2010) Editorial: Sport and the New Media. *Convergence: The International Journal of Research into New Media Technologies*, 16, 259–262.

Butterworth, M. (2008) Fox Sports, Super Bowl XLII, and the affirmation of American civil religion. *Journal of Sport and Social Issues*, 32, 318–323.

Chun, S., Gentry, J. W. and McGinnis, L. P. (2005) Ritual aspects of sports consumption: How do sports fans become ritualized? *Asia Pacific Advances in Consumer Research*, 6, 331–336.

Cooper, C. G. and Cooper, B. D. (2009) NCAA website coverage: Do athletic departments provide equitable gender coverage on their athletic home web pages? *The Sport Journal*, 12(2). Retrieved from http://www.thesportjournal.org/article/ncaa-website-coverage-do-athletic-departments-provide-equi-table-gender-coverage-their-athlet

Crawford, G. (2004) *Consuming Sport: Fans, Sports and Culture*. London: Routledge.

Dart, J. J. (2009) Blogging the 2006 FIFA World Cup Finals. *Sociology of Sport Journal*, 26, 106–126.

Denham, B. E., Billings, A. C. and Halone, K. (2002) Differential accounts of race in broadcast commentary of the 2000 NCAA Men's and Women's Final Four Basketball Tournaments. *Sociology of Sport Journal*, 19, 315–332.

Duncan, M. C. and Messner, M. A. (1998) The media image of sport and gender. In L. A. Wenner (ed.), *MediaSport* (pp. 170–185). New York: Routledge.

Fielding-Lloyd, B. and Meân, L. J. (2008) Standards and separatism: The discursive construction of gender in English football coach education. *Sex Roles*, 58, 24–39.

Foucault, M. (1972) *The Archaeology of Knowledge*, London: Tavistock.

Graham, P. and Hearn, G. (2001) The coming of post-reflexive society: Commodification and language in digital capitalism. *Media International Australia Incorporating Culture and Policy*, 98, 79–90.

Gray, J., Sandvoss, C. and Harrington, C. L. (eds) (2007) *Fandom: Identities and communities in a mediated world*. New York: New York University Press.

Hardin, M. (2005) Stopped at the gate: Women's sports, "reader interest", and decision making by editors. *Journalism and Mass Communication Quarterly*, 82, 62–77.

Hardin, M. and Whiteside, E. A. (2006) Fewer women, minorities work in sports departments. *Newspaper Research Journal*, 27, 38–51.

Hardin, M. and Whiteside, E. A. (2009) Token responses to gendered newsrooms: Factors in the career-related decisions of female newspaper sport journalists. *Journalism*, 10, 627–646.

Horne, J. (2006) *Sport in consumer culture*. Basingstoke: Palgrave Macmillan.

Huffingtonpost.com (October 12, 2012) *Breast cancer awareness month NFL campaign gives just 5% to charity.* http:// huffingtonpost.com/2012/10/12/nfl-breast-cancer-pink-campaign_n_1961307.html

Hur, Y., Ko, Y. J. and Valacich, J. (2011) A structural model of the relationship between sport website quality, E-satisfaction, and E-loyalty. *Journal of Sport Management*, 25, 458–473.

Hutchins, B., Rowe, D. and Ruddock, A. (2009) "It's fantasy football made real": Networked media sport, the internet, and the hybrid reality of *MyFootballClub*. *Sociology of Sport Journal*, 26, 89–106.

Leonard, D. J. (2009) New media and global sporting cultures: Moving beyond the clichés and binaries. *Sociology of Sport Journal*, 26, 1–16.

Meân, L. J. (2001) Identity and discursive practice: Doing gender on the football pitch. *Discourse and Society*, 12, 789–815.

Meân, L. J. (2010) Making masculinity and framing femininity: FIFA, soccer and World Cup websites. In H. Hundley and A. C. Billings (eds), *Examining Identity in Sports Media* (pp. 65–86). Thousand Oaks, CA: Sage Publications.

Meân, L. J. (2011) Sport, identities, and consumption: The construction of sport at ESPN.com. In A. C. Billings (ed.), *Sports Media: Transformation, Integration, Consumption* (pp. 162–180). New York: Routledge.

Meân, L. J. (2012) Empowerment through sport? Female fans, women's sport and the construction of gendered fandom. In K. Toffoletti and P. Mewett (eds), *Sport and its Female Fans* (pp.169–192). New York: Routledge.

Meân, L. J. and Kassing, J. W. (2008) "I would just like to be known as an athlete": Managing hegemony, femininity, and heterosexuality in female sport. *Western Journal of Communication,* 72(2), 126–144.

Mewett, P. and Toffoletti, K. (2011) Finding footy: Female fan socialization and Australian rules football. *Sport in Society,* 14, 553–568.

Oates, T. P. (2009) New media and the repackaging of NFL fandom. *Sociology of Sport Journal,* 26, 31–49.

Rowe, D., Ruddock, A. and Hutchins, B. (2010) Cultures of complaint: Online fan message boards and networked digital media sport communities. *Convergence: The International Journal of Research into New Media Technologies,* 16, 298–315.

Sanderson, J. (2010) Weighing in on the coaching decision: Discussing sports and race online. *Journal of Language and Social Psychology,* 29, 301–320.

Scherer, J. (2007) Globalization, promotional culture and the production/consumption of online games: Emerging Adidas's "Beat Rugby" campaign. *New Media and Society,* 9, 475–496.

Suh, Y. I. and Pedersen, P. M. (2010) Participants' service quality perceptions of fantasy sports websites: The relationship between service quality, customer satisfaction, attitude, and actual usage. *Sport Marketing Quarterly,* 19, 78–87.

Van Dijk, T. A. (1993) Principles of critical discourse analysis. *Discourse and Society,* 4, 249–283.

Wenner, L. A. (1991) One part alcohol, one part sport, one part dirt, stir gently: Beer commercial and television sports. In L. R. Vande Berg and L. A. Wenner (eds), *Television Criticism: Approaches and Applications.* New York: Longman.

Wolter, S. M. (2012) *Serving, Informing, and Inspiring Today's Female Athlete and Fan Postfeminist, Neoliberal Discourse: A Critical Media Analysis of EspnW.* Unpublished Ph.D. Dissertation, University of Minnesota.

Zhang, Z. and Won, D. (2010) Buyer or browser? An analysis of sports fan behaviour online. *International Journal of Sports Marketing and Sponsorship,* 11, 124–139.

341

30

EXAMINING GAYS AND LESBIANS IN SPORT VIA TRADITIONAL AND NEW MEDIA

Edward M. Kian

OKLAHOMA STATE UNIVERSITY

John Vincent

UNIVERSITY OF ALABAMA

In April 2013, basketball player Jason Collins became the first openly gay active athlete in any of the four major professional male team sport leagues in the United States: Major League Baseball (MLB), National Basketball Association (NBA), National Football League (NFL), National Hockey League (NHL). Only six athletes from these four leagues had ever announced they were gay or bisexual, none of whom were well known and all announcing after their careers were over (Kian and Anderson, 2009). However, it remains to be seen at the time of this writing whether Collins will become the first active gay athlete in the NBA and thus face the in-season media attention that would come with such standing.

Collins – a 34-year-old largely unknown reserve throughout his career at the time of his announcement – still has to sign a contract and make an NBA roster for the 2013–14 season to become the first gay male athlete to play in one of the four major US professional team sports. That may prove challenging, since Collins averaged less than 2 points per game during an injury-plagued 2012–13 season. Regardless, both traditional media and the Internet anointed Collins with historical significance following his announcement (Doyle, 2013).

Even if he never plays in the NBA again, Collins' announcement served as yet another historic accomplishment for the gay rights movement, one of many this decade. In 2010, the US Congress repealed the official "Don't ask, don't tell" policy of the US military, which prohibited openly gay, lesbian, or bisexual individuals from serving in the armed forces. After being defeated every previous time a gay marriage measure was on a ballot in the US, gay rights advocates celebrated victories in all four states that cast votes on gay marriage in the 2012 election. These results coincided with the re-election of Barack Obama, who became the first sitting US president to publicly express support for gay marriage. More accepting views toward homosexuality and advancements in the gay rights movement have not been limited to the US in recent years, but instead have become commonplace in Western democracies. Public-opinion surveys showed continually increasing acceptance of homosexuality among the adult populations in 27 of 31 countries each polled five times from 1988–2008 (Nemenov, 2011).

Until recently, though, sport remained one cultural institution where there had been less visible progress for gays and lesbians, particularly within professional male team sports, which have long received the vast majority of media coverage throughout the world (Duncan, 2006). However, the advent of the Internet as a dominant medium has thrust homosexuality and gay rights into the media spotlight. In 2012 a watershed moment appeared to break from the National Football League (NFL), which American media frame as rugged and masculine, and is by far the most popular and publicized of all professional US male team sport leagues (Anderson and Kian, 2012). The website for *US Weekly* was one of many online outlets that reported a former NFL player came out as gay (Ravitz, 2012). Soon the Internet was abuzz with news that Wade Davis, described as an "NFL star" by many reports, had told the gay-focused website *OutSports.com* that he went to great lengths to keep his homosexuality private while in the NFL (Zeigler, 2012).

Not only was Davis not an "NFL star," he never actually played in a regular-season game or appeared on an NFL roster. Instead, Davis spent a few weeks on the Washington Redskins' practice squad and had tryouts with two other NFL teams. His name does not appear in the extensive databases of past and present players on NFL.com or *ProFootballReference.com*. However, the list of gay athletes is so sparse that Internet blogs seized on this chance to report a significant outing while seemingly failing to fact-check the athlete making the declaration.

Davis' self-outing, however, was essentially a non-story among traditional media, which is not surprising since media have long ignored male athletes who do not conform to ideal forms of masculinity (Lenskyj, 2013). It only became a news story due to the advent of the Internet, which – in part due to its unlimited space– has resulted in increased media coverage of athletes and sports largely ignored by the more traditional mass media (Kian, Mondello and Vincent, 2009).

The announcement by Jason Collins received coverage from all types of media. *Sports Illustrated* rushed to publish this story on its website, *SI.com*, for fear of another Internet site first reporting Collins' decision to come out publicly (Haughney, 2013).

Other examples of the media treatment of gay athletes will be discussed later in this chapter. First we will define and explain the acronym LGBT (lesbian, gay (males), bisexual, and transgender community) before looking at possible reasons why most gay athletes remain closeted. We briefly outline the extensive research on the types of male and female sports receiving the most media coverage, which correlates with how media frame athletes in accordance with desired characteristics of masculinity and femininity. Finally, we examine the limited research on sport media coverage of gays and lesbians in sport, with a focus on new media and its potential to change the framing of LGBT athletes in the future.

Understanding LGBT

Historically, most researchers concluded that homosexuals composed less than 10 percent of individuals, although those identifying as gay men or lesbians tallied just 3 percent in the vast majority of surveys (Laumann, Gagnon, Michael and Michaels, 1994). However, as society has become more accepting of homosexuality, a recent comprehensive survey showed that 8 percent of adult men and 7 percent of adult women in the US identified as gay, while 15 percent of US men admitted to having at least one gay sexual experience before the age of 50 (Indiana University Center for Sexual Health Promotion, 2010). However, a person's sexual orientation is never absolute. Gender identity and sexual desires are fluid (Halberstam, 2005).

Most people identify as heterosexuals, including the majority of those who acknowledge having homosexual experiences with others (Laumann *et al.*, 1994). However, it may be most difficult for bisexuals to reveal their orientations due to not only *homophobia* (the fear and intolerance of gays and lesbians), but also *biphobia* (an aversion toward bisexuality), the latter of which is prevalent within some gay circles (Griffin, 2012).

Professional journalists and academics often incorrectly utilize the terms "sex" and "gender" synonymously. Historically *gender* differentiated between men and women, who were thought to be easily distinguishable through biological traits (i.e. the binary contrast). But gender implies an identity that can easily be altered, whereas one's *sex* is commonly believed to be biologically determined at birth (Halberstam, 2005). *Transgender* is the newest classification in LGBT. Not surprisingly, it is the group least likely to be protected through anti-discrimination policies and the most discriminated against by both heterosexuals and gays (Lucas-Carr and Krane, 2012). Transgender means that an individual's gender identity does not match their biological sex (Halberstam, 2005). Transgender individuals could conceivably change their gender identities throughout each day. In contrast, *transsexuals* consistently identify with a gender opposite of their biological sex, with some undergoing medical procedures in efforts to alter their sex (Devor, 1997).

There is confusion about these terms. Of the two, more media coverage has centered on transsexuals in sport, perhaps most notably Renee Richards, who tried to continue her professional tennis career but was initially prohibited from entrance into the 1976 women's US Open Championships after legally changing her name from Richard Raskind and undergoing sexual reassignment surgery (Birrell and Cole, 1990). The New York Supreme Court, allowing her to resume a professional career on the female circuit, eventually overturned Richards' denial by the United States Tennis Association. More recently, media often report mixed martial arts fighter Fallon Fox as transgender. Fox, who was born Boyd Burton, had gender reassignment surgery and now identifies as a woman. Her attempts to fight as a woman have generated tremendous controversy (Gregory, 2013). South African female track star Caster Semenya has also been a major news topic, with a few stories wrongly identifying Semenya as transgender or transsexual (Ellison, 2012). Semenya – like some other muscular, athletic women with masculine physical characteristics (Sykes, 2006) – has been dogged by innuendo that she was a man. The International Association of Athletics Federations (IAAF) ordered her to undergo gender verification tests. The IAAF did not release specifics but did announce three months later that Semenya was "innocent," clearing her to compete as a woman (Ellison, 2012).

Athletes in the closet

The closeting of gay male team sport athletes has not been just an American problem, but a global phenomenon. Soccer is the world's most popular sport, evident by an estimated 2.2 billion television viewers of the 2010 FIFA World Cup (FIFA, 2011). However, no openly gay past or present footballer competed in the Barclays (English) Premier League (EPL) or the Spanish La Liga, which are ranked as the world's top two leagues by the International Federation of Football History and Statistics. The most prominent team sport professional athlete to come out during his career was probably Justin Fashanu, who was more recognized for being the first Black soccer player in the United Kingdom to sign a contract worth at least a million pounds (King, 2004). Fashanu's career faltered after he publicly revealed his homosexuality in 1990, before the EPL's creation, subjecting him to scorn from fans and fellow soccer players, including some of his teammates (King, 2004). Other former gay professional European footballers came out after retirement, but none were well known among casual fans.

Robbie Rogers became the first openly gay male athlete to play in US Major League Soccer (MLS) in 2013. Rogers had played professional soccer in the US and UK before revealing that he is gay and subsequently retiring from the sport at the age of 25 (Grautski, 2013). However, he decided to return to soccer a few months later as a member of the LA Galaxy. Welshmen Gareth Thomas, a rugby star, came out publicly in 2009 near the end of his athletic career but while still a professional. Orlando Cruz, a boxer from Puerto Rico, came out in 2012 and still competes professionally. Brittney Griner, a 6-foot-8-inch American basketball superstar, said she was asked to hide her lesbianism while competing at the college-level for a religious-affiliated institution, Baylor University (Hill, 2013). Griner, however, came out publicly since joining the Women's National Basketball Association (WNBA). Whereas the number of athletes who publicly disclose that they are gay is sure to increase, the likes of Cruz, Griner and Rogers remain relative rarities, because few gay athletes come out publicly while active in their sports. Homophobia has historically been so entrenched in male team sports that former MLB pitcher Kazuhito Tadano publicly claimed he was heterosexual and apologized to teammates for his past "mistakes" after it was anonymously revealed on an Internet message board that he engaged in homosexual acts while filmed in pornography in his native Japan (Hancock, 2009). Of course, Kazuhito only came to the US to compete after his acting history was uncovered, resulting in his apparent blackballing by all Japanese professional teams (Hancock, 2009). The few famous openly gay male athletes (e.g. figure skater Rudy Galindo, diver Greg Louganis) competed in individual sports that media have historically construed as more appropriate for women (Messner, 2002). Whereas certainly not in abundance, there have been more known lesbians in high-profile sport. For example, tennis legends Billie Jean King and Martina Navratilova revealed that they were lesbian while ranked among the sport's top players. The vast majority of academic scholarship on LGBT in sport has focused on lesbian athletes and coaches (Lenskyj, 2013).

Sport, like much of the rest of society, is becoming increasingly more accepting of gays and lesbians as well as alternate forms of gender identity. Recent scholarship and surveys on athletes from all levels of sport (Anderson, 2011; Fink, Burton, Farrell and Parker, 2012; Wertheim, 2005), coaches (Adams, Anderson and McCormack, 2010), administrators (Cunningham, 2010), advertisers and marketers (Vincent, Hill and Lee, 2009), and fans (Cashmore and Cleland, 2011) have shown increasing rates of acceptance for LGBT and non-traditional gender identities. The four major US professional male team sport leagues all added sexual orientation to their non-discrimination policies in the past decade (Griffin, 2012). The NBA launched a public service campaign against the use of gay slurs, highlighted by several Internet advertisements and a television commercial featuring then-Phoenix Suns star Grant Hill.

A few other notable athletes have spoken out for gay rights, including Hill's former team-mate, Steve Nash, who campaigned for marriage equality in New York, and Baltimore Ravens football player Brendon Ayanbadejo, who served as a key public speaker on behalf of the successful 2012 gay marriage equality vote in Maryland (Himmelsbach, 2012). The NFL's Chris Kluwe, an outspoken and heterosexual gay-rights proponent, posed shirtless for *Out*, a magazine catering to gay men. These are just three of the most active among the rapidly increasing number of athletes who use Twitter and other forms of social media to support gay rights to thousands of followers. However, at least until this decade, mainstream media have been slow to report on changes within sport culture, maybe because of a lack of openly gay athletes, or possibly due to a culture within the sport media workforce that is resistant to social change.

Hegemonic masculinity

In her analysis on gender power relations, Connell (2005) noted that multiple femininities and masculinities co-exist in a socially constructed hierarchy that generally favors men. Connell (1987, 2005) defined *hegemonic masculinity* as the configuration of gender practices that assist in maintaining and strengthening the societal dominance of men over women. Hegemonic masculinity rewards those who exhibit the most desired masculine traits and qualities such as power, assertiveness, independence, and aggression (Connell, 2005). At or near the bottom of the hegemonic masculine social hierarchy are openly gay men, who challenge traditional definitions of masculinity through their sexual orientation (Anderson, 2002). Many authors theorized that mass media and sport are two of the primary forces helping to maintain hegemonic masculinity in Western societies (e.g. Kian, Fink and Hardin, 2011; Vincent, 2004). Men have long dominated both the ranks and power positions within all realms of the sport media industry throughout the world (e.g. Capranica and Aversa, 2002; Claringbould, Knoppers and Elling, 2004; Lapchick, 2013). The dominance of men in covering sport extends to Internet journalism, both at the most popular sites (Kian and Hardin, 2009) and smaller blogs (John Curley Center for Sports Journalism, 2009). The proportional dominance of men in the industry may explain why a hegemonic male culture is pervasive within many sport media outlets (Gee and Leberman, 2011; Pedersen, Whisenant and Schneider, 2003; Schoch and Ohl, 2011).

Women who compete in sports like gymnastics receive more media attention than male athletes in those sports, which media generally frame as inappropriate (not masculine enough) for men (Billings, Angelini and Duke, 2010; Bruce, Hovden and Markula, 2010). Male athletes in gender-inappropriate sports are often framed as effeminate through the limited mass media coverage they do receive (Adams, 2011). In turn, men and women in gender-inappropriate sports are suspected of being gay by many, whereas those in gender-appropriate sports are generally assumed to be heterosexual (Anderson, 2005). Women who have more masculine physical characteristics (such as large size), but compete in feminine sports are the prime exception, in that they receive less coverage than men in the same sports (Griffin, 1998). Duncan (2006) concluded that when female athletes "appear to have mannish qualities, the threat of lesbianism is greater so heterosexuality must be defended that much more vigorously" (p. 241).

Via their sexual orientation alone, gay male athletes are gender inappropriate when measured by the most desired notions of masculinity, with heterosexuality ranking at or near the top of that list (Kian, Clavio, Vincent and Shaw, 2011). Their lack of coverage is significant, because the most prominent gay male athletes compete in sports that are commonly framed as feminine, such as gymnastics and diving (Lenskyj, 2013). Only one published scholarly article has examined attitudes of sport journalists toward homosexuality. A majority of newspaper sport reporters surveyed by Hardin and Whiteside (2009) agreed that homophobia is a problem within sport. But most respondents disagreed with the notion that a gay professional male athlete would be accepted if he came out during his playing career.

Media framing

In the only published survey on sport journalists' attitudes toward gays and lesbians, 74 percent of respondents either *strongly agreed* or *agreed* with the statement, "I do not think it is appropriate to ever ask an athlete about his or her sexual orientation" (Hardin and Whiteside, 2009). Only 1 percent *strongly disagreed*. The authors theorized that these attitudes are a key reason why there are so few well-known gays in sport, concluding, "reporters are likely to help athletes stay in the closet" (p. 67). This "don't ask, don't tell" media approach toward LGBT athletes helps keep society ignorant about issues of importance toward LGBT in sport and society (Plymire and Forman, 2000; Staurowsky, 2012). Calhoun, LaVoi and Johnson (2011) provided a stronger denunciation, contending that by ignoring the personal lives of gay and lesbian athletes, media reinforce *heteronormativity*, which affirms heterosexuality as natural and creates a culture where gays and lesbians are not respected as equals. Lenskyj (2013) noted this is further strengthened by hypersexualized media images of female athletes.

While criticizing media, these scholars may ignore the fact that prominent athletes are not willfully coming out. They direct blame at media for not covering what – at least on the surface – is not news. They also may not account for journalistic ethics and respect for individual privacy, which call for a wall of separation where most reporters do not dig into athletes' personal lives without due cause. This distinguishes legitimate reporters from the paparazzi, although that line is deteriorating with Internet blogs becoming more prevalent while the newspaper industry struggles in countries like the US (Kian and Zimmerman, 2012).

In his ethnography on female professional golf, Crossett (1995) was critical of media for delving into the sexual orientations of suspected lesbians, which he attributed largely to male writers' jealousy of the golf skills of these women. However, more researchers found media either ignored or did not report on relationships of known or suspected gay athletes (Dworkin and Wachs, 1998; Wright and Clarke, 1999) For example, although she initially denied its veracity, the allegation that Billie Jean King was a lesbian first surfaced in a civil suit brought forth by her former secretary and lesbian lover, which occurred while King was in a heterosexual marriage and after she attained fame for defeating Bobby Riggs in the famous "Battle of the Sexes" tennis match (Nelson, 1984). Despite television cameras regularly showing images of athletes' celebrity wives or girlfriends, the sporting press rarely investigates the personal lives of most heterosexual athletes, thus supporting Kramer's old-but-still-poignant (1987) contention that "there is a vast difference between digging up dirt and reporting on the dirt dished up by the athletes themselves" (¶ 16).

Until 2013, the two biggest US media sport stories related to the sexuality of athletes were based on rumors of prominent athletes being homosexual. The ongoing Skip Bayless–Troy Aikman feud serves as a cautionary tale: Bayless, a former sportswriter, indicated in his 1996 book on the NFL's Dallas Cowboys that Aikman – then the star quarterback for a squad that had won three Super Bowls in four years – was gay. Bayless offered no factual evidence, but speculated that Aikman was gay since he was among the most eligible bachelors in Texas but remained unmarried (Bayless, 1996). Aikman, who later wed a woman and fathered children with her, denied the report. Bayless capitalized on the attention to help launch a career as a combative sport talk-show host. Meanwhile, widespread rumors in popular culture have centered on Aikman's sexual orientation since Bayless' report, intensifying after Aikman filed for divorce from his wife in 2011. Aikman recently implied he might physically injure Bayless if he saw him in person, while also insinuating that Bayless is gay (Buzinski, 2011).

The other major media story surfaced after Brendan Lemon, an editor at gay lifestyle magazine *Out*, wrote that he had an affair with an unnamed professional baseball standout, adding that the player would come out publicly (Butterworth, 2006). Talk-radio and Internet message boards quickly centered upon then-New York Mets catcher Mike Piazza. Piazza called a press conference to proclaim his heterosexuality but attempted to deflect away the newsworthiness of an athlete's sexual orientation. However, newspapers framed Piazza as effeminate after he did not initiate a physical altercation upon being beamed with a pitch by the Los Angeles Dodgers' Guillermo Mota (Butterworth, 2006).

A few scholarly articles have analyzed media content after athletes publicly revealed their homosexuality. Two studies on media framing of former NBA player John Amaechi's decision to come out while promoting his autobiography found both international and US sport coverage highly supportive of Amaechi's decision (Kian and Anderson, 2009), or at least not expressing overt homophobia (Hardin, Kuehn, Jones, Genovese and Balaji, 2009). Media also positively framed the announcement of bisexual basketball star Sheryl Swoopes and lesbian golfer Rosie Jones, although Swoopes received significantly more attention since she was pregnant at the time with a child that she said was conceived through sex with a man (Chawansky and Francombe, 2011). Other recent research showed sport media supportive of LGBT athletes (Nylund, 2004) while denouncing homophobia as archaic (Hardin and Whiteside, 2010). However, even while they professed support for LGBT athletes and gay rights, these sport journalists still framed heterosexuality as the norm or basis of comparison for all sexual orientations (Hardin *et al.*, 2009; Nylund, 2004).

New media

Because of its vast potential for content creation free from corporate constraints and traditional ideology, much of the Internet has emerged as more hospitable for coverage on men and women in what media historically construed as gender-inappropriate sports, as well as openly LGBT athletes (Kian and Clavio, 2011). For example, Newhall and Buzuvis (2008) found that former Penn State women's basketball coach Rene Portland was eviscerated on Internet blogs and message boards for her homophobic, anti-lesbian policy. Traditional media followed suit in their condemnation of Portland, which resulted in Lenskyj (2013) wondering "why these progressive media professionals had been relatively silent from 1980–2007" (p. 143). In an analysis of European soccer message boards, Cleland (2013) found most anonymous posters rejected homophobia, instead accepting more inclusive forms of masculinity.

Athletes, such as Robbie Rogers, and coaches have recently started using the Internet and social media to publicly come out as gay. The defense attorney for Kwame Harris, who last played in the NFL in 2008, acknowledged his client is gay after Harris was charged for allegedly assaulting an ex-boyfriend. In an article titled, "Kwame Harris is gay. It's OK, you can say it," *Outsports.com* co-founder Cyd Zeigler, Jr. (2013) noted that traditional media did include the "ex-boyfriend" in stories. However, Zeigler pointed out that "none of them talked about the fact that Harris is gay," (¶ 4), adding that the ESPN Internet network left out that Harris was charged with domestic violence against another man in its headline. Most of the stories on Harris' sexual orientation came from websites outside of the mainstream.

The future for research

There is minimal research on LGBT in sport, in part because so few notable athletes have come out. That will change due to recent announcements of notable athletes such as Collins and Griner. Public acceptance of homosexuality and support for gay rights has increased dramatically over the past two decades in most Western societies, thus propelling the LGBT community into the mainstream. Whereas sport media largely ignored LGBT issues until very recently, homosexuality and gay rights have been covered extensively by news outlets over the past decade and instilled into popular culture via television sitcoms like *Will and Grace* in the US.

Cultural changes may have material benefits for gay athletes. Whereas King lost most of her sponsorships after allegations surfaced that she was a lesbian (Griffin, 2012), recent research indicates that marketing openly gay sporting women or female athletes with more masculine physical characteristics does not affect consumers' perceptions of products (Parker and Fink, 2012). Moreover, openly gay athletes are likely to earn more money in endorsements due to the affluence of the LGBT community and gay rights advocates (Anderson, 2011; Butterworth, 2006). Thus, the time is right for more gay athletes to come out on their own volition, which will generate media coverage. That content, in turn, would lead to needed scholarship on the framing, images, and effects of sport media coverage of LGBT in sport.

However, great challenges still exist for LGBT in sport, which should also be examined by scholars. Anti-gay ordinances and rampant homophobia are becoming more commonplace in Russia and other former Soviet-bloc countries, making the 2014 Winter Olympic Games in Sochi, Russia, likely a chilly place for LGBT athletes (Nemenov, 2011; Whiteside 2013). This chapter largely focused on lesbians and gays due to the scant academic research examining bisexual athletes in sport media coverage and because scholars have essentially ignored coverage of transgender athletes in sport media. However, that will likely soon change, especially after *Sports Illustrated* published an in-depth series of articles on the future of transgender athletes (Torre and Epstein, 2012). Regardless, early research indicates that societal acceptance of bisexual, transgender, and transsexual athletes and coaches will be even slower than for gays and lesbians, including among gay and lesbian sport fans (Griffin, 2012).

References

Adams, A., Anderson, E. and McCormack, M. (2010) Establishing and challenging masculinity: The influence of gendered discourses in organized sport. *Journal of Language and Social Psychology*, 29(3), 278–300.

Adams, M.L. (2011) *Artistic Impressions: Figure Skating, Masculinity, and the Limits of Sport.* Toronto, Canada: University of Toronto Press.

Anderson, E. (2002) Contesting hegemonic masculinity in a homophobic environment. *Gender and Society,* 16(6), 860–877.

Anderson, E. (2005) *In the Game: Gay Athletes and the Cult of Masculinity.* New York: State University of New York Press.

Anderson, E. (2011) Updating the outcome: Gay athletes, straight teams, and coming out at the end of the decade. *Gender and Society,* 25(2), 250–268.

Anderson, E. and Kian, E.M. (2012) Examining media contestation of masculinity and head trauma in the National Football League. *Men and Masculinities,* 15(2), 152–173.

Bayless, S. (1996) *Hell-bent: The Crazy Truth About the "Win or Else" Dallas Cowboys.* New York: HarperCollins.

Billings, A.C., Angelini, J.R. and Duke, A.H. (2010) Gendered profiles of Olympic history: Sportscaster dialogue in the 2008 Beijing Olympics. *Journal of Broadcasting and Electronic Media,* 54(1), 9–23.

Birrell, S. and Cole, C.L. (1990) Double fault: Renee Richards and the naturalization of difference. *Sociology of Sport Journal,* 7(1), 1–21.

Bruce, T., Hovden, J. and Markula, P. (2010) *Sportswomen at the Olympics: A Global Content Analysis of Newspaper Coverage.* Rotterdam, The Netherlands: Sense.

Butterworth, M.L. (2006) Pitchers and catchers: Mike Piazza and the discourse of gay identity in the national pastime. *Journal of Sport and Social Issues,* 30(2), 138–157.

Buzinski, J. (2011, September 1) Troy Aikman: I'm not gay, but Skip Bayless might be. *Outsports.com.* Retrieved from http://outsports.com/jocktalkblog/2011/09/01/troy-aikman-im-not-gay-but-skip-bayless-might-be/

Calhoun, A.S., LaVoi, N.M. and Johnson, A. (2011) Framing with family: Examining online coaches' biographies for heteronormative and heterosexist narratives. *International Journal of Sport Communication,* 4(3), 300–316.

Capranica, L. and Aversa, F. (2002) Italian television sport coverage during the 2000 Sydney Olympic Games. *International Review for the Sociology of Sport,* 37(3–4), 337–349.

Cashmore, E. and Cleland, J. (2011) Grasswing butterflies: Gay professional football players and their culture. *Journal of Sport and Social Issues,* 35(4), 420–436.

Chawansky, M. and Francombe, J.M. (2011) Cruising for Olivia: Lesbian celebrity and the cultural politics of coming out in sport. *Sociology of Sport Journal,* 28(4), 461–477.

Claringbould, I., Knoppers, A. and Elling, A. (2004) Exclusionary practices in sport journalism. *Sex Roles,* 51(11/12), 709–718.

Cleland, J. (2013) Discussing homosexuality on association football fan message boards: A changing cultural context. *International Review for the Sociology of Sport.* Advance online publication.

Connell, R.W. (1987) *Gender and Power.* Stanford, CA: Stanford University Press.

Connell, R.W. (2005) *Masculinities* (2nd edn.). Berkeley, CA: University of California Press.

Crosset, T. (1995) *Outsiders in the Clubhouse: The World of Professional Women's Golf.* Albany, NY: State University of New York Press.

Cunningham, G.B. (2010) Predictors of sexual orientation diversity in intercollegiate athletics departments. *Journal of Intercollegiate Sport,* 3(2), 256–269.

Devor, H. (1997) *FTM: Female-to-Male Transsexuals in Society.* Bloomington, IN: Indiana University Press.

Doyle, G. (2013, April 29) Jason Collins no longer has to live a lie, and that's worth celebrating. *CBSSports.com.* Retrieved from http://www.cbssports.com/nba/story/22167239/jason-collins-no-longer-has-to-live-a-lie-and-thats-worth-celebrating

Duncan, M.C. (2006) Gender warriors in sport: Women and the media. In A.A. Raney and J. Bryant (eds), *Handbook of Sports and Media* (pp. 231–252). Mahwah, NJ: Lawrence Erlbaum.

Dworkin, S.L. and Wachs, F.L. (1998) "Disciplining the body": HIV-positive male athletes, media surveillance, and the policing of sexuality. *Sociology of Sport Journal,* 15(1), 1–20.

Ellison, J. (2012, July 26) Caster Semenya and the IOC's Olympics Gender Binder. *The Daily Beast.* Retrieved from http://www.thedailybeast.com/articles/2012/07/26/caster-semenya-and-the-ioc-s-olympics-gender-bender.html

FIFA.com (2011, July 11) *Almost Half the World Tuned in at Home to Watch 2010 FIFA World Cup South Africa.* Retrieved from http://www.fifa.com/worldcup/archive/southafrica2010/organisation/media/newsid=1473143/index.html

Fink, J.S., Burton, L.J., Farrell, A.O. and Parker, H.M. (2012) Playing it out: Female intercollegiate athletes' experiences in revealing their sexual identities. *Journal for the Study of Sports and Athletes in Education,* 6(1), 83–106.

Gee, B.L. and Leberman, S.I. (2011) Sports media decision making in France: How they choose what we get to see and read. *International Journal of Sport Communication,* 4(4), 321–343.

Grautski, A. (2013, May 24) Robbie Rogers coming back as first active openly gay player in Major League Soccer, has reportedly agreed to terms with LA Galaxy. *New York Daily News* [online]. Retrieved from http://www.nydailynews.com/sports/more-sports/robbie-rogers-coming-back-active-openly-gay-player-mls-article-1.1354323

Gregory, S. (2013, May 24) Should a former man be able to fight women? *Time* [online]. Retrieved from http://keepingscore.blogs.time.com/2013/05/24/should-a-former-man-be-able-to-fight-women/

Griffin, P. (1998) *Strong Women, Deep Closets: Lesbians and Homophobia in Sport.* Champaign, IL: Human Kinetics.

Griffin, P. (2012) LGBT equality in sports: Celebrating our successes and facing our challenges. In G.B. Cunningham (ed.), *Sexual Orientation and Gender Identity in Sport: Essays from Activists, Coaches, and Scholars* (pp. 1–12). College Station, TX: Center for Sport Management Research and Education.

Halberstam, J. (2005) *In a Queer Time and Place: Transgender Bodies, Subcultural Lives.* New York: New York University Press.

Hancock, D. (2009, February 11) Baseball player's gay porn past. *CBS News* [online]. Retrieved from http://www.cbsnews.com/stories/2004/01/28/entertainment/main596540.shtml

Hardin, M., Kuehn, K.M., Jones, H., Genovese, J. and Balaji, M. (2009) 'Have you got game?' Hegemonic masculinity and neo-homophobia in US newspaper sports columns. *Communication, Culture, and Critique,* 2(2), 182–200.

Hardin, M. and Whiteside, E.A. (2009) Sports reporters divided over concerns about Title IX; *Newspaper Research Journal,* 30(1), 58–80.

Hardin, M. and Whiteside, E.A. (2010) The Rene Portland case: New homophobia and heterosexism in women's sports coverage. In H.L. Hundley and A.C. Billings (eds), *Examining Identity in Sports Media* (pp. 17–36). Thousand Oaks, CA: Sage.

Haughney, C. (2013, April 29) How *Sports Illustrated* broke the Jason Collins story. *The New York Times* [online edition]. Retrieved from http://www.nytimes.com/2013/04/30/business/media/how-sports-illustrated-broke-the-jason-collins-story.html?_r=0

Hill, J. (2013, April 25) Brittney Griner's inspiring message. *ESPN Internet.* Retrieved from http://espn.go.com/wnba/story/_/id/9189749/brittney-griner-clear-inspirational-message

Himmelsbach, A. (2012, September 8) Players' support of gay marriage alters NFL image. *The New York Times* [online]. Retrieved from http://www.nytimes.com/2012/09/09/sports/football/players-support-of-gay-marriage-alters-nfl-image.html?_r=0

Indiana University Center for Sexual Health Promotion (2010) *National survey of sexual health and behavior.* Retrieved August 15, 2011, from http://www.nationalsexstudy.indiana.edu/

John Curley Center for Sports Journalism (2009, July) *From outside the press box: The identities, attitudes, and values of sports bloggers.* Retrieved from http://news.psu.edu/story/175617/2009/07/10/report-sports-bloggers-believe-attitude-approach-set-them-apart#rss61

Kian, E.M. and Anderson, E. (2009) John Amaechi: Changing the way reporters examine gay athletes. *Journal of Homosexuality,* 56(7), 799–818.

Kian, E.M. and Clavio, G. (2011) A comparison of online media and traditional newspaper coverage of the men's and women's US Open tennis tournaments. *Journal of Sports Media,* 6(2), 55–84.

Kian, E.M., Clavio, G.,Vincent, J. and Shaw, S.D. (2011) Homophobic and sexist yet uncontested: Examining football fan postings on Internet message boards. *Journal of Homosexuality,* 58(5), 680–99.

Kian, E.M., Fink, J.S. and Hardin, M. (2011) Examining the impact of journalists' gender in online and newspaper tennis articles. *Women in Sport and Physical Activity Journal,* 20(1), 3–21.

Kian, E.M. and Hardin, M. (2009) Framing of sport coverage based on the sex of sports writers: Female journalists counter the traditional gendering of media content. *International Journal of Sport Communication,* 2(2), 185–204.

Kian, E.M., Mondello, M. andVincent, J. (2009) ESPN – The women's sports network? A content analysis of Internet coverage of March Madness. *Journal of Broadcasting and Electronic Media,* 53(3), 477–495.

Kian, E.M. and Zimmerman, M.H. (2012) The medium of the future: Top sports writers discuss transitioning from newspapers to online journalism. *International Journal of Sport Communication,* 5(3), 285–304.

King, C. (2004) Race and cultural identity: Playing the race game inside football. *Leisure Studies,* 23(1), 19–30.

Kramer, S.D. (1987, August 23) The rewritten rules of sports journalism. *The New York Times* [online]. Retrieved from http://www.nytimes.com/1987/08/23/sports/the-rewritten-rules-of-sports-journalism.html?pagewanted=all&src=pm

Laumann, E., Gagnon, J.H., Michael, R.T. and Michaels, S. (1994) *The Social Organization of Sexuality: Sexual Practices in the United States.* Chicago, IL: University of Chicago Press.

Lapchick, R. (2013, March 1) *The 2012 Associated Press Sports Editors Racial and Gender Report Card.* Retrieved from http://www.tidesport.org/RGRC/2012/2012_APSE_RGRC.pdf

Lenskyj, H.J. (2013) Reflections on communication and sport: On heteronormativity and gender identities. *Communication and Sport,* 1(1/2), 138–150.

Lucas-Carr, C.B. and Krane,V. (2012) Troubling sport or trouble by sport: Experiences of transgender athletes. *Journal of the Study of Sports and Athletes in Education,* 6(1), 21–44.

Messner, M.A. (2002) *Taking the field: Women, Men, and Sports.* Minneapolis, MN: University of Minnesota Press.

Nelson, J. (1984) The defense of Billie Jean King. *Western Journal of Speech Communication,* 48(1), 92–102.

Nemenov, A. (2011, May 30) More countries accepting homosexuality: Study. *Yahoo! News.* Retrieved from http://ph.news.yahoo.com/more-countries-accepting-gay-lifestyle-study-031409308.html

Newhall, K. and Buzuvis, E. (2008) (e)Racing Jennifer Harris: Sexuality and race, law and discourse in Harris v. Portland. *Journal of Sport and Social Issues,* 32(4), 345–368.

Nylund, D. (2004) When in Rome: Heterosexism, homophobia, and sports talk radio. *Journal of Sport and Social Issues,* 28(2), 136–168.

Parker, H.M. and Fink, J.S. (2012) Arrest record or openly gay: The impact of athletes' personal lives on endorser effectiveness. *Sport Marketing Quarterly,* 21(2), 70–79.

Pedersen, P.M.,Whisenant,W.A. and Schneider, R.G. (2003) Using a content analysis to examine the gendering of sports newspaper personnel and their coverage. *Journal of Sport Management,* 17(4), 376–393.

Plymire, D.C. and Forman, P.J. (2000) Breaking the silence: Lesbian fans, the Internet, and the sexual politics of women's sport. *International Journal of Sexuality and Gender Studies,* 5(2), 141–153.

Ravitz, J. (2012, June 7) Wade Davis, NFL star, reveals he's gay. *US Weekly* [online]. Retrieved from http://www.usmagazine.com/celebrity-news/news/wade-davis-nfl-star-reveals-hes-gay-201276

Schoch, L. and Ohl, F. (2011) Women sports journalists in Switzerland: Between assignments and negotiation of roles. *Sociology of Sport Journal,* 28(2), 189–209.

Staurowsky, E.J. (2012) Sexual prejudice and sport media coverage: Exploring an ethical framework for college sports journalists. *Journal of the Study of Sports and Athletes in Education,* 6(2), 121–140.

Sykes, H. (2006) Transsexual and transgender policies in sport. *Women in Sport and Physical Activity Journal,* 15(1), 3–13.

Torre, P.S. and Epstein, D. (2012, May 28) The transgender athletes. *Sports Illustrated* [online]. Retrieved from http://sportsillustrated.cnn.com/vault/article/magazine/MAG1198744/index.htm

Vincent, J. (2004) Game, sex, and match: The construction of gender in British newspaper coverage of the 2000 Wimbledon Championships. *Sociology of Sport Journal*, 21(4), 435–456.

Vincent, J., Hill, J.S. and Lee, J.W. (2009) The multiple brand personalities of David Beckham: A case study of the Beckham brand. *Sport Marketing Quarterly*, 18(3), 173–180.

Wertheim, J. (2005, April 18) Gays in sports: A poll. *Sports Illustrated*, 102(16), 64–66.

Whiteside, K. (2013, February 7) Sochi Olympics will test gay rights. *USA Today* [online]. Retrieved from http://www.usatoday.com/story/sports/olympics/2013/02/06/russia-gay-rights-sochi-olympics/1897021/

Wright, J. and Clarke, G. (1999) Sport, the media and the construction of compulsory heterosexuality. *International Review for the Sociology of Sport*, 34(3), 227–243.

Zeigler, Jr., C. (2012, June 5) Wade Davis talks for the first time about being gay in the NFL, working with LGBTQ youth. *Outsports.com*. Retrieved from http://outsports.com/jocktalkblog/2012/06/05/wade-davis-talks-about-being-gay-former-nfl-player-working-with-lgbtq-youth-for-the-first-time/

Zeigler, Jr., C. (2013, January 30) Kwame Harris is gay. It's OK, you can say it. *Outsports.com*. Retrieved from http://newsle.com/article/0/57720710/

31

COMMUNICATING LEGITIMACY, VISIBILITY, AND CONNECTIVITY

The functions of new media in adapted sport

Kurt Lindemann

SAN DIEGO STATE UNIVERSITY

James L. Cherney

WAYNE STATE UNIVERSITY

New media has been used by disabled persons for many years and for a variety of reasons. In fact, new media[1] has a long history of connecting marginalized groups. In the 1920s and 1930s, radio – at the time the "newest" media in existence – provided physically disabled people unable to attend social gatherings the ability to connect with the larger world outside their homes (Kirkpatrick, 2012). Of course, the role of new media for physically disabled people, particularly athletes, has changed considerably. Today it seems to function, as with most able-bodied sports, primarily as a way for athletes to market themselves and their accomplishments to a wider audience (McNary and Hardin, 2013).

More than simply making disabled sports available to new and diverse audiences, however, new media serves several important functions. It not only increases perceived legitimacy and visibility among mainstream audiences, it connects disabled athletes to each other in distinct and important ways. First, it provides a channel for athletes to negotiate the informal rules of competition and inclusion that generate tension in highly competitive sports like wheelchair rugby. Second, it enables athletes to discuss health issues associated with their physical disabilities and their sport in a context that is relatively free from the often constricting medicalized model of disability. In exploring these functions of connectivity, this chapter draws on a case study of message board communication among wheelchair rugby athletes. We argue that the notion of community illuminated by an examination of new media use in wheelchair rugby provides insight into the problems associated with identity politics in disability rights activism; ultimately, we argue that athletic identity as communicated via new media might be a more productive way in which to investigate the intersections of community and identity. Below, we briefly explore the dimensions of social media with regard to adapted sport before examining in-depth one instance of a nuanced and complex use of social media to sustain a community of wheelchair athletes.

General media coverage of disabled athletes seems to coalesce around several similar, often stereotypical themes. Because of this, social media has emerged as an effective way to control the content and tenor of messages about athletes' own participation. Media coverage of competitors in the Special Olympics often include a focus on an athletes' participation as inspiring, as a boost to their own self-esteem, and as reframing what it means to be "disabled" (Tanner, Green and Burns, 2011). The "inspiring" frame in media coverage of disabled athletes, termed as the "supercrip" stereotype (Hardin and Hardin, 2004), positions athletes as courageous for overcoming their disability and for succeeding in competition despite their "inabilities" to function as a "normal" athlete. In such frames, disability is almost always visibly attached to these athletes; the images are presented with a reference to disability (Hargreaves and Hardin, 2009). As such stereotypical images and frames can encourage a discriminatory perspective (Brittain, 2004; Cherney and Lindemann, 2009; Longmore, 1987; Nelson, 2003) social media presents an attractive alternative to mainstream media when it comes to representation of disability and sport.

The functions of new media in disabled sport

This new media functions in three ways when it comes to disabled sport: it serves to legitimize for mainstream audiences disabled sport as a "real" sport, it provides visibility for the athletes, and it enables athletes to connect to their fans and to each other. We briefly address each of these functions, using contemporary examples as illustrations, before exploring implications of the third in the context of a wheelchair rugby message board.

The case of the 2012 London Paralympics

First, the use of new media, or social media, seems to legitimize disabled sport as a "real"[2] sport relative to its able-bodied counterparts. The founder of the Paralympic games, neurosurgeon Ludwig Guttman, always intended the Paralympics, first billed as the Stoke Mandeville Games for the Paralyzed, to be staged more or less side-by-side with the Olympics. His decision to encourage English Word War II veterans to participate in wheelchair polo just hours from the 1948 London Olympics speak to this desire for legitimacy (Chappell, 2012). Use of online media helped make the 2012 London Paralympics into what the Associated Press (2012) notes was the most popular, best viewed, and most widely attended to date. The Paralympic web page illustrates this legitimating function; like the 2012 Olympics web page, found on the same site, the Paralympic web page represents each sport it features with icons consisting of the silhouette of an athlete participating in a particular sport.

Some of these Paralympic icons, including those for Judo and Swimming, are the same icons used for these sports in the Olympics. Others, such as Equestrian and Cycling-Track, differ from the Olympic icons but display no clear visual reference to disability. As opposed to the Olympic icon, the horse in the Paralympic Equestrian icon is walking instead of jumping, and the Paralympic Cycling-Track icon shows two people cycling instead of the single person used in the Olympic icon.[3] A third group of icons explicitly display characteristics related to disability. For example, the icons for Wheelchair Rugby and Wheelchair Tennis both include a wheelchair, the icons for Goalball and 5-A-Side Football display the eye covering worn by competitors in these sports, and Powerlifting and Sitting Volleyball show figures in a prone or sitting posture (The London Organising Committee of the Olympic Games and Paralympic Games, 2012b). Certainly, some disability-rights advocates might read either of the first two types of icons as purposely hiding or obscuring an athlete's disability, thereby promoting an ableist perspective on sport in general and the Paralympics specifically. Conversely, disabled athletes "passing" as more able-bodied can be a form of resistance against both the medical model of disability and regulations of sport that classify bodies based on that model (Cherney, 2003; Lindemann, 2008). The tension created by such alternative reading of these icons reveals the sedimented ableism still facing Paralympic athletics in the attempt to ensure credible, ethical, and inclusive new media representations.

In addition to similar-looking icons, much of the text of the 2012 Paralympic site, including its placement and wording, matches the London Olympics site. Perhaps most notable is the tag line that appears at the top of all pages for *both* the Olympic and Paralympic pages: "inspire a generation" (The London Organising Committee of the Olympic Games and Paralympic Games, 2012a). This function of new media not only provides a visual linkage of able-bodied and disabled sport, it also captures the desire of disabled competitors to be taken seriously as athletes.

Presenting media messages about disabled sport in parallel with messages about able-bodied sport seems to suggest that both able-bodied and disability sport should be treated as equally legitimate. Additionally, organizing committees for events like the Olympics and Paralympics may capitalize on the visual components of new media to ensure that disabled sport websites "look legitimate," which may mean they mimic other professional sports organizations or, in the case of the London Paralympics, bear no discernible difference to its able-bodied counterpart. This sort of legitimacy has a symbiotic relationship with visibility that can be both beneficial and detrimental to disabled sport.

The effects of new media on disability sport

New media has great potential in garnering visibility for disabled sports and its athletes (Hargreaves and Hardin, 2009; Lindemann and Cherney, 2008; Manderson and Peake, 2005). While the study of social media use within and among disabled athletes is still nascent, its use has already catapulted some athletes into the same media stories as their able-bodied counterparts. For example, mono skier Josh Dueck, who completed the first back flip by a disabled skier, gained fame when the YouTube video of this feat went viral (McNary and Hardin, 2013). Clearly, Dueck's use of social media has afforded him, and his sport, a certain degree of visibility it did not have before his venture into the world of social media. Similarly, the Twitter feed of Paralympic and Olympic sprinter Oscar Pistorius, arguably the most high-profile disabled athlete in the world at this time, exceeded 300,000 followers after he was arrested for the alleged murder of his girlfriend, Reeva Steenkamp, in February 2013 (Levs, Karimi and Mabuse, 2013). As of the writing of this chapter, the effects of Pistorius' trial on disability sport, on its representations in the media, and on his visibility (including his number of Twitter followers) remains murky.

In a symbiotic fashion, visibility of disabled athletes and their respective sports is closely linked to the legitimacy with which mainstream media and sports fans view those athletes. For example, the visibility garnered by Dueck's YouTube video has given him and the sport of mono skiing a certain degree of legitimacy. While YouTube features stunts many might deem wacky or downright foolish, it is often the only place many "underground" sports like skateboarding, motocross, and parkour or "free running" can gain visibility. The fact that Dueck's video exists alongside other displays of athletic prowess from able-bodied athletes communicates to viewers the equally difficult nature of such a feat. For example, Dueck was interviewed alongside able-bodied X-Games skiers about the Games' decision to eliminate the ski and snowboard cross events (in which skiers race each other down a hill, as opposed to a timed solo run) (Mackenzie, 2012). The news story mentions Dueck simply as another X-Games athlete with only a passing mention of his disability or that he is a mono skier. And even in stories as disturbing as those about Pistorius, he is referred to alternately as an "admired Olympian" (Levs *et al.*, 2013, para. 1) and a "Paralympic runner" (Levs *et al.*, 2013, para. 2).

Unfortunately, visibility can also threaten a sport's legitimacy. Scott Hogsett, a wheelchair rugby athlete prominently featured in the Oscar-nominated documentary *Murderball*, lamented the fact that the film harmed the sport's status as a competitive, elite sport for quadriplegic people, inviting everyone in a wheelchair to play, when this was just not the case (Mandel and Shapiro, 2005). On the heels of the film's success, the subsequent saturation of the athletes and their images throughout multiple media platforms (Cherney and Lindemann, 2009; Henson, 2012) increased the sport's visibility to the point that disabled people of all kinds wanted to become a wheelchair rugby athlete. Not everyone possesses the qualifications (impairment in all four limbs) let alone the physical skills and sport experience to become an elite athlete like those featured in the film. If viewers interpret the film as suggesting that anyone could roll in off the street and excel at wheelchair rugby, it calls into question the sport's status as a "real" sport comparable to able-bodied "extreme sports." This tension between inclusion and competition is present in many disabled sports played at a level like the Paralympic or X-Games, and is something we explore further later in this chapter.

Interestingly, Dueck's backflip on YouTube did not seem to have the same effect as the widespread, more mainstream media representations of wheelchair rugby. This may be, in part, because new media like YouTube caters to more specific audiences (McNary and Hardin, 2013) and may be less likely to appeal to people with little interest and experience in a particular sport. With new media, as McNary and Hardin (2013) argue, disabled athletes can control not only the messages about themselves and their sport, but their audiences as well. Such control may be beneficial as these athletes are able to use new media regulate the visibility and, in effect, how they are portrayed. In any case, new media allows the athletes to connect with fans and non-fans in particular ways.

Communicating negotiated and contested meanings

Finally, new media offers a connection between fans, athletes, and even the officials of a particular sport. The use of new media can create and sustain a feeling of community across space and time. For disabled persons, this connection may be particularly crucial in helping develop a sense of belonging. Networking sites like LinkedIn, in which business professionals post profile information, published works, resumes and vitas, and connect with others in similar fields, are poised to connect disabled persons and marginalized groups, especially around work groups and organizations (Baker, Bricout, Moon, Coughlan and Pater, 2013). Surprisingly, this sense of community is not always the case for other common uses of new media in sports, like fantasy football. Fans often report a sense of community as less of a driving force for participation in these online sports than other factors like thrill-seeking and entertainment (Farquhar and Meeds, 2007). However, for fans who want to keep track of and communicate with a favorite or hated athlete, social media is the most effective, albeit unpredictable, channel in which to do so (Hutchins, 2011; McNary and Hardin, 2013). In the case of adapted sport, the ability of social media to allow players and fans to connect and interact points to potential insight into how new media allows participants to negotiate the formal and informal rules of their sport.

We focus on wheelchair rugby[4] in this particular section for several reasons. The visibility and media attention the sport has received in the wake of the Oscar-nominated documentary *Murderball* (Mandel and Shapiro, 2005), its featured athletes' subsequent appearances on television shows like *Jackass* and *Friday Night Lights*, and the US team's success on the international stage, including winning the bronze medal in the 2012 London Paralympics, signals a sort of media saturation not enjoyed by other such disabled sports. This level of media attention allows us to bypass more obvious new media channels like Twitter and Facebook and delve deeper into the ways new media shapes understanding of disability and participation in that particular sport.

The use of new media in the sport offers insight into two important facets of adapted sport in general, and of wheelchair rugby participation in particular. First, examining the use of new media in such a potentially rough and injurious sport like quad rugby provides access to the ways athletes discuss the injuries that result from their sport participation in the context of their disability. Previous research shows that participation in quad rugby not only alters meanings of disability but what it means to live life as a disabled athlete, including handling sport injuries (Lindemann and Cherney, 2008). Second, new media interaction enables a deeper look into one of the more pervasive qualities of competitive disabled sport: the tension between the notion of inclusion on which such sports were founded, and the strive for legitimacy and visibility by becoming an elite, high competitive sport (Cherney, 2003; Lindemann, 2008; Lindemann and Cherney, 2008; Promis, Erevelles and Matthews, 2001). We explore each of these facets in more depth.

New media and the negotiation of injury and medical advice

In examining the role new media plays in the discussion of health among athletes, we turned to the website discussion board for the United States Quad Ruby Association (USQRA). Here, coaches and players discuss upcoming tournaments, argue about the rules of the game, relive past matches, rank the top players in the sport, and engage the sort of fan talk one would generally expect to find on such a site. Players also ask for medical advice about injuries, seek advice on sports equipment, and engage in a dialogue indicative of what Coopman (2003) calls "disability as community" (p. 376), or online social practices that form connections and relationships.

Sports injuries that seem commonplace for able-bodied persons can have dire consequences for physically disabled persons whose bodies have already suffered traumatic blows to the nervous, skeletal, and immune systems. For example, simple bruises acquired from playing quad rugby could lead to severe skin infections, due to athletes' lessened sensation and healing capabilities. Stories of this kind of experience populate the USQRA online discussion board. For example, a player with the online user name "generals" described how rugby participation prompted him to have his elbow's bursa sac, a fluid-filled sac that protects soft tissue from being damaged by nearby bones, surgically removed:

> I believe I continually caused trauma to my forearms and elbow while playing quad rugby, specifically, pushing with elbows while protecting the ball. The repeated trauma and lack of sensation led to a staph infection. I've had the entire bursial sac [*sic*] can be taken out to prevent future infection [*sic*].
>
> *(generals, 2004)*

Likewise, user "J. Ezell" asks for advice about a recurring infection, writing:

> Ok guys, I realize this is a 'sore' subject, but it's become part of my reality and I'm wondering what others are doing to combat recurring staph [infection]" acquired by "cuts on my hands where they've cracked open from pushing [wheelchair rims].
>
> *(Ezell, 2012)*

Like "generals," this user receives some immediate advice which may or may not match a doctor's medical advice: applying lotion to the affected area (stigwrq, 2012).

The connection among players provided by this social media channel enables the athletes to better play their sport; one would imagine such infections interfering with a player's ability to participate. More interestingly, new media enables athletes to share stories in order to better live life with a disability. For example, "J.Ezell" is happy to share his "quad tricks," things he's learned about living life with quadriplegia: "Well, it's been almost 14 years now since I became a quad. One thing I've learned is to ask others and experiment to find better, more efficient ways of doing things." (Ezell, 2010). The rest of this thread includes responses from other athletes about how to more efficiently accomplish their daily routines. While such talk is common among players on the same team (Lindemann and Cherney, 2008), discussion board posts allow for a wider variety of people and advice.

Communicative negotiations of adapted sport's rules and regulations

Quad Rugby was originally started in the 1970s to offer quadriplegics a more inclusive recreation alterative to the then-dominant sport of wheelchair basketball, played by paraplegics who have a less severe spinal cord injury than quads (QuadRugby.Com, 2005a). Quad rugby is currently one of only two organized team sports available for quadriplegics; the other team sport is power soccer, played by severely disabled quads who use motorized wheelchairs. The USQRA welcomes male and female players of all skill levels but frames the sport as an intense, "tough, give-no-quarter game" (QuadRugby.Com, 2005b, para. 11), implying that players must be willing to engage in hard-hitting physical contact. This may intimidate and subsequently exclude players who do not feel up to the challenge. Some claim that including more severely disabled persons in the same category as less severely disabled persons dilutes the competitive quality of sport participation (Brasile and Hedrick, 1996). Others, however, argue that inclusion must be re-conceptualized to provide opportunities for all to experience the transformative qualities of sport. Promis *et al.* (2001) found that accommodating persons of varying physical impairments led to social segregation and isolation, in both able-bodied athletes as well as among disabled athletes. Promis *et al.* (2001) therefore recommend a radical reconceptualization of inclusiveness and competitive equality, one that will, "transform the very notion of sport [that] is committed to idealized notions of bodily perfection, physical prowess, and sexual appeal" (p. 48). The tension that lays at the foundation of adapted sports, inclusion versus competition, is played out in the USQRA discussion board.

Discussions about inclusiveness come up with surprising frequency on the USQRA discussion board. These discussions sometimes turn into debates centered on the question of whether paraplegics or other similarly mobile athletes should play the sport. The responses vary, but most fall into two categories: the detrimental effect of such players on the integrity of the sport, and the ongoing "sandbagging" that such players already commit.

Quad rugby players are rated on a 0.5–3.5 point scale, graded in 0.5 increments, which measure their degree of mobility (0.5 is least mobile, 3.5 is the most). A player classified as a 3.5 is thought to possess the maximum mobility, agility, and strength for a quadriplegic person. Each team is only allowed four players on the court at a time whose classifications must total no more than 8 points. This rule is meant to ensure that more severely disabled players classified at 1.5, for example, are not excluded from play. Debates about changing the classification system occur with regular frequency on the USQRA online discussion board. A player with the screen name "ChipD" suggested a wider definition of disability to include more players:

I realize that quad rugby started as just that, "Quad Rugby." With that said, I would like to... propose the addition of a 4.0 player to Wheelchair Rugby. This gives great potential for growth of newer teams and will help developing teams become more competitive, face it, there are a lot of teams that don't have the impact 3.0 or 3.5 player which are hard to find.

(ChipD, 2003)

Generally, the only wheelchair athletes more mobile than a 3.5 quad are paraplegics. For some, the inclusion of such players would be detrimental to the sport in a practical way. The online user "Tom Hamill" speculated that the strength of paraplegics would damage other players' equipment:

Wearing my team manager hat, I already spend too much quality time with my local welder and we went through 2 dozen tubes [for tires] and at least 3 axles [for rear wheels] at Sectionals. In fact, we lost our lead over S. Fla because of equipment issues. If we add that much more power on the court, we'll have to look at carrying spare chairs to tournaments. I look at what [high pointer] players in the system... can do and I get concerned about liability issues. I don't think we can keep our sport a contact sport if we add a new class of more powerful players.

(Hamill, 2003)

To others, a proposal to include higher classed, and presumably more mobile, players runs counter to the reason quad rugby was created, a point the online user named "hotwheels" argued:

I'm... too fat and slow to chase a 4.0 player. Jesus, some 3 and 3.5 are almost like para's [sic], now you want to put actual para athletes out there? Why not add a hoop and eliminate the contact and it'll be basketball [a popular paraplegic sport] yey-freakin-hoo!

(hotwheels, 2003)

Similarly, "QRforLife" responded to another's query about paraplegics playing quad rugby:

There's competitive skiing, basketball, football and other sports for you to play, but QUAD rugby will always be for quads. Although I have seen to my amazement that a para can "hurt" his hand playing basketball (make sure it's not your dominant hand) and play with that hand in a club-like brace, tell everyone that your [sic] a quad, get a bigger back for your chair, and be sure your [sic] fat enough so no-one sees your stomach muscles [quads have usually lost most function of their torso]. Put all these together and not only can you play in the USQRA you can make it to team USA and fool the world!

(QRforLife, 2009)

The above responses not only communicate possessiveness, warranted or not, about the sport of quad rugby, they also point to a community response to the practice commonly called "sand-bagging": people "faking" more disability than they might actually possess to get a favorable classification (Lindemann, 2008). Through these social media interactions, players come to an agreement about the interpretation of the sport's rules and regulations, as well as engage in consciousness-raising about what it means to be a quadriplegic athlete. While some might argue that paraplegics have their own sports to play and should not be "muscling in" on quad rugby, ChipD's concern is that quad rugby's exclusion of paraplegics hinders competition. In his view, developing teams are limited to low pointer quads; their lack of players with a much rarer 3.0 or 3.5 injury level hinders their competitiveness because those players, being stronger and more mobile, are the "impact" players. A paraplegic would likely be classified as a 4.0 or above in the quad rugby system. Given the statistics on spinal cord injuries (NSCIA, 2003), there are more paraplegics than there are high-functioning quads. Including paraplegics, according to ChipD, would actually foster inclusion and competitive equality.

For several reasons, these discussions might be best conducted online. Although a relatively small community, the anonymity afforded users might help them feel freer to speak their mind. This feeling of anonymity is a common occurrence with social media (Farquhar and Meeds, 2007), and while it can sometimes result in flaming, or excessively insulting others, it may also serve to foster open and honest discussions about potentially sensitive subject matter. At the same time, social media has the capability to bring geographically isolated groups of people, important for disabled people who may themselves be limited in their ability to travel and looking to connect with like-minded individuals (Baker *et al.*, 2013).

Our examination of the connectivity function of new media in wheelchair rugby also provides insight into an oft-contested topic, and one made more volatile with the introduction of social media into a sports fan base: community (Farquhar and Meeds, 2007; McNary and Hardin, 2013). In interrogating this notion of community in the context of disability, we employ Coopman's (2003) discussion of metaphors of disability in communication research. Coopman (2003) presents several metaphors for disability studies that may simultaneously empower and oppress the disabled population. She distinguishes between disability as cognition, in culture, as culture, as politics, and as community, noting that the last metaphor provides the most complex and comprehensive view of disability. However, as our discussion of connectivity and new media above illustrates, it is one that is still not free from politics and fragmentation. The above discussion suggests the value of theorizing community as a multi-layered concept: i.e. the community of quad rugby within the community of disabled sport within the community of sport. Empowering communication strategies may be hard to come by and, despite being negotiated online, such strategies still seem to be limited by the materiality of the disabled body; in other words, by the "quad versus para" debate over ability.

New media and adapted sport participation

In our analysis, use of new media serves several functions in adapted sport participation: it increases legitimacy, fosters visibility, and facilitates athletes' connections between themselves and their fans. By mirroring the form and content of other sport-oriented sites, new media can position disability sports as an equal counterpart rather than less-than-equal by comparison. New media can also foster visibility of adapted sport. And, perhaps most in line with social media's unique characteristics, the use of new media in adapted sport can increase a sense of community among athletes. It is this last function of new media that, arguably, complicates the concepts of community and identity in disabled sport.

New media use complicates the notion of community, fostering connections while and preventing what some might call a "real" or "true" connection. In short, social media can increase connections among people and at the same time it alienates people from each other (Turkle, 1995). For wheelchair rugby, the use of new media does not so much foster alienation as it simply explodes the notion that a sport community coalesces around the sport itself. In the case of quad rugby, two topics frequently discussed are athlete health and the rules of the sport. As disability issues, these conversations extend beyond the immediate concerns of the sport itself; discussions about injury become lessons about living with disability and debates over the rules engage the larger question of inclusion within the disability community. This use of new media offers insight into the unique characteristics of the wheelchair rugby community. Athletes' concerns transcend the sport even as their concerns are directly tied to participation in the sport, like playing-time exacerbating an existing injury that might be less problematic for an able-bodied athlete. This connectivity function of new media in the world of quad rugby suggests scholars should consider community as a multi-layered concept that incorporates the various communities that intersect around a shared activity, and that such an exploration is enhanced and complicated by a consideration of new media. Additional work is needed to further the investigation of and development of such a theory, but our study suggests the potential of new media use for clarifying the ways communication impacts processes of inclusion and exclusion among disability communities. Such work might contribute to reconceiving the political possibilities of disability and disability rights.

Additionally, the use of new media in adapted sport offers insight into the complex notion of identity. Contemporary disability politics remains strongly tied to identity (Linton, 1998), but these ties can be complicated by the range of possible identities that any one person can claim at the same time. Davis (2002) argues that choosing among possible identities limits the ultimate impact of identity politics for people with disabilities because it forms an unstable foundation for activism and social change. We suggest that the notion of community (as conceived here) may prove more useful: since virtually everyone always occupies multiple communities at the same time, the multi-layered community facilitated by new media in adapted sport might provide a model for disability politics that avoids the potential limitations of grounding it in identity. Whether activists and scholars pursue this possibility, the ways social media facilitate communities centered on adapted sport have and will continue to effect the impact such activities have on living with disability.

Notes

1. In this chapter, we use "social media" and "new media" interchangeably. Some use the term "new media" only to distinguish it from "old media" like television, radio, and newspapers, and specifically use "social media" to may refer to technology that allows people to connect and interact. We assume that most new media, save for DVDs, contain a social component such as a message board or comments section.
2. We use the term "real" not as derogatory but merely to capture the ableist sentiment about disabled sport that is often present in mainstream media coverage.
3. The implications of such differences remain debatable, as they accurately represent events in those sports. For example, Paralympic Cycling-Track does include events with tandem cyclists, and Olympic Cycling-Track includes events with solo cyclists. But Olympic Cycling-Track also includes tandem events and Paralympic Cycling-Track has events that feature solo cyclists. Good arguments can be made on either side of the question as to whether or not displaying two cyclists in the Paralympic icon instead of one reveals and/or encourages an ableist perspective of the sport.
4. We use the terms "wheelchair rugby" and "quad rugby" interchangeably. There is currently no adapted rugby sport for paraplegic athletes, and organized wheelchair rugby sport is played by quadriplegic athletes exclusively.

References

Associated Press (2012, August 28) *Pioneering Doctor Remembered for Paralympic Idea*. Retrieved from http://www.npr.org/templates/story/story.php?storyId=160151285

Baker, P. M. A., Bricout, J. C., Moon, N. W., Coughlan, B. and Pater, J. (2013) Communities of participation: A comparison of disability and aging identified groups on Facebook and LinkedIn. *Telematics and Informatics, 30*, 22–34. doi: 10.1016/j.tele.2012.03.004

Brasile, F. M. and Hedrick, B. N. (1996) The relationship of elite wheelchair basketball competitors to the International Functional Classification System. *Therapeutic Recreation Journal, 30*, 114–127.

Brittain, I. (2004) Perceptions of disability and their impact upon involvement in sport for with disabilities at all levels. *Journal of Sport and Social Issues, 28*, 429–452.

Chappell, B. (2012, August 29) Paralympics begin In London, near 'spiritual home' of Games. *The Two-Way: NPR's News Blog.* Retrieved from http://www.npr.org/blogs/thetwo-way/2012/08/29/160249876/paralympics-set-to-begin-in-london-near-spiritual-home-of-games

Cherney, J. L. (2003) Sport, (dis)ability, and public controversy: Ableist rhetoric and Casey Martin v. PGA Tour, Inc. In R. S. Brown and D. J. O'Rourke III (eds), *Case Studies in Sport Communication* (pp. 81–104). London: Praeger.

Cherney, J. L. and Lindemann, K. (2009) Sporting images of disability: Murderball and the rehabilitation of identity. In A. C. Billings and H. Hundley (eds), *Examining Identity in Sport Media* (pp. 195–216). Thousand Oaks, CA: Sage.

ChipD. (2003, March 20) 4.0 player/8.0 system [Msg 234]. Message posted to http://quadrugby.com/cgi-bin/ultimatebb.cgi?ubb=get_topic&f=1&t=000234

Coopman, S. J. (2003) Communicating disability: Metaphors of oppression, metaphors of empowerment. In P. J. Kalbfleisch (ed.), *Communication Yearbook, 27*, 337–94. Mahwah, NJ: Lawrence Erlbaum Associates.

Davis, L. J. (2002) *Bending Over Backwards: Disability, Dismodernism and Other Difficult Positions.* New York: New York University Press.

Ezell, J. (2010, May 25) Quad tricks [Msg 1]. Message posted to http://www.quadrugby.com/node/1501

Ezell, J. (2012, June 24) No title [Msg 1]. Message posted to http://www.quadrugby.com/node/2046

Farquhar, L. K. and Meeds, R. (2007) Types of fantasy sports users and their motivations. [Article]. *Journal of Computer-Mediated Communication, 12*(4), 1208–1228. doi: 10.1111/j.1083-6101.2007.00370.x

generals. (2004, February 24) Septic bursitis in forearm [Msg 371]. Message posted to http://quadrugby.com/cgi-bin/ultimatebb.cgi?=get_topic&f=1&t=000371

Hamill, T. (2003, March 20) 4.0 player/8.0 system [Msg 236]. Message posted to http://quadrugby.com/cgi-bin/ultimatebb.cgi?ubb=get_topic&f=1&t=000234

Hardin, M. and Hardin, B. (2004) The 'Supercrip' in sport media: Wheelchair athletes discuss hegemony's disabled hero. *Sociology of Sport Online, 10.* Retrieved from http://physed.otago.ac.nz/sosol/v7i1/v7i1_1.html

Hargreaves, J. A. and Hardin, B. (2009) Women wheelchair athletes: Competing against media stereotypes. *Disabilities Studies Quarterly, 29*(2). Retrieved from http://dsq-sds.org/article/view/920/1095

Henson, M. (2012, September 5) Paralympics 2012: How Murderball film changed view of disabled sport. *BBC Sport.* Retrieved from http://www.bbc.co.uk/sport/0/disability-sport/19484847

hotwheels. (2003, March 20) 4.0 player/8.0 system [Msg 235]. Message posted to http://quadrugby.com/cgi-bin/ultimatebb.cgi?ubb=get_topic&f=1&t=000234

Hutchins, B. (2011) The acceleration of media sport culture [Article]. *Information, Communication and Society, 14*(2), 237–257. doi: 10.1080/1369118x.2010.508534

Kirkpatrick, B. (2012) "A blessed boon": Radio, disability, governmentality, and the discourse of the "shut-in," 1920–1930. *Critical Studies in Media Communication, 29*(3), 165–184. doi: 10.1080/15295036.2011.631554

Levs, J., Karimi, F. and Mabuse, N. (2013, February 18) 'Blade runner' Pistorius charged with murder of model girlfriend. *CNN.com.* Retrieved from http://www.cnn.com/2013/02/14/world/africa/south-africa-blade-runner-shooting

Lindemann, K. (2008) "I can't be standing up out there": Communicative performances of (dis)ability in wheelchair rugby. *Text and Performance Quarterly, 28*(1/2), 98–115. doi: 10.1080/10462930701754366

Lindemann, K. and Cherney, J. L. (2008) Communicating in and through "Murderball": Masculinity and disability in wheelchair rugby. *Western Journal of Communication, 72*, 107–125. doi: 10.1080/10570310802038382

Linton, S. (1998) *Claiming Disability: Knowledge and Identity.* New York: New York University Press.

Longmore, P. K. (1987) Screening stereotypes: Images of disabled people in television and motion pictures. In A. Gartner and T. Joe (eds), *Images of the Disabled, Disabling Images* (pp. 65–78). New York: Praeger.

Mackenzie, E. (2012, August 30) X Games drops ski, snowboard cross races. *The Whistler Question.* Retrieved from http://www.whistlerquestion.com/article/20120830/WHISTLER02/308309955/-1/

WHISTLER/x-games-drops-ski-snowboard-cross-races

Mandel, J. and Shapiro, D. A. (Writers) and H. A. Rubin and D. A. Shapiro (Directors) (2005) *Murderball* [Motion picture]. United States: Thinkfilm, Inc.

Manderson, L. and Peake, S. (2005) Men in motion: Disability and the performance of masculinity. In C. Sandhal and P. Auslander (eds), *Bodies in Communication: Disability and Performance* (pp. 230–242). Ann Arbor, MI: University of Michigan Press.

McNary, E. and Hardin, M. (2013) Subjectivity in 140 characters: The use of social media by marginalized groups. In P. M. Pedersen (ed.), *Handbook of Sport Communication* (pp. 238–247) London: Routledge.

National Spinal Cord Injury Association (NSCIA) (2003) *More About Spinal Cord Injury*. Retrieved from http://64.224.255.232/html/factsheets/spinstat.shml

Nelson, J. (2003) The invisible cultural group: Images of disability. In P. Lester and S. Ross (eds), *Images that Injure: Pictorial Stereotypes in the Media* (pp. 175–184). Westport, CT: Greenwood Publishing.

Promis, D., Erevelles, N. and Matthews, J. (2001) Reconceptualizing inclusion: The politics of university sports and recreation programs for students with mobility impairments. *Sociology of Sport Journal*, 18, 37–50.

QRforLife (2009, December 1) Sorry [Msg 963]. Message posted to http://www.quadrugby.com/node/1311#comment-963

QuadRugby.Com (2005a) Frequently asked questions about Murderball. Retrieved from http://www.murderball.quadrugby.com/faqs.html

QuadRugby.Com (2005b) Smashing stereotypes. Retrieved from http://www.murderball.quadrugby.com/quadrugby.html

stigwrq (2012, June 24) Lotion, lotion, lotion [Msg 2]. Message posted to http://www.quadrugby.com/node/2046

Tanner, S., Green, K. and Burns, S. (2011) Media coverage of sport for athletes with intellectual disabilities: The 2010 Special Olympics national games examined. *Media International Australia*, 140, 107–116. Retrieved from http://libproxy.sdsu.edu/login?url=http://search.ebscohost.com/login.aspx?direct=true&db=ufh&AN=66210912&site=ehost-live

The London Organising Committee of the Olympic Games and Paralympic Games (2012a) [Home page]. Retrieved from http://www.london2012.com/index-olympic.html

The London Organising Committee of the Olympic Games and Paralympic Games (2012b) *Sports*. Retrieved from http://www.london2012.com/paralympics/sports/

Turkle, S. (1995) *Life on the Screen: Identity in the Age of the Internet*. New York: Simon & Schuster.

INDEX

Endnotes are given with an italic '*n*' followed by the endnote number e.g. '*Deadspin.com*' 40*n*1.
Figures are given with an italic '*f*' followed by the figure number e.g. 'eye tracking, split screen presentation' 277*f*24.5.
Tables are given with an italic '*t*' followed by the table number e.g. 'Facebook, content of Olympic Games' posts' 162*t*14.3.

3DTV 262
1966 World Cup 301, 302–3
2008 Beijing Summer Olympic Games 153, 304; IOC and social media 156
2010 Vancouver Winter Olympic Games: hockey final 11; social networks 156; VANOC 156; website 156
2010 World Cup Final 24
2012 London Paralympic Games 82, 354–5
2012 London Summer Olympic Games 9, 11–12; communication campaign 157–8; fencing Incident 84; first social media Olympics 85, 305; IOC social media regulations 138; multiculturalism 305, 306; official website 157–8; Opening Ceremony 82, 83, 306; Open Water Warfare 78; revenue generating streams 230; sponsorship 80, 135; website feed to social networks 158
2012 NFL Super Bowl 12, 247, 264; media upload content 16, 215

ABC (American Broadcasting Company) 91
accelerated culture 67–8
Adam, Brad 110
Adams, Guy 13
Agricultural Age of sports journalism 89–90
Aikman, Troy 347
Allen & Company 45
Allen (Texas) 230
Amaechi, John 347–8
Amazon Kindle 76

American Idol 10
American Turf Register 89
APIs (Applied Programming Interfaces) 231
apps: APIs 231; sports information 231
Arab Spring 37
Aristotle 34
Arledge, Roone 91
Armitage, John 68
Armstrong, Lance 252
Asen, R. 34
Aston Villa Football Club 250
Astrojumper 292–3
athletes *see* sportspeople
athletics departments *see* collegiate athletics
Atlanta Journal-Constitution 107
Auburn University 280
Avery, Sean 38
Ayanbadejo, Brendon 38–9, 345

Bagdikian, Ben 94–5
Bailey, Richard 127, 138
Baltimore Ravens 32, 38–9
Barton, Joey 126–7
Barwell, Gary 306
Baseball Hall of Fame 89
Basking in Reflected Glory (BIRGing) 167, 168, 169, 225
Baudrillard, Jean 68–9, 73
Bayless, Skip 347
Benoit, William 178–9
Bentham, Jeremy 55
Berens, Ricky 15
Berry, Matthew 243
The Big Ten 148
Bio-Games 78
bio-politics 64, 65*n*3
bisexuality *see* homosexuality
Blake, Steve 264
The Bleacher Report 49, 115, 315
BleacherReport.com 105